Sherlock Holmes on Screen

The Complete Film and TV History

Sherlock Holmes on Screen

THE COMPLETE FILM AND TV HISTORY

Alan Barnes

REYNOLDS & HEARN LTD
LONDON

For Sim, for stuff

Frontispiece: *Basil Rathbone in character*
Contents page: *Jeremy Brett and David Burke in* **The Adventures of Sherlock Holmes**: The Final Problem *(1985)*

First published in 2002 by
Reynolds & Hearn Ltd
61a Priory Road
Kew Gardens
Richmond
Surrey TW9 3DH

A CIP catalogue record for this book is available from the British Library.

ISBN 1 903111 78 1

Designed by Peri Godbold.

Printed and bound by Biddles Ltd., Kings Lynn, Norfolk.

Contents

Acknowledgments

The author would like to thank all of his many Irregulars, without whom ...

First and foremost: Andy Lane (AL) and Jonathan Rigby (JR), who supplied a number of witty, erudite and faultlessly researched entries for this book, all of which are credited within the text – and none of which the author could improve upon, much to his embarrassment. Sincerest gratitude for their insight, enthusiasm and charity.

Thanks also to: Adrian Rigelsford; Donald Tosh, whose recollections cast new light on Peter Cushing's BBC Holmes; Peter Griffiths, who interviewed *Baker Street Boys* creator Anthony Read on my behalf; my German associates Robert N Bloch, Rainer Engelhard, Gerhard Lindenstruth and Uwe Sommerlad, who supplied invaluable information; the BBC Written Archives Centre, the British Film Institute library, the British Library Newspaper Library and Westminster Central Library; Anthony Brown, Gavin Collinson, Neil Corry, Sue Cowley, Robert Dick, Andrew Englefield, Joel Finler, Gary Gillatt, James Goss, Derek Handley, Julian Knott, David Miller, Steven Moffat, Peter Nicholson, Andrew Pixley, Charles Prepolec, Steve Roberts and Gary Russell, for assorted favours, thoughts and loans; Peri Godbold, long-suffering designer; and finally Richard Reynolds, who commissioned the book in the first place.

As ever, apologies to Jane, my 'one fixed point in a changing age'. Hello to Julian Alexander and Oliver Nathaniel. Love to Isabella Astrid.

Introduction

'I shall write a monograph some day on the noxious habit of accumulating useless trivia'
– Sherlock Holmes (Basil Rathbone) in **Sherlock Holmes in Washington**

Buster Keaton projects himself into Holmes' place in **Sherlock Jr** *(1924)*

It could easily be argued that Sherlock Holmes was the first pop icon of the modern age. Instantly identifiable by his silhouette alone, even the slightest of visual prompts lead to the Great Detective: deerstalker, Meerschaum pipe, violin, hansom cab, Watson, housekeeper, Hound. This book notes the importance of all these signifiers in establishing the myth of perhaps the foremost hero of the post-Darwinian era – for Holmes could surely not have evolved until science had punctured the myth of the Creation. When Arthur Conan Doyle's detective uses forensic, analytical method in his quest to disprove the existence of the phantom hounding the Baskerville clan, or the speckled horror slithering after the Stoner girls of Stoke Moran, he is bringing reason to bear on the oldest of monsters – superstition, ignorance, fear. And, as we shall see, Sherlock Holmes and his methods have been called upon by filmmakers to banish seemingly invulnerable and inexplicable demons of the latter day – serial killers like Jack the Ripper, the state-sanctified madness of the Nazis.

The Sherlock Holmes stories peaked in popularity as the film medium came to be – and, necessarily, Holmes has enjoyed a big screen

By royal appointment: Sherlock Holmes (Basil Rathbone) defends the Crown Jewels in **The Adventures of Sherlock Holmes** *(1939)*

1990s (**The Adventures of Sherlock Holmes**, 1984-5, *et al*). Although this book adopts an A to Z format, a chronology at the rear indexes all the films listed in order of release.

Any survey of such a vast subject has to be curbed at some point, and I have, albeit reluctantly, limited the scope of this book to live-action fiction films and TV programmes which contain characters or stories originated in the Sherlock Holmes stories of Doyle. There are a number of sub-genres that have been only selectively addressed, taking only remarkable examples of each: silent parodies, animations, films about Sherlock Holmes fantasists (**They Might Be Giants**, for example) and those which feature Doyle himself. Areas I've left untouched include documentaries, advertising and TV show sketches (a definitive list of every two-bit comedian who's ever sucked a pipe and muttered 'Elementary...' would fill at least half of these pages). Nor have I been able to study those particular films that owe a tangentially interesting debt to Holmes – *The Name of the Rose* (1985) for one, with its Holmes and Watson in the guise of mediaeval monk and apprentice.

As with millions of others, my first experience of Sherlock Holmes was of Holmes as a moving-picture phenomenon. When I was eight or nine years old, the 1940s Basil Rathbone films were repeated on BBC2 in the early evenings – and so, when I came to read the Doyle stories a few years down the line, in my head Holmes and Watson always spoke with the voices of Rathbone and Nigel Bruce. In that case, which, for me, was the original – the incredibly old Universal films, or the only slightly older Doyle stories? So although *Sherlock Holmes on Screen* assumes a very general acquaintance with the 60 adventures comprising 'the canon', as it's rather portentously termed in Sherlockian circles, it's not been written for Doyle purists – those who fetishise textual authenticity above fundamental film priori. I note, for example, where a TV or film adaptation has diverted from Doyle, but I do so without prejudice: I want to know why, what effect it has, and whether the change is interesting or amusing or entertaining in its own right.

Like Dracula again, or James Bond, the idea of Sherlock Holmes has become far larger, and now means far more, than the letter of the texts that inspired it.

career rivalled only by Bram Stoker's Count Dracula (another invention of late-Victorian England, and in many respects the anti-Holmes). The confluence between the creation of Holmes and the coming of film means that it would be possible, if one so desired, to observe almost every historical, cultural and technological development in the moving image purely through the changing representations of Sherlock Holmes – from a jerky picture on a 'What the Butler Saw' machine (**Sherlock Holmes Baffled**) through pre-copyright exploitation (**Sherlock Holmes i Livsfare** *et al*), the arrival of sound (**The Return of Sherlock Holmes**, 1929), the arrival of television (**The Three Garridebs**), wartime propaganda (**Sherlock Holmes and the Voice of Terror** *et al*), 'X'-rated horror (**A Study in Terror**), postmodern reconceptualisation (**The Seven-Per-Cent Solution**), and finally the transformation of the low culture of the 1880s and 1890s into the high culture of the 1980s and

Author's note

In the A to Z listing, details of film and TV productions are given thus:

● **Title** [in country of origin, exactly as spelled out on original print and/or supported, where applicable, by contemporaneous documentation]

● *tr* '**literal translation of title**' [where applicable]

● *at* **alternate title(s)** [in country of origin, where applicable]

● *aka* **also known as** [alternate English language titles, where applicable]

● *country of origin*

● *year* [usually date given in copyright details on film print]

● *TV format* [television productions only: stand-alone TV movies are *TVM*; *TV series/serial*s are preceded by number of episodes, where applicable, and approximate duration of each standard episode]

● *type* [either *adaptation*, meaning 'a dramatisation of one of the Sherlock Holmes stories written by Arthur Conan Doyle'; *pastiche*, meaning 'a new story, using characters drawn from the Sherlock Holmes stories written by Arthur Conan Doyle'; or *parody*, meaning 'a burlesque of the Sherlock Holmes story written by Arthur Conan Doyle, designed primarily for comic effect']

● *production company* [wherever possible, as given in copyright details on film print]

● *duration if sound film* [in minutes, wherever possible as per original release print in country of origin]

● *length if silent film* [in feet. Early cinema films were manufactured in a number of formats and shown at various projection speeds; it is therefore unsatisfactory to attempt to calculate the running time of silent films from their length alone]

● *bw/colour/silent* [black and white/colour/silent, where applicable. All pre-colour films given as *bw*, regardless of tint effects]

● *tx* [TV productions only: date of first transmission in country of origin, plus broadcaster]

● *w* **screenwriter**

● *p* **producer**

● *d* **director**

● *cast* character name: **performer** [in order given on original print. Performers uncredited on the original print are denoted with an **asterisk**＊ and listed in alphabetical order. Characters' names are given verbatim, except those that have been standardised according to house style – so 'Dr Watson' is used throughout, not 'Doctor Watson', 'Dr. Watson', etc]

Occasionally, additional production credits may be given; these are spelled out in full.

Cross-references to entries elsewhere in this book are given in **bold type**, with date of production in brackets where necessary to identify particular versions, eg: **The Hound of the Baskervilles** (1959). To distinguish between films/TV series and Sherlock Holmes stories with the same title, references to 'the canon' of adventures written by Arthur Conan Doyle are given in SMALL CAPITALS, eg: THE HOUND OF THE BASKERVILLES.

Synopses are provided for all *pastiches*, with the exception of **The Private Life of Sherlock Holmes**, where the film's story is relayed while detailing the even more convoluted story behind the film. The more complex synopses are divided into three-act sections: The Mystery, The Investigation, The Solution. Synopses are only provided for *adaptations* of Doyle originals when the adaptations are deemed sufficiently 'free' to warrant them.

Throughout, the magnificent Oxford World's Classics texts of Doyle's Sherlock Holmes stories (general editor Owen Dudley Edwards, 1993) have been consulted for all titles and quotes (hence THE SIGN OF THE FOUR, not 'The Sign of Four', etc). Especially useful sources included: *Universal Horrors* (Michael Brunas, John Brunas and Tom Weaver, 1990); *A Study in Celluloid* (Michael Cox, 1999); *Bending the Willow* (David Stuart Davies, 1996); *The World Bibliography of Sherlock Holmes and Dr Watson* (Ronald Burt De Waal, 1976); *Damned in Paradise: The Life of John Barrymore* (John Kobler, 1977); *The Uncollected Sherlock Holmes* (ed Richard Lancelyn Green, 1983); *The Television Sherlock Holmes* (Peter Haining, 1996); *The Great Northern Adventures of Sherlock Holmes* (Bjarne Nielsen, 1997); *Conan Doyle in the Cinema* (Scott Allen Nollen, 1996); *The Sherlock Holmes File* (Michael Pointer, 1976); and *The Films of Sherlock Holmes* (Chris Steinbrunner and Norman Michaels, 1978). Of the many periodicals consulted, the *Bioscope*, *Kine Weekly*, *Moving Picture World* and *Scarlet Street* proved essential.

The Adventure of Sherlock Holmes' Smarter Brother

*US 1975 parody Twentieth Century-Fox Film
Corporation 91m colour*

wd **Gene Wilder** *p* **Richard A Roth**
cast Sigerson Holmes: **Gene Wilder** Jenny Hill: **Madeline
Kahn** Orville Sacker: **Marty Feldman** Gambetti: **Dom De
Luise** Moriarty: **Leo McKern** Moriarty's assistant: **Roy
Kinnear** Lord Redcliff: **John Le Mesurier** Sherlock Holmes:
Douglas Wilmer Dr Watson: **Thorley Walters**
Bruner: **George Silver** Hunkston: **Nicholas Smith**
Moriarty's gunman: **John Hollis** coach driver: **Aubrey
Morris** Fred: **Tommy Godfrey** Queen Victoria: **Susan Field**
Russian: **Joseph Behrmannis** Frenchman: **Wolfe Morris**
man in tails: **Julian Orchard** butler: **Kenneth Benda**
Renato: **Michael Crane** opera conductor: **Tony Sympson**

THE MYSTERY

An important state document passed on by Queen
Victoria herself is stolen from the bedroom of
Home Secretary Lord Redcliff; its theft could cause
war by Thursday. Not wishing to alert 'every
murderer and petty thief in England' to their
investigation, Sherlock Holmes and Dr Watson
conspire to 'disappear', apparently *en route* to Paris
– but not before Holmes has arranged to have 'one
or two of his less urgent assignments' passed on to
his insanely jealous younger brother, Sigerson...

THE INVESTIGATION

Aided by memory man Sergeant Orville Stanley
Sacker of Scotland Yard, Sigerson investigates the
case of music hall singer 'Bessie Bellwood', who
claims to be a victim of blackmail. 'Bessie',
however, turns out to be one Jenny Hill, a
pathological liar who also happens to be governess
to widower Lord Redcliff's children – and has
since become his fiancée. Meanwhile, villain
Professor Moriarty and his henchmen dog
Sigerson's progress. Moriarty is arranging to sell
the stolen document to hostile foreign powers –
but he does not yet have it in his possession...

THE SOLUTION

Corrupt opera singer Eduardo Gambetti has the
document, which he had forced the unfortunate
Jenny, his stage co-star, to steal for him. The incriminating scroll is to be handed over to Moriarty's
chief crony during Gambetti's next performance,
but the plot is foiled and, following a perilous duel
with Sigerson, Moriarty ends up in the Thames.
Holmes and Watson – who, heavily disguised, have
shadowed Sigerson and Sacker all along – return
the document into the care of the Crown.

✦ ✦ ✦

Beginning with a dumpy, bethroned Queen
Victoria muttering 'Shit!' and concluding with
a touching romantic adieu in a sun-dappled park,
The Adventure of Sherlock Holmes' Smarter Brother
veers wildly between the wilfully vulgar and the
near-sublime throughout – and although it would

*Sigerson Holmes (Gene Wilder) demonstrates the skills that made
him school champion at the Patricia Seddon Fencing Salon for Girls
in **The Adventure of Sherlock Holmes' Smarter Brother** (1975)*

be grossly unfair to label it a vanity project as such, it certainly never fails to highlight the omnipresence of writer, director and leading man Gene Wilder (1934-).

The film was born of a lunch Wilder had enjoyed with producer Richard A Roth sometime in 1973. 'He asked me if I had ever thought of doing a Sherlock Holmes film,' Wilder told the *Guardian* two years later, 'and I said I had – every other week for a year. But I couldn't see making fun of such a well-loved character in a 140-minute movie. So every other week I'd pace around and ask myself, is there some way, is there some way? ... About a week later I saw Richard again and he said, "I don't suppose you've given Sherlock Holmes another minute's thought." I said, "No, but I have given a great deal of thought to Sherlock's insanely jealous brother Sigi." That was the starting point...'

It seems entirely possible that Roth had envisaged a Holmes parody in the same vein as Wilder's previous script *Young Frankenstein*, a rich evocation of Universal Pictures' 1930s horror sequence. Whether or not Roth had intended this follow-up to likewise work over the Twentieth Century-Fox/Universal Basil Rathbone/Nigel Bruce series beginning with **Sir Arthur Conan Doyle's The Hound of the Baskervilles** remains tantalisingly unrecorded. What he got, however, was an entirely different creature.

The Adventure of Sherlock Holmes' Smarter Brother had been intended for director Mel Brooks, Wilder's long-term filmic conspirator. The pair had first worked together on Brooks' *The Producers* (1967), in which Lee Strasberg-trained Method actor Wilder had played an early lead. Later Wilder-headlining pictures, notably the whimsical *Willy Wonka and the Chocolate Factory* (1971), had died at the box-office, and it was only with Brooks' raucous *Blazing Saddles* (1974) that Wilder made a seriously big impression with his turn as burned-out gunfighter the Waco Kid. As a result, Wilder's *Frankenstein* parody became immediately bankable (he'd been writing unproduced scripts since 1968); that, again, was directed by Brooks. It would mark a break in their association, however. Brooks 'made it clear he didn't want to direct anything else that wasn't his own conception. In a way it would be a waste of his time' – and promptly decamped to make a TV-only Robin Hood spoof. Wilder signed a deal with Fox to write, direct and star in three films,

of which *Smarter Brother* was to be the first.

Roles were written specially for other members of Brooks' informal repertory company – Madeline Kahn, Dom De Luise – plus, significantly, a reprisal of Wilder's double-act with pop-eyed British actor Marty Feldman, his primary on-screen foil throughout *Young Frankenstein*. The name given Feldman's character, Orville Sacker, betrays an in-depth acquaintance with Doyle unplumbed elsewhere in the script. 'Ormond Sacker' was the name given the Watson figure in ACD's earliest draft of A STUDY IN SCARLET; likewise, Wilder's 'Sigerson' is derived from the alias Holmes uses while exploring Tibet in Norwegian guise following his 'death' in THE FINAL PROBLEM. However, Wilder's lengthy drafting process (some four versions) saw the piece alter in tone: 'As I kept working on it, I realised the film was turning into a romance. I was happy about that, because where my soul is at now is not just jokes and funnies. By romance I mean I'm less funny and the others are more funny ... It's a special world you've got to create. I want people to take Gene Wilder's romance seriously.'

The film was shot at England's Shepperton Studios, its remaining cast comprised of thoroughly respectable British thespians, notably Leo McKern, Roy Kinnear and John Le Mesurier, who had previously appeared in an episode of the 1951 TV series **We Present Alan Wheatley as Mr Sherlock Holmes in...** and in Hammer Films' 1959 version of **The Hound of the Baskervilles**. Although their casting would have meant little to American audiences, the film's 'real' Holmes and Watson were Douglas Wilmer and Thorley Walters; the former had made a significant impression as the Great Detective in BBC TV's 1965 **Sherlock Holmes** series, while the latter had played Watson to Christopher Lee's Holmes in **Sherlock Holmes und das Halsband des Todes** (1962). Forever lurking on the periphery beyond an amusing early scene at 221B Baker Street, the pair are not allowed much gravitas, particularly when dragged up as elderly women in a sequence that bears a passing similarity to Tony Curtis' and Jack Lemmon's similarly attired locomotive boarding in *Some Like it Hot*.

Hugely positive notices on both sides of the Atlantic heralded the film's release in December 1975. *Variety* called it 'a total delight'; *Films and Filming*'s Gordon Gow went further, claiming that: 'A smile hardly ever left my face, and for much of the time I absolutely shook with pleasure.' Wilder's star was very much in the ascendant, and it now seems odd to record that the man later responsible for *The Woman in Red* and *Haunted Honeymoon* was once compared to Charlie Chaplin in the 'respectable' press: 'The last screen comedian [pre-Wilder] who consistently succeeded in creating hilarious but poignant characters ... At this current rate of advancement, Wilder will wind up owning United Artists in about three years,' reckoned the *Guardian*; 'demonstrates a Chaplinesque tendency,' ruminated *Monthly Film Bulletin*.

Its prime mover's desire to be viewed as a jack-of-all-trades renders *The Adventure of Sherlock Holmes' Smarter Brother* a distinctly mixed bag, consistently falling out of its own reality. Good-natured puerility (mentions of 'your handling of the Case of the Three Testicles'; Sigi and Sacker unintentionally fondling each other's unknowingly exposed buttocks at a society ball; camp male housekeeper 'Hunkston') gives way to anachronistically ragtime-inflected song-and-dance numbers (the gratingly jolly 'Kangaroo Hop') and soft-focus set-ups featuring Madeline Kahn's Jenny, whose never-clarified character renders her much-touted 'romance' with Sigi mostly baffling.

Cursed by his 'urge to do something absolutely rotten every 24 minutes' (and keeping a coin-operated priest churning out tokens reading 'Absolved'), Leo McKern's snake-fondling, mathematically incompetent and hokey-Oirish Moriarty steals the show from romantic hero *manqué* Wilder. Towards the climax, one of the spectators at Gambetti's soon-to-be-curtailed rendition of Verdi's *Un ballo di maschera* turns to the viewer and asks, 'Is this rotten, or wonderfully brave?' Which, for chutzpah alone, surely earns *The Adventure of Sherlock Holmes' Smarter Brother* the benefit of the doubt.

The Adventures of Sherlock Holmes

aka **Sherlock Holmes; or Held for Ransom** [GB]
US 1905 adaptation [THE SIGN OF THE FOUR]
The Vitagraph Company of America 725 feet bw silent

A milestone, being the first film known to have been taken directly from one of Doyle's detective stories, this was described in a late 1905

Sherlock Holmes (Douglas Wilmer) and Dr Watson (Thorley Walters) effect their 'disappearance' in **The Adventure of Sherlock Holmes' Smarter Brother** (1975)

edition of *The Optical Lantern and Cinematograph Journal* as 'an episode in seventeen scenes, dealing with one of the most startling of Sir Conan Doyle's marvellous conceptions, culled from the series of adventures of the bandits who designate themselves "The Sign of Four".' Screened in the UK at the Alhambra under the title *Sherlock Holmes; or Held for Ransom*, the *Optical Lantern* asserted that 'The detail of this film is wonderful, and it is realistic to the highest degree.'

Many sources nominate Maurice Costello (1877-1950), a genuine heart-throb of the silent era, as the man who played Sherlock Holmes, thereby making Costello the first actor known to have portrayed the detective on film. Sadly, this is impossible to substantiate. Certainly, the wavy-haired, effete-looking Costello – aka 'Dimples' – did become one of the Vitagraph Company of America's major players, and therefore one of the first 'known' screen actors (it's said that he was the first film star to receive fan mail), but he is not known to have made reference to the film in any later interview. In fact, he is on record as saying that he didn't actually join Vitagraph until 1907.

Vitagraph was founded in New York circa 1898 by Sheffield-born newspaper illustrator J [James] Stuart Blackton (1875-1941) and Albert E Smith (1875-1958). Legend has it that Blackton's interest in filmmaking was sparked by a meeting with Thomas Edison, who used his newly invented Kinetograph camera to film Blackton at work drawing pictures under the title *Blackton, The Evening World Cartoonist*. Fascinated by the new technology, the first film made by Blackton and Smith under the Vitagraph banner was *The Burglar on the Roof* (1898), photographed atop the company's premises in the Morse Building, 116 Nassau Street, New York. Newsreels – including pictures from the Galveston flood of 1900 and the Presidential inauguration of 1904 – also provided a large part of Vitagraph's output until the summer of 1905, when the foundations were laid for a glasshouse studio at the corner of East 15 Street and Locust Avenue in Flatbush, Brooklyn.

According to Vitagraph historian Anthony Slide, the first film made at Flatbush entered production before building work had even been completed. This was the crime thriller *The Adventures of Raffles, the Amateur Cracksman*, produced by arrangement with actor (Cosmo) Kyrle Bellew (1885-1948) and Liebler and Company – who, as star and producers respectively of a 1903 Broadway play representing E W Hornung's gentleman thief, claimed dramatic rights in the character. The Vitagraph version ('contains sufficient sensationalism to satisfy the most ardent seeker after thrills,' reckoned the *Optical Lantern*) featured not Bellew but J Barney Sherry (1874-1944).

Perhaps significantly, many of the sources that nominate Costello as the star of the Holmes picture also claim that both Bellew and Sherry appeared alongside him in the film, which was supposedly written by Theodor A Liebler Jr of the aforementioned Liebler and Company. Whereas Blackton, Liebler and Costello would work together in later years, notably on an ambitious production of *Julius Caesar* (1908), it seems extremely unlikely that all these people should have first been united on the Sherlock Holmes film.

In the absence of any first-hand evidence, all one can assume with a reasonable degree of certainty about the production of *The Adventures of Sherlock Holmes* is that it was quite possibly directed by Blackton, most likely had exterior scenes filmed at Flatbush and interiors photographed back at Nassau Street, and very probably featured a cast of unknowns and now-forgottens – such as William Shea (1862-1918), who remembered that, around the time that *The Adventures of Sherlock Holmes* was recorded, 'Moving picture actors were scarce in those days and many a time I doubled, several times in the same picture. *The Servant Girl Problem* [1905] is one I call to mind in which I played five different parts, three separate and distinct old maids and two character parts, a Jew and a Dutchman...'

Shea was one of the first actors to become part of Vitagraph's repertory company of recurring players, alongside men such as Paul Panzer (1872-1958), who featured in *The Escape from Sing-Sing*, released in tandem with the company's Raffles film. If one is seeking to speculate who might have been the first true Holmes, or maybe Watson, or Jonathan Small, or Mordecai Smith, or Tonga – or, indeed, all of the above! – then these are among the names that ought to be considered.

No print survives.

The Adventures of Sherlock Holmes

GB 1921 15 x film series adaptations Stoll Picture Productions Ltd silent bw
scenarios/w **William J Elliott** [except where stated]
chief of production/p **Jeffrey Bernerd**
production/d **Maurice Elvey**
regular cast Sherlock Holmes: **Eille Norwood**
Dr Watson: **Hubert Willis**

THE DYING DETECTIVE
2274 feet
regular cast, plus Culverton Smith: **Cecil Humphries**
his servant: **J R Tozer** housekeeper: **Mdme d'Esterre**

THE DEVIL'S FOOT
2513 feet
regular cast, plus Mortimer Tregennis: **Harvey Braban**
Dr Sterndale: **Hugh Buckler**

A CASE OF IDENTITY
2612 feet
regular cast, plus Mary Sutherland: **Edna Flugrath**
Hosmer Angel: **Nelson Ramsey**

THE YELLOW FACE
2021 feet
regular cast, plus Grant Munro: **Clifford Heatherley**
Effie Munro: **Norma Whalley** the Negress: **L Allen**
the child: **Master Robey**

THE RED-HEADED LEAGUE
2139 feet
regular cast, plus Jabez Wilson: **Teddy Arundell**
Spalding: **H Townsend**

THE RESIDENT PATIENT
2405 feet
regular cast, plus Percy Trevelyan: **C Pitt Chatham**
Blessington: **Judd Green** Moffat: **Wally Bosco**
Inspector Lestrange [sic]: **Arthur Bell** Trevelyan's maid:
Beatrice Templeton

A SCANDAL IN BOHEMIA
2100 feet
regular cast, plus King of Bohemia: **Alfred Drayton**
Irene Adler: **Joan Beverly**

THE MAN WITH THE TWISTED LIP
2411 feet
regular cast, plus Mrs Hudson: **Mdme d'Esterre**
Hugh Boone/Neville St Clair: **Robert Vallis**
Mrs St Clair: **Paulette del Baye**

THE BERYL CORONET
2339 feet
regular cast, plus Mrs Hudson: **Mdme d'Esterre**
Alexander Holder: **Henry Vibart** Mary: **Mollie Adair**
Arthur: **Laurence Anderson** Sir Geo Burnwell [sic]:
Jack Selfridge

THE NOBLE BACHELOR
2100 feet
regular cast, plus Lestrade: **Arthur Bell**
Mrs Hudson: **Mdme d'Esterre** St Simon: **Cyril Percival**
Hetty Doran: **Temple Bell** Doran: **Mr Arlton**
Miss Millar: **Middleton** [sic] Moulton: **Frederick Earle**

THE COPPER BEECHES
2191 feet
regular cast, plus Violet Hunter: **Madge White**
Rucastle: **Lyell Johnson** Mrs Rucastle: **Lottie Blackford**
Mr Toller: **F Raynham** Mrs Toller: **Eve McCarthy**
Japhat: **W J Elliot Junr** Ada Repson: **Madge White**
Miss Sloper: **C Nicholls**

'Really the resemblance to the figure of the imagination is uncanny': silent maestro Eille Norwood in **The Adventures of Sherlock Holmes** *(1921)*

THE EMPTY HOUSE
1801 feet
regular cast, plus Mrs Hudson: **Mdme d'Esterre** Inspector
Lestrade: **Arthur Bell** Ronald Adair: **Austin Fairman**
Mrs Adair: **J Gelardi** Sir Charles Ridge: **Cecil Kerr**

THE TIGER OF SAN PEDRO
adaptation [WISTERIA LODGE]
2080 feet
regular cast, plus Mrs Hudson: **Mdme d'Esterre** Inspector
Lestrade: **Arthur Bell** Scott Eccles: **George Harrington**
Murillo: **Louis Gilbert** Garcia: **Arthur Walcott**
Dolores: **Valia Venitshaya**

THE PRIORY SCHOOL
2100 feet
w **Charles Barnett**
regular cast, plus Mrs Hudson: **Mdme d'Esterre** Dr
Huxtable: **Leslie English** Duke of Holderness: **C H Croker-
King** Duchess of Holderness: **Irene Rooke** Lord Saltire:
Patrick Kay Wilder: **Cecil Kerr** Reuben Hayes: **Tom Ronald**
Dr Castulet: **Alien Learny**

THE SOLITARY CYCLIST
2139 feet
regular cast, plus Carruthers: **R D Sylvester**
Violet Relph: **Violet Hewitt** Woodley: **Allen Jeayes**

For many commentators, the story of Sherlock
Holmes on the screen proper begins with

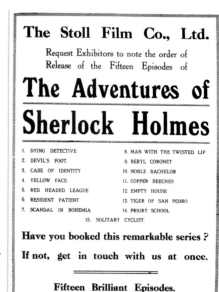

The Stoll Film Co., Ltd.

Request Exhibitors to note the order of
Release of the Fifteen Episodes of

The Adventures of
Sherlock Holmes

1. DYING DETECTIVE
2. DEVIL'S FOOT.
3. CASE OF IDENTITY
4. YELLOW FACE.
5. RED HEADED LEAGUE
6. RESIDENT PATIENT
7. SCANDAL IN BOHEMIA

8. MAN WITH THE TWISTED LIP
9. BERYL CORONET
10. NOBLE BACHELOR
11. COPPER BEECHES
12. EMPTY HOUSE
13. TIGER OF SAN PEDRO
14. PRIORY SCHOOL

15. SOLITARY CYCLIST.

Have you booked this remarkable series ?

If not, get in touch with us at once.

Fifteen Brilliant Episodes.

Stoll's full-page advertisement for the first series of Eille Norwood adventures, as printed in the Bioscope

Stoll Picture Productions was chaired by Sir Oswald Stoll, an Australian-born Irish entrepreneur-cum-theatrical impresario who'd gone from running provincial music halls to establishing one of the grandest West End stages at the London Coliseum, built in 1904. Following the Great War, and fearing the public's taste for music hall was on the wane, Stoll elected to get into moving pictures, which he considered the medium of the future. In 1919, he opened several cinemas and, more significantly, purchased a disused aircraft factory in Cricklewood, north-west London, turning it into what was then the largest film studio in Britain. The managing directors of Stoll's new enterprise, which would come to boast capital reserves of a staggering £400,000, were W S Gordon Michie and Jeffrey Bernerd; the latter would be intimately involved in the production of the Holmes pictures.

Stoll's series, known as *The Adventures of Sherlock Holmes*, comprised 15 Holmes adaptations, three taken from the most recent collection of stories, *His Last Bow*, first published in 1917. Bernerd hired Maurice Elvey (1887-1967) to direct. Today, Elvey is remembered as the most-credited British film director of all time, with over 300 features and shorts to his name. Born William Seward Folkard, Elvey began a brief career as a stage actor at 17 but soon graduated to become one of Britain's first 'name' film directors. His earliest features included a version of the crime shocker *Maria Marten* (1913), an adaptation of Robert Louis Stevenson's *The Suicide Club* (1914) and *The Life Story of David Lloyd George* (1918), a biography of the then-Prime Minister which was immediately suppressed and only rediscovered in 1996. For Stoll, Elvey had directed an English Civil War adventure, *The Tavern Knight*, in 1920 – in which Eille Norwood had appeared as a Cavalier lord.

Despite Stoll's resources and Elvey's abilities, *The Adventures of Sherlock Holmes* remains significant because of Norwood's obsessive determination that his Holmes should be true to the character created by Doyle. Like Elvey's, Norwood's was an assumed name; he had been born Anthony Edward Brett, taking 'Eille', bizarrely, from a girlfriend called Eileen, and 'Norwood' from the south London suburb where he lived. He'd made his stage début around 1884 but didn't rack up his first film appearance until 1911, in a period

actor Eille Norwood (1861-1948), who, between 1921 and 1923, played the Great Detective in 45 shorts and two features, a record number of appearances that stands to this day. Indeed, bearing in mind that ten of the Doyle stories had not yet been published by the time Norwood retired from the role, he came very close to featuring in an adaptation of every story in the canon as it then stood (leaving only A STUDY IN SCARLET, THE VALLEY OF FEAR and THE FIVE ORANGE PIPS). In that context, the Norwood films can be seen as a quite remarkable, and still unparalleled, achievement.

Prior to Norwood's first series of 15 shorts, the only 'authorised' Holmes adaptations had been the Éclair productions ... **From the Adventures of Sherlock Holmes** (1912), plus the two Samuelson pictures, **A Study in Scarlet** (1914) and **The Valley of Fear** (1916). It seems likely that Doyle was dissatisfied with the Éclair efforts, since it's claimed he bought the film rights back for ten times the amount he'd sold them for. The stories adapted by Samuelson were not included in any of the Norwood series, suggesting that rights in these were retained by Samuelson for some time. The next recipient of a licence to produce Sherlock Holmes films was Stoll Picture Productions Ltd in 1920, a company that had only been set up in 1919. Not that Doyle's faith in this industry newcomer was misplaced...

melodrama titled *Princess Clementina*; apparently, he also featured in Bert Haldane's 1915 screen version of Doyle's *Brigadier Gerard*.

The story goes that, when Elvey asked Norwood to do an impromptu screen test for Sherlock, the actor disappeared into a dressing room to apply his make-up and, 'within the space of a very few minutes', returned and 'astonished' Elvey: 'He had done very little in the way of make-up, and he had no accessories, but the transformation was remarkable – it *was* Sherlock Holmes who came in that door.' Make-up, in fact, was a particular passion of Norwood's. Another much-repeated anecdote has Jeffrey Bernerd attempting to have a 'common-looking' cabby removed from the set of *A Scandal in Bohemia*, completely unaware that the insalubrious 'cabby' was none other than Norwood wearing one of Holmes' many disguises. Bernerd's embarrassment was compounded by his earlier claim that Norwood would never be able to alter his stature and physique to the extent this particular disguise demanded. Norwood is also supposed to have 'contrived a new and original bald pate' that did not show the joins when applied to the crown.

But Norwood's greatest contribution was his sheer diligence: he re-read all the Holmes stories to date prior to beginning work, learned scratch violin-playing and would study *Strand* magazine artist Sidney Paget's Holmes illustrations for clues to costume and even posture. In a Baker Street scene in the Stoll version of *The Man With the Twisted Lip*, Norwood's Holmes draws his feet up to the edge of his seat, his knees up to his chest and his arms around his shins exactly as per a particular Paget depiction.

In a May 1921 edition of *Stoll's Editorial News* – a weekly for cinema-owners – Norwood recorded his own impression of Holmes: 'My idea of Holmes is that he is absolutely quiet. Nothing ruffles him, but he is a man who intuitively seizes on points without revealing that he has done so, and nurses them with complete inaction until the moment when he is called upon to exercise his wonderful detective powers. Then he is like a cat – the person he is after is the only person in all the world, and he is oblivious of everything else till his quarry is run to earth. The last thing in the world that he looks like is a detective. There is nothing of the hawk-eyed sleuth about him. His powers of

observation are but the servant of his powers of deduction, which enable him, as it were, to see round corners, and cause him, incidentally, to be constantly amused at the blindness of his faithful Watson, who is never able to understand his methods.'

The Adventures of Sherlock Holmes began shooting in November 1920; the photography was credited to Germain Burger, and the series would be edited by Leslie Britain. Elvey planned to film several exteriors on Baker Street itself, but found his progress hampered by crowds of onlookers. Nevertheless, most episodes enjoyed a substantial amount of location work, mostly in and around London's suburbia (a pawnshop in Westbourne Park figured in *The Red-headed League* and *The Yellow Face* called for the use of a house in leafy Chorleywood), but occasionally further afield (a coastal clifftop makes a striking backdrop early in the Cornish-set *The Devil's Foot*). For *The Man With the Twisted Lip*, actor Robert Vallis filmed scenes showing the bent-faced Hugh Boone begging for money at Piccadilly Circus, where he apparently 'collected fourpence from pitying people who saw him there'.

A semi-permanent Baker Street interior was constructed at Cricklewood under the supervision of art director Walter W Murton. Hubert Willis – who, circa 1904, had played 'John Forman' in a special one-off matinée performance of William Gillette's play *Sherlock Holmes*, performed in front of Gillette himself at London's Duke of York's Theatre – made a white-haired and slightly redundant Dr Watson. ('Mr Willis laudably resists the natural temptation to burlesque this character,' noted a contemporary reviewer.) Other actors to appear in more than one instalment were Arthur Bell as Inspector Lestrade and Mdme Catherine d'Esterre as a fussy, comic relief Mrs Hudson. (The character is credited simply 'Housekeeper' on the surviving print of *The Dying Detective*, but Hudson's name is used by Holmes in a later text caption – and spelled out in most of the *Stoll's Editorial News* listings, too.) Amusingly, Mrs Hudson's below-stairs speech patterns are rendered phonetically on the caption cards: she refers to 'one of them desprit [desperate] messenger boys' in *The Dying Detective*, for example.

By all accounts, Norwood's Holmes, first seen in early summer 1921, proved a huge hit with cinemagoers. In the UK, the *Bioscope* ran out of superlatives when reviewing *The Dying Detective*, *The Devil's Foot* and *The Yellow Face*: 'As popular attractions, *The Adventures of Sherlock Holmes* are, in our opinion, considerably the best things yet shown by Stoll. They represent a complete change from the conventional screen story, and technically ... are achievements of which any firm might be proud ... they should give full satisfaction to picturegoers of almost all classes.' Released by Alexander Film in the US early in 1922, Stoll's adaptations were no less rapturously received by Laurence Reid in *Motion Picture News*: 'Classics of literature, they automatically become classics of the silver-sheet ... The stories have been translated to the screen with remarkable fidelity ... A great deal of the success of the offerings is due to the remarkable impersonation of Holmes by Eille Norwood. Really the resemblance to the figure of the imagination is uncanny. It is much more genuine than William Gillette's characterisation.'

All the instalments bar *The Noble Bachelor* have survived as 'preservation material'; at the time of writing, however, only five are available to view (*The Dying Detective*, *The Devil's Foot*, *A Case of Identity*, *The Man With the Twisted Lip* and *The Beryl Coronet*). Watch-ing them, it's not hard to see why the films were so popular. The performances are vastly more understated than in, say, the Éclair series of just nine years previously. The narratives are full and detailed, employing some surprisingly sophisticated devices (flashbacks are frequently used), though it's difficult not to be amused by some of the more strained efforts to tell the tales without sound. Holmes' terribly eager note to himself re Culverton Smith's motives in *The Dying Detective* is a case in point, and his sworn threat to Smith in the same episode – 'As sure as my name is Sherlock Holmes, I'll get you yet!' – lacks a certain finesse.

It's true, too, that these films clearly date from a time before Eisenstein, when the grammar of filmmaking had not yet been fully developed; some shots and reverses of the eponymous 'Man With the Twisted Lip' are particularly difficult for the modern eye to make logical sense of. Nevertheless, Norwood's hawk-nosed, dangerous-looking Sherlock, a study of pent-up energy barely contained beneath a menacing widow's peak, has a real, formidable presence, and certain sequences

retain tremendous power despite their relative crudeness and age: the grotesque after-dinner tableau that Holmes and Watson stumble upon at the Tregennis household in *The Devil's Foot*, for instance, or Norwood/Holmes removing his opium addict's face in *The Man With the Twisted Lip*.

The series would continue in 1922, with **The Further Adventures of Sherlock Holmes**; before that, however, Elvey would mount a feature-length version of **The Hound of the Baskervilles** (1921). 1921 would also see Elvey cast Norwood and d'Esterre in another Stoll production written by William J Elliott: an adventure entitled *A Gentleman of France*. Norwood, however, missed out on the same year's other Stoll-produced Elvey/Elliott/d'Esterre picture, a romance called *Innocent* in which a young stage actor made his film début in the role of Amadis de Jocelyn. His name? Basil Rathbone.

The Adventures of Sherlock Holmes

aka **Sherlock Holmes** [GB]
US 1939 pastiche Twentieth Century-Fox Film Corporation 85m bw

w **Edwin Blum**, **William Drake** *source* **Sherlock Holmes** [play by **William Gillette**] *assoc p* **Gene Markey** *d* **Alfred Werker**

cast Sherlock Holmes: **Basil Rathbone** Dr Watson: **Nigel Bruce** Ann Brandon: **Ida Lupino** Jerrold Hunter: **Alan Marshal** Billy: **Terry Kilburn** Professor Moriarty: **George Zucco** Sir Ronald Ramsgate: **Henry Stephenson** Inspector Bristol: **E E Clive** Bassick: **Arthur Hohl** Mrs Jameson: **May Beatty** Lloyd Brandon: **Peter Willes** Mrs Hudson: **Mary Gordon** Justice: **Holmes Herbert** Mateo: **George Regas** Lady Conyngham: **Mary Forbes** Dawes: **Frank Dawson** stranger: **William Austin** Tony: **Anthony Kemble Cooper**

THE MYSTERY

1894: in a London courtroom, Professor Moriarty is acquitted of murder – despite a last-minute intervention on the part of Sherlock Holmes. Moriarty vows to 'break' Holmes before retiring from a life of crime, and later sends two letters... both of which end up being brought to Holmes by potential clients. The first is to Sir Ronald Ramsgate, Constable of the Tower of London, warning that a priceless emerald, the Star of Delhi, will never be delivered into his hands, as scheduled for the next weekend; Holmes promises to observe its handover. The second, depicting a man with an albatross around his neck, is sent to one Ann Brandon, who believes it to portend the death of her brother, Lloyd (her father had received an identical note exactly ten years before in South America – and he was killed on the same date specified, May 11th). Watson follows Ann's solicitor fiancé, Jerrold Hunter, to his office – where he sees him meeting with Moriarty. But by the time Watson catches up with Ann and Holmes, Lloyd has been found dead outside his home, strangled by unknown means...

THE INVESTIGATION

Studying the scene, Holmes concludes that Lloyd's assassin was club-footed. Meanwhile, Ann has been alarmed by a beggar playing an ancient Inca funeral dirge on a flute; she heard the same music the night her father died. Soon, Ann receives another 'albatross' picture; this time the date is May 13th and seems to be meant for her. That night, Ann is due at a garden party thrown by Lady Conyngham – where Holmes shadows her, sending Watson in his place to the Tower of London. There, disguised as policemen, Moriarty and his men seize the Star of Delhi, but drop it in their flight. Thinking the day saved, Watson goes

Holmes (Basil Rathbone) searches the Tower of London for the arch-criminal Professor Moriarty in **The Adventures of Sherlock Holmes** *(1939)*

A candid shot of Nigel Bruce (1895-1953), taken some ten years before he adopted his signature role as Dr Watson

to Lady Conyngham's – unaware that Moriarty has contrived to have himself locked in with the Crown Jewels...

THE SOLUTION

Holmes saves Ann from the whirling bolas of Mateo, the gaucho assassin sent after Ann – and discovers he was sent by 'the Professor'. Realising that Ann's case has been but a sideshow to distract him, and that the real crime has yet to be committed, Holmes races to the Tower to stop Moriarty from seizing the Crown Jewels. Holmes and Moriarty fight on the Tower's battlements, and the Professor falls to his doom. Safe, Holmes reveals that Jerrold was innocently entangled in Moriarty's web.

✦ ✦ ✦

After **Sir Arthur Conan Doyle's The Hound of the Baskervilles** (1939), the second of Twentieth Century-Fox's two Basil Rathbone/Nigel Bruce pictures is an altogether more brassy piece that revels in its own absurdities and still manages to convince – but only just.

Ostensibly drawn from the William Gillette play (see **Sherlock Holmes**, 1916), *The Adventures of Sherlock Holmes* retains next-to-nothing of the original: an intellectual duel between Holmes and Moriarty; the characters Billy and Bassick; plus, most tenuously, a subplot involving an attractive young woman with a suspect fiancé. What it *does* resemble, however, is **Conan Doyle's Master Detective Sherlock Holmes** (1932), an earlier in-name-only adaptation of the Gillette play that opens with Moriarty being tried for his many crimes and ends with his attempting to rob a seemingly impregnable fortress – the Faulkner bank in the first instance, the Tower of London for Fox. Screenwriters Edwin Blum and William Drake have clearly recalled THE SIGN OF THE FOUR, too – carbon-copying Tonga in the form of Mateo, another foreign assassin who uses a weapon unknown in the West and whose footprints are somehow distinctive.

For its first quarter-hour, *The Adventures of Sherlock Holmes* is simply wonderful. We open in a London courtroom – the Old Bailey, presumably, crowded full in a fashion unfamiliar to the other, cheaper, Rathbone pictures – where Moriarty is begrudgingly found not guilty of the murder of one 'Lorait', the police having simply been unable to prove their case. Holmes then barges in on proceedings, having worked out how the Professor actually did it. It's not revealed on screen, but a follow-on scene in the script would have seen Holmes demonstrating how Moriarty had, ingeniously, tampered with Greenwich Mean Time in order to furnish himself with an alibi for the slaying of Lorait. The detective was supposed to have been assisted in this by chief astronomer Dr Gates, as played by Ivan Simpson – and since Simpson is indeed seen chasing Holmes' entrance in the finished film, it's entirely probable that the scene was filmed and then cut to keep an already lengthy piece down.

Outside, Moriarty offers to share his cab with Holmes, giving rise to perhaps the single most memorable line unique to a century's worth of the celluloid detective's exploits: 'You've a magnificent brain, Moriarty. I admire it. I admire it so much I'd like to present it pickled in alcohol to the London Medical Society.' In turn, the Professor vows to finish Holmes by bringing off 'the crime of the century' right under his nose. They then go their separate ways, not to meet again until the film's final moments – an intriguing structural touch, but misguided, given the quality of their all-too-brief dialogue here.

Next, we follow Moriarty home – where, while plotting 'a crime that children will read about in history books!', he discovers that his butler, Dawes, has allowed one of his flowers to die: 'You've murdered a flower ... To think that for merely murdering a man I was incarcerated for six whole weeks in a filthy prison cell!' And so to Baker Street, where Holmes is plucking his violin for the benefit of bluebottles trapped in a brandy glass, hoping to observe 'the reaction on the common housefly of the chromatic scale': 'If I can find the note that annoys the housefly ... one need only play that note and all the houseflies disappear!'

So why doesn't the remainder of the film live up to this blackly funny, boldly painted, beautifully realised opening? While it has no shortage of highpoints – Watson pretending to be a corpse for Holmes' benefit, and being quizzed by a bemused passer-by; Ann Brandon shivering at the sound of the gaucho music ('There's death in every note of

it!'); Holmes, in vaudeville guise, performing 'Oh I Do Like To Be Beside the Seaside' – the central 'mystery' is at once dreary and (albeit purposefully) redundant, revolving entirely around the rather winsome Ann and her stiff fiancé, Jerrold.

The problem, perhaps, is that we know from Scene Three that the Ann plot is a tedious blind, concocted by Moriarty to distract Holmes from his attempt on the Crown Jewels – and so the revelation of the fact towards the end is no real revelation at all. The Professor's despatch is cursory and the wrap-up risible, leaving various story threads frayed and untidy – again, a result of script fiddling. The first of three possible endings had Holmes explaining how the vengeful Mateo believed that Ann's father had been responsible for the death of his own, and had stolen the mine that made the Brandons rich; meanwhile, Brandon family lawyer Jerrold's shifty behaviour had been caused by his desire to shield Ann from the truth about her dead father. None of this crucial background information is conveyed in the finished piece.

Moriarty was originally intended for Lionel Atwill, whose Dr Mortimer had made such a sinister red herring in **Sir Arthur Conan Doyle's The Hound of the Baskervilles**. Atwill would get his chance at the Professor, to fabulous effect, in **Sherlock Holmes and the Secret Weapon** three years later, but for now the role went to George Zucco (1886-1960), a Manchester-born actor who came to *The Adventures of Sherlock Holmes* fresh from appearing as the the the top-hatted, bespectacled villain 'the Stinger' in Paramount's *Arrest Bulldog Drummond* (1939). The most measured of crazies, Zucco's Moriarty makes a significant impression, enjoying another standout scene in which he dares the bullied Dawes to let slip a razor while shaving him: 'You're a coward, Dawes. If you weren't a coward you'd have cut my throat long ago...'

The Adventures of Sherlock Holmes began filming in June 1939; by July, there was talk of Fox releasing one Rathbone/Bruce Holmes and Watson film a year. It seems, however, that indifferent British reviews of the Fox **Hound**, coupled with the Doyle estate's reluctance to permit the studio to concoct all-new pastiches, put paid to any such plans. Of the *Adventures*, released on 1 September 1939 (two days ahead of an especially weighty announcement by British Prime Minister Neville Chamberlain), *New York Times* critic Frank S Nugent remarked,

The terrified Ann Brandon (Ida Lupino) flanked by Sherlock Holmes (Basil Rathbone) and Dr Watson (Nigel Bruce) in a lobby card for **The Adventures of Sherlock Holmes** (1939)

with unintentional foresight, 'Nothing dates Conan Doyle so terribly these days as the fact that his villainous Professor Moriarty persists in declaring war on Scotland Yard instead of just making it.' War would indeed impinge upon Holmes' world the next time Rathbone picked up his pipe, in **Sherlock Holmes and the Voice of Terror**.

The Adventures of Sherlock Holmes

GB 1984-5 13 x 50m approx TV series adaptations
Granada UK colour
developed for television by **John Hawkesworth** *p* **Michael Cox**
regular cast Sherlock Holmes: **Jeremy Brett**
Dr Watson: **David Burke**

A Scandal in Bohemia

tx 24 April 1984 ITV
w **Alexander Baron** *d* **Paul Annett**
regular cast, plus Irene Adler: **Gayle Hunnicutt** King of Bohemia: **Wolf Kahler** Godfrey Norton: **Michael Carter** John: **Max Faulkner** cabby: **Tim Pearce** Mrs Hudson:

Rosalie Williams Mrs Willard: **Tessa Worsley** clergyman: **Will Tacey** 1st loafer: **Tom Watt** 2nd loafer: **Paul Elsam** 1st big man: **David Bauckham** 2nd big man: **Edward York** 1st young man: **John Graham Davies** 1st burglar: **John Carr**

The Dancing Men

tx 1 May 1984 ITV
w **Anthony Skene** *d* **John Bruce**
regular cast, plus Hilton Cubitt: **Tenniel Evans** Elsie Cubitt: **Betsy Brantley** Inspector Martin: **David Ross** Abe Slaney: **Eugene Lipinski** Mrs King: **Lorraine Peters** Saunders: **Wendy Jane Walker** Walker: **Paul Jaynes** Dr Carthew: **Bernard Atha** cabbie: **Tommy Brierley**

The Naval Treaty

tx 8 May 1984 ITV
w **Jeremy Paul** *d* **Alan Grint**
regular cast, plus Percy Phelps: **David Gwillim** Joseph Harrison: **Gareth Thomas** Annie Harrison: **Alison Skilbeck** Lord Holdhurst: **Ronald Russell** Charles Gorot: **Nicholas Geake** Mrs Tangey: **Pamela Pitchford** Tangey: **John Malcolm** Inspector Forbes: **David Rodigan** Miss Tangey: **Eve Matheson** Mrs Hudson: **Rosalie Williams** Dr Ferrier: **John Taylor**

THE SOLITARY CYCLIST

tx 15 May 1984 ITV
w **Alan Plater** *d* **Paul Annett**
regular cast, plus Violet Smith: **Barbara Wilshere**
Carruthers: **John Castle** Woodley: **Michael Siberry**
Williamson: **Ellis Dale** Sarah Carruthers: **Sarah Aitchison**
Peter: **Simon Bleackley** Mrs Dixon: **Penny Gowling**
landlord: **Stafford Gordon** Mrs Hudson: **Rosalie Williams**

THE CROOKED MAN

tx 22 May 1984 ITV
w **Alfred Shaughnessy** *d* **Alan Grint**
regular cast, plus Henry Wood: **Norman Jones**
Nancy Barclay: **Lisa Daniely** James Barclay: **Denys
Hawthorne** Miss Morrison: **Fiona Shaw**
Major Murphy: **Paul Chapman** Jane: **Shelagh Stephenson**
young Henry Wood: **Michael Lumsden** young Nancy:
Catherine Rabett young Barclay: **James Wilby**
Mrs Fenning: **Maggie Holland** Private Bates:
Colin Campbell pianist: **David Graham Jones**

THE SPECKLED BAND

tx 29 May 1984 ITV
w **Jeremy Paul** *d* **John Bruce**
regular cast, plus Dr Grimesby Roylott: **Jeremy Kemp**
Helen Stoner: **Rosalyn Landor** Julia Stoner: **Denise
Armon** driver: **John Gill** Mrs Hudson: **Rosalie Williams**
Thorne: **Timothy Condren** Percy Armitage: **Stephen
Mallatratt**

THE BLUE CARBUNCLE

tx 5 June 1984 ITV
w **Paul Finney** *d* **David Carson**
regular cast, plus Inspector Bradstreet: **Brian Miller**
Mrs Hudson: **Rosalie Williams** the Countess of Morcar:
Rosalind Knight John Horner: **Desmond McNamara**
James Ryder: **Ken Campbell** Catherine Cusack: **Ros
Simmons** Henry Baker: **Frank Middlemass**
Windigate: **Don McCorkindale** Jennie Horner:
Amelda Brown Peterson: **Frank Mills** Breckenridge:
Eric Allan Mrs Oakshott: **Maggie Jones**

THE COPPER BEECHES

tx 25 August 1985 ITV
w **Bill Craig** *d* **Paul Annett**
regular cast, plus Jephro Rucastle: **Joss Ackland**
Violet Hunter: **Natasha Richardson** Mrs Rucastle: **Lottie
Ward** Miss Stoper: **Patience Collier** Mrs Toller: **Angela
Browne** Toller: **Peter Jonfield** Fowler: **Michael Loney**
Alice: **Rachel Ambler** Edward: **Stewart Shimberg**

THE GREEK INTERPRETER

tx 1 September 1985 ITV
w **Derek Marlowe** *d* **Alan Grint**
regular cast, plus Mycroft Holmes: **Charles Gray**
Mr Melas: **Alkis Kritikos** Wilson Kemp: **George Costigan**
Harold Latimer: **Nick Field** Paul Kratides: **Anton Alexander**
Sophy Kratides: **Victoria Harwood** Inspector Gregson:
Oliver Maguire Mrs Stern: **Rita Howard** ticket inspector:
Peter MacKriel

THE NORWOOD BUILDER

tx 8 September 1985 ITV
w **Richard Harris** *d* **Ken Grieve**
regular cast, plus Mrs Lexington: **Rosalie Crutchley** Lestrade:
Colin Jeavons John Hector McFarlane: **Matthew Solon** Jonas
Oldacre: **Jonathan Adams** Mrs McFarlane: **Helen Ryan**
Mrs Hudson: **Rosalie Williams** constable: **Andy Rashleigh**
tramp: **Anthony Langdon** seafaring tramp: **Ted Carroll**

*Jeremy Brett (Holmes) and David Burke (Watson) strike a classic
pose for Granada's* **The Adventures of Sherlock Holmes** *(1984-5)*

Cubitt housemaids Saunders (Wendy Jane Walker) and Mrs King (Lorraine Peters) are cross-questioned by Inspector Martin (David Ross), Sherlock Holmes (Jeremy Brett) and Dr Watson (David Burke) in **The Adventures of Sherlock Holmes**: The Dancing Men (1984)

THE RESIDENT PATIENT

tx 15 September 1985 ITV

w **Derek Marlowe** *d* **David Carson**

regular cast, plus Dr Percy Trevelyan: **Nicholas Clay**
Blessington: **Patrick Newell** Russian Count: **Tim Barlow**
Count's son: **Brett Forrest** Cartwright: **Charles Cork**
Inspector Lanner: **John Ringham** Mrs Hudson: **Rosalie
Williams** Fenton: **David Squire** detective: **Norman Mills**
Nora: **Lucy Anne Wilson** carpenter: **Dusty Young**

THE RED HEADED LEAGUE

tx 22 September 1985 ITV

w **John Hawkesworth** *d* **John Bruce**

regular cast, plus Jabez Wilson: **Roger Hammond**
John Clay: **Tim McInnerny** Duncan Ross: **Richard Wilson**
Sarasate: **Bruce Dukov** Mr Merryweather: **John Woodnutt**
Athelney Jones: **John Labanowski** doorman: **Reg Stewart**
accountant: **Ian Bleasdale** Archie: **Malcolm Weaver**
Professor Moriarty: **Eric Porter**

THE FINAL PROBLEM

tx 29 September 1985 ITV

w **John Hawkesworth** *d* **Alan Grint**

regular cast, plus Professor Moriarty: **Eric Porter** Mrs
Hudson: **Rosalie Williams** Director of the Louvre: **Olivier
Pierre** Minister of the Interior: **Claude Le Sache** the artist:

Michael Goldie American millionaire: **Robert Henderson**
young art expert: **Paul Sirr** porter at Victoria: **Jim Dunk**
Herr Steiler: **Paul Humpoletz** Swiss youth: **Simon Adams**

W here did *The Adventures of Sherlock Holmes*, unquestionably the most important series of Doyle adaptations yet produced for television, begin? With Sebastian Flyte's teddy bear, is as good an answer as any. The bear was central to *Brideshead Revisited* (1981), a no-expense-spared summoning-up of a lost 1930s idyll based on the novel by Evelyn Waugh and produced by Manchester's Granada Television for the independent ITV network. The critical and commercial success of *Brideshead*, shot entirely on film and with a budget of some £5 million, redefined the nature of British television production. Suddenly, it was possible – desirable, even – for the independent companies to indulge themselves in literary, languidly paced and lavishly mounted evocations of a mostly mythical English past, and yet still make a profit from overseas sales. Heritage TV was born.

British copyrights in Sherlock Holmes had expired in 1980, 50 years after Doyle's death. Noting this anniversary, and the fact that monies would no longer have to be paid to the Doyle estate, Granada producer Michael Cox had proposed making 'the definitive series, in colour, for a new generation of viewers'. The company had only just finished production of the Victorian police series *Cribb* (1979-81) – made, as was standard, on video in a multi-camera electronic studio, with a limited amount of location filming telecined in. Had it not been for *Brideshead*, and the willingness of Granada's managing director, David Plowright, to risk making more of its ilk, Cox's 'definitive' Holmes would merely have replicated the methods used in the production of the BBC series of 13 years before, **Sir Arthur Conan Doyle's Sherlock Holmes** (1968).

Brief consideration was given to the possibility of casting either of *Brideshead*'s young leads, Anthony Andrews and Jeremy Irons, as Holmes; when Cox demurred, Plowright suggested 'someone like Jeremy Brett'. Born Jeremy Huggins in 1933, Brett, a former National Theatre player, had most recently worked for Granada as the ill-fated Edward Ashburnham in a version of Ford Madox Ford's *The Good Soldier* (tx 15 April 1981). His previous television roles included Dorian Gray, Lord Byron and the cruel Maxim de Winter in a 1978 BBC serialisation of *Rebecca* (also featuring his first wife, Anna Massey, from whom he had long since separated). Reviewing the stories prior to accepting Granada's offer, Brett discerned something Puckish about Holmes: 'I remember I read: "He wriggled in his chair and roared with laughter." I had never thought of Holmes as laughing.'

Brett's Holmes would indeed owe a little to Shakespeare's 'Robin Goodfellow' – a 'shrewd and knavish sprite', an otherworldly mischief-maker who often carries out his business in disguise. (Holmes' revelling in the lordly King of Bohemia's discomfort in the first episode and his sneering at the avowedly provincial Hilton Cubitt in the second indicate the two extremes of this impish tendency: a good pixie in the former, a bad fairy in the latter.) He also had an actorly desire to do the stories right, to interpret the words of Doyle as he might the text of *King Lear*. Principally, however, Brett saw an opportunity to explore a richly detailed but little-understood character: 'He's chilling ... If I saw him walking down the street I'd say, "Poor soul ... What a tortured creature. He's not a happy man." Who *could* be happy who falls apart when he's not working or has to be drugged in order to go to sleep?' If, at this early stage, Brett

thought there was something of himself to be found in these darker recesses of Holmes' psyche, he wasn't letting on.

A legal dispute involving the backers of a sequence of rival TV movies caused a hiatus in production (see **Sir Arthur Conan Doyle's The Hound of the Baskervilles**, 1983), during which time the world in which the series would function was made solid by John Hawkesworth, a writer-producer who'd overseen the phenomenally successful Edwardian-set *Upstairs Downstairs* (1971-5). While Hawkesworth developed the 13 scripts that would comprise the first series (an unused 14th, Bill Craig's *The Reigate Squires*, was commissioned as a reserve), an extensive Baker Street exterior was being built on a former railway yard adjacent to the permanent set constructed for the soap opera *Coronation Street* (1960-). David Burke, with whom Cox had worked on a 1972 serial called *Holly*, was hired to play Watson, predetermined as being significantly younger than the television norm, a straight man to warm a sometimes cold and erratic Holmes – as in *The Crooked Man*, where he is physically pained by Holmes' bad-tempered outburst to the evasive Major Murphy, closing his eyes in shame while a purged Holmes adopts a beatific smile.

Jeremy Brett (Sherlock Holmes) and Eric Porter (Professor Moriarty) rehearse the fatal struggle at the Reichenbach Falls for **The Adventures of Sherlock Holmes:** *The Final Problem (1985)*

Jeremy Brett strikes a Sidney Paget pose in **The Adventures of Sherlock Holmes***: A Scandal in Bohemia (1984)*

The series would fetishise fidelity to both Doyle (key production staff were issued with a 77-page dossier of facts gleaned from the stories, ranging from a list of Holmes' pipes to an inventory of articles found inside 221B) and to artist Sidney Paget's *Strand* magazine illustrations. Viewers first glimpse Brett perched in a chair, knees drawn up to his chest, in a precise recreation of a particular Paget tableau, and not an episode goes by without some similar effort being made – efforts ostenta-tiously underlined by the Paget versions being reproduced on the caption cards beginning and ending the ad breaks. Such fastidiousness would not go unnoticed, and the series immediately established itself as a fan's dream.

It's interesting, therefore, that many of the series' finest moments come when the episodes read between the lines of the text – the standout scene in the first episode recorded, *The Solitary Cyclist*, being a case in point. Here, Holmes has a set-to in a Surrey pub with the repulsive Jack Woodley, his enquiries of whom have suggested that the latter is not considered a gentleman. Hearing this, Woodley launches himself at Holmes, bellowing: 'I'm as much a gentleman as you are.' Holmes picks himself up, removes his jacket, addresses the room – 'Everyone here will bear witness to the fact that I am acting in self-defence' – and puts his fists up, nimbly rocking back and forth, shuffling his toes, before delivering Woodley three sharp blows: 'Only a ruffian deals a blow with the back of the hand. A gentleman uses the straight – *left!* [whack] – and I, sir, am a gentleman!' Woodley is floored; Holmes steps forward, smug, and accepts applause. The 'delicious' encounter is only fleetingly reported in Doyle; its mechanics here are entirely invented, inviting us to view Holmes first as an effete, faintly ridiculous presence, to refute this idea immediately by virtue of his success, and then to depict him as a crowing triumphalist, reliving the moment back in 221B for Watson's benefit. In just one minor sequence, Peter Cushing's arch superman, John Neville's self-righteous physicality and Basil Rathbone's sharp superiority are fused into a fascinating whole.

A Scandal in Bohemia, the first episode broadcast, confidently improves on Doyle by having Gayle Hunnicutt's game Irene Adler (pronounced 'Ee-rain-er Ard-ler') throw her compromising picture of the King of Bohemia into the sea, giving the story the firm conclusion it otherwise lacks. Likewise, THE GREEK INTERPRETER undergoes a thoroughly modern makeover, turning Doyle's hapless damsel-in-distress Sophy Kratides into a woman with 'a cold heart and not a single shred of compassion', as illustrated in an entirely new finale in which Holmes, Watson and Mycroft Holmes apprehend the villains as they flee on the boat-train to the Continent. The corpulent, leathery Mycroft of Charles Gray (1928-2000), best known for his fey Blofeld in the James Bond film *Diamonds Are Forever* (1971), is but one of a number of outstanding guest turns, from Tenniel Evans' cringing Cubitt in *The Dancing Men* to Joss Ackland's predatory Rucastle in *The Copper Beeches*. Most remarkable of these, however, is the monstrous Professor Moriarty of Eric Porter (1928-95), famous for his brooding Soames in the BBC's *The Forsyte Saga* (1967).

It's well-known that the penultimate episode of the *Adventures, The Red Headed League* [sic], establishes that Moriarty is behind the attempted robbery of gold Napoleons from the City and Suburban Bank; knowledge of the fact tends to diminish the size of the revelation, which comes while Holmes and Watson await intruders in the vaults. 'This is much bolder and larger in conception than I first thought,' murmurs Holmes, perhaps commenting simultaneously on John Hawkesworth's fabulous adaptation. 'A mastermind has been at work...' Doyle's rather outré tale is transformed into a worrying prologue to THE FINAL PROBLEM, the lines twisted from the merely throwaway into the grimly portentous – especially when Holmes hears Sarasate play the afternoon before the attempt on the bank and Watson fears 'an evil time' might be coming. Granada's *Final Problem* has its own legend, principally concerning the jaw-dropping shots showing stuntmen Marc Boyle and Alf Joint plummeting 365 feet on cables before the torrential Reichenbach Falls, realised *in situ* in Switzerland. Hawkesworth's audacious script adds the theft of the Mona Lisa to the story – an aptly grand scheme to be foiled by Holmes and lead, with sickening inevitability, to the two antagonists' endgame in the Alps. The finale, in fact, is subtly telegraphed throughout all 12 preceding episodes: above the Baker Street mantel is not a mirror, as instructed by Doyle, but an etching of a Reichenbach-like cascade.

The Adventures of Sherlock Holmes is not perfect: *The Crooked Man*, for example, is distinctly anaemic, all rep-theatre lightning effects and no

Jeremy Brett, guest star Gayle Hunnicutt and David Burke promote the first episode of **The Adventures of Sherlock Holmes**: A Scandal in Bohemia *(1984)*

Maestro!
Jeremy Brett in
**The Adventures
of Sherlock
Holmes**: The
Resident Patient
(1984)

mystery whatsoever, and Holmes' already-bizarre NAVAL TREATY soliloquy – 'What a lovely thing a rose is!' – is grandly, soullessly reproduced near-verbatim in the TV version, without any consideration being given to the possibility that it's merely a peculiar metaphysical non-sequitur that would be better cut. It's a misnomer, too, to describe the series as a staggering success: of the first lump of seven episodes, broadcast in 1984, only *The Blue Carbuncle* rose above eight million viewers; of the final six, shown in 1985, *The Copper Beeches'* encouraging opening score of 11.23 million plunged to just 7.22 for the next week's *Greek Interpreter*, only recovering by a million or so for the remainder. **The Return of Sherlock Holmes** (1986-8) was not, therefore, guaranteed. If it had not appeared, viewers might have been left with the despairing endnote of *The Final Problem* – not the detective's demise in the Falls, but an entirely unexpected and typically bold flourish in which David Burke's Watson turns from his writing-desk to the camera and addresses the first and last lines of Doyle's story direct to the audience: 'It is with a heavy heart that I take up my pen...' Non-naturalistic it may be, but like all the episodes of the *Adventures*, the ending has a bigger truth about it; more real, perhaps, than Doyle's words can ever be.

Alfred Hitchcock Presents: My Dear Watson

*US 1988 TV pastiche AHF Film Productions Inc
30m colour
tx 22 April 1989*
w **Susan Woollen** *p* **Mary Kahn** *d* **Jorge Montesi**
cast Mycroft: **Graeme Campbell** Sherlock Holmes: **Brian Bedford** Dr Watson: **Patrick Monckton** Lestrade/Moriarty: **John Colicos** Grimes: **Robert Nicholson** Mrs Hudson: **Bunty Webb** Liz: **Lori Lansens** himself: **Alfred Hitchcock***

THE MYSTERY

London, 1895: returning to Baker Street some years after his near-fatal encounter with arch-enemy Professor Moriarty at the Reichenbach Falls, Sherlock Holmes re-encounters Dr Watson and Inspector Lestrade, who has just been released from a sanatorium near Reading; the hapless policeman has suffered from the stress of the 'public humiliation' he encountered following the release of Watson's accounts of Holmes' exploits. That night, Watson is kidnapped by a bogus coachman...

THE INVESTIGATION

The kidnapper, a 'Mr Warder', sends a note

requesting an assignation in Whitechapel. There, Lestrade – delighted to be of some use – is told by a streetwalker that 'Warder' wants all of Holmes' criminal files delivered the next evening. Together with his brother Mycroft, Holmes works through the night forging a set of false files – but when Mycroft makes the East End rendezvous, he is killed...

THE SOLUTION

The killer is tracked down, but he too has been murdered. However, the impression of a Beefeater's regimental ring leads Holmes and Lestrade to a series of gas-filled tidal tunnels beneath the Tower of London, where Watson is found. 'Lestrade' then reveals himself to be none other than the still-very-much-alive Moriarty, delighted to have successfully foxed Holmes again. Holmes is unimpressed; he has been going along with the ruse from the outset, and the sham-dead Mycroft waits with the police above. Moriarty and Holmes duel with swordsticks, and the Professor is wounded. Holmes and Watson make their escape – but the Napoleon of Crime refuses to lie down...

✦ ✦ ✦

A 1980s revival of the near-legendary late fifties/early sixties anthology series, the 'new' *Alfred Hitchcock Presents*, made by Paragon Motion Pictures Inc in association with Michael Roberts Productions, used garishly colourised archive clips of the long-dead director's to-camera introductions to set the scene for all-new suspense tales – albeit with only a fraction of the black wit and menace of the originals. *My Dear Watson* was among the last episodes in the fourth and final series.

Plodding and predictable, the sheer pointlessness of *My Dear Watson* might have been a virtue in a play with parodic intent. Some of the ideas buried within Susan Woollen's slender teleplay are intriguing enough, principally the suggestion that the put-upon Inspector Lestrade might have suffered a breakdown brought about by the embarrassment of being outwitted by Holmes at every turn. Unfortunately, the possibility that an insane and lusting-for-glory Lestrade might be the villain responsible for Watson's incarceration is only tacitly invoked, if at all, and it is Professor Moriarty's unveiling which makes up the underwhelming conclusion instead. Like so many pastiches, the play appears to be founded on the delusion that, like

comic strip sidekicks, both Lestrade and Moriarty made frequent appearances in the Holmes canon.

Although bookended with moderately amusing moments of parody (an irritated Mrs Hudson complaining that Holmes has listened to her climbing the stairs to announce the arrival of an individual whose identity he has already deduced, for example), such diversions are sidelined in favour of an entirely po-faced and resolutely unamusing presentation. And despite the fact that the actors' English accents are beyond reproach, transatlantic phrasing still works its way in. Brian Bedford's long-haired Holmes asks a cabby to take him to 'two twenty-one' Baker Street, for example.

Given the *Alfred Hitchcock Presents* format, there's absolutely no reason why *My Dear Watson* should not have revelled in iconoclasm, but even its principal 'shock' moment – the killing of Mycroft – is later exposed as a silly and altogether purposeless scam. Which serves well enough as an epitaph for the play as a whole.

Arsène Lupin contra Sherlock Holmes

tr 'Arsène Lupin versus Sherlock Holmes'
Germany 1910-11 5 x film series pastiche Vitascope GmbH silent bw
d Viggo Larsen
known cast Arsène Lupin: **Paul Otto**
Sherlock Holmes: **Viggo Larsen**

[1] DER ALTE SEKRETÄR
tr 'The old secretaire'
aka **Arsene Lupin** [GB]
1115 feet

An old gentleman decides to purchase an antique secretaire from a dealer – but soon after is approached by a mysterious stranger who wants the item for himself. The buyer refuses to sell, and the secretaire is duly delivered to the old man's home. Inside, he finds a note ordering him to send the desk back within two days, or 'something will happen'; it is signed 'Arsène Lupin'. Two days later, the buyer's daughter goes missing – and the man receives another note, telling him that the girl is well but will remain so only if the secretaire is sent back. The old man summons Sherlock

Holmes and his 'friend' – who, disguised, seek out Lupin in a restaurant. Lupin, however, recognises the pair and cuts the restaurant's telephone wires as he makes his escape, so Holmes is unable to call the police. In the street, Holmes sees an old, bearded man trip, and helps him home – only to find himself the prisoner of Lupin, as much a master of disguise as Holmes himself. The detective is rescued when his friend climbs over the roof of the house to free him. Meanwhile, the kidnapped girl is being driven by car down to the river, where a boat is waiting. But Holmes arrives in another car, accompanied by the police, to intercept both Lupin and the girl. After 'a fusillade of revolver shots', Holmes 'dashes in the river after Lupin'; the girl is returned to her waiting father, who congratulates Holmes on his 'wonderful detective powers'.

[2] DER BLAUE DIAMANT
tr 'The blue diamond'
1411 feet
[synopsis unavailable]

[3] DIE FALSCHEN REMBRANDTS
tr 'The fake Rembrandts'
aka **The Two Rembrandts** [GB]
968 feet

A treacherous doorkeeper helps Arsène Lupin break into a wealthy man's house at night and steal two Rembrandt paintings, substituting good forgeries in their place – but the doorkeeper's daughter hears the deed being done and fires her gun at Lupin, causing his arm to be broken. She hides the wounded Lupin in the cellar of her father's house. Sherlock Holmes is summoned to view the scene of the presumed aborted robbery – and declares the Rembrandts to be false. He questions both the doorkeeper and his daughter, afterwards following the girl and eavesdropping as Lupin gives her his instructions. Holmes writes a note to the chief of police, telling him to meet him at the house in 24 hours' time, when he will reveal the thief – but Holmes is captured by Lupin's accomplices and tied up in the cellar for a day. Meanwhile, Lupin has disguised himself as Holmes and is about to receive the chief of police, telling him that he, 'Holmes', has failed – but, after a fight, Holmes has overpowered his captors and arrives on the scene just in time to reveal the

disguised Lupin's true identity. Smiling, Lupin allows himself to be arrested.

[4] DIE FLUCHT
tr 'The escape'
[synopsis unavailable]

[5] ARSÈNE LUPINS ENDE
at **Arsène Lupins Tod**
tr 'The end/death of Arsène Lupin'
aka **The End of Arsene Lupin** [GB]
902 feet

Stealing in through Sherlock Holmes' window, the vengeful Arsène Lupin attempts to shoot his detective nemesis; they struggle, Lupin escapes, and Holmes resolves to take a holiday. Switching places with a cab driver, the disguised Lupin then attempts to ensnare Holmes *en route*, but Holmes, realising what has happened, leaps out of the cab and takes another, disappearing into an opium den. When Lupin arrives, the den's proprietor, 'The Celestial', refuses to tell him where Holmes has gone. Knocking him senseless, Lupin has an assistant show him the window through which Holmes made his exit. He follows Holmes to a train and by nightfall is standing on the balcony outside the room where Holmes is staying. Lupin 'slips into the room, and is raising his pistol to fire when the detective springs on him. Backwards and forwards they sway in a death struggle, and slowly Holmes forces his enemy back. Then the detective raises Lupin high above his head, and sends him crashing down to the ground beneath.'

✦ ✦ ✦

In 1909, following production of **Den Grå Dame**, Viggo Larsen, the writer/director/actor behind almost every aspect of the Nordisk Films Holmes series beginning with **Sherlock Holmes i Livsfare**, turned his back on the Danish film industry and moved to Berlin.

German readers were no strangers to Holmes, and translations of various of the stories were readily available: *Späte rache* (A STUDY IN SCARLET) and *Das Zeichen der Vier* (THE SIGN OF THE FOUR) had actually been issued by the Stuttgart-based publisher Robert Lutz as early as 1894. Indeed, the public was so keen on Holmes that Lutz would go on to release a magazine series comprising 230 new, anonymously written Holmes stories between 1907 and 1911, with titles ranging from the ridiculous to the ridiculous: *Der Vampir von London, Der Mord im Harem, Admiral Nelson als Detektiv*.

Germany had also become the principal foreign market for Nordisk's film exports – indeed, the company would soon find itself making several pictures specifically tailored to Teutonic tastes – and demand for new product was exceptionally high, due in no small part to the activities of a Berlin-based kinematograph entrepreneur named Jules Greenbaum (1867-1924). Greenbaum (born Julius Grünbaum) had seen the potential of the new Bioscope equipment while living briefly in Chicago – and, over a ten-year period, had gone from importing cameras and projectors to becoming both a major manufacturer of moving-picture machinery and a cinema owner. Seeking to expand his empire by initiating a programme of commercial feature film production, Greenbaum duly hired experienced hands – including Larsen, whose 'Detektivfilms' had proved hugely successful in Greenbaum's homeland.

The first production to be released under the banner of Greenbaum's Vitascope GmbH, filmed in a state-of-the-art studio in the Markgrafenstraße, was a new five-part Holmes adventure directed by and starring Larsen. This would not pit Sherlock against gentleman thief Raffles, in the manner of the first two Nordisk releases; this time the Great Detective would face Raffles' closest Gallic counterpart – Arsène Lupin, the invention of author Maurice Leblanc (1864-1941). As before, the production was authorised by neither of the characters' creators. But unlike before, the characters' meeting was not a total flight of fancy on Larsen's part, Leblanc himself having already brought Lupin and Holmes together in print.

The Arsène Lupin stories first appeared in 1905 in the pages of the French magazine *Je sais tout*, and Maurice Leblanc's rogue *cambrioleur* – more errant knight than knight errant – went on to achieve massive popularity in France and most of Europe. A friend suggested to Leblanc that Lupin and Holmes ought to cross swords in a future tale and, despite Conan Doyle's refusal to grant Leblanc his blessing, meet they would, albeit with the detective wearing the absurdly thin disguise of 'Herlock Sholmes' ('Holmlock Shears' in the earliest English translations).

A German ad block, circa 1911, advertising screenings of both Nordisk's **Million-testamentet** *and, further down the bill,* Die Flucht – *the fourth episode of* **Arsène Lupin contra Sherlock Holmes**

The young Lupin and Sholmes had their first encounter in *Herlock Sholmes arrive trop tard* ('Herlock Sholmes arrives too late'), published in 1906 and collected a year later in the book *Arsène Lupin, Gentleman Cambrioleur* ('Arsène Lupin, gentleman burglar'). Sholmes' associate 'Dr Wilson' was introduced in two further tales, *La Dame blonde* ('The blonde woman') and *La Lampe Juive* ('The Jewish lamp'), both anthologised in the 1908 volume *Arsène Lupin contre Herlock Sholmes* ('Arsène Lupin versus Herlock Sholmes'). A nine-part serial, *L'Aiguille creuse* ('The hollow needle', later published as a novel), concluded with Sholmes accidentally shooting dead Lupin's second wife, Raymonde de Saint-Veran. Sholmes would also be mentioned in the next Lupin epic, titled simply *813*.

Unlike Leblanc, Larsen, cavalier as ever regarding copyright, evidently saw no reason to Spoonerise Holmes' name – his filmic Lupin/Holmes confrontation was boldly entitled *Arsène Lupin contra Sherlock Holmes*. The first episode, released in August 1910, detailed Lupin's desperate efforts to secure an antique writing-desk, although the precise reason why the thief needs to stoop to kidnapping in order to secure the item goes unrecorded. Clearly set in a contemporary milieu, the plot took in telephones, cars and gunplay. Frustratingly, the synopsis published in the *Bioscope* on 1 September 1910, shortly before this first episode's British release, does not actually identify the 'friend' who clambers over rooftops to rescue Holmes from Lupin's clutches as Dr Watson – or, indeed, 'Wilson'.

No storyline is known to have survived detailing the events of episode two (likewise the fourth instalment) – but the detective did not appear to have had a comrade-in-arms by the time of episode three, released in England on 8 January 1911. This time round, Holmes was forced to rely on his own physical resources, according to the breathless account of his escape from Lupin's allies published in the *Bioscope*: 'Holmes lowers his head and butts [one of Lupin's men] in the chest. Then securing his opponent's knife between his teeth, Holmes cuts his hands free, and grasping the other's pistol, compels him to throw down his weapons...' Having presumably escaped from the clutches of the police in episode four, Lupin would swear to kill the detective at the time of their next meeting. But, following one final episode's worth of extended chase, clearly with shades of THE FINAL PROBLEM, it was the slippery Lupin who suffered a terminal fall in the closing reel of the fifth part, set before British picturegoers from 22 April 1911.

So successful had the series been that a second Viggo Larsen/Vitascope opus, **Sherlock Holmes contra Professor Moryarty**, was in preparation even as Arsène Lupin met his *Ende*. Paul Otto (1878-1943), who had played Lupin throughout, would enjoy a lengthy film career – writing, directing and starring as a vengeful Tibetan prince in *Der Tod und die Liebe* ('Death and Love', 1921), in addition to straightforward acting duties on pictures including *Rasputin, Dämon der Frauen* (1930: *Rasputin, Demon With Women* in the US).

Lupin, too, would enjoy a lengthy film career. Georges Tréville (possibly Holmes in the 1912 Éclair series detailed under **... From the Adventures of Sherlock Holmes**) took the lead in the earliest Lupin picture proper, *Arsène Lupin*, written and directed by Émile Chautard. Many more would follow in later years, with actors like John Barrymore, Melvyn Douglas, Robert Lamoureux and Jean-Claude Brialy playing the burglar-hero. Lupin would tangle with Sherlock Holmes again: in 1945, in the Italian *Arsenio Lupin*, starring actor/producer Ramón Pereda as Lupin and featuring José Baviera as Holmes; and in a little-seen Japanese animation of the early 1980s, *Lupin vs Holmes*. This was the second of several cartoons detailing the adventures of the master thief, took in the slaying of one Baron Autrech, the theft of a blue diamond and a confrontation between Lupin and Holmes on a sinking boat (the latter a scene taken from *La Lampe Juive*).

Herlock Sholmes would also reappear, in various instalments of several French television series. Henri Virlojeux featured occasionally as the detective in *Arsène Lupin* (1971-74), 26 hour-long instalments starring George Descrières. The Sholmes episodes were: *Arsène Lupin contre Herlock Sholmes: Le Diamant bleu* ('Arsène Lupin versus Herlock Sholmes: the blue diamond', tx 1 April 1971); *Herlock Sholmes lance un défi* ('Herlock Sholmes sets a challenge', tx 18 December 1973); *Le Secret de l'aiguille* ('The secret of the needle', tx 25 December 1973); and *L'Homme au chapeau noir* ('The man in a black hat', tx 27 December 1973).

More than 20 years later, Sholmes returned, this time played by Joseph Sartchadjiev, in one of eight 90-minute TV films under the title *Les nouveaux exploits d'Arsène Lupin* ('The new adventures of Arsène Lupin'): *Herlock Sholmes s'en mêle* ('Herlock Sholmes meddles', tx 9 December 1995) was an original story by Jacques Avanac, Albert Kantof and Philippe Delannoy. The next year brought Sholmes' final appearance to date, this time in a children's animated series, *Les Exploits d'Arsène Lupin* ('The adventures of Arsène Lupin'), aka *Nighthood*. The first episode went under the title *Élémentaire, mon cher Lupin*, which the reader can translate for himself.

The Baker Street Boys

GB 1983 8 x 25-30m TV series pastiches
BBC Television colour
p **Paul Stone**
regular cast Wiggins: **Jay Simpson** Beaver: **Damion Napier**
Shiner: **Adam Woodyatt** Sparrow: **David Garlick**
Queenie: **Debbie Norris** Rosie: **Suzi Ross**

THE ADVENTURE OF THE DISAPPEARING DISPATCH CASE

2 episodes tx 8, 11 March 1983 BBC1
w **Anthony Read** *d* **Marilyn Fox**
regular cast, plus Sherlock Holmes: **Roger Ostime**
Sir Alfred Connyngham: **Barrie Cookson** Orlov: **Cyril Shaps**
Bukovsky: **Michael Poole** Dr Watson: **Hubert Rees** [1]
Merriman: **Eric Francis** [1] PC Boot: **Ray Burdis** [1]
Bert: **Roger Avon** [1] Stanley: **Lee Chappell** [1]
Freddie Connyngham: **Paul Critchley** [2]
butler: **William Lawford** [2] railwayman: **Gordon Salkild** [2]
footman: **Paul Gale** [2]

The 'Baker Street Boys' – Wiggins, Beaver, Shiner, Sparrow, Queenie and Rosie – are Sherlock Holmes' 'Irregulars', a gang of mostly orphaned children who carry out occasional street-level investigations for the Great Detective. When Sir Alfred Connyngham is attacked in the street by a 'red-bearded brute', the Boys give chase – only to find the assailant has apparently disappeared into thin air. Sir Alfred's dispatch case, containing vital diplomatic documents, is missing; the Boys soon conclude that it was seized by an accomplice disguised as an old woman. The conspirators are Bukovsky and Orlov, a master illusionist-turned-anarchist revolutionary. They are plotting to trace the secret movements of the Archduke Alexander, a visiting foreign dignitary – and blow up the train carrying him on his way to sign a peace treaty. The Boys race to Canterstone Mills station to avert the assassination and so prevent war breaking out in Europe.

THE GHOST OF JULIAN MIDWINTER

2 episodes tx 15, 18 March 1983 BBC2/BBC1
w **Richard Carpenter** *d* **Michael Kerrigan**
regular cast, plus Dr Watson: **Hubert Rees** Inspector
Lestrade: **Stanley Lebor** Hopkins: **Iain Ormsby-Knox**
Julian Midwinter: **Robert Swann** Charley Telfer: **Andrew
McCulloch** Sherlock Holmes: **Roger Ostime** [1]
Mrs Hudson: **Pat Keen** [1] Stanley: **Lee Chappell** [1]
Stanley Fluff: **Michael Ripper** [2]

Accused of the murder of playboy gambler Julian Midwinter, underworld debt collector Charley Telfer is on the run from Inspector Lestrade. Telfer maintains that all he did was find Midwinter's body in his library, and the Boys agree to investigate on his behalf. They break into Midwinter's Hampstead home, where Rosie sees what she believes to be Midwinter's ghost. However, shell-shocked Light Brigade veteran Stanley Fluff testifies to recent changes in the habits of Julian's reclusive cello-playing brother, Jasper – leading the Boys to the conclusion that Julian killed Jasper and stole his identity.

Artful dodgers Shiner (Adam Woodyatt), Beaver (Damion Napier) and Wiggins (Jay Simpson) in **The Baker Street Boys** *(1983)*

A Mountford Museum attendant (Sidney Livingstone) surrounded by all but one of the Irregulars – Shiner (Adam Woodyatt), Queenie (Debbie Norris), Beaver (Damion Napier), Sparrow (David Garlick) and Rosie (Suzi Ross) – in **The Baker Street Boys**: The Adventure of the Winged Scarab (1983)

THE ADVENTURE OF THE WINGED SCARAB

2 episodes tx 22, 25 March 1983 BBC1
w Richard Carpenter d Marilyn Fox
regular cast, plus Dr Watson: **Hubert Rees** Professor
Moriarty: **Colin Jeavons** Colonel Moran: **Michael Godley**
Professor Flanders: **Michael Burrell** Sherlock Holmes:
Roger Ostime museum attendant: **Sidney Livingstone** [1]
Mrs Hudson: **Pat Keen** [1] German Professor: **Alan
Downer** [1] Stanley: **Lee Chappell** [1] Inspector Lestrade:
Stanley Lebor [2] Hopkins: **Iain Ormsby-Knox** [2]

Sherlock Holmes has Wiggins deliver a message to Professor Flanders at the Egyptian Gallery of the Mountford Museum: Holmes' arch-rival Professor Moriarty is planning to steal the priceless, jewel-encrusted Winged Scarab of Amenhotep I, as discovered by Flanders one year previously. At the Museum, a visitor is pushed downstairs by two mystery attackers and killed; Wiggins and Beaver find cracked plaster pieces beside the body. Meanwhile, Moriarty calls on Dr Watson at 221B. Queenie and Rosie eavesdrop as Moriarty tells Watson that he has kidnapped Holmes, and he intends to steal the Scarab – and if the police learn that Holmes is missing before Moriarty is safely in Switzerland with the precious artefact, Holmes will die. Refusing to believe that Moriarty won't kill Holmes regardless, Wiggins plots to steal the Scarab before the Professor, exchanging it for the detective's safe return. Shiner's theft of the Scarab is successful, and the swap duly takes place – but the Professor later throws the Scarab in a river. Meanwhile, Inspector Lestrade, believing the Boys to have been bribed by Moriarty to act as accomplices, has Wiggins arrested for the theft – but soon the rest of the gang recall the cracked plaster pieces, realising that they form a mould for the Scarab. The Boys confront Flanders, who reveals the plot he has fallen into: the Scarab was a fake, made by the man 'silenced' by Moriarty and his accomplice Colonel Moran at the Museum. Posing as the American millionaire who owns the 'priceless' Scarab, Moriarty had hoped to claim £50,000 insurance on the worthless piece.

THE CASE OF THE CAPTIVE CLAIRVOYANT

2 episodes tx 29 March, 1 April 1983 BBC1
w Anthony Read d Michael Kerrigan
regular cast, plus Marvin: **Ed Bishop** Mary: **Siobhan
O'Carroll** Sam Trump: **Don Henderson** T J O'Neill: **Blain
Fairman** Bert: **Roger Avon** Mme Pompadour: **Christine**

Ozanne Gorgeous Gertie: **Jean Selfe** Signor Maccarelli: **Mario McCarthy** Horace – a villain: **Ron Flanagan** Sherlock Holmes: **Roger Ostime** [2] Dr Watson: **Hubert Rees** [2] Inspector Lestrade: **Stanley Lebor** [2] Hopkins: **Iain Ormsby-Knox** [2] Mrs Hudson: **Pat Keen** [2]

While working at Trump's Music Hall, Sparrow attempts to help the unhappy Mary Ashley, who makes up half of a popular mind-reading act with her stepfather, the cruel Marvin. They have only recently left their home in New York, and Marvin has offered Mary no explanation for their sudden emigration. 'Not even Sherlock Holmes can help me,' Mary tells Sparrow – and, together with the Boys, they hatch a plan to manage Mary's 'disappearance'. In a bid to learn more about Mary's business, Queenie contrives to stand in for Mary at the next performance – during which Marvin is horrified to receive a piece of paper bearing a spot of blood. After the show, Marvin is stabbed and Queenie kidnapped. Pinkerton's detective T J O'Neill helps the Boys solve the riddle: unknowingly, Mary carries a locket containing a stolen ticket for a safety deposit box which holds a hoard of gangster's loot – so the 'Iron Fist' gang, desperate to retrieve the ticket, put a price on ex-member Marvin's head. Queenie escapes the clutches of the villainous Horace and his mystery, rasping boss. Meanwhile, Wiggins helps out with Mary's farewell performance, which is designed to draw the murderers into the open: the boss is Sam Trump himself, whose attempted escape from the police on a flying trapeze is foiled by a very distinguished member of the audience – Sherlock Holmes.

✦   ✦   ✦

This twice-weekly children's series chronicled the further adventures of the 'Baker Street Irregulars', the gang of street urchins and ragamuffins employed as freelance scouts by Doyle's Holmes in A STUDY IN SCARLET, THE SIGN OF THE FOUR and THE CROOKED MAN (referred to as Holmes' 'Baker Street boys' in the latter). Shot on video with occasional film inserts, *The Baker Street Boys* was produced by the BBC in association with Lella Productions and Talbot Television.

The format was devised by Anthony Read, formerly one of the two script editors on the BBC's highly acclaimed 1965 **Sherlock Holmes** series

starring Douglas Wilmer, for which he'd adapted THE RED-HEADED LEAGUE. Also associated with its 1968 follow-up, the Peter Cushing-headlining **Sir Arthur Conan Doyle's Sherlock Holmes**, Read would go on to work on *Doctor Who* and *Hammer House of Horror*, among others. *The Baker Street Boys* was, he says, 'a concept I'd had for ages … I'd had this thought at the back of my mind about what happened with the Irregulars – it could run alongside or whatever. What happened when Sherlock Holmes wasn't around? The mysteries were solved by the boys. It just seemed a smashing idea, and happily I managed to get it away.'

The series came about when Read was approached by independent producer Paul Knight, later to oversee fire-fighting soap *London's Burning*. At the time, London Weekend Television was soliciting formats from independents for 'a new series for Saturday night along the lines of [adult crime show] *The Professionals*'. 'I'd written the first episode of *The Professionals*, and Paul came to me and said, "Let's get together and talk about this." I came up with a few ideas, but they were a bit young for London Weekend and not really their cup of tea.

'Paul said that as an independent producer he was trying to set up a separate serial as well, and did I have any ideas with an international kind of name to hang it on? I said, "Yeah, I've got one." It had to involve children, check, and it had to be period – check! I said, "Yes, it's got all of that," and explained the idea for *The Baker Street Boys*. He said, "Well well well, fantastic. Let's do it!" He ran off and found the money. The idea originally was to make it as a fully independent production and a long-running show, but when they looked around, London Weekend wasn't in the market for family programmes. They then took it to the BBC, who decided to make it in-house with BBC Children's [department]. I was disappointed by that decision because it would lose out, and I think in the end it did in many ways. It didn't have the extra polish that you needed. It had the stamp of children's series on it, whereas I thought of it as 'family'. That was a big part of my object...'

Read penned two of the four two-part *Baker Street Boys* adventures himself, with *Catweazle* and *Robin of Sherwood* creator Richard Carpenter responsible for the remainder. Sherlock Holmes makes only fleeting, briefly glimpsed appearances throughout, camera shots being carefully positioned to avoid showing his face. Although almost always indisposed (in disguise and hunting for Professor Moriarty, for example, or even confined to bed with flu – the foggy mists of the Grimpen Mire, as visited in THE HOUND OF THE BASKERVILLES, being said to have undermined his constitution), he does leave occasional words of advice for the gang. Dr Watson, Mrs Hudson and a particularly bungling Inspector Lestrade are more often seen, the latter accompanied by a junior, Hopkins.

As per the Doyle canon, the Boys have a spokesman/leader in the eldest member, Wiggins (here given the first name Arnold), who idolises Holmes. (Amusingly, it's hinted that Wiggins and Holmes' pageboy, Stanley, have a jealous loathing of one another.) The other members of the gang, all aptly named, are bookish proto-Watson Beaver, shoeshine boy Shiner, stage-struck Sparrow – plus,

A **Baker Street Boys** photo opportunity outside the Sherlock Holmes pub, London: Hubert Rees (Dr Watson, centre) and juvenile co-stars (clockwise from left) Suzi Ross, Adam Woodyatt, Jay Simpson, Damion Napier, David Garlick and Debbie Norris

oddly enough, two girls, mumsy Queenie and flower-seller Rosie. All the Boys, who live together in a cellar hideout-cum-headquarters, wear a shilling hung round their necks as a badge. The six young leads are all pretty effective, despite their stage-school cock-er-nee accents grating from time to time; lines like 'I've 'ad enuff of this blinkin' fog!' don't help. Adam Woodyatt, who played Shiner, would go on to portray chip-shop mogul Ian Beale in the long-running BBC soap opera *EastEnders*.

The Boys' escapades, ranging from uncovering anarchist assassination plots to attempting to rescue the kidnapped Sherlock, bring them into conflict with a number of nefarious no-goods – including, in *The Adventure of the Winged Scarab*, a rat-faced Professor Moriarty played by Colin Jeavons, later cast as Inspector Lestrade opposite Jeremy Brett's Sherlock in several episodes of the Granada-produced **The Adventures of Sherlock Holmes** (1984-5) and sequels. *The Adventure of the Winged Scarab* – in which Moriarty is partnered by his THE EMPTY HOUSE acolyte Colonel Moran – is easily the most engaging, sophisticated and well-plotted of the four adventures. Its success is due in no small measure to Jeavons' smashing, sword-stick-waving Moriarty, who enjoys a particularly fine confrontation with Hubert Rees' paternalistic Watson: 'We have fought a long, secret battle, he [Holmes] and I. It is on the whetstone of his intellect that my genius has been sharpened...'

Broadly pleased with the result, Read was disappointed that a second series wasn't commissioned: 'I have a feeling that the Children's Department, as it then was, were a bit miffed. It wasn't their idea, and they didn't regard it as being 'wholesome' or educational enough. Also, it didn't sell as well as we'd hoped – as well as the American co-producers had hoped – in the States, because the cockney accents were unintelligible to Americans. I'd said all along to the producers, "Make them speak slower! This is period stuff, so it's got to be more stage cockney." It was very difficult. When the Guild Awards came up the next year, the BBC didn't enter the series for them – they entered a dramatisation that had been made completely in-house called *The Machine Gunners*. Someone on the awards committee had seen *The Baker Street Boys* and wondered why it wasn't on the list, and so they called it in. It won.'

The Case-book of Sherlock Holmes

GB 1990-91 6 x 50m approx TV series adaptations
Granada Television colour
p **Michael Cox**
regular cast Sherlock Holmes: **Jeremy Brett**
Dr Watson: **Edward Hardwicke**

THE DISAPPEARANCE OF LADY FRANCES CARFAX

tx 21 February 1991 ITV
w **T R Bowen** *d* **John Madden**
regular cast, plus Lady Frances Carfax: **Cheryl Campbell**
Albert Schlessinger: **Julian Curry** Miss Calder: **Mary Cunningham** the Hon Philip Green: **Jack Klaff**
hotel manager: **Nicholas Fry** the Earl of Rufton: **Michael Jayston** vicar: **Anthony Benson** Mrs Hudson: **Rosalie Williams** bank official: **Anthony Schaeffer**
woman in undertakers: **Margot Stanley**

THE PROBLEM OF THOR BRIDGE

tx 28 February 1991 ITV
w **Jeremy Paul** *d* **Michael Simpson**
regular cast, plus J Neil Gibson: **Daniel Massey**
Maria Gibson: **Celia Gregory** Grace Dunbar: **Catherine Russell** Marlow Bates: **Niven Boyd** Sergeant Coventry: **Andrew Wilde** Mr Ferguson: **Stephen MacDonald** Mr Joyce Cummings QC: **Philip Bretherton** Billy: **Dean Magri**

THE BOSCOMBE VALLEY MYSTERY

tx 7 March 1991 ITV
w **John Hawkesworth** *d* **June Howson**
regular cast, plus John Turner: **Peter Vaughan** Inspector Summerby: **Jonathan Barlow** Alice Turner: **Joanna Roth**
William McCarthy: **Leslie Schofield** James McCarthy: **James Purefoy** Crowder the gamekeeper: **Cliff Howells**
Patience Crowder: **Makala Saunders** George: **Mark Jordon**
coroner: **Will Tacey**

THE ILLUSTRIOUS CLIENT

tx 14 March 1991 ITV
w **Robin Chapman** *d* **Tim Sullivan**

regular cast, plus Baron Gruner: **Anthony Valentine**
Baroness Gruner: **Carol Noakes** Sir James Damery: **David Langton** Miss Violet Merville: **Abigail Cruttenden**
Mrs Hudson: **Rosalie Williams** Jarvis: **John Pickles**
Kitty Winter: **Kim Thomson** Shinwell Johnson: **Roy Holder**
first thug: **Andy Bradford**

SHOSCOMBE OLD PLACE

tx 21 March 1991 ITV
w **Gary Hopkins** *d* **Patrick Lau**
regular cast, plus Sir Robert Norberton: **Robin Ellis**
Lady Beatrice Falder: **Elizabeth Weaver** John Mason: **Frank Grimes** Carrie Evans: **Denise Black** Stephens: **Michael Bilton** Sandy Bain: **Martin Stone** Josiah Barnes: **Michael Wynne** Samuel Brewer: **James Coyle** Mrs Hudson: **Rosalie Williams** Joe Barnes: **Jude Law** Harvey: **Alan Pattison**

THE CREEPING MAN

tx 28 March 1991 ITV
w **Robin Chapman** *d* **Tim Sullivan**
regular cast, plus Professor Presbury: **Charles Kay**
Edith Presbury: **Sarah Woodward** Jack Bennett: **Adrian Lukis**
Alice Murphy: **Anna Mazzotti** Macphail: **James Tomlinson**
Wilcox: **Peter Guinness** Jenkins: **Steve Swinscoe** Inspector Lestrade: **Colin Jeavons** Secretary of the Zoological Society: **Anthony Havering** great ape: **Peter Elliott**

'I salute your powers of improvisation, sir, and your effrontery,' Jeremy Brett's Sherlock Holmes tells 'Major Albert Schlessinger', aka Holy Peters, in *The Disappearance of Lady Frances Carfax*, 'but it *will not do*!' In the circumstances, adapter T R Bowen's line is a choice portion of cod Doyle, for the third series of Granada Television's dramatisations presents us with six convincingly cobbled-together imitations of the originals, some more amusing than others, but also demonstrates a turning-aside from the company's original mission: to bring an authentically realised Sherlock Holmes to television.

Given that the feature-length **The Hound of the Baskervilles** (1988) ended up financially compromised after various of the later episodes of **The Return of Sherlock Holmes** (1988) went

Jeremy Brett and Edward Hardwicke on location for **The Case-book of Sherlock Holmes** *(1991)*

disastrously over budget, one queries the wisdom of attempting to open the next series with a story set largely on the shores of Lake Geneva – and so, sensibly, the locale of THE DIS-APPEARANCE OF LADY FRANCES CARFAX is amended to the Lake District in the Granada version, with a holidaying Watson witnessing events leading up to the titular vanishing at first hand. Whereas this seems eminently practical in dramatic terms too – and pleasing, even, given the sumptuous location filming at Derwent Water in Cumbria – the reason for turning Doyle's 'rather pathetic' Lady Frances into a feisty, skiff-sailing adventuress-of-sorts is less comprehensible.

Every bit as baffling is the decision to hire an actor of the quality of *Quiller*'s Michael Jayston and then waste him in less than a handful of scenes playing a character only ever reported dead in the original; Jayston, surely, would have made a more natural Sir Robert Norberton than *Poldark*'s Robin Ellis in *Shoscombe Old Place*, an episode chiefly pleasurable for the *schadenfreude* inherent in seeing latterday 'Britpack' heart-throb Jude Law make an early appearance in old biddy drag as the inconveniently expired Lady Beatrice.

The selection of stories dramatised in *The Case-book* is questionable not merely because some of them are 'difficult', requiring significant alteration or broadening-out for the purposes of commercial television – in fact, not revealing from the outset that THE CREEPING MAN's Professor Presbury has developed animalistic traits, for example, makes for a far more satisfying narrative. Instead, one

queries the production team's choices on the grounds of repetition: both THE DISAPPEARANCE OF LADY FRANCES CARFAX and SHOSCOMBE OLD PLACE build to finales centred around old women in coffins, and both SHOSCOMBE OLD PLACE and THE CREEPING MAN – like SILVER BLAZE, the previous season – turn on the changed behaviour of a domestic dog. One wonders, too, whether or not the series' most trivial recurring theme, the state of Holmes' breakfast eggs – as referred to in *The Problem of Thor Bridge* and *Shoscombe Old Place*, and used as an impromptu ashtray in *The Creeping Man* – was intended as a running gag.

Then again, the whole of *The Creeping Man* is a joke, what with its science-fiction outcome and its spate of 'monkey thefts'. When Holmes' search of a broken-in zoo cage leads to a set of conclusions like 'The primate was quietened by a pad of chloroform, administered by someone who lavishes their hair with Mr Brewster of Jermyn Street's pomade, which would suggest that he also sports a waxed moustache ... If this was so, Lestrade, you could do worse than have a word with Harry 'the tache' Wilcox of Soho,' one suspects that the scriptwriter has long since stopped taking his business seriously.

The Illustrious Client does, at least, mark a temporary return to the standard of the earlier Granada episodes, being both intelligently refined – Kitty Winter is partly justified in throwing vitriol over the vile Baron Gruner, having been acid-scarred on the chest and neck by Gruner long before – and performed with real intensity, especially by Kim Thomson (also in the rather less auspicious **Hands of a Murderer**) as a luminously vengeful Kitty and Anthony Valentine (Yorkshire TV's *Raffles* of the mid-1970s) as a commandingly unpleasant Gruner. It also contains one of the Brett Holmes' most enjoyably acerbic lines, when he warns the cigar-puffing Baron: 'If you aspire to be accepted into English society, you'd do well to remove the band from your Havana first – otherwise you'll be put down for a bounder.'

Filmed after Brett and Hardwicke had spent over a year appearing on stage in Granada screenwriter Jeremy Paul's two-handed pastiche *The Secret of Sherlock Holmes*, including a residency at Wyndham's Theatre in the West End, *The Case-book of Sherlock Holmes* was widely promoted as marking Brett's retirement from the role. He'd change his mind in time for **The Master**

Blackmailer, the first of three stand-alone productions in a TV movie format which would continue to move the Granada shows further from the declared intentions of original producer Michael Cox. Perhaps tellingly, *The Case-book* was the last of the Granada sequence to have Cox at the helm.

The Case of the Whitechapel Vampire

Canada 2002 TVM pastiche White Chapel Productions (Muse) Inc 88m colour

tx 25 October 2002 Hallmark Channel [US]

wd **Rodney Gibbons** *p* **Irene Litinsky**

cast Sherlock Holmes: **Matt Frewer** Dr Watson: **Kenneth Welsh** Brother Marstoke: **Shawn Lawrence** Dr Chagas: **Neville Edwards** Sister Helen: **Cary Lawrence** Signora de la Rosa: **Isabel Dos Santos** The Thing: **Jere Gillis** Sister Margaret: **Jane Gilchrist** Inspector Jones: **Michel Perron** Hector de la Rosa: **Danny Bianco Hall** Brother Caulder: **Joel Miller** Brother John: **Matthew Tiffin** Brother Abel: **Tom Rack** Brother Sinclair: **Norris Domingue** lamplighter: **John Dunn-Hill** Mrs Hudson: **Kathleen McAuliffe** Inspector Lestrade: **Julian Casey** Policeman #1: **Philip Pretten** Mrs Duncan: **Emma Stevens** workman: **Terry Simpson** Mme Karavsky: **Kathleen Fee** street vendor: **Sam Stone** lady with cape: **Maria Bertrand**

THE MYSTERY

At the abbey of St Justinian's in Whitechapel, Anglican monk Brother Sinclair is found dead, two puncture wounds in his neck. Gossip says he has fallen victim to a vampire – and, despite a coroner's pronouncement of death by heart failure, the order's Head, Brother Marstoke, summons a sceptical Sherlock Holmes to solve the business 'in the name of God'. Some of the order were formerly missionaries in Guyana, where an outbreak of rabies had claimed many local lives. Believing a colony of vampire bats to blame, Marstoke had ordered the creatures exterminated. Soon after, Brothers Lee and Thomas were killed – apparently by a demon, Desmodo, who had left a bloody message 'From Hell': 'As you have sinned against me, so shall I exact my revenge. The blood of yours for the blood of mine.'

THE INVESTIGATION

The finger of suspicion falls first on the naturalist Dr Chagas, who had opposed Marstoke's killing of the bats and is now resident in Whitechapel. Guyanese emigrant the Signora de la Rosa recounts talk of Chagas being a 'dhampiro', the spawn of a vampire male and a human female. Holmes is not persuaded by such talk of the supernatural, but cannot account for a sudden earth tremor felt inside the church. When Brother John is killed and Sister Helen attacked by a cowled 'demon' in a Whitechapel alley, local anger forces Inspector Athelney Jones to arrest Chagas, but the doctor escapes. Returning from the salon of spiritualist Madame Karavsky – whose brother is a declared opponent of Marstoke's liberal views – a hooded figure attempts to push Holmes under a speeding horse and cart ...

THE SOLUTION

After proving Chagas' innocence to Jones, Holmes adopts a monk's habit to draw out the killer – one Brother Abel in a Desmodo mask, demented ever since being infected with rabies himself. Abel, whose modified garden claw has made the 'bite marks' in his victims' throats, is prevented from killing Holmes when another 'earth tremor' sends a statue of St Justinian falling. This is not divine intervention, however – subsidence from the Underground railway construction works beneath the church has been Holmes' salvation.

✦ ✦ ✦

Pointedly making use of a three-pronged garden weeder as a weapon, *The Case of the Whitechapel Vampire* – last in the line of Muse Entertainment's Frewer/Welsh films, following on from **The Hound of the Baskervilles** (2000), **The Sign of Four** (2001) and **The Royal Scandal** – would seem to seek to summon up the spirit of the Rathbone/Bruce cycle, specifically invoking **The Scarlet Claw**. And, for the most part, writer/director Rodney Gibbons makes a fair fist of the job, conflating *Dracula* and Umberto Eco's *The Name of the Rose* with no little style. But whereas the Bram Stoker references have charm (Dr Chagas lives at 4 Renfield Place, and 'the Thing' attacks Brother John and Sister Helen just off Demeter Street), it's going a shade too far to throw in Jack the Ripper too. Blood-scrawl spelling out 'From Hell', the Whitechapel setting and the silhouette of Dr Chagas carrying his Gladstone bag all make up a highly specific allusion, but the Ripper is a red herring for the audience alone, not the characters involved – an in-joke, just like naming the author of the fictional tome *Bats of the Ancient World* after producer Irene Litinsky.

It takes considerable *chutzpah* to square a *deus ex machina* ending with a firm rebuttal of the existence of God, but Gibbons gets away with it. It is a shame, however, that his climax should resort to the *Scooby-Doo* standby of a minor character wearing a rubber mask. The pedantic may pause to wonder if Brother Abel's motives are well-defined enough to be detectable by Holmes; how Abel could be certain that all of his victims would die of heart attacks; whether or not Abel was responsible for one or both of the killings in Guyana; and quite how several minutes' worth of clunky exposition at the end could possibly fail to bring up, let alone resolve, any of these questions. Gibbons does, at least, refuse to give into temptation and leave open any real possibility of supernatural agencies at work – a factor that mars, say, **The Last Vampyre**, or even **Murder By Decree**. Indeed, Holmes is so ardent about his rationalism throughout – 'The great hereafter! Pah! I can assure you there is nothing but the great here and now!'; 'I have no fear of offending the gods, Watson, for I know there are no gods to offend' – that it has a touch of crusading zeal about it.

Filmed in and around Montreal between 25 November and 21 December 2001, *The Case of the Whitechapel Vampire* saw director of photography Serge Ladouceur nominated for an American Society of Cinematographers Award for his atmospheric work.

So ends Matt Frewer's last bow – an acquired taste as Holmes, for sure, but it'd be the greatest disappointment to learn that no more are in the planning. It is not *The Scarlet Claw*, but it is as close an approximation of the Universal Pictures approach as we're ever likely to see again.

Children's Mystery Theater: The Treasure of Alpheus T Winterborn

aka **The Clue According to Sherlock Holmes**
[video release]
US 1980 TV pastiche Asselin Productions Inc 46m colour

tx 26 December 1980 [CBS]
w **Kimmer Ringwald** *source* **The Treasure of Alpheus Winterborn** [novel by **John Bellairs**] *p* **Diane Asselin, Paul Asselin** *d* **Murray Golden**
cast Miss Eells: **Dody Goodman** Anthony Monday: **Keith Mitchell** Sherlock Holmes: **Keith McConnell** Dr Watson: **Laurie Main** Philpotts: **Matthew Tobin** Gegenfurtner: **Al Lewis** Loomis: **Louis Guss** other roles: **Art Kassul, Hale Porter, Stanley Grover, Claire Mallis, Frank Dent**

London, circa 1980: Sherlock Holmes uses a story in the *Winterborn Mirror*, a newspaper from somewhere in smalltown America, to prove to Dr Watson that 'a mystery may pop up in any nook and cranny of the world'. The newspaper report relates the tale of a young treasure-hunter called Anthony Monday who, with the help of librarian Miss Eells, went in search of the lost treasure of long-dead local philanthropist Alpheus T Winterborn. Riddles left by Winterborn led Monday to the weathervane atop the local library, which was stuffed full of gold pieces. However, a mystery man with squeaky shoes had been shadowing Monday's every move...

Pity the youth of America. *The Treasure of Alpheus T Winterborn* was, we learn, 'Recommended by The National Education Association' – an organisation which evidently thought nothing of teaching the nation's preteens that, just 20 years short of the 21st century, their English cousins still got about their capital city in horse-drawn carriages. Being, in fact, an entirely feeble children's 'mystery' in which a bland, blond-haired goody-two-shoes goes in search of a golden hoard found by solving Musgrave Ritual-style 'riddles', it holds as much interest to Sherlockians as it does educational value – ie, none whatsoever.

Keith McConnell's sun-tanned detective looks more like a retired playboy than a plausible Holmes, and Laurie Main's jigsaw-loving sidekick is a dimwit with a gleaming bald pate; the film cuts back to the pair every now and again, their dismal dialogues underscoring events for the sake of the remedial class. The level of sophistication in their repartee may be gauged from the following excerpt: says Watson, 'Holmes, when did you know you were going to devote your life to solving mysteries?' 'As a young lad at school,' says Holmes. 'School, eh?' muses Watson. 'Don't tell me – Elementary!' 'Kindergarten, actually,' replies Holmes.

Surprisingly, this wretchedly insipid piece was based on a highly acclaimed, hugely atmospheric 1978 children's book by John Bellairs (1938-91), author of many Gothic-style detective thrillers for adolescents such as *The House With a Clock in its Walls* (1973). Producers Asselin Productions added Holmes and Watson to the TV version, which is no more satisfying to Bellairs fans than Doyle devotees. (The characters Anthony Monday and Miss Eells appear in other Bellairs novels, too.) This was not the first time that Dublin-born McConnell (1923-87) and Main (1929-) had played the detective and the doctor on screen, having first appeared together in a 1973 TV ad for Schlitz Malt Liquor. Main would go on to provide the voice of Watson – playing against the long-dead Basil Rathbone – in the Disney cartoon **The Great Mouse Detective** (1986).

Classics Dark and Dangerous: Silver Blaze

GB/Canada 1977 TV adaptation
Highgate Associates Ltd/HTV/OECA 30m colour
w **Julian Bond** *p* **William Deneen** *d* **John Davies**
tx 27 November 1977 ITV
cast Sherlock Holmes: **Christopher Plummer**
Dr Watson: **Thorley Walters** Colonel Ross: **Basil Henson**
Inspector Gregory: **Gary Watson** Straker: **Richard Beale**
Fitzroy-Simpson: **Donald Burton** Silas Brown: **Barry Lineham** Edith: **Julia Chambers** groom: **Malcolm Rogers**
Mrs Straker: **Josie Kidd** Ned: **Clive Woodward** first stable
boy: **Daniel Hill** second stable boy: **Nigel Hicks**

*C*lassics Dark and Dangerous was an umbrella title under which six half-hour adaptations of horror/mystery short stories, produced by independents Highgate Associates Ltd in tandem with Bristol-based regional broadcasters Harlech Television (HTV) and Toronto's Ontario Educational Communications Authority (OECA), would eventually be packaged. Only four appear to have been transmitted in the UK, this version of Doyle's SILVER BLAZE being the second. The other films were: D H Lawrence's *Rocking Horse Winner*, starring Kenneth More and directed by Peter Medak (broadcast August 1977); L P Hartley's *The*

Watson (Thorley Walters) escorts a narcotically addled Holmes (Christopher Plummer) in **Classics Dark and Dangerous: Silver Blaze** (1977)

Island, with John Hurt and Charles Gray, directed by Robert Fuest (broadcast April 1978); E F Benson's vampire tale *Mrs Amworth*, featuring Glynis Johns and directed by Alvin Rakoff (broadcast June 1978); Isaac Asimov's *Ugly Little Boy*, directed and co-produced by and starring Barry Morse; plus a version of *Psycho* author Robert Bloch's *Mannikin*.

The presence of Toronto-born Christopher Plummer (1927-) at the head of the cast list would have ensured that *Silver Blaze* held a little local interest for Highgate's Canadian partners. A cousin of Nigel Bruce, Watson to Basil Rathbone's Holmes from **Sir Arthur Conan Doyle's The Hound of the Baskervilles** (1939) on, Plummer's considerable achievements on the Shakespearean stage remain overshadowed by his appearance as the head of the all-singing von Trapp family in *The Sound of Music* (1965). His rather dry, distant Holmes would be partnered by Thorley Walters' overgrown-schoolboy Watson. The faithful Walters had already supported Great Detectives played by

Christopher Lee and Douglas Wilmer in **Sherlock Holmes und das Halsband des Todes** (1962) and **The Adventure of Sherlock Holmes' Smarter Brother** (1975), plus a 'bit' with Peter Jeffrey in *The Best House in London* (1968).

Silver Blaze was filmed in the summer of 1976 at locations that included the steam-run Severn Valley Railway, which only the previous year had been utilised in **The Seven-Per-Cent Solution**. During production, Plummer told *Photoplay* that he hoped *Silver Blaze* would be 'the first of a mini-series of six of the best [Sherlock Holmes] stories which have not been done before'. He also told *TV Times* reporter Stewart Knowles, who was putting together what would become a cover feature for the magazine, that 'since the subject of drugs is so topical', he had chosen to stress Holmes' cocaine addiction – principally, it seems, by requesting the application of a daringly pallid layer of foundation.

The film remained stuck in HTV's vaults for nearly 18 months, eventually airing late on a Sunday evening in November 1977 – by which time all thoughts of a follow-on series seem to have vanished. Hazel Holt, reviewing the production in *The Stage and Television Today*, thought it 'a pity that HTV's production of *Silver Blaze* should have been brought out of the deep freeze at last in the very week that brought us another look at the first of the Basil Rathbone Sherlock Holmes movies', for this latest version didn't make for a favourable comparison. 'Christopher Plummer played Holmes as a restless neurotic, made up very pale to emphasise the drug addiction. Actually, he looked a sort of acid pink to me and no amount of fiddling with the set improved matters – the colour, in fact, was decidedly bad. This was symptomatic of the attitude of the whole production: Conan Doyle is old-hat, so we'll emphasise the drugs bit to jazz it up ... Exploiting the brand-name, as it were, while basically despising the product.'

Plummer's Great Detective would be positively golden-skinned, glowing with health, when he filmed the Holmes-versus-Jack the Ripper feature *Murder By Decree* the following summer. As with all the *Classics Dark and Dangerous* shorts, this all-round-competent but otherwise unengaging crack at SILVER BLAZE has vanished from view.

Comedy Playhouse Presents: Elementary, My Dear Watson

GB 1973 TV parody BBC 30m colour
w N F Simpson p Barry Took d Harold Snoad

THE STRANGE CASE OF THE DEAD SOLICITORS

tx 18 January 1973 BBC1
cast Sherlock Holmes: **John Cleese** Dr Watson: **William Rushton** Frank Potter (alias Moriarty): **Bill Maynard** Lady Cynthia: **Josephine Tewson** Inspector Street: **Norman Bird** the Constable: **Chic Murray** Fu Manchu: **Larry Martyn** the Prime Minister: **John Wells** Supt Truscott: **Michael Gover** Rupert: **Michael Knowles** the Secretary: **Helen Lambert** Mabel: **Rosemary Lord** the Airport Loader: **Ivor Salter** other roles: **Rose Hill, Colin Bean, Gordon Faith** the *Call My Bluff* teams: **Frank Muir, Dawn Addams, Alan Coren, Patrick Campbell, Morag Hood, John Carson** referee: **Robert Robinson**

THE MYSTERY
London, 1973: the 'indestructible' Sherlock Holmes and Dr Watson receive a letter from Lady Cynthia Bellingham-Datchet asking them to investigate the reappearance of the family curse – a poisonous rattlesnake. However, *en route* to Euston Station, they are accosted by Inspector Street of New Scotland Yard, who requests their assistance in solving the mystery of the bizarre deaths of five prosperous Old World solicitors who shared an office in Cockfosters; all five have been found slumped over their desks in an identical position, a dagger protruding from their backs...

THE INVESTIGATION
One of the solicitors' corpses is later stolen, complete with his desk; this macabre tableau is subsequently found to be the 'Mystery Object of the Week' in a round of TV game show *Call My Bluff*, where the 'Dead Solicitor' is defined as a much-prized conversation piece in 19th century China...

THE SOLUTION
The culprit is the nefarious Oriental, Fu Manchu, whose efforts to retrieve the solicitors' bodies and transport them to China as an offering to the People's Palace, Peking are eventually halted at an airport... but only after Holmes has filled up five

minutes' screen time in a completely irrelevant scrape involving arch-enemy Moriarty who, under the alias of a reformed piano tuner named Fred Potter, is found in drag as panto character Mother Goose. Meanwhile, all the Bellingham-Datchets, and their pets, have fallen victim to the Curse.

✦ ✦ ✦

Between 1961 and 1974, *Comedy Playhouse*, a half-hour strand devised by BBC Head of Light Entertainment Tom Sloan, had functioned as a 'try-out' slot for pilot editions of putative comic series. Shows which first went out under its banner include such enduring successes as *Steptoe and Son*, *Till Death Us Do Part*, *The Liver Birds* and *Last of the Summer Wine*.

Subtitled *The Strange Case of the Dead Solicitors*, *Elementary, My Dear Watson* was broadcast on the same day as the final episode of the third series of *Monty Python's Flying Circus* – and the last instalment to feature the long-limbed John Cleese. Although the remaining five members of the Python team would limp on through a lacklustre fourth series, Cleese had quit, feeling 'very constricted' by their 'marriage'. Having recorded that final *Python* on 18 May 1972, he was searching for a new comedy project. Under producer Barry Took, the man who'd brought the Pythons together four years previously, Cleese was duly cast opposite William Rushton – a major player in the early sixties satire boom, intimately involved with both the magazine *Private Eye* and the seminal *That Was the Week That Was* – in this *Comedy Playhouse* effort.

Much of the show seems tailored to the style of postmodern parody pioneered by Python, leading one to suspect it was written for Cleese. The characters are aware that they are participating in a constructed fiction, first signposted when Holmes and Watson step into modern Baker Street's busy motor traffic to hail an anachronistic hansom cab; on seeing various bystanders' baffled reactions, Holmes observes, 'I suspect we're a figment of these people's imagination, Watson. They've been reading too much Conan Doyle.'

In addition, there's a lengthy sequence presenting an edition of the BBC panel game *Call My Bluff*, featuring that show's 'real' cast. The getaway of the villain, Sax Rohmer's Fu Manchu, is foiled when Holmes orders the film to be reversed, thus sending the bad guy backwards into the arms

of the police; and the inconsequential pursuit of Moriarty is dismissed by Holmes as 'a simple device to fill out the script, which would otherwise have been short by fully five minutes.' However, as evinced by the steadily diminishing guffaws of the studio audience on the 'laugh track', the show isn't all that funny, exchanging Python's crueller excesses (a poisoned tortoise excepted) and intellectual pretensions for a rather more cosy iconoclasm, if such a thing's possible.

Unsurprisingly, a full series of *Elementary, My Dear Watson* failed to appear; Cleese's next comic role for the BBC would prove rather more fruitful – playing a manic and monstrous Torquay hotelier in his own *Fawlty Towers*. A few years later, he burlesqued the Great Detective once more in an hour-long TV special, **The Strange Case of the End of Civilisation As We Know It**.

Conan Doyle's Master Detective Sherlock Holmes

US 1932 pastiche Fox Film Corporation 71m bw
w **Bertram Millhauser** *source* **Sherlock Holmes** [play by **William Gillette**] *pd* **William K Howard**
cast Sherlock Holmes: **Clive Brook** Alice Faulkner: **Miriam Jordan** Professor James Moriarty: **Ernest Torrence** George, the publican: **Herbert Mundin** Dr Watson: **Reginald Owen** Little Billy: **Howard Leeds** Colonel Gore-King: **Alan Mowbray** Judge: **Montague Shaw** [character unknown]: **Frank Atkinson** Mr Faulkner: **Ivan Simpson** Homer Jones: **Stanley Fields** Manuel Lopez: **Roy D'Arcy*** Al, Jones' henchman: **Eddie Dillon*** Gaston Roux: **Robert Graves*** secretary to Erskine: **Brandon Hurst*** chaplain: **Arnold Lucy*** Sir Albert Hastings: **Claude King*** Hans, the Hun: **Lucien Prival***

THE MYSTERY

Arch-criminal Professor James Moriarty is convicted of murder and sentenced to hang; from the dock, he swears that prosecutor Erskine, police officer Gore-King and Sherlock Holmes, all of whom helped incriminate him, shall die before he does. Soon after, Holmes, who is preparing to retire from detection prior to marrying Alice Faulkner, hears that Erskine has gone missing, and discovers the prosecutor hanged. Although an attempt had been made to suggest that Erskine's death was self-inflicted, Holmes finds a secret message hidden in

'Oh, get out, Watson!' Reginald Owen's Watson contemplates a high-handed Holmes (Clive Brook) in a studio shot for **Conan Doyle's Master Detective Sherlock Holmes** *(1932)*

Erskine's 'suicide note': 'Moriarty'. Police commissioner Sir Albert Hastings has kept the fact of the Professor's escape from prison secret. Gore-King and Holmes are next on Moriarty's blacklist...

THE INVESTIGATION

Moriarty has assembled a group of international criminals – American gunman Homer Jones plus the Frenchman Gaston Roux, the Spaniard Manuel Lopez and the German Hans Dreiaugen – and the gang plan to introduce 'American methods' to London's streets: protection rackets and the like. Meanwhile, a plot is hatched to fool Holmes into murdering Gore-King, believing him to be Jones; this is, it appears, successful, and Holmes is arrested. While newspapers trumpet details of Holmes' confession, the gang's racketeering begins in earnest...

THE SOLUTION

Moriarty kidnaps Alice plus Holmes' page, Billy – then goes to Alice's father to inform him that his gang are robbing the vault of his bank, and he is to co-operate if he wishes to ensure Alice's safety. However, Holmes, disguised in drag as the elderly 'Aunt Matilda', is at the Faulkner house; Gore-King's 'death' has been a ruse to lure Moriarty off-guard. Holmes leads an assault on the bank and, while Scotland Yard's finest engage in a shoot-out with the gang, he pursues Moriarty, who is eventually gunned down. Holmes and Alice are now ready to begin a new life as a farmer and his wife.

✦ ✦ ✦

'PUBLIC'S IDOL DEGRADED' proclaims a fake *Observer* headline seen at one point in the ostentatiously titled *Conan Doyle's Master Detective Sherlock Holmes*. The charitably inclined might view the wording as the Fox Film Corporation's covert apology to readers of Doyle; the cynical will, however, see it as an expression of the studio's contempt. For the lead character, a disdainful, gun-toting inventor who spurns even the label 'detective', bears no real resemblance to the Sherlock Holmes put forward by Doyle (or even Gillette, the ostensible source for the piece). The offence is compounded by the film's full title, a six-word lie. Most reference works, in fact, choose to reduce the title to simply 'Sherlock Holmes'; perhaps their authors found the film's proper appellation too incredible, or insulting.

Following 1929's **The Return of Sherlock Holmes** and the versus-Fu Manchu skit in **Paramount on Parade**, lead actor Clive Brook defected to Fox to appear in this, the last of his Holmes efforts – but he might as well be playing a different character altogether, so removed is the Fox Holmes from the Paramount model. We first meet Holmes in his Baker Street headquarters (seemingly a house, as opposed to rooms) where, from a well-appointed laboratory, this self-declared 'mastermind' is perfecting an electromagnetic 'motor-wrecking ray' intended to incapacitate criminals' getaway cars – his 'farewell gift' to Scotland Yard.

'Little Billy' (a Canadian, for reasons unexplained) is now more a general assistant to Holmes than a houseboy, following his master even to a crime scene. Reginald Owen's not-bad Watson is, in fact, so marginalised that he appears in two scenes only, Brook's Holmes seemingly having no time for the duffer. Faced with American hoodlums exporting protection rackets and mob rule to sleepy London, Holmes tells Watson that, 'There's only one way to deal with these alien butchers … Their own way. Shoot first, investigate afterwards.' 'But is it sporting, old chap?' protests the appalled doctor. 'Oh, get out, Watson,' sneers Holmes. And so Watson gets out, and is never seen again, sending a message to say that family illness means he can't be best man at Holmes' wedding to the upper-crust Alice Faulkner. 'Family illness' indeed; after such treatment, the old boy must be heartbroken.

The Moriarty-led 'alien invasion' plot is far and away the most ingenious and pleasing of the film's inventions. Irrespective of his crimes against Holmes himself, screenwriter Bertram Millhauser (mis-spelled 'Milhauser' in the credits) revels in transporting the scum of 1930s Chicago gangland to the film's quasi-Victorian England, and there's fun to be had in the scenes where slow-witted salt-of-the-Earth East Enders attempt to come to grips with firebombings and other 'American methods' (although the presentation stops short of

'machine-guns turned on little children in the streets!', as an over-emotional Holmes prophesise). Ernest Torrence's beady-eyed mutant Moriarty is a powerful presence, too – a hunched-up and entirely malevolent old buzzard who claims to be 'distinguished' by Holmes' enmity.

Production values are high – arguably the finest in any Holmes film up to this point – and William K Howard's direction is both striking and sprightly. The silhouetted opening shot, showing Moriarty being led to trial, is especially noteworthy, as is the grotesque funfair montage, all grinning carny types shot in close-up. (American-born Howard had traversed similar territory before, in 1930's *Scotland Yard*, aka *Detective Clive Bart*; perhaps this helps explain the film's fascination with the Yard's top brass.) It's a shame that the otherwise attractive production design is so incompetently researched, though; this is a London where long-girdered Brooklyn-style bridges cross the Thames, and dank public houses have become glass-fronted 'saloons'.

In the space of a year, Reginald Owen would have graduated to playing Holmes himself in 1933's **A Study in Scarlet** (alongside Alan Mowbray as Inspector Lestrade, formerly Brook-Holmes' Yard rival Gore-King). Millhauser would pursue his fascination with hoods and racketeers in a number of subsequent pictures, including James Cagney comedy *Jimmy the Gent* (1934) and the tellingly titled *Nick Carter, Master Detective* (1939),

Alice Faulkner (Miriam Jordan) in thrall to her detective fiancé (Clive Brook) in a posed shot for **Conan Doyle's Master Detective Sherlock Holmes** *(1932)*

before writing the first of several fine Universal Holmes films with **Sherlock Holmes in Washington** (1943). Soon after describing Hollywood as 'a chain gang ... we lose the will to escape. The links of the chain are forged not with cruelties but with luxuries', Brook returned to the English stage. He died in 1974, but not before confessing that the last of his Holmes pictures was 'a terrible film'. 'Sherlock Holmes Says Humiliation Cause of Killing', runs another of those mocked-up headlines. 'Self-admitted Slayer Avers Series of "Insufferable Insults".'

The Crucifer of Blood

US 1991 TVM adaptation [THE SIGN OF THE FOUR]
Turner Pictures Ltd 120m colour
tx 4 November 1991 TNT
wpd **Fraser C Heston** *source* play by **Paul Giovanni**
cast Sherlock Holmes: **Charlton Heston** Dr Watson: **Richard Johnson** Irene St Claire: **Susannah Harker** Alistair Ross: **Edward Fox** Neville St Claire: **John Castle** Inspector Lestrade: **Simon Callow** Jonathan Small: **Clive Wood** Birdy Johnson: **James Coyle** Durga Dass: **Kaleem Janjua** Wali Dad: **Stefan Kalipha** PC Hopkins: **Lloyd McGuire** Tonga: **Kiran Shah** Mordecai Smith: **Sidney Livingstone** leper: **Roly Lamas**

Purporting to document the 'true' story of the case that came to be written up by Watson in bowdlerised form as THE SIGN OF THE FOUR, *The Crucifer of Blood* is an utterly intriguing revision of the second Sherlock Holmes adventure, undone by an excessively theatrical and static presentation style – unsurprisingly, since it's based on a stage play.

Writer, director and rock musician Paul Giovanni (immortalised for horror fans by his extraordinary score for the 1972 film *The Wicker Man*) first staged *The Crucifer of Blood* at the Studio Arena Theater, Buffalo, New York, where it opened on 6 January 1978 with Paxton Whitehead and Timothy Landfield as Holmes and Watson respectively. In its original form, the names of Major Sholto and Mary Morstan were retained; Glenn Close took the Morstan role, here reconfigured as a cold femme fatale. Again directed by Giovanni, the play then opened at London's Theatre Royal Haymarket on 21 March 1979, with Keith Michell, David Horovitch and Susan Hampshire; Michell and Hampshire were subsequently replaced by

Gerald Harper and Kate O'Mara. Later still, in 1980, the show was staged at Los Angeles' Ahmanson Theater, where the part of the Great Detective was taken, surprisingly, by Charlton Heston – whose starring roles in pictures such as *The Ten Commandments* (1956) and *Ben-Hur* (1959) had once made him Hollywood's choicest Epic lead. In a pleasing twist, Heston's Watson was English actor Jeremy Brett, later acclaimed as one of the finest of all screen Sherlocks for the Granada-produced TV adaptations which would commence with **The Adventures of Sherlock Holmes** in 1984.

Come the late eighties, US cable channel TNT initiated an extensive programme of relatively highbrow TV movie production; prominent among these was a version of Robert Louis Stevenson's *Treasure Island* (itself cited by Arthur Conan Doyle Society founder Christopher Roden, in his introduction to the 1993 Oxford University Press edition of THE SIGN OF THE FOUR, as a largely unacknowledged influence on Doyle's original). TNT's *Treasure Island* was filmed in Cornwall and Jamaica with a (mostly British) cast headed by Heston, here under the first-time direction of his son, Fraser C Heston. Its success presumably led directly to the screen version of *The Crucifer of Blood* – which again employed both Hestons, plus English actors Richard Johnson (as a distinctly repressed Watson) and Clive Wood (later a regular in fire brigade soap opera *London's Burning*).

Shot in the UK in association with Agamemnon Films and British Lion, the film was first broadcast on 4 November 1991. Its portentous opening scene lays out Watson's manuscript for 'The Adventure of the Crucifer of Blood' – the full and unexpurgated text of which, the author tells us, must remain suppressed: 'If, in future years, some other eye should read this memoir, it will become apparent why I myself consider it best to leave unpublished ... the heart of this appalling story.' Amusingly, a copy of *Beeton's Christmas Annual* 1887 – in which A STUDY IN SCARLET was first published – can be glimpsed on the doctor's desk.

The action flashes back to the Indian Mutiny of 1857, recounting the murderous circumstances which bind the British soldiers Jonathan Small, Neville St Claire and Major Alistair Ross in a compact signed in blood in the shape of an encircled cross – the 'crucifer' of the title. (St Claire and Ross are conflations of the Doyle characters of

Major Sholto and Colonel Morstan, given the names and some of the habits of characters from THE MAN WITH THE TWISTED LIP and SILVER BLAZE respectively.) The narrative then moves forward 30 years, where it bobs and weaves its way through THE SIGN OF THE FOUR. Here, the opium-addicted St Claire is financially dependent on the wheel-chair-bound Ross (a marvellously OTT Edward Fox, previously in **Dr Watson and the Darkwater Hall Mystery**), who is murdered by the savage Tonga in a blood-and-thunder set-piece straight out of the 'Beginners' Guide to Gothic Melodrama'. See also the crass prosthetic shock-horrors of the treasure-carrying leper, plus Small's dream-sequence removal of a glass eye from its gaping socket.

The hysteria continues in a lengthy sequence within a Limehouse opium den, where Holmes – disguised as a Mandarin drug-peddler! – attempts to extract the story behind the Crucifer from the addle-headed St Claire. The Indian treasure which the vengeance-fixated Small has reclaimed from its hiding-place inside Ross' wheelchair is recovered during Holmes' pursuit of the *Gloria Scott* (not *Aurora*) along the River Thames, whereupon the story plunges headlong into *film noir* territory with the revelation that St Claire's butter-wouldn't-melt daughter Irene, with whom Watson has fallen helplessly in love, is, in fact, a mur-derous Jezebel. She has employed Holmes and Watson for the sole purpose of leading her to the treasure, which she plans to then seize for herself. (This plot twist is painfully signalled by Irene's changing from prim, buttoned-up gentlewoman's corsetry to a plunging-necklined scarlet get-up.) Following a showdown with Watson ('Give me one last kiss of unspeakable hatred!'), the treasure is retrieved and delivered to Buckingham Palace. Here, the ostensible reason for Watson's withholding of the facts becomes apparent; the Agra hoard sent to Queen Victoria is, indeed, cursed. 'You think it might destroy Her Majesty – and even the British Empire itself?' gasps Inspector Lestrade. 'Give it to her and see,' pouts Irene.

This 'true' account does, of course, raise some fascinating questions regarding the original – if Watson's beloved Irene ended up in chokey, then was he ever married to THE SIGN OF THE FOUR's Mary Morstan at all? Is a more accurate depiction of Ms St Claire seen in the form of her Christian-namesake, A SCANDAL IN BOHEMIA's villainous Irene Adler? *The Crucifer of Blood* is equally playful

Charlton Heston (Sherlock Holmes) consults his writer/ producer/director son Fraser on location for **The Crucifer of Blood** *(1991)*

elsewhere. In the closing scene, Mordecai Smith, captain of the here-unseen *Aurora*, presents himself at 221B Baker Street with a mystery concerning a giant rat of Sumatra – this, of course, being the tale of the outsized rodent referred to in THE SUSSEX VAMPIRE as 'a story for which the world is not yet prepared.'

The notion that Watson's published reminis-cences may be every bit as apochryphal as the Giant Rat of Sumatra is a tantalising one, and its deft execution excuses *The Crucifer of Blood*'s plain failings – the fact that it simply has not been 'opened out' from its stage origins, for example. Fundamentally, the film comprises five studio-bound scenes – at the Red Fort at Agra, at 221B, at Pondicherry Lodge, at the opium den and back to 221B – bridged by a couple of minor location sequences, and no attempt has been made to disguise the characters' clumsy entrances and exits.

But what of Charlton Heston's Sherlock? If anything, he's a little too uptight and reverential, playing the part over-cautiously, and, obviously, he's way too old. The curiously uncompelling and lethargic leads are not the film's worst acting offence, however. That distinction goes to the normally estimable Simon Callow, whose Lestrade is a snickering simpleton rightly described by Holmes as a 'mental deficient'.

Detective: The Speckled Band

GB 1964 TV adaptation BBC Television 50m bw
tx 18 May 1964 BBC1

w **Giles Cooper** *p* **David Goddard** *d* **Robin Midgley**
cast Sherlock Holmes: **Douglas Wilmer** Dr Watson: **Nigel
Stock** Dr Grimesby Roylott: **Felix Felton** Helen Stoner:
Liane Aukin Julia Stoner: **Marion Diamond** Percy
Armitage: **Donald Douglas** Mrs Hudson: **Mary Holder**
Annie: **Nan Marriott-Watson** Maigret: **Rupert Davies***

Sometime early in 1963, 12 years on from **We Present Alan Wheatley as Mr Sherlock Holmes in…**, the BBC's second essay into the works of Doyle, BBC staff producer Vere Lorrimer entertained Light Entertainment head Tom Sloan with the idea of adapting more Holmes stories for television. Out of interest, Sloan asked the Corporation's copyright department to determine whether rights were currently available from the Doyle estate – and was surprised to learn that they were.

Recognising television rights in the Holmes stories as 'a valuable property which might be snapped up by the opposition' (the BBC's state monopoly on British television broadcasting had been broken in 1955, with the establishment of the independent ITV group of companies), late in July Sloan recommended a Holmes series to Drama head Sydney Newman. At this point, Sloan envisaged 'someone like Bernard Archard' in the lead. (Archard had been made famous as gaunt interrogator Lt-Col Pinto in the BBC's *Spycatcher*, which had come to an end two years previously.) Newman, however, was able to trump Sloan with the news that his Drama group was actively preparing a new anthology series, *Detective*, which had been devised in order to showcase the adventures of several fictional characters in 50-minute try-out instalments – the most successful of which were to be given follow-up series of their own. 'Sherlock Holmes will not be forgotten,' Newman promised.

The probable reason for the establishment of *Detective* was the BBC's need to find a replacement for the immensely popular *Maigret* (1960-63), which had adapted the exploits of novelist Georges Simenon's Parisian sleuth. Accordingly, each instalment of *Detective* was to be introduced by *Maigret* actor Rupert Davies 'in character'. The first series of 18 50-minute dramatisations commenced on 30 March 1964 with a version of Edmund Crispin's *The Moving Toyshop*, featuring Richard Wordsworth as Professor Gervase Fen; other investigators highlighted in this initial run included Geoffrey Horne's Caleb Cluff, E C Bentley's Philip Trent, Ngaio Marsh's DCI Alleyn, G K Chesterton's Father Brown... and, in week eight, as Newman had predicted, Doyle's Sherlock Holmes.

Early in 1964, the BBC had signed a contract with the Doyle estate to purchase rights in any five Holmes stories with an option to buy a further eight, then a further 13, and 13 more beyond that, each option becoming increasingly expensive. It seems, however, that these rights excluded adapting THE HOUND OF THE BASKERVILLES (which remained tied to Hammer Film Productions until 1965, following the company's 1959 film version), plus A SCANDAL IN BOHEMIA, THE FINAL PROBLEM and THE EMPTY HOUSE (rights in which had almost certainly been taken by the producers of the soon-to-open Broadway musical *Baker Street*). With this in mind, *Detective*'s producer David Goddard focused on another of the better-known short stories, the snake-down-the-bellpull mystery THE SPECKLED BAND, as a try-out for Holmes. *Maigret* adapter/script editor Giles Cooper was to provide the teleplay.

Although Holmes had not been seen on BBC television for many years, the Corporation had been broadcasting a variety of radio dramatisations of the Great Detective's exploits since 1943 – latterly on the Light Programme, and starring Carleton Hobbs and Norman Shelley as Holmes and Watson respectively. Between 1960 and 1962, Robin Midgley had produced and directed 18 instalments in the series – including, on 17 July 1962, a version of THE SPECKLED BAND with Felix Felton and Liane Aukin as the terrible Dr Grimesby Roylott and his hapless stepdaughter Helen. Midgley was approached to direct *Detective*'s take on the story; both Felton (who had long been associated with the radio series, as both adapter and actor, in addition to featuring in the Corporation's very first Holmes effort, **For the Children: The Adventure of the Mazarin Stone**) and Aukin would also be retained for the television version.

As early as August, Newman had noted that 'each detective should be played by a star or an outstanding individual performer who may be prepared to stay with the idea should it later on become a series'. Cast as Holmes was Douglas Wilmer (1920-), a respected character actor of stage and screen soon to be seen in Anthony Mann's rambling Technicolor epic *The Fall of the Roman Empire*. His Watson was to be Nigel Stock (1919-86), a stage performer from the age of 12 whose film credits included *Brighton Rock* (1947), *The Dam Busters* (1954) and *The Great Escape* (1963). Both had worked on many BBC dramas previously, at least as far back as 1947 (Stock) and 1952 (Wilmer), and had appeared together in Powell and Pressburger's *The Battle of the River Plate* (1956).

Studio sequences were videotaped at the BBC's Birmingham outpost on 17 April, following three days' location filming in Surrey between 1 and 3 April (in the grounds of and on the approaches to Tilling Bourne House, Wootton, near Dorking, which doubled as Stoke Moran). *The Speckled Band* was transmitted on BBC1 on Monday 18 May, gaining a spectacularly high Reaction Index figure (a measure of audience appreciation): 76, as opposed to *Detective*'s overall series average of 60. Typical of the viewer response was a letter in *Radio Times* in June, from Alex Lynch of Bedford: 'I am sure [Doyle] would have been highly delighted could he have witnessed such a faithful reproduction of his story. Douglas Wilmer (unknown to me) was the best Sherlock Holmes ever, whilst Nigel Stock as Dr Watson was just as Conan Doyle intended him to be... More please, BBC!'

Further episodes were, by this time, guaranteed. On 21 May, just three days after transmission, Director of Television Kenneth Adam informed Newman that the BBC's Board of Governors had 'unanimously and unreservedly praised the *Sherlock*

Holmes episode in *Detective*, on grounds of style, faithfulness and good casting.' He continued: 'They very much hoped there might be more...' BBC1 chief Donald Baverstock lost no time in inviting drama series head Elwyn Jones to discuss further Holmes instalments from the same team. By 29 May, Jones was happy to report that: 'Both Douglas Wilmer and Nigel Stock, our Holmes and Watson, are willing to go on, and Giles Cooper, adapter of *The Speckled Band*, is more than interested in continuing, too.' A series of 12 episodes, titled simply **Sherlock Holmes**, would begin on 20 February 1965; that, however, is another story. *Detective* would go on to beget the series *Cluff* (1964-65) and *Thorndyke* (1965); the strand was revived in 1968, with 27 more mysteries being broadcast over the next two years.

The Speckled Band's popularity was such that it was retransmitted just four months after its initial airing, on 25 September 1964 – albeit this time under the banner of *Encore*, a mystifyingly eclectic BBC2 repeat slot. (The previous week's presentation, for example, had been Federico Fellini's 1953 film *I vitelloni*.) Late in March 1965, a new set of opening and closing titles, exactly matching the now-ongoing series, was recorded, to enable *The Speckled Band* to be sold abroad as part of a 13-episode Wilmer/Stock package. This is the only version that remains in the BBC's film and television library today, its original *Detective* titles and 'Maigret' introduction now thought lost.

Opening with a stylish and atmospheric replay of the two-years-past death of Julia Stoner, *The Speckled Band* revels in the grim, Gothic gloom of Stoke Moran – all the more remarkable, seeing that the limitations of 'as live' television production mean that the presentation of the house is restricted to just two rooms and a hallway. Giles Cooper's intelligent adaptation plays up the presence of the gypsies on Dr Roylott's land: in a remarkably well-played sequence, Holmes attempts to question the utterly silent, sullen travellers at their encampment, leaving the scene having observed that one of their number wears a spotted neckerchief... or speckled band. Less successful is the attempt to make Roylott's 'old and foolish' housekeeper a suspect by presenting a cracked and cackling crone.

Douglas Wilmer's Holmes is a stout-hearted, oddly benevolent gent with a slightly aristocratic manner. He's engaging enough, but there are moments when Holmes' smile suggests not a passion for the Game but the self-congratulation of the insufferably smug; there's far too much business with his pipe, too, which is swapped from one side of his mouth so often in several sequences that it's impossible for the viewer not to be distracted. With such an approachable Holmes, Nigel Stock's Watson has little to do except chunter away to himself in the background, but he does it agreeably enough. Felix Felton's poker-bending Doctor is quite perfect, however – a fierce, toad-faced ogre at the mercy of his own horrid demons.

Dr Watson and the Darkwater Hall Mystery: A Singular Adventure

GB 1974 TVM pastiche BBC Television 73m colour tx 27 December 1974 BBC2
w **Kingsley Amis** *p* **Mark Shivas** *d* **James Cellan Jones** cast Dr Watson: **Edward Fox** Sir Harry: **Christopher Cazenove** Emily: **Elaine Taylor** Miles: **Jeremy Clyde** Bradshaw: **John Westbrook** Carlos: **Terence Bayler** Dolores: **Carmen Gomez** Black Paul: **Anthony Langdon** Black Paul's woman: **Anne Cunningham** Mrs Hudson: **Marguerite Young** Maddocks: **Derek Deadman**

THE MYSTERY

An overworked Sherlock Holmes has been sent away for a fortnight's rest cure – and when Lady Emily Fairfax calls at 221B asking for Holmes' assistance, she persuades Dr Watson to help her in the detective's stead. Rumour has it that her magistrate husband, Sir Harry Fairfax, is in mortal danger, one 'Black Paul', a local poacher whom he'd convicted, having sworn to revenge himself on Fairfax after being released from jail...

THE INVESTIGATION

Watson goes to stay at Darkwater Hall, the Fairfax ancestral home, and meets the rest of the household: Harry's bitter, absinthe-drinking, Oscar Wilde-quoting twin brother Miles, who missed out on inheriting the family title and estate because he was born 20 minutes too late; Major Jack Bradshaw (ret), a hard-up and wholly dependent ex-army comrade of the Fairfaxes' father; Spanish

servants Carlos and Dolores; and an imbecile groundsman, Maddocks. At breakfast, it is noticed that one of Fairfax's antique rifles has gone missing – and is presumed stolen. Watson calls on the violent-tempered Black Paul, but begins to doubt Paul's homicidal intentions. Taking tea with Emily, he observes that Miles and Bradshaw, both of whom love Emily from afar, have reasons to want Fairfax dead – and that Paul's threats might have given another would-be murderer the opportunity to strike, possibly during the next day's grouse shoot, and avoid suspicion. A shot rings out, shattering Emily's teacup...

THE SOLUTION

Emily is unharmed, and the grouse shoot goes ahead – where Fairfax is felled by a bullet fired by Black Paul from the stolen rifle. Watson strides purposefully towards Paul, telling him to aim for his heart; Paul does so – and misses, enabling Watson to knock him to the ground. As the wounded Fairfax recovers back at the Hall, Watson reveals that he recognised the rifle as being a type notoriously unreliable at short range, his suspicions being confirmed when the assassin had shot off-target at himself and Emily the day before. Returning to 221B, Watson is told by Mrs Hudson that another young lady wishes to see him...

✦ ✦ ✦

Things are exactly what they seem in *Dr Watson and the Darkwater Hall Mystery: A Singular Adventure*, a part-deconstruction, part-parody of Doyle by Kingsley Amis (1922-95). Best known for his first novel, *Lucky Jim* (1956), Amis' love of British pulp fiction had led him to pen a full-length Ian Fleming pastiche, *Colonel Sun* (1968), under the guise of 'Robert Markham'. *Darkwater Hall* isn't as much fun, despite a confident opening scene in which Lady Fairfax asks Dr Watson if there are any other detectives in London whom she might approach: 'Well, yes, it's true that in the last few years, a number of, ah – what shall I call them? – rivals of Sherlock Holmes have sprung up,' mumbles Edward Fox's young fogey doctor. 'For instance, Carnacki – or however it's pronounced. But they're very slight and unsatisfactory fellows. I couldn't recommend you to a single one...' Followers of William Hope

Sir Harry Fairfax (Christopher Cazenove) and Dr Watson (Edward Fox) examine some suspicious stonework in **Dr Watson and the Darkwater Hall Mystery: A Singular Adventure** *(1974)*

Hodgson's occult detective Carnacki ('the Ghost-Finder') would presumably disagree.

Indeed, the first 20 minutes or so promise a fannishly knowledgeable spoof, rich in supplementary detail: a note reading 'RACHE' is pinned above the Baker Street mantel (after A STUDY IN SCARLET); the name of 'Black Paul' is invoked (a nod to the likewise foul-tempered BLACK PETER); and Watson recounts THE MUSGRAVE RITUAL as an after-dinner turn. It's established that Watson has not yet begun to publish his reminiscences of the adventures of Sherlock Holmes, but he has written up the story of what transpired at Stoke Moran; we see a snakeskin-covered folder bearing the title 'The Adventure of the Deadly Cobra' – which Watson suddenly crosses out and replaces with THE SPECKLED BAND.

Matters take a rather morose turn, however, as the denizens of Darkwater Hall stop behaving like caricatures and their characters take over. Amis' 'big idea' appears to be that tangled plots are found only in fiction, with the result that the piece ends up resembling a long drawn-out shaggy dog story. The viewer is led to expect a showdown in which Miles' grievances, or the Major's bitterness – or even Carlos' jealousy at Watson being bedded on consecutive nights by Dolores, or the night-time dressing-up games in which Sir Harry impersonates a witch-hunting Cavalier and, er, 'prosecutes' Emily with a riding crop – will come into play. They don't: instead, Watson hollers 'Aim here!' at the rifleman Paul and strides, unblinking, towards him. It's a fabulous set-piece for the redoubtable, steadfast doctor, but there's an awful lot of effort wasted in getting there.

In retrospect, it's easy to see that the conclusion is determined at the outset, where Watson, in a number of voice-overs, announces that he could see the various characters' true personalities 'straight away' (viz, his first encounter with swarthy butler Carlos on the platform of Darkwater Halt: 'I could tell straight away that the feller was a foreigner, probably a Spaniard. Not that I've got anything against 'em – honest, solid chaps ... This specimen was obviously one of the best of them'). Doubtless the most controversial aspect of the piece is the nature of the relationship between Watson and Dolores; happily, it's all very tastefully done, with no heaving unpleasantness (and since there's no reason to assume that the story takes place after THE SIGN OF THE FOUR, Watson need not have feared the wrath of the former Mary Morstan).

Fox (1937-), best known at the time as the titular assassin in *The Day of the Jackal* (1973), makes a personable enough Watson, whose silly-ass delivery masks a thoroughly decent and quite humane cove. He's not given quite enough to do, although his muddled attempts to stand in for Holmes from beneath a deerstalker provide some real amusement. Fox would go on to make an appearance as the crippled Alistair Ross in **The Crucifer of Blood** (1991). Elaine Taylor, playing the 'devilish pretty' Emily, married Christopher Plummer, Holmes in both **Classics Dark and Dangerous: Silver Blaze** (1977) and **Murder By Decree** (1978).

Amis went on to adapt the script as a short story, *The Darkwater Hall Mystery*, first published in the saucy magazine *Playboy* in May 1978; it was later included in his *Collected Short Stories* (Hutchinson, 1980).

Dressed to Kill

aka **Sherlock Holmes and the Secret Code** [GB]
US 1946 pastiche Universal Pictures Company Inc
72m bw

w **Leonard Lee** story **Frank Gruber** pd **Roy William Neill**
cast Sherlock Holmes: **Basil Rathbone** Dr Watson: **Nigel Bruce** Hilda Courtney: **Patricia Morison** Julian Emery: **Edmond Breon** Colonel Cavanaugh: **Frederic Worlock** Inspector Hopkins: **Carl Harbord** Evelyn Clifford: **Patricia Cameron** Ebenezer Crabtree: **Holmes** Herbert Hamid: **Harry Cording** tour guide: **Leyland Hodgson** Mrs Hudson: **Mary Gordon** Scotland Yard Commissioner: **Ian Wolfe** tourist: **Lillian Bronson*** Detective-Sergeant Thompson: **Tom P Dillon*** Kilgour Child: **Topsy Glyn*** cab driver: **Charlie Hall*** Alfred: **Olaf Hytten*** Joe Cisto: **Delos Jewkes***

THE MYSTERY
Three musical boxes made by Dartmoor prisoner Paul Davidson are put up for auction at the Gaylord Art Gallery. A prospective buyer, Colonel

Cavanaugh, arrives too late to put in a bid but he manages to acquire the names of two of the three purchasers from auctioneer Crabtree. Not long after, Dr Watson's old school friend Julian 'Stinky' Emery, a collector of musical boxes, presents an odd circumstance to Sherlock Holmes: he has been burgled, but of all the antique pieces that could have been taken, only a solitary box worth £2 was seized. Holmes concludes that the burglar may have targeted the similar-looking box Emery bought from Gaylord's, and memorises its remarkable tune. Later, Emery is visited by a glamorous acquaintance, Hilda Courtney, who is also interested in the box – and Emery is killed by Hilda's chauffeur, Hamid. Hilda and her associate, Cavanaugh, now want the other two boxes...

THE INVESTIGATION
Noting the theft, Holmes traces the box to Gaylord's and visits the second purchaser, one Mr Kilgour – only to find the box taken, Hilda having got there before him. Holmes, however, manages to beat Hilda to the third box, which was sold to a Golders Green gift-shop proprietor. Stationed at the shop to follow Hilda, Detective-Sergeant Thompson is soon run over and killed by the gang. The Commissioner of Scotland Yard reveals to Holmes that manufacturer Davidson has consistently refused to reveal the location of the Bank of England printing plates he stole; were the plates to be found, perfect £5 notes would flood the British economy. Holmes suspects that the boxes play significant variations (a fact confirmed by a loyal busker, Joe Cisto) and Watson provides the clue that enables Holmes to decode two-thirds of the message contained in the boxes, indicating something to do with a 'Dr S'. 221B Baker Street is burgled, but Hilda's gang cannot find the concealed box. A hand-made cigarette stub left behind finally gives Holmes Hilda's name – but Hilda, having read Holmes' monograph on tobacco ash, had left the stub behind as a deliberate enticement. Holmes is left to be gassed in an underground garage; when he escapes, he learns that Hilda has re-entered 221B and contrived to steal the third box from Watson. All seems lost...

THE SOLUTION
...until Watson unwittingly solves the riddle: 'Dr S' is a reference to Dr Samuel Johnson. Hilda's gang

Poster for **Dressed to Kill** *(1946), highlighting mink-lined gangstress Hilda Courtney (Patricia Morison)*

duly find the £5 plates behind shelves in the famous lexicographer's London house – but Holmes, and the police, catch them in the act.

✦ ✦ ✦

Much can be commended about *Dressed to Kill* – but despite its serious-minded and sincere approach to Holmes and Watson, its Doyle-like premise and a particularly lovely reversal (the villain using Holmes' infamous paper on tobacco ash to entrap him), it's a desperately low-key and disappointing end to the Universal sequence that began with **Sherlock Holmes and the Voice of Terror**. When tried-and-tested plot devices seen in previous films falter (the divided message from **Sherlock Holmes and the Secret Weapon**, the tracking-down of newly purchased antiques from **The Pearl of Death** – not to mention the implacable *femme fatale* adversary from **The Spider**

Woman and **The Woman in Green**), the story simply fizzles out, leading to a cursory and unexciting climax. We've seen it all before, and better.

Rathbone and Bruce's rather joyless last hurrah opens with the pair in oddly reflective vein, publication of Watson's retelling of the Irene Adler affair in the *Strand* under the title A SCANDAL IN BOHEMIA inspiring uncharacteristically moody reminiscence in Sherlock. (Watson refers to the case of THE SOLITARY CYCLIST, too.) Like the business with the tobacco ash, it's deeply satisfying to note that Hilda has bamboozled Watson by borrowing the 'smoke bomb' trick she's read about in A SCANDAL IN BOHEMIA – but the story stops short of presenting Hilda as 'The *Other* Woman'.

These touches suggest that it's no coincidence the finale takes place in the home of Dr Johnson, whose biographer, Boswell, Watson is explicitly compared to by Doyle. Minor literary pretension is

Holmes (Basil Rathbone) demonstrates the forensic deconstruction of tobacco ash to Hilda (Patricia Morison) in **Dressed To Kill** *(1946)*

all very well, but it doesn't make up for the gaping holes in the plot. If the convict Davidson is unable to get a message to the outside world, how do Hilda's gang learn about the boxes? Why doesn't Holmes share Hilda's name with the police – or Watson, even? An attempt is made to explain why the Bank of England hasn't simply changed its £5 note, but it's not exactly convincing – and suggesting that Davidson is trying to reveal the £5 plates' location to Hilda's gang because he fears that they will be discovered by accident merely underlines how incredible it is that the plates have not been found already.

Shot as *Prelude to Murder* (every bit as inapt a title as *Dressed to Kill*, which renders the change rather baffling), Universal's last Holmes film premiered in the US on 7 June 1946. The weary Rathbone, aware that his identification with Sherlock had cost him work, had elected not to renew his contract long beforehand. Some thought was given to replacing him with Tom Conway (1904-67), then playing 'The Falcon' for RKO in what would amount to 13 second features. Though Conway later took Rathbone's place opposite Bruce in one season's worth of radio adventures, Universal apparently elected to discontinue the Holmes series with Rathbone's retirement, despite its screen rights being valid for another three years. Whatever the truth, the

company was soon to dispense with its roster of B-pictures altogether. Roy William Neill, the producer-director responsible for all but the first of the Universal run, suffered a heart attack and died in England in October 1946. If an era ever ended, it ended here.

Saddest of all: Rathbone was unable to maintain his resolve, eventually returning to Holmes, seemingly out of desperation, in a TV one-off, **Suspense: The Adventure of the Black Baronet**.

Droske Nr. 519

aka **Cab No. 519** [GB], **Cab Number 519** [US]
*Denmark 1909 pastiche Nordisk Films Kompagni
1125 feet bw silent*
wd **Viggo Larsen**
known cast Sherlock Holmes: **Viggo Larsen**
Mr B, the heir: **Elith Pio** H, the villain: **Gustav Lund**

Mr B inherits £200,000 from his uncle – but his jealous friend, H, in cahoots with one John Smith, hatches a plan to get the money for himself.

A bogus cab kidnaps B from outside a leather-seller's. However, B has left his wallet inside the shop; the proprietor notes down the cab's number – 519 – and, on finding that B has gone missing, takes the details of the case to Sherlock Holmes. Posing as the driver of cab 519, Holmes traces the drugged B to a berth aboard a steamer, where the insane Smith attempts to throw B overboard. Smith is arrested, and Holmes and B go to confront H at a solicitor's office – where the latter, having taken B's identity, is about to take possession of B's inheritance. Found out, H attempts to kill himself, but is foiled by Holmes and duly taken to prison.

According to *Moving Picture World*, this fifth Nordisk Holmes, in which 'the excitement rises to its greatest height on the deck of the steamer', was 'the best of its kind'. The follow-up to **Sangerindens Diamanter**, *Droske Nr. 519* was released in Denmark on 30 April 1909, in Britain in May and in the US in June. Nordisk's series continued with **Den Grå Dame**.

The Eligible Bachelor

1992 TVM adaptation [THE NOBLE BACHELOR]
Granada Television 106m colour
tx 3 February 1993 ITV
w **T R Bowen** *p* **June Wyndham Davies** *d* **Peter Hammond**
cast Sherlock Holmes: **Jeremy Brett** Dr Watson: **Edward Hardwicke** Mrs Hudson: **Rosalie Williams** Inspector Montgomery: **Geoffrey Beevers** Lord Robert St Simon: **Simon Williams** Henrietta Doran: **Paris Jefferson** Lady Helena/Agnes Northcote: **Anna Calder-Marshall** Lady Florence: **Mary Ellis** Lady Mary: **Phillada Sewell** Lady Blanche: **Elspeth March** Hon Amelia St Simon: **Heather Chasen** Aloysius Doran: **Bob Sessions** Flora Miller: **Joanna McCallum** Thomas Floutier: **Myles Hoyle** Gallagher: **Bruce Myers** Alice: **Tres Hanley** Esther: **Joyce Grundy** Oswald: **Robin Hart** George Tidy: **Peter Graves** Moulton: **Peter Warnock** butler: **Don Blaylock** waiter: **Aubrey Phillips** stage doorkeeper: **Vincent Worth**

There is something perverse about a production team which takes two Doyle stories and squashes them together to make a 50-minute TV episode (*The Mazarin Stone*, in **The Memoirs of Sherlock Holmes**), and yet stretches out another short story, THE NOBLE BACHELOR, well beyond its natural length to fill more than 100 minutes' screen time. (Admittedly, THE VEILED LODGER is also touched upon, but only in passing.) It is instructive to note that the only crime in Doyle's NOBLE BACHELOR is bigamy, committed by Hetty Doran against Lord Robert St Simon, and it goes unpunished. Here, the wounded party has been pumped up into a full-blown Gothic villain, but the transformation is unconvincing.

It has to be said that **The Eligible Bachelor** is, using whatever critical criteria one chooses, appallingly bad television. Ponderously slow, insanely illogical, it engenders something like slow-motion disbelief in the viewer. It takes fully 39 minutes before St Simon consults Holmes regarding the disappearance of his third bride, Henrietta Doran, and even then Holmes never quite seems to take the supposed crime seriously. Not long after, Holmes is visited by the veiled figure of Agnes Northcote – whose sister, Helena, was the second Lady St Simon. That marriage was annulled when Helena was committed to a madhouse, but Agnes alleges that St Simon hired an actress named Flora Miller to impersonate his wife and feign her insanity; when Agnes visited St Simon's ancestral home, Glarvon, to discover the truth, she was mauled by one of the creatures in St Simon's Grimesby Roylott-esque roaming menagerie.

It becomes apparent to Holmes that St Simon is a serial monogamist who marries rich heiresses and then kills them when their money is used up. Soon, Henrietta (who had run away from the wedding service after learning that her previous, presumed dead husband is still alive) reappears and makes her way to Glarvon. Holmes and Watson follow, rescuing her from a grisly fate and stumbling across a pit in which St Simon has been keeping the 'insane' Helena like an animal. She is sane enough, however, to have set a trap for him, and he dies in a rockslide.

As with one or two other Granada adaptations around this time, attempts are made to tie the action to contemporaneous events (Holmes attends a performance of Henrik Ibsen's *Ghosts* and makes reference to 'Oscar Wilde's latest play', *The Importance of Being Earnest*) and to place

Jeremy Brett as Sherlock Holmes in **The Eligible Bachelor**

Above: Holmes (Jeremy Brett) tries to apprehend the mysterious veiled lady

Below: The disfigured Agnes Northcote (Anna Calder-Marshall) reveals her identity to Sherlock Holmes in **The Eligible Bachelor**

Holmes within his own history, dreaming of Reichenbach Falls and mentioning both Professor Moriarty and the Grimpen Mire. Here – another characteristic of the Granada productions of the time – the supernatural rears its ugly head when Holmes dreams repeatedly of a room filled with cobwebs and chairs with ripped covers. He later discovers the same room in Glarvon (the tears being caused by the claws of St Simon's big cat), so the dream is obviously precognitive. It's also quite pointless; it's there, but it doesn't enable Holmes to draw any conclusions or take any actions that he wouldn't have done otherwise – foresight without insight, as it were.

Deservedly reviled at the time of transmission, **The Eligible Bachelor** also earned the disapprobation of Estate inheritor Dame Jean Conan Doyle. Such responses led producer June Wyndham Davies to contemplate presenting out-and-out pastiches, but Jeremy Brett, stung by the Estate's rebuke, refused to countenance the idea. Granada's schedulers subsequently dropped tentative plans to make two further TV films and it seemed the sequence might simply disappear in ignominy. An impromptu decision in the early summer of 1993 to make six one-hour episodes in the old style saved some of the reputation of Brett's Holmes, but **The Memoirs of Sherlock Holmes** would prove a less than glorious valediction. (AL)

Den Forklædte Guvernante

tr 'The bogus governess'
at **Den Forklædte Barnepige** ['The bogus nurse']
aka **The Bogus Governess** [GB/US]
Denmark 1910 pastiche Nordisk Films Kompagni
1050 feet silent bw
known cast Sherlock Holmes: **Otto Lagoni**
the father: **Poul Welander**

W hen a wealthy father advertises for a
governess for his young daughter, a
criminal gang espies an opportunity – and one of
them obtains the post by disguising himself as a
woman. The father soon receives a letter
demanding a large sum of money to ensure that
his daughter is not murdered; he hires Sherlock
Holmes, who places an envelope stuffed with
paper at the drop-off point specified and hides
nearby. Holmes observes the governess leaving a
message for the gang, warning them that the
detective is on their trail and telling them where
and when they can kidnap the child – who is duly
seized. Having observed a razor among the
governess' possessions, Holmes sends the police a
telegram, telling them to send officers to the
gang's hideout, a timber-framed hut where he is
himself ambushed and tied to a tree with a ticking
time bomb attached; he soon escapes, however.
The police arrest the gang, and Holmes returns
the child home – where he promptly unmasks the
bogus governess.

Otto Lagoni replaced Viggo Larsen in this,
Nordisk's follow-up to **Den Grå Dame** – another
daft melodrama with a cross-dressing theme.
Lagoni's pipe-smoking detective was rather more
stout than Larsen's, and often seen with an
outsized golfing cap teetering on his head.

The *Bioscope* reckoned that 'some thrilling
incidents make the film most exciting' on its
release in the UK on 7 January 1911; *Moving
Picture World* noted the 'impossibilities' of *Den
Forklædte Guvernante*'s plot on its release in

America midway through June. Next in the series
was **Sherlock Holmes i Bondefangerkløer**.

For The Children: The Adventure of the Mazarin Stone

GB 1951 TV adaptation [THE MAZARIN STONE]
BBC Television 30m bw tx 29 July 1951
w **Anthony Cope** *p* **Alan Bromly**
cast Billy: **Jeremy Spenser** Dr Watson: **Philip King**
Sherlock Holmes: **Andrew Osborn** Count Negretto
Sylvius: **Frank Cariello** Sam Merton: **Martin Boddey**
Lord Cantlemere: **Felix Felton**

T he first-ever British television adaptation of a
Sherlock Holmes story was a half-hour's
Sunday teatime treat for juniors. Broadcast from
London by the state-owned British Broadcasting
Corporation (the only channel in the country at the
time) at half-past five in the afternoon, and introduced by D A Smith, this adaptation of THE
MAZARIN STONE formed the final part of an hour's
entertainment labelled *For the Children*; it followed
on directly from *Puppet Party* (15 minutes' worth of
the creations of H W Whanslaw, President of the
British Puppet and Model Theatre Guild) and a
Children's Newsreel (including 'Aerial Thrills at
Hendon'). *For the Children*, the strand that first
introduced wooden marionette Muffin the Mule
and once presented slapstick character Mr Pastry,
dated back to April 1937. Most broadcasts of the
time were staged at the BBC's Alexandra Palace
studios near Muswell Hill, north London.

Confined solely to Holmes' Baker Street sitting
room, THE MAZARIN STONE would have made an
ideal candidate for adaptation, given early
television's 'live' limitations (indeed, Doyle's tale
was itself a rewrite of a brief, one-act 'playlet', *The
Crown Diamond*). Although no footage has
survived (it's highly unlikely that the production
was ever recorded), an indication of *The Adventure*

of the *Mazarin Stone*'s relative fidelity to the
original text is given by the fact that violinist
Stanley Kamine was hired to play a section of Max
Woltag's arrangement for violin of Jacques
Offenbach's 'Barcarolle'. A gondolier's song from
Offenbach's posthumously produced 1881 operetta
Contes d'Hoffmann ('Tales of Hoffmann'), this is
exactly the piece that Doyle specifies Holmes
should announce he is going to 'try over' in his
bedroom while villain Count Negretto Sylvius and
his partner-in-crime Sam Merton confer. One
other piece of music was heard in this presentation:
a barrel-organ tune titled 'Over the Waves'.

Holmes was played by Andrew Osborn, a frequent BBC television actor whose credits went back
at least as far as 1938; his roles to date had been as
varied as Water Rat in *Toad of Toad Hall* (1946) and
Alexander the Great in Terence Rattigan's *Adventure
Story* (1950). By the sixties, Osborn had moved into
production, overseeing the popular *Maigret* and
ultimately influencing the direction of the 1968
BBC TV series **Sir Arthur Conan Doyle's Sherlock
Holmes**. At the time of broadcast, young Jeremy
Spenser, playing Holmes' pageboy Billy, was
appearing in *His House in Order* at London's New
Theatre. Felix Felton, here the virtuous Lord
Cantlemere, would go on to play a particularly
repulsive Dr Grimesby Roylott in the Corporation's
1964 try-out, **Detective: the Speckled Band**.

The Adventure of the Mazarin Stone would
prove to be the one and only Holmes adaptation
performed as part of *For the Children* – and within
the space of just a few months, the Corporation
would mount a full, six-part series for grown-ups,
**We Present Alan Wheatley as Mr Sherlock Holmes
in...** Although ostensibly unconnected to the
Osborn play, it might be significant that the
Wheatley series took a recording of 'Barcarolle' for
its opening theme.

... From the Adventures of Sherlock Holmes

France circa 1912 8 x 20m approx film series
adaptations Éclair silent bw
Produced under the personal supervision of the Author,
Sir A Conan Doyle

The Speckled Band

Silver Blaze

The Beryl Coronet

The Musgrave Ritual

The Reygate Squires
adaptation [The Reigate Squires]

The Stolen Papers
adaptation [The Naval Treaty]

The Mystery of Boscombe Vale
adaptation [The Boscombe Valley Mystery]

The Copper Beeches

Circa 1911, Arthur Conan Doyle sold film rights
in his Sherlock Holmes stories to the French
company Éclair, which that year produced a two-
reel silent melodrama entitled *Les Aventures de
Sherlock Holmes*, written and directed by Victorin-
Hippolyte Jasset (1862-1913) with an actor named
Henri Gouget in the lead. Éclair's output of the
time included the moving picture adventures of the
newspaper-cartoon crime lord Zigomar, as played
by Alexandre Arquillière (1870-1953) in several
Jasset-directed films including *Zigomar* (also 1911,
and with Gouget in the cast), *Zigomar contre Nick
Carter* and *Zigomar, Peau d'anguille* (both 1912).
Some of these featured Charles Krauss as
investigator Nick Carter; Éclair's first Carter film
had been *Nick Carter, le roi des détectives* (1908).

Far less obscure are Éclair's eight Holmes
shorts of 1912, produced by Georges Tréville, an
actor-director in the film industry since 1903.
Although Éclair had established a studio in Paris
four years previously, interiors for this octet were
recorded at the Kursaal in the English resort of
Bexhill-on-Sea (not far from Dover, the main
point of entry to the Continent), with exteriors
presumably found elsewhere in the Sussex
countryside. Tréville is supposed to have played the
hero-detective himself, although a *Kinematograph
Weekly* writer of June 1921, reporting on Tréville's
arrival in Britain to direct a version of *All Sorts and
Conditions of Men* for Ideal, noted his association
with the earlier Holmes series and added: 'It was
these pictures which gave Cameron Carr his first
introduction to film acting.'

Englishman Carr would be a noted film player throughout the twenties and early thirties; in his mid-thirties at the time of the Éclair films, Carr shared the dark colouring and sallow, slightly sunken features of the actor playing Holmes, but the condition of the surviving film, *The Copper Beeches*, makes it impossible to positively identify one or the other in the lead. Title cards claim the series to have been produced under Doyle's 'personal supervision'; British trade paper the *Bioscope* would later note that the films were 'taken amidst the surroundings which have been so graphically described by the author', leading one to speculate that British-based filming may have been a condition of the rights being assigned in the first place. The director may have been one Adrien Caillard, or possibly Tréville himself.

Although a date for the films' original French release has not been established, America received them late in 1912 – with British distribution, through the Fenning Film Service Ltd of Regent Street, London, commencing a year later. The *Bioscope* stated that Britain would, in fact, be receiving nine pictures in the series (a fact confirmed by Fenning's later ad blocks), the last having been 'taken in America'; a 2000-feet film, *The Sign of Four*, is listed as being produced by Éclair for release after *The Copper Beeches*, leading to the assumption that this was actually Thanhauser's **Sherlock Holmes Solves 'The Sign of Four'** (1913). It should also be noted that accounts of the various films' lengths differ between contemporary US and UK journals, all bar two being measured at 2000 feet in Britain.

First to be issued in the UK, on 27 October 1913, was *The Speckled Band*, which the *Bioscope* asserted was 'in no respect founded on the play which was produced in London recently ... Except for the omission of Dr Watson, who has always been a somewhat colourless individual on the stage, the film follows the story pretty much on the original lines.' In fact, the Éclair version has Holmes disguising himself as 'a foreigner of good position' in order to infiltrate the country house of 'Dr Grimsby Rylott' [sic], whose step-daughter has asked the detective to investigate the death of her sister shortly after the announcement of her engagement. Holmes then 'makes a formal offer of marriage' to the stepdaughter, the girl 'seemingly consenting'; Rylott 'has no pretext for

An Autumn 1913 Bioscope ad promoting distribution of Éclair's Sherlock Holmes films in the UK

refusal, and, as Holmes anticipated, matters are brought to a crisis.'

Silver Blaze was released on 24 November, with the remaining films being sent out at a rate of one a month until the summer of 1914. As a surviving example of the series *The Copper Beeches* has not dated well. The tyrannical Rucastle, infuriated by his daughter's choice of fiancé, is a swaggering Bluebeard prone to wild over-gesticulation, while his hapless daughter is a swooning damsel in distress locked in a barn for refusing to sign away her inheritance. Rucastle hires a governess, Miss Hunter, from the Westaway Agency; she, perturbed by the various goings-on in and around Rucastle's house, goes to see Holmes, a scarf-wearing, trilby-hatted type in baggy riding breeches and knee-length boots, later seen swishing a horsewhip and carrying a pistol. The finale has Holmes riding to the scene to prevent the shotgun-toting Rucastle from killing the fiancé; he then helps to free the daughter from her prison.

Doyle's story is barely related, but the production is handsome for its time, using four nicely detailed interior rooms and a total of nine different set-ups in various exterior locations. As per *The Speckled Band*, no Watson appears, nor is he mentioned in the American *Moving Picture World* write-up of *Silver Blaze*; a 'Mr Moyse' is reported to have played the character in various of the instalments, but since there is little evidence to support this assertion, it ought to be treated with caution.

Back in 1913-14, British business for all nine films was, according to cinema-owners as far afield as Handsworth, Hulme, Sunderland and Clapham Common, phenomenal. The Holmes films were mostly considered 'top-liners' by the trade, going out alongside such draws as *Fantomas, the False Magistrate* in Stoke Newington, for example. Perhaps the most vivid example of their impact was provided by the *Bioscope*'s Birmingham correspondent, who wrote on 22 January 1914 in response to a prominent Scottish librarian's comments on 'the deleterious effects of the cinema on reading': 'I should like to note here that the sale of the various editions of Conan Doyle's works has been visibly augmented during the screening of the pictures in the town. This statement is made, not from theory, but from considerable research ... to my mind, it shows that the cinema convinces the public of the quality of a book – that instead of borrowing a copy for a week or two [from a library] they prefer to expend 6d, and make the volume a lasting friend.'

Fu Er Mo Si Yu Zhong Guo Nu Xia

aka **Sherlock Holmes and the Chinese Heroine,
Sherlock Holmes in China**
China 1994 pastiche Beijing Film Studio 82m colour
w **Ke Zhanghe, Li Changfu, Wang Fengkui**
d **Liu Yun-Zhou, Wang Chi**
cast includes Sherlock Holmes: **Fan Ai Li** [aka **Alex Vanderpor**] Furong [aka 'Fu Yong']: **Xiulan Limei** Jin Mazhang: **Wang Chi** Tu Wu: **Zhang Chunzhong** Du Wencai: **Wang Hongtao**
Watson: **Xu Zhongquan** Henry: **Hanson**

The early 20th century: travelling in China, Sherlock Holmes and Dr Watson stay the night at a hotel where they meet the outgoing British ambassador, who is transporting Chinese treasure to England. The ambassador is murdered in the night; a local government representative asks Holmes to investigate, despite his masters' certainty that the deed was done by the rebel Boxers. Holmes discovers that Furong, the young woman who runs the hotel, is one of the Boxers – and, convinced of the rebels' innocence, Holmes con-spires with the Boxers to set a trap for the guilty party.

The prospect of a period-set Sherlock Holmes film produced by the largest and oldest film studio in Asia remains an intriguing one, for *Fu Er Mo Si Yu Zhong Guo Nu Xia* is not known to have been seen in the West. The film takes place against the backdrop of the Boxer Rebellion of 1900-1, a peasant uprising designed to force all foreigners from China – and so the idea that Holmes should side with the 'righteous and harmonious fists' of the martial arts-trained Boxers is quite fascinating.

Female lead Xiulan Limei has been seen as Wenrui, the Princess Lui, in the period romance *Strange Love in the Forbidden City* (also 1994).

The Further Adventures of Sherlock Holmes

GB 1922 15 x film series adaptations Stoll Picture Productions Ltd silent bw
w **Geoffrey H Malins, Patrick L Mannock** [except where stated] *chief of production/p* **Jeffrey Bernerd**
d **George Ridgwell**
regular cast Sherlock Holmes: **Eille Norwood**
Dr Watson: **Hubert Willis**

Charles Augustus Milverton
1900 feet
regular cast, plus Detective Insp Hopkins: **Teddy Arundell**
Mrs Hudson: **Mdme D'Esterre** Charles Augustus Milverton: **George Foley** butler to Milverton: **Harry J Worth** well-dressed woman: **Tony Edgar-Bruce** cook: **Annie Hughes** housemaid: **Edith Bishop**

The Abbey Grange
2193 feet
regular cast, plus Det Insp Hopkins: **Teddy Arundell** Mrs Hudson: **Mdme D'Esterre** Lady Brackenstall: **Madeline Seymour** Sir Eustace Brackenstall: **Lawford Davidson** Captain Croker: **Leslie Stiles** Theresa, Lady Brackenstall's maid: **Madge Tree**

THE NORWOOD BUILDER

2067 feet

regular cast, plus Jonas Oldacre: **Fred Wright** John
McFarlane: **Cyril Raymond** Mrs McFarlane: **Laura Walker**
Det Insp Hopkins: **Teddy Arundell** Mrs Hudson: **Mdme
D'Esterre**

THE REIGATE SQUIRES

1885 feet

regular cast, plus Det Insp Hopkins: **Teddy Arundell**
Mrs Hudson: **Mdme D'Esterre** Alec Cunningham:
Richard Atwood Squire Cunningham: **Teddy O'Neil**
William Kirwan: **C Sequin** Col Hayter: **Arthur Lumley**

THE NAVAL TREATY

1536 feet

regular cast, plus Percy Phelps: **Jack Hobbs** Joseph
Harrison: **Francis Duguid** Miss Harrison: **Nancy May**

THE SECOND STAIN

2179 feet

regular cast, plus Det Insp Hopkins: **Teddy Arundell** Lord
Bellinger: **Cecil Ward** Mrs Hope: **Dorothy Fane** Mrs Hudson:
Mdme D'Esterre Eduardo Lucas' wife: **Maria Minetti**

THE RED CIRCLE

1770 feet

regular cast, plus Amelia Lucca: **Sybil Archdale**
Mrs Hudson: **Mdme D'Esterre** Det Insp Hopkins: **Teddy
Arundell** Gorgiano: **Maresco Marisini** Gennaro Lucca:

Bertram Burleigh Leverton, New York Private Detective:
Tom Beaumont Mrs Warren: **Esme Hubbard**

THE SIX NAPOLEONS

1753 feet

regular cast, plus Mrs Hudson: **Mdme D'Esterre**
Det Insp Hopkins: **Teddy Arundell** Beppo: **George Bellamy**
Pietro Venucci: **Jack Raymond** Lucretia Venucci: **Alice Moffat**

BLACK PETER

1776 feet

regular cast, plus Mrs Hudson: **Mdme D'Esterre**

*Reginald Musgrave (Geoffrey Wilmer) watches on as Watson (Hubert
Willis) and Holmes (Eille Norwood) lift the lid on the 'Musgrave
Ritual'. From* **The Further Adventures of Sherlock Holmes** *(1922)*

According to Arthur Conan Doyle himself, Eille Norwood's Holmes had 'that rare quality which can only be described as glamour...'

Det Insp Hopkins: **Teddy Arundell** Patrick Cairnes: **Hugh Buckler** Peter Carey: **Fred Paul** Mrs Carey: **Mrs Hubert Willis** Miss Carey: **Miss Willis** Neligan, Jnr: **Jack Jarman** Neligan, Snr: **Fred Raines**

THE BRUCE-PARTINGTON PLANS
2130 feet
regular cast, plus Det Insp Hopkins: **Teddy Arundell**
Colonel Valentine Walter: **Ronald Power**
Oberstein: **Edward Sorley** Cadogan West: **Malcolm Todd**
Mycroft Holmes: **Lewis Gilbert** Sidney Johnson: **Leslie Brittain**

THE STOCKBROKER'S CLERK
1830 feet
regular cast, plus Pycroft: **Olaf Hytten** Pinner: **Aubrey Fitzgerald** Beddington: **George Ridgwell**

THE BOSCOMBE VALLEY MYSTERY
2410 feet
regular cast, plus Charles McCarthy: **Hal Martin**

James McCarthy: **Ray Raymond** John Turner: **Fred Raynham** Miss Turner: **Thelma Murray**

THE MUSGRAVE RITUAL
1698 feet
w **George Ridgwell**
regular cast, plus Brunton (Musgrave's butler):
Clifton Boyne Rachel Howells (Musgrave's maid):
Betty Chester Musgrave: **Geoffrey Wilmer**

THE GOLDEN PINCE-NEZ
1630 feet
regular cast, plus Coram: **Cecil Morton York** Det Insp
Hopkins: **Teddy Arundell** Anna Coram: **Norma Whalley**

THE GREEK INTERPRETER
1796 feet
regular cast, plus Mr Melas: **Cyril Dane** Latimer: **J R Tozer**
Wilson Kemp: **Robert Vallis** Sophy Katrides: **Edith Saville**
Paul Katrides: **L Andre** Det Insp Hopkins: **H Wheeler**
Mrs Hudson: **Mdme D'Esterre**

By the autumn of 1921, that year's British-made series of Stoll Picture Productions shorts **The Adventures of Sherlock Holmes** had been seen as far afield as Japan and Australia; a recently released feature, **The Hound of the Baskervilles**, would meet with similar success. Further adventures were guaranteed – and, indeed, 15 *Further Adventures of Sherlock Holmes* were duly issued to Stoll's picture palaces from March 1922. All 15 have survived, but only five in a viewable format: *The Abbey Grange, The Red Circle, The Bruce-Partington Plans, The Stockbroker's Clerk* and an impressively detailed *The Musgrave Ritual*.

Director Maurice Elvey was replaced by George Ridgwell (d 1935), some of whose earliest picture credits, such as *The Mystery in Room 13* (1915), had been for America's Edison organisation. In 1920, he'd made several features for the British & Colonial Kinematograph Company before defecting to Stoll to direct, among others, a version of Edgar Wallace's *The Four Just Men* (1921). This featured Edward 'Teddy' Arundell as Inspector Falmouth; Arundell, who'd been Jabez Wilson in the first series instalment *The Red-headed League*, would be cast as Doyle's Detective-Inspector Hopkins in most of the *Further Adventures*, replacing Arthur Bell's Lestrade. Arundell's death from heart disease in November 1922 would lead

The FURTHER ADVENTURES of SHERLOCK HOLMES

A New Series of Holmes Pictures. From Sir A. Conan Doyle's Immortal Stories. Eille Norwood as the great Detective Stoll Picture Productions.

Hubert Willis and Eille Norwood feature in another Stoll ad block for **The Further Adventures of Sherlock Holmes** *(1922)*

to another Inspector, played by Tom Beaumont, becoming the police liaison to Eille Norwood's Holmes in the following year's final series of films, **The Last Adventures of Sherlock Holmes**.

Arundell's illness may also explain Hopkins being portrayed by 'H Wheeler' in the last of the *Further Adventures*, *The Greek Interpreter*, an episode which is distinguished by Norwood's Holmes disguising himself as an old woman at one point. (The next Sherlock to employ such a tactic would be Clive Brook in **Conan Doyle's Master Detective Sherlock Holmes**.) It's worth noting that Lewis Gilbert became the first actor to portray Sherlock's brother, Mycroft Holmes, on screen in Stoll's version of *The Bruce-Partington Plans* – a distinction often erroneously accorded Robert Morley in **A Study in Terror**, made 43 years later.

As before, Norwood's Holmes was seen in a wide variety of London locations, mostly tracked down by young Stoll employee Baynham Honri – who not only persuaded the officers of the Metropolitan Line to allow Stoll to use the railway for the *Bruce-Partington Plans* scene in which a body is thrown onto the roof of a passing train, but also got the company to lay on a train from Neasden, free of charge, and cast one of the Line's own ticket inspectors in a sequence filmed at Gloucester Road. Even more remarkable, Honri gained permission from the Foreign Office to use part of its St James' Park premises, plus Horse Guards Parade, for shots in *The Naval Treaty* – a first for a state department, apparently. 'It looks like Stolls make history as well as pictures,' crowed the company's *Editorial News*.

Not that Norwood was always out and about – one or two episodes, it seems, were partly filmed at his own home. And when not performing, Stoll's renaissance man continued to pursue his talents in other areas: one of the musical pieces recommended to cinema-owners as accompaniment for the films was the 'very taking' 'Dance des Follettes', published by Chappell and composed by Eille Norwood.

Den Grå Dame

at **Af Sherlock Holmes Oplevelser IV**
['Of Sherlock Holmes' Memoirs IV']
aka **The Grey Lady** [GB], **The Grey Dame** [US]
Denmark 1909 pastiche Nordisk Films Kompagni
1007 feet bw silent
wd **Viggo Larsen**
known cast Sherlock Holmes: **Viggo Larsen**
Lord Beresford: **Gustav Lund** Lord Beresford's son, Willy:
Elith Pio John, Lord Beresford's nephew: **Poul Welander**

Accepting an invitation to visit his uncle and cousin, Lord Beresford and son Willy, John goes to the ancient Beresford Castle. At dinner, the legend of the ghostly Grey Dame is told; whenever her spectral form is seen, the eldest Beresford son in the house shall die. The ghost duly appears, and Lord Beresford is found dead. Soon after, Willy sees the apparition – but survives, and sends a telegram to Sherlock Holmes, requesting assistance. Holmes arrives and, surviving being cast into the dungeons, discovers a number of secret doors and passageways – plus the very real dress of the 'Grey Dame'. By impersonating Willy, the detective traps the 'ghost' – revealing it to be none other than the scoundrel John, who has been determined to remove all other heirs to the estate.

Released in Denmark on 27 August 1909, *Den Grå Dame*, the sequel to **Droske Nr. 519**, was the sixth in the Nordisk sequence – and the last to involve writer/director/actor Viggo Larsen who, apparently in the wake of a disagreement with company founder Ole Olsen, shortly thereafter decamped to Germany to make the serial **Arsène Lupin contra Sherlock Holmes**. With its HOUND OF THE BASKERVILLES-style storyline – an ancient castle, a spectre heralding the death of the family heir revealed to be a contrivance of the villain – *Den Grå Dame* proved to be the most widely distributed of the Danish Holmeses since **Raffles Flugt Fra Fængslet**; 100 copies were sold abroad with, variously, German, English, Spanish, French, Italian and Swedish captions. Praising the 'splendid story' underpinning this latest effort, *Moving Picture World*'s correspondent related, sweetly, that 'later when we told a small boy of nine what we had seen, he clapped his hands and said, "Oh, how I wish I could have seen that picture ..."' Nordisk's series continued with **Den Forklædte Guvernante**.

Sherlock Holmes (Viggo Larsen) pops up from the hidden crannies of Beresford Castle in **Den Grå Dame** *(1909)*

Die graue Dame

tr 'The grey lady'
Germany 1937 pastiche Neue Film KG 92m bw
w **Erich Engels**, **Hans Heuer** *source* **Die Tat des Unbekannten** ['The deed of the unknown',
stage play by **Muller-Puzika**]
d **Erich Engels**
cast 'Jimmy Ward' [Sherlock Holmes]: **Hermann Speelmans** Maria Iretzkaja: **Trude Marlen** Lola: **Elisabeth Wendt** Baranoff: **Edwin Jürgensen** Harry Motel: **Theo Shall** Inspector Brown: **Ernst Karchow** John, diener bei Ward: **Werner Finck** Jack Clark: **Werner Scharf** James Hewitt: **Hans Halden** Archibald Pepperkorn: **Henry Lorenzen** Wilson: **Reinhold Bernt** Fra Miller: **Eva Tinschmann** other roles: **Ursula Herking**, **Charles W Kayser**, **Maria Loja**, **Paul Schwed**

A bizarre cash-in, *Die Graue Dame* is a quasi-Holmes picture based on a theatrical play entirely unrelated to the works of Doyle and released shortly after the Bruno Güttner-starring **Der Hund von Baskerville** (1937). Here, young Jimmy Ward – played by Hermann Speelmans (1906-60), who'd featured in the vile Nazi propaganda feature *Hitlerjunge Quex: ein Film vom Opfergeist der Deutschen Jugend* (1933), an immorality tale designed to drum up recruitment into the Hitler Youth – infiltrates a criminal gang, only to reveal at the last moment that he is, in fact, none other than an undercover Sherlock Holmes. One can only presume that the 'John' – who, according to the credits list, acts as Holmes' 'servant' – was intended to be none other than the hapless Dr Watson.

The Great Mouse Detective

at **The Adventures of the Great Mouse Detective**
[1992 reissue]
aka **Basil the Great Mouse Detective** [GB]
US 1986 animation The Walt Disney Company 71m colour
w **Pete Young, Vance Gerry, Steve Hulett, Ron Clements, John Musker, Bruce M Morris, Matthew O'Callaghan, Burny Mattinson, Dave Michener, Melvin Shaw** *source* **Basil of Baker Street** and sequels [book series by **Eve Titus** and **Paul Galdone**] *p* **Burny Mattinson** *d* **John Musker, Dave Michener, Ron Clements, Burny Mattinson** *voice cast* Professor Ratigan: **Vincent Price** Basil: **Barrie Ingham** Dawson: **Val Bettin** Olivia: **Susanne Pollatschek** Fidget: **Candy Candido** Mrs Judson: **Diana Chesney** the Mouse Queen: **Eve Brenner** Flaversham: **Alan Young** Sherlock Holmes: **Basil Rathbone** Watson: **Laurie Main** lady mouse: **Shani Wallis** bar maid: **Ellen Fitzhugh** citizen: **Walker Edmiston** Bartholomew: **Barrie Ingham** thug guards: **Wayne Allwine, Tony Anselmo, Val Bettin, Walker Edmiston**

THE MYSTERY
London, 1897: while the human world sleeps, a widowed mouse toymaker, Flaversham, is kidnapped from his workshop by a one-legged bat with a crippled wing. War veteran Dr David Q Dawson, recently returned from Afghanistan, is searching for lodgings when he comes across Flaversham's young daughter, Olivia, who has

'Jimmy Ward' (Hermann Speelmans) reveals himself to be Sherlock Holmes in **Die graue Dame** (1937)

become lost while searching for the famous mouse detective Basil. Dawson takes Olivia to 221 Baker Street, where they meet the eccentric Basil – who recognises the bat kidnapper as Fidget, henchman of his arch-enemy, the evil Professor Ratigan...

THE INVESTIGATION
Ratigan, who is plotting to become the supreme ruler of all mousedom on the occasion of the Queen's diamond jubilee one day hence, sends Fidget out to collect component parts that Flaversham must use to build some sort of automaton – and orders him to find Olivia, too, the better to ensure Flaversham's co-operation. Fidget fails to swipe Olivia from Basil's home, leaving his cap behind – and also a trail of scent which Toby, the bloodhound owned by the human detective who lives above Basil, can follow. Basil, Dawson and Olivia follow Toby to a human toyshop, where Fidget is collecting both mechanical gears and Royal Guard uniforms from a troop of clockwork soldiers; after a struggle, Olivia is grabbed by Fidget. The list of instructions that Ratigan had given Fidget contains enough forensic evidence to point Basil and Dawson in the

direction of a seedy bar on the Thames waterfront
– where, disguised as Irish sailors, they spot and
pursue the wicked Fidget to Ratigan's secret lair in
a human pub cellar. But the detective has been
duped: Ratigan is ready and waiting for him.

THE SOLUTION

The Professor has forced Flaversham to build a
clockwork double of the Queen, which he plans to
substitute for the real ruler – and it is the double
which will announce that Ratigan is to become her
consort, enabling the Professor to seize power and
instigate an oppressive tax regime (among other
fiendish policies). Leaving Basil and Dawson
strapped into a particularly elaborate and deadly
mousetrap, Ratigan leaves, by airship, for
Buckingham Palace – where his lackeys, wearing
Royal Guard uniforms, have already captured the
real Queen. Basil and Dawson contrive to escape
the trap, freeing Olivia and racing on Toby's back
to the Palace, just in time to gain control of the
clockwork Queen, which Basil then uses to
denounce Ratigan before the Queen's subjects.
Ratigan takes to the air with Olivia in tow while
Basil and Dawson pursue the villain to Big Ben in
a jerry-built balloon. Ratigan's airship crashes into
the clock face – and, after an almighty tussle with
Basil, the evil Professor falls to his doom. Olivia
and Flaversham are re-united and Basil teams up
with Dawson on a permanent basis.

✦ ✦ ✦

Firstly, yes, Sherlock Holmes, played by the
inimitable Basil Rathbone, *is* seen in *The Great
Mouse Detective* – as a violin-scraping silhouette
pacing the upper floors of 221 Baker Street, telling
Watson that he needs loud German music, the
better to 'introspect'. The line is taken from an
episode of the 1940-46 Rathbone/Nigel Bruce
radio series, although here Watson is given voice
by one Laurie Main (who'd previously essayed the
role in **Children's Mystery Theater: The Treasure of
Alpheus T Winterborn**). Toby the bloodhound, as
borrowed by Holmes in THE SIGN OF THE FOUR,
makes an even more substantial appearance.
Having therefore satisfied ourselves that *The Great
Mouse Detective* meets all the proper Holmes film
criteria, we can now address an entirely joyful,
well-observed piece that numbers among the very
best of Doyle-inspired parodies.

The Great Mouse Detective was derived from a
series of children's books written by Eve Titus and
illustrated by Paul Galdone: the first, *Basil of Baker
Street*, published in 1958, was followed by titles
like *Basil and the Lost Colony*, *Basil and the Pygmy
Cats*, *Basil in Mexico* and *Basil in the Wild West*.
Titus' rodent investigator was named in tribute to
Rathbone; accordingly, the Walt Disney Company's
animators clearly based their visualisation of his
Watson type on Nigel Bruce, hence the portly,
blustering and endlessly goodhearted 'Dawson'.
Basil, more charismatic than any two-dimensional
anthropomorphic cheese-muncher has any right to
be, displays all the essential characteristics of the
man upstairs in his first scene alone: he's a master
of disguise, entering in the costume of an inflated
mandarin, a Fu Manchu; he's a scientific/deductive
genius, conducting ballistics tests; and he's prone
to operatic mood swings, plunging into the depths
of despair when said tests fail. Frankly, Basil
makes for a more acceptable and engaging lead
than many human Sherlocks.

Basil's Moriarty is the scheming, silver-tongued
Professor Ratigan, who claims to be a mouse but
is, in fact, a 'slimy, contemptible' sewer rat with
ideas above his station; he reverts to type in the
closing moments of the film and it's a startling,
almost horrible transformation. One of the piece's
many pleasing inversions is the idea that Ratigan
keeps a cat – the corpulent, pampered Felicia, who
functions as the Professor's chief whip, dispensing
fanged justice to members of the gang who step
out of line (indeed, the eating of the drunken
Bartholomew makes for the film's cruellest
moment). Horror movie demi-god Vincent Price
(1911-93), doubtless best known to *The Great Mouse
Detective*'s target audience as the voice of Michael
Jackson's 'Thriller', plays this other Napoleon of
Crime. Price would apparently nominate Ratigan
among his favourite roles, and only the resolutely
po-faced could resist smiling as Cinema's Scariest
Man launches into his renditions of the songs
'The World's Greatest Criminal Mind' and
'Goodbye, So Soon'.

Produced relatively cheaply, *The Great Mouse
Detective* grossed a very respectable $38.6 million on
release in summer 1986 – by way of comparison,
the previous winter had seen the vastly more
expensive **Young Sherlock Holmes** gather just a
fraction of Basil's take – but, despite broadly happy

reviews, and the fact that the closing scene has Dawson reveal that he and Basil shared many further adventures together, no sequel has been forthcoming. (A Basil statuette could, however, be glimpsed in several episodes of Disney's 1991-92 TV series *Darkwing Duck*.) The film is now obscure enough to have spawned a cult following of its very own, a plethora of internet sites being devoted to the indefatigable Basil. And that's not in the least bit surprising, for *The Great Mouse Detective* rewards re-watching, every frame being packed with detail: Disney's flying elephant Dumbo can be glimpsed in the human toyshop; there's the news-sheet, *The Illustrated London Mouse*; there's a disarmingly sexualised rodent whore in the waterfront tavern; there's the fact that the closing battle on Big Ben references the 1978 remake of *The Thirty-nine Steps*. There's even a hidden Mickey Mouse.

In 1990, the altogether less sophisticated Roland Rat, a gurning glove puppet popularised by breakfast television, would attempt to seize the mantle of mousedom's premier detective in *Tales of the Rodent Sherlock Holmes*. Needless to say, Basil of Baker Street's reputation remains intact.

Back in 1984, incidentally, a more straightforward (and rodent-free) attempt at 'animating' Sherlock Holmes was made by the Australian company Pacific Arts, for whom Eddy Graham produced four canonical adaptations aimed at children: *Sherlock Holmes and a Study in Scarlet*, *Sherlock Holmes and the Sign of Four*, *Sherlock Holmes and the Valley of Fear* – each of which ran 48 minutes – plus a 70-minute *Sherlock Holmes and the Baskerville Curse*. Earle Cross voiced Dr Watson and Peter O'Toole, no less, brought his tranquillised tones to Sherlock Holmes.

Hands of a Murderer

aka **Sherlock Holmes and the Prince of Crime**
US 1990 TVM pastiche Green Pond Productions Inc
120m colour
w/co-p **Charles Edward Pogue** *p* **Robert E Fuisz**
d **Stuart Orme**
tx 16 May 1990 CBS TV
cast Sherlock Holmes: **Edward Woodward** Doctor Watson:
John Hillerman Professor Moriarty: **Anthony Andrews**
Sophy de Vere: **Kim Thomson** Mycroft Holmes: **Peter
Jeffrey** Colonel Booth: **Warren Clarke** Inspector Lestrade:
Terence Lodge Stubb: **Christopher Fairbank**
Richard Farrington: **Harry Audley** Finch: **David Sibley**
Oberstein: **Nickolas Grace** Berton: **John Tordoff**
Wiggins: **Danny Newman** Mrs Hudson: **Faith Kent**
Minister: **David Neal** policeman: **Steve Ellis** police driver:
David Arlen ballad singer: **Graham Gill** Wilkes: **Jimmy
Flint** old drunk: **Ronald Nunnery** preacher: **Geoffrey Rose**
hangman: **Peter Brace** Queen Victoria: **Honora Burke**
the Baker Street Irregulars: **Ben Waters**, **Matthew Baker**,
Ben Davis, **Tony Vaughn**, **David King**

THE MYSTERY

At the hangman's scaffold, Professor Moriarty
evades execution with the help of a gang of his
followers disguised as a Salvation Army band. Soon
after, Sherlock Holmes, who had been responsible
for Moriarty's conviction, receives a cryptic message
from the Professor informing him that 'the day of
my vengeance is at hand...' To divert his brother
from his 'pathetic obsession', Mycroft Holmes
summons him to his club, where war hero Colonel
Booth reveals that a series of mysterious leaks
from within the Whitehall establishment have
compromised national security...

THE INVESTIGATION

Under the hypnotic influence of the ravishing
'Baroness Angela de Vere' – actually a failed
actress named Sophy, now Moriarty's consort –
Mycroft's aide, Farrington, allows a safe-cracker,
Stubb, access to Mycroft's office, where a hugely
sensitive coded message is stolen. Moriarty plans
to sell this on to German agent Oberstein, but still
lacks the key to breaking the cipher. The Thuggee
Berton is dispatched to kidnap Mycroft; caught,
Mycroft pretends to succumb to Sophy's
mesmerism, leading Stubb to mount a doomed
attempt to raid the safe at 221B. A stalemate
develops between Holmes and Moriarty, broken
only when Holmes reveals to Booth that he has
deduced that the key to cracking the code is
contained within a marked volume of Voltaire.
Booth is, of course, a traitor; Holmes, Watson and
Lestrade follow him to the deserted church where
Moriarty is keeping his appointment with
Oberstein. Mycroft is freed, and Oberstein is shot
by Watson. Taking flight with Sophy, Moriarty sets
a bomb covering his exit; the resulting explosion
kills both Booth and Sherlock Holmes...

THE SOLUTION

Moriarty cannot resist attending Holmes' funeral –
but his disguise does not fool Holmes, whose
'death' had been staged in a bid to trap the
Professor. Holding Holmes hostage, Moriarty
attempts to escape in a hansom cab, with Sophy
steering; however, as Moriarty and Holmes
struggle, Sophy is shot, and the cab runs out of
control. Holmes contrives to escape at the last
moment, and the cab plunges into a lake. Although
Moriarty's body is not found, the state's secrets are
safe once more, and Holmes is duly summoned to
a meeting with 'his biggest fan' – Queen Victoria.

✦ ✦ ✦

Saddled with a meaningless title – excluding
the possibility of its being an extremely sly
reference to the many and various acolytes who
undertake Moriarty's dirty work throughout –
Hands of a Murderer, filmed in England in
association with Yorkshire Television, is no more
than a number of high-concept set-pieces linked by
the flimsiest of stories. Thrill – to Moriarty's daring
escape from the gallows! See – the beautiful
mesmerist cast her wicked spell over the great and

good! Gasp – as Holmes and Moriarty fight to the death aboard a runaway coach! Groan – as yet another plot thread is left unexplained and unexplored! True, the set-pieces are often very impressive indeed, and the overall production is extremely handsome (some iffy blue-screen work in that runaway coach sequence apart). But, founded on a premise which starts big (Moriarty's ultimate revenge on Holmes) then dwindles to virtually nothing (endless gubbins about a secret document of little import), the whole ends up a great deal less than the sum of its parts.

Seemingly, *Hands of a Murderer*'s *raison d'etre* is to underline the duality of, and the never-ending duel between, Holmes and Moriarty; its key scene, where the pair meet over a symbolic chessboard, is about as bald, blatant and unsubtle an exposition of their contest as could possibly be contrived. Studying the position of the various pieces, the Professor – who, at this point, has Mycroft and Watson held captive by his goons – spells out Holmes' dilemma with the line, 'If you want to take the black King, first you must sacrifice a Knight and a pawn.' Which would be a fascinating development if it were true, but the dark, brooding and pathologically obsessive Holmes needed to make the situation interesting is simply not there. We are never left in any doubt that Edward Woodward's stiff, grouchy Sherlock is too all-round decent to succumb to the desire to see Moriarty undone at any price, however often he might utter dire threats in the Professor's direction. Put plainly, he simply doesn't play the game; for the notion to work, Holmes must operate in shades of grey, not pristine white.

Anthony Andrews' Moriarty is just as flawed a realisation, but rather more interesting for all that. Young, cruel, libidinous and utterly mad, the interpretation suggests a James Bond villain. He surrounds himself with exotic killers; he's a traitor with a fascination for 'bad' Orientalism; he merrily disposes of failed henchmen in cruel and unusual ways (one dies from the bite of a pet cobra); he's smart, slicked-back, buttoned-up and, rather like Joseph Wiseman's filmic Dr No, has black-gloved hands at all times; he even has a luxurious hidden 'base' adorned with stolen works of art (here, the Mona Lisa, whereas the aforementioned No could only manage Goya's Duke of Wellington in the 1962 film). What he lacks is a real plan – the

actual project which should swing into action in the film's final third. Instead, his plotting is cursorily foiled and he's nothing left to do but turn up at Holmes' 'funeral' just in time to be despatched in the picture's rather underwhelming epilogue/finale. It's been suggested that Andrews should have played Holmes and Woodward Moriarty, and it's not hard to imagine how much more striking the actors could have been in each other's shoes.

The remaining cast are uniformly good, nonetheless: John Hillerman's avuncular-but-canny Watson is a special delight. (In his guise as regular character Jonathan Quayle Higgins, Hillerman had already played proxy Watson to a man convinced he is Sherlock Holmes – as portrayed by Patrick Macnee, himself a frequent Holmesian TV face – in *Holmes is Where the Heart Is*, a 1984 episode of long-running US detective show *Magnum, PI*.) Redhead Kim Thomson (shortly thereafter Kitty Winter in Granada's **The Case-book of Sherlock Holmes**: *The Illustrious Client*) makes the underwritten Sophy aptly bewitching at every turn, and Oberstein actor Nickolas Grace would also turn up in Granada's Holmes sequence, playing Bertrand in the controversial **Sherlock Holmes The Master Blackmailer**.

Amusingly, *Hands of a Murderer*'s script does make an effort to articulate the position of its askew take on the Baker Street mythos – not to mention Woodward's portly Holmes! – in relation to the Doyle canon. At one point, the latest edition of the *Strand* arrives in Holmes' hands; flicking through the newly published THE ENGINEER'S THUMB, Holmes huffs, 'Hmph! Appropriately accompanied by irrelevant and inaccurate illustrations, I see!' (It even transpires that Moriarty is an eager reader of Watson's reminiscences: 'I enjoy a cheap penny-dreadful now and again...') One nice touch is the inclusion of the German spy Oberstein, as mentioned in THE SECOND STAIN and committed to gaol for 15 years at the conclusion of THE BRUCE-PARTINGTON PLANS. That adventure occurs in 1895; publication of THE ENGINEER'S THUMB, however, dates *Hands of a Murderer* to March 1892 – which not only means that Oberstein survives and makes his escape, but that Watson later writes up THE BRUCE-PARTINGTON PLANS with no reference to their earlier encounter! Unless, of course, given the involvement of Mycroft in a plot concerning highly sensitive government papers in both, Watson's THE BRUCE-PARTINGTON PLANS is, in itself, a hugely fanciful reworking of the 'true' events related in this film...

Deft execution cannot prevent *Hands of a Murderer* from running out of steam, and off the rails, before its pithy conclusion. For the most part, however, it remains undemanding, pulpy fun – something much less than was surely intended.

Det Hemmelige Dokument

tr 'The Secret Document'
aka **Sherlock Holmes in the Gas-Cellar** [GB],
Sherlock Holmes III: The Detectives Adventure in the Gas Cellar [sic: US]
Denmark 1908 pastiche Nordisk Films Kompagni
902 feet bw silent
wd **Viggo Larsen**
known cast Sherlock Holmes: **Einar Zangenberg**
other roles **Julie Henriksen, August Blom**

With the help of his wife, a scoundrel named Snapper obtains an important state document which has been stolen from a safe in the 'Intelligence Department' and attempts to sell it back to the Department for thousands of pounds. Unable to raise the ransom, the Intelligence chief calls in Sherlock Holmes, who identifies Snapper via graphology and duly calls at the villain's home, fixing a rendezvous for the document's return – a gas cellar, where Holmes is later attacked, tied up and left for dead while gas floods the room. Holmes is rescued by his boy, Billy, and captures the villains at gunpoint.

A *Nordisk Films advert for* **Sherlock Holmes in the Gas-Cellar** *which appeared in The Bioscope (17 December 1908)*

This third entry in the Nordisk Films sequence was released in Great Britain midway through December 1908 alongside the supposedly 'comic' *Badger Hunting*; US release followed in March 1909. The 'gas cellar' climax seems to have been swiped from Act Three of William Gillette's stage play *Sherlock Holmes* (first filmed in 1916). A new Holmes, Einar Zangenberg, replaced writer/ director Viggo Larsen in the lead, although Larsen would return to the role in the fourth film, **Sangerindens Diamanter**, while Zangenberg would get another crack at the character in the later **Hotelrotterne**. *Moving Picture World* was less impressed with this second sequel to **Sherlock Holmes i Livsfare**, claiming that 'The action is not especially spirited and there are instances where the characters move like wooden puppets.'

Hotelrotterne

tr 'The Hotel Rats'
at **Hotelmysterierne**
tr 'The hotel mystery'
aka **Hotel Thieves** [US/GB]
Denmark 1910 pastiche Nordisk Films Kompagni
837 feet bw silent
known cast Sherlock Holmes: **Einar Zangenberg**
male 'Rat': **H C Nielsen**

'The Hotel Rats' are a man and a woman who book themselves into expensive hotels and then, at night, rob the other residents' rooms. Baffled by a spate of thefts, a hotel manager asks Sherlock Holmes to stay at his establishment in an effort to identify the thieves and their methods. The chimney of Holmes' room is blocked up by one of the Rats, and the detective nearly suffocates – but is saved when a common-or-garden burglar breaks the window of his room! Holmes give chase to the Rats, catching the man on a train – but he is surprised by the woman and thrown onto the railway line. The detective eventually traces the pair to Switzerland, where he disguises himself as a mountain guide in order to lead the Rats up a mountain – at the top of which he unmasks himself. After a struggle, the male Rat falls over a precipice.

With shades of THE FINAL PROBLEM, *Hotelrotterne* ('Sherlock Holmes' sidste Bedrift' –

the detective's latest adventure, as a Danish ad block had it) debuted in Copenhagen on 7 February 1911, and in the UK the next day. Following his role as the arch-criminal Dr Mors in Nordisk's previous Holmes effort, **Milliontestamentet**, *Hotelrotterne* marked a once-only return to the lead role for actor Einar Zangenberg, Holmes in 1908's **Det Hemmelige Dokument**. Approximately 246 feet worth of *Hotelrotterne*, detailing a rooftop gunfight and an escape by boat, was discovered in Aalborg in 1984, but the rotting nitrate film is supposed to have disintegrated before a copy could be made.

The next Nordisk short, the last of the company's Sherlock Holmes films, was **Den Sorte Hætte**.

'I say, Holmes, this script's a stinker': Watson (John Scott-Paget) and Holmes (Patrick Macnee) in **The Hound of London** (1993)

The Hound of London

Canada 1993 TVM pastiche Intrepid Productions 71m colour
wp **Craig Bowlsby** *source* **The Hound of London** [stage play by **Craig Bowlsby**] *d* **Gil Letourneau, Peter Reynolds-Long**
cast Sherlock Holmes: **Patrick Macnee** Dr Watson: **John Scott-Paget** Insp Lestrade: **Colin Skinner** Moriarty/Rex: **Jack Macreath** Lance Sterling: **Craig Bowlsby** Mrs Hudson: **Sophia Thornley** Irene Norton: **Carolyn Wilkinson** Campbell: **Drew Kemp** Stonegrimble: **Ned Lemley** Striker: **Ed Belanger** Gadsby: **Dale Kelly** King of Bohemia: **Rob Vanderbrink** Queen of Bohemia: **Colleen Bignell** the body: **David Wood**

THE MYSTERY
Backstage at the Strand Theatre, caretaker Stonegrimble discovers the bodies of an actor, Gadsby, and a theatrical agent, Striker, who appear to have shot one another dead. Investigating, Inspector Lestrade concludes that Gadsby was blackmailing Striker, who seems to have been having an affair with an actress in the company. But producer Colin Campbell insists on hiring the services of Sherlock Holmes for just one day. Holmes, coming down from a long cocaine binge, only becomes interested when he learns that the actress involved is one Irene Norton – whom he knew 12 years earlier as the adventuress Irene Adler.

THE INVESTIGATION
Director Rex London has stepped into Gadsby's

shoes, and he is rehearsing a shooting scene with actor Lance Sterling when Holmes, Watson and Lestrade arrive at the theatre. While Holmes is interviewing the now-widowed Irene, a mystery gunman shoots him down – but Holmes is saved when the bullet impacts into a metal cigarette case in his jacket pocket. Twists of cotton found in the stalls lead Holmes to conclude that someone has been shooting at a dummy in seat A7 – which is booked in the name of a 'Mr King'. It transpires that Sterling is planning to fire a live bullet during the performance, 'accidentally' killing 'Mr King' – actually the King of Bohemia, who still follows Irene's career. But before Lestrade can arrest Sterling, 'Rex London' reveals himself to be none other than Professor Moriarty...

THE SOLUTION
Moriarty, now resident in Bohemia, murdered Irene's husband as part of his plot to assassinate the King; Gadsby and Striker, two untrustworthy confederates, were slain by the Professor too. Holmes gambles his life against the outcome of a game of a chess; when Moriarty loses, he departs – but not before instructing the loyal Sterling to slay Holmes, Watson and Irene. Sterling duels with both Watson and Holmes, but is ultimately despatched by Irene.

✦ ✦ ✦

Cheap, nasty and painful to watch, *The Hound of London* – a reference, presumably, to

Moriarty's alias of 'Rex London', although the Professor himself describes Holmes as 'a determined hound' at one point – is as woeful a piece of fan fiction as one will ever encounter, its only real plus being its sheer obscurity.

Derived from a play first performed in Burnaby, British Columbia, in September 1987, the television version, written, produced by and featuring Craig Bowlsby (also one of two sword masters on the production) quite fails to disguise its roots, the vast proportion of its length being played out against theatre flats. Although minor roles were found for both the director of the original, Dale Kelly, and its Irene Adler, Colleen Bignell, the recorded *Hound* was, bar Bowlsby, completely recast, Patrick Macnee taking the place of Steve Barrett's Holmes.

Macnee was merely bad as Roger Moore's Watson in **Sherlock Holmes in New York** and only terrible as Christopher Lee's sidekick in **Sherlock Holmes and the Leading Lady** and **Incident at Victoria Falls** – but he makes a truly dreadful Holmes, wheezing out every line while resembling nothing less than an unshelled tortoise poured into a monkey suit. True to the early nineties zeitgeist, this is a Holmes first seen in the throes of a cocaine-induced paranoid depression: thrashing a cast-off tie which he believes to be a SPECKLED BAND swamp adder with a poker, holding a pistol to his head and threatening to blow his own brains out. It's all terribly, terribly embarrassing. The central plot idea – that Moriarty is using Irene Adler in a bid to assassinate the King of Bohemia – might be pulpy enough to amuse, were it not for the clumsy reading of the beyond-parody script by such a patently unskilled cast. In fact, the quantifiably bad bits, such as Moriarty's accounting for his appearance having changed since he and Holmes last met – 'Facial reconstruction, they call it. After Reichenbach Falls, I needed quite a lot of that sort of thing' – come as some relief from the tedium.

As if *The Hound of London* wasn't more than enough, at the 1996 Cannes Film Festival Associated Television International touted Macnee as playing the lead in a future production, *Sherlock Holmes: The Case of the Temporal Nexus*. Written by Rick Hull and due to be directed by David L Stanton, this would apparently have seen a series of unexplained deaths in a small Scottish village leading Holmes into a confrontation with 'beings from another dimension' who are seeking to plunge Planet Earth into a new Ice Age.

So far, the thing has gone unmade. Pray God it stays that way.

The Hound of the Baskervilles

GB 1921 adaptation Stoll Picture Productions Ltd
5500 feet bw silent
w **Maurice Elvey, William J Elliott, Dorothy Westlake**
chief of production/p **Jeffrey Bernerd**
production/d **Maurice Elvey**
cast Sherlock Holmes: **Eille Norwood** Dr Watson: **Hubert Willis** Dr Mortimer: **Allen Jeayes** Sir Henry Baskerville: **Rex McDougall** James Stapleton: **Lewis Gilbert** Beryl Stapleton: **Betty Campbell** Barrymore [US: Osborne]: **Fred Raynham** Mrs Barrymore [US: Mrs Osborne]: **Miss Walker** Sir Charles Baskerville: **Robert English** housekeeper: **Mdme d'Esterre** the convict: **Robert Vallis**

Filmed in the wake of the 15-part series **The Adventures of Sherlock Holmes** (1921) and some time prior to **The Further Adventures of Sherlock Holmes** (1922), this was only the second 'true' attempt to film Doyle's most famous novel – and although a print has survived, the loss of the first moving picture adaptation, episode one of **Der Hund von Baskerville** (1914-20), robs us of a potentially intriguing comparison.

Adventures overseer Maurice Elvey appears to have taken more liberties with the source material in presenting this feature-length adaptation than he did in putting together the first set of Eille Norwood-starring shorts. Here, the Hound, whose flickering 'phosphorescent' outline was achieved by scratching the surface of the stock, dogs Sir Charles Baskerville long before it slays him, causing the knight to bemoan how it never leaves him alone; the Baskervilles are declared to have been distantly related to the notorious hangman's friend, Judge Jeffreys; and Beryl Stapleton is given something of a Pearl White role, escaping from her brother's ropes with the aid of a candle and abseiling out of a window after tying her bedsheets together. The Stapletons' residence is called Merripet, rather than Merripit, House (maybe just an intertitle writer's typo, but an amusing pun nevertheless) and it is left to Watson to shoot the beast while Holmes gets all too literally bogged down elsewhere, trying to fish Stapleton out of the Grimpen Mire.

Prior to shooting, Elvey issued a press appeal for 'a hound of gigantic proportions' to appear in the film. Some 30 dogs were auditioned, and a particularly formidable creature was cast – which, on arriving at Stoll's Cricklewood studio, promptly bit 'clean through' the hand of the assistant producer, Ian Beverley, with the result that Beverley had to be taken to hospital. The creature was duly sacked, and a more placid specimen selected. Although several sources have claimed that the film was shot on Dartmoor itself, the moorland scenes were mounted close to the village of Thursley, near Guildford, Surrey. Dartmoor-esque stone tors were transported by lorry to the location, with Stoll's use of two new 'Sunlight Arc' lamps to illuminate the night-time sequences attracting much local comment. Other scenes were filmed at Indian Farm, Effingham, near Leatherhead; 'Baskerville Hall', meanwhile, was just seven miles away, being a property owned by Sir Francis Barker.

The Norwood *Hound* was released in the UK on 8 August 1921. The aforementioned night filming caught the attention of the *Bioscope*: 'As an instance of sustained night photography it is probably unique. Some of the twilight effects, showing the moon hanging above the dusky moor at sunset, are also remarkably novel and beautiful. The sense of vague horror created by these original pictorial methods adds vastly to the thrilling quality of the story, and provides noteworthy evidence of the real imagination and technical skill with which the subject has been handled by Mr Elvey and his camera-artist, Germain Burger.'

The film didn't arrive in the US for 14 months, with the Barrymores renamed the Osbornes, presumably to avoid confusion with the John Barrymore-starring **Sherlock Holmes** (1922), released the same year. The *New York Times* was critical of the film's failing to 'reveal the real Holmes': 'Holmes doesn't solve any mystery. It solves itself.' No such reservations were expressed by Doyle himself – who, at a celebratory Stoll dinner held at the Trocadero, Piccadilly, on 27 September 1921, toasted 'Mr Eille Norwood, whose wonderful personation of Holmes has amazed me. On seeing him in *The Hound of the Baskervilles* I thought I had never seen anything more masterly.'

Sir Henry Baskerville (John Stuart) pinioned by the Hound (Champion Egmund of Send) in The Hound of the Baskervilles *(1931)*

The Hound of the Baskervilles

GB 1931 adaptation Gainsborough Pictures Ltd 75m bw
w **Edgar Wallace**, *V* **Gareth Gundrey** *p* **Michael Balcon**
d **V Gareth Gundrey**
cast Sir Henry Baskerville: **John Stuart** Stapleton: **Reginald Bach** Sherlock Holmes: **Robert Rendel** Dr Watson: **Frederick Lloyd** Beryl Stapleton: **Heather Angel** Dr Mortimer: **Wilfred Shine** Sir Hugo Baskerville: **Sam Livesey** Barrymore: **Henry Hallett** Mrs Barrymore: **Sybil Jane** Laura Lyons: **Elizabeth Vaughan** Cartwright: **Leonard Hayes** the Hound: **Champion Egmund of Send***

Michael Balcon (1896-1977), the producer of this second British stab at filming THE HOUND OF THE BASKERVILLES, would later become chief of production at Ealing during its halcyon years, so the chorus of critical raspberries directed at his single Holmes project represents only a minor blip in a remarkable career.

Dismissing the film as an 'average second feature booking' and 'a complicated story lacking any real thrills,' the *Bioscope* pronounced on 29 July 1931 that 'To follow this story ... with any degree of accuracy will call for an effort in concentration from the majority of audiences. It is upon the dialogue of Edgar Wallace rather than sustained action that the producer relies to hold his audience, and the development becomes tedious in the attempt to piece together the various phases of the mystery.' The film aroused so little interest in the trade that general release only followed in February 1932, when *Picturegoer's* Lionel Collier insisted that 'This picture fails to do justice to Conan Doyle's thrilling Sherlock Holmes story. While production qualities are good, there is an absence of suspense or thrill, and it is very pedestrian in the unfolding of its rather vague plot ... It seems to me that a great chance has been missed in the filming of this story.'

The same issue of *Picturegoer* carried an Ealing set report titled 'Return of Sherlock (Wontner) Holmes', detailing the in-production Wontner vehicle **The Sign of Four: Sherlock Holmes' Greatest Case** (directed, coincidentally, by Balcon's fellow Gainsborough founder, Graham Cutts). But the authenticity of Wontner's Holmes is nowhere to be seen in the Gainsborough *Hound*, with Robert Rendel and Frederick Lloyd portraying Holmes and Watson as well-fed, clubbable, 'hail-fellow-well-met' types, rather than, as specified in the film's script, 'The Czar of all the sleuths' and 'An assistant sleuth'. 'Once again,' sniffed *Picturegoer*, 'a type that fails to look like the original has been chosen for Sherlock Holmes. Robert Rendel acts well, but he is not at all the conception of fiction's most famous detective.'

The film originated in a Gainsborough appeal in the pages of *Film Weekly* for cinemagoers to nominate the kind of talkie they'd like to see. Given the recent death of Conan Doyle, it was appropriate that the man engaged to collaborate on the script with director V Gareth Gundrey was Edgar Wallace (1875-1932), the wildly popular thriller writer who was enjoying a great vogue in British studios. (Balcon, for instance, would film *The Frightened Lady* first thing in 1932.) Though incorporating a fair amount of Doyle dialogue, Gundrey and Wallace brought the story up-to-date (in common with all Holmes pictures of the early 1930s) and granted centre stage to Sir Henry Baskerville, 'a light-hearted, slightly frivolous young man ... [who] combines the role of hero with that of comedy relief but is never a buffoon.' The role of this self-confessed 'fat-headed chump' was assigned, together with top billing, to John Stuart (1898-1979), a Scottish-born heart-throb of the silent screen whose marathon career only ended with Richard Donner's *Superman* shortly before his death. An unthreatening mastiff called Champion Egmund of Send was cast as the Hound and shooting was divided between the Gainsborough studio in Islington's Poole Street and Lustleigh Hall near Dartmoor itself.

Wallace and Gundrey obviously had big plans for the Hound. 'The effect of eeriness,' they wrote, 'must be heightened by an unusual lighting effect (in combination with oil on the Hound's body) and by a curious camera angle. It is only by these devices that we can make our screen beast approximate to the weird and wonderful beast described in the book. A distorting lens might prove helpful.' Cinematographer, and future director, Bernard Knowles fails miserably here, but elsewhere lends the film some visual graces foreshadowing his creepy work on *Gaslight* (1940).

Try as one might to look at this film in context, however, the modern viewer is likely to be alternately bored and convulsed by the stuffed-shirt solemnity of the proceedings and the laughable ineffectiveness of Gundrey/Wallace innovations like sending Stapleton (who, as played by Reginald Bach, might as well have a placard reading 'VILLAIN' slung round his neck) over a ravine in a climactic car wreck. Once Holmes has smugly announced that 'Only one thing remains to complete the case' and flourishes Sir Henry's missing boot, the credits roll on a film impossible to reconcile with other Gainsborough thrillers of the period like Walter Forde's dazzling *Rome Express*. (JR)

The Hound of the Baskervilles

GB 1959 adaptation Hammer Films 87m colour
w **Peter Bryan** *p* **Anthony Hinds** *d* **Terence Fisher**
cast Sherlock Holmes: **Peter Cushing** Dr Watson: **André Morell** Sir Henry: **Christopher Lee** Cecile: **Marla Landi** Sir Hugo: **David Oxley** Dr Mortimer: **Francis De Wolff** Bishop: **Miles Malleson** Stapleton: **Ewen Solon** Barrymore: **John Le Mesurier** Mrs Barrymore: **Helen Goss** Perkins: **Sam Kydd** Lord Caphill: **Michael Hawkins** servant girl: **Judi Moyens** convict: **Michael Mulcaster** servant: **David Birks*** Mrs Goodlippe: **Elizabeth Dott*** Lord Kingsblood: **Ian Hewitson*** the Hound: **Colonel***

If there was an inevitability about the fact that Hammer Films would be the first to shoot a Sherlock Holmes film in colour, and if there was a high probability that the company would choose to adapt the Gothic horror-scented THE HOUND OF THE BASKERVILLES, then it was surely a certainty that Hammer's Holmes would be Peter Cushing

At Baskerville
Hall, Watson
(André Morell)
and Holmes
(Peter Cushing)
compare notes in
**The Hound of
the Baskervilles**
(1959)

(1913-94), an actor plainly born to play the part.

Until 1955, Hammer Film Productions Ltd, formed in 1949 as a production wing of the Exclusive group of companies, had been primarily a moderately successful producer of 'quota quickies' – cheap and cheerful Britflicks with titles like *Wings of Danger* and *Murder by Proxy*, designed to satisfy an act of Parliament which decreed that a certain percentage of all pictures exhibited in the UK should be originated at home. *The Quatermass Xperiment*, a creepingly horrible adaptation of a 1953 BBC TV science fiction serial that flaunted its adults-only 'X' rating, changed all that, bringing the Hammer name to wider attention within the industry and pointing the company in a new direction. Soon after, *The Curse of Frankenstein* (1956) and *Dracula* (1958), lavishly coloured and oddly classy exploitation films which made international stars of both Cushing and Christopher Lee (1922-), helped catapult the company into the big league on both sides of the Atlantic.

Kenneth Hyman, the son of one of Hammer chairman James Carreras' most frequent investors, first suggested that THE HOUND OF THE BASKERVILLES, part-financed by America's United Artists, might fit in well alongside Hammer's Mary Shelley and Bram Stoker adaptations. The monster, and the fact that THE HOUND qualifies as a horror classic in its own right, was what attracted Hammer to the project; Holmes himself was never the main selling point (a fact evinced by the poster, which depicted only a slavering dog with bloodied fangs). Carreras (1901-90), a showman with an eye for the main chance, seems to have feared that a stuffily faithful leading character might have diluted Hammer's sensational intent, maintaining that the actor playing Holmes would have to 'sex it up a bit'. Cushing, who had inherited a collection of *Strand* magazines from the uncle who had read him the Holmes stories as a boy, would surely have blanched.

Oddly enough, the screenplay was by Peter Bryan, previously a camera operator for the company. Although designed to suit an all-welcome 'A' certificate, Bryan's broadly faithful script would attempt to beef up, if not sex up, the

Peter Cushing draws attention to Holmes' Persian slipper in this posed shot from **The Hound of the Baskervilles** *(1959)*

original, painting it over with typically Hammer-esque strokes. Early on, an attempt is made on Sir Henry Baskerville's life by means of a tarantula spider; Stapleton's virtuous 'sister' becomes his black-hearted, flighty, half-Spanish daughter Cecile; an attempt is made on Holmes' life deep within the disused tin mine where the Hound has its lair; and, bizarrely, Stapleton's right hand is monstrously webbed. The escaped convict Selden fares worst of all: once just 'the Notting Hill murderer', he now seems to have become the Notting Hill Ripper, having killed 'a number of street women'. Even Selden's accidental death provides no escape, for his body is later found horribly mutilated, 'some revolting sacrificial rite' having been performed upon it.

The tone is set in the opening sequence, when the vile Sir Hugo hurls one of his servants through a window of Baskerville Hall, has him dragged out of the moat and then thrusts the hapless lackey's head into an open fire while his drooling 'herd of rams' look on. Hollering 'May the hounds of Hell take me if I can't hound her down!', Hugo then chases the servant's escaped daughter to a ruined

abbey – where, for no readily apparent reason, he stabs her to death on an altar-like stone... and a huge, unseen, maybe-spectral beast claims him.

In preparation, Cushing covered his script in reams of pernickety notes and even sketches relating to the character, ranging from how to smoke Holmes' pipes to the precise extent of his 'top quiff'. He even asked for the 221B set to be modified in accordance to a particular Holmes trait: 'Holmes had this habit of keeping all his correspondence 'stabbed' on the mantelpiece with his jack-knife. Well, that wasn't in the script, so I said, "Let's do that." Little things like that are all-important to a character.' But – save a couple of minor additions, such as the THOR BRIDGE line about not varying his professional charges – Cushing did not query Bryan's dialogue for Holmes, some of which suggests a detective with an appreciation and acceptance of the supernatural. 'There is more evil around us here than I have ever encountered before,' he tells Watson; to clergyman Bishop Frankland, he declares, 'I am fighting evil – fighting it as surely as you do.' Indeed, upon Holmes' self-confessed 'dramatic entrance' at the ruined abbey, he cuts a truly sinister figure, emerging from the shadows in a black, full-length, Dracula cloak.

If this is not an entirely rational, sceptical Holmes, then those qualities are found in abundance in his dogged Watson, played with assurance by André Morell (1909-78), a one-time Major in the Royal Welsh Fusiliers whose next engagement would be as the third, and definitive, TV incarnation of Nigel Kneale's Professor Quatermass in the BBC's *Quatermass and the Pit*. Morell had already appeared opposite Cushing, playing torturer O'Brien to Cushing's Winston Smith, in Kneale's 1954 BBC adaptation of George Orwell's *Nineteen Eighty-Four*, as realised by Quatermass director Rudolph Cartier, producer of **The Man Who Disappeared**.

Clever enough to work out when Barrymore is being economical with the *actualité*, shocked by tenant farmer Stapleton's use of a gin-trap and brave enough to return, alone, to the night-shrouded moor after sighting the mysterious figure who turns out to be Holmes, Morell's Watson marks a significant and largely unheralded departure from the type established by Nigel Bruce in **Sir Arthur Conan Doyle's The Hound of the Baskervilles**

(1939) and sequels. His finest moment undoubtedly comes after the potty, sherry-guzzling entomologist Frankland (played by Miles Malleson for comic relief, in the manner of his appearance as a comedy undertaker in the earlier *Dracula*) tells him: 'I knew a Watson in Capri. A notorious white slaver. Nice fellow, though. Relation of yours?' Replies Watson, deadpan: 'No, sir. Not that I know...'

Hammer's *Hound* was filmed between 13 September and 31 October 1958 under the eye of director Terence Fisher (1904-80), who'd largely defined Hammer's macabre stock-in-trade after putting together the breakthrough Frankenstein and Dracula films. Hedging their bets, the company cast their other 'name', Christopher Lee, as a curt, arrogant but strangely feeble jodhpur-clad Sir Henry. (Some four years later, Lee would get the chance to play Sherlock himself, again directed by Fisher, in **Sherlock Holmes und das Halsband des Todes**.) Surrey's Chobham Common and Frensham Ponds doubled for Dartmoor, although brief inserts of both Dartmoor itself and Holyport would be spliced into the film. Other parts of the moor were created inside Hammer's Thames-side home, Bray Studios, where production designer Bernard Robinson incorporated parts of the Castle Dracula exteriors into the frontage of Baskerville Hall.

The appearance of the Hound in the final reel caused difficulties: an attempt had been made to trick the scale of the beast by having it pounce not on Christopher Lee, but instead a small boy called Robert, dressed in Lee's costume. The unlovely footage was scrapped, and the scenes reshot with Lee and a Great Dane wearing a rabbit-skin mask made by Margaret Carter, Robinson's future wife. In the film, Holmes reveals that the beast has been wearing a mask all along, to make it look more terrifying.

The British Board of Film Censors required three minor cuts to be made to the final print before it could receive an 'A' certificate: in Reel 1, a shortening of 'the scene in which a servant is held against the fire', plus the deletion of a shot showing Sir Hugo 'smelling girl's garment and his words "Insolent cow!"' ('The bitch has got away!' remained, however); and, in Reel 9, a reduction of the number of shots showing the Hound 'worrying Stapleton's throat'. The film won only a lukewarm response upon release at Easter 1959: critics were startled by Cushing's 'impish, waspish, Wilde-ian' Holmes (*Films and Filming*), and disinterested in

Hammer's souped-up presentation. 'Any freshly entertaining possibilities in this much-filmed story have been lost in a welter of blood, love interest and mood music,' moaned the *Monthly Film Bulletin*. 'The dialogue is indifferent. The producer, having reasonably cast Peter Cushing to play Holmes, need not have cast two of the tallest men on the English screen, Francis de Wolff and Christopher Lee, to dwarf him,' remarked Campbell Dixon, snidely, in the *Daily Telegraph*.

Hammer's sumptuous, sweeping, hugely entertaining and beyond-camp *Hound* is a synthesis of many talents, swathed in very lovely colour. Cushing would perfect his enjoyably affected Holmes a decade on, in the BBC TV series **Sir Arthur Conan Doyle's Sherlock Holmes** – but there was never any question of his reprising the part for Hammer. Despite respectable box-office takings, it seems the demands of the Doyle estate went beyond the (admittedly, probably tight) limits of the Carreras purse, and further films were not once considered. Nonetheless, we can still dream of a parallel world where Hammer followed its *Hound* with a SPECKLED BAND, a SUSSEX VAMPIRE, perhaps a CREEPING MAN...

The Hound of the Baskervilles

US 1972 TVM adaptation Universal City Studios Inc 90m colour tx 12 February 1972 ABC-TV
w **Robert E Thompson** p **Stanley Kallis** d **Barry Crane**
cast Sherlock Holmes: **Stewart Granger** Dr Watson: **Bernard Fox** George Stapleton: **William Shatner** Dr John Mortimer: **Anthony Zerbe** Laura Frankland: **Sally Ann Howes** Beryl Stapleton: **Jane Merrow** Sir Henry Baskerville: **Ian Ireland** Arthur Frankland: **John Williams** Inspector Lestrade: **Alan Caillou** John Barrymore: **Brendan Dillon** Mrs Barrymore: **Arline Anderson** messenger: **Liam Dunn** constable: **Michael St Clair** manager: **Barry Bernard** eel monger: **Constance Cavendish** Cartwright: **Billy Bowles** Higgins: **Arthur Malet** Mrs Mortimer: **Karen Kondan** maid servant: **Elaine Church** peasant girl: **Jenifer Shaw** chestnut salesman: **Terence Pushman** porter: **Eric Brotherson** Seldon [sic]: **Chuck Hicks***

First broadcast on Saturday 12 February 1972 in ABC-TV's *Movie of the Weekend* slot, The

Hound of the Baskervilles was one of three pilots for a series of TV movies alternating the adventures of three literary sleuths – Sherlock Holmes, Nick Carter and Hildegard Withers. All executive-produced by Richard Irving, *Hound* was the first to be transmitted. *The Adventures of Nick Carter*, starring Robert Conrad, followed on 20 February, with Eve Arden assuming the role of Withers in *A Very Missing Person*, networked on 4 March. And if the Carter and Withers films were even a fraction as insulting to the memory of their literary progenitors as this Holmes, it's deeply unsurprising that the mooted tripartite film sequence never happened...

Universal Studios' first foray into Sherlockiana following the conclusion of its run of mostly magnificent Basil Rathbone-headlining features, the film may be largely true to the letter of Doyle's original HOUND but the minor adjustments made are so fundamentally flawed in spirit as to render the rest unutterably fatuous. For example, in an especially crass sequence unworthy even of *Scooby Doo*, the Barrymores are hunted through a trick-brick-activated secret passageway to the window where they signal to the wretched Selden. Less comprehensible still is the scriptwriter having Stapleton paint over the portrait which reveals his own incriminating resemblance to Sir Hugo with a mole appearing to show instead Dr Mortimer's descent from the Baskerville line. This begs so many questions of even the most listless and unconcerned viewer – when did this happen? did the Barrymores not notice? why didn't Stapleton simply steal the portrait, or destroy it? wouldn't anything which encouraged further investigation of the portrait, even in using it to cast suspicion on another man, be an extremely unwise move in the circumstances? – that its addition beggars belief.

We're also treated to a side-trip to the Natural History Museum, an attempt on Sir Henry's life in London, and finally the sight of villain Stapleton being forced to his ultimate doom beneath a particularly unconvincing, studio-bound Grimpen Mire by the mortally wounded Hound itself – a sequence presumably intended to satisfy through hoist-by-his-own petard irony. It doesn't.

The production design alone would be hilariously funny if it was simply the case that the behind-the-scenes team had got it wrong – but,

given that a hotch-potch of left-over sets on the Universal backlot is supposed to serve as Holmes' London, one can only presume that they just didn't care. So we're presented with a Baker Street baking under Californian sun, looking like a sort of tangled mittel-European town square built to plans drawn up by the architect of Dodge City, its roadways intersecting around leaning embankments dotted with emaciated-looking trees. Miles into the far distance is St Paul's Cathedral, towering imposingly atop an enormous hill. No, it's not necessary that every filmic 221B should stand on a painstakingly exact reproduction of the Baker Street thoroughfare, taken straight from the pages of the *Strand*. But it's not unreasonable to expect that the visual setting could conceivably belong in the correct city, country, continent and century.

Into this grim scenario strolls Stewart Granger's tepid, torpid Holmes, pausing only for a bag of hot chestnuts (oh, very Sherlockian... not). Granger's glory days as a dashing British lead in good-natured Hollywood adventure pics of the early fifties (*King Solomon's Mines*, *The Prisoner of Zenda* etc) had long since expired. Here, he's aloof and adrift playing a Great Detective scripted as a stuffy, brandy-guzzling gourmand who describes his Baker Street lodgings as his, quote, 'flat' – all these foibles, like the chestnuts, written in to make the character more likeable and human to the folks gathered around their TV sets in Boisie, Idaho. (If, that is, they were placed purposefully at all; like the sets, chances are that no-one gave a damn.) Heading the list of the show's 'Guest Stars' is William Shatner as a stocky and unconvincing Stapleton, three years after his regular employment as Captain James T Kirk in the original *Star Trek* series had been curtailed. The remaining cast phone in performances equal to the quality of the dialogue apportioned them.

On this leadenly directed show's début, *Variety*'s 'Bok' was relatively kind: 'the pilot-feature failed to generate much interest or suspense above and beyond what the viewer nostalgically brought to the home set,' he wrote on 16 February. '*Hound* came in on tippytoes where it should have been taking giant steps.' It's some small mercy that one might now say that it's some small mercy that this production-line pap was not expanded into a full series.

Sir Henry
Baskerville
(Kenneth
Williams) and Dr
Watson (Dudley
Moore) wring
more lame jokes
out of Doyle in
**The Hound of
the Baskervilles**
(1977)

The Hound of the Baskervilles

... YET ANOTHER ADVENTURE OF SHERLOCK HOLMES AND DR. WATSON BY A. CONAN DOYLE

GB 1977 parody Michael White Ltd 84m
w **Peter Cook, Dudley Moore, Paul Morrissey**
executive p **Michael White, Andrew Braunsberg**
p **John Goldstone** *d* **Paul Morrissey**
cast Sherlock Holmes: **Peter Cook** Dr Watson/Mrs Ada
Holmes/Mr Spiggot: **Dudley Moore** Stapleton: **Denholm
Elliott** Beryl Stapleton: **Joan Greenwood** Frankland: **Hugh
Griffith** Mrs Barrymore: **Irene Handl** Dr Mortimer:
Terry-Thomas Arthur Barrymore: **Max Wall** Sir Henry
Baskerville: **Kenneth Williams** Ethel Seldon: **Roy Kinnear**
Mary Frankland: **Dana Gillespie** Iris: **Lucy Griffiths**
receptionist at massage parlour: **Penelope Keith**
Mrs Tindale: **Jessie Matthews** Glynis: **Prunella Scales**
nun: **Josephine Tewson** masseuse: **Rita Webb** shopkeeper:
Henry Woolf policeman: **Spike Milligan** Mrs Oviatt: **Molly
Maureen** Enid: **Helena McCarthy** Perkins: **Geoffrey Moon**
sausage and mash lady: **Anna Wing** nuns: **Vivien Neve,
Jacquie Stevens** Marsha: **Ava Cadell** rail passengers:
Sidney Johnson, Pearl Hackney masseuses: **Mohammed
Shamsi*, Patsy Smart*** the Hound: **Hamish***

In August 1976, Island Records issued *Derek and Clive (Live)*, a scatological series of much-bootlegged Peter Cook and Dudley Moore sketches that sold 100,000 copies in Britain alone. Cook (1937-1995) and Moore (1935-) were suddenly 'hot' again, so much so that producer Michael White initiated a Pete and Dud film project. By the end of 1976, the pair were shuttling between their respective homes in Hampstead and Los Angeles, working flat-out on a script inspired by one of their old sketches, 'Sherlock Holmes Investigates ... The Case of the One-Legged Dog', which had appeared in their ATV series *Goodbye Again* in August 1968.

The resulting film, *The Hound of the Baskervilles*, met with unanimous critical derision when belatedly released on 5 November 1978. 'All the elements seem so promising; but the outcome is awful,' lamented the *Times*. The *Guardian* called it 'extraordinarily cack-handed in conception', the *Financial Times* 'a Grimpen Mire of comic enervation' and *Time Out* 'truly one of the crummiest movies ever made.' What went wrong?

The chosen director, New Yorker Paul Morrissey, had acquired notoriety as the man responsible for the Andy Warhol-sponsored underground shockers *Flesh* (1968), *Trash* (1970) and *Heat* (1972). In summer 1973, he had decamped to Italy at the behest of Carlo Ponti and Roman Polanski's production associate, Andrew Braunsberg, to make two 'splatter' comedies back-to-back: *Il mostro è in tavola... barone Frankenstein* (aka *Flesh for Frankenstein*) and *Dracula vuole vivere: cerca sangue di vergine!* (*Blood for Dracula*). Both films were released with Warhol's name tenuously attached and the Frankenstein film, in particular, was a smash hit. But the striking contrast between the sick-bag Grand Guignol proficiency of these films and the shattering ineptitude of *The Hound of the Baskervilles* lends credence to rumours that the Frankenstein/Dracula pictures were 'ghost'-directed by exploitation master Antonio Margheriti.

If Morrissey seems an odd choice as director, it's worth noting that the comedy dismemberment featured in his Italian films is in much the same vein as Michael White's 1975 hits, *Monty Python and the Holy Grail* and *The Rocky Horror Picture Show*. Morrissey was also a devotee of the Carry On films. As Colin Vaines testified in his *Screen International* 'Production Beat' column, the director's absorption in British popular culture was complete. 'He was more interested in reading the *Sun* than having to talk about his latest film,' Vaines lamented. 'His high nasal voice, which irresistibly reminds one of a certain wisecracking cartoon rabbit, trails off as he starts reading about

Arsenal considering paying £500,000 for Trevor Francis ... Before he reaches Page Three, I decide to ask why he's directing the film. "Oh, you know, there are so many reasons..."'

Given Morrissey's interest in the *Sun*, it's hardly surprising that Page Three favourite Vivien Neves was included in the cast, playing a thoroughly covered-up nun (one of the few good jokes in the whole picture). The other actors constituted a mouth-watering collection of the great and good of British comedy: Kenneth Williams (lynchpin of the Carry On series), Terry-Thomas (rapidly succumbing to Parkinson's Disease), Irene Handl (previously Mrs Hudson in **The Private Life of Sherlock Holmes**), Max Wall, Spike Milligan, even 1930s musical comedy legend Jessie Matthews. Peter Cook himself facetiously announced that 'This film is to be the authentic version that Sir Arthur Conan Doyle always wanted ... We have seen the Basil Rathbone and Peter Cushing versions. I've even seen a couple of silent German films. But this time we are doing it from the Hound's point of view.'

Shooting began on 11 July 1977, alternating between Bray Studios and the neighbouring Oakley Court. Bray had previously housed Hammer's **The Hound of the Baskervilles**, while

Stapleton (Denholm Elliott) presents Watson (Dudley Moore) with a prodigiously micturating chihuahua in **The Hound of the Baskervilles** *(1977). 'You'll p*** yourself laughing!' ran the poster tagline*

Oakley Court, having appeared in innumerable British horror films, here stood in for Baskerville Hall both inside and out. On 3 August, however, Morrissey came down with hepatitis and filming only resumed on 5 September, cinematographer Dick Bush having defected to a Ken Russell TV project and been replaced by John Wilcox. Initial enthusiasm by this time had ebbed away. Kenneth Williams privately referred to the film as a 'hotch-potch of rubbish'; publicly, he reported that 'It is being played for absolute reality. It's not a Carry On. Everything has to be sincere and every reaction has to be honest. That's what makes it so screamingly funny.' He was being disingenuous, of course. In fact, Morrissey was urging his actors to inflate their characterisations to the limit. In a *South Bank Show* special devoted to the shooting of the film (finally broadcast on 8 April 1978), Cook confessed, with visible disquiet, that 'Paul Morrissey has made me as grotesque as I've ever been – apart from in private life.'

As the *New Statesman* concluded, 'The Warhol man, Paul Morrissey, is known for his devotion to our Carry Ons; clearly, he has totally misread them.' The pervading impression left by the film is of gifted comedians who have completely lost the plot. Cook plays Holmes as a lisping Jew, first seen in whalebone corset and Ena Sharples hair-net, while Moore gives Watson an excruciating Welsh accent and doubles, in some conspicuously laugh-free sequences, as Holmes' mother Ada. She's a phoney spiritualist (possibly a gesture to the spiritualism subplot grafted onto the Basil Rathbone version), and assaults her vacantly smiling associate with the line, 'I like to strike a happy medium.' Few of the gags rise above this level, and even those that do are hopelessly mistimed. When Terry-Thomas mutters 'I wouldn't send a dog out on a night like this,' he can actually be seen to raise his eyebrows in despair at the quality of the script.

There are a few moments of inspired lunacy, with Cook and Moore solving the structural problem of Holmes' prolonged absence from the investigation by sending him to the 'Piccadilly Health and Relaxation Spa de Paree', where he is belaboured by flame-haired cockney loudmouth Rita Webb. The porcelain beauty Joan Greenwood plays a devil-possessed Beryl Stapleton, spewing green bile à la *The Exorcist* and defenestrating Watson with her demonic power, only to hilariously

Not only a Jewish Holmes (Peter Cook) but also a Welsh Watson (Dudley Moore) feature in **The Hound of the Baskervilles** *(1977)*

re-fenestrate him a moment later. (Greenwood's husband, André Morell, had played Watson in the Hammer version some 19 years earlier; what he thought of this new version is unknown.) And Denholm Elliott's Stapleton cradles an incontinent chihuahua that sprays everything within reach, especially Watson, with an unending stream of urine – a kind of lavatorial equivalent of the spurting jets of blood featured throughout Morrissey's comic horrors.

But the experience is otherwise a dismally depressing one, with our last views of Cook (spewing coffee) and Moore (being pelted with vegetables) seeming unusually apt. As a miserable symbol of the British film industry sinking into its very own late-1970s Grimpen Mire, it's hard to beat. (JR)

The Hound of the Baskervilles

GB 1982 4 x 30m TV serial adaptation BBC Television colour
tx 3-24 October 1982 BBC1
w **Alexander Baron** *p* **Barry Letts** *d* **Peter Duguid**
cast Sherlock Holmes: **Tom Baker** Dr Watson: **Terence**

From time travel to train travel: Tom Baker as Holmes in **The Hound of the Baskervilles** *(1982)*

Rigby Sir Henry Baskerville: **Nicholas Woodeson**
Dr Mortimer: **Will Knightley** [1-3] Barrymore: **Morris Perry**
[1-3] Mrs Barrymore: **Gillian Martell** [1-3] Sir Charles
Baskerville: **John Boswall** [1] Sir Hugo Baskerville: **Terry
Forrestal** [1] girl: **Joanna Andrews** [1]
Stapleton: **Christopher Ravenscroft** [2-4] Beryl Stapleton:
Kay Adshead [2-4] Clayton: **Mike Kemp** [2]
Perkins: **Norman Tyrrell** [2] waiter: **Gideon Kolb** [2]

reception clerk: **Brian de Salvo** [2] Laura Lyons: **Caroline
John** [3-4] Frankland: **William Squire** [3] Selden: **Michael
Goldie** [3-4] Inspector Lestrade: **Hubert Rees** [4]

Fourteen years after first presenting the story as part of the Peter Cushing-starring series **Sir Arthur Conan Doyle's Sherlock Holmes** (1968), the BBC broadcast a rather redundant second

HOUND, this time in its Sunday teatime 'classic adaptations' strand. And Sunday teatime is the note struck throughout; it's as traditional as crumpets and as unthreatening as jam.

Always considered a stand-alone Sherlock, *The Hound of the Baskervilles* was produced out of the Corporation's Birmingham studios, with film inserts shot mostly on Dartmoor. Although it's true to say that Alexander Baron's doggedly faithful scripts generate little excitement (the episode endings – Holmes and Watson rushing by coach to Sir Henry's hotel, Watson and Sir Henry catching Barrymore signalling to Selden, and finally the death of Selden – are less cliffhangers than abrupt breaks in the narrative), the production's key failing is its anonymous cast.

Terence Rigby (1937-), soon to appear as Inspector Layton in **Sir Arthur Conan Doyle's The Sign of Four** (1983), seems rather lost as a mumbling Watson, and quite why the distinctly diminutive Nicholas Woodeson could ever have been considered an authoritative Sir Henry is a mystery. Once a part for a matinée idol, a Richard Greene or a Christopher Lee, Woodeson's casting is all too literal an indicator of how this pivotal character had shrunk in stature over the years.

The principal attraction, however, is Tom Baker (1934-) as Holmes. Baker had been made famous in 1974, after *Hound* producer Barry Letts had cast him as the fourth incarnation of *Doctor Who*. Having hung up the Doctor's unfeasibly long scarf early in 1981, *The Hound of the Baskervilles* marked Baker's return to TV. It's often said that one of Baker's *Doctor Who*s, the 1977 six-parter *The Talons of Weng-Chiang*, sees him impersonating Holmes. But although his Time Lord character does indeed don deerstalker and cape to stalk a giant rat – albeit not necessarily Sumatran – through the sewers of Victorian London, the story is principally a Fu Manchu pastiche.

Physically a throwback to a William Gillette or an Eille Norwood type, Baker's loud Holmes dominates each scene he's in – but his necessary absence from the screen for half of Episode Two and almost all of Episode Three leaves a void that no other performer is able to fill. Although Baker would come to consider himself to have failed in the part – and, indeed, the part of Professor Moriarty, when he later doubled as both Holmes and his arch-enemy on the Dublin stage in Hugh

More than one string to his bow? Tom Baker on the fiddle in **The Hound of the Baskervilles** *(1982)*

Leonard's *The Mask of Moriarty* – the serial's failure isn't his; he simply isn't around enough to carry the piece alone.

When the Hound finally pounces on Sir Henry, and Holmes fires a round of bullets into its hide, the film is blurred into slow motion. How ironic, then, that this should be one of the few scenes where the pace actually picks up.

The Hound of the Baskervilles

GB 1988 TVM adaptation Granada Television 105m colour tx 31 August 1988 ITV
w **Trevor Bowen** *executive p* **Michael Cox**
p **June Wyndham Davies** *d* **Brian Mills**
cast Sherlock Holmes: **Jeremy Brett** Dr John Watson: **Edward Hardwicke** Sir Charles Baskerville: **Raymond Adamson** Dr Mortimer: **Neil Duncan** Barrymore: **Ronald Pickup** Mrs Barrymore: **Rosemary McHale** Sir Henry Baskerville: **Kristoffer Tabori** purser: **Edward Romfourt** Stapleton: **James Faulkner** pageboy: **Philip Dettmer**

Kenneth Welsh and Matt Frewer, take to the London streets in **The Hound of the Baskervilles** *(2000)*

Perkins: **Stephen Tomkin** Beryl Stapleton: **Fiona Gillies** Frankland: **Bernard Horsfall** vicar of Grimpen: **Donald McKillop** Selden: **William Ilkley** postmistress: **Myrtle Devenish** Laura Lyons: **Elizabeth Spender** manservant: **Donald Bisset** the Hound: **Kahn**∗

With the second leg of Granada's The Return of Sherlock Holmes spiralling over-budget, it was decided to scrap the final two instalments and to concoct a cut-price, feature-length version of THE HOUND OF THE BASKERVILLES instead. The signs of financial belt-tightening in the finished product are clear: a spoken account of the Baskerville curse designed to dodge an expensive 17th century flashback, a cramped studio set for the moor (plus location shots at Brimham Rocks in Yorkshire, easily accessible from Granada's Manchester base), Colin Jeavons' weaselly Inspector Lestrade written out of the script prior to shooting, etc. The dead hand of corporate constraints, often extolled by zero-budget filmmakers as a spur to creativity and imaginative corner-cutting, seems to have had the opposite effect here: the whole project is dreary, enervated, spiritless – in fact, more or less dead.

Sadly, the enervation at the barely pulsing heart of this *Hound* proceeds not only from the straitened budget but from Jeremy Brett himself. There are glimpses of the old vim – notably his uproarious response to Dr Mortimer's phrenological flirtation on their first meeting ('Behave and sit down, Dr Mortimer...') – but elsewhere we're all too obviously watching an actor trying desperately to redefine his role in order not to be consumed by it. Rendered more owl-like than hawk-like by the various medications he was subject to (a change underscored by some unflattering close-ups), Brett's characterisation is just as softened around the edges as his appearance. But this newly relaxed and mellifluous approach is also paralysingly slow, killing several sequences – notably the restaurant scene in the Northumberland Hotel – stone dead. To make matters worse, the rather unprepossessing supporting cast picks up Brett's torpid pace, holding pauses for unfeasibly long periods that should have been smartly cut short in the editing process. In particular, the scenes of Watson's arrival at Baskerville Hall are so somnolently acted and directed they seem like some kind of underwater ballet.

There are a few nice touches, notably the sinister, black-gloved acquisition of Watson's letters at Grimpen Post Office and the revelation that the fugitive Selden was lobotomised prior to his escape. ('He's a broken man,' stammers Mrs Barrymore. 'They done surgery, sir – to tame him. He's like a child, sir.') Director Brian Mills uses a vertiginous, high-angle shot of banisters as people rush down stairs not once but twice (a trick presumably derived from Alfred Hitchcock's *The Lodger*, 1926), and Brett introduces an intriguing detail of his own, cradling the Hound-ravaged Sir Henry with his gloved hand to the younger man's head, moments later cradling the similarly brutalised Beryl Stapleton but thinking better of the hand-to-head bit. But apart from these brief moments, and an engaging Frankland from the whiskery Bernard Horsfall, this *Hound* is conspicuously lacking in tension, excitement and, most damagingly, atmosphere.

For a production team so proud of their fidelity to Doyle's original stories, to have got the most famous of them so disastrously wrong seems inexplicable – and it was a mis-step the Brett sequence never fully recovered from. (JR)

The Hound of the Baskervilles

Canada 2000 TVM adaptation Muse Entertainment (Baskervilles) Inc 90m colour
tx 21 October 2000 Odyssey Channel [US]
w **Joe Wiesenfeld** *p* **Irene Litinsky** *d* **Rodney Gibbons**
cast Sherlock Holmes: **Matt Frewer** Dr Watson: **Kenneth Welsh** Sir Henry Baskerville: **Jason London** Beryl: **Emma Campbell** Dr Mortimer: **Gordon Masten** Stapleton: **Robin Wilcock** Mr Barrymore: **Arthur Holden** Mrs Barrymore: **Leni Parker** Sir Hugo: **Benoit Gauthier** Frankland: **John Dunn-Hill** Perkins: **Joe Cobden** Selden: **Jason Cavalier** Mrs Laura Lyons: **Linda Smith** Sir Charles: **Barrie Baldaro** maiden: **Nathalie Girard** Grimpen man #1: **Greg Kramer** the Hound: **Eno***

Given the Doylean literalism of the various Jeremy Brett-headlining Granada series beginning with **The Adventures of Sherlock Holmes** (1984-5), a mildly iconoclastic approach was perhaps the only way forward for the next major television Holmes. This, the fourteenth live-action version of THE HOUND OF THE BASKERVILLES, presents a number of intriguing and refreshing diversions from the source text – not to mention a boldly uncompromising variation on Holmes, as played by Matt Frewer (1958-).

American-born but British-trained, Frewer's remarkably geometric features led many 1980s children to believe that his 'video jockey' character Max Headroom was, in fact, computer-generated. Fruity of diction and flighty of mood, there is much about Frewer's Holmes to aggravate stuffier Sherlockians, from his playful over-gesticulation to his amusingly idiosyncratic choices of loungewear. 'There will certainly be Holmes aficionados who will say it's a bastardisation,' Frewer told *Scarlet Street* magazine, 'but that's part of the territory...' Past the over-ripe vowel sounds, however, there are some rich undercurrents: alone, at night, in Baker Street, Holmes spreads out his map of Dartmoor in an attempt to divine his unknown adversary's intent. 'It shall be a pleasure running you to ground, sir,' he murmurs.

Fortunately for those unconvinced by the Frewer Holmes, the production has the foursquare credibility of Kenneth Welsh's Watson to lean on. Welsh, most familiar to TV viewers as the sinister Windom Earle in David Lynch's *Twin Peaks* (1990-1), is given a substantially expanded role, carrying the story right into its closing stages. It's Watson who learns that Selden is Mrs Barrymore's brother, Watson who tracks down the mysterious Laura Lyons (here, the estranged daughter of grumpy Scots curtain-twitcher Frankland), and Watson who witnesses Stapleton reveal himself as the villain. Holmes only steps out of the shadows once matters have run out of hand, emptying a bullet into the Hound, which is savaging young Jason London's Ivy League Sir Henry while Watson is engaged in scrapping with Stapleton.

Holmes needs to have conspired with Beryl to make this adjustment work – the only plot thread left flapping being the question of when and how Holmes sees the picture of Sir Hugo that so resembles Stapleton – and it does enable Watson to angrily accuse Holmes of treating him like 'a tethered goat' and allowing Sir Henry to come to harm: 'This is worse than arrogance, Holmes, this is hubris!' Even the Cerberene Hound has come in for revision: no longer coated in phosphorus, its supernatural origin is here suggested by glowing red eyes, the result of being blinded by its master – who presumes it will therefore enjoy a heightened sense of smell.

Shot on a 22-day schedule in pretty but most un-Dartmoorlike rolling fields and hills at Harrington, Quebec, with various 17th and 18th century streets in Old Montreal standing in for London, *The Hound of the Baskervilles* (the only real failing of which is its clodhopping, straight-to-video slasher movie score) was judged successful enough to beget several sequels, the first being **The Sign of Four** (2001).

The Hound of the Baskervilles

GB 2002 TVM adaptation Tiger Aspect Productions/BBC 99m colour

tx 18 November 2002 CBC [Canada]
26 December 2002 BBC1 [GB]

w **Allan Cubitt** *p* **Christopher Hall** *d* **David Attwood**
cast Sherlock Holmes: **Richard Roxburgh** Watson: **Ian Hart**
Stapleton: **Richard E Grant** Sir Henry Baskerville: **Matt Day** Dr Mortimer: **John Nettles** Mrs Mortimer: **Geraldine James** Miss Stapleton: **Neve McIntosh** Barrymore: **Ron Cook** Mrs Barrymore: **Liza Tarbuck** Selden: **Paul Kynman** Inspector Lestrade: **Danny Webb** Clayton: **Richard Hawley** coroner: **Jim Norton** hotel porter: **David McNeill** warder 1: **Caspar Zafer** warder 2: **Stephan Bessant** Knight/choreographer: **Malcolm Shields** Father Christmas: **Tom Freeman** Hound: **Eddie Brittain** Perkins [Baskerville groom]: **John Maude*** Sir Charles Baskerville: **Peter Roberts***

Doyle's HOUND OF THE BASKERVILLES can easily be recalled as a classic of Gothic fiction in its own right, separate from the Holmes canon. Its phantom dog stalking Dartmoor has entered into cultural mythology, a companion of those other great nineteenth-century literary terrors – Frankenstein's Monster, Count Dracula and the bestial Mr Hyde. The fact that the tale also features the character of Sherlock Holmes is surely incidental to its endurance: it may not have been quite so widely read if its rationalist hero had been AN Other, but it would have nevertheless survived. (Only the sheer potency of the Hound myth can account for popularity of the multiple **Der Hund von Baskerville** films made in Weimar-era Germany.)

But after some 16 principal live-action retellings, there is little new to wring from the myth. To his credit, screenwriter Allan Cubitt breaks new ground in his version – the third to be made for the BBC – returning to the tale an edge of unpredictability, of danger and surprise. That his screenplay is also sympathetic to the story's essence is a very considerable achievement. He shuns the well-worn business of Dr Mortimer's cane; telegraphs a significant part of the mystery's resolution by introducing a photograph showing a gathering of Baskervilles Sir Charles, Sir Henry (senior) and the rotten Roger; has Sir Henry confront Selden in the kitchens of Baskerville Hall; eliminates the character of Laura Lyons, making Beryl Stapleton Sir Charles' bait; and sets the piece at Christmas, with the legend being staged as a mystery play at the Hall, complete with a hobby-horse Knight, a demonic Santa and an anthropomorphised Hound. He even swipes the séance scene from the Basil Rathbone version (**Sir Arthur Conan Doyle's The Hound of the Baskervilles**, 1939), enabling the wonderful Geraldine James to give us her best Linda Blair, as medium Mrs Mortimer channels the dead Sir Charles ('The Hound! The Hound! Its eyes ... weeping red fire!').

All these are but minor embellishments compared to Cubitt's adjustments around the character of Stapleton, to whom he ascribes a new motivation – revenge upon the Baskervilles for their casting out his father (not unreasonably, Holmes wonders how Stapleton could possibly hope to avoid engendering suspicion in staking his claim to the Estate, after having lived in the area under another identity for two whole years beforehand). He also chooses to inflate Stapleton's villainy, but Holmes' declaration 'I tell you, Watson, we have never had a foe more worthy of our steel' has too much hyperbole about it to wholly convince. The detective returns early from his self-imposed exile in the wilderness to state the identity of the Baskervilles' malefactor; and the film's second half now concerns Holmes' efforts to prove his unsubstantiated case. Inevitably, Cubitt opens up fresh plot holes in his quest to plug Doyle's; the viewer may well be left wondering why Holmes doesn't simply burst into the Baskerville Ball waving the photograph he's just discovered showing Stapleton's father with his brothers, and end the business then and there without recourse to setting up poor Sir Henry as a Judas goat. This would, of course, mean that Beryl would not be found hanged on Christmas Day, strung up in the stables by her husband; meaning that Ian Hart's emotional yo-yo of a Watson would not find it necessary to attempt to shoot the arrested Stapleton dead; meaning that Holmes would not have to chase the villain through the Grimpen Mire; and meaning that Holmes wouldn't (in an especially pleasing inversion of the traditional denouement) fall into the swamp, leaving himself a sitting duck for Stapleton's bullets. (Fortunately, Watson has regained his composure enough to follow the pair, and shoots the skull-coveting Stapleton dead through his own parietal fissure.)

There's an obvious question to be asked in the light of such a radical reworking: why bother? If it's so necessary to twist the story through so many contortions just to keep it interesting, aren't you just kicking against the fact that you shouldn't be bothering with such a hoary old chestnut in the first place? Why not go for something less well-worn but equally spooky, like THE DEVIL'S FOOT? In context, this was a commission for a classic to be a centrepiece of the BBC's Christmas 2002 schedule, occupying the place of Tiger Aspect's version of Doyle's *The Lost World* the previous year (a show also managed by former *Poirot* associate producer Christopher Hall – and another high-profile opportunity to work animatronic and CGI techniques developed by the much-acclaimed Crawley Creatures/Framestore teams for the award-winning documentary series *Walking With Dinosaurs* into a drama, although the lumpen Hound generated here comes as the most tremendous disappointment). The production is extraordinarily handsome – filmed over six weeks on location in the Isle of Man, Liverpool, London, Keighley and Cumbria – and edited with zest, exerting maximum shock effect from its opening moments (showing Sir Charles' rictus form laid out on a mortuary slab) to its last. It also employs some of the finest acting talents available, with Richard E Grant (a bizarre Mycroft in the woeful **Sherlock**, 2001) giving an uncharacteristically measured performance ...

... but as Stapleton, not Holmes, which must surely be one of the most perverse casting choices in a century of Sherlock Holmes films. Producer Hall told the *Sydney Morning Herald*: 'We knew what [Grant would] do with Sherlock Holmes and it wasn't what we wanted. Whereas with Richard Roxburgh, there was no baggage and we could reinvent the character.'

Late in the proceedings, Stapleton turns on Holmes, describing him as 'Conceited, opinionated, egotistical, vain – all disembodied mind and cold calculation! You're no match for me!' The second half of his statement is certainly true, but the character outlined in the first sentence simply isn't there. Roxburgh's Holmes is a smooth, presentable, moderately debonair, coke fiend; his closest relative is probably Christopher Plummer's Holmes (in **Classics Dark and Dangerous: Silver Blaze** and **Murder By Decree**), but minus the passion that made Plummer's depiction so credible. Again according to the *Sydney Morning Herald*, Australian-born Roxburgh, best known for his portrayal of the Duke in Baz Luhrmann's *Moulin Rouge* (1999), was cast alongside Matt Day after producer Hall and director David Attwood had seen the pair together in *Doing Time For Patsy Cline* (1997):

'"We turned to each other and said, 'There's our Holmes and there's our Baskerville'," Hall says. Roxburgh and Day remain mystified, though gratified, at their insight. As Roxburgh points out, in *Patsy Cline*: "I played a drug-dealing conman in a Jag and Matt Day played the starry-eyed wannabe country-music star."'

A Holmes minus the dreary accoutrements of deerstalker, Meerschaum and violin is all well and good; a Holmes who jacks up cocaine in a train station toilet is at least different; but neither in themselves are the making of a character. Neither Roxburgh (soon to be a desperately uninspiring Moriarty in **The League of Extraordinary Gentlemen**, 2003) nor Cubitt bring to Holmes any real substance, leaving a yawning gap at the heart of the piece. Nor is this Holmes especially distinct from Ian Hart's ferret-faced Watson, and it's impossible to perceive just why the pair hang out together – especially since the script makes a point of establishing the fact that Watson cannot ever trust Holmes. One supposes that the ramifications of this conclusion might have been elaborated upon in a follow-up – at the time of this latest *Hound*'s transmission, there was some speculation that another Holmes-versus-the-Ripper tale might be forthcoming from the same team – but this now seems unlikely to emerge. THE HOUND OF THE BASKERVILLES' plot may indeed be in need of fine-tuning, but you tinker with Holmes at your peril.

The House of Fear

US 1944 adaptation [THE FIVE ORANGE PIPS]
Universal Pictures Company Inc 69m bw
w **Roy Chanslor** pd **Roy William Neill**
cast Sherlock Holmes: **Basil Rathbone** Dr Watson: **Nigel Bruce** Alastair: **Aubrey Mather** Lestrade: **Dennis Hoey** Simon Merrivale: **Paul Cavanagh** Alan Cosgrave: **Holmes Herbert** John Simpson: **Harry Cording** Mrs Monteith: **Sally Shepherd** Chalmers: **Gavin Muir** Alison MacGregor: **Florette Hillier** Alex MacGregor: **David Clyde** Ralph King: **Dick Alexander*** Guy Davies: **Wilson Benge*** Angus: **Alec Craig*** Stanley Raeburn: **Cyril Delevanti*** Sergeant Bleeker: **Leslie Dennison*** Bessie: **Doris Lloyd***

THE MYSTERY
Insurance underwriter Chalmers relates the tale of 'the Good Comrades', a seven-strong club of middle-aged men with no next of kin gathered at Drearcliff, a 'grim old house perched high on a cliff on the west coast of Scotland'. One night, at dinner, Comrade Ralph King receives an envelope containing just seven orange pips; soon after, his car goes over the cliff and explodes. Later, another Comrade, Stanley Raeburn, receives six pips; he, too, meets a grisly end. Chalmers' company underwrites the Comrades' unique life insurance; each of the Comrades stands to inherit the worth of the others' policies, up to £100,000. Fearing foul play, Chalmers sets out the Comrades' story to Sherlock Holmes – whose interest is piqued when he sees that one of their number is Dr Simon Merrivale, a Harley Street surgeon who vanished upon being acquitted of the suspected murder of his bride 20 years previously. In Scotland, Holmes and Dr Watson hear the local legend relating to Drearcliff – the house where 'no man goes whole to his grave'...

THE INVESTIGATION
News of the death of another Comrade – Guy Davies, found 'burned to a crisp' in the furnace after being delivered five pips – brings Holmes and Watson to Drearcliff, where they meet the four surviving members of the group: the beaming,

nerveless Bruce Alastair, who has inherited the house; Merrivale, who has a morbid interest in murder (and, indeed, the exploits of Holmes); gruff former Naval officer John Simpson; plus Alan Cosgrave. At dinner, Cosgrave is sent four pips and becomes the next to die, dynamited in a shed while the rest of the household is distracted by various nocturnal goings-on. The newly arrived Inspector Lestrade attempts to take charge, but fails to prevent the pips-foretold death of Simpson, whose torso is found on the beach. Lestrade is sent a note by local tobacconist MacGregor, who had apparently seen the ghost of one of the dead men – but MacGregor is found shot dead before Holmes can interrogate him. In the meantime, Merrivale has been crushed beneath a boulder, leaving just one suspect: Alastair, whom Lestrade arrests.

THE SOLUTION
Dr Watson disappears after observing that Simpson's supply of tobacco has been exhausted. Holmes, who has noticed a discrepancy between the exterior and interior dimensions of the house, leads Lestrade and Alastair down a secret staircase to an old smuggler's cave – where they save Watson from all six of the 'dead' Comrades, who had faked their own deaths in turn, disinterring corpses from a local cemetery to mutilate and then 'identify' as their own. Having framed Alastair for their 'murders', the collaborators planned to escape with the pool of insurance money. Back in London, Holmes gives the grateful Chalmers' cheque to Alastair, who had told Holmes what Watson had noticed about Simpson's tobacco jar, so saving the doctor's life.

✦   ✦   ✦

Historically, the plot of *The House of Fear* most resembles that of Agatha Christie's novel *Ten Little Niggers* (1939), first filmed as *And Then There Were None* in 1945, the same year as *The House of Fear*'s release. (In Nollen (1996), MGM's *The Unholy Night* (1929) is nominated as another source for the story.) Viewed in Britain in the summer of 2001, however, one is inescapably reminded of the format of 'reality TV' sensation *Big Brother*: seven diverse housemates are nominated one-by-one for permanent eviction until just one is left to scoop a prize of exactly

Sinister servant
Mrs Monteith
(Sally Shepherd)
is questioned by
Watson (Nigel
Bruce) and
Holmes (Basil
Rathbone) in **The
House of Fear**
(1945)

£100,000. So if *The House of Fear* fails both as a Sherlock Holmes film and a properly satisfying murder-mystery, its premise is at least enduring.

Before filming this, the follow-up to **The Pearl of Death**, under the title *The Murder Club* in May 1944, Basil Rathbone and Nigel Bruce had taken a break from their Holmes and Watson personae by appearing together as the Lords Rockingham and Godolphin in Paramount's pirate melodrama *Frenchman's Creek*. Retitled *The House of Fear*, Universal's eighth Holmes film divided critics on the occasion of its release in March 1945. For all those who thought it 'one of the better pictures in the series' (*New York Daily News*), 'exceedingly neat' (*New York Post*) and 'a return to the authentic Holmes manner' (*New York World-Telegraph*), another – Bosley Crowther in the *New York Times* – considered it 'wearily produced' and a sign that 'Sherlock Holmes has certainly gone to the bow-wows in the clutches of Hollywood'.

A frequent complaint – one that endures to this day – is that Holmes has too little to do and solves the problem too late. Close analysis suggests that this isn't really the case. On entering Drearcliff for the first time, Holmes declares that he suspects

'no one but everyone', and if one views the film in the light of his merely trying to prove a thesis he has formulated from the outset, there is absolutely no harm in his sitting back and waiting for each 'murder' to take place in anticipation of the conspirators eventually making a conclusive mistake. Certainly, he doesn't step up his efforts to settle the matter until the one unforeseeable happening: the killing of tobacconist MacGregor. It's a shame that this is not made explicit.

While Sherlock treads water, there's much to enjoy: an unsettling, weird ambience, underlined by some remarkably dramatic camera angles and Virgil Miller's deep-focus cinematography; some very black humour, as in the cut from discussion of Simpson's mutilated torso to a shot of Merrivale carving a roast chicken; even a neat little 'post-modern' joke whereby Holmes fan Merrivale is seen reading a book entitled 'Murder in the Fog', jacketed with the poster artwork for **The Scarlet Claw**. The atmosphere is helped by some rather ostentatious performances, from Aubrey Mather's creepy, beaming Alastair and Paul Cavanagh's oleaginous Merrivale to Sally Shepherd's housekeeper, a living portent of doom who brings each of the pip-laden envelopes to the Good Comrades' table.

Screenwriter Roy Chanslor's lines are most effective when revelling in the lurid, from an arresting opening voiceover delivered by Chalmers to Holmes' quite marvellous assertion that 'Murder's an insidious thing ... Once a man has dipped his fingers in blood, sooner or later he'll feel the urge to kill again.' As always, it's best not to consider the mechanics of the plot too closely, but one cannot help wondering exactly how the conspirators are intending to collect their payout even if Alastair is convicted of their murders.

Despite furnishing Holmes with the one last vital piece of evidence, Nigel Bruce's Watson does not fare well, being a source of irritation to the detective (Holmes loudly informs the entire household that Watson snores 'like a pig') and the butt of a semi-jokey five-minute sequence in which, guarding downstairs on his own, he flaps hither and thither while attempting to track down the source of a number of strange noises. (He shoots a suit of armour and a cat before asserting, 'They've got me completely surrounded!') Nevertheless, Holmes' concluding sentiments are directed entirely towards a 'long and happy association' with Watson. In fact, the only truly irksome presence is that of Dennis Hoey's now entirely unsubtle Lestrade, whose attendance at the scene is both unnecessary and bizarre. It's baffling that his beat should here extend to the remotest part of Scotland, when his services are not required back in London for the next in the Universal series, **The Woman in Green**.

Der Hund von Baskerville

tr 'The hound of the Baskervilles'
Ger 1914-20 7 x film series bw silent

[1] DER HUND VON BASKERVILLE
tr 'The hound of the Baskervilles'
1914 adaptation Union-Vitascope GmbH
4386 feet/35mm
w **Richard Oswald** sources THE HOUND OF THE
BASKERVILLES and **Der Hund von Baskerville** [stage
adaptation by **Ferdinand Bonn**] p **Jules Greenbaum**
d **Rudolf Meinert**
known cast Sherlock Holmes: **Alwin Neuß** Stapleton:
Friedrich Kühne Miss Lyons: **Hanni Weisse** Henry von

Baskerville: **Erwin Fichter** Barrymore: **Andreas von Horn**

[2] DAS EINSAME HAUS
tr 'The lonely house'
1914 pastiche Union-Vitascope GmbH
3412 feet/35mm
w **Richard Oswald** p **Jules Greenbaum** d **Rudolf Meinert**
known cast Sherlock Holmes: **Alwin Neuß** Stapleton:
Friedrich Kühne Henry von Baskerville: **Erwin Fichter**
Miss Lyons: **Hanni Weisse** Barrymore: **Andreas von Horn**

[3] DAS UNHEIMLICHE ZIMMER
at **Das geheimnisvolle Zimmer**
tr 'The uncanny room'/'The mysterious room'
1915 pastiche Greenbaum-Film GmbH
wd **Richard Oswald** p **Jules Greenbaum**
known cast Sherlock Holmes: **Alwin Neuß** Stapleton:
Friedrich Kühne Henry von Baskerville: **Erwin Fichter**
Barrymore: **Andreas von Horn** other roles: **Tatjana Irrah**

[4] DIE SAGE VOM HUND VON BASKERVILLE
at **Wie entstand der Hund von Baskerville**
tr 'The saga of the hound of the Baskervilles'/'How
the hound of the Baskervilles appeared'
1915 adaptation Greenbaum-Film GmbH
2654 feet/35mm
wd **Richard Oswald** p **Jules Greenbaum**
known cast Sherlock Holmes: **Alwin Neuß**
Stapleton: **Friedrich Kühne** Von Baskerville: **Erwin Fichter**
Barrymore: **Andreas von Horn** other roles: **Hilde Bork**

[4A] DAS DUNKLE SCHLOß
tr 'The dark castle'
1915 pastiche Projektions-AG Union
3773 feet/35mm
wp **unknown** d **Willy Zeyn**
known cast Sherlock Holmes: **Eugen Berg**
Stapleton: **Friedrich Kühne** Miss Lyons: **Hanny** [sic]
Weisse other roles [**Frederic**] **Zelnik**

[5] DR MACDONALDS SANATORIUM
tr 'Dr Macdonald's sanatorium'
1920 pastiche Greenbaum-Film GmbH 4501 feet
w **Robert Liebmann** from a story by **Irene Daland**
p **Jules Greenbaum** d **Willy Zeyn**
known cast Sherlock Holmes: [**Erich**] **Kaiser-Titz**
Stapleton: **Friedrich Kühne** Henry von Baskerville: **Erwin
Fichter** von Baskerville's wife: **Hanni Weisse**
Holmes' assistant: **Lya Sellin**

[6] DAS HAUS OHNE FENSTER
tr 'The house without windows'
1920 pastiche Greenbaum-Film GmbH 5682 feet
w **unknown** *p* **Jules Greenbaum** *d* **Willy Zeyn**
cast unconfirmed

The first of the umpteen film and television versions of the best-known Sherlock Holmes story – a story which has, arguably, come to transcend the Holmes canon, rightly establishing itself as one of the finest examples of the Gothic genre – was, in many ways, the most extraordinary. Central to the seven-year saga of *Der Hund von Baskerville*, a shadowy epic with the most unlikely of twists, are just two characters. The first is Jules Greenbaum, the entrepreneur behind **Arsène Lupin contra Sherlock Holmes**, a man who'd spent a decade building up his German kinematograph empire. The name of the second is Richard Oswald (1880-1963).

Oswald, the son of a Jewish businessman, was born Richard Ornstein in Vienna, Austria. As a young actor, he toured Austria-Hungary with several small companies, graduating to the Viennese stage in 1907. Two years later, now a budding director, he mounted a version of THE HOUND OF THE BASKERVILLES at a small theatre in the Praterstraße, quite possibly based on the text of *Der Hund von Baskerville: Schauspiel in vier Aufzügen aus dem Schottischen Hochland. Frei nach motiven aus Poes und Doyles Novellen* ('*The Hound of the Baskervilles*: a play in four acts set in the Scottish Highlands. Freely adapted from the stories of Poe and Doyle'). This had originally premiered at Ferdinand Bonn's Berliner Theater on 17 January 1907; written by and starring actor/impresario Bonn himself, it followed on from a four-act Sherlock Holmes 'Detektivkömedie' first staged in June 1906. Bonn's fanciful version – which transported 'Schloß Baskerville' from Dartmoor to the Highlands, added a subplot concerning a treasure hoard belonging to Bonnie Prince Charlie and renamed the wicked Stapleton 'Argyll' (it's uncertain which of Edgar Allan Poe's tales of mystery and imagination were also added to the mix) – had proven a big hit with audiences, including none other than Kaiser Wilhelm II.

Moving to Düsseldorf to escape anti-Semitic attacks, Oswald became engaged on the fringes of

Hanni Weisse played 'Miss Lyons' in several instalments of **Der Hund von Baskerville** *(1914-20)*

the burgeoning film industry, making his first on-screen appearances in 1911. A childhood friend, Hermann Fellner, had also entered the movie business, becoming a senior partner in Greenbaum's Vitascope company – and, early in 1914, Oswald found himself employed as a script and advertising supervisor at the new 'Union-Vitascope' studios in the Berlin-Weißensee.

In a bid to stave off foreign competition, principally from the French Pathé Frères group, Vitascope had since entered into a merger with Paul Davidson's all-powerful PAGU ('Projektions-Aktiengesellschaft Union'), an association with over 800 employees. Boasting substantially increased resources, Union-Vitascope was now able to up its production slate. 'Detektivfilms' were still a sure winner at the German box-office (much to the dismay of the intellectual establishment, which blamed the ever-popular Nick Carter, Nat Pinkerton and Miss Nobody series, among others, for 'diverting the workers from the quest for moral uplift and educational advancement'), and Oswald soon found himself scripting a feature-length *Der Hund von Baskerville* as Union-Vitascope's response.

Oswald's *Hund*, which blended both Doyle's original and Bonn's stage interpretation, was realised in lavish, blood-and-thunder style by director Rudolf Meinert (1882-1945). Meinert would later supervise production of the massively influential and still-nightmarish *Das Cabinet des Dr Caligari* (1919) – and it was on *Der Hund von Baskerville* that he first worked with set designer Hermann Warm, the man who would be credited with *Caligari*'s 'insane' backdrops. Another figure intimately involved with *Der Hund* would also become feted for his contribution to fantasy cinema: cameraman Karl Freund (1890-1969), whose artistry would grace pictures as significant as *Der Golem: wie er in die Welt kam* (1920), *Metropolis* (1926) and Universal Pictures' *Dracula* (1931), eventually directing *The Mummy* (1932) and *Mad Love* (1935), among others. One surviving hint of *Der Hund von Baskerville's* visual impact comes in a contemporaneous description of the dog itself – 'a monstrous Great Dane with flaming eyes and fire emerging from its mouth'.

Alwin Neuß, who'd played a stern-faced Sherlock in the Nordisk Films Kompagni's **Milliontestamentet** (1910), would reprise his role in *Der Hund*. He had also played both Dr Jekyll and Mr Hyde twice, first in Nordisk's *Den Skæbnesvangre Opfindelse* ('The ill-fated device', 1910) and then in *Ein seltsamer Fall* ('A strange case'), another Oswald-scripted Vitascope film made in 1914 – and which co-starred Hanni Weisse (1892-1967), cast in the 'Laura Lyons' role in *Der Hund*. Friedrich Kühne (1869-1958) made an older-than-usual Stapleton, supported by Erwin Fichter as the young von Baskerville heir and Andreas von Horn as Barrymore, the family retainer. It is not generally believed that a Watson figure appeared anywhere in *Der Hund*, from which it may be inferred that Oswald's script departed significantly from Doyle's Watson-intensive narrative.

Der Hund von Baskerville premiered in Berlin on 12 June 1914 at the Union-Theaters in Kurfürstendamm and Friedrichstraße – and it's a mark of the film's astonishing success that a sequel was released little over four months later. *Das einsame Haus* picked up where *Der Hund* left off, with Stapleton escaping his condemned cell the night before his planned execution. For reasons presumably connected to the disputed legacy at the heart of Doyle's story, he then captures Henry von Baskerville and Miss Lyons and imprisons them inside a mysterious house which can be sunk 'by an ingenious mechanism' beneath the surface of a lake. Holmes attempts to

rescue Stapleton's prisoners, but the three of them only narrowly escape the sunken house as it floods with water.

Reuniting the cast and crew responsible for the original (bar Freund, whose place was taken by Werner Brandes), *Das einsame Haus* was hailed as 'a miracle of German technology and art direction [that] puts everything up to now in the shade'. Indeed, *Der Kinematograph* went on to claim that the scenes in which the specially constructed three-storey house of the title is repeatedly immersed in water cost over 60,000 marks alone, making it apparently the most expensive film yet produced in Germany. Subtitled *Der Hund von Baskerville. 2*, it debuted in Berlin on 30 October, this time at three Union-Theaters.

Plans for further instalments were already underway, but *Das einsame Haus* would be the last in the series to be directed by Rudolf Meinert. Tantalisingly, however, it's just possible that Meinert *did* direct a third Oswald-scripted Neuß-starring Holmes picture for Union-Vitascope. Various filmographies suggest that *Detektiv Braun*, a picture with the alternate title *Sherlock Holmes contra Dr Mors*, was submitted to the German film censor's office in December 1914; 'Dr Mors', the villain of Ferdinand Bonn's first Holmes play, had also appeared in *Milliontestamentet*, Neuß's sole Holmes film for Nordisk. Bonn himself is supposed to have featured as the evil Mors, with Freidrich Kühne reprising his role as Stapleton. However, no contemporaneous evidence has yet been unearthed to corroborate any of this – and press reports would clearly number the next known instalment in the *Baskerville* series 'III'. Meinert also wrote and produced *William Voss, der Millionendieb* (1916, see Appendix), reviewed as a Sherlockian film in the press of the day.

Meanwhile, bloody war broke out in Europe. Union-Vitascope had only just completed a complex series of international distribution and sale agreements with Pathé, part of which had involved the sale of the Weißensee facility to their competitors-turned-partners, when Germany declared war on France on 3 August. Overnight, everything changed. The Weißensee studio was placed under official administration – but, suddenly free of the threat from foreign competition, and sensing an opportunity to become established as the single largest force in the domestic trade, Greenbaum elected to buy the facility for himself. In November 1914, Greenbaum divorced himself from his 11 months' marriage to PAGU – and set up a new company, Greenbaum-Film GmbH. Greenbaum took most of the Union-Vitascope talent with him – and, with Oswald, Warm, Neuß, Kühne, Fichtner and von Horn on his side, doubtless he believed that the *Baskerville* series was his by right.

Oswald would both write and direct the next two instalments, *Das unheimliche Zimmer* and *Die Sage vom Hund von Baskerville*, which were completed in rapid succession and submitted to the censor in the early summer of 1915. The third episode would see Stapleton attempt to exact his revenge on Holmes, and the fourth ('a costume drama with Knights', according to a censor's note) would apparently flash back to the story of the wicked von Baskerville ancestor who murdered his wife and her favourite dog, after which the phantom hound first arose – which, if correct, represents an interesting, and rather neat, refinement of the original text.

PAGU, outraged by what was viewed as Greenbaum's theft of a valuable money-spinner, had other ideas. The story goes that the mighty Union contrived to have the films – already *jugendverbot*, forbidden for exhibition to children – banned by the censor for the duration of the war, presumably on spurious grounds regarding their sentiment. Until the cessation of hostilities, Greenbaum-Films' latest *Hund* episodes could only be sold to neutral territories, including the USA. PAGU did, however, have an ace up its sleeve – and, in August 1915, the Union released its own continuation of *Der Hund von Baskerville: Das dunkle Schloß*.

Filmed at the PAGU studios in the Berlin-Tempelhof, *Das dunkle Schloß* featured Eugen Berg, hitherto known mostly for comedy roles, as Holmes, and 'Zelnik' (probably Frederic Zelnik, 1885-1950, later a producer/director) as his main adversary, a master of disguise. Friedrich Kühne and Hanni Weisse were the only cast members to have also appeared in the Union-Vitascope pictures; Weisse is thought to have been under exclusive contract to PAGU, meaning that she had been replaced in the third and fourth Greenbaum instalments by Tatjana Irrah and, possibly, Hilde Bork.

The story concerned the murder of a rich colonel in his castle; his young bride is arrested for the crime – but Holmes, convinced of her

Teutonic terror Fritz Rasp played 'Stapelton' and then Barrymore in the 1929 and 1937 versions of **Der Hund von Baskerville**

innocence, searches for another explanation. He discovers that, by night, the colonel's elderly manservant becomes 'an elegant man-about-town', enjoying a double life as a baron in the gambling clubs of a nearby city. The detective finds proof of the servant's guilt in the castle, but ends up trapped in the building as it burns. Rescued by the fire brigade, Holmes rushes to a nearby magistrate's office, where a long-lost cousin of the victim is asserting his rights of inheritance; Holmes exposes this false-bearded fraudster as none other than the wicked manservant in disguise. *Der Kinematograph* was impressed by Berg's Holmes, comparing him favourably to other actors to have essayed the role – but reserved the highest praise for Zelnik, a 'master of the mask art' whose disguises were thought utterly convincing. The paper did, however, note that the supposedly dark castle was actually 'brilliant white'.

The Armistice of November 1918 meant that Greenbaum was, at last, free to release *Das unheimliche Zimmer* in Germany – but, come May 1919, the film would meet a decidedly less enthusiastic public. One Egon Jacobsohn, writing in *Der Kinematograph*, expressed the opinion that despite the fact that this was undoubtedly one of the best detective films he'd ever seen, a fourth instalment would be surplus to requirements, the cinema now being saturated with such productions. *Der Film* had reservations about the 'not always clear' photography, but nonetheless recognised Oswald's fine directorial skills.

Oswald, however, had long since moved on, separating from Greenbaum in 1915 and transferring his allegiances to the distributor Lothar Stark, for whom he created a new, patriotically German detective: Engelbert Fox, as played by Erich Kaiser-Titz, who then took the title role in Oswald's adaptation of *Hoffmanns Erzählungen* ('Tales of Hoffmann', 1916, also featuring Kühne, von Horn and Ferdinand Bonn). In the spring of that year, Oswald set up in business on his own, forming Richard Oswald-Film-Gesellschaft, under which banner he continued to write, produce and direct commercially successful mystery/horror films and literary adaptations: *Zirkusblut* ('Circus of blood', 1916, again with Kühne); *Das Bildnis des Dorian Gray* ('The picture of Dorian Gray', a 1917 version of the Oscar Wilde novel, also with von Horn); plus *Unheimliche Geschichten* ('Uncanny tales', a 1919 anthology film starring Conrad Veidt).

Meanwhile, *Es werde Licht!* ('Let there be light!', 1917) was a dramatised treatise warning the public of the dangers of syphilis. Sponsored by the Society for the Combating of Venereal Diseases, it led to several sequels and ultimately a trend for *Aufklärungsfilme* – sex education films with a prurient bent, a booming genre exploited by Oswald in the two *Prostitution* pictures (both 1919) and *Anders als die Andern* ('Different from the Others', a film about homosexuality, also 1919). Oswald's 1920s would be turbulent, surviving several high-profile failures and ultimately bankruptcy before he was hired by Erda-Film to direct a new adaptation of Doyle's HOUND, again as **Der Hund von Baskerville**, in 1929.

Greenbaum's destiny was altogether different. PAGU's answer to the eventual release of Greenbaum-Films' third and fourth *Hund* instalments was to reissue the first two films compiled together as a single feature. Greenbaum then elected to make his parts five and six, *Dr Macdonalds Sanatorium* and *Das Haus ohne Fenster*. The first of these required a new Holmes to replace Alwin Neuß, who was then beginning to establish himself as a director, and his place was duly taken by Oswald's Engelbert Fox, Erich Kaiser-Titz, whom Greenbaum had since employed as the arch-criminal Fantômas in a series of films borrowed from the

novels of Marcel Allain and Pierre Souvestre.

Another newcomer was Lya Sellin as Holmes' female assistant, who is required to disguise herself as a nurse in order to infiltrate the sanatorium of the fifth episode's title. Kühne, Weisse and Fichtner all returned to the series – as did Willy Zeyn, director of *Das dunkle Schloß*, in a move that must, surely, have been one in the eye for PAGU. *Dr Macdonalds Sanatorium* premiered in September 1920, when *Der Film* praised Robert Liebmann's well-constructed script, the cinematography of 'Gottschalk' and the tasteful production design of one S Wroblewsky. Almost nothing is known about *Das Haus ohne Fenster*, which was sent before the censor in the same month as episode five's release, implying that the two films were shot back-to-back.

This time, PAGU chose not to retaliate; after all, the time of the sensational mystery-adventure had passed, replaced by the more realistic 'psychologically credible' dramas featuring gentleman detective Stuart Webbs (as played by the clean-cut Ernst Reicher in 50 films between 1914 and 1926) – and, on the other hand, the more dubious pleasures of Oswald's *Aufklärungsfilme*. And so, the book of *Der Hund von Baskerville* was closed... at least, for the time being.

In a 1922 court case relating to payments due from film exports to the Balkan countries over 1918-19, Greenbaum-Film GmbH was held liable for vast amounts of damages, existing in name only for another ten years. Jules Greenbaum did not, however, live to see the last remnants of his once-mighty empire enter liquidation. By the autumn of 1924 he had been confined to a mental hospital, where he died on 1 November, following an illness. Greenbaum was buried in a Jewish churchyard on the Weißensee, close to the studio where his greatest pictures had been made. According to the trade press, the film industry was poorly represented at his funeral.

Der Hund von Baskerville

Germany 1929 adaptation [THE HOUND OF THE BASKERVILLES] *Erda-Film-Produktions-GmbH 7815 feet silent bw*
w **Herbert Juttke**, **G C Klaren** p **Fred Lyssa**
d **Richard Oswald**

cast Lord Charles Baskerville: **Alexander Murski** Sir Henry Baskerville, sein Erbe: **Livio Pavanelli** Beryl: **Betty Bird** Mr Stapelton [sic]: **Fritz Rasp** Sherlock Holmes: **C Blackwell** Dr Watson, sein Freund und Gehilfe: **Georges Seroff** Barrymore, Verwalter im Schloß Baskerville: **Valy Arnheim** Frau Barrymore: **Alma Taylor** Laura Lyons, Stapeltons Geliebte: **Carla Bartheel** Dr Mortimer, Hausarzt von Baskerville: **Jaro Fürth** Frankland, ein Gast auf Baskerville: **Robert Garrison**

L ast of the Sherlock Holmes films to be made in the silent era, *Der Hund von Baskerville* – despite being directed, once again, by Richard Oswald – was not a 'remake' of parts of the 1914-20 serial of the same name, proclaiming itself to be a straight adaptation of the original novel instead.

The latter part of the twenties had seen Oswald form a new production company in association with Heinrich Nebenzahl (Nero GmbH) and direct the politically risky *Feme* (1927), about a murder committed by right-wing activists. This, plus the next year's *Cagliostro*, were both scripted by the writing team of Herbert Juttke and Georg C Klaren, to whom Oswald turned when he was asked to direct a new *Hund von Baskerville* for Erda-Film-Produktions-GmbH. The film was shot in Berlin with an international cast including: the American-born Carlyle Blackwell (1884-1955), a former Vitagraph player who had enjoyed leading roles in *Bulldog Drummond* (1923) and *She* (1925), as Holmes; the Italian Livio Pavanelli (1881-1958) as Sir Henry; and Briton Alma Taylor (1895-1974), known to the earliest picturegoers as young 'Tilly the Tomboy' in literally dozens of comic shorts, as Barrymore's 'frau'. Casting Fritz Rasp (1891-1976) as 'Mr Stapelton' was not going to fool audiences for one second, former comedian Rasp having become notorious as the face of German screen scoundrelhood in pictures such as G W Pabst's *Die Liebe der Jeanne Ney* (1927); he could also be seen in Fritz Lang's enduring *Metropolis* (1926).

Despite being (apparently) a very faithful retelling realised in good, menacing fashion, Oswald's new *Hund*, which premiered at Berlin's Capitol on 28 August 1929, proved a failure at the box-office, submerged beneath a tsunami of novelty sound films – and, although a print was claimed in the mid-seventies to be in held in an archive in Soviet Russia, no copies are known to

have survived in the West. Nevertheless, Rasp's popularity was enough to ensure that he would reappear in yet another *Hund*, directed by Karl Lamac in 1937 – albeit this time playing Barrymore.

Oswald would score a major hit with the musical *Ein Lied geht um die Welt* (1933, aka *My Song Goes Round the World*), featuring the tenor Joseph Schmidt – but he would soon flee Germany, fearing the rise in anti-Semitic feeling under the banners of National Socialism. After flitting around Europe, he eventually settled in the US – where, despite remaining in work, he never again met with quite the same success as he had in Germany, the country to which he finally returned in 1962. Richard Oswald died in Düsseldorf on 11 September 1963.

Der Hund von Baskerville

Germany 1937 adaptation [THE HOUND OF THE BASKERVILLES] *Ondra-Lamac-Film-GmbH 82m bw w* **Carla von Stackelberg** *d* **Karel Lamač** *[as* **Carl Lamac***] cast* Lord Henry Baskerville: **Peter Voss** Lord Charles Baskerville: **Friedrich Kayssler** Beryl Vendeleure: **Alice Brandt** Sherlock Holmes: **Bruno Güttner** Dr Watson: **Fritz Odemar** Barrymore: **Fritz Rasp** Barrymore's Frau: **Lilly Schönborn** Stapleton: **Erich Ponto** Dr Mortimer: **Ernst Rotmund** wirtin von Sherlock Holmes: **Gertrud Wolle** Sträfling: **Paul Rehkopf** notar: **Klaus Pohl** telefonistin: **Ilka Thimm** hoteldirektor: **Ernst Schaah** other roles: **Horst Birr, Kurt Lauermann** Lady Baskerville: **Hanna Waag** Lord Hugo Baskerville: **Artur Malkowski** voice of Sherlock Holmes: **Siegfried Schürenberg***

O ne of the many films which Adolf Hitler screened as after-dinner entertainment at his so-called 'Eagle's Nest' – the Berghof, in the Nazis' Obersalzburg complex in the Alpine retreat of Berchtesgaden. The third German version of THE HOUND OF THE BASKERVILLES has become infamous for this reason alone. The piece was put together by Czech-born Karel Lamač (1887-1952). Lamac, in 1932, had directed the 86-minute Elektafilm comedy-drama *Lelíček ve službách Sherlocka Holmese* (literally, 'Lelicek in the service of Sherlock Holmes'), which featured Vlasta Burian as both Fernando XXIII, the King of 'Portorico', and his doppelgänger, František

Lelíček. However, the role of Holmes, as played by Mac Frič (principally a writer and director, sometimes known as 'Martin Fric', 1902-68), was little more than an extended cameo in a piece that is not known to have any other Sherlockian connections – and does not, therefore, fall within the remit of this book.

Producers Ondra-Lamac-Film had been founded by Lamač and the popular actress Anny Ondra (Anna Sophie Ondráková, 1902-1987); previous productions had included the Edgar Wallace adaptations *Der Zinker* (1931) and *Der Hexer* (1932), both jointly directed by Lamač and Frič, and both starring Fritz Rasp. Rasp had, of course, featured as Stapelton [sic] in the 1929 *Der Hund von Baskerville*. But his previous association with Lamač perhaps better explains his Barrymore being given a larger-than-usual role, grappling to seize the reins of Stapelton's horse and cart as the villain tries to make his escape at the last. Little is known about Lamač's turtleneck-wearing, leather-greatcoated Holmes, Bruno Güttner, who was dubbed by Siegfried Schürenberg (Siegfried Wittig, 1900-93), the German-speaking voice of stars such as Clark Gable and Herbert Lom.

The most part of this first 'talkie' version of the story to be made in a language other than English fails to live up to its *sturm und drang* prologue. This is a flashback to the sixteenth century, in which bad Lord Hugo – a demagogue with a passing resemblance to Henry VIII – slays his wife's lover in public. He is busy throttling his fickle Lady when her dappled wolfhound leaps to his mistress's aid, savaging him. The main action is updated to a telephone-connected, motor car-driving 1930s England, and so Holmes is able to establish a link between Erich Ponto's owlish Stapleton and Schloss Baskerville resident Beryl Vendeleure, after uncovering a snapshot of the pair together on what appears to be a palm beach! Given the time and place of the film's production, it may be instructive to note that Holmes employs an Aryan blond houseboy straight out of *Hitlerjunge Quex* (1935). It's oddly chilling, too, to observe Fritz Odemar's portly but nonetheless raffishly natty Watson having his identity papers examined by British bobbies hunting escaped convict Strafling (not Selden). But once the very shaggy Hund has been shot dead by Holmes and Stapleton's cart has sunk into the Mire, the most lasting impression is made by the music used as a backing to several of the Dartmoor scenes – the souped-up histrionics of Modest Mussorgsky's Hallowe'en-inspired *Night on Bare Mountain* (1867), a very ostentatious soundtrack for such a mundane adaptation.

Der Hund von Baskerville

Germany 1955 TV adaptation [THE HOUND OF THE BASKERVILLES] *Hessischer Rundfunk 80m bw tx 16 August 1955*
wd **Fritz Umgelter**
cast Sir Charles Baskerville: **Werner Xantry** Sir Henry Baskerville: **Ernst-August Scheppmann** Jack Stapleton: **Axel Ivers** Beryl Stapleton: **Hedi Reich** Dr James Mortimer: **Christian Schmieder** Benjamin Frankland: **Gerhard Ritter** Barrymore: **Hans Epskamp** Sarah Barrymore: **Annelotte von Obstfelde** Sherlock Holmes: **Wolf Ackva** Dr Watson: **Arnulf Schröder**

Eighteen years after the Ondra-Lamac-Film-GmbH **Der Hund von Baskerville** (1937), the title was revived, this time as a television play that aired for the first and only time on 16 August 1955. Produced by the Hessischer Rundfunk, it featured Wolf Ackva (1911-2000) as Holmes; set mostly in the Great Hall of a Scottish Schloß Baskerville, it was performed live but, sadly, never recorded. (The same goes for a version of THE DYING DETECTIVE thought to have been transmitted the previous year, presumably under the title *Der sterbende Detektiv*.) Holmes next appeared on West German television in the guise of actor Erich Schellow in the series **Sherlock Holmes** (1967-8).

Incident at Victoria Falls

*US/Italy/GB 1991 TVM pastiche Harmony Gold/
Banque et Caisse d'Epargne de l'Etat Luxembourg/
Banque Parabis Luxembourg/Silvio Berlusconi
Communications 175m colour*
no known tx; released to video with on-screen prefix:
Sherlock Holmes The Golden Years
w **Bob Shayne** *story:* **Gerry O'Hara** *exec p* **Harry Alan
Towers** *p* **Frank Agrama, Daniele Lorenzano, Norman
Siderow** *d* **Bill Corcoran**
cast Sherlock Holmes: **Christopher Lee** Dr John Watson:
Patrick Macnee Lillie Langtry: **Jenny Seagrove** King
Edward: **Joss Ackland** Lord Roberts: **Richard Todd**
Theodore Roosevelt: **Claude Akins** Khumalo: **John Indi**
Gugliamo [sic] Marconi [aka Bantini]: **Stephen Gurney**
Maharani: **Sunitha Singh** Mavropolis: **Anthony Fridjhon**
Amelia Morrison: **Claudia Udy** Captain James Morrison:
Neil McCarthy Chandra Sen: **Pat Pillay** Van Meer: **Dale
Cutts** Stanley I Bullard [aka Raffles]: **Alan Coates** Mrs
Hudson: **Margaret John** Mycroft: **Jerome Willis** Ram
Dhulup: **Kessie Govendor** Lord Milner: **Hywell Williams**
Inspector Lestrade: **Kenway Baker** Uma: **Sangeeta Jina**
Themba: **Dominic Makuvachuma** Lt Grisholm: **Ron
Smervzak** Colonel Thornbury: **Michael Brunner** hotel
manager: **Trevor Keeling** telegrapher: **Patrick Cadman**
waiter on train: **Steve Chigorimbo** chief cook: **Jones
Muguse** officer: **Anthony Fairclough** conductor: **Brian
Cooper** Sergeant Fuller: **Lawford Sutton-Price** maitre d':
Michael Parker neighbour woman: **Kala Jina** desk clerks:
Tafi Chiota, Andrew Whaley Connery: **Trevor Pugh**
Anglican minister: **Paul Tingay** coachman: **Barry McCurdy**

The Mystery

Making ready for retirement, Sherlock Holmes is
sent to Cape Town by King Edward VII to ensure
the safe passage of a precious diamond known as
the Star of Africa. With Watson in tow, Holmes
arranges (or seems to) for the jewel to be exchanged
for a fake until the official presentation ceremony.
At the ceremony, however, a safecracker, Ram
Dhulup, is found murdered and the valuable 'Star'
has gone. A hotel employee is exposed by Holmes

as the notorious thief Raffles and, against Holmes'
wishes, is arrested by the fatuous Van Meer.

The Investigation

A train ticket among the dead man's effects leads
Holmes to Victoria Falls, though a youthful
Thuggee assassin, Chandra Sen, is himself
murdered en route. On a safari organised by ex-US
president Theodore Roosevelt, venal businessman
Mavropolis is strangled, while Roosevelt's winsome
third cousin Amelia is struck by a poisoned dart
and mangled by crocodiles. Holmes discovers that
Amelia's husband, Captain James Morrison, is the
son of the man who first discovered the Star back in
1896, and that Morrison is now intent on finding
the larger hoard of which the Star was just a part.

The Solution

When the hoard is uncovered, Morrison and his
lover – a beautiful Indian woman who has been
masquerading as the Maharani but is in fact
Chandra Sen's sister – are both killed in a cave-in
from which Holmes and Watson only narrowly
escape. Returning to England for the funeral of
King Edward, Holmes exposes the real culprit as
Italian fraudster Bantini, a fellow safari member
passing himself off as telegraphy pioneer
Guglielmo Marconi. The Star is retrieved from a
secret compartment in Bantini's moving picture
camera but, quizzed by Watson, Holmes remains
inscrutable as to whether it was the real Star or the
one he apparently substituted for it.

✦ ✦ ✦

*I*ncident at Victoria Falls was the second of two
cable TV capers devised by Harry Alan Towers
and starring Christopher Lee as an autumnal but
still lively Holmes. The first, **Sherlock Holmes and
the Leading Lady**, finished filming on 20 October
1990, after which Lee had a mere two days back in
London to receive the relevant jabs before starting
Incident at Victoria Falls in Zimbabwe.

Bill Corcoran took over as director from Peter
Sasdy, but the film labours under many of the same

*Christopher Lee's
Holmes on safari
in* **Incident at
Victoria Falls**
(1991)

and Watson. Patrick Macnee was cast only after Towers' original choices, Nigel Stock and Gordon Jackson, had died, but the fact that he had been at prep school with Lee in the early 1930s gives a certain 'second childhood' zest to their scenes together. Though irredeemably flawed, *Incident at Victoria Falls* has an epic, exotic sweep about it that puts it a few notches above **Sherlock Holmes and the Leading Lady**. The plot bears traces of THE SIGN OF THE FOUR and is more engaging than the hash of Bosnian anarchists featured in the previous film; the Star of Africa, meanwhile, seems like an echo of the Star of Delhi featured in **The Adventures of Sherlock Holmes** (1939). Lee himself, despite having roasted in African temperatures of over 100° Fahrenheit during the shoot, appears to be enjoying himself hugely. Treating the script as if it were a comedy of manners by Pinero, he succeeds in making Holmes a gently absurd figure without in any way diminishing his intellectual glamour. In one extraordinary sequence, Holmes and Theodore Roosevelt are seen sitting nonchalantly on the pointed nose of a moving steam locomotive, both Lee and Claude Akins clearly having disdained doubles for the scene. Other scrapes Lee's Holmes gets into include a tense face-off with a charging lioness – his rifle jams as a leonine hearth-rug is flung at him from off-camera – and a nocturnal scene in which he fishes the too-inquisitive Watson out of a snake-pit. He also tricks himself out, very engagingly, as a shuffling Sikh at one point.

Raffles, previously invoked by Shayne in **The Return of Sherlock Holmes**, here turns up in person, a late manifestation of a Holmes/Raffles face-off first seen in **Sherlock Holmes i Livsfare** in 1908. Mycroft Holmes, in the lean and grey-faced form of Jerome Willis, reappears at Lee's side, too, but Shayne is chiefly concerned to emulate **The Seven-Per-Cent Solution** in stuffing the cast list with historical personages. Having put Sigmund Freud, Elliott Ness and the Emperor Franz Joseph into the first film, he now drags on Roosevelt, Lord Roberts, Lillie Langtry, a bogus Marconi and Edward VII himself. As Lillie Langtry, the luminous Jenny Seagrove (previously Mary Morstan in Granada's **The Sign of Four**) has her romantic overtures to Holmes summarily rejected; even more summarily, her entire performance was cut out of the much-abbreviated US video. (JR)

drawbacks as its predecessor: a variable set of supporting actors, an equally variable notion of period authenticity, lumbering plots that are likely to defeat even the most attentive viewer and, worst of all, a grotesquely rinky-dink score that adds musical 'stings' to comic vignettes which, by and large, aren't funny in the slightest. Screenwriter Bob Shayne had previously written the 'Holmes thawed out in the 1980s' tale, **The Return of Sherlock Holmes** (1986), but for these more 'authentic' adventures he called on the British crime writer H R F Keating for assistance, though Keating would only be credited on **Sherlock Holmes and the Leading Lady**.

Keating cited Shayne's script-conference suggestion that Holmes might find a clue in a cocktail umbrella as an instance of his complete lack of a 'sense of history'. Despite Keating's intervention, this historical uncertainty, smacking of filmmakers who simply aren't paying attention, crops up several times in *Incident at Victoria Falls*. Struggling with his collar stud, Watson complains that 'Someone should invent a collar attached to the shirt.' 'Bizarre idea,' replies Holmes. Yet elsewhere in the film they can be seen in soft-collared, one-piece shirts on regular occasions.

There remains a great deal of charm, however, in the crusty interplay between the elderly Holmes

The Last Adventures of Sherlock Holmes

GB 1923 15 x film series adaptations Stoll Picture Productions Ltd silent bw
w **Geoffrey H Malins, Patrick L Mannock** [except where stated] *chief of production/p* **Jeffrey Bernerd**
d **George Ridgwell**
regular cast Sherlock Holmes: **Eille Norwood**
Dr Watson: **Hubert Willis**

SILVER BLAZE
2077 feet
regular cast, plus Straker: **Sam Marsh** the groom: **Bert Barclay** Straker's wife: **Norma Whalley** Colonel Ross: **Knighton Small** Silas Brown: **Sam Austin**
Inspector Gregory: **Tom Beaumont**

THE SPECKLED BAND
1804 feet
regular cast, plus housekeeper: **Mdme d'Esterre**
Helen Stoner: **C Murtaugh** Dr Grimsby Roylott: **Lewis Gilbert** the baboon: **H Wilson**

THE GLORIA SCOTT
2070 feet
regular cast, plus James Trevor: **Fred Raynham**
Victor Trevor: **Reginald Fox** Hudson: **Laurie Leslie**
Prendergast: **Ray Raymond** Evans: **Ernest Shannon**
Ship's Doctor: **Charles Barrett**

THE BLUE CARBUNCLE
1864 feet
regular cast, plus Peterson: **Douglas Payne**
Henry Baker: **Sebastian Smith** Mrs Oakshott:
Mary Mackintosh Breckinridge: **Archie Hunter**
Ryder: **Gordon Hopkirk**

THE ENGINEER'S THUMB
1991 feet
regular cast, plus Hatherley: **Bertram Burleigh**
Colonel Stark: **Latimer** [sic] Ferguson: **Ward McAllister**
the girl: **Mercy Hatton**

HIS LAST BOW
1539 feet
regular cast, plus Von Bork: **Nelson Ramsay**
Baron Herling: **Van Courtland** Martha: **Kate Gurney**
naval officer: **Watts Phillips**

THE CARDBOARD BOX
1801 feet
regular cast, plus Inspector Lestrade: **Tom Beaumont**
Miss Cushing: **Maud Wulff** Sarah Cushing: **Lewellyn** [sic]
Mary Browner: **Hilda Anthony** James Browner: **J Butt**
Alec Fairbairn: **Eric Lugg**

THE DISAPPEARANCE OF LADY FRANCES CARFAX
1818 feet
w **George Ridgwell**
regular cast, plus Lady Frances Carfax: **Evelyn Cecil**
Hon R Green: **David Hawthorne** 'Holy Peters': **David Morton York** Mrs Peters: **Madge Tree** Marie Devine:
Wilkins [sic] Gregory: **Tom Beaumont**

THE THREE STUDENTS
2448 feet
regular cast, plus Hilton Soames: **William Lugg**
Bannister: **A Harding Steerman** Gilchrist: **L Verne**

THE MISSING THREE-QUARTER
2201 feet
regular cast, plus Cyril Overton: **Hal Martin**
hotel porter: **Jack Raymond** Dr Leslie Armstrong:
Albert E Rayner Godfrey Staunton: **Leigh Gabell** Lord
Mount-James: **Cliff Davies** housekeeper: **Mdme d'Esterre**

THE MYSTERY OF THOR BRIDGE
adaptation THOR BRIDGE
2070 feet
regular cast, plus Mr Gibson: **AB Imeson**
Miss Dunbar: **Violet Graham** Mrs Gibson: **Noel Graham**
Inspector: **Harry J Worth** housekeeper: **Mdme d'Esterre**

THE MAZARIN STONE
1873 feet
regular cast, plus Inspector Gregory: **Tom Beaumont**

Watson (Hubert Willis) witnesses a Baker Street face-off between Moriarty (Percy Standing) and Holmes (Eille Norwood) in **The Last Adventures of Sherlock Holmes**: The Final Problem (1923)

Count Sylvius: **Lionel d'Aragon** Merton: **Laurie Leslie**
housekeeper: **Mdme d'Esterre**

THE DANCING MEN
2382 feet
regular cast, plus Hilton Cubitt: **Frank Goldsmith**
Slaney: **Wally Bosco** Mrs Cubitt: **Dezma du May**

THE CROOKED MAN
2228 feet
regular cast, plus Henry Wood: **Jack Hobbs**
Mrs Barclay: **Gladys Jennings** Miss Morrison:
Dora de Winton Major Murphy: **Richard Lindsay**

THE FINAL PROBLEM
1686 feet
regular cast, plus Professor Moriarty: **Percy Standing**
Inspector Taylor: **Tom Beaumont** scout: **P Francis**

As with all but one of the first 30 Stoll Picture Productions/Eille Norwood shorts beginning with **The Adventures of Sherlock Holmes** (1921), the final sequence of 15, *The Last Adventures of Sherlock Holmes*, survives *in toto*; only ten, however, are currently available for viewing: *The Gloria Scott, His Last Bow, The Cardboard Box, The Disappearance of Lady Frances Carfax, The Three Students, The Missing Three-quarter, The Mystery of Thor Bridge, The Mazarin Stone, The Dancing Men* and *The Final Problem*. Generally considered superior to the Maurice Elvey-directed episodes, they benefit from George Ridgwell's relatively dynamic direction, the mutiny aboard the *Gloria Scott* and the 'Cambridge' sequences in *The Three Students* being particularly noted. They also reveal the extent to which colour tinting was used on their original release (starting in March 1923) –

red/amber and green in parts of *The Gloria Scott*, *The Missing Three-quarter* and *The Mystery of Thor Bridge*, blue in parts of *His Last Bow*.

This time round, roadworks in Baker Street forced Ridgwell to film the 221B exteriors at Stoll's Cricklewood facility. In addition to Cambridge filming for *The Three Students* and the wooden frigate moored at Greenhithe seen in *The Gloria Scott*, *Silver Blaze* called for location work at Epsom racecourse and *The Cardboard Box* was partly shot in Brighton, partly at the Royal Albert Docks. The final episode, however, required Ridgwell's crew to travel even further afield, Eille Norwood's Holmes meeting his doom at the hands of arch-rival Professor Moriarty in *The Final Problem* over the edge of Somerset's Cheddar Gorge, rather than Switzerland's Reichenbach Falls – making this the only film or TV sequence to date brave enough to end the detective's exploits on such an admirably grim note.

An admirably grim ending, that is, if one is prepared to overlook the fact that Norwood would reprise the role on film one last time, in the feature-length **The Sign of Four**, released later the same year – and the fact that he also produced and starred in a Doyle-endorsed play, *The Return of Sherlock Holmes*, which ran for 130 performances at the Prince's Theatre, London, between October 1923 and January 1924. (The script, co-written by Norwood's nephew J E Harold Terry, conflated elements from THE DISAPPEARANCE OF LADY FRANCES CARFAX, CHARLES AUGUSTUS MILVERTON and THE EMPTY HOUSE, among others.) Norwood never made a 'talkie', supplementing stage appearances with compiling cryptic crosswords for the *Daily Express* – but he was still giving interviews about his time as Holmes well into his eighties. He died on Christmas Eve 1948.

At the Stoll dinner given in 1921 at which Doyle raised an effusive toast to Norwood, the actor replied with a speech ending in a self-penned epitaph: 'Lies Sherlock Holmes beneath the soil/His still remains disarmed, destroyed/But thanks to Stoll and Conan Doyle/He still remains in celluloid.' Despite the perishability of nitrate film stock, all but one of Norwood's 47 Holmes pictures do indeed remain; only 22 of these are currently available, but we can nevertheless nominate Eille Norwood – with no real fear of contradiction, save a respectful nod in the direction of theatrical titan William Gillette – as the first truly great Great Detective.

The Last Vampyre

GB 1992 TVM adaptation [THE SUSSEX VAMPIRE]
Granada Television 108m colour
tx 27 January 1993 ITV
w **Jeremy Paul** *p* **June Wyndham Davies** *d* **Tim Sullivan**
cast Sherlock Holmes: **Jeremy Brett** Dr Watson: **Edward Hardwicke** John Stockton: **Roy Marsden** Rob Ferguson: **Keith Barron** Carlotta: **Yolanda Vasquez** Rev Merridew: **Maurice Denham** Jack: **Richard Dempsey** Dolores: **Juliet Aubrey** Michael: **Jason Hetherington** Mrs Mason: **Elizabeth Spriggs** Mr Gresty: **Peter Geddis** Mrs Gresty: **Kate Lansbury** Vera Gresty: **Maria Redmond** pedlar: **Freddie Jones** Miss Ruddock: **Hilary Mason** PC Ware: **Stephen Tomlin** Mrs Carter: **Eileen O'Brien** Mr Carter: **Andy Abrahams** Tom Carter: **Marcello Marascalchi** Albert, the page boy: **Paul Parris** Ricardo, the baby: **Anthony Price**

*T*he Last Vampyre – the second of the three early nineties Granada/Jeremy Brett TV movies, following on from **The Master Blackmailer** – was transmitted just as Francis Ford Coppola's *Bram Stoker's Dracula* was doing the rounds in British cinemas. Equally portentous in (presumed) intent, they share the same pretentiousness in execution.

Toothless: Holmes (Jeremy Brett) in the shadow of John Stockton (Roy Marsden) in **The Last Vampyre** *(1993)*

Jeremy Brett as Holmes attempts to exorcise **The Last Vampyre** *(1993)*

Ostensibly based on THE SUSSEX VAMPIRE (the setting was altered when location shooting was arranged for the Cotswolds village of Stanton), *The Last Vampyre* actually owes something to THE HOUND OF THE BASKERVILLES; the production appears to be targeting the same triumvirate of Sherlock Holmes, bleak landscapes and the supernatural. The give-away, of course, is the pre-title sequence. Most modern versions of THE HOUND begin with a prologue set a hundred or so years before Holmes' time in which an evil landowner hunts down a poor gypsy girl and has his wicked way with her before being killed by a gigantic hound symbolising the spirit of retribution. *The Last Vampyre* begins with a prologue set over a hundred years before Holmes' time in which an evil landowner impregnates a local girl, kills her, dumps her body at the local church and then is burned alive by local villagers in a completely non-symbolic act of vengeance.

In the original, tea broker Bob Ferguson asks Holmes to investigate his South American wife, who for several months has been seen abusing his son from a previous marriage – and now she has been found kneeling over their own baby with blood on her mouth. Ferguson cannot believe she is a vampire, but what other explanation can there be? Holmes, too, cannot believe she is a vampire, and centres his enquiries on Ferguson's older son. At Ferguson's farmhouse, Holmes notes that Ferguson's dog has become paralysed – poisoned, it transpires, for the toxin was tried out on the dog

by the jealous, spiteful son before he scratched his baby half-brother's neck and poisoned the wound. The mother, seeing what had happened, attempted to suck the venom out, and was caught with blood around her mouth. Case closed.

Doyle is a much misunderstood writer. It is commonly accepted, for instance, that he was writing detective stories, and yet in many of them there are three main characters: the person who has been injured, the person who has been wrongfully accused and the person who eventually turns out to be guilty. Frequently either the first or the second of those characters is absent, narrowing the field of suspects considerably. Doyle wasn't writing puzzles either – most of his solutions revolve around observation or coincidence rather than deduction. In fact, he is writing little tableaux of criminality, showing how even the most respectable streets and villages can hide villainy at their heart.

The writers working on the various Jeremy Brett series discovered this problem pretty early on: they had crimes, they had a detective, they had clues, but they had an obvious suspect who then turned out to be guilty. No surprise there, and so no drama. In order to beef up the stories, they needed to introduce red herrings, suspects who have means, motive and opportunity but who, in the end, turn out to be innocent.

In *The Last Vampyre* the red herring is John Stockton, a recent arrival in Ferguson's village who claims to be descended from the Sinclair family of evil memory; local lore has it that Stockton's ancestor drank blood, and that Stockton himself is a vampire. The Reverend Merridew (a part originally offered to Peter Cushing) contacts Holmes when Ferguson's young son dies following a dinner party at which Stockton was present. Holmes and Watson arrive in the village concerned that an innocent man might be the victim of a witch-hunt, but feelings are running high: Ferguson's wife's maid is attacked, Stockton is killed in a carriage accident and people fall ill all over the village. Finally, Stockton's corpse is dug up and staked down to keep him at rest – all to no avail.

The interesting thing is that no crime has actually been committed – the baby died of influenza (which is what the villagers are suffering from), and Stockton's accident was just that. Everything else is hysteria. The point of the script, if there is a point, is that people like Stockton, who act differently from the norm, automatically attract suspicion, and that suspicion can grow into violence. In a vague concession to the original, Ferguson's crippled older son Jack actually believes himself to be a vampire (influenced by Stockton's dark charisma) and attacks his mother's maid, whom he desires sexually – leading to a relocated scene in which Ferguson's wife sucks the poison out of her maid's neck, rather than her baby's. But Jack's problem is just a symptom, not a cause, of the rabid hysteria. It's all rather fragmentary and odd.

Beneath the plot's 'supernatural' elements lies a substratum of sensible English logic, and yet beneath that is a substratum of the supernatural again. Holmes appears to see a ghost at one point, and also gains glimpses of the future; he believes he may have been hypnotised by Stockton, but we are never vouchsafed an explanation as to when or indeed why. Asked if he admits to the existence of the inexplicable, Holmes responds, 'Oh yes, there's plenty of evidence for that,' in direct contradiction to his solidly materialistic stance in the original: 'The world is big enough for us. No ghosts need apply.'

The film ends tragically, with Ferguson's deluded son attempting to fly, and accidentally hanging himself with his makeshift cape. Nobody is responsible, and it's hard to see how this could be a retributive punishment. Holmes and Watson return to London in a rather sombre frame of mind.

Before filming the next Granada TV movie, **The Eligible Bachelor**, Brett and Edward Hardwicke recorded the first instalment of *The Four Oaks Mystery*, one of four linked sketches featuring various ITV detectives (Taggart, Van der Valk, Inspector Wexford) broadcast in June 1992 as part of the charity-fundraising *ITV Telethon* weekend. Also starring Phyllis Calvert as Holmes' godmother, the segment was written and directed by the *Last Vampyre* pairing of Jeremy Paul and Tim Sullivan. (AL)

The League of Extraordinary Gentlemen

US 2003 pastiche Twentieth Century-Fox Film Corporation 110m colour
w **James Dale Robinson** *source comic mini-series by* **Alan Moore, Kevin O'Neill** *p* **Trevor Albert, Don Murphy** *d* **Stephen Norrington**

cast Allan Quatermain: **Sean Connery** Captain Nemo: **Naseeruddin Shah** Mina Harker: **Peta Wilson** Rodney Skinner: **Tony Curran** Dorian Gray: **Stuart Townsend** Tom Sawyer: **Shane West** Dr Henry Jekyll/Edward Hyde: **Jason Flemyng** Moriarty (Fantom): **Richard Roxburgh** Dante: **Max Ryan** Sanderson Reed: **Tom Goodman-Hill** Nigel: **David Hemmings** Ishmael **Terry O'Neill** Draper: **Rudolf Pellar** Constable Dunning: **Robert Willox** running officer: **Robert Orr** copper #1: **Michael McGuffie** copper #2: **Joel Kirby** soldier: **Marek Vasut** Toby: **Ewart James Walters** assassin #3: **Michal Grün** elderly hunter: **Robert Vahey** old traveler: **Sylvester Morand** Edgar Shreave: **Mariano Titanti** hansom cab driver: **Huggy Leaver** marksman #1: **Pavel Bezdek** marksman #2: **Stanislav Adamickij** marksman #3: **James Babson** terrified crewman: **San Shella** recordist: **Ellen Savaria** Venice conning tower crewman: **Riz Meedin** Rocket Room crewman: **Sartaj Garewal** crewman Patel: **Neran Persaud** headphones crewman: **Andrew Rajan** stunned guard: **Daniel Brown** breathless crewman: **Aftab Sachak** signal crewman: **Guy Singh Digpal** crewman Chandra: **Harmage Singh Kalirai** guard #1: **Brian Caspe** valet: **Robert Goodman** flame thrower: **Rene Hajek** witch doctor: **Semere-Ab Etmet Yohannes**

THE MYSTERY

1899: following a series of terror attacks conceived by a masked figure calling himself 'the Fantom', retired African adventurer Allan Quatermain is persuaded to travel to London to meet with a mysterious British official, 'M', who is assembling a 'League of Extraordinary Gentlemen' to combat the Fantom menace. Joining Quatermain in this latest of several Leagues are the pirate Captain Nemo; invisible thief Rodney Skinner; chemist and vampiress Mina Harker; immortal aesthete Dorian Gray; American boy agent Tom Sawyer; and man/monster hybrid Henry Jekyll/Edward Hyde. According to M, the Fantom next plans to strike at a gathering of world leaders in Venice …

THE INVESTIGATION

Travelling in Nemo's vast futuristic submersible *Nautilus*, the League begin to suspect that one of their own is a traitor … and soon after, Skinner disappears. The League arrive in Venice as the ancient city is ripped apart by a series of explosions – but their efforts to break this wave of bombs are frustrated by the Fantom's gunmen. In a Venetian graveyard (!), Quatermain grapples with the Fantom, exposing him as none other than M.

The villain escapes, as does his accomplice, Gray. Back aboard the *Nautilus*, the League listen to a gramophone recording left behind by Gray, in which M describes his plan to assemble the League in order to obtain their secrets – Nemo's science, Skinner's skin sample, Jekyll's potion and Mina's blood ...

THE SOLUTION

Skinner leads his fellow League members to a remote Mongolian factory complex where M is mass-producing items derived from the League's own secrets to be sold as weapons of war to the highest bidder: rows of *Nautili* are under construction; armies of superhuman Hydes, invisible spies and vampiric assassins are in the making. While Mina confronts and kills Gray, forcing him to gaze upon his own portrait, Quatermain meets with M – in fact, none other than the fabled Professor Moriarty, the so-called 'Napoleon of Crime' thought to have perished at the Reichenbach Falls. As his hideaway is destroyed, Moriarty makes his escape, mortally wounding Quatermain in his flight – but is shot dead from a seemingly impossible distance by Quatermain's protégé, Sawyer.

✦ ✦ ✦

Let the manifold idiocies of this cynically manufactured multiplex software bother us only a little: the fact that Mark Twain's Tom Sawyer, blatantly inserted as a sop to American interest, ought to be in his sixties in 1899; that any Victorian lady, even a vampiric one, would deport herself in public as a dominatrix; that the sunken Venice (almost entirely decimated in the course of the picture) is filled with roadways convenient for high-speed automobile excursions, and its inhabitants bury their dead underground ...

No, let us instead turn to the source text: Volume 1 of Alan Moore and Kevin O'Neill's deft, iconoclastic but nonetheless affectionate *League of Extraordinary Gentlemen* comic books, published in six instalments over 1999-2000. Here, we find a cadaverous Professor Moriarty who has all along been a British Intelligence operative, a crime lord manufactured by an MI5 seeking to control and monitor the underworld themselves. 'When you begin shadowboxing, sometimes the shadows become real,' ruminates Moore's Moriarty, as he prepares to raze the East End of London in an effort to purge himself of his only rival, an inscrutable 'devil doctor' of Limehouse. 'Am I, for example, a director of military intelligence posing as a criminal ... or a criminal posing as a director of military intelligence ... or both?' Here, we find a glorious re-enactment of THE FINAL PROBLEM, making us at last privy to the conversation shared by Holmes and Moriarty above the tumult of the Falls: 'As closing acts go, I'll allow the scenery is more than adequate'; 'Why, sir, it is Olympian! We tread the very borders of mythology!'

But in *this*, the first major motion picture of Sherlockian interest to have been released in eighteen long years (since **Young Sherlock Holmes**, in fact), we find only a silly spiv delivering his silly plan in a silly Dick Van Dyke Enger-lish accent. One can hardly blame actor Richard Roxburgh alone, so recently an at-least diverting Sherlock in **The Hound of the Baskervilles** (2002); it cannot, after all, have been Roxburgh's decision to so utterly emasculate both Moore's and Doyle's Moriartys, leaving but a Generic Action Movie Baddie. But since no trace remains of the Professor's character, nor his appearance, and there is only the briefest mention of his history, which has not the slightest bearing on the picture's (admittedly, paper-thin) plot – well then, why bother naming the villain at all?

Ah well. The revelation is lost in a closing cacophony of explosions and gunfire, drowning out the most terrible sound – that of Messrs Doyle, Haggard, Stoker, Twain, Verne, Wells and Wilde, all spinning and wailing in their lonely graves.

The Loss of a Personal Friend

GB 1987 pastiche 14m colour
wd **N G Bristow** *p* **Michael S Ostrow**
cast Dr John Watson: **Ian Price** Sherlock Holmes/the bookseller: **Peter Harding** Mrs McKinnley: **Maggie Ellis**

The Reichenbach Falls, Switzerland: fearing that his friend, Sherlock Holmes, has been lured into a trap by his nemesis, Moriarty, Dr Watson races, too late, to Holmes' aid. He finds only Holmes' cane and cigarette case at the scene, his friend having, presumably, perished... Cut to black. A gunshot is heard. Bring up: it is some years later, and Watson is writing secretly to his publisher, regarding an extraordinary encounter earlier that day... In Baker Street, Watson bumps into a stooped bookseller; soon after, the bookseller comes knocking at the door of 221B, carrying Holmes' cigarette case – the very case that Watson had recovered at the Falls. Watson sees Holmes, disguised, as the bookseller; he passes out. When Watson comes to, Holmes relates the tale of how he survived his struggle with Moriarty – and declares his intention to leave in search of the assassin he believes to be on his trail. Although shocked by the manner in which Holmes has deceived him, Watson wants to protect Holmes, and seizes his revolver. Later: Watson is telling Holmes how glad he is that Holmes has changed his mind and stayed at 221B, where he's safest. The camera pans to the mirror above the hearth, showing the true image of the room; the bookseller lies dead in Holmes' place, a gunshot wound to his head.

At once a sophisticated meditation on grief and a deeply macabre joke, *The Loss of a Personal Friend* – its title taken from a column written by *Strand Magazine* editor George Newnes in reference to the public's response to Sherlock Holmes' 'death' in THE FINAL PROBLEM – is ten times as effective a piece of drama as a great many Holmes films ten times its length. Despite a token appearance by Watson's housekeeper, bafflingly named 'Mrs McKinnley', it's a two-hander, filmed mostly in a fire-lit gloom on a budget of, presumably, next-to-nothing. Writer/director N G Bristow has worked on episodes of television series including *Ballykissangel* and *The Bill*.

The mood is set in the pre-credits scene (shot on location in North Wales), showing Watson at the Reichenbach Falls; thinking his friend destroyed, Watson howls out Holmes' name in mortal anguish, like a faithful hound whose master has failed to return home.

The most part of this little-seen oddity, however, is given over to a rewrite of the scene in THE EMPTY HOUSE where the thought-dead Holmes returns to 221B. 'I've missed you, so very much. That is to say, my life has been very dull,' sobs Ian Price's choked Watson. 'Why did you send me no message, that you were still alive?' Peter Harding's cruel, lupine Holmes sneers in reply: 'Forgive me, but you would not have written so convincingly of my death had you not thought it was true.' The pivotal moment

comes with Watson's betrayed rejoinder: 'You really are an automaton, aren't you? A calculating machine!' – a paraphrase from THE SIGN OF THE FOUR, but delivered with utter despair.

This quite inspired 14-minute piece is best viewed, therefore, in the light of latterday efforts to rescue Watson from the shadow of Nigel Bruce, bumbling counterpoint to Basil Rathbone's Sherlock in the Paramount/Universal pictures of the thirties and forties. In Granada Television's **The Adventures of Sherlock Holmes** and sequels, plus films such as **The Crucifer of Blood** and even **Without a Clue**, a younger, more 'authentic', more emotionally deep Watson is depicted – but the Ian Price version is probably the darkest ever, a man tortured by grief and ultimately driven homicidally insane by the need to be released from his bereavement (or alternatively, desperate to rid himself of this unfeeling user of a Holmes). When the camera reveals that Watson is hallucinating Holmes in the hapless, absurdly accented bookseller's place, it's a truly numbing disclosure. Despite the fact that the doctor's deluded, *The Loss of a Personal Friend* ought to be feted as 'the one where Watson murders Holmes'.

Killer: a grief-stricken Watson (Ian Price) shoots dead a harmless bookseller (Peter Harding) in **The Loss of a Personal Friend** *(1987)*

The Man Who Disappeared

GB/US 1951 adaptation [The Man With the Twisted Lip] Vandyke/Dryer & Weenolsen Productions Inc 26m bw
p **Rudolph Cartier** *d* **Richard M Grey**
cast Sherlock Holmes: **John Longden** Dr Watson: **Campbell Singer** Neville St Clair: **Hector Ross** Kate, his wife: **Ninka Dolega** Doreen: **Beryl Baxter** Luzatto: **Walther Gotell**

Ahopelessly dreary early fifties effort featuring one of the least charismatic Holmeses of all, *The Man Who Disappeared*, advertised in US trade paper *Variety* as a pilot for a full television series, ultimately limped out as a B-feature. Filmed on location in London and against a handful of very flat studio flats, this uninspiring piece attempts to beef up the story of The Man With the Twisted Lip by having the well-to-do Neville St Clair forced into adopting the role of ragged beggar Hugh Boone after becoming involved in the affairs of a former sweetheart, Doreen, whose husband has been killed by the swarthy Luzatto, proprietor of the opium den known as the 'Bar of Gold'.

The business is, in fact, all so wretchedly convoluted that it comes as some relief when a particularly empty-headed Watson is whisked from 221B Baker Street by Luzatto's henchmen, who – having seen the bored doctor don a deerstalker and enunciate 'Elementary, my dear Watson' into a mirror – have mistaken him for Holmes. Held hostage in Luzatto's den, Watson is rescued when Holmes climbs through an upstairs window while – hurrah! – the good old Boys in Blue raid the Bar of Gold. Our heroes then join in a perfunctory brawl with fists and guns, helping to give the ghastly foreign types the thrashing they deserve.

John Longden (1900-71), who plays his prematurely aged Sherlock more like a battleship commander than a detective, was famous for appearing in several early Hitchcock features and turned up later as Inspector Lomax in Hammer Film Productions' *Quatermass 2* (1957). (His greatest contribution to the cinema, however, was his uncredited voiceover – 'This is the universe. Big, isn't it?' – which introduces Powell and Pressburger's 1946 *A Matter of Life and Death*.) Playing Luzatto was German actor Walther Gotell (usually credited 'Walter'; 1924-97), who would continue to portray dastardly overseas types in a succession of British and American features – and is now most often recognised for his role as KGB spymaster General Gogol in no less than five of the Eon-produced James Bond films, from *The Spy Who Loved Me* (1977) on.

Although mostly third-rate, *The Man Who Disappeared* does manage one nearly lovely moment. When Holmes and Watson first enter the Bar of Gold, the doctor is appalled: 'Heavens, Holmes – it's an opium den!' he gasps. Replies Longden's Holmes: 'If your nose had been as sensitive as your eyes, you'd have known that 30 seconds ago...'

The Masks of Death

GB 1984 TVM pastiche Tyburn Productions Ltd 78m colour
tx 23 December 1984 Channel 4
w **N J Crisp** *story* **John Elder** [pseudonym for **Anthony Hinds**] *p* **Norman Priggen** *d* **Roy Ward Baker**
cast Sherlock Holmes: **Peter Cushing** Dr Watson: **John Mills** Irene Adler: **Anne Baxter** Home Secretary: **Ray Milland** Graf Udo Von Felseck: **Anton Diffring** Alec MacDonald: **Gordon Jackson** Miss Derwent: **Susan Penhaligon** Anton Von Felseck: **Marcus Gilbert** Mrs Hudson: **Jenny Laird** Alfred Coombs: **Russell Hunter** Frederick Baines: **James Cossins** Lord Claremont: **Eric Dodson** Lady Claremont: **Georgina Coombs** chauffeur: **James Head** boot boy: **Dominic Murphy**

The Mystery

London, 1913: the River Police drag a body from beneath a Thames wharf. Two others, found not far away in Whitechapel, are similarly distinguished – their faces contorted in terror, but their bodies bearing no obvious signs of violence. Scotland Yard's Inspector MacDonald calls in the semi-retired Sherlock Holmes, who goes to Whitechapel with Dr Watson. Near a closed-down pub called the Crown, Holmes interrogates a rambling down-and-out who claims to have seen 'devils incarnate' with 'holes for eyes and snouts for noses'. Holmes makes little progress, however – and, some weeks later, drops the case after the Home Secretary calls at 221B with Graf Udo Von Felseck, an emissary of Kaiser Wilhelm II, in tow. Von Felseck reveals that an un-named young gentleman, whom Holmes is led to believe must be the German Crown Prince, has vanished from the Graf's Buckinghashire retreat. This distinguished visitor had travelled incognito to England in a bid to avert war with Germany and the Home Secretary fears that his disappearance may be part of a plot to engineer the outbreak of hostilities...

THE INVESTIGATION

In Buckinghamshire, Holmes and Watson recognise one of Von Felseck's house guests, an American known as Mrs Norton, as none other than Irene Adler, an adventuress who bested Holmes some 25 years before. Mysterious comings and goings at night lead Holmes to a nearby chalk pit, where he enters a hut containing mechanical apparatus; realising that he has walked into a trap, he flees just before a rockfall causes the hut's combustible contents to explode. The business of the Crown Prince, deduces Holmes, has been an utter fabrication – the 'royal' traveller being Von Felseck's son, Anton. Holmes and Watson return to London by train, foiling another assassination attempt *en route* thanks to their being forewarned by Irene. Back home, they pick up the trail of the Whitechapel bodies, the mystery they were distracted from solving...

THE SOLUTION

Inspired by both a faltering gas lamp and his recollection that he once saw Von Felseck give a lecture in Heidelberg on the subject of the extermination of vermin, Holmes leads Watson back to the Crown, to which 'beer barrels' are still being delivered. A secret passage in the cellar leads to an abandoned sewer, where white-hooded German fifth columnists – the 'demons' seen earlier – are treating poison gas, intending to leave every home in

London connected to a gas main ready to be flooded with lethal fumes upon the outbreak of war (the same vapours caused the contorted faces of those accidentally exposed to it). Discovered, the infiltrators flee through another tunnel, leading them into the arms of MacDonald's officers. Soon afterwards, Holmes is summoned to Windsor Castle, there to receive a 'signal honour' from the King.

✦ ✦ ✦

Since finishing work on **Sir Arthur Conan Doyle's Sherlock Holmes**, the 1968 BBC TV series which left him shell-shocked by the 'terrible pressure' of modern television production, the now-widowed Peter Cushing had thrown himself into a succession of largely undistinguished film/TV projects – including *The Great Houdini*, a 1976 American TV movie in which he appeared in an extended cameo role as Holmes creator Doyle himself, attempting to convince Paul Michael Glaser's escapologist hero of the merits of the spiritualist life (and afterlife). Most of Cushing's work in the seventies and eighties, however, attempted to trade off his reputation as the acceptable face of horror cinema – among them *The Ghoul* and *Legend of the Werewolf* (both 1975), two modestly budgeted pieces from Tyburn Films, a tiny would-be rival to the by-now ailing Hammer organisation.

Tyburn was run by Kevin Francis (1944-), the son of director/cinematographer Freddie; in 1979, Freddie had flown to Poland to supervise several episodes of the ill-fated series **Sherlock Holmes and Dr Watson** alongside three other ex-Hammer directors, Val Guest, Peter Sasdy and Roy Ward Baker. Around the same time, Kevin Francis had attempted to raise finance for a new film version of THE HOUND OF THE BASKERVILLES – one that was intended to give Cushing a third brush with the beast of Dartmoor, albeit this time with the dog realised as a 'stop-motion' model courtesy of animator Ray Harryhausen. Although this project came to nothing, it did lead to Francis discussing an original Holmes script with former Hammer producer-turned-freelance writer Anthony Hinds (who, as 'John Elder', had written both of the above-mentioned Tyburn horrors). Cushing's advancing years had suggested a Holmes-in-retirement scenario, a companion-piece to HIS LAST BOW; television writer N J (Norman) Crisp polished Hinds' story treatment, adding many Doyle touches in a bid to avoid antagonising the ever-vigilant Cushing.

The combined ages of all those associated with *The Masks of Death*, as the resultant film was entitled, must surely have come close to equalling Methuselah's: Cushing was 71; Roy Ward Baker, whom Francis had hired to direct, was 68; John Mills, an eager Watson whose professional association with Baker dated back to 1947, was 76; and Anton Diffring, cast, as ever, as a steely, warmongering German nasty, was 66. Ray Milland, Anne Baxter and Gordon Jackson were hardly spring chickens, either. Filmed in the summer of 1984 at Twickenham Studios and on location in Buckinghamshire and London, *The Masks of Death* debuted as part of Channel 4's Christmas 1984 schedule, when it was warmly received by both viewers and critics, who thought it a 'peculiarly English combination of genuine horror and spirited comedy' (the *Times*) and 'a jolly confection ... *Dad's Army* Conan Doyle' (the *Observer*).

Opening in 1926 (by which time Watson's arthritis prevents him from transcribing Holmes' memoirs, being forced to employ a pretty young secretary, Miss Derwent), but set primarily in the run-up to the Great War, *The Masks of Death* sees the reappearances of both Scotland Yard's Alec MacDonald (from THE VALLEY OF FEAR) and adventuress Irene Adler (A SCANDAL IN BOHEMIA). Obviously, given a sexagenarian lead played by a septuagenarian actor, the film doesn't dare even to hint at any kind of romantic interest between Holmes and Irene; instead, Cushing's ultra-crotchety Sherlock seems to view her as a blasted nuisance. Watson describes the two of them, rather nicely, as 'two fencers'. The script, however, is distinctly lopsided: both Irene and the villainous Graf Udo von Felseck simply vanish from the piece a good while before the slightly cursory ending, accentuating the fact that the whole of the plodding middle section struggles to remain relevant to the main plot. All the same, the scene in which a flickering gas-lamp causes Holmes to cotton on to what's actually been happening in Whitechapel while he's been distracted elsewhere is beautifully realised, giving a real hint as to the detective's skewed insights, and the sight of the hooded 'demons' manufacturing poison gas in London's sewers makes for a striking conclusion.

Plans were made to film a follow-up in 1986, *The Abbot's Cry*, again written by Hinds and Crisp

and part-derived from an unused Hinds horror script, *The Satanist*. The story, consciously styled to mimic the narrative structure of THE HOUND OF THE BASKERVILLES, was to begin with a vicar leaping to his death from the top of his church, an event that ties into a local legend dating back to Henry VIII's dissolution of the monasteries. The mid-eighties was not, however, a good time for the British film industry – capital was hard to come by – and this, coupled with Cushing's declining health, meant that *The Abbot's Cry* never met its prospective starting date. Once it was clear that Cushing would never again be fit enough to endure even the most sympathetic filming schedule, efforts were made to recast him. Ian Richardson, who'd played Holmes in two ill-fated TV movies, **Sir Arthur Conan Doyle's The Sign of Four** and **Sir Arthur Conan Doyle's The Hound of the Baskervilles** (both 1983), has recalled discussing the part with Cushing at his house in Whitstable, but nothing concrete ever came of this.

As it turned out, *The Masks of Death* was to provide Cushing with his final leading role. Although a slightly faltering lap of honour, it would be hard to imagine a more fitting way to bring down the curtain on such a remarkable career: bearing this hero of another age, with honours, to a far-off, turreted castle in an open-topped carriage.

The Master Blackmailer

1991 TVM adaptation [CHARLES AUGUSTUS MILVERTON] *Granada Television 102m colour tx 2 January 1992 ITV*
w **Jeremy Paul** *p* **June Wyndham Davies** *d* **Peter Hammond** *cast* Sherlock Holmes: **Jeremy Brett** Dr Watson: **Edward Hardwicke** Charles Augustus Milverton: **Robert Hardy** Lady Diana Swinstead: **Norma West** the Dowager: **Gwen Ffrangcon-Davies** Inspector Lestrade: **Colin Jeavons** Bertrand: **Nickolas Grace** Lady Eva Blackwell: **Serena Gordon** the Hon Charlotte Miles: **Sarah McVicar** Colonel Dorking: **David Mallinson** Harry, Earl of Dovercourt: **Brian Mitchell** Hebworth (alias Veitch): **Hans Meyer** Agatha: **Sophie Thompson** Stoker: **Stephen Simms** Lillie: **Belinda Peters** Daphne: **Henrietta Whitson-Jones** Tronson, the butler: **Alan Rothwell** Lewis, Dorking's batman: **Howard Gay** art gallery owner: **David Scase** Hubbs, the painter: **Jimmy Hibbert** auctioneer: **Tony Broughton** Emile: **Lee Clarke** cabaret artiste: **Simon Fogg**

'Do you feel a creeping, shrinking sensation, Watson, when you stand before the serpents in the Zoo, and see the slithery, gliding, venomous creatures, with their deadly eyes and wicked, flattened faces? Well, that's how Milverton impresses me...' With these words, Doyle has Holmes describe 'the worst man in London'. In Jeremy Paul's much-expanded adaptation, Holmes' unflattering description is replaced with a scene in the reptile house at London Zoo where Holmes and Watson discuss Charles Augustus Milverton, 'the master blackmailer', while watching the snakes curl and hiss. It's an ideal replication of Doyle's intention: a scene that preserves his aim while transferring the aural to the visual. In other words, a perfect example of adapting the written word to the screen.

Following Granada's **The Case-book of Sherlock Holmes**, *The Master Blackmailer* was an experiment in presenting Jeremy Brett's Holmes in a TV movie designed for a two-hour slot – a format which had seen Central Television's John Thaw-starring Inspector Morse mysteries meet with wild success from 1987 on. And in many ways, *The Master Blackmailer* is the best of the later Granada/Brett adaptations – the script uses as much of Doyle's dialogue as is humanly possible (including, unfortunately, Milverton's last words – 'You done me!') and adds scenes only to enrich, rather than alter, the original.

The casting is splendid, with Robert Hardy (1925-) playing rather against type as the repressed Milverton. Brett has rarely been better as Holmes, his distaste for the repellent extortionist being plain in every scene. Daringly, he's given a sort-of love interest ('Sherlock shows he's no Holmo!', as the *Sun*'s headline in advance of transmission had it): having inveigled himself into the fortress-like Milverton household in the guise of a plumber, Holmes is required to romance Milverton's flighty maid, Aggie, and his heartfelt reply to her 'Give us a kiss' – 'I don't know how' – is all too believable. Watson has a big moment, too – being moved to strike Milverton in a lengthy 221B scene pregnant with menace. Unlike some of the 50-minute episodes, which seem to have too much plot for their running time, and the subsequent TV films **The Last Vampyre** and **The Eligible Bachelor**, which seem padded with unnecessary material, *The Master Blackmailer* is just the right length.

'Give us a kiss': Aggie (Sophie Thomson) has her wicked way with Holmes (Jeremy Brett) in The Master Blackmailer *(1992)*

There will be those who complain that Holmes seems to switch employers halfway through, forgetting about the elderly Dowager who first called upon his services when Lady Eva Blackwell's reputation is threatened. More substantial is the loss of the original's wry little coda, in which Inspector Lestrade asks Holmes' assistance in tracking down the black-clad burglars seen fleeing Milverton's home on the night of his murder. But then, given such a bloodily dramatic showdown – in which Lady Eva's aunt, Diana Swinstead, revenges herself on the blackmailer by shooting him repeatedly before (presumably) stamping out his eyes with her heel, all the while Holmes and Watson look on from their place of concealment – perhaps it's as well to leave the drama undiluted. (AL)

The Memoirs of Sherlock Holmes

GB 1994 6 x 50m approx TV series adaptations
Granada Television colour
p June Wyndham Davies
regular cast Sherlock Holmes: **Jeremy Brett**
Mrs Hudson: **Rosalie Williams**

THE THREE GABLES

tx 7 March 1994 ITV
w Jeremy Paul *d* Peter Hammond
regular cast, plus Dr John Watson: **Edward Hardwicke**
Isadora Klein: **Claudine Auger** Douglas Maberley:
Gary Cady Duke of Lomond: **Benjamin Pullen**
Dowager Duchess: **Caroline Blakiston** Mary Maberley:
Mary Ellis Langdale Pike: **Peter Wyngarde**
Haines-Johnson: **Michael Graham** Steve Dixie:
Steve Toussaint Susan: **Barbara Young** Mr Sutro: **John Gill**
Dora: **Emma Hardwicke**

THE DYING DETECTIVE

tx 14 March 1994 ITV

w **T R Bowen** *d* **Sarah Hellings**

regular cast, plus Dr John Watson: **Edward Hardwicke**
Culverton Smith: **Jonathan Hyde** Adelaide Savage:
Susannah Harker Victor Savage: **Richard Bonneville** John
Gedgrave: **Roy Hudd** Charles Damant: **Trevor Bowen**
Inspector Morton: **John Labanowski** Colonel Carnac:
Rowland Davies Mrs Carnac: **Caroline John** Penrose
Fisher: **Shaughan Seymour** Benson: **Keiran Flynn** Staples:
Malcolm Hebden Chinese lady: **Mary Ten Pow** Marina
Savage: **Rachel Rice** police sergeant: **Colin Stevens**

THE GOLDEN PINCE-NEZ

tx 21 March 1994 ITV

w **Gary Hopkins** *d* **Peter Hammond**

regular cast, plus Mycroft Holmes: **Charles Gray**
Professor Coram/Sergius: **Frank Finlay** Inspector Hopkins:
Nigel Planer Anna: **Anna Carteret** Susan Tarlton: **Natalie
Morse** Abigail Crosby: **Patricia Kerrigan** Willoughby Smith:
Christopher Guard Mrs Marker: **Kathleen Byron**
Alexis: **Roger Ringrose** Vladimir: **Daniel Finlay**
Mortimer: **Harry Kirkham**

THE RED CIRCLE

tx 28 March 1994 ITV

w **Jeremy Paul** *d* **Sarah Hellings**

regular cast, plus Dr John Watson: **Edward Hardwicke**
Mrs Warren: **Betty Marsden** Mr Warren: **Kenneth Connor**
Gorgiano: **John Hallam** Gennaro Lucca: **James Coombes**
Emilia Lucca: **Sophia Diaz** Inspector Hawkins: **Tom
Chadbon** Leverton: **Kerry Shale** Firmani: **Joseph Long**
Vera: **Louise Heaney**

THE MAZARIN STONE

tx 4 May 1994 ITV

w **Gary Hopkins** *d* **Peter Hammond**

regular cast, plus Dr John Watson: **Edward Hardwicke**
Mycroft Holmes: **Charles Gray** Agnes Garrideb: **Phyllis
Calvert** Emily Garrideb: **Barbara Hicks** Count Sylvius: **Jon
Finch** Lord Cantlemere: **James Villiers** Inspector
Bradstreet: **Denis Lill** John Garrideb/James Winter: **Gavan
O'Herlihy** Princess of Wales: **Helen Ryan** Nathan
Garrideb: **Richard Caldicott** Ikey Sanders: **Harry Landis**
Commissionaire Jenkins: **Michael Wynne**

THE CARDBOARD BOX

tx 11 May 1994 ITV

w **T R Bowen** *d* **Sarah Hellings**

regular cast, plus Dr John Watson: **Edward Hardwicke**

Jim Browner: **Ciaran Hinds** Susan Cushing: **Joanna David**
Sarah Cushing: **Deborah Findlay** Mary Browner: **Lucy
Whybrow** Inspector Hawkins: **Tom Chadbon** Marcel
Jacottet: **Thierry Harcourt** Mr Bradbrook: **Richard Dixon**
Murdoch Gull: **Renny Krupinski** postman: **Andrew
Readman** Mrs Clyde: **Ann Rye** Lucy: **Rachel Smith**
policeman: **Andy Tomlinson**

When the Granada production team came to plan *The Memoirs of Sherlock Holmes* – which they did hastily, the series being commissioned just six months before its intended transmission – they were faced with two problems. On the one hand, beginning with **The Adventures of Sherlock Holmes** (1984-5), they had turned more of Doyle's stories into television episodes than anyone else, and were now left, broadly speaking, with the dregs – the stories Doyle wrote to fulfil contractual obligations or churned out in a rush between patients. On the other, just when they needed a charismatic lead who could carry the series through a weak patch with skill and charm, they found themselves having to write around an actor who was effectively dying before their eyes. The solution was obvious, and unfortunate: if the material is dross and the performer incapable, then the only thing that can save the day is style, lots of it. And padding.

The Memoirs of Sherlock Holmes is styled to within an inch of its life. Peter Hammond and Sarah Hellings directed three episodes each, and whereas the former can't let a polished surface go past without reflecting something in it, the latter has a penchant for candles, gas lamps and other sources of light. Every veneered surface is lingered over, every costume is scrutinised in detail, every face lovingly lit in an attempt to divert our attention from the shortcomings of the episodes themselves.

The adapters, all experienced in the ways of Holmes, have to work harder than ever. The material they have is sparse, and their additions clash both with Doyle's own style and with the Victorian era in general. Worst of these encumbrances is the half-buried theme of the supernatural that permeates the series – a theme that Doyle himself, despite his strong spiritualist beliefs, kept out of his Holmesian work, and which here hangs over from the TV movie **The Last Vampyre**, shown some two years beforehand. 'I shall be watching you with my third eye!' Holmes tells Watson in

The Mazarin Stone; later, his brother Mycroft manages to appear and disappear several times in the fog without moving across the intervening ground. It's all smoke and mirrors, quite literally.

Sadly, Holmes himself is a shadow of his former self. Jeremy Brett was seriously ill, of course – he collapsed during filming of the third episode, *The Three Gables*, after a prescription for lithium had caused fluid to build up in his lungs, and he collapsed again following shooting of the next, *The Dying Detective*, when a chronic heart problem was diagnosed – but even the detective seems to bumble through the episodes in a daze. When the only piece of deductive reasoning in six episodes involves Holmes' identification of a dog's owner purely *because the dog looks like her*, it's time to hang up the deerstalker in disgust.

Let's consider the episodes in turn. THE THREE GABLES is, in many ways, the weakest of Doyle's stories; there is no real crime for Holmes to investigate, there is no detection, there are some major lapses in logic and the antagonist goes unpunished. And yet Granada chose to launch the series with this thin gruel.

The story involves an elderly woman, Mary Maberly, who receives an impressive offer for her house, The Three Gables, on condition that she abandons everything in it. Holmes learns that Mary's recently deceased son, Douglas, had an affair with a noted society beauty, Isadora Klein – who eventually admits that Douglas had written a novel in which she appeared, thinly disguised and in a most unflattering light. Fortunately for her, Douglas died before he could send the manuscript to his publisher, and all that remained was for her to secretly obtain it (rather than just, say, burning the house down, of course).

Some flashbacks to the story of Klein and her diplomat lover (who is now Mary Maberley's grandson) are included in the TV version, but these are minor changes compared with what else has been done to the story. Firstly, Watson is now given the task of staying at the Gables overnight in case a burglary is attempted; when it occurs, he is badly beaten up. Secondly, gossip columnist Langdale Pike – a throwaway reference in Doyle – is given form and voice. (As played by cult sixties icon Peter Wyngarde – previously Baron Grüner [sic] in the BBC's **Sherlock Holmes** series of 1965 – Pike is more than a match in overt theatricality

Mycroft Holmes (Charles Gray) stood in for Sherlock in two episodes of **The Memoirs of Sherlock Holmes** *(1994)*

for the Brett Holmes.) Thirdly, and most importantly, we now have a crime where Doyle had none – the manslaughter of Douglas Maberly. In the original, he died of pneumonia brought on by a broken heart; here, he dies of pneumonia brought on by a ruptured spleen following a beating by his former lover's hired thugs.

The events that take up Doyle's THE DYING DETECTIVE occupy some ten minutes or so at the end of the televised version: Holmes is discovered, seriously ill and delirious, in his rooms; he enjoins Watson to fetch an expert on tropical diseases, Culverton Smith. Hidden, according to Holmes' instructions, behind the detective's sickbed, Watson is party to Culverton Smith's examination of Holmes and subsequent confession that he himself has infected the detective with the disease in reprisal for Holmes' accusing him of murdering his own nephew, young Victor Savage.

According to adapter T R Bowen, however, it is Savage's wife who goes to Holmes and Watson, worried that Savage is being led astray by his cousin, Culverton Smith, who has introduced her husband to the opium dens of the Limehouse district. (Holmes is discomfited by all the talk of addiction, as well he might be.) Holmes and Watson are invited to dinner *chez* Savage, but during the meal Savage falls fatally ill; under the terms of a complicated will, everything is left to Culverton Smith. Holmes accuses Smith of infecting Savage, and then Holmes himself is taken ill... The rest of the story is as Doyle wrote it.

Apart from Mrs Savage and a clutch of friends – introduced, presumably, as potential suspects – the major addition is John Gedgrave, a procurer and arranger who, under Culverton Smith's instructions, takes Savage around Limehouse. The part is ripe, and comedian Roy Hudd does it justice. Bowen also throws in an appearance by the 'Baker Street Irregulars' – the gang of ragamuffins that serves as Holmes' intelligence-gathering arm.

The Granada version of THE GOLDEN PINCE-NEZ (a title referring to a clue discovered in a dead man's hand – one that leads precisely nowhere) sticks more-or-less faithfully to Doyle's plot, bar flashbacks set in Russia, a subplot involving a suspicious suffragette and the inclusion of Mycroft Holmes – played, as in Granada's versions of THE GREEK INTERPRETER and THE BRUCE-PARTINGTON PLANS, by Charles Gray. Here, Mycroft replaces Watson – Edward Hardwicke having had a prior commitment to appear in the C S Lewis biopic *Shadowlands* – but, alas, he acts merely as a foil to Holmes, displaying little of the fruity character we have come to expect. He also shares a handful of appalling scenes in which the Holmes brothers display an unedifyingly juvenile sibling rivalry.

Like THE GOLDEN PINCE-NEZ, THE RED CIRCLE is one of several stories in which international intrigues reach a dramatic conclusion in Doyle's somewhat prosaic, fog-bound London. Unusually for this season of the Granada adventures, the adaptation takes few liberties with the text, the plot plainly considered dramatic enough to sustain 50 minutes' television without being bulked up by extraneous material. The same cannot be said of *The Mazarin Stone*, arguably the oddest of all the Jeremy Brett episodes. Never before have we seen two Doyle stories collide and Holmes disappear, bar a few seconds at the beginning and the end.

The episode incorporates elements from the eponymous tale, and also from THE THREE GARRIDEBS. In the former (adapted into a short story by Doyle himself from his own stage play *The Crown Diamond*), Holmes lures the man he suspects of stealing the famous Mazarin Stone – Count Negretto Sylvius – to Baker Street, along with a confederate. Holmes threatens them, then leaves them to talk while he apparently plays the violin next door; in fact, the violin is a recording and he is actually in the room with them, listening to them reveal the location of the diamond. THE

THREE GARRIDEBS, by contrast, is a much more solid adventure in which Holmes is approached by a man named Nathan Garrideb who, along with an American named John Garrideb, is searching for a third man with the same surname in a bid to fulfil the provisions of a rather odd will. Holmes realises instantly that the American is lying about almost everything, and suspects that his aim is to lure the reclusive Nathan away from his home. Holmes and Watson lie in wait when Nathan leaves in search of a bogus Birmingham Garrideb, and surprise 'John Garrideb' – actually one 'Killer' Evans – when he breaks into the supposedly deserted house. The house had previously been occupied by a particularly brilliant forger, he admits, and the cellar still contains a printing press and tools.

It's difficult to know which direction to approach the television version from, the changes are so wide-ranging. Perhaps the most obvious is the total removal of Holmes himself. Jeremy Brett being too ill to work at the time, his place is taken by Charles Gray's Mycroft. Signs of rapid rewriting are everywhere, unfortunately, with Mycroft rushing hither and thither in blithe contradiction of his previously established character, displaying powers of disguise which are usually the province of his brother and openly chatting in the supposedly silent precincts of the Diogenes Club. By the end of the episode, Mycroft has mutated into a supernatural presence, dodging bullets and appearing from clouds of fog like some Asian demon.

The plot begins with THE MAZARIN STONE, diverts into THE THREE GARRIDEBS and ends in previously uncharted territory. The Mazarin Stone has been stolen, and Mycroft suspects Count Sylvius – but his pursuit of the scoundrel is diverted when two sisters named Garrideb consult him regarding a strange American who has entered their lives... From here events proceed pretty much as per the story, with Mycroft and Watson staking out the house and catching the American as he breaks in. The cellar is not, however, a forger's paradise – it is a jewel thief's workshop, containing tools to break a large diamond into smaller pieces. Mycroft makes the connection, and forces the American to tell him where Count Sylvius will be taking the Mazarin Stone. A confrontation ensues, following which Sherlock appears through the mist to thank his brother for filling in for him. It's a bizarre, nightmarish confection – acceptable, perhaps, as the pilot for a new show starring Charles Gray as 'Mycroft Holmes, Master Detective', but almost laughable as a serious Sherlock Holmes drama.

Fortunately, *The Cardboard Box*, although hardly unadulterated (the scene in which Holmes and Watson make a rather embarrassed visit to the Metropolitan Police Christmas Party, not to mention Holmes' cry of 'Mrs Hudson, how dare you take my aspidistra!', are quite unlike anything Doyle ever wrote), at least concludes the series – *all* the series – in rather more fitting mode. Indeed, such is the quiet despair underlying Holmes' closing elegy about 'this circle of misery and violence and fear' – a downbeat alternative to 'There's an east wind coming' – that it now seems the only possible way for Brett to make his last bow. He was dead within 18 months, his heart having finally given out – a grim hangover from the drugs used to treat his depression.

In conversation with the prominent Sherlockian David Stuart Davies not long beforehand, when it was clear that he would never again play the role, Brett dismissed the idea that his was the definitive Holmes: 'I had a crack at him. I never actually saw him, you know – he was always a few steps ahead and I never actually caught up with him...' Brett's butterfly portrayal, flitting between brilliant understatement and painful histrionics, was never going to win the major awards his fans so wanted for him; at his best, he was touched by genius, at his worst, simply touched. Many of the later Granada productions are blighted, blunted by their sometimes-enforced reversal into the undramatic, un-Doylean devices which the earlier **Adventures** tried so hard to deny. But perhaps that's just as well. Perfection, after all, can be rather boring; and being boring is not what Jeremy Brett's Sherlock Holmes was all about. (AL)

Milliontestamentet

tr 'The million [kroner] testament'
at **Millionobligationen**
tr 'The million [kroner] legacy'
at **Den Stjålne Millionobligation**
tr 'The stolen million [kroner] legacy'
aka **The Stolen Legacy** [GB/US]
*Denmark 1910 pastiche Nordisk Films Kompagni
1017 feet bw silent*

Baker Street boy Billy (Anton Seitzberg) and his boss (Alwin Neuß) with bungling bobbies in **Milliontestamentet** *(1910)*

known cast Sherlock Holmes: **Alwin Neuß** Dr Mors: **Einar Zangenberg** the Countess: **Mrs Zangenberg** Billy: **Anton Seitzberg** a police constable: **Victor Fabian**

On his deathbed, a Count makes a will in favour of his wife; it is placed in a safe. However, the notorious criminal Dr Mors masquerades as a medical attendant, taking a wax impression of the safe's keyhole, making a key and giving it to his accomplice, a woman who is posing as the Count's nurse. When the Count dies, Mors gets his hands on the will. Sherlock Holmes is called in and after a number of adventures – in which Holmes is shadowed by Mors' associates and the Countess is kidnapped and delivered into the custody of a 'horrible little hunchback' who has instructions to kill her on the stroke of midnight – eventually retakes the will on the Countess' behalf.

The follow-up to **Den Sorte Haand**, this was the only Nordisk picture to feature Alwin Neuß (Carl Heinrich Neuß, Kondeutz, 1879) as Holmes. Neuß would later play the detective for Germany's Union-Vitascope in four of the semi-serialised **Der Hund von Baskerville** films (1914-20). The pepper-throwing, motor car-owning 'criminal king' Dr Mors – as played by the gangling Einar Zangenberg, Holmes in the earlier Nordisk entry, **Det Hemmelige Dokument**, and Holmes once again in the next of the company's detective films, **Hotelrotterne** – is almost certainly related to the legacy-stealing villain of German actor/impresario Ferdinand Bonn's play *Sherlock Holmes: Detektivkömedie in vier Aufzügen*, first staged in

Berlin in July 1906 (see also **Der Hund von Baskerville**, 1914-20).

Milliontestamentet was released in Denmark on 14 January 1911, and in Britain exactly one week later. The film's American issue didn't come until April/May of the same year, when *Moving Picture World* noted, albeit not exactly disapprovingly, that 'Some of the methods utilized by thieves like these in obtaining access to safes and the means they take to rid themselves of troublesome relatives are clearly shown'. The reference to 'troublesome relatives' is the only surviving hint as to Dr Mors' exact intention regarding the purloined will; he is, presumably, linked by blood to the deceased Count.

The Missing Rembrandt

GB 1932 adaptation [CHARLES AUGUSTUS MILVERTON] *Twickenham Film Studios Ltd 84m bw*
w **Cyril Twyford, H Fowler Mear** *p* **Julius Hagen**
d **Leslie Hiscott**
cast Sherlock Holmes: **Arthur Wontner** Dr Watson: **Ian Fleming** Baron von Guntermann: **Francis L Sullivan** Mrs Hudson: **Minnie Rayner** Claude Holford: **Miles Mander** Lady Violet Lumsden: **Jane Welsh** Carlo Ravelli: **Dino Galvani** Pinkerton man: **Ben Welden** Inspector Lestrade: **Philip Hewland** Marquess de Chaminade: **Antony Holles** Manning: **Herbert Lomas** Chang Wu: **Takase**

Arthur Wontner's first Holmes vehicle, **The Sleeping Cardinal**, had been a big hit in America as well as the UK. 'This one picture brought me offers from Hollywood,' Wontner explained in *Film Weekly* (19 December 1931), 'and two more adventures of Sherlock Holmes [are] to be made shortly in British studios. I start one at Twickenham almost immediately, and later will make *The Sign of Four*.'

The first of these, *The Missing Rembrandt*, was a pretty free adaptation of CHARLES AUGUSTUS MILVERTON and got underway shortly before Christmas. Wontner was fresh from a more offbeat Twickenham project, Walter Forde's *Condemned to Death*, which had reunited him with several collaborators from **The Sleeping Cardinal** – producer Julius Hagen, screenwriter H Fowler Mear, cinematographers Sidney Blythe and William Luff, art director James Carter, editor Jack Harris – on a quasi-horror subject based on the

play *Jack O'Lantern*. As a judge possessed by the spirit of a man he sent to the gallows, Wontner headed what *Picturegoer* called an 'exceedingly capable cast' in a film typical of Twickenham's penchant for (*Picturegoer* again) 'murder-mystery-horror-thrill specialities'.

The new Holmes subject, *The Missing Rembrandt*, was in similar bloodcurdling vein and by August 1932 was drawing high praise from *Picturegoer*'s Lionel Collier. 'The tracking down of a master criminal who hides his activities under the cloak of a respectable art dealer is intriguing,' he reported, 'and Holmes's deductions are well pointed. [Leslie] Hiscott has, perhaps, failed to get much movement into his story, but this deficiency is amply made up for by the excellent way in which he has directed Arthur Wontner, on whom the main interest is continually focused. The atmosphere of Baker Street and Limehouse are realistic, and all through respect has been paid to the tradition with which this famous character is inseparable.'

If even *Picturegoer* could draw attention to Hiscott's viscid approach to pace and staging, *The Missing Rembrandt* might seem a daunting prospect. It's hard to say, however, as the film, like the Rembrandt, appears to be missing – a 'lost' film. It's redeemed, apparently, by some nicely atmospheric glimpses of a Limehouse opium den, a couple of off-the-wall disguises adopted by Holmes (an old biddy and a meddling clergyman with a revolver handily concealed in his copy of *The Collected Sermons of the Rev Erasmus Peabody*), and a heavyweight master-criminal from the always watchable Francis L [Loftus] Sullivan (1903-1956). Best known for playing Jaggers in two versions of *Great Expectations* (1934 and 1946), the massive Sullivan brought reptilian style to films as diverse as the Conrad Veidt vehicle *The Wandering Jew* (1933) and the Edgar Wallace thriller *The Four Just Men* (1939).

The Missing Rembrandt was Sullivan's second film appearance, playing an American Milverton clone called Baron von Guntermann. Holmes discovers that the Baron has cajoled a doped-up painter, Claude Holford (Miles Mander, a weasel-faced actor-manager later to resurface in Universal's Basil Rathbone sequence), into springing a Rembrandt from the Louvre and a series of embarrassing love letters from Lady Violet Lumsden. (Jane Welsh, retained from

Showing off his Paget profile, Arthur Wontner's Holmes returns some embarrassing correspondence to Lady Violet Lumsden (Jane Welsh) in **The Missing Rembrandt** *(1932)*

Wontner's previous adventure, **The Sleeping Cardinal**, had also featured in *Condemned to Death*.) The blackmail plot is administered, not by the snivelling Holford, but by the Baron's Latin lover-type secretary, Carlo Ravelli (Dino Galvani).

The highlight of the picture reportedly takes the form of a tense stand-off between Guntermann and the disguised Holmes. The Baron isn't fooled by the detective's clerical get-up and corners him in a subterranean vault; this is where Holmes' hidden pistol comes in handy. Holmes and Watson subsequently attempt to retrieve Lady Violet's compromising correspondence by breaking into the Baron's Hampstead home. A Pinkerton agent on Guntermann's trail is murdered by him, however – Holmes himself is nearly collared for the crime – and the miserable Holford later succumbs to a Guntermann-induced overdose. Holmes finally

Cane scrutiny: Arthur Wontner as Holmes in **The Missing Rembrandt** *(1932)*

reveals, with a theatrical flourish of turpentine, that Holford's latest watercolour is in fact the errant Rembrandt, whereupon the odious Baron has to face the vengeance of Lady Violet herself.

Wontner's impact as Holmes was great enough by this stage for Associated Radio Pictures to lure him into making a rival Holmes picture, **The Sign of Four: Sherlock Holmes' Greatest Case**, which Graham Cutts loaded with the kind of narrative zip Leslie Hiscott habitually passed over in favour of stately atmospherics. Wontner's impact also emboldened Leslie Collier, in his *Picturegoer* assessment of *The Missing Rembrandt*, to come right out with it and state that 'Arthur Wontner *is* Sherlock Holmes, and in this picture he is excellent, giving a characterization which makes Conan Doyle's famous detective 'live' on the screen.' (JR)

Murder By Decree

GB/Canada 1978 pastiche Saucy Jack Inc 112m
Panavision colour
w **John Hopkins** *source* **The Ripper File** [book by **Elwyn**

Jones and **John Lloyd**] *p* **Rene Dupont** and **Bob Clark**
d **Bob Clark**
cast Sherlock Holmes: **Christopher Plummer** Dr Watson:
James Mason Inspector Foxborough: **David Hemmings**
Mary Kelly: **Susan Clark** Sir Charles Warren: **Anthony
Quayle** the Prime Minister: **John Gielgud** Inspector
Lestrade: **Frank Finlay** Robert Lees: **Donald Sutherland**
Annie Crook: **Genevieve Bujold** Dr Hardy: **Chris Wiggins**
Mrs Lees: **Teddi Moore** William Slade: **Peter Jonfield**
Sir Thomas Spivey: **Roy Lansford** Carrie: **Catherine Kessler**
Makins: **Ron Pember** Annie Chapman: **June Brown**
dock guard: **Ken Jones** Danny: **Terry Duggan** Catherine
Eddowes: **Hilary Sesta** Lanier: **Anthony May** Mrs Hudson:
Betty Woolfe Elizabeth Stride: **Iris Fry** Home Secretary:
Geoffrey Russell Lees' housekeeper: **PeggyAnn Clifford**
Jane: **Ann Mitchell** Molly: **Katherine Stark** Ellen: **Elaine
Ives Cameron** Betty: **Stella Courtney** Emily: **Judy Wilson**
Carroll: **Roy Pattison** Prince of Wales: **Victor Langley**
Princess Alexandra: **Pamela Abbott** Duke of Clarence
'Eddy': **Robin Marshall** doctor: **Richard Pescuid**
nurse: **Pat Brackenbury** Constable Long: **Dan Long**
Constable Watkins: **Michael Cashman**

THE MYSTERY

London, 1888: at the opera, Sherlock Holmes and Dr Watson see the Prince of Wales heckled for arriving late. Meanwhile, in seedy Whitechapel, Elizabeth Stride becomes the third prostitute to fall victim to the so-called 'Jack the Ripper', a vicious murderer who travels the East End's back streets in a well-appointed coach. That night, a 'Citizens' Committee' – in fact, concerned Whitechapel shopkeepers – sends a delegation to 221B Baker Street to ask for Holmes' assistance in apprehending the killer. Holmes appears disinterested, but soon after receives an anonymous tip-off that a fourth whore has been slain...

THE INVESTIGATION

Holmes meets police inspectors Foxborough and Lestrade at the crime scene, where he discovers the stem from a bunch of grapes near the mutilated body of Catherine Eddowes – but his investigation is forcibly curtailed by the intervention of Sir Charles Warren, Commissioner of the Metropolitan Police. As Holmes leaves, he catches sight of a 'strangely haunting' woman bystander. A message reading 'The Juwes are not the men that will be blamed for nothing' is found freshly chalked to a nearby wall; claiming to fear a race riot, Warren orders the lettering erased. Holmes' secret informant asks to meet him at the Elizabeth Wharf, where he is told to seek out a medium called Robert Lees; as Holmes and Watson depart the dock, the informant – Makins, ostensible head of the Citizens' Committee – is slain by the Ripper.

Later, Holmes and Watson uncover the erased writing. Makins' body is found, and Sir Charles attempts to have Holmes arrested for the murder – but a witness at the docks is able to give Holmes an alibi. Holmes exposes Sir Charles as a Freemason, suggesting that 'Juwes' is a reference to three figures in a Masonic ritual that refers to bodily evisceration. Disguising himself as a chimney sweep, Holmes visits Robert Lees, whose house is under police guard; having revealed that he had seen the killer in a vision, Lees had been instructed to follow the killer's trail... and led the police to Sir Charles' house. Meanwhile, Watson has discovered that the dead women were all friends of one Mary Kelly, the woman whom Holmes had noticed at the scene of Eddowes' murder. Holmes pursues Mary from Eddowes' funeral, but a coach appears and runs them down. Mary flees, but not before revealing the involvement of one Annie Crook, a woman who not long before was committed to an asylum near Reading by Sir Thomas Spivey, physician to the court of none other than Queen Victoria herself, and a man fond of a particularly expensive variety of grape – the type found near Eddowes' corpse.

Holmes speaks with the disturbed Annie, driven insane only since her incarceration commenced. It seems that soon after giving birth to the child of her secret husband, 'Eddy' (a man from the highest echelons of society), associates of Eddy had tried to track her down, locking her up when she refused to reveal where the child was hidden. Mary Kelly alone knows where the child is; the Ripper has been working his bloody way through Mary's associates in his search for the child – and Holmes must find Mary before he does...

THE SOLUTION
Foxborough, who has been Holmes' secret informant all along, distracts Holmes and Watson from their search of Whitechapel; the Inspector heads a cell of radicals (which included the dead Makins) who are sworn to overthrow the Establishment. Too late, Holmes and Watson find

Mary gutted by *two* Rippers, one of whom is the deranged Spivey. The other, the coachman – one William Slade – thrusts a red-hot iron into Watson's shoulder and slays Foxborough in his flight; Holmes pursues Slade to the docks, where the killer becomes ensnared in netting and strangles himself. Recovered, Holmes meets the Prime Minister, the Home Secretary and Sir Charles at a palatial Masonic temple, where he reveals that Spivey and Slade had believed themselves to be acting in the Establishment's interests by tracking down the secretly born, Catholic child of 'Eddy' – actually the Duke of Clarence, son of the Prince of Wales. Learning of Annie's suicide, an outraged Holmes denounces the great and the good for their complicity in the Ripper killings. Unknowingly third in line to England's throne, Annie's daughter remains in the care of nuns.

✦ ✦ ✦

Conspiracy theories come and go, but one of the most enduring is the idea that the Royal House of Saxe-Coburg was intimately connected to the 'Jack the Ripper' murders of autumn 1888. The first Sherlock Holmes-versus-the-Ripper movie, 1965's **A Study in Terror**, had been content to flirt with the notion of an aristocratic link to the murders, co-producer Herman Cohen claiming to have heard tell of documentary evidence implicating Queen Victoria herself. Thirteen years later, the producers of the second Sherlock/Jack team-up, *Murder By Decree*, would have a small library's worth of 'real-life' investigative efforts to draw on –

Whitechapel, 1888: on the trail of Jack the Ripper, Dr Watson (James Mason) meets a prostitute and falls victim to a 'clipping' scam in **Murder By Decree** *(1978)*

Watson (James Mason) and Holmes (Christopher Plummer) en route to an asylum near Reading, there to meet the pitiful Annie Crook, in **Murder By Decree** *(1978)*

and would be able to stir police corruption, radical *agents provocateur* and Freemasonry into an already heady brew.

The 'Prince Eddy' theory propounded in *Murder By Decree* – which describes itself by means of an on-screen caption as 'a fictional dramatisation based on recent theories concerning the infamous crimes committed by the alleged "Jack the Ripper"' – was first popularised in the BBC television serial *Jack the Ripper*, a spin-off from the police series *Barlow and Softly, Softly: Task Force* (sequels to/spin-offs from the long-running police series *Barlow at Large* and *Softly, Softly*, themselves sequels to/spin-offs from the even longer-running police series *Z Cars*). Over six consecutive Friday nights in July and August 1973, fictional present-day Detective Chief Superintendents Charlie Barlow and John Watt (Stratford Johns and Frank Windsor) reopened the case of the Whitechapel Murders in a bizarre hybrid of drama and documentary scripted by Elwyn Jones and John Lloyd from notes supplied by researchers Wendy Sturgess, Ian Sharp and Karen de Groot. (Jones was a former BBC drama head involved in the set-up of the Corporation's 1965 Douglas Wilmer series: see **Detective: The Speckled Band**.) In the final instalment, *The Highest in the Land?*,

Joseph Sickert put forward his explanation for the whole bloody business.

The gist of Sickert's story, which would be developed over several years, goes as follows: Joseph alleged that his father, the noted artist Walter Sickert, had been a close friend of 'Prince Eddy', the Duke of Clarence – Queen Victoria's grandson. 'Eddy', he claimed, had secretly sired a daughter, Alice, with a Catholic commoner named Annie Elizabeth Crook. On discovering this, a furious Queen Victoria instructed the Prime Minister, Lord Salisbury, to deal with the matter. Crook was sent to an asylum and effectively lobotomised by Sir William Gull, the Queen's personal physician. However, Alice had been hidden by her nanny, Mary Kelly, who later fell into prostitution. A number of Mary's streetwalking associates attempted to persuade her to blackmail both the government and the Crown with her knowledge of the affair between Annie and the Duke – and so Gull, together with a coachman called John Netley, sought out the girls and murdered them one by one in a manner drawn from Masonic lore. Joseph Sickert would also claim that Walter had later married Alice – making Joseph himself, one supposes, a distant heir to the throne.

In fact, 'Prince Eddy' had himself been nominated as the killer in an article by a Dr Thomas Stowell published in an issue of the *Criminologist* five years previously. Stowell's theory also has Gull intimately involved with the business, and draws attention to a psychic named R J Lees, who supposedly suffered visions of the Ripper. Lees would be given a whole subplot to himself in *Murder By Decree*, albeit with much of his supposed story amended. Director and co-producer Bob Clark later confirmed that the Stowell hypothesis was what first attracted him to the subject: 'I first came up with the idea of the film when I heard about that very first theory printed by a British journalist saying the Duke of Clarence was the killer. I thought, "What an incredible notion for a movie." That theory was soon discredited and the theories that we're following are much later ones ...'

Jones and Lloyd novelised their six 50-minute teleplays as *The Ripper File*, first published by Arthur Barker Ltd in 1975 – and it is this that became the basis for *Murder by Decree*, which was written by *Z Cars*' first script editor John Hopkins (1931-98) from a story by Clark. Hopkins' cinema credits included co-authoring the fourth James Bond picture, *Thunderball* (1966), and adapting his own play *This Story of Yours* for director Sidney Lumet under the title *The Offence* (1972).Meanwhile, Stephen Knight, a journalist who had interviewed Sickert for the *East London Advertiser*, elaborated upon the 'Prince Eddy' saga in his bestselling *Jack the Ripper: The Final Solution*, first published by George G Harrap & Co in 1976. Knight's book remains in print 25 years on, its appeal undiminished despite its central thesis having been thoroughly disembowelled by a great many so-called 'Ripperologists' since. Further discussion of this fascinating subject is way beyond the scope of this book – but, for the record, the author is utterly unconvinced by the Sickert story, finding Stewart Evans and Paul Gainey's 1995 nomination of one Francis Tumblety, the only police suspect, as the Ripper, far more persuasive: see their *The Lodger: The Arrest and Escape of Jack the Ripper*.

Hopkins' ambitious screenplay plunges Holmes into a world where the Metropolitan Police are not so much bungling as institutionally corrupt, where no-one's motives can be trusted and where even the State itself is threatened by tensions from both within and without. Oddly, a number of 'real-life' names are altered, but Hopkins' renaming of Gull and Netley as Spivey and Slade seems strangely coy; those whom the producers earnestly believe to have been the Ripper are given the cover of pseudonyms, but no such sympathy is shown, for example, to the hapless Annie Crook – who, if innocent of any connection to the murders, is cruelly libelled throughout. It's equally inconsistent to mercilessly castigate police chief Sir Charles Warren, but refuse to identify the person whom anarchist infiltrator Foxborough is based on. The best guess is that the part played by otherwise absent CID Inspector Abberline is split between the fictional characters of Foxborough and Lestrade. Again, are we to assume that Abberline was actually some kind of covert anti-Establishment activist?

To be fair, Clark would deny that *Murder By Decree* was intended to be taken as any kind of semi-documentary piece: 'I really didn't want to make a film to prove any history ... I'm not trying to prove anything. I'm just doing a "what if" history. That's why I brought Sherlock Holmes into it, who is a semi-fictional character. He's not real, but so many think he is. By bringing him into the story, we're saying in effect that we're not claiming this is fact.' Nonetheless, it's impossible to deny that *Murder By Decree* has played a reasonably substantial part in perpetuating a long-since-discredited series of suppositions. In later years, products such as 1988's 'centenary celebration' TV mini-series *Jack the Ripper*, starring Michael Caine, would continue, unreasoningly, to implicate the hapless Gull.

Like 1977's **Classics Dark and Dangerous: Silver Blaze**, the first piece of Holmesiana to feature actor Christopher Plummer as Sherlock, *Murder By Decree* was an Anglo-Canadian production (part-financed, in fact, by the Canadian Film Development Corporation). Bob Clark's pedigree included horror movies *Children Shouldn't Play with Dead Things* (1972) and *Black Christmas* (1974), plus Mafia thriller *Breaking Point* (1976). In addition to Canadian resident Clark and the Toronto-born Plummer, other Canadian talents involved in *Murder By Decree* included the barely-known-in-the-UK Susan Clark (also 'Madge Larrabee' in 1981's televised revival of the William Gillette play *Sherlock Holmes*, starring Frank

Christopher Plummer as an impassioned, socially conscious Holmes in **Murder By Decree** (1978)

area; and in Barton Street, Westminster, where an exterior fitting 221B Baker Street was found. The most part, however, was filmed at Shepperton Studios, Middlesex, where the Docklands wharf set was constructed, and at EMI Elstree Studios, Borehamwood, where release hyperbole would have it that production designer Harry Pottle's network of fog-shrouded Whitechapel alleyways – an effort to conjure up the London of the 19th century French artist Gustave Doré – represented the largest set built in a British film studio up to that point.

Clark, Hopkins, Plummer and Mason shared a desire to present Holmes and Watson in a new, 'humanised' light – a less aloof, more emotionally engaged Holmes paired with a less crusty, more intellectually involved Watson. 'The relationship between the two men appealed to me deeply,' confirmed Hopkins. 'This is a passionate and caring Holmes; I wanted to get through his traditional reserve.' 'It's easy to play [Holmes] as supercilious, rather snobbish,' reckoned Plummer, 'but that's not what I intended to do...'

This new, impassioned approach to Sherlock finds its ultimate expression in the scene where the detective finally unearths the unfortunate Annie Crook in a lunatic asylum: appalled by her cruel treatment, Holmes lashes out at a warder and is restrained; as he gazes back at the wretched girl, there is a tear in his eye. There is no inner darkness in the Plummer model: early on, he uses one of Watson's needles to clean his pipe, pointedly not putting it to any more dubious application. Like John Neville's version in *A Study in Terror*, this is a gung-ho Holmes, carrying a weighted Thuggee scarf with which to disarm assailants. Not that this style of presentation is entirely without problems: the testimony of the spiritualist Robert Lees is accepted uncritically by this non-sceptic Holmes – and, unsurprisingly, this subplot quite fails to convince as a result.

Mason's Watson plays against type, too: watching Holmes examine the mutilated body of Annie Chapman, he cries out, 'For God's sake, Holmes – must you dwell on the beastly matter?' He's also a game sort: following a very funny scene in which the eternally stiff doctor falls foul of a 'clipping' scam while attempting to procure information from a tart, he wrestles an assailant to the ground. It's immensely pleasing that *Murder*

Langella), here credited fourth for her relatively brief appearance as Mary Kelly; Chris Wiggins as Dr Hardy; Donald Sutherland in a 'special guest' turn as psychic Robert Lees; and, most notably, Genevieve Bujold as the pathetic, near-incoherent Annie Crook, whose single asylum-set scene is powerful enough to overshadow the remainder of the film.

Two *A Study in Terror* alumni took major roles: Frank Finlay reprised his Inspector Lestrade, and Anthony Quayle played the corrupt Warren. Given actors of this calibre, plus David Hemmings (wasted in the underwritten role of Foxborough), John Gielgud (in another single-scene turn, Gielgud plays the Prime Minister, by implication Lord Salisbury, whom Holmes confronts in the finale) and James Mason (1909-84) as a humane and clever Watson, *Murder By Decree* distinguishes itself as having surely the single most impressive cast list of any Holmes picture before or since.

Budgeted at $5 million Canadian, *Murder By Decree* was shot entirely in the UK over 12 weeks, beginning on 24 June 1978. Location work took place at the Royal Academy and at Wyndham's Theatre (where exteriors and interiors respectively for the opera house seen early in the film were shot); at the Royal Naval College, Greenwich; around Clink Street, in Southwark's Bankside

By Decree makes room to suggest some real warmth between the two, most obviously where Holmes amuses himself by thwarting Watson's efforts to fork the last pea on his plate.

Having discovered his own intellect to have been used as a tool of darker agencies ('We've unmasked madmen, Watson, wielding sceptres. Reason run riot. Justice howling at the moon,' as the script, rather beautifully, puts it), Holmes denounces Warren, the Home Secretary and the Prime Minister at a grand Masonic lodge in a fascinating 13-minute coda. Whereas Foxborough and his anarchists could 'expect no mercy', here Holmes lets the government stand so long as Annie Crook's child remains safe. 'You know what you risk, Mr Holmes,' intones Gielgud's bushy-faced Prime Minister. 'The ruin of your own society, and the substitution of a radical Anarchist ideology.' 'I care nothing about that,' returns Holmes. 'You're all the same to me. You, Prime Minister, Foxborough and the radicals – all of you equally to blame. God knows if I could prove your complicity I would not hesitate – but I was not a party to your secret councils. Only you know to what extent you are responsible.' A Holmes who barters his silence for the safety of a child is a novelty indeed.

Murder By Decree was released in February 1979 in both Canada and the USA, with British exhibition not following until March 1980. It was received more-or-less ecstatically in Canada, where it garnered five 'Genie' awards – for direction, editing, music, plus acting gongs for Plummer and Bujold – as granted by the Academy of Canadian Cinema. One dissenting view was expressed by *Cinema Canada* critic John Hofsess, who described *Murder By Decree* as 'a bad movie that is currently making a lot of money and has drawn favourable reviews based on mental laxity'. Some British critics were also unimpressed: in *Films and Filming*, Julian Fox described the film as 'overblown and weighted down with guest stars to the exclusion of the kind of wit and tension one used to find in the low-budgeted, admittedly anachronistic Universal series of the forties ... Here, Holmes is played by the physically right but temperamentally wrong Christopher Plummer ... [who] reduces the clear-cut, highly observant Holmes of tradition to something very nearly akin to a bumbling ass.'

It seems odd to note that Bob Clark's next film was the infantile frathouse sex comedy *Porky's*

(1981), about as great a departure from the brooding and (literally) dreadful atmosphere of *Murder By Decree* as it's possible to imagine. Unlike *A Study in Terror*, *Murder By Decree* is not romanticised in any way, or made 'safe'; its desperate whores are properly raddled, and its 'true' villains are not allowed the get-out of being simply mad. No-one wins. A repeated motif has movement and sound slurring to a crawl as the black coach of Spivey and Slade clatters through Whitechapel; the killings are horrible, squalid rituals, filmed in such a way as to convey the utmost repulsion with the minimum of exploitation. So if this is a far-from-conventional Holmes and Watson, so be it; few could remain unaffected and unchanged by the events that have their grim unfolding here. *Murder By Decree* is a film that dares to care deeply about its characters, about the terrible forces that shape the world of its fiction. No, it's not the perfect Holmes picture, nor is it the consummate Ripper flick; it's a thriller with a conscience, and that makes it more rare and more necessary than either of these.

Murder Rooms: The Dark Beginnings of Sherlock Holmes

GB/US 2000-1 2 x 60m/4 x 90m TV series pastiches
BBC Films/WGBH Boston
assoc p/series created by **David Pirie**
regular cast Dr Joseph Bell **Ian Richardson**

MURDER ROOMS: THE DARK BEGINNINGS OF SHERLOCK HOLMES
tx 4-5 January 2000 BBC2
w **David Pirie** *p* **Ian Madden** *d* **Paul Seed**
regular cast, plus Arthur Conan Doyle: **Robin Laing**
Sir Henry Carlyle: **Charles Dance** Elspeth: **Dolly Wells**
Lady Sarah Carlyle: **Ruth Platt** Inspector Beecher: **Sean McGinley** Summers: **Laurie Ventry** Crawford: **Joel Strachan**
Neill: **Alec Newman** Stark: **Andrew John Tait** Sophia: **Tamsin Pike** Mary Doyle: **Sarah Collier** Charles Doyle: **John Bett** Waller: **Matthew Macfayden** Dr Gillespie: **Stephen MacDonald** Canning: **Ewan Stewart** Canning's maid: **Julie Wilson Nimmo** Strand editor: **Ralph Riach** fiddler: **Aly Bain** medical lecturer: **Alan Sinclair** Baxter: **David MacDowell** Madame Rose: **Linda Duncan McLaughlin**

Hazel: **Anne Marie Kennedy** sobbing woman:
Mary Goonan PC Murdoch: **Eric Barlow** Dr Latimer:
Patrick Hannaway Crawford senior: **Bernard Horsfall**
Kate: **Jenny Foulds** Marie: **Coral Preston**

THE PATIENT'S EYES

tx 4 September 2001 BBC1
w **David Pirie** *p* **Alison Jackson** *d* **Tim Fywell**
regular cast, plus Heather: **Katie Blake** Conan Doyle:
Charles Edwards Turnavine: **Alexander Armstrong** Baynes:
Simon Quarterman Hettie: **Gem Durham** fainting man:
Paul Butterworth nearby man: **Michael Webber**
Blythe: **Malcolm Sinclair** Greenwell: **Andrew Woodall**
Coatley: **Dragan Micanovic** Inspector Warner: **Simon
Chandler** Agnes: **Sarah Peirse** Horler: **David Maybrick**

THE PHOTOGRAPHER'S CHAIR

*tx 18 September 2001 BBC1 [postponed from
11 September]*
w **Paul Billing** *p* **Alison Jackson** *d* **Paul Marcus**
regular cast, plus Conan Doyle: **Charles Edwards**
Elspeth/Helena Petchey: **Claire Harman** De Meyer: **Henry
Goodman** sailor: **Paul McNeilly** Polly: **Amber Noble**
Inspector Warner: **Simon Chandler** Sgt Richards: **Morgan
Jones** Mrs Williams: **Mossie Smith** Dr Ibbotson: **Roger
Lloyd Pack** Elkins: **Dermot Crowley** Rhodes: **Tim
Woodward** distressed woman: **Karen Meagher** Mrs Casey:
Caroline Pegg young girl: **Cassandra Compton** Mrs
Berkley: **Sarah Badel** Bolton: **Tim Potter** Judd: **Jake Wood**
Mitchell: **David Hayman** respectable gent: **Stuart Richman**

THE KINGDOM OF BONES

*tx 25 September 2001 BBC1 [postponed from
18 September]*
w **Stephen Gallagher** *p* **Alison Jackson** *d* **Simon Langton**
regular cast, plus Everard IM Thurn: **Miles Richardson**
Arthur Conan Doyle: **Charles Edwards** Reuben Proctor:
Crispin Bonham-Carter Innes Doyle: **Ben MacLeod**
Mrs Williams: **Mossie Smith** senior mover's man:
Robert Ashe Professor Rutherford: **John Sessions**
local newspaperman: **Nick Haverson** Inspector Warner:
Simon Chandler Heywood Donovan: **Ian McNeice**
Gladys Donovan: **Caroline Carver** Randolph Walker:
Warwick Davis pitchwoman: **Sonia Ferrugia** Walter Ward:
Randal Herley Jasper the boxer: **Charles Cork** dowager:
Daphne Oxenford Reverend Smoot: **Cyril Shaps**
tattooed man: **John Paul Connolly** mortuary desk clerk:
Sean Wightman Superintendent Mulford: **John Stahl**
verger: **Hugh Dickson** Mrs Proctor: **Belinda Carroll**
Elizabeth Proctor: **Jessica Brooks**

THE WHITE KNIGHT STRATAGEM

tx 2 October 2001 BBC1
w **Daniel Boyle** *p* **Alison Jackson** *d* **Paul Marcus**
regular cast, plus Alicia Craine: **Lucy Allen** Arthur Conan
Doyle: **Charles Edwards** Innes Doyle: **Ben MacLeod**
Doyle senior: **Hugh Ross** asylum doctor: **Gregory Fox-
Murphy** Blaney: **Rik Mayall** Sgt Clark: **Henry Ian Cusick**
Fergusson: **Ron Donachie** Sir John Starr: **Ronald Pickup**
Orde: **Michael J Jackson** Mrs Troy: **Margo Gunn**
Margaret Booth: **Annette Crosbie** Lyla Milburn: **Beatie
Edney** Milburn: **Anton Lesser** Alexander Cameron: **David
Gant** Cross Bros assistant: **William Petrie** Mrs Kitson:
Barbara Rafferty Frank D'Arcy: **Gregor Truter** cricket boy:
Thomas Edward Wansey Ned Ball: **Paul Malcolm**

'This edgy Victorian thriller,' explained the first
Radio Times of the 21st century, 'is based on
the true story of forensic pathologist Dr Joseph
Bell, who taught Arthur Conan Doyle at
Edinburgh medical school and was actually the
model for Sherlock Holmes ... There were no
complete preview tapes available, but the snippets
we have seen look excellent (if occasionally gory).
The programme's pedigree is such that it should
be top-quality. Written by David Pirie (who
specialises in these dark, Gothic thrillers) and
directed by Paul Seed (*A Rather English Marriage*
and *House of Cards*), it stars the always watchable
Ian Richardson as Bell, Robin Laing (*The Lakes*) as
Conan Doyle and Charles Dance as Sir Henry
Carlyle.'

That David Pirie should specialise in 'dark
Gothic thrillers' is hardly surprising, given his
authorship of the books *A Heritage of Horror* (1973)
and *The Vampire Cinema* (1977). His cerebral BBC
frighteners include *Rainy Day Women* (1984), a
controversial adaptation of *The Woman in White*
(1997; controversial because radically altered from
the Wilkie Collins original) and the J S Le Fanu
adaptation, *The Wyvern Mystery* (2000). The latter
followed hot on the heels of *Murder Rooms: The
Dark Beginnings of Sherlock Holmes*, a two-part Pirie
speculation which caused some discomfort in the
quality press about the dangers of so-called 'faction'.

'It's a producer's dream,' wrote Maxton Walker
in the *Guardian* of 4 January 2000, 'a Sherlock
Holmes mystery and high-class costume drama
rolled into one, without the need to go through the
palaver of reinventing the detective for the small
screen. But there's one problem: *Murder Rooms* is

Medical student Arthur Conan Doyle (Robin Laing) assists his tutor Joseph Bell (Ian Richardson) in **Murder Rooms: The Dark Beginnings of Sherlock Holmes** *(2000)*

[a] mixture of fiction and supposition ... Many viewers will believe it's an accurate depiction of Conan Doyle's early years. But Sherlock Holmes was a fictional creation, undoubtedly influenced by Bell, but still a character that owed everything to Conan Doyle's imagination. *Murder Rooms* implies that Holmes was a virtual clone of Bell ... [which] only reinforces the misconception that writers' ideas are always drawn directly from their own experiences (do people *really* believe writers are incapable of making things up?) ... In the end ... one doubts that the great Sherlock Holmes, a celebrated champion of truth, could possibly have approved of something that depends so heavily on deception.'

The vexed question of viewer gullibility aside, *Murder Rooms* bears all the classic hallmarks of the British shockers Pirie had celebrated in *A Heritage of Horror*: a venal aristocrat, a spunky heroine balanced by a wilting one (sisters on this occasion), a whorehouse with attendant fulsome prostitutes, a white-haired investigator, his wet-behind-the-ears sidekick, doltish coppers and an American villain who, in the old days, would have provided the film-makers with the perfect opportunity to cast a fading Hollywood star. Pirie even succeeds at the end in planting a very obvious invitation to expect a

sequel. Indeed, despite the production's striving for gritty realism – the wilting heroine, for example, is wilting from syphilis rather than the symbolic attentions of a vampire – the film which *Murder Rooms* recalls most strongly is *The Plague of the Zombies* (1965), itself a very Holmes-inflected Hammer horror. *Plague* has all the English Gothic standbys enumerated above (except the whorehouse and American villain) and a beautifully played quasi-Holmes in André Morell, previously a spot-on Watson in Hammer's **The Hound of the Baskervilles** (1959).

In Ian Richardson, Pirie was lucky to have a white-haired investigator of André Morell calibre. Despite the snowy Afro he's required to act under, Richardson's proto-Holmes is consistently exciting to watch; more so, even, than his bona fide Holmes in **Sir Arthur Conan Doyle's The Sign of Four** and **Sir Arthur Conan Doyle's The Hound of the Baskervilles** (both 1983). The scene in which he challenges Charles Dance's cold-eyed Sir Henry Carlyle to taste his own strychnine tablets is played in the grand manner and is genuinely electrifying. It leads directly, however, to the story's rather hasty and unsatisfying conclusion.

The plot revolves around a series of apparently motiveless poisonings, with cruel Sir Henry as the

Dr Joseph Bell (Ian Richardson), in **Murder Rooms: The Dark Beginnings of Sherlock Holmes** (2000)

and whose name is still attached to that of Jack the Ripper.

This final comment is not only palpably untrue – Cream was eliminated from the Ripper inquiry over a century ago – but it's also a slightly lame attempt to account for the vein of unintegrated Ripper-style imagery which runs through *Murder Rooms*. The blood-drenched bordello bedroom is an obvious nod to the horrific police photo of the Ripper's one-and-only indoor victim ('Contains strong images,' warned *Radio Times* solemnly), while the neat piles of coins found beside the victims is another Ripper gesture, reminding one of Stephen Knight's gripping (but since discredited) account of the murders, *Jack the Ripper: The Final Solution*. (See also the 1978 Holmes/Ripper film **Murder by Decree**.)

Knight's conviction, from various ritualistic signs and symbols at the crime scenes, that the Masons were behind the Ripper, and Pirie's suggestion in *Murder Rooms* that some arcane ritual is being played out by the killer, point very firmly towards Sir Henry as the culprit, and we're intrigued to know what his strange *modus operandi* might mean. But we never find out, because the killer turns out to be a motiveless nutter who was in reality a 'mere' poisoner, not a ripper. Pirie tries to get around this problem by having Cream snip the ears off one poisoned victim and send them through the post, an echo not only of Doyle's THE CARDBOARD BOX but also of one of the Ripper's more flamboyant gestures in 1888. But the hash of Gothic motifs with real-life facts never properly gels, and one is reminded of Pirie's own judgment on *Dracula Has Risen from the Grave* in *A Heritage of Horror*, where he drew attention to the film's 'inability to relate the poetry and atmosphere of vampirism to the rest of the plot' and to the fact that it is 'ultimately reduced to an inconsequential splurge of arbitrary ... motifs.'

Though it can't sustain the whole narrative, Pirie's characteristic exploration of the horrid truths underlying Gothic imagery is still fascinating stuff. The above-mentioned syphilitic heroine, for instance, points to the grim reality behind the Victorians' fondness for pallid damsels in distress. Pirie is also very good at weaving Holmes situations into the mix; Bell and Doyle's first investigation involves a lethal gas which functions very like the snake in THE SPECKLED BAND, while Bell's analysis

chief suspect, and as Bell's investigation finally seems to be getting into high gear halfway through Episode Two, the viewer could be forgiven for wondering how on earth Pirie is going to resolve the whole thing in 25 minutes flat. The truth is, he doesn't. One red herring – a gimlet-eyed misogynist student called Crawford – has just been eliminated (by hanging himself), when the horrible mutton-chopped aristo is also revealed as a red herring.

Now there's only about ten minutes left. Very hurriedly, the villain is revealed as Doyle's fellow student Neill, whom we vaguely remember for his theories about the 'imp of the perverse' (purloined, without acknowledgment, from Edgar Allan Poe) way back at the beginning of Episode One. He then gets away, Scot-free, and a concluding title informs us that he was the real-life serial killer Dr Thomas Neill Cream, who really *did* study medicine with Doyle, who was executed in 1892 of a fob-watch is lifted direct from the opening of THE SIGN OF THE FOUR. The latter scene was perhaps developed by Pirie from a hint in the most thorough Doyle biography, Owen Dudley Edwards' *The Quest for Sherlock Holmes*.

Murder Rooms also benefits greatly from its use of 1870s Edinburgh as a background. The stark contrast between its Old Town and New Town, very vividly present here, has been suggested by cultural historian Christopher Frayling as the inspiration for Stevenson's *Dr Jekyll and Mr Hyde* and also enlivens one of the best British horror films, a Burke and Hare shocker called *The Flesh and the Fiends* (1959). Stevenson himself, incidentally – in receipt of Doyle's first Holmes opus while domiciled in the South Seas – reportedly remarked, 'But surely this is my old friend Joe Bell...'

Despite an unconvincing resolution, the sequel hinted at in the closing moments of *Murder Rooms* remained a welcome prospect. It duly followed in the shape of four 90-minute films that went into production in November 2000, wrapping early in June the following year. The production base was Bray Studios, peculiarly apt given the facility's origin as the home of Hammer Films. '*Murder Rooms* took me completely by surprise when it came along the first time,' Ian Richardson claimed in *Sherlock Holmes The Detective Magazine*. 'And quite frankly I didn't think that much would come of it.'

He also suggested that further sequels might need to be produced sooner rather than later. 'Let me be perfectly honest with you. I am too old for the part. Bell was in his late forties, very early fifties at this period and I'm in my sixties. Nobody else ... [seems] to think that this is a problem. Perhaps it isn't, but it is constantly at the back of my mind. If there is another series, I shall be another year older at least. Having said that, I would enjoy going through another series provided they don't do that awful thing of 'doing it for less'. In other words, cut back on the budget and the length of time that they give ... If they start talking about it in those terms I shall just walk away.'

The four instalments of this new *Murder Rooms*, broadcast in September and October 2001, replaced Robin Laing's Doyle with the rather more rugged, but equally vulnerable, Charles Edwards. There had also, apparently, been some vacillation over the series title, though in the end the pilot

title was retained. *The Patient's Eyes* is an elaborate riff by Pirie on THE SOLITARY CYCLIST, with Doyle taking up his medical duties in Portsmouth and becoming involved with a local heiress who is harrowed at regular intervals by a shrouded figure on a bicycle. (Damp with autumn leaves, these scenes are agreeably spooky.) Soon Bell is involved, too – Richardson's fright-wig hair-piece from the original *Murder Rooms* has been judiciously exchanged here for a smoother model – and tells Doyle that it was the younger man's account of 'Miss Heather Grace and the solitary cyclist' that 'brought me south'.

Doyle becomes romantically involved with the winsome Heather, a young man is found buried upright in the forest with weighted feet, and Heather's ambiguous fiancé Greenwell is climactically murdered, in best *Cat and the Canary* tradition, moments before divulging crucial information. The killer is revealed as yet another Heather admirer, Horler, an ex-Captain of Marines posted overseas who 'became fanatically

Dr Joseph Bell (Ian Richardson), unwittingly on the trail of the man who will become Jack the Ripper, in **Murder Rooms: The Dark Beginnings of Sherlock Holmes** *(2000)*

jealous of the woman he left here.' In one of Pirie's niftier bits of dialogue, Bell explains grimly that, out in Natal, Horler 'lost half his face and most of his mind, it would seem.'

But the workings of Pirie's pastiche machinery begin to grind almost audibly in this instalment, with the Doyle/Heather romance proving particularly wet, its stick-figure protagonists engaging little audience sympathy. TV critic Nancy Banks-Smith was agreeably disposed towards the production, however. 'David Pirie has concocted a rich, possibly over rich, mix based on *The Solitary Cyclist*,' she wrote. 'A scorpion would take off its hat to the sting in the tail of this new version ... Posh production values have been poured over the film like warm brandy over plum pudding. The writing and acting are better than strictly necessary, the lighting is downright seductive and where did they find those charming bats. Someone has taken a lot of trouble.'

The remaining episodes were turned over to other writers: Paul Billing for *The Photographer's Chair*, horror novelist Stephen Gallagher for *The Kingdom of Bones* and Daniel Boyle for *The White Knight Stratagem*. The titular chair in the first of these, explained Gareth McLean in the *Guardian*, 'was being used by a crazy Masonic aristocrat to seat his victims while he mechanically garotted them and took photographs in an attempt to commit their departing soul to film ... What with the involvement of a foxy spiritualist, a syphilitic photographer, his feral sidekick, a brothel madam, her Barclay Horse (don't ask), a ghost called Elspeth, an alcoholic police surgeon who had accidentally sawed off his own fingers (along with the leg and testicles of a patient) and Elsie 'Meningitis' Casey, *The Photographer's Chair* met all the criteria to be judged as a Tricky One by Dr Bell and Arthur Conan. I half expected the Phantom Raspberry Blower of Old London Town to pitch up until it was made clear that *Murder Rooms* is set in Portsmouth.'

As McLean's litany indicates, *The Photographer's Chair* is somewhat over-egged, though its premise (lifted in part from a 1972 shocker called *The Asphyx*) furnishes a chilly basis for Doyle's latter-day interest in spiritualism, when Dolly, the Titian-haired love interest cruelly taken from him in the original *Murder Rooms*, puts in a posthumous appearance. More *The Ring of Thoth* than Sherlock Holmes, *The Kingdom of Bones* packs an agreeably old-fashioned wallop, with a suicidal museum curator, a kidnapped Egyptian mummy concealing a more recently deceased body, assorted Fenian outrages, even a surreal instance of 'exit pursued by an elephant'. And *The White Knight Stratagem* brought *Murder Rooms* full circle, returning Doyle and Bell to Edinburgh for a run-in with Bell's old antagonist Lieutenant Blaney, who manipulates people like pawns in an effort – unsuccessful, naturally – to discredit Bell.

By this stage the mechanical convolutions of the plots were exacerbated by a severe attack of over-familiar telly faces (Roger Lloyd Pack, John Sessions, Rik Mayall, Annette Crosbie etc), evincing a surprising lack of faith in the power of the basic format to keep the capricious TV viewer interested. Hard to credit when the central pillar of that format was the never-less-than-mesmerising Ian Richardson, his characterisation enriched by a crucial discovery he had made in the interim between the pilot and the subsequent series: Bell's son, Benjamin, had succumbed to the same disease, peritonitis, that had previously robbed Bell of his wife. And, as the original *Murder Rooms* made very clear, Doyle had effectively lost his father when he was forced to commit him to a mental home. 'This,' Richardson concluded in Holmesian mode, 'is the key. Here is a man who has lost his son and heir, and here is young Doyle, who has lost his father.' This 'key' ensures that the *Murder Rooms* saga has a piquancy at its heart that more than makes up for its imperfections. (JR)

1994 Baker Street: Sherlock Holmes Returns

at **Sherlock Holmes Returns**
aka **Sherlock Holmes: The Adventure of the Tiger Murders** *[GB video release]*
US 1993 TVM Paragon Entertainment Corp/Kenneth Johnson Productions Inc 97m colour
tx 12 September 1993 CBS
wpd **Kenneth Johnson**

cast Sherlock Holmes: **Anthony Higgins** Amy Wilmslow: **Debrah Farentino** Zapper: **Mark Adair Rios** Mrs Hudson: **Joy Coghill** Detective Griffin: **Julian Christopher** James Moriarty Booth: **Ken Pogue** Lt Ortega: **Eli Gabay** Lt Civita: **Jerry Wasserman** Mrs Ortega: **Kerry Sandomirsky** Pavon: **Fabricio Santin** Slick: **Jorge Vargas** Rancho: **Jason Diablo** Ronald Hunt: **Gerry Therrien** resuscitation nurse: **Catherine Lough** respiratory therapist: **Peter Kelamis** nurse #1: **Susan Lee Appling** old man Moriarty: **John Wardlow** Mr Hudson: **Daniel Chambers** young Mrs Hudson: **Tish Heaven** Lefty: **Tom Heaton** night watchman: **John Blackwell** Destry Max: **Philip Hayes** Father Moriarty: **Norman Armour** rookie cop: **Thomas Cavanagh** Sergeant: **Ken Camroux** cop #1: **Alvin Sanders** DA Weis: **Scott Nicholson** Curly: **Lee Sollenberg**

THE MYSTERY

San Francisco trauma unit doctor Amy Wilmslow drives to Marin County to visit Mrs Hudson, the widow of a former patient, at the estate her family has looked after for its original owner, an eccentric English émigré named 'Captain Basil', since 1899. Mrs Hudson has been forced to consider selling the estate, despite the fact that the Captain's main stipulation in leaving the house to the Hudsons – that its supply of electricity must be maintained, unbroken, until 1 January 2000 – remains in force. Mrs Hudson offers Amy the house at a knock-down price, but Amy cannot afford even that. Later, Amy enters the wine cellar – where she discovers a secret room containing a strange, coffin-shaped device. An electrical short-circuit sends Mrs Hudson into a panic ... and a bearded figure staggers out of the cellar's gloom, claiming to be none other than Sherlock Holmes.

THE INVESTIGATION

Recovering from a cardiac arrest, Holmes, for whom 'Captain Basil' was an alias, tells Amy he had placed himself in a form of cryogenic suspension of his own invention after falling prey to an all-consuming melancholy in the aftermath of his despatch of Professor Moriarty in 1899 (the process required the use of an extract derived from a now-extinct black fish of the Bering Sea). Tracks in the cellar's dust lead Holmes to conclude that sometime in the 1940s, his resting-place was disturbed by the Professor's brother, Henry, and his grandson, the club-footed James Moriarty Booth – who stole jewels and papers Holmes intended to use to help reintegrate himself into society following his revival. Holmes removes himself to Amy's house at 1994 Baker Street, San Francisco, and before long confronts the grown-up Booth, now a crime lord of fearsome reputation – only to learn that Booth's whole empire was founded upon the loot ransacked from Holmes' cellar.

THE SOLUTION

Associates of a kidnapped police lieutenant, Ortega, have been slaughtered by first a tiger, then piranhas, beetles, and a venomous snake. Holmes' observation that these breeds are commonly known as tiger fish, tiger beetles and the tiger snake lead him to conclude that Booth has committed the murders on behalf of fellow criminal Pavon – whose brother, killed by Ortega, was known as 'El Tigre'. Having made an ally of a technologically minded petty criminal known as 'Zapper', beaten off a lethal serpent and pursued his quarry on the back of Amy's motorbike, Holmes eventually rescues Ortega from the harbourside, furnishing the police with fingerprint evidence linking Booth to the killings. Back at 1994 Baker Street, and joined by Mrs Hudson, Holmes sets himself up in practice as a consulting detective.

Life in the freezer: Dr Amy Wilmslow (Debrah Farentino) resuscitates the mysterious 'Captain Basil' (Anthony Higgins) in **1994 Baker Street: Sherlock Holmes Returns** *(1993)*

The CBS network has twice attempted to present a defrosted Sherlock at large in present-day America, accompanied by an attractive female doctor. Just like **The Return of Sherlock Holmes** (1987) before it, *1994 Baker Street: Sherlock Holmes Returns* failed to develop into a full series – but it would be unfair to label this occasionally amusing effort as simply a rip-off of the earlier Michael Pennington vehicle; not when it borrows equally from 1979's delightful *Time After Time*, in which Victorian adventurer-novelist HG Wells pursues Jack the Ripper to contemporary San Francisco. Indeed, Anthony Higgins' flowing-locked, frock-coated Sherlock claims to have put himself into deep freeze after finding inspiration in his friend Wells and his *Time Machine*!

1994 Baker Street begins well, with Holmes emerging from his tomb looking rather like Monty Python's 'It's ...' man. Higgins' Holmes is an arrogant pig with a fine line in put-downs ('Bravo, Wilmslow, bravo! Isn't it rewarding to use the senses the good Lord gave us?'), but he's given a few moments of quiet introspection for contrast, notably where he realises that he must now refer to his 'late brother Mycroft', and makes much of his redundancy after gaining a glimpse of the busy SFPD Forensics division ('Now there is an entire wing at police headquarters dedicated to that

which I once did alone ...'). But his charms begin to grate after the umpteenth protracted demonstration of his awesome powers of observational deduction, and the dreary join-the-dots plotting of the main story is not interesting enough in itself to hold the viewer's attention. A couple of fan references intrigue, however: isn't that a lifebuoy from the *SS Friesland* (see **Pursuit to Algiers**) on the cellar walls; and surely that can't be Doyle himself standing alongside Holmes in the yellowed photograph held by Booth?

Shot in Vancouver, British Columbia, *1994 Baker Street* enjoyed a fine pedigree: writer-producer-director Kenneth Johnson (1942-) had been intimately involved in the production of science fiction-flavoured primetime series for 20 years, including *The Six Million Dollar Man* and spin-off *The Bionic Woman*, *The Incredible Hulk*, *V* and *Alien Nation*; British-born leading man Anthony Higgins (1947-), noted for youthful appearances as 'Anthony Corlan' in 1970s Hammer horror movies *Taste the Blood of Dracula* and *Vampire Circus*, had played Holmes' engagingly villainous tutor Rathe (aka Moriarty) in **Young Sherlock Holmes** (1985) before giving his Sherlock in Lyric Theatre comedy *The White Glove* early in 1993; even proxy Watson Debrah Farentino (1959-) would have been familiar with the territory, having enjoyed a major role in the previous year's TV movie *Back to the Streets of San Francisco* (1992). Trade mag *Variety* did not, however, give much for *1994 Baker Street*'s future prospects, listing its deficiencies as: 'derivative premise, thin content and production values, awkward dialogue, bad jokes ... and consistent overacting.'

Viewers of the 1996 TV movie revival of *Doctor Who* may have had fun spotting its coincidental similarities with *1994 Baker Street: Sherlock Holmes Returns*: a velvet frock-coated hero (Paul McGann) is brought to life in San Francisco in 1999, soon teaming up with an attractive female doctor (Daphne Ashbrook) and a good-natured street kid (Yee Jee Tso) and taking to a motorbike to foil the millennial crimes of his arch enemy the Master (Eric Roberts), who sometimes takes the form of a large snake...

An on-ice Sherlock would be reconstituted in the 1999 animated series **Sherlock Holmes in the 22nd Century**, proving that the concept still appeals.

Paramount on Parade

US 1930 parody Paramount Pictures 102m bw/colour
w **various** p **Elsie Janis** d **various** [including **Rowland V Lee**, **Frank Tuttle**]
cast includes himself/Sherlock Holmes: **Clive Brook**
himself: **Jack Oakie** himself/Dr Fu Manchu: **Warner Oland**
himself/Sergeant Heath: **Eugene Pallette**
himself/Philo Vance: **William Powell**

A poor excuse for studio heads to show off the talent they had under contract, the all-star revue, typically a compendium of skits, sketches, musical numbers and various after-dinner turns, was a short-lived Hollywood fad of the late twenties and early thirties. Among the earliest examples were Metro-Goldwyn-Mayer's *The Hollywood Revue of 1929* (nominated as Best Picture in that year's Academy Awards) and Warner Bros' *Show of Shows* (also 1929, and shot entirely in crude, developmental Technicolor). Players roped in for *Paramount on Parade*, Paramount Pictures' 1930 answer to the MGM and Warners efforts, included Clara Bow, Maurice Chevalier and Gary Cooper.

Of particular interest, however, is a 7'40" black and white comedy sequence sometimes referred to as 'Murder Will Out', which brought together three of Paramount's popular pulp/thriller stars: Warner Oland as the nefarious Dr Fu Manchu, William Powell as the snob sleuth Philo Vance and Clive Brook as a superior Sherlock Holmes. Oland had played Sax Rohmer's Oriental 'devil doctor' in *The Mysterious Dr Fu Manchu* (1929) and *The Return of Dr Fu Manchu* (1930), both directed by Rowland V Lee. Alongside Eugene Pallette as his police officer patsy Sergeant Heath, Powell had featured as SS Van Dine's stuffy sophisticate in *The Canary Murder Case*, *The Greene Murder Case* (both 1929) and *The Benson Murder Case* (1930, director Frank Tuttle). And, finally, Brook had debuted as the first speaking Sherlock in **The Return of Sherlock Holmes** (1929). The writer and director of the 'Murder Will Out' segment are

unknown, but it may be significant that both Lee and Tuttle are credited for directorial work on *Paramount on Parade*.

The sequence opens in the Paramount canteen, where vaudeville compere Jack Oakie greets Oland, Brook, Powell and Palette in turn, all of whom are out to lunch and all of whom believe they are about to appear in 'a mystery play written especially for me'. Cut to the 'mystery play' itself: we open in an enclosed vault of some description, on a shot of Dr Fu Manchu writing a threatening message on the back of the corpse of a man he has just killed. Flatfoot Sergeant Heath enters, apparently because the Chinaman has telephoned him to tell him that a murder has been committed; contendedly, Heath goes to handcuff a smiling Fu. Suddenly, an upright Ancient Egyptian sarcophagus trundles into the chamber; Philo Vance emerges, and disputes the notion that Fu may have killed the shot and stabbed body – despite Heath having found Fu holding a gun and a knife.

Sherlock Holmes enters, muttering to an off-screen Watson. When Holmes also suggests that Fu might not be the killer, Fu shoots Vance in the buttocks (he falls dead, clutching his chest) and then fires at Holmes, hitting him first in the wrist and then in the breast (he, too, dies unconvincingly). 'I had to do it,' Fu tells Heath, 'it was the only way I could convince them that I am a murderer.' Trapdoors help dispose of the bodies of Vance and Holmes – and then Fu literally flies away, leaving Heath alone with the gun and the corpse... and ready to be arrested by the several policemen who suddenly burst onto the scene. And the punchline? The 'corpse' sits up and removes a fake moustache, revealing the features of none other than Jack Oakie himself. 'It's a mystery play written especially for *me*,' he tells the viewer, shaking with forced hysterics. Boom, boom.

It's been said that the most noteworthy aspect of this sequence is that, for the first and only time, Holmes dies on screen. It's not actually true, since it is clearly Brook playing Holmes who acts out a stage death in a section flagged up as a constructed fiction. Oland, Powell and Brook would each play their respective characters just once more on film, in *Daughter of the Dragon* (1931, Paramount), *The Kennel Murder Case* (1933, Warner Bros) and **Conan Doyle's Master Detective Sherlock Holmes** (1932, Fox Film) in turn.

The Pearl of Death

US 1944 adaptation [THE SIX NAPOLEONS] *Universal Pictures Company Inc 68m bw*
w **Bertram Millhauser** *pd* **Roy William Neill**
cast Sherlock Holmes: **Basil Rathbone** Dr Watson: **Nigel Bruce** Lestrade: **Dennis Hoey** Naomi Drake: **Evelyn Ankers** Giles Conover: **Miles Mander** Amos Hodder: **Ian Wolfe** Digby: **Charles Francis** James Goodram: **Holmes Herbert** Bates: **Richard Nugent** Mrs Hudson: **Mary Gordon** the Creeper: **Rondo Hatton** Sgt Bleeker: **J Walsh Austin*** Constable: **Billy Bevan*** housekeeper: **Lillian Bronson*** George Gelder: **Harry Cording*** boss: **Harold DeBecker*** Constable Murdock: **Leslie Denison*** customs officer: **Leyland Hodgson*** bearded man: **Charles Knight*** Ellen Carey: **Connie Leon*** teacher: **Audrey Manners*** Thomas Sandeford: **Arthur Mulliner*** chauffeur: **Eric Wilton*** guards: **Al Ferguson***, **Colin Kelly*** stewards: **Wilson Benge***, **Arthur Stenning***

THE MYSTERY

Disguised as a vicar, Sherlock Holmes foils an attempt by Naomi Drake to steal the priceless Borgia Pearl as it is being transported into the UK. Drake is working for the international criminal Giles Conover, who vows to steal the Pearl from its case in the Royal Regent Museum, seizing his chance to do so when Holmes disconnects the Museum's alarm system to demonstrate lapses in security. Conover is arrested, but the Pearl is found nowhere on his person – and Inspector Lestrade is eventually forced to release him. Holmes, meanwhile, is ridiculed in the press for allowing the Pearl to be taken. His reputation is in tatters.

THE INVESTIGATION

A retired Major, Horace Harker, is found murdered in his home – his back broken, a *modus operandi* favoured by Conover's henchman, the so-called 'Hoxton Creeper'. Holmes is intrigued by the fact that the killer has paused to smash every

item of china in the room, and pursues his own enquiries. Conover attempts to assassinate Holmes by delivering to him a fake folio of Dr Johnson's dictionary holding a spring-loaded blade. Two more victims of the Hoxton Creeper are found, again surrounded by broken china. Sorting through porcelain debris from all three crime scenes, Holmes and Watson identify plaster fragments from three identical busts of Napoleon, and soon realise what Conover is up to. Fleeing the Museum, Conover must have ducked into the workshop of an ornamental plasterer, George Gelder – and placed the pearl into one of six freshly cast, still-wet Napoleon heads.

THE SOLUTION

The heads went to an art shop owned by Amos Hodder; there, Holmes sees Naomi Drake posing as Hodder's assistant, 'Miss Bettinger'. Searching for the Pearl, Drake has smashed two other of the busts, leaving just one outstanding – but Holmes manages to discover the name of the last buyer, a Dr Julian Boncourt, before having Naomi arrested. Holmes impersonates Boncourt, and awaits the arrival of the Creeper at Boncourt's surgery; he meets both the killer and his master soon enough. Playing on the Creeper's feelings for Naomi, Holmes succeeds in turning the Creeper against Conover – but is forced to shoot the homicidal horror dead. The police, and Watson, arrive to see the Borgia Pearl recovered.

✦   ✦   ✦

P erhaps in a bid to produce the consummate Universal Holmes flick, *The Pearl of Death* is positioned almost exactly between the pulp adventure of **The Spider Woman** and the horror mechanics of **The Scarlet Claw** – but lacks both the sense of fun of the former and the bug-eyed conviction of the latter. The villain, Giles Conover, is a sort of Moriarty without the class (he 'pervades Europe like the plague!') and his henchman's preferred method of despatch (breaking backs, or so we're told; the on-screen presentation falls far short of demonstrating it) jars with Conover's jolly, gung-ho thieving. This clash of styles mars the perfunctory finale, too, in which a flustered Holmes guns down the brutish ''Oxton 'Orror' in the coldest of blood (a scene that was queried, probably rightly, by the public censor).

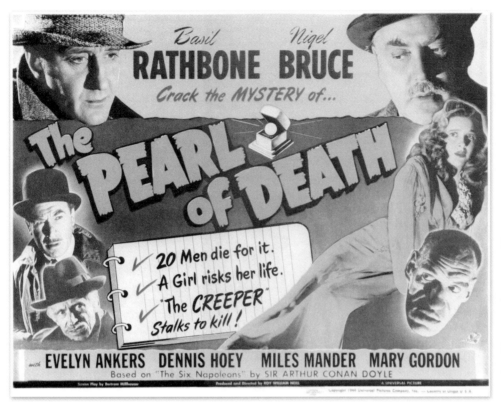

A lurid poster for **The Pearl of Death** *(1945), featuring: right, Lestrade (Dennis Hoey) and Giles Conover (Miles Mander); and left, an uncharacteristically fearful Naomi Drake (Evelyn Ankers) plus the brutish Creeper (Rondo Hatton)*

The chief plot innovation is the rather odd 'disgrace' of Holmes, a story element barely exploited beyond Lestrade's gloating and Watson's reported punching of a reporter in the teeth – a shame, for such an idea might, by now, have carried one of the Universal pictures by itself, with no need to resort to such crude devices as the hulking Creeper. Principal pleasures are the underused Evelyn Ankers (on the side of the angels in **Sherlock Holmes and the Voice of Terror**) as Conover's agent Naomi (the scene where Ankers is costumed as a coarse fag-ash Lil, scrubbing plates in a kitchen, is a minor revelation), plus the surprisingly suspenseful sequence in which Watson is repeatedly distracted from opening the bogus dictionary that contains the means of his instant doom.

Holmes' closing speech-cum-homily, crashingly pretentious though it is, has a certain something about it, too: 'What's Conover? No more than a symbol of the greed and cruelty and lust for power that have set men at each other's throats down the centuries. And the struggle will go on, Watson – for a pearl, kingdom, perhaps even world domin-ion, until the greed and cruelty are burned out of every last one of us. And when that time comes, perhaps even the Pearl will be washed clean again.'

Filmed between 11 April and 1 May 1944, and released on 1 August, *The Pearl of Death* rewarded Miles Mander for his scene-stealing **Scarlet Claw** turn as the reclusive Judge Brisson with the much larger role of Conover. Mander (also in the Arthur Wontner-starring **The Missing Rembrandt**) would be dead two years later – as would Creeper actor Rondo Hatton, a minor cult figure whose remarkable features, caused by a glandular condition, Universal was quick to exploit, rather tastelessly, in films such as *House of Horrors* (1945), *The Spider Woman Strikes Back* and the reprehensible *The Brute Man* (both 1946). Before being cast as the Creeper, Hatton, a former journalist for the *Tampa Tribune*, had played bit parts – as a leper in *The Moon and Sixpence* (1942), for example.

Throughout, *The Pearl of Death* hints at the Creeper's King Kong-like admiration for Naomi – indeed, the assumption of this fact is central to the climax – but neglects to give the pair a proper scene together. It's tempting to view this omission as symptomatic of the film: coy, and somehow incomplete.

Priklyucheniya Sherloka Kholmsa i doktora Vatsona

tr 'The adventures of Sherlock Holmes and Dr Watson'
USSR 1979-86 5 x TV serials USSR Gostelradio/Lenfilm Studio colour
d **Igor Maslennikov**
regular cast Sherlock Holmes: **Vasily Livanov** Dr Watson: **Vitaly Solomin** Mrs Hudson: **Rina Zelenaya**

SERIES I
tx 1979
w **Yuly Dunskoy, Valery Frid**

[1]
tr 'Introduction'
adaptation [A STUDY IN SCARLET/THE SPECKLED BAND] *67m*
guest cast includes Ellen Stoner/Julia Stoner: **Maria Solomina** *other roles:* **Gennady Bogachev, Feodor Odinokov**

[2]
tr 'A study in scarlet'
1979 adaptation [A STUDY IN SCARLET] *67m*
guest cast includes Inspector Lestrade: **Borislav Brondukov** Inspector Gregson: **Igor Dmitriev** Jefferson Hope: **Nikolay Karachentsov** *other roles:* **V Aristov, V Baganov, A Ilyin, L Tischenko, O Khromenkov**

SERIES II
tx 1980
w **Vladimir Valutsky**

[1]
tr 'The king of blackmail'
adaptation [CHARLES AUGUSTUS MILVERTON] *65m*
guest cast includes Inspector Lestrade: **Borislav Brondukov** *other roles:* **Valentina Panina, Boris Ryzhukhin, Boris Klyuev, Anatoly Podshivalov**

[2]
tr 'Mortal fight'
adaptation [THE FINAL PROBLEM] *65m*

guest cast includes Inspector Lestrade: **Borislav Brondukov** *other roles:* **Victor Evgrafov, Alexander Zakharov, Boris Klyuev, Nikolai Kryukov, Alexei Kozhevnikov, Ignat Leirer, I Andronnikov, Anatoly Podshivalov, Y Eller, Dima Khrilyev**

[3]
tr 'Tiger hunt'
adaptation [THE EMPTY HOUSE] *65m*
guest cast includes Inspector Lestrade: **Borislav Brondukov** Inspector Gregson: **Igor Dmitriev** *other roles:* **Victor Evgrafov, Alexander Zakharov, Alexei Kozhevnikov, Boris Klyuev, Nikolai Kryukov, Anatoly Podshivalov, I Kraslavskaya, E Kharkevich, A Zakharov** [sic], **V Smolyakov**

SERIES III
SOBAKA BASKERVILEJ
tr 'The hound of the Baskervilles'
1981 2 x episodes adaptation [THE HOUND OF THE BASKERVILLES] *75/70m*
w **Igor Maslenikov, Yuri Veksler**
guest cast includes Beryl Stapleton: **Irina Kupchenko** Sir Henry Baskerville: **Nikita Mikhalkov** Laura Lyons: **Alla Demidova** Mrs Barrymore: **Svetlana Kruchkova** Barrymore: **Aleksandr Adabashian** Inspector Lestrade: **Borislav Brondukov** Dr Mortimer: **Evgeny Steblov** Stapleton: **Oleg Yankovsky** *other roles:* **Sergei Martinson, O Belov, D Bessonov, O Palmov, A Hudeyev, R Chirov**

SERIES IV
SOKROVISHCHA AGRY
tr 'The treasures of Agra'
1983 2 x episodes adaptations [THE SIGN OF THE FOUR/A SCANDAL IN BOHEMIA]
wd **Igor Maslennikov**
guest cast includes Inspector Lestrade: **Borislav Brondukov** Thaddeus Sholto: **Viktor Proskurin** Jonathan Small: **Sergei Shakurov** *other roles:* **Yekaterina Zinchenko, Pavel Kadochnikov**

SERIES V
DVADTSATYJ VEK NACHINAYETSYA
tr 'The 20th century begins'
1986 2 x episodes adaptations [THE ENGINEER'S THUMB/THE SECOND STAIN/HIS LAST BOW/THE BRUCE-PARTINGTON PLANS]
wd **Igor Maslennikov**
guest cast includes Inspector Lestrade: **Borislav Brondukov** Prime Minister: **Innokenti Smoktunovsky** Mycroft Holmes: **Boris Klyuev** Lady Hilda Trelawney Hope: **Larisa Guzeyeva**

Von Bork: **Leonid Kuravlyov** other roles: **Viktor Koretsky, Arkadi Koval, Yevgeni Platokhin, Aleksandr Romantsov, Yelena Safonova, Igor Yefimov**

It's chastening to realise that some of the finest Sherlock Holmes adaptations ever broadcast on television have languished in almost total obscurity for a quarter-century; and were it not for the advent of internet shopping, the 11 episodes of *Priklyucheniya Sherloka Kholmsa i doktora Vatsona* might never have found their way to the West from the former Soviet Union at all – remaining at best a footnote where the details of such minor works as **The Strange Case of the End of Civilisation As We Know It** have been faithfully transcribed. For the record, then: the pairing of Vasily Livanov (1935-) and the late Vitaly Solomin (1941-2002) ought to figure in the higher reaches of the Holmes/Watson pantheon – up there with Rathbone and Bruce, Brett and Burke, Cushing and Stock – and their five series of *Adventures* can stand alongside both **Sir Arthur Conan Doyle's Sherlock Holmes** (1968) and **The Adventures of Sherlock Holmes** (1984-5) as examples of sympathetic-but-never-slavish adaptations, perfectly in tune with their audience of the time, but still rewarding to the viewer of today.

Russia was never immune to the Great Detective's charms, Doyle's works having always available in translation – but nothing is known of any film or television adaptations prior to the early 1970s, when a version of THE HOUND OF THE BASKERVILLES was first broadcast on state television. Featuring Nikolay Volkov (1934-2003) as Holmes alongside Lev Krugly (1931-) as Watson and Oleg Shklovsky (1947-) as Sir Henry Baskerville, this two-and-a-half hour production was apparently repeated several times over the next decade.

The Livanov/Solomin episodes aired to far greater acclaim. The first two instalments, broadcast in 1979, conflate A STUDY IN SCARLET with THE SPECKLED BAND. Here, we are privy to Watson's rarely-filmed first encounter with Holmes, when the rightly youthful, red-headed ex-military doctor pitches up at 221B Baker Street in search of lodgings. He soon begins to suspect, on the 'evidence' furnished by the comings and goings of several strange visitors, a set of skeleton keys and a murder victim's eyeball found dropped

in a glass of water, that his peculiar new room-mate is no less than 'the brain of the criminal world!' – and challenges him to a boxing bout. The essential parts of Holmes' nature are all on display, his wilful ignorance of anything outside his immediate sphere of concern bringing out Watson's latent romanticism: 'How awful it would be to live in a world where you can't talk to anyone about poetry, about art or politics.' As with all these Lenfilm adaptations, the takes are long and the pace languorous, almost solely dependent on the on the two leads' performances; indeed, a full half-hour goes by before Holmes' true profession is revealed, and they take up their first shared exploit with the arrival of the mortally-afraid 'Ellen Stoner' [sic] at 221B.

DVD copies of the films are plagued by a number of quirks in their English subtitling, the most evident of which comes as Miss Stoner of 'Sarray' regales Holmes and Watson with the terrible tale of what transpired to her (twin) sister Julia in the house of 'Stock-Moron', concluding with her immortal description: 'A ribbon! ... A motley ribbon!' At least the building that stands in for Stoke Moran might plausibly be situated in leafy Surrey; throughout, the series' producers struggle to find locations evocative of nineteenth-century England, giving rise to the use of a cramped, curving Baker Street exterior, its walls painted ochre yellow; not to mention the Steppes of Dartmoor on display throughout *Sobaka Baskervilej*. A charmingly silly error is made in the Series II adaptation of THE EMPTY HOUSE, where 'Sir Ronald Ader' returns to his house in London's Park Lane – which is, quite reasonably, a grand detached residence situated amid a green country park! (Meaning that there can be no villa opposite from where Colonel Moran is required to shoot the unfortunate Sir Ronald ...)

But these are minor difficulties, and much is translated with great clarity. The next instalment opens with Holmes shooting a 'VR' crest in the wall of 221B, and sees the room-mates conducting a game of speed-chess as a prelude to the SIGN OF THE FOUR business in which Holmes surmises the sorry tale of Watson's elder brother from the state of his pocket-watch. Livanov and Solomin play this sequence with heart, Watson's hurt being palpable. The sophistication and depth of characterisation here is clearly comparable to the approach taken by Jeremy Brett and David Burke in the Granada **Adventures**, made some five years later; indeed, Solomin's fastidious, tidy, nattily-dressed Watson is, on occasion, a dead ringer for Burke's. (In a later episode, Holmes will wound Watson again, laughing at the doctor for failing to see through one of his many disguises. Solomin's Watson blinks, blurry-eyed, and hurries away, ashamed more of his 'friend' than himself.) Once the business of A Study in Scarlet is concluded, the killer Jefferson Hope being led away, nobly, to his self-determined fate, Watson vows to be Holmes' chronicler, a self-reflexive note being struck in his closing declaration: 'Yes, they'll read my stories in all the different languages – in Austria, in Japan ... in Russia!'

The second series is the high-water mark, linking Charles Augustus Milverton to The Final Problem and The Empty House to create a single epic adventure in three distinct movements. The tale of the 'King of Blackmail' takes in a few portions of The Greek Interpreter, where Holmes' brother Mycroft attempts to intervene in the matter of the disgrace of Lady Eva Brackwell (in the Diogenes Club, we are afforded a glimpse of a members' lounge resembling no less than a half-lit waxworks) – but the most daring of the screenplay's inventions is to connect Milverton to Professor Moriarty, whose monogram (made of four crossed swords) is seen among Milverton's papers. (A not-dissimilar trick would be pulled in Granada's **Adventures**, where *The Red-headed League* would segue into *The Final Problem*.) As the second episode progresses, it becomes clear that Holmes' intervention in Milverton's affairs is of the gravest concern to the Professor, for Holmes now possesses a coded document detailing the most secret workings of London's underworld. The Professor is utterly terrifying: a sneering, red-eyed hunchback whose key henchman, Price, is a fanged monstrosity with a startling similarity to Lon Chaney Jr as Universal Pictures' Wolf Man. (As an aside, an early glimpse inside Holmes' rooms shows a series of framed horror portraits all around – presumably models for Holmes' various make-ups – one of which is clearly a still of Lon Chaney Sr as a grinning, skull-headed Phantom of the Opera, from the 1925 silent version of the Gaston Leroux novel.)

And so to Reichenbach, where Holmes' 'demise' is realised in thrilling *sturm und drang* style, with the spiderish Professor scuttling and snarling around the brink of the abyss in his efforts to send Sherlock plunging to his doom. One minor conceit is to have innkeeper Peter Steiler Jr – now a reformed thief of Holmes' former acquaintance – return with Watson to the Falls, where Holmes' fate becomes clear. As Watson sinks to the ground in tears, Steiler Jr hollers a heart-felt eulogy over the roar of the torrent: 'What tragedy! What misfortune! Mr Holmes was the only one who treated me with respect. If not for him, I wouldn't be living here now. I wouldn't be admiring this beautiful scenery! ... Poor Mister Holmes!'

The final instalment picks up the thread one month later: the assassination of Sir Ronald Ader (Doyle's Ronald Adair) has been prefigured in the second episode, with Holmes' last request to Watson being to take care of the unlucky Hon. Watson, of course, muffs it – after 'disguising' himself as an Italian padre with an all-too-English red moustache, the better to follow Ader's movements, he succeeds only in becoming personally implicated in Ader's death. Re-enter Sherlock Holmes, who weeps after revealing to Watson his deception.

Perhaps the highest compliment one might pay the Livanov/Solomin series is that, bar the occasional cross-cultural hiccough, to watch them is to experience the adventures afresh: broadly untainted by 75-odd years of Sherlock Holmes films and television presentations, they carry no baggage. Their joys are many: Vlademir Dashkevich's mock-baroque theme music (performed by the Leningrad State Philharmonic Orchestra); Rina Zelenaya's Mrs Hudson, for whom the scriptwriters manage to find plenty of business (there's a lovely sequence where she practices her own version of Holmes' logical deduction, correctly discerning through untrained intuition that a messenger is a retired naval sergeant); a genuinely frightening Baskerville Hound, made horrifying by the simplest device (by painting a dog's skull over its own head) ... Livanov himself does not doubt what made the series work, telling a Russian magazine in 2000: 'The Conan Doyle stories had been made into many films before us, but, as I see it, our characters are remarkable in being very human and convincing.' He went on to claim: 'This is probably why the

'Any emotional involvement warps your judgement and clouds your reason': Holmes (Robert Stephens) and Gabrielle Vallodon (Geneviève Page) in **The Private Life of Sherlock Holmes** *(1970)*

British recognised our film to be the best European version of its kind.'

Not yet, they haven't. But in time – who knows?

The Private Life of Sherlock Holmes

GB/US 1970 pastiche Phalanx Productions/Mirisch Productions/Sir Nigel Films 125m colour
w **Billy Wilder, I A L Diamond**
associate p **I A L Diamond** *pd* **Billy Wilder**
cast Sherlock Holmes: **Robert Stephens** Dr John H Watson: **Colin Blakely** Gabrielle Valladon [aka Ilsa von Hoffmansthal]: **Geneviève Page** Mycroft Holmes: **Christopher Lee** Madame Petrova: **Tamara Toumanova** Rogozhin: **Clive Revill** Mrs Hudson: **Irene Handl** Queen Victoria: **Mollie Maureen** gravedigger: **Stanley Holloway** woman in wheelchair: **Catherine Lacey** Von Tirpitz: **Peter Madden** cabby: **Michael Balfour** guide [at Urquhart Castle]: **James Copeland** carters: **John Garrie, Godfrey James** hotel manager: **Robert Cawdron** baggageman: **Alex McCrindle** porter [at Diogenes Club]: **Frank Thornton** monk: **Paul Hansard** Cassidy: **Michael Elwyn*** minister [at graveside]: **Kenneth Benda*** Wiggins [Mycroft's manservant]: **Graham Armitage*** 2nd gravedigger: **Eric**

Francis* Petrova's maid: **Ina de la Haye*** submarine crew [the Tumbling Piccolos]: **Ismet Hassan*, Charlie Young Atom*, Teddy Kiss Atom*, Willie Shearer*** lady in waiting: **Daphne Riggs*** equerry: **John Gatrell*** scientists [at Jonah presentation]: **Martin Carroll*, John Scott*** Lt Commander: **Philip Anthony*** McKellar: **Phillip Ross*** secretary: **Annette Kerr*** sleeping old man at Diogenes Club: **Kynaston Reeves*** conductor: **Miklos Rozsa***
actors in deleted scenes included: Mr Havelock-Smith: **John Williams** Inspector Lestrade: **George Benson** Mr Plimsoll: **David Kossoff** ship's captain: **Noel Johnson** honeymoon bride: **Nicole Shelby** honeymoon bridegroom: **Jonathan Cecil** Oxford beauty: **Jenny Hanley**

'Now don't ask me why I'm making a film about Sherlock Holmes, like all the people who've visited me,' Billy Wilder warned John Gillett of *Sight and Sound.* 'The answer is, I love him, and I wanted to.'

Wilder (1906-), the acerbic Austrian-born director of such classics as *The Lost Weekend, Sunset Boulevard, Some Like It Hot* and *The Apartment,* had read the Conan Doyle stories in German translation as a boy. In 1954, he toyed with the idea of mounting a Broadway musical based around the character, a notion which by the early 1960s had

Watson (Colin Blakely) enters into 'The Dance of the Little Swans' in 'The Singular Affair of the Russian Ballerina', one of the surviving segments of **The Private Life of Sherlock Holmes** *(1970)*

been exchanged for a proposed *screen* musical. By 1963, however, he was working with his usual collaborator, I A L ('Izzy') Diamond, on what he called 'a serious study of Holmes. Here is a most riveting character. A dope addict and a misogynist, yet in all the movies made about him nobody has ever explained why. I want to change the image of him. He'll still be tall, ascetic and cerebral, but he'll be real.'

By the time *The Private Life of Sherlock Holmes* began filming at Pinewood Studios on 5 May 1969, it was a $10,000,000 production sponsored by the Mirisch Brothers. Having at one time earmarked Peter O'Toole and Peter Sellers for Holmes and Watson, Wilder later considered stage star Nicol Williamson as Sherlock and rejected the overtures of Rex Harrison outright. (Harrison's signature role in both the stage and screen versions of *My Fair Lady* – the all-knowing but emotionally stunted phoneticist Henry Higgins – had been partly intended by George Bernard Shaw as a Holmes parody, so Harrison's aspiration to play Holmes himself was a reasonable one.) Wilder settled instead for National Theatre players Robert Stephens (1931-1995) and Colin Blakely (1930-1987), who had come to prominence five years before in the original production of Robert Bolt's

The Royal Hunt of the Sun, in which they had played Atahualpa and Pizarro respectively. Other major roles were taken by the French actress Geneviève Page, recently seen as the Madame in Luis Buñuel's *Belle de Jour* (1967), and Christopher Lee, formerly Sherlock himself in **Sherlock Holmes und das Halsband des Todes** (1962), cast here as a conspicuously lean Mycroft after George Sanders proved too ill to take part.

Celebrated production designer Alexandre Trauner (1906-93) was engaged to construct an extraordinarily elaborate Baker Street set, 150 yards of it, to the tune of some £80,000; construction work had begun before the end of 1968 and Trauner's painstaking attention to detail was extended to a briefly glimpsed reproduction of the Diogenes Club on Pinewood's D Stage. 'He built houses, not sets,' scoffed the film's equally celebrated cinematographer, Christopher Challis (1919-). (The set remained in place, nevertheless, until being 'struck' after flood damage in 1973; in the meantime, it had been seen in pictures as diverse as *Hands of the Ripper* and *Carry On At Your Convenience*, both in 1971.) The production was just as profligate in other departments, including an expensive location stint at Inverness, during which a mock-up monster constructed by special effects veteran Wally Veevers was irretrievably lost in Loch Ness, necessitating a studio reconstruction of the sequence at MGM Elstree.

As the film raced over-budget and over-schedule, the pressure on the actors (with co-writer Diamond, mouthing the lines out-of-shot even as they spoke them, insisting on letter-perfect reproduction of the scripted dialogue) became so intense that, shortly after the unit's return from Inverness, Robert Stephens suffered a nervous breakdown and the production ground to a halt for ten days or so. By the time the film was in its nineteenth week of production, Wilder was filming a group of midgets in a Home Counties graveyard. Surveying the tombstones, he muttered, 'The people around here died so old. They can't have had anything to do with the movie industry.'

As was his usual practice, Wilder had written the script literally to music, with Miklos Rozsa's 'Violin Concerto Opus 24' forming a blueprint for the film's structure. In the graveyard, he confided to Mark Shivas that the assembled midgets were involved in 'the fourth of four stories 'discovered' in 221B Baker Street in a tin box. The fourth movement of our symphony. But they're not exactly separate movements. You've seen *La Dolce Vita*? Well, that's like a lot of separate stories running together...'

As originally conceived, the first movement was called 'The Case of the Upside-Down Room', in which a jaded Holmes is called by Inspector Lestrade to a Limehouse dive to investigate the murder of a Chinaman, found sprawled in a room where all the furniture has been nailed to the ceiling. Holmes rapidly dismisses the whole thing as an elaborate set-up designed by Watson to distract him from his use of cocaine. 'The Singular Affair of the Russian Ballerina' has Holmes propositioned by the fêted Madame Petrova, who has decided that her beauty and his brains will yield the perfect baby. Holmes cites his 'relationship' with Watson as an impediment, makes his excuses and leaves – much to Watson's homophobic horror.

'The Dreadful Business of the Naked Honeymooners' puts Holmes and Watson on board a boat returning from Constantinople in the summer of 1886, literally swopping hats as Watson determines to crack a case on his own. He blunders into the wrong cabin, however, and theorises at length over two 'corpses' which turn

out to be slumbering newly-weds. Finally, 'The Adventure of the Dumbfounded Detective' involves a beautiful Belgian client called Gabrielle Valladon, whose search for her engineer husband takes Holmes to Scotland, where Mycroft is overseeing the development of a revolutionary new submersible disguised, for the time being, as the Loch Ness Monster.

'*The Private Life of Sherlock Holmes* is not a comedy and it's not serious,' Wilder concluded. 'It should keep audiences in the theatre for around three hours.' This was not to be, however. Despite having the right to final cut in his contract, Wilder bowed to corporate demands that the first and third episodes should be dropped altogether, together with a modern-day prologue, some material establishing Holmes' dissipation prior to Lestrade's arrival, a lengthy flashback to a failed Oxford romance of Holmes' (originally embedded in the 'Dumbfounded Detective' section), and a return visit from Lestrade at the end of the picture, asking for assistance in tracking down Jack the Ripper. Much truncated, the film emerged on 28 October 1970 and was cold-shouldered by the public, despite critical endorsements like that of Tom Milne in the *Observer*: 'Paradoxical as always, in upsetting the Sherlock applecart Wilder has made a film which comes full circle through a generous helping of his acid wit to become an affectionate hommage ... *The Private Life of Sherlock Holmes* goes straight into my Ten Best of 1970 list.'

Though bits and pieces of the excised material came to light in the 1990s, the whereabouts of the rest remains a mystery. Even in its truncated form, however, *The Private Life of Sherlock Holmes* is an uncommonly charming and atmospheric picture. As a Holmes pastiche, it is realised with all the exquisitely phrased humour expected of Wilder

Watson (Colin Blakely) and Holmes (Robert Stephens) swop hats, literally, in 'The Dreadful Business of the Naked Honeymooners', a segment dropped from **The Private Life of Sherlock Holmes** (1970)

Holmes as whey-faced malcontent: Robert Stephens in **The Private Life of Sherlock Holmes** *(1970)*

and Diamond. (As the credits unfold, a selection of Holmes artefacts finally yields a hypodermic syringe, the needle of which is directed squarely at Wilder and Diamond's writing credit as if to emphasise the droll pointedness of their script.) And Challis' muted Scope photography (soft browns predominating) combines with Trauner's meticulous production design to make *Private Life* arguably the most seductive-looking Holmes picture ever made.

Stripped of its surrounding structure, the ballerina episode acts as a hilarious prelude to the 'Dumbfounded Detective' story, which now forms the main body of the film. Clive Revill's hook-nosed Rogozhin, conceited interpreter for the imperious Madame Petrova, is a delightful comic creation in miniature, matched later on by the lofty hauteur of Christopher Lee's sardonic Mycroft and the expertly maintained ambiguity of Geneviève Page's Gabrielle Valladon. (Of the film's four female characters, incidentally – Gabrielle, Queen Victoria, the wheezing wheelchair-bound old lady and Mrs Hudson – all but the latter appear to have been dubbed by the ubiquitous Olive Gregg.) The wild contrivances of the main story, from a Belgian engineer interred with a scattering of bleached canaries to a prototype submarine with a Loch

Ness Monster headpiece, push the outré details beloved of Conan Doyle ever so gently into the realms of the absurd, while the silhouetted perambulations of several monks (actually German spies in disguise) maintain a breath of the sinister even when the film is at its funniest.

The heart of the film, however, is the plangent relationship between Holmes and Watson. Colin Blakely's brilliant comic performance as a wiry, pugnacious, touchingly naïve Watson is geared around a perplexed interior monologue we're privy to as the 'Dumbfounded Detective' section gets underway. 'What indeed *was* his attitude towards women?' he ponders in the face of Holmes' grave inscrutability on the subject. 'Was there some secret he was holding back? Or was he just a thinking machine, incapable of any emotion?'

Robert Stephens plays Holmes as a whey-faced malcontent labouring under some unspecified melancholia. Fey and theatrical, he seems, superficially, like a Holmes reconfigured by Oscar Wilde or even Aubrey Beardsley, an effete poseur unable to come to terms with the emotions he has so long suppressed. The question of which sex those emotions might be directed towards becomes an irrelevance. Wilder later told his biographer Ed Sikov that 'I should have been more daring. I wanted to make Holmes a homosexual ... That's why he's on dope, you know.' Thank God for Wilder's reticence, for it makes the film as ambivalent on the subject as Holmes himself, and magically so. No graphic portrait of an uncompromisingly gay Sherlock Holmes would have been even half as effective.

Holmes trots out the usual gently misogynist stuff – 'Actually, I don't dislike women,' he tells Watson, 'I merely distrust them: the twinkle in the eye and the arsenic in the soup' – but much of it rings hollow. And when his emotions are unexpectedly stirred by Gabrielle, a woman whose pluck and acumen he admires even when Mycroft reveals that she is in reality a German spy called Ilsa von Hoffmansthal, his world begins to totter, the faintly ludicrous details of the wild goose chase she's led him on receding into insignificance. He fails to solve the mystery, much to Mycroft's delight ('Am I going too fast for the best brain in England?'), and is shattered when Mycroft informs him by letter that Ilsa has been executed by the Japanese; here Miklos Rosza's original violin theme is gently reinstated to point up the tragedy. Stephens was an actor given to rather camera-unfriendly performances in films like *Lunch Hour* (1961) and *The Asphyx* (1972), but his mournful Holmes is a triumph. It's by no means the standard-issue Sherlock of the popular imagination, but remains much the most human and affecting interpretation on film. (JR)

Pursuit to Algiers

US 1945 pastiche Universal Pictures Company Inc
65m bw
w **Leonard Lee** *pd* **Roy William Neill**
cast Sherlock Holmes: **Basil Rathbone** Dr Watson: **Nigel Bruce** Sheila: **Marjorie Riordan** Agatha Dunham: **Rosalind Ivan** Mirko: **Martin Kosleck** Jodri: **John Abbott** Prime Minister: **Frederic Worlock** Sanford: **Morton Lowry** Nikolas: **Leslie Vincent** Kingston: **Gerald Hamer** Gregor: **Rex Evans** Gubec: **Wee Willie Davis** clergyman: **Wilson Benge*** Johansson: **Sven Hugo Borg*** steward: **Ashley Cowan*** customer: **James Craven*** restaurant proprietor: **Tom Dillon*** furtive man: **Alan Edminston** Ravez: **Gregory Gaye*** Stimson: **Olaf Hytten*** fuzzy-looking woman: **Dorothy Kellogg*** Reginald Dene: **George Leigh*** aides: **James Carlisle***, **Sayre Dearing***

THE MYSTERY
Setting out for a shooting holiday in Scotland, Sherlock Holmes and Dr Watson find themselves led, by a number of carefully placed intrigues, to 26 Fishbone Alley, there to be greeted by a most distinguished prospective client: the Prime Minister of the Mediterranean state of Rovenia. It transpires that the King of Rovenia has recently been assassinated and the Prime Minister wants Holmes to help him transport the Crown Prince safely from school in England back to his homeland. Holmes agrees but, when he and Watson meet the aircraft chartered to take the Prince, informs Watson of a change of plan: the doctor will now take the *SS Friesland* to rendezvous with the detective at Algiers. Early in the voyage, Watson learns that Holmes' plane has crashed in the Pyrenees – with no survivors.

THE INVESTIGATION
Called to attend to a sick passenger, Watson finds himself facing both Holmes and the Crown Prince, neither of whom ever boarded the plane. The Prince will instead be travelling as the doctor's nephew, 'Nikolas Watson', a deception intended to wrongfoot would-be assassins. A number of passengers arouse suspicions in the pair, but it is only when three dubious characters – mute Gebec, knife-thrower Mirko and their leader, Gregor – board at Lisbon that Nikolas is placed in mortal danger. Holmes sees off several attempts to kill Nikolas – by knife, by poison, by a bomb concealed in a novelty cracker. Shortly before the ship comes into port at Algiers, Holmes is finally caught off-guard; Nikolas is seized by the conspirators and taken ashore to his certain death...

THE SOLUTION
All is not lost, however – for Holmes reveals that 'Nikolas' was but a decoy; the real Prince has all along been travelling as the steward Sanford. The conspirators are arrested.

✦ ✦ ✦

There is no mystery to solve in *Pursuit to Algiers*, save exactly how Universal thought it was ever going to pass off this sub-Buchan chase melodrama as a Sherlock Holmes film. Even **Sherlock Holmes in Washington**, the series entry it most closely resembles, had called upon some of

Aboard the cruise liner SS Friesland, Holmes (Basil Rathbone), 'Nikolas' (Leslie Vincent) and Watson (Nigel Bruce) become involved with pianist and unwitting diamond smuggler Sheila (Marjorie Riordan) in **Pursuit to Algiers** (1945)

the detective's intellectual powers some of the time. Since the case here is no case at all, the story is forced to fall back on a number of contrivances – most pleasingly, the fact that singer Sheila Woodbury is unwittingly carrying the Duchess of Brookdale's stolen emeralds, the theft of which is fleetingly invoked at the very beginning of the film.

Least satisfactory is the revelation that the conspirators have been targeting the wrong passenger all along – which, after over an hour's wait for the thrilling finale, comes as not so much a twist in the tale, more an outright con. In between, we are 'treated' to the sight of Holmes driving a car, Watson's rendition of 'Loch Lomond' (one of four songs included in the picture, the others being Sheila's 'There Isn't Any Harm in That', 'Flow Gently, Sweet Afton' and 'Cross My Heart'), the case of the Giant Rat of Sumatra being recounted as an after-dinner turn and Holmes' deadpan assertion that 'the late Professor Moriarty was a virtuoso on the bassoon'.

The villains are colourless, the supporting characters either nondescript or robbed of red-herring potential way too soon. The opening

sequence, in which Holmes and Watson are called upon to decode a series of quite absurd indicators and present themselves before the Prime Minister of Rovenia, would not seem out of place in a full-on parody. Bizarrely, it's Nigel Bruce's Watson who is responsible for the film's only serious, affecting moment; on learning that Holmes' plane has crashed, he turns his back to the camera and looks out to sea, murmuring to a steward, 'I can't see anyone now.' It's as if his life has ended, too.

Known in production as *The Fugitive*, this dreary bill-filler, the sequel to **The Woman in Green**, debuted in the US on 26 October 1945. Perceptively, the *New York Post* remarked: 'the Sherlock Holmes series finds itself marking time on the dull outskirts of a mythical kingdom until someone guesses where public interest has shifted with the end of the war ... *Pursuit to Algiers* does nothing but keep the Sherlock Holmes franchise for Universal and lessen its value.' Although the next film would retain the idea of an adventure in transit, **Terror by Night** could hardly fail to be an improvement on this, the least rewarding picture in the whole Universal series by far.

Raffles Flugt Fra Fængslet

tr 'Raffles' escape from prison'
aka **More Sherlock Holmes: Mr Raffle's** [sic]
Attempt on His Life [GB], **Raffles Escape From
Prison**, **Sherlock Holmes II** [GB/US]
*Denmark 1908 pastiche Nordisk Films Kompagni
689 feet bw silent*
wd **Viggo Larsen**
known cast Sherlock Holmes: **Viggo Larsen** Raffles: **Holger
Madsen** other roles **Poul Gregaard**

*Left: Holmes
(Viggo Larsen) on
the trail of a
master thief in*
**Raffles Flugt Fra
Fængslet** *(1908)*

*Below: a
grammatically
suspect Bioscope
ad for* **Raffles
Flugt Fra
Fængslet** *(1908)*

Raffles escapes prison after sending a telegram to his allies. Determined to revenge himself on Holmes, he employs a 'pretty but depraved girl' to lure Holmes to an old house where, disguised as an old woman, Raffles hurls the detective into an old sewer. With 'superhuman strength' Holmes drags himself along the pipes until he hears footsteps overhead, and is drawn up to the surface. Raffles duly plans a second murder bid, taking up lodgings directly opposite Holmes' house, intending to assassinate the detective at his leisure. However, Holmes' boy Billy identifies the house's new tenant, alerts Holmes and, placing a dummy in Holmes' place beside his window, the two conspire to catch Raffles in the act of shooting 'Holmes'. Raffles is collared once more...

Direct sequel to **Sherlock Holmes i Livsfare**, possibly filmed back-to-back with its precursor; one contemporaraneous review claims that

Professor Moriarty returned to plague Holmes alongside the indefatigable Raffles, but this remains uncertain. With a central plot device bearing a more-than-passing similarity to events in THE EMPTY HOUSE, **Raffles Flugt Fra Fængslet** arrived in the UK late in November 1908 and in the US late in February 1909. The *New York Dramatic Mirror* thought it outranked only by an unspecified 'cavalry picture' and *The Last Days of Pompeii*, while *Moving Picture World* held it to be 'as much a masterpiece as its predecessor'.

Raffles actor Holger Madsen (1878-1943) would go on to acquire over 30 directorial credits for pictures as enticingly titled as *Opiumsdrømmen* ('Opium dreams', 1914), *Den Hvide Djævel* ('The White Devil', 1916) and *Das Himmelskibet* (aka *A Trip to Mars*, 1917). The next Nordisk Holmes was **Det Hemmelige Dokument**.

The Return of Sherlock Holmes

*US 1929 pastiche Paramount-Famous Players-Lasky
Corporation 79m* [sound version]
6376 feet [silent version] *bw*
w **Basil Dean, Garrett Fort** *exec p* **David O Selznick**
d **Basil Dean**
cast Sherlock Holmes: **Clive Brook** Dr Watson: **H Reeves-
Smith** Mary Watson: **Betty Lawford** Captain Longmore:
Charles Hay Roger Longmore: **Phillips Holmes** Professor

Holmes (Clive Brook) disguised as an Austrian violinist in **The Return of Sherlock Holmes** (1929)

Moriarty: **Harry T Morey** Colonel Moran: **Donald Crisp**
Sergeant Gripper: **Hubert Druce** other roles: **Arthur Mack**

THE MYSTERY

On the day of the wedding of Dr Watson's daughter, Mary, the groom's father, Captain Longmore, is visited by his associate, Professor Moriarty – head of a criminal 'radio-tapping' organisation. Moriarty uses a booby-trapped cigarette case to poison the conscience-stricken Longmore, who has written out a lengthy confession. Dying, Longmore tells his son, Roger, what has befallen him. The Professor has taken Longmore's confession, and so

Roger goes in pursuit of Moriarty, ending up on an ocean liner where Moriarty's henchman, Colonel Moran, is serving as ship's doctor. The Professor uses the boat as his headquarters, eavesdropping on the international telephone circuit in collaboration with the ship's radio operator.

THE INVESTIGATION

When Longmore's body is discovered, the police automatically assume that Roger must have killed his father and fled. Disbelieving, Mary asks her father's friend, Sherlock Holmes, to come out of retirement to find her fiancé and clear his name.

Holmes, Watson and Mary follow a trail of clues to Cherbourg, France, from where Moriarty's ship is about to sail to New York. Aboard, Holmes adopts the guise of an Austrian violinist and magician to steal Longmore's confession from Moriarty – but Roger is still nowhere to be seen, having been caught, drugged and hidden away by the criminals.

THE SOLUTION

Holmes paints Moran's shoes with phosphorence and follows the Colonel to a secret cabin where the hapless Roger is imprisoned. Moriarty invites Holmes to a lavish dinner where he attempts to prick the detective with the poisoned needle hidden in the bogus cigarette case. But Watson, listening in on events via a concealed radio, is alert to Moriarty's plans. As the ship docks in New York, Moriarty vanishes over the side rather than face arrest.

✦ ✦ ✦

'You've read about this relentless crime tracker,' ran a Paramount press block of 1929. 'See him – thrillingly active, talking, in *The Return of Sherlock Holmes...*' *The Return* may indeed be the first of the detective's talking pictures, but it owes much to the tropes of his silent film career – Clive Brook's Holmes being more a dilettante master of disguise than an intellectual investigator. The lead character's in-name-only resemblance to Holmes was not lost on contemporaneous reviewers, who, hugely disappointed by this sound début, poured scorn on 'Sherlock Brook'. 'Anyone more alien to the character of Holmes would be difficult to find,' wrote *Film Weekly*'s Randolph Carroll Burke.

Suave in appearance and brusque in delivery, the London-born Brook (1887-1974) had made his film début as a murder suspect in Stoll Picture Productions' version of *Trent's Last Case* (1920); contracted to Paramount in 1924, he became known as 'the perfect Englishman' through pictures such as *The Four Feathers* (1929). Head of production David O Selznick is supposed to have cast Brook as Holmes, who was – bafflingly, given Brook's age and debonair appearance – presented in bee-keeping retirement in a scenario part-constructed by writer-director Basil Dean (1887-1978), whom Brook knew from their days together in Liverpool rep.

The plot, however, is surprisingly modern, revolving around the surreptitious interception of radio messages, and perhaps borrowing as much from the real-life arrest of the murderer Hawley Harvey Crippen (1862-1910) as Doyle. (Crippen was apprehended while attempting to flee Europe aboard a transatlantic liner, the suspicious captain of which radioed Scotland Yard for help.) It's unsurprising, therefore, that Moriarty's preferred method of dispatch is poison, although the mechanics of his hidden needle appears to be swiped from Dr Culverton Smith in THE DYING DETECTIVE.

Filmed at Paramount's Astoria Studios on Long Island, the picture benefited from location sequences aboard a docked cruise ship and a view of the Manhattan skyline. Local interest did not, however, fool *New York Times* man Mordaunt Hall who, reviewing the film upon its release on 18 October 1929, pointed out that 'the fun it elicits is not always intended'. Brook managed to rationalise the audience's amusement: 'I remember going to the preview of *The Return of Sherlock Holmes* with members of our studio and to our amazement there was laugh after laugh after laugh – a little bit because I

'Perfect Englishman' Clive Brook as a very youthful post-retirement Holmes in **The Return of Sherlock Holmes** *(1929)*

*Dr Watson
(H Reeves-Smith)
and Sherlock
Holmes (Clive
Brook) sail into
New York in* **The
Return of
Sherlock Holmes**
(1929)

exaggerated [Holmes], and I was rather pleased with the film in a way, because it had gone down well.' Object of ridicule or not, Brook's Holmes would reappear in cameo in **Paramount on Parade** (1930) before being entirely reimagined in **Conan Doyle's Master Detective Sherlock Holmes** (1932).

The Return of
Sherlock Holmes

*GB 1986-8 11 x 50m approx TV series adaptations
Granada UK/Granada Television colour
p* **June Wyndham Davies**
regular cast Sherlock Holmes: **Jeremy Brett**
Dr Watson: **Edward Hardwicke**

THE EMPTY HOUSE
tx 9 July 1986 ITV
w **John Hawkesworth** *d* **Howard Baker**
regular cast, plus Professor Moriarty: **Eric Porter**
Colonel Sebastian Moran: **Patrick Allen** coroner: **James Bree** Inspector Lestrade: **Colin Jeavons** Sir John Hardy: **Richard Bebb** Mr Murray: **Robert Addie** the Countess of Maynooth: **Naomi Buch** the Hon Ronald Adair: **Paul Lacoux** Mrs Hudson: **Rosalie Williams** Ivy: **Elizabeth Ritson** butler: **Roger Rowland** policeman: **John Palmer**

THE PRIORY SCHOOL
tx 16 July 1986 ITV
w **TR Bowen** *d* **John Madden**
regular cast, plus the Duke of Holdernesse: **Alan Howard** Dr Huxtable: **Christopher Benjamin** James Wilder: **Nicholas Gecks** Lord Arthur Saltire: **Nissar Moti** Aveling: **Michael Bertenshaw** Reuben Hayes: **Jack Carr** Mrs Hayes: **Brenda Elder** Mrs Hudson: **Rosalie Williams** Rivers: **William Abney** Caunter: **Mark Turin** choir: **the Choristers of Westminster Abbey** master of the Choristers: **Simon Preston**

THE SECOND STAIN
tx 23 July 1986 ITV
w **John Hawkesworth** *d* **John Bruce**
regular cast, plus Lord Bellinger: **Harry Andrews** Lady Hilda Trelawney Hope: **Patricia Hodge** Rt Honourable Trelawney Hope: **Stuart Wilson** Inspector Lestrade: **Colin Jeavons** Constable MacPherson: **Sean Scanlan** Eduardo Lucas: **Yves Beneyton** Madame Henri Fournaye: **Yvonne Orengo** Mrs Hudson: **Rosalie Williams** Bates: **Alan Bennion**

THE MUSGRAVE RITUAL
tx 30 July 1986 ITV
w **Jeremy Paul** *d* **David Carson**
regular cast, plus Richard Brunton: **James Hazeldine**

Sir Reginald Musgrave: **Michael Culver** Rachel Howells:
Johanna Kirby Janet Tregallis: **Teresa Banham**
Inspector Fereday: **Ian Marter** Tregallis: **Patrick Blackwell**

The Abbey Grange
tx 6 August 1986 ITV
w **Trevor Bowen** *d* **Peter Hammond**
regular cast, plus Inspector Hopkins: **Paul Williamson**
Sir Eustace Brackenstall: **Conrad Phillips**
Lady Mary Brackenstall: **Anne Louise Lambert**
Theresa Wright: **Zulema Dene** Captain Croker: **Oliver
Tobias** Mr Viviani: **Nicholas Chagrin**

The Man With the Twisted Lip
tx 13 August 1986 ITV
w **Alan Plater** *d* **Patrick Lau**
regular cast, plus Neville St Clair: **Clive Francis**
Mrs St Clair: **Eleanor David** Inspector Bradstreet: **Denis
Lill** Mrs Whitney: **Patricia Garwood** Isa Whitney: **Terence
Longdon** Mrs Hudson: **Rosalie Williams** Lascar: **Albert
Moses** constable: **Dudley James**

The Six Napoleons
tx 20 August 1986 ITV
w **John Kane** *d* **David Carson**
regular cast, plus Harker: **Eric Sykes** Inspector Lestrade:
Colin Jeavons Venucci: **Steve Plytas** Beppe: **Emile Wolk**
Morse Hudson: **Gerald Campion** Lucretia: **Marina Sirtis**
Beppo's cousin: **Nadio Fortune** Mr Sandeford: **Jeffrey
Gardiner** Mr Brown: **Michael Logan** Pietro: **Vincenzo
Nicoli** Mandelstam: **Vernon Dobtcheff**

The Devil's Foot
tx 6 Apr 1988 ITV
w **Gary Hopkins** *d* **Ken Hannam**
regular cast, plus Dr Leon Sterndale: **Dennis Quilley**
Mortimer Tregennis: **Damien Thomas** Reverend
Roundhay: **Michael Aitkens** Mrs Porter: **Freda Dowie**
Owen Tregennis: **Norman Bowler** George Tregennis: **Peter
Shaw** Brenda Tregennis: **Christine Collins** Dr Richards:
John Saunders police inspector: **Frank Moorey**

Silver Blaze
tx 13 Apr 1988 ITV
w **John Hawkesworth** *d* **Brian Mills**
regular cast, plus Colonel Ross: **Peter Barkworth** John
Straker: **Barry Lowe** Fitzroy Simpson: **Jonathan Coy**
Mrs Hudson: **Rosalie Williams** Inspector Gregory:
Malcolm Storry Edith Baxter: **Manda-Jayne Beard**
Ned Hunter: **David John** Mrs Straker: **Sally Faulkner**

Silas Brown: **Russell Hunter** Dawson: **Nicholas Teare**
bookmaker: **Marcus Kimber** race official: **Geoffrey Banks**
King's Pyland grooms: **Sean Lee*, Kieron Smith***

Wisteria Lodge
tx 20 Apr 1988 ITV
w **Jeremy Paul** *d* **Peter Hammond**
regular cast, plus Inspector Baynes: **Freddie Jones**
Miss Burnet: **Kika Markham** Scott Eccles: **Donald
Churchill** Henderson: **Basil Hoskins** Lucas: **Trader
Faulkner** Garcia: **Arturo Venegas** Luis: **Guido Adorni**
the mulatto: **Sonny Caldinez** Henderson's daughters:
Abigail Melia, Lorna Rossi

The Bruce Partington Plans
tx 27 Apr 1988 ITV
w **John Hawkesworth** *d* **John Gorrie**
regular cast, plus Mycroft Holmes: **Charles Gray**
Inspector Bradstreet: **Denis Lill** Mrs Hudson: **Rosalie
Williams** Colonel Valentine Walter: **Jonathan Newth** Sidney
Johnson: **Geoffrey Bayldon** Violet Westbury: **Amanda
Waring** Cadogan West: **Sebastian Stride** clerk at Woolwich
station: **Robert Fyfe** Underground officer: **John Rapley**
butler: **Simon Carter** Hugo Oberstein: **Derek Ware**
1st platelayer: **Stephen Crane** 2nd platelayer: **John Laing**

Having successfully concluded the adventure of
The Second Stain – returning the Rt Hon
Trelawney Hope's lost letter, averting war and
bamboozling the Prime Minister, no less – Jeremy
Brett's Sherlock Holmes canters into the street
outside and leaps three feet into the air with a triumphant 'Wa-hey!' Cocksure exuberance underlines
all of the first seven instalments following **The
Adventures of Sherlock Holmes** (1984-5); whereas
those episodes were manufactured in the dark,
without praise or plaudits, the next set would be
produced by a team assured of their own brilliance.

And it shows. It shows in *The Second Stain*,
with its dazzlingly choreographed single shot in
which, while Hope and the Premier cluster round
Hope's despatch box, Holmes exits the frame in
the background, slips a lost letter into the pile out
of shot and circles the tableau to re-enter the
picture in close-up, coolly lighting a cigarette as the
document is discovered. It shows in the coda to a
cheeky, blackly comic revision of THE MUSGRAVE
RITUAL, in which the body of the disappeared maid
Rachel Howells resurfaces in the Musgrave lake,
frozen in precisely the pose of John Everett Millais'

Holmes (Jeremy Brett) tracks down a missing racehorse on the Wessex moors in **The Return of Sherlock Holmes**: Silver Blaze (1988)

pre-Raphaelite drowned Ophelia. It shows in *The Man With the Twisted Lip*, with Clive Francis' fey and unhappy Neville St Clair turning Doyle's rather dubiously motivated tale of a man who lives a double life as a beggar into a metaphor for sublimated homosexuality.

A new Watson, Edward Hardwicke – son of the celebrated Sir Cedric, who'd played Holmes in a 1945 BBC radio adaptation of THE SPECKLED BAND – would feature throughout *The Return*, David Burke having received an offer from the RSC. The join is seamless, with Hardwicke's older, wearied doctor trudging a lonely path as a part-time police surgeon at the opening of *The Empty House*. In a significant improvement on Doyle's faintly incredible original, John Hawkesworth's deft adaptation has Watson called to examine the body of airgunned aristo Ronald Adair at the outset, giving Holmes rather more reason to choose this moment to reveal to his friend that he did not, after all, die in the Reichenbach spume three years before.

The flashback to the scene of Holmes' presumed demise is heartbreaking: from the concealed detective's point of view, we see a tiny Watson, his face imperceptible, realise that Holmes must have perished; we then watch a crestfallen Holmes struggling not to call out the name of his friend in reply, his cry of 'Wa-' dying in his throat. Of course, *The Final Problem* had already established sniper's sights (Colonel

Moran's, presumably) being trained on Holmes' back in Switzerland three years before. A further indication of the degree of pre-planning involved is given by the new shots of Brett at Reichenbach. More, involving Burke, was also apparently filmed at the time of the *Final Problem* shoot, but Watson's recasting meant that additional material had to be recorded in Wales.

Brett's Holmes is clearly a little more worldly, a little more cynical, throughout these first seven, broadcast in 1986. 'And how is the dear wife?' he asks Reginald Musgrave, only to respond with a tart 'How wise' when informed that the Musgrave heir is not married. Of the purloined letter in *The Second Stain*, he comments: 'If it's on the market, I'll buy it – if it means another penny on income tax.' Elsewhere in the same episode, however, he proves himself as manically focused as before, diving frenziedly to the parquet floor of Eduardo Lucas' house and snorting – *snorting* – when the secret compartment he finds there proves to be empty.

So the difference between the energised Holmes of these episodes (plus the next year's TV movie, **The Sign of Four**) and the morose, brooding creature who figures in the final four instalments of *The Return*, broadcast in 1988, is shocking, and it's impossible not to bear in mind Brett's own story in accounting for it. Brett's second wife, Joan Wilson, had fallen victim to cancer before filming commenced on *The Return*; shortly after completing work on *The Six Napoleons*, Brett suffered a nervous breakdown and was admitted to London's Maudsley Hospital for ten weeks, a turn of events crassly revealed in one of the most prominent red-tops under the banner 'TV SHERLOCK IN A MENTAL HOME: Actor Brett goes crazy with grief'. Years would pass before Brett could publicly acknowledge the manic depression that dogged him throughout the remainder of his career, by which time a regimen of powerful drugs had entailed dire consequences for his physical well-being.

It would be trite to observe that the brutal, self-inflicted haircut and the cumbersome black scarf sported by Brett's Holmes in the four 1988 episodes must be some sort of signifier of his illness, but aspects of the episode with which he returned to the role – *The Devil's Foot* – are, at the very least, worrying: Holmes is taken on a rest-cure to Cornwall, abandons cocaine but then chooses to observe the effect of the Devil's Foot root on himself, hallucinating that he is running through Neolithic ruins, blood pouring from his eyes. In the remainder, he often seems out of sorts, if not completely out of character: in one scene in *The Bruce Partington Plans* [sic], Holmes claims that his brother Mycroft 'writes like a drunken crab' – and then, on finding his map-reading impeded by his landlady, complains: 'Mrs Hudson, you're *hideously* in my way!'

The Bruce Partington Plans demonstrates a second symptom of the Granada adaptations' sudden decline: it's all words and no action, director John Gorrie being forced to extraordinary lengths to disguise the lack of adequate London locations – not easy, in a story that follows the route of the Metropolitan Line. (Just two years before, *The Second Stain* had enjoyed much inessential location work in Whitehall.) The story goes that huge overspends on both *The Devil's Foot* (which was shot entirely on location in Cornwall) and *Silver Blaze* (for which the Wessex Cup steeplechase was lavishly recreated at Bangor racecourse, replete with a positively decadent number of costumed extras) forced the Granada team into the terrible economy of writing off the two further hour-long episodes they had planned for *The Return*, then making up the deficit with a two-hour **The Hound of the Baskervilles** (1988) – and a compromised HOUND at that, one restricted in scale and scope.

The Return of Sherlock Holmes

US 1986 TVM pastiche CBS Inc 92m colour
tx 10 January 1987 CBS
w **Bob Shayne** *p* **Nick Gillott** *d* **Kevin Connor**
cast Jane Watson: **Margaret Colin** Mrs Houston: **Lila Kaye**
Violet Morstan: **Connie Booth** Tobias Gregory: **Nicholas**
Guest Sherlock Holmes: **Michael Pennington**
Carter Morstan: **Barry Morse** Spellman: **William Hootkins**
the doctor: **Tony Steedman** Hopkins: **Paul Maxwell** Stark:
Shane Rimmer Hampton: **Olivier Pierre** Kitty: **Sheila Brand**
Singer: **Ray Jewers** Ross: **Daniel Benzali** *with* **John Sterland**,
Miles Richardson, Sneh Gupta, Ricco Ross, Nancy Paul,
Debora Weston, Hubert Tucker, Howard Swinson

THE MYSTERY

It is 1987. Following her father's death, Jane Watson takes over his Boston-based private investigation agency. Short of cash, she travels to England to sell the country pile that originally belonged to her great-grandfather, Dr John H Watson. On her arrival, she is handed a sealed box held by the family's representatives for decades, with instructions to deliver it to the next Watson to enter the house. Inside is a letter telling her to enter the cellar, where she discovers a complex mechanical apparatus housing the frozen-alive body of John H Watson's associate, the great detective Sherlock Holmes. Thawed out, Holmes reveals that he interred himself in this device of his own invention in 1901, after being infected with then-incurable bubonic plague by a brother of his arch-enemy Professor Moriarty. Holmes and Jane steal drugs to cure the disease. Meanwhile, back in Boston, a threatening letter is left in Jane's office: 'Your father is dead. First of the four. The others will soon follow. Small.'

THE INVESTIGATION

It transpires that the menacing letter has been delivered to the wrong address, and its intended recipient was one Violet Morstan – a woman whose father, Carver, was recently killed by a mystery assailant in his home, his body being set alight. Carver was a former FBI investigator, and it seems that 'Small' was an aeroplane hi-jacker whom Carver's friends had helped prosecute. Another FBI man, Bart Sholto, is killed – and, assisted by undercover FBI man Tobias Gregory, Holmes and Jane discover that the million-dollar proceeds of Small's hi-jack were exchanged for counterfeit money by a conspiracy of FBI investigators: 'the four', another of whom is soon shot dead. Small, gaoled for passing the fake notes, has recently been released. Holmes drives into the Arizona desert in search of the last of the four – but his car is forced off the road by a jeep marked 'Tonga', and he is left for dead in the wilderness...

THE SOLUTION

Holmes is saved when he stumbles across the original London Bridge at Lake Havasu, as famously bought and shipped out by a wealthy eccentric. He and Jane trace Ross, the last of the gang, and put him into hiding, but have no further leads – until Holmes realises that Jane's office has been bugged all along, and that they have been leading the killer to each of the four. At Morstan's

Jeremy Brett on exuberant form while working on **The Return of Sherlock Holmes** *(1986-8)*

house, Holmes and Jane confront the innocent Violet... but now Carver reveals himself: it was Small who was shot and burned in his place, Carver killing his co-conspirators to keep his guilty secret. But Holmes has had the house surrounded by the FBI, and Carver is led away. Holmes, Jane and Tobias walk off arm-in-arm.

✦ ✦ ✦

Having spent most of the twentieth century frozen in sleep, a caped detective-adventurer is awakened in a brash modern world that bears little relation to the genteel Victorian age of his heyday. Allying himself with a liberated young woman, he brings his crime-fighting skills into the present-day, confounding the criminal and vanquishing the vulgar... It's a great pitch for a continuing series of television adventures, as was ably demonstrated by the BBC in the 29 episodes of *Adam Adamant Lives!* broadcast between June 1966 and March 1967. And 20 years later, some bright spark at America's giant CBS corporation had much the same idea – albeit with Sherlock Holmes himself revived from 'Arctic sleep', and Dr

Watson's feisty great-grand-daughter at his right hand. Surely it couldn't possibly fail... ?

The Return of Sherlock Holmes, a try-out for a possible continuing series, was filmed in the UK at Lee International Studios, Shepperton, with location scenes at the real London Bridge in Lake Havasu, Arizona, among others. The story, a cheeky update of THE SIGN OF THE FOUR with 'sky-jack' revenue standing in for the Agra hoard, a jeep doubling for the venomous Tonga and an undercover FBI computer programmer substituting for the bloodhound Toby, was by Bob Shayne, a veteran of seventies and eighties detective shows including *Hart to Hart*, *Magnum PI* and CBS's *Murder, She Wrote*. Amusingly, in the pilot, Jane Watson's secretary/housekeeper Mrs Houston is seen reading *The Corpse Danced at Midnight*, a novel by 'J B Fletcher' – the crime-fighting crime writer played by Angela Lansbury in the latter show. Had *The Return* gone to a full series, could a CBS TV 'tec team-up have been on the cards?

Michael Pennington (1943-), a much-garlanded British stage actor largely unknown in the States (a small role in 1983's *Star Wars: Return of the Jedi* notwithstanding), took the part of Holmes; early in 1986, he'd co-founded the English Shakespeare Company. Pennington's Sherlock is an innocent abroad, bemoaning 'I know nothing of the modern world. A babe in the woods. A walking anachronism.' Indeed, his wide-eyed, almost child-like response to his situation is underlined by his having to go to a toyshop to purchase the microscope, handcuffs and disguise kits he'll employ in the field.

The Holmes stories written by John H Watson were, we learn, 'prone to exaggeration and romanticism'; since this Holmes was frozen in 1901, vast chunks of the Doyle canon are excluded from his biography. (But not THE SIGN OF THE FOUR, usually dated to 1888; since Holmes sees no parallel with the Small case unfolding in 1987, presumably THE SIGN OF THE FOUR never occurred in the world of The Return. In which case, John H Watson *didn't* marry Mary Morstan... so who was Jane's great-grandmother?) There are, however, a few references to opera singer Irene Adler, whose name he cries out when feverish (A SCANDAL IN BOHEMIA is Jane's favourite story), and a nod towards his cocaine addiction when Jane hands him a syringe containing the plague cure, saying she doesn't know how to use it. He rolls up his sleeve and injects himself, murmuring 'I've had some experience of these things.' It's the TV movie's sole dark moment. And, oddly, Holmes claims to have learned the trade of burglary from a relative who 'wrote a book on it – name of Raffles...'

It was clearly intended that Holmes and Watson would share equal billing in a series descended from The Return of Sherlock Holmes, their 'will-they-or-won't-they' relationship being not dissimilar from that shared by Cybill Shepherd's Maddy and Bruce Willis' David in the then-huge comedy-thriller series *Moonlighting*. (There's a suggestion, in fact, that Tobias Gregory, whom Watson dates during the course of the pilot, would have become a third lead, establishing a grisly 'love triangle' in future episodes... although given the way that Holmes recoils from Violet Morstan's kiss after their date at the opera, Watson might have found him a very cold fish.) In 1986, Margaret Colin (1957-), cast as Watson, was best known for her role as a District Attorney in CBS sitcom *Foley Square*; following The Return, she won a leading role as a private detective in CBS show *Leg Work*. Although largely wasted in their roles, the main guest stars for The

Return were Barry Morse (famous for The Fugitive in the US and Space: 1999 in the UK), plus *Fawlty Towers* co-creator Connie Booth, as seen in **The Strange Case of the End of Civilisation As We Know It** and the 1983 version of **The Hound of the Baskervilles**.

The Return of Sherlock Holmes begins in fine style – the moment where Holmes discovers that 221B Baker Street is now a branch of McDonald's is both striking and funny – but the same gags (everything's a 'Watergate', Holmes is terrified of flying and sex) are endlessly regurgitated throughout the final hour, the thin plot of which holds very little interest. Slickly made but almost entirely bland, it's amazing that it didn't score a massive hit with US TV audiences of the late eighties. Not that CBS gave up on the core concept; six years later, they'd revive the idea of a Sherlock revived in contemporary America in **1994 Baker Street: Sherlock Holmes Returns**.

Michael Pennington would go on to play Professor Moriarty opposite Clive Merrison's Holmes in two 1992 episodes of BBC Radio 4's acclaimed series of adaptations from the canon.

The Return of the World's Greatest Detective

US 1976 TVM parody Universal City Studios, Inc 78m colour
tx 16 June 1976 NBC-TV
wp **Roland Kibbee, Dean Hargrove** *d* **Dean Hargrove** *cast* Sherman Holmes: **Larry Hagman** Watson: **Jenny O'Hara** Lt Tinker: **Nicholas Colasanto** Himmel: **Woodrow Parfrey** landlady: **Helen Verbit** Spiner: **Ivor Francis** Judge Clement Harley: **Charles Macaulay** Dr Collins: **Ron Silver** Vince Cooley: **Sid Haig** psychiatrist: **Booth Colman** Mrs Slater: **Lieux Dressler** detective: **Fuddle Bagley** Klinger: **Benny Rubin** manager: **Robert Snively** caretaker: **Jude Farese** Sergeant: **George Brenlin** bailiff: **Al Dunlap** delivery man: **Jefferson Kibbee**

THE MYSTERY
Temporarily suspended from duty as a result of his incompetence, Los Angeles motorcycle cop Sherman Holmes is lying in a park, reading a volume of Sherlock Holmes stories, when his badly-parked motorbike topples over onto his head. Three months later, psychiatric social worker Joan

'Doc' Watson – in whom Sherman had confided his desire to be a detective – agrees to supervise the delusional Sherman on his release from a state mental hospital. Not only does Sherman now believe himself to be the actual Sherlock Holmes, he has acquired uncanny powers of deduction – and believes his 'accident' to have been caused by Professor Moriarty and his henchmen.

THE INVESTIGATION

Dressed by Watson in deerstalker and cape, 'Sherlock' takes up rooms at a boarding-house in LA's Baker Street, which he sends Watson to furnish with books and chemistry equipment. A newspaper article on the presumed-accidental death of an embezzler named Edward Kagle in a ravine off Mulholland Drive attracts Holmes' eye – and he soon convinces homicide detective Lt Tinker that Kagle was actually strangled with his own car's seatbelt. When a conman named Roy Ballinger dies in similar fashion, Holmes follows a trail of murder leading to a small-time crook named Vincent Cooley, who is due to plead guilty to an arson attack ...

THE SOLUTION

In the courtroom of Judge Clement Harley, Holmes attempts to question Cooley, but is rebuffed by the Judge. Suddenly, a smoke bomb is let off – and, in the confusion, someone tries to shoot Cooley dead. When the smoke clears, Holmes unmasks the culprit: the Judge himself, who has given a number of crooks bail in exchange for information which would lead him to the missing $1/2 million stolen by Kagle ... and then murdered his informants.

✦ ✦ ✦

At a press conference called by America's NBC network on 23 June 1975, it was announced that plans were afoot to develop a new series of Holmes adaptations starring Robert Shaw – whose latest role, as a shark-hunter named Quint, was in the film *Jaws*, released just three days earlier. The project never materialised – scuppered in the wake of the shark film's success, perhaps – but NBC would go on to air two entirely dissimilar Holmes-related projects in 1976, both co-produced by Universal. The first of these was a comedy-drama starring Larry Hagman as a demented former motorcycle cop, convinced that he is none other than the great detective; the

second was the unlovely **Sherlock Holmes in New York**, starring Roger Moore.

Then still best-remembered as the lead in the top-rated sitcom *I Dream of Jeannie* (1965-70), Larry Hagman's worldwide fame as oil tycoon JR Ewing in *Dallas* (1978-91) was yet to come; between the two, he had been reduced to the level of an appearance in the wretched horror sequel *Beware! The Blob* (1972). His lighter-than-air but not disagreeable Holmes was hired by writer/producers Roland Kibbee and Dean Hargrove, mystery specialists who had worked together on many instalments of the hugely popular *Columbo*. *The Return of the World's Greatest Detective*, as the project was ultimately titled, would be realised in a similar style to the adventures of Peter Falk's mac-wearing supertec.

Commissioned as a pilot for an ongoing series, the 90-minute opener recycles the central premise of the 'fantasist' Holmes film **They Might Be Giants** (1971), but Hagman's happily deranged detective bears no real resemblance to the damaged Justin Playfair in the latter. The script brazenly rejects any serious analysis of the mental disorder suffered by its protagonist: we're cheerfully informed that Holmes is a 'classic case of schizophrenia', and utterly incurable. There's an odd little scene in which 'psych soc' Watson is cautioned by her superior, Spiner: 'You're supposed to help your cases cure their delusions, not encourage them! ... If he suddenly doubted he was Sherlock Holmes, would you try to persuade him he is? ... You'd better hope that never happens because if it does, you're fired!' Any darker developments along the lines hinted go unexplored in the pilot, however, which occupies itself with a plodding little mystery enlivened only by a sudden lunge into Doylean territory, when Holmes realises that a mystery villain has borrowed the plot of THE RED-HEADED LEAGUE in pursuit of loot buried at a construction site (Himmel, the manager of the coin-op laundry next door, is lured away from his premises to a useless but highly-paid job as a market researcher ... and while Himmel is absent, his newly-appointed assistant is tunnelling through to the site from the laundry's basement).

There's one good laugh to be had, where Holmes' landlady tells Watson: 'I gotta go down the drug store and get him a syringe' – to which Watson replies, 'Mrs Hudson, I think that's humouring him a little too far ...'. But, all in all, this comedy-drama is neither funny enough to amuse, nor dramatic enough to enthral. A full series was never commissioned.

The Royal Scandal

Canada 2001 TVM adaptation [A Scandal in Bohemia/The Bruce-Partington Plans] Bohemia Productions (Muse) Inc 90m colour tx 19 October 2001 Hallmark Channel [US]
w Joe Wiesenfeld *p* Irene Litinsky *d* Rodney Gibbons
cast Sherlock Holmes: **Matt Frewer** Dr Watson: **Kenneth Welsh** Irene Adler: **Liliana Komorowska** Wiggins: **Daniel Brochu** Meisener: **Seann Gallagher** Mycroft Holmes: **RH Thomson** Crown Prince: **Robin Wilcock** PC Trevor: **Alain Goulem** Cadogan West: **Jacob Richmond** Mrs Hudson: **Kathleen McAuliffe** burly #1: **Alan Legros** burly #2: **Kevin Ryder** Inspector Lestrade: **Julian Casey** Professor Morgan: **Noël Burton** Jenkins: **David Francis** Lord Hareford: **Harry Hill** Sir James Walter: **Edward Langham** BSI #1: **Aaron Hancox** BSI #2: **Sam Tevel** Timothy Carter: **Sean Devine** signalman: **Philip Spensley** chimney sweep: **Sam Holden** Countess Maria: **Una Kay** Sigismund: **Arthur Holden** officer: **Laurent Imbault** intruder #1: **Jean-Marc Bisson** intruder #2: **Sven Eriksson**

Matt Frewer's third shot at Holmes (after **The Hound of the Baskervilles**, 2000, and **The Sign of Four**, 2001) serves as notice that there is considerably more to his interpretation than a ludicrously affected tone of voice, pitched somewhere between art critic Brian Sewell and Maggie Smith's Miss Jean Brodie. Indeed, *The Royal Scandal*'s two standout moments come where he's playing it straighter than straight ...

Joe Wiesenfeld's ambitious but never entirely convincing treatment marries A Scandal in Bohemia to The Bruce-Partington Plans. Most of the former is duly replayed, from the visit of the scandal-fearing German Crown Prince to Baker Street, to Holmes' method for discerning the location of the compromising photograph held by adventuress/opera singer Irene Adler, through to the detective gazing upon a picture of the departed Irene. The latter is essayed by means of a series of tortuous contrivances leading to the revelation that Irene has been in cahoots with Holmes' brother Mycroft from the start, helping British Intelligence

pass error-strewn technical plans to the Germans via the treacherous-minded Cadogan West, whose corpse duly ends up dumped onto the roof of a Metropolitan Railway train. No secret agent Oberstein appears, however, and much of this portion of the plot becomes horribly convoluted in the telling. The point of it all is to draw Holmes into conflict with his brother. The two Holmes' showdown is worth the price of admission alone, a visibly wounded Sherlock being moved to barely controlled anger when RH Thomson's weathered and worldly Mycroft reveals the full extent of his culpability in the death of Cadogan West: 'And if in the course of your duty, I betrayed your secrets, would you also have me thrown headfirst down a flight of stairs?' It's an intriguing angle on Sherlock's under-examined relationship with his elder brother, and one well worth exploration.

Wiesenfeld's other innovation is to have Holmes and Irene previously acquainted, a flashback to a Strasbourg opera house six years earlier relating how Holmes had been used by her to escort a diamond stolen from her patron from the scene of the crime. Holmes sees her first as a diva, bringing tears to his eyes as she brings down the curtain on a production of *Magdelena*: 'I must confess, she had the most profound effect on me. That face; that voice ...' The fact that Holmes is moved to something like love by her song distances their carefully choreographed duologues from the base business of sex (or, for that matter, romance). Comparisons with the 'Singular Affair of the Russian Ballerina' portion of **The Private Life of Sherlock Holmes** are almost merited. (Almost.)

As for the remainder, Kenneth Welsh's Watson gets a few decent moments – and, in contradicting police surgeon Professor Morgan's findings at the autopsy of Cadogan West ('I'm afraid the facts do not support your hypothesis ...'), he even manages a draw a nicely underplayed nod of approval from Holmes. The pair also encounter Inspector Lestrade for the first time – who, in a pleasing move aside from the Dennis Hoey stereotype of a practical Plod, is presented as a diminutive keener barely out of short trousers. 'Well, that was certainly a change,' remarks Watson, 'A Scotland Yard inspector who's honoured to meet Sherlock Holmes!' 'Yes,' muses Holmes, 'he's obviously new ...'

The Royal Scandal was succeeded by **The Case of the Whitechapel Vampire**.

Sangerindens Diamanter

tr 'The singer's diamonds'
aka **The Theft of the Diamonds** [US]
Denmark 1909 pastiche Nordisk Films Kompagni
591 feet bw silent
wd **Viggo Larsen**
known cast Sherlock Holmes: **Viggo Larsen**

Dissolute heir John Baxter is shown a diamond bracelet that his uncle intends to give a noted opera diva. He breaks into the singer's dressing room but cannot find the bracelet, and instead follows the singer home. He uses a rope to gain entrance to the singer's house, but is spotted; thinking that Baxter has not seen her, the singer telephones Sherlock Holmes, who hears only a scream at the end of the line as Baxter knocks her down and seizes the bracelet. Holmes traces the call, drives to the house, climbs the rope and arrests Baxter after a rooftop chase.

With *Sangerindens Diamanter*, writer/director Viggo Larsen reclaimed the mantle of Holmes from Einar Zangenberg, who'd appeared in its altogether more inspiring-sounding precursor, **Det Hemmelige Dokument**. Released in Denmark in January 1909, it wasn't until March 1910 that this, the fourth in the Nordisk series, finally reached the US – where its two successors, **Droske Nr. 519** and **Den Grå Dame**, had played during the previous year. Supplied in the States as a split reel with another Nordisk short, *A Quiet Honeymoon*, here *Moving Picture World* hailed acting so 'sympathetic' that 'the audience becomes absorbed in the picture and regrets when it closes'.

The Scarlet Claw

US 1944 pastiche Universal Pictures Company Inc
74m bw
w **Edmund L Hartmann**, **Roy William Neill** *story* **Paul Gangelin**, **Brenda Weisberg** *pd* **Roy William Neill**

cast Sherlock Holmes: **Basil Rathbone** Dr Watson: **Nigel Bruce** Potts, Tanner, Ramson: **Gerald Hamer** Lord Penrose: **Paul Cavanagh** Emile Journet: **Arthur Hohl** Judge Brisson: **Miles Mander** Marie Journet: **Kay Harding** Sergeant Thompson: **David Clyde** Drake: **Ian Wolfe** Nora: **Victoria Horne** storekeeper: **Harry Allen*** Lady Penrose: **Gertrude Astor*** attendant: **Al Ferguson*** Inspector: **Clyde Fillmore*** Sir John: **Charles Francis*** hotel clerk: **Olaf Hytten*** Father Pierre: **George Kirby*** Assistant Inspector: **Charles Knight*** page boy: **Norbert Muller*** cab driver: **Frank O'Connor*** Trent: **Peter Sosso*** musician: **Tony Travers*** night clerk: **Eric Wilton***

THE MYSTERY
In La Morte Rouge, a remote village in Canada, the unexpected tolling of the church bell alerts Father Pierre to a grisly discovery in his nave... Sherlock Holmes and Dr Watson, meanwhile, are in Quebec, attending a meeting of the Royal Canadian Occult Society where La Morte Rouge resident Lord Penrose describes supposedly supernatural occurrences in the vicinity. A century before, a monster is said to have slain three villagers, tearing out their throats – and now a number of sheep have been found with their gullets ripped. Holmes is sceptical, but the meeting is abruptly ended when Penrose receives a telegram informing him that his wife has been found dead in the church... her throat slashed. Penrose spurns Holmes' offer of assistance, but the next morning Holmes receives a letter written by Lady Penrose before her death, telling him of the mortal dread she feels – and summoning him to the town.

THE INVESTIGATION
At Penrose Manor, Holmes identifies 'Lady Penrose' as Lilian Gentry, a noted actress who unexpectedly retired from the stage five years previously. Meeting the local police, Holmes speculates that the 'claw' that slew Gentry might have been a five-pronged garden weeder. Holmes and Watson set up base at the hotel-café run by the recently arrived Emile Journet and his young daughter Marie. That night, while Watson attempts

Holmes (Basil Rathbone) and Watson (Nigel Bruce) face up to the Gothic horrors of La Morte Rouge in **The Scarlet Claw** *(1944)*

to interview the locals, including postman Potts, Holmes sneaks out to survey the marshland where Lady Penrose was killed – and is pursued by an ethereally glowing 'spectre' which leaves behind a shred of cloth soaked in phosphorous. The fabric comes from a shirt belonging to the paranoid Judge Brisson, a retired magistrate who lives a hermit-like existence. Brisson confirms that the worn shirt was given to Tanner, an itinerant labourer who sometimes stays in a derelict hotel nearby. There, Holmes and Watson confront Tanner, but he escapes through a window into the river...

THE SOLUTION

Among Tanner's belongings, they find one half of a publicity picture of Lilian Gentry, signed 'To Alastair Ramson – a great actor'. From Penrose, Holmes learns that Ramson had been in Gentry's last theatre company; obsessed with the actress, he had killed a rival and precipitated her retirement. Holmes realises that Ramson, who has since escaped from prison, will next target Brisson, the man who sentenced him. They arrive too late. The last to be killed will be Journet, formerly Ramson's prison guard – but Journet has gone into hiding,

and Holmes, who has deduced that Ramson must have another personality under which he mingles freely with the villagers, finds that Ramson has killed Marie instead. Holmes and Watson make their imminent departure known, but Holmes disguises himself as Journet to lure Ramson into action. The ploy succeeds; postman Potts is the killer's other identity. The police pursue Ramson across the marshes, where he meets his end at the hands of Journet... and that seemingly innocuous five-pronged garden weeder.

✦ ✦ ✦

The antithesis of the previous film in Universal's Holmes sequence, the breathlessly playful **The Spider Woman**, *The Scarlet Claw* is a doomy mood piece owing much to THE HOUND OF THE BASKERVILLES: a remote marshland setting; a painted-phosphorescent but thought-supernatural terror; an escaped convict on the loose; a cold killer ingratiating himself with everyone in the vicinity; a subplot involving cast-off clothing; plus, of course, Holmes' method of unmasking the murderer, making to return home but actually remaining behind to catch the villain red-handed (or, indeed, scarlet-clawed).

Holmes (Basil Rathbone) helps Watson (Nigel Bruce) recover from a dunking in the marshes of La Morte Rouge in **The Scarlet Claw** (1945)

Dourness, sobriety and lack of invention (except in the name of the village, which suggests that at least one of the four credited writers was familiar with the works of Edgar Allan Poe) have led *The Scarlet Claw* to acquire a reputation among Holmes fans as the best of Universal's Basil Rathbone pictures, but it's quite atypical of the series – an exception, yes, but hardly exceptional. To praise its grim credibility is to overlook the absurdity of its central premise: that the only three people in the world whom cracked actor Alastair Ramson wants dead have, quite independently, chosen to settle in the same tiny hamlet. As with **Sherlock Holmes Faces Death**, 'uncanny' plot threads are left dangling – the bell that tolls for Holmes when he sees the glowing 'monster' in the marshes, for example – and it's never explicitly stated that Ramson has been ripping sheep in order to establish an ambience of dread. But at least Holmes is made to seem rightly sceptical from the very first.

That said, *The Scarlet Claw* is a very fair approximation of a psycho-thriller; it's amusing to note that Ramson, who's based in a tumbledown hotel, drags up as a dowdy, bewigged spinster in order to slaughter Judge Brisson 16 years before

Anthony Perkins' Norman Bates went on the rampage in his mother's best frock. Ramson's entirely gratuitous killing of young Marie Journet gives the last few scenes a jarringly horrible kick, and Holmes' appalled response – 'Poor innocent little child. I should have prevented this' – is memorable. Welshman Gerald Hamer (1886-1972), who'd played hapless courier Pettibone in **Sherlock Holmes in Washington** and traumatised ex-POW Major Langford in **Sherlock Holmes Faces Death**, is consistently impressive as the various identities of the rodent-faced Ramson, particularly in his confrontation with Holmes in the darkened upper room of the De La Porte hotel.

The mostly unsympathetic supporting characters – the sham-crippled Brisson, the cold and lofty Penrose and the gruff child-beater Journet – are portrayed with enough relish to distinguish themselves from the Gothic *mise-en-scène*, inspiring in the viewer precisely the same distaste registered on the face of Nigel Bruce's Watson as he first casts his eye over a saloonful of the snaggle-toothed inbreds who populate La Morte Rouge. The murky ambience appears, in fact, to go to Watson's head, leading the doctor to complain bitterly about

Holmes' treatment of him to the local police sergeant ('It's very unfair of him, keeping me in suspense like this. He knows how worried I become. He continues to do it. And do you know why? He actually enjoys making me miserable!'), and snapping at those who dare consider him merely Holmes' dogsbody ('I'm not his assistant!').

Beginning life, oddly enough, as another Holmes-versus-Moriarty story by writers Paul Gangelin and Brenda Weisberg, the piece was reworked under the title *Sherlock Holmes in Canada* by **Sherlock Holmes and the Secret Weapon** co-writer Edmund L Hartmann in association with series producer Roy William Neill and the unacknowledged Tom McKnight. Shot over 19 days beginning in January 1944, *The Scarlet Claw* enjoyed, untypically, a small amount of location filming at Nagana Rocks, California; a 'special photography' credit was arranged for John P Fulton, who supervised the of-their-time 'glowing monster' sequences. As with **Sherlock Holmes in Washington**, Rathbone's Holmes ends the film with a piece of rousing Winston Churchill oratory – this time a eulogy to Canada ('the link that joins together these great branches of the human family'), extracted from a speech given at a lunch in honour of Canadian Prime Minister Mackenzie King at London's Mansion House on 4 September 1941.

A few good notices notwithstanding, *The Scarlet Claw* earned some scathing reviews on its release in May 1944. Howard Barnes of the *New York Herald Tribune* called it 'a generally dreary pipe-dream ... When Holmes bores one and Watson is not even faintly amusing, it is high time to switch to something more substantial in the way of melodrama.' He continued: 'the others in the cast try hard, but unsuccessfully, to get some animate drama out in front of the conventional background of fog and haunted houses. It is time, I think, that the whole cycle should be dropped.' The cycle could not, however, be stopped: by now, **The Pearl of Death**, the first in Universal's third block of Holmes pictures, had already wrapped.

The Seven-Per-Cent Solution

US 1976 pastiche Universal Pictures 113m colour
w **Nicholas Meyer** executive p **Arlene Sellers, Alex Winitsky**
pd **Herbert Ross**

cast Sigmund Freud: **Alan Arkin** Lola Deveraux: **Vanessa Redgrave** Dr Watson: **Robert Duvall** Sherlock Holmes: **Nicol Williamson** Prof Moriarty: **Laurence Olivier** Lowenstein: **Joel Grey** Mary Watson: **Samantha Eggar** Baron von Leinsdorf: **Jeremy Kemp** Mycroft Holmes: **Charles Gray** Mrs Freud: **Georgia Brown** Madame: **Régine** Freda: **Anna Quayle** Mrs Holmes: **Jill Townsend** Berger: **John Bird** Mrs Hudson: **Alison Leggatt** Marker: **Frederick Jaeger** butler [Jenkins]: **Erik Chitty** Dr Schultz: **Jack May** Pasha: **Gertan Klauber** Squire Holmes: **Leon Greene** young Holmes: **Michael Blagdon** young Freud: **Ashley House** nun: **Sheila Shand Gibbs** station master: **Erich Padalewski** train engineer: **John Hill** Toby: **Midas***

THE MYSTERY

Spring 1891. In the throes of cocaine-induced delusions, Sherlock Holmes is persecuting his timid old maths tutor, Professor Moriarty, convinced that he is a criminal mastermind. Dr Watson and Holmes' brother Mycroft concoct a false 'Moriarty' trail which leads the demented Holmes to the Vienna surgery of Sigmund Freud. Having undergone treatment, Holmes accompanies Freud on a visit to another of his patients, the flame-haired actress Lola Deveraux, who claims to have been kidnapped and force-fed drugs to keep her compliant.

*Dr Watson (Robert Duvall) steps out in **The Seven-Per-Cent Solution** (1976)*

THE INVESTIGATION

On the trail of a weasely suspect called Lowenstein, Holmes, Watson and Freud realise too late that they have been decoyed away while Lola is abducted a second time. They follow a trail of white lilies and, in a high-class brothel, discover the corpse of the nun who was nursing Lola. Together, Freud and Holmes deduce that the culprit is the odious Baron von Leinsdorf, who has agreed to supply Lola to the Turkish Pasha in exchange for settling the Baron's gambling debts.

THE SOLUTION

In pursuit of von Leinsdorf, Holmes hijacks a steam train and impales the Baron in a duel. Lola is restored, while Freud finally solves the mystery of Holmes' obsession: as a small boy, he witnessed his father's murder of his mother when she was caught *in flagrante* with Moriarty. Holmes elects to stay behind in Europe, assuming the guise of itinerant musician Sigerson, and urges Watson to account for his absence in any way he wishes.

✦ ✦ ✦

In 1974, Nicholas Meyer's novel, *The Seven-Per-Cent Solution*, earned rave reviews and became a surprise Number One bestseller. With its witty attempt to provide the 'true' story behind Holmes'

three-year disappearance – a story 'bowdlerised' by Watson in THE FINAL PROBLEM – it caused a degree of controversy among committed Holmes aficionados, particularly for its modish emphasis on Holmes' cocaine dependency. It nevertheless initiated a trend for elaborate Holmes pastiches supposedly found among the late John Watson's unpublished papers.

Universal's film version went into production on 29 September 1975, the schedule divided between Pinewood and Vienna, with former dancer-cum-choreographer Herbert Ross (1927-2001) at the helm. 'The problem of the film is that the principal characters are of mythical proportions,' Ross explained. 'I had to have strong actors who never succumb to posturing; there must be no preconceived Rathbone ideas. Yet at the same time we must go for style and a touch of theatricality. Probably that is what persuaded me to go for a primarily British cast ... The model, if we want to find a model, could be *Around the World in 80 Days*. It's a movie Nick Meyer likes a great deal and I do too. I want to see Holmes a little soft, a little quizzical, a bit like Leslie Howard.'

As Holmes, Ross cast Nicol Williamson, a giant of the Royal Shakespeare Company who had previously been offered the lead in **The Private Life of Sherlock Holmes**. 'I'd been offered Holmes

Primal scream: Holmes' mother (Jill Townsend) is murdered while in bed with her lover, Professor Moriarty (Laurence Olivier), in **The Seven-Per-Cent Solution** *(1976)*

Holmes (Nicol Williamson) and Watson (Robert Duvall) consult psychoanalyst Sigmund Freud (Alan Arkin) in **The Seven-Per-Cent Solution** (1976)

before, by Billy Wilder,' Williamson confirmed, 'but I turned it down because the character seemed too corny. This Holmes is different: below the surface there is a fractured little boy chasing after a butterfly.'

Blond and conspicuously non-aquiline, Williamson does indeed resemble the ill-fated matinée idol Leslie Howard – whose son Ronald, coincidentally, had played Holmes in Sheldon Reynolds' 1954 TV series, **Sherlock Holmes**. Williamson's Holmes is convincingly demented in the earlier part of the film, 'analysing' Sigmund Freud to the manner born ('a private study is an ideal place for observing facets of a man's character') but betraying his unbalanced condition by a twitchy display of hand-wringing and thumb-twiddling as he does so. The cold turkey sequences, in which Holmes achieves a precarious freedom from 'the fiendish coils of drug addiction', are handled in straightforward Grand Guignol style (a slavering Baskerville hound lurks in the wardrobe, the snake from THE SPECKLED BAND slithers down the bell-pull), and are succeeded by a touching apology from Holmes for calling the war-wounded Watson an 'insufferable cripple'.

We're presented, as per Williamson's prescription, with 'a living man to whom things are happening, not just a hat and a pipe'. But the things that happen subsequently aren't happily integrated with the first half of the film. Holmes' grovelling need for further hypnosis just when the game is (finally) afoot creates some suspenseful moments (notably when Freud, Watson and Holmes are assailed by a team of six white stallions in a Vienna riding school), but none of them can disguise the fact that the Lola Deveraux intrigue, as David Castell put it in *Films Illustrated*, is 'a piffling trifle that PC Dixon could have solved without leaving Dock Green.' And the climactic train chase, lifted in part from the Marx Brothers' *Go West* (1940), is done with a swashbuckling brio that seems to come out of nowhere.

If *The Seven-Per-Cent Solution* is a film of two distinct halves, it merely follows the book upon which it's based. Though omitting to fix this structural discrepancy, screenwriter Nicholas Meyer took considerable liberties with his own novel elsewhere, ditching a great deal of expository detail, altering the villainous von Leinsdorf's age, occupation and motivation, and revealing Moriarty as the man who cuckolded Holmes' father, rather than just the man who let him know about Mrs Holmes' extramarital dalliance. This makes for a satisfactory 'primal scene' conclusion, as Freud coaxes the images from Holmes' subconscious and Laurence Olivier's haunted Moriarty scuttles half-dressed from Mrs Holmes' blood-drenched bed.

The presence of Olivier in the relatively small Moriarty role is an indication of the deluxe treatment lavished on the film, ranging from Alan Arkin's wonderfully relaxed turn as Freud to meticulously detailed, yellow-suffused sets designed by Ken Adam. Two actors later to feature in Granada's Jeremy Brett sequence, starting with **The Adventures of Sherlock Holmes** in 1984, also put in appearances: Charles Gray as a suitably massive Mycroft (he would play the same role opposite Brett) and Jeremy Kemp, whose von Leinsdorf is just as loathsome as his later Dr Roylott in Granada's version of THE SPECKLED BAND. Meyer's scraps of incidental pastiche are consistently engaging, too, as when Watson enlists the olfactory talents of Toby, acknowledging the dog's role in THE SIGN OF THE FOUR but also letting on that 'More recently, Holmes had employed Toby to trace an orang-utan through the sewers of Marseille.' It's also tempting to interpret the Pasha's Titian-haired harem as a kinky nod to THE RED-HEADED LEAGUE.

The film's most conspicuous flaw remains the casting of American actor Robert Duvall, fresh from *The Godfather Part II*, as Watson. Having turned down the Chief Brody role in *Jaws*, Duvall was particularly keen for *The Seven-Per-Cent Solution* to do well. 'Watson is too often played as a bumbling buffoon,' he pontificated. 'I want to emphasise the solid decency of the man, the loyalty to his friend.' Duvall does this well enough, but saddles Watson with a strangulated English accent (apparently modelled on the famous conductor Sir Adrian Boult) that has to be heard to be believed. *Films and Filming* compared these excruciating sounds to those of 'some badly programmed computer', while John Coleman in the *New Statesman* wrote off Duvall's performance with the phrase, 'I feah the fawg hez delayed arse.'

The film opened in the US on 24 October 1976, appearing in the UK the following May. Pauline Kael's encouraging assessment in the *New Yorker* ('Movies don't often splurge on such a clever idea,

and it's very pleasurable to see the casting and the details brought off without stinting') was not echoed by British critics. 'A turgid concoction which draws no life from the Holmes/Freud confrontation and seems particularly ill-plotted,' said the *Times*. 'The tale drags on for reel after reel before we cotton on to the fact that it is meant to be funny,' added the *Daily Telegraph*, and the *Sunday Times* concluded that 'the basic conflicts in Conan Doyle's original dissipate into whimsy, cuteness and slow, period-laden self-indulgence.'

The film failed to achieve the kind of box-office takings Universal had in mind, putting paid to a proposed film version of Meyer's second Holmes pastiche, *The West End Horror* (1976). The film's uncertainty of tone had seemingly caught cinemagoers on the hop; was this a straight 1890s melodrama or a sly send-up? Meyer himself summed up the problem in its simplest terms when he pointed out that 'It was not a Sherlock Holmes movie. It was a movie about Sherlock Holmes. Not the same thing.' (JR)

Sherlock

aka Sherlock: Case of Evil [DVD release]
GB/Switzerland 2002 TVM pastiche Box Film (Baker Street) Ltd/Pueblo Film AG 91m colour
tx 25 October 2002 USA Network [US]

w/co-p **Piers Ashworth** p **Tim Bradley** d **Graham Theakston** cast Sherlock Holmes: **James D'Arcy** Dr Watson: **Roger Morlidge** Rebecca Doyle: **Gabrielle Anwar** Moriarty: **Vincent D'Onofrio** Inspector Lestrade: **Nicholas Gecks** Henry Coot: **Peter-Hugo Daly** Mycroft: **Richard E Grant** Ben Harrington: **Struan Rodger** Sergeant Cox: **Mihai Bisericanu** Dr Cruickshank: **Mihai Gruia Sandu** captor #1: **Costi Barbulescu** captor #2: **Doru Dumitrescu** Goldie Duggan: **Constantin Vasilescu** Chinese proprietor: **Corneliu Tigancu** Anna: **Fritha Goodey** Victoria: **Ioana Abur** pretty young hopeful: **Natalie Ester** debutante #1: **Oana Ardelean** debutante #2: **Cristina Teodorescu** burlesque girl: **Andreea Balan** theatre manager: **Mihai Dinvale** young Holmes: **Stefan Veronca** killer: **Valentin Popescu** pianist: **Radu Captari** nurse: **Anca Androne*** surgeon: **Adrian Huluban***

THE MYSTERY

October 1886: following a case commissioned by the widowed Lady Isabella De Winter, youthful private detective Sherlock Holmes becomes publicly feted after shooting England's most wanted man, multiple murderer Professor Moriarty, through the heart. Although no body is found, Holmes' new-found celebrity leads him to be visited by opium importer Ben Harrington, who fears he may yet become the next victim in a series of gangland slayings related to his illicit trade. Holmes first meets mortuary technician Dr Watson, who is conducting an autopsy on an earlier victim of the so-called 'Opium Wars'. Together, they lead police inspector Lestrade to the killer: a pint-sized, hook-handed, Afghan war veteran named Dr Cruickshank, who appears to have committed suicide.

THE INVESTIGATION

Acting on impulse, Holmes persuades Watson to cut up Cruickshank's corpse. After discovering the victim's brain to be suffused with an unknown alkaloid, and learning that Harrington, too, is dead, Holmes realises that he has been fooled. In the course of an alcoholic bender, Holmes divines the hand of Moriarty by seeing a figure 'M' in the various puncture-marks in Harrington's arm. Still alive, the Professor had used Holmes to 'kill' him, thus giving him an alibi for some criminal venture – but what? Watson takes Holmes to visit the detective's elder brother, Mycroft, crippled after an earlier encounter with Moriarty – and it is Mycroft who puts Holmes on the trail of the bogus 'Isabella De Winter', the girl who first lured Holmes into Moriarty's charade. Holmes identifies her as a Whitechapel actress named Rebecca Doyle, saving her from a Moriarty assassin and taking her to his Baker Street flat. Moriarty kidnaps Holmes, injecting him with massive doses of a morphine derivative of his own recipe – heroin, with which he intends to dominate the drugs trade.

THE SOLUTION

The addled Holmes escapes, and is helped through the process of withdrawal by Rebecca, with whom he begins having sex. Cured, Holmes leads Lestrade to make an armed raid of Moriarty's headquarters – but the Professor has gone to Baker Street, to kidnap Rebecca. Holmes follows them into the under-construction tunnels of London's Underground railway, where Moriarty forces Holmes to witness his cold-blooded murder

of the girl. Above ground, the pair fight a final battle inside the clock-face of Big Ben, where Holmes thrusts a blade into Moriarty's heart, slaying the villain at last.

✦ ✦ ✦

'Forget all the clichés you've been used to in Sherlock Holmes stories and movies,' claimed the PR guff for *Sherlock*, 'this is where the legend begins. The famous detective is not the mature hero and flawless detective depicted by Sir Arthur Conan Doyle ...' Too damn right, he's not. Leaving aside some neophiliac hypemonger's efforts to excite interest in a Sherlock Holmes TV movie by claiming it contains nothing recognisable as Sherlock Holmes – a unique selling point, yes, but what a monumentally inane strategy! – we find *Sherlock*, sometimes given the lumpen subtitle *Case of Evil* (bringing to mind a Pandora's box of some description, although no such McGuffin is involved) to be little more than a bad photocopy of **Young Sherlock Holmes** sexed up with lashings of absinthe, slices of eviscerated brain and an ever-priapic lead in dire need of a very cold shower. The similarities are obvious: both purport to detail the first meeting of Holmes and Watson; both see Holmes engaged in hitherto unreported confrontation with Professor Moriarty; both see Holmes falling victim to a grim narcotic, bringing forth hallucinogenic sequences; in both, Holmes's lady-love is shot dead by Moriarty before he and Holmes settle their quarrel in a vicious swordfight; and both would seem to assert that these experiences would leave Holmes incapable of love. (Not that there are no other precedents to set against *Sherlock*: something is surely very wrong when the exact manner of Moriarty's demise – plummeting to his doom through the shattered face of Big Ben – was done first, and better, in **The Great Mouse Detective**.)

Oh – but forget all the clichés you've been used to, *Sherlock* has got all of the following, too: Watson, an occasional inventor and frequent Cassandra, sawing open murder victims' skulls and slicing cerebella like paté; a baby-faced Holmes who hangs about at society balls, where he brags to adoring debutantes about killing Moriarty; a Mycroft who (for no stated reason), was injected with an unidentified substance by Moriarty an unknown number of years before, which (for no good reason) left him a calliper-legged cripple on walking sticks; a Moriarty who chooses the title 'drug baron' for himself; a script riddled with anachronisms ('drug dealer' and the 'street name' for an illegal narcotic; not to mention 'serial killer', 'Health Service', 'clinical trials', 'reckless driving' and traffic 'congestion'); plus a lengthy set-piece in which Holmes, frustrated by his inability to penetrate the mystery, downs a bottle of gin and a bottle of claret, hits the town for a bottle of absinthe, then collects three more bottles to share with two wide-eyed groupies, with whom he proceeds to enjoy a threesome beneath his Baker Street mantel.

Sauce makes this stodgy Euro-pudding, filmed on location in Bucharest and at the Castel Film Studios, Romania, between 5 November and 16 December 2001, no more digestible – and that's without the mountainous cheese-board brought to the table by Vincent D'Onofrio's stovepipe-hatted Moriarty, all thuggish Bill Sikes swagger. The arrival of Richard E Grant (soon to be a Moriarty-quoting Stapleton in the BBC's third **Hound of the Baskervilles**, 2002) as Mycroft may be no more than a sop to traditionalists, but where he and Sherlock paraphrase their GREEK INTERPRETER game, each outdoing the other with ever-more-outlandish deductions about passers-by, one is given a sole, slight indication that writer/co-producer Piers Ashworth enjoys anything more than a layman's knowledge of Sherlockian lore. It's not that it's *wrong* to seek to strip an icon of redundant baggage – but for the whole of its length, the self-important *Sherlock* doesn't once suggest just what these 'clichés' are it's rebelling against, still less arrive at any viable alternatives.

Sherlock Holmes

US 1916 pastiche Essanay Film Mfg Co 7 reels bw silent
w **H S Sheldon** source **Sherlock Holmes** [play by **William Gillette**] d **Arthur Berthelot**
cast Sherlock Holmes: **William Gillette** Alice Faulkner: **Marjorie Kay** Professor Moriarty: **Ernest Maupain** Dr Watson: **Edward Fielding** Benjamin Forman: **Stewart Robbins** Sir Edward Leighton: **Hugh Thompson** Count von Stalburg: **Ludwig Kreiss** James Larrabee: **Mario Majeroni** Sidney Prince: **William Postance** Craigin: **Chester Beery** Tim Leary: **Frank Hamilton** 'Lightfoot' McTague:

Fred Malatesta Madge Larrabee: **Grace Reals** Theresa: **Miss [Leona] Ball** Billy: **Burford Hampden** a suffragette: **Marion Skinner**

'The story of Alice Faulkner and the papers she holds relating to some Prince of Royal Blood, the blackmailer Larrabee, and the great criminal Moriarty, Sherlock Holmes and his faithful followers, Billy and Dr Watson, have become such familiar figures as almost to lose the charm of novelty,' noted the *Bioscope* on the occasion of the British release of the film version of *Sherlock Holmes: A Drama in Four Acts*, the play so crucial to the development of Sherlock Holmes on film.

As the 19th century drew to a close, Connecticut-born William Gillette (1853-1937) had become one of the most prominent actor-managers of his generation. Nominated (apparently) by Doyle as the author's ideal theatrical Holmes – and urged on by his manager, impresario Charles Frohman – late in 1898 Gillette found himself sitting down to write a play inspired by Doyle's characters, later receiving from Holmes' creator a telegram telling him he might 'marry the detective, or murder him, or do anything he pleased with him'.

Gillette's script, which drew primarily upon A SCANDAL IN BOHEMIA and THE FINAL PROBLEM, related the tale of young Alice Faulkner, who has come into possession of various letters belonging to her dead sister which might disgrace a prominent VIP. She is incarcerated by the Larrabees, married associates of the scheming Professor Moriarty, who is desperate to have these documents for himself. Holmes, who has become progressively more enamoured of Alice, confronts Moriarty first at 221B Baker Street and later in a Stepney gas-chamber, where the Professor's henchmen fail to execute him. After Holmes' rooms have been burned down at Moriarty's instigation, Holmes repairs to Dr Watson's consulting-room in Kensington, where he finally ensnares the Professor... and gets the girl.

The play opened at the Star Theatre, Buffalo on 23 October 1899, transferring to the Garrick, New York on 6 November, where it ran until June the following year. Its impact cannot be overestimated. Gillette himself took the show to the Lyceum, London, between September 1901 and April 1902 (the performance of 1 February being attended by King Edward VII), returning to England in 1905 (where, at the Duke of York's Theatre, the 15-year-old Charles Chaplin took the role of pageboy Billy) and again, briefly, in 1910.

Versions of the play ran in Oslo, Stockholm and Gothenburg (all in 1902), Malmo (1905), Munich (1906) and Paris (1907). It became a touchstone for the fledgling filmmakers of the Scandinavian countries; in Copenhagen, the Nordisk Films Kompagni ran out two-reelers featuring Moriarty, Billy, and scenes set in 'gas-cellars' (see **Sherlock Holmes i Livsfare** etc). Gillette even gave the world the now-obligatory curved Meerschaum pipe and a painfully familiar expression based on the line, 'Oh, this is elementary, my dear Watson!'

Given the sheer volume of Sherlock Holmes film production in the 1910s, it was inevitable that Gillette would be asked to lend his features to a cinematic Holmes – and, sure enough, rights in the play were picked up by Essanay, an outfit founded by George K Spoor and actor 'Broncho Billy' Anderson (Gilbert Maxwell Aronson, 1880-1971). Essanay ('S and A', after the bosses' initials) had started out as a producer of Westerns, but by 1915 – with a new studio set-up at Niles, California – had diversified into other areas (including comedy, finding a star in the now-adult 'Charlie' Chaplin and his new-found Tramp persona). The partnership of screenwriter H S Sheldon (1877-1925) and director Arthur Berthelet (1879-1949) would be exercised not only on *Sherlock Holmes* but also on two other Essanay productions that year, *The Havoc* and *The Misleading Lady*.

Not long before shooting Essanay's film, Gillette – who first claimed to have retired from the role in 1910 – had been engaged in yet another New York production, this time at the Empire Theatre between 11 October and 6 November 1915. Several members of this latest company were asked to join him on the film, including Edward Fielding (1875-1945) as Watson, Stewart Robbins as Benjamin Forman, Burford Hampden as Billy and Grace Reals as Madge Larrabee. French actor Ernest Maupain (c 1881-1949), who had appeared in Essanay's quasi-biographical Edgar Allan Poe adaptation *The Raven* (1915), would see his Moriarty lauded in the pages of *Moving Picture World* following *Sherlock Holmes*' release on 15 May 1916: 'Mr Gillette never had a stronger opposite.'

British release, however, was delayed by over a year, by which time Essanay was bankrupt. The

Actor/writer William Gillette distilled his famous stage play into the Essanay feature **Sherlock Holmes** *(1916)*

Bioscope was unimpressed. 'It is perhaps not quite so fortunate,' ran its review, 'that the action of the play should in some respects date back to 15 years, almost as much as the costumes and the hansom-cabs. To tell the truth, there is much of it which seems a little old-fashioned at the present time, when every week we get some new and original crook drama, thoroughly up to date, and each with some new and original sensation which has never been exploited before.' Its harshest words were reserved for Gillette, 63 years old at the time of the film's production: 'It is rather curious to note that an actor who has made his reputation to so great an extent by the quietness and restraint of his methods should appear a little hurried and spasmodic when seen through the medium of the camera...'

Despite noting the 'large gathering' of Scottish patrons at the film's Sauciehall Street showings, the paper only identified the reason for its dissatisfaction two weeks later, in an early example of a complaint common to the next 85 years of Holmes film reviews: 'It presents Sherlock Holmes, not as he is generally known, but in a different light ... as a photo-play depicting the character created by Sir Arthur Conan Doyle and popularised through the *Strand Magazine* ... it falls far short of the ideal which will be, and rightly so, expected by the public.'

Gillette would continue to revive the play well into his seventies, his 'Farewell Tour' lasting from 1929 to 1932. (Burford Hampden was still playing Billy the teenage pageboy at the time of Gillette's last performance.) Even at the age of 82, Gillette wasn't quite finished with Holmes. Having already played the lead in the first ever Sherlockian radio dramatisation (of THE SPECKLED BAND, broadcast by NBC on 20 October 1930), he summoned up enough of the old spirit to read some of his now 36-year-old lines for WABC's *Lux Radio Theatre* on 18 November 1935. Gillette's playscript would continue to be performed well after his death in 1937 and was filmed four more times – excitingly, in 1922, with John Barrymore; loosely, in 1932, as **Conan Doyle's Master Detective Sherlock Holmes**; unrecognisably, in 1939, as **The Adventures of Sherlock Holmes**; and diligently, in 1981, with Frank Langella. But the Essanay version is long since lost, and with it, one supposes, any permanent record of Gillette's portrayal.

There's a sense, however, that Gillette's Holmes will be with us always; there's something immortal about the idea of the detective as hero-adventurer, Meerschaum in mouth. Something elementary.

Sherlock Holmes

aka **Moriarty** [GB]
US 1922 pastiche Goldwyn Pictures Corp [9 reels]
bw silent

w **Earle Brown, Marion Fairfax** *source* **Sherlock Holmes** [play by **William Gillette**] *p* **F J Godsol** *d* **Albert Parker**
cast Sherlock Holmes: **John Barrymore** Professor Moriarty: **Gustav von Seyffertitz** Alice Faulkner: **Carol Dempster** Dr Watson: **Roland Young** Prince Alexis: **Reginald Denny** Forman Wells: **William Powell** Madge Larrabee: **Hedda Hopper** Rose Faulkner: **Peggy Bayfield** James Larrabee: **Anders Randolf** Craigin: **Louis Wolheim** Billy: **Jerry Devine*** Otto: **Robert Fischer*** Dr Leighton: **Lumsden Hare*** Terese: **Margaret Kemp*** Sid Jones: **Percy Knight*** Alf Bassick: **Robert Schable*** Count von Stalburg: **David Torrence*** Inspector Gregson: **John Willard***

P erversely, the epic intention of what was almost certainly the most prestigious Sherlock Holmes film of the silent era is what makes it such hard work today – and at over 100 minutes,

the John Barrymore version of the William Gillette play [see above] will not be easily endured by the casual student of Sherlockian cinema.

Barrymore (John Sidney Blythe, 1882-1942) should, of course, need no introduction – the 'Great Profile' himself; the black sheep of America's foremost acting dynasty; reportedly the finest Hamlet of his generation; wilful abuser of his own talents; the man who once said, 'The good die young – because they see no point in living if they have to be good.' Etcetera. Before Sherlock Holmes, Barrymore's most renowned film personae included the 'Amateur Cracksman' in *Raffles* (1917) and both title roles in *Dr Jekyll and Mr Hyde* (1920). According to director Albert Parker (1887-1974), who'd harboured a desire to film the Gillette play ever since appearing as Sidney Prince alongside the author in an October 1910 revival of the show: 'I went to see John Barrymore in his theatre dressing-room when he was appearing on the stage ... He didn't want to do the film. I had to talk him into it. He didn't like the part, because it was such a trade mark ... In the end he said he'd do it. So immediately I took a train all the way to Chicago to see about getting the rights...'

Parker's picture was set up with the studio of the equally legendary Samuel Goldwyn (Samuel Goldfish, 1882-1974) – and the first Holmes film with a transatlantic schedule began filming in London in summer 1921. Barrymore, who joined the project in the final leg of a turbulent European vacation with his second wife, went AWOL upon landing in England; Parker eventually traced his leading man to an attic room at the Ritz, where he was found 'sitting up in bed, stoned. Gin bottles lay everywhere, even inside his shoes' (Kobler, 1977). Drunk throughout production, Barrymore's continual wrangling drove a despairing Parker to warn his star that he was killing himself – an appeal which appeared to have some (temporary) effect. 'Jack and I became great friends,' recalled Parker. 'But he was absolutely crazy, mad as a hatter, not good for himself at any time, but lovable.' The film was completed in Switzerland (the only named character seen in the Swiss sequences being Rose Faulkner, who throws herself off a mountainside after being rejected by the cruel Crown Prince Alexis) and on Goldwyn's Stateside stages.

Sherlock Holmes is not an entirely straightforward translation of Gillette's text. Opening with a

Holmes (John Barrymore) confronts an unwelcome visitor – Professor Moriarty (Gustav von Seyffertitz) – in **Sherlock Holmes** (1922)

for-its-time remarkable aerial shot of London, it first establishes Professor Moriarty – 'in whose heart the blood is as cold as a corpse' – by superimposing his mis-shapen face in the centre of a spider's web. We cut to Cambridge, where young Prince Alexis has been falsely accused of stealing Athletic Funds. Alexis' friend, Watson, recommends he seek out a fellow undergraduate, Sherlock Holmes – 'a marvel at digging out things'. Holmes, a long-limbed swain, 'whiles away his working hours in country lanes, entering philosophical observations in his notebook'; these include A STUDY IN SCARLET-like notes on his own limitations ('Politics – rotten. Chemistry – profound') and the rather more pithy enquiry, 'What is love?'

The latter is answered rather suddenly when, having fallen off the side of a house he's been climbing, a prostrate Sherlock finds himself in the arms of Alice Faulkner, sister of Alexis' fiancée. A discarded cufflink sets Holmes on the trail of the thief – one Forman Wells, who reveals himself to be a sleeping agent sent to infiltrate Cambridge academe by the master criminal Moriarty. Appalled, Holmes steals inside Moriarty's London HQ (which, with a touch of the Fu Manchus, is found behind a Chinese

shopfront in Limehouse) to confront the Professor in a dialogue that will confound any modern viewers who refuse to believe that silent film captions are, by necessity, devoid of wit. 'I merely wanted to know you a little better,' says Holmes, who claims to be just an interested student. 'Several Scotland Yard Inspectors tried that. Their lifeless bodies were found floating in the Thames,' menaces Moriarty. 'Of course if you're as difficult to know as all that,' counters Holmes, 'I'd better be getting back to my microbes...' Back at college, Holmes announces that he has found his life's vocation: 'to rid the world of that gigantic menace – Moriarty'.

The story then jumps forward several years to take up Gillette's narrative proper, following its turns more-or-less accurately to a rather fluffed finale. That said, the focus on the Professor – a top-hatted, stooped grotesque played with significant authority by the Viennese actor Gustav von Seyffertitz (1863-1943) – makes it entirely explicable why the film's British title was changed to simply *Moriarty*. As a grown-up, Barrymore's Holmes is a brooding soul, tormented by 'a world of strange complexities'. Reviewing the film in August 1922, *Motion Picture* stated that: 'If we

John
Barrymore
in
SHERLOCK
HOLMES

Directed by **Albert Parker** . *Adapted from*
William Gillette's *stage play founded on*
Sir **Conan Doyle's** *stories*

A Goldwyn Picture

The 'Great Profile' figures heavily in this poster for **Sherlock Holmes** *(1922)*

nurtured a belief in witchcraft we would believe that Barrymore transmitted the psychology of his characters to his audience by supernatural means. He sways his audience as the winds sway slender reeds.' His performance is potent and powerful still; in the scene where Holmes refuses to take the letters he's been seeking unless Alice gives them to him of her own free will, the most exquisite agonies are writ large in his *manner*, with no need for the slightest gurning of the face. It's interesting to note that Barrymore met with Constantin Stanislavski, grandfather of 'the Method', in London while working on *Sherlock Holmes*.

Thought lost for many years, the film was reconstructed in the 1970s from a muddle of rolls of negative by Kevin Brownlow (1938-), initially with Parker's help. Clearly, some material is still missing – most notably, a large enough chunk of the 'gas chamber' sequence is lost to render its unfoldment quite baffling. The plot is tangled enough as it stands, without any omissions – a fact not lost on the film's original critics. ('The story is badly handled, the continuity leaping along by fits and starts,' reckoned *Variety*.) So if those with the requisite stamina won't uncover a rare masterpiece, they will at least view an intriguing take on the detective, played with passion as a hero of romance. And those in the mood for cold, scholarly analysis may wish to compare and contrast **Young Sherlock Holmes**, made more than six decades later, with the Barrymore film – a very obvious source.

Sherlock Holmes

*US 1954-5 39 x 25m approx TV series pastiches/
adaptations Motion Pictures For Television bw
p* **Sheldon Reynolds** *assoc p* **Nicole Milinaire**
regular cast Sherlock Holmes: **Ronald Howard**
Dr Watson: **H Marion Crawford**

The Case of the Cunningham Heritage

*tx 18 October 1954 NBC
w* **Sheldon Reynolds** *d* **Jack Gage**
guest cast includes Inspector Lestrade: **Archie Duncan**
Mrs Cunningham: **Meg Lemonnier** Joan: **Ursula Howells**

Lord Stamford: **Richard Bartrop** Ralph: **Pierre Gay**

THE CASE OF LADY BERYL

tx 25 October 1954 NBC
w **Sheldon Reynolds** *d* **Jack Gage**
guest cast includes Lady Beryl: **Paulette Goddard**
Inspector Lestrade: **Archie Duncan** Lord Beryl: **Peter**
Copley Bobby: **K Richard Larke** Ross: **Duncan Elliott**

THE CASE OF THE PENNSYLVANIA GUN

tx 1 November 1954 NBC
wd **Sheldon Reynolds**
guest cast includes Macleod: **Russell Waters**
Morelle: **Maurice Teynac** Sergeant: **Frank Dexter**

THE CASE OF THE TEXAS COWGIRL

tx 8 November 1954 NBC
w **Charles and Joseph Early** *d* **Steve Previn**

THE CASE OF THE BELLIGERENT GHOST

tx 15 November 1954 NBC
w **Charles Early** *d* **Sheldon Reynolds**
guest cast includes Inspector Lestrade: **Archie Duncan**
Van Bentham: **Lou Van Burg** Maggie Blake: **Gertrude**
Flynn Bobby: **Cecil Brock**

THE CASE OF THE SHY BALLERINA

tx 22 November 1954 NBC
w **Charles Early** *d* **Sheldon Reynolds**
guest cast includes Mrs Chelton: **Natalie Schafer**

THE CASE OF THE WINTHROP LEGEND

tx 29 November 1954 NBC
w **Sheldon Reynolds** *story* **Harold Jack Bloom** *d* **Jack Gage**
guest cast includes Harvey Winthrop: **Ivan Desny**
John Winthrop: **Peter Copley** Alice: **Meg Lemonnier**
Peg: **Karen** [sic] Constable: **Charles Perry**

THE CASE OF BLIND MAN'S BLUFF

tx 6 December 1954 NBC
w **Lou Morheim** *story/d* **Sheldon Reynolds**
guest cast includes Inspector Lestrade: **Archie Duncan**
Vickers: **Eugene Deckers** Jocko Farraday: **Gregoire Aslan**
Sergeant: **Richard K Larke** Docteur Jonas [sic]: **Colin Drake**
Pitt: **Yves Brainville** barmaid: **Margaret Russell**

THE CASE OF HARRY CROCKER

tx 13 December 1954 NBC
w **Harold Jack Bloom** *d* **Sheldon Reynolds**

THE MOTHER HUBBARD CASE

tx 20 December 1954 NBC
w **Lou Morheim** *d* **Jack Gage**

THE RED HEADED LEAGUE

tx 27 December 1954 NBC
w **Lou Morheim** *d* **Sheldon Reynolds**
guest cast includes Inspector Lestrade: **Archie Duncan**
Jabez Wilson: **Alexander Gauge** Vincent Spaulding:
Eugene Deckers Duncan Ross: **Colin Drake**
Mr Merryweather: **M Seyford**

THE CASE OF THE SHOELESS ENGINEER

tx 3 January 1955 NBC
w **Harold Jack Bloom** *d* **Steve Previn**
guest cast includes Haterley: **David Oxley**

THE CASE OF THE SPLIT TICKET

tx 10 January 1955 NBC
w **Lou Morheim** *d* **Steve Previn**
guest cast includes Brian O'Casey: **Harris** [Harry] **Towb**
Belle Rogers: **Margaret Russell** Albert Snow: **Colin Drake**

THE CASE OF THE FRENCH INTERPRETER

tx 17 January 1955 NBC
w **Lou Morheim** *d* **Steve Previn**

THE CASE OF THE SINGING VIOLIN

tx 24 January 1955 NBC
w **Kay Krause** *d* **Steve Previn**
guest cast includes Betty: **Delphine Seyrig** Guy Durham:
Arnold Bell Jimmy: **Colin Mann** Dr Moreno: **Ben Omanoff**

THE CASE OF THE GREYSTONE INSCRIPTION

tx 31 January 1955 NBC
w **Gertrude and George Fass** *d* **Steve Previn**
guest cast includes Inspector Lestrade: **Archie Duncan**
John Cartwright: **Tony Wright**

THE CASE OF THE LAUGHING MUMMY

tx 7 February 1955
w **Charles and Joseph Early** *d* **Sheldon Reynolds**
guest cast includes Reggie Taunton: **Barry Mackay**
Rowena: **June Elliott** Aunt Agatha: **Lois Perkins Marechal**
Prof Caulkins: **Frederick O'Brady** Porter: **Colin Maun**

THE THISTLE KILLER

tx 14 February 1955 NBC
w **Charles and Joseph Early** *d* **Steve Previn**

THE CASE OF THE VANISHED DETECTIVE

tx 21 February 1955 NBC

w **Charles and Joseph Early** *d* **Steve Previn**

guest cast includes Inspector Lestrade: **Archie Duncan**
Wilkins: **Kenneth Richards** John Carson: **Cecil Brock**
Helene: **Judith Haviland** Judge Westlake: **Colin Drake**

THE CASE OF THE CARELESS SUFFRAGETTE

tx 28 February 1955 NBC

w **Sheldon Reynolds** *d* **Jack Gage**

guest cast includes Inspector Lestrade: **Archie Duncan**
Doreen: **Dawn Addams** Sergeant: **Kenneth Richards**
Henry: **David Thomson** Agatha: **Margaret Russell**
Boris Turgoff: **Frederick O'Brady**

THE CASE OF THE RELUCTANT CARPENTER

tx 7 March 1955 NBC

w **Gertrude and George Fass** *d* **Steve Previn**

guest cast includes Bricker: **Pierre Gay**

THE CASE OF THE DEADLY PROPHECY

tx 14 March 1955

w **Gertrude and George Fass** *d* **Sheldon Reynolds**

guest cast includes Marie Grande: **Nicole Courcel**
Docteur Dimanche: **Jacques François**
Henri Carolan: **Yves Brainville** Comte de Passevant:
Maurice Teynac Mrs Soule: **Helena Manson**
Manelli: **Robert Le Beal**

THE CASE OF THE CHRISTMAS PUDDING

tx 4 April 1955 NBC

w **George & Gertrude Fass** *d* **Steve Previn**

guest cast includes John Norton: **Eugene Deckers**
Bess Norton: **June Rodney** Warden: **Richard Watson**

THE CASE OF THE NIGHT TRAIN RIDDLE

tx 11 April 1955 NBC

w **Lou Morheim** *d* **Steve Previn**

guest cast includes Lydia: **Roberta Haynes** Paul: **James
Doran** Cecil: **Duncan Elliott** Coco: **Billy Beck**

THE CASE OF THE VIOLENT SUITOR

tx 18 April 1955 NBC

w **Lou Morheim** *d* **Steve Previn**

guest cast includes Inspector Lestrade: **Archie Duncan**
Susan Dearing: **Marie Sinclair** Jack Murdock:
E Micklewood Alex Doogle: **Brookes Kyle**
Tilda: **Rolly Bester**

THE CASE OF THE BAKER STREET NURSEMAIDS

tx 25 April 1955 NBC

w **Hamilton Keener** *d* **Sheldon Reynolds**

THE CASE OF THE PERFECT HUSBAND

tx 2 May 1955 NBC

w **Charles and Joseph Early** *d* **Steve Previn**

guest cast includes Janet Partridge: **Mary Sinclair**
Russell Partridge: **Michael Gough**

THE CASE OF THE JOLLY HANGMAN

tx 9 May 1955

w **Charles and Joseph Early** *d* **Steve Previn**

guest cast includes Inspector MacDougal: **Archie Duncan**
Jessie Hoper: **Alvys Maben** Baxter: **Philip Leaver**

THE CASE OF THE IMPOSTER MYSTERY

tx 16 May 1955 NBC

w **Roger E Garris** *d* **Steve Previn**

guest cast includes Sir Arthur Treadley: **Basil Dignam**

THE CASE OF THE EIFFEL TOWER

tx 23 May 1955

w **Roger E Garris** *d* **Steve Previn**

guest cast includes Inspector Lestrade: **Archie Duncan**
Nana de Melimar: **Martine Alexis** Gustav: **Sacha Pitoeff**
Bayard: **O'Brady** [sic]

THE CASE OF THE EXHUMED CLIENT

tx 30 May 1955 NBC

w **Charles and Joseph Early** *d* **Steve Previn**

guest cast includes Inspector Lestrade: **Archie Duncan**
Elizabeth Farnsworth: **Alvys Maben** George Farnsworth:
Alan Adair Sylvia Taylor: **Judith Haviland** Dr Reeves:
Michael Turner

THE CASE OF THE IMPROMPTU PERFORMANCE

tx 6 June 1955 NBC

w **Joe Morhaim** *d* **Steve Previn**

guest cast includes Inspector Lestrade: **Archie Duncan**
Wilkins: **Kenneth Richards** Brighton: **Patrick Shelley**
Pettyfoot: **Eugene Deckers**

THE CASE OF THE BAKER STREET BACHELORS

tx 20 June 1955 NBC

w **Roger E Garris** *story* **Joseph Victor** *d* **Steve Previn**

guest cast includes Inspector Lestrade: **Archie Duncan**

Pamela: **Alvys Maben** Edna: **Penny Portrait**
Oliver: **Duncan Elliott** Mason: **Seymour Green**

THE CASE OF THE ROYAL MURDER
tx 27 June 1955 NBC
w **Charles and Joseph Early** *d* **Steve Previn**
guest cast includes King Conrad: **Jacques Decqmine**
Princess Antonio: **Lise Dourdin** Prince Stephan:
Maurice Teynac Count Magor: **Jacques Francois**
gypsy: **Christine Paray**

THE CASE OF THE HAUNTED GAINSBOROUGH
tx 4 July 1955 NBC
w **Charles and Joseph Early** *d* **Steve Previn**
guest cast includes Malcolm MacGregan: **Archie Duncan**
Heather: **Cleo Rose** MacLeish: **John Buckmaster**
Archibald Ross: **Zach Matalon** Sam Scott: **Roger E Garris**

THE CASE OF THE NEUROTIC DETECTIVE
tx 11 July 1955 NBC
w **Lou Morheim** *d* **Steve Previn**
guest cast includes Inspector Lestrade: **Archie Duncan**
Commissioner: **Seymour Green** Jennifer Ames: **June M
Crawford** Toby Judson: **Russ Caprio** Dr A Fishblade:
Eugene Deckers young man: **James R Richman**

THE CASE OF THE UNLUCKY GAMBLER
tx 18 July 1955 NBC
w **Lou Morheim** *d* **Steve Previn**
guest cast includes Andy Fenwick: **Richard O'Sullivan**
Jack Driscoll: **Duncan Elliot** bartender: **John Buckmaster**
Briggs: **Zach Metalone** manager: **Russ Caprio**
Herbert Fenwick: **Rowland Bartrop** patron: **J Seyfort**

THE CASE OF THE DIAMOND TOOTH
tx 19 September 1955 NBC
w **Lou Morheim** *d* **Sheldon Reynolds**
guest cast includes Inspector Lestrade: **Archie Duncan**

THE CASE OF THE TYRANT'S DAUGHTER
tx 17 October 1955 NBC
w **Roger E Garris** *d* **Steve Previn**

History has not been kind to the first full series of televised Sherlock Holmes pastiches, its more whimsical moments (*The Case of the Texas Cowgirl*, *The Mother Hubbard Case*) being repeatedly recalled when its outright triumphs (*The Case of Blind Man's Bluff*, *The Case of the Deadly Prophecy*)

pass by unremarked. Associate producer Nicole Milinaire – her French accent phonetically transcribed when interviewed by the *New York Herald-Tribune* as the series aired in 1955 – was quite prepared to admit that, out of all the 39 episodes, 'we only have five stinkaires'. Fair enough; after all, the various Jeremy Brett-starring Granada-produced series of three to four decades later are not judged solely on, for example, **The Eligible Bachelor** or **The Memoirs of Sherlock Holmes:** *The Mazarin Stone*. So why should this Ronald Howard-starring, Sheldon Reynolds-produced sequence be damned simply for containing a title like *The Case of the Baker Street Nursemaids*?

The series was the brainchild of producer (and, on occasion, writer/director) Sheldon Reynolds, previously responsible for the popular espionage series *Foreign Intrigue* (1951-5). Although produced with American money for the American market, to keep production costs down *Foreign Intrigue* had been filmed in a studio in Stockholm. Reynolds' next project, *Sherlock Holmes*, would also be based in a European capital – this time Paris. Milinaire was hired to help oversee operations on the Continent. A curved, cobblestoned Baker Street exterior and a 221B interior, designed by the man who'd built the same as a Festival of Britain exhibit, stood throughout the year's filming. Some mute, oft-repeated establishing shots were filmed in and around familiar London landmarks, but very little location work would be undertaken in France (episodes including *The Case of the Deadly Prophecy* and *The Case of the Eiffel Tower* being notable exceptions). The majority of the series was directed by Steve Previn (1925-93), who'd worked with Reynolds on *Foreign Intrigue*.

Reynolds' object had been to present the Holmes of A STUDY IN SCARLET: 'I was suddenly struck by the difference between the character in that book and that of the stage and screen. Here, Holmes was a young man in his thirties, human, gifted, of a philosophic and scholastic bent, but subject to fateful mistakes which stemmed from his overeagerness and lack of experience ...' It made sense to present a younger Holmes, one easily distinguishable from that of Basil Rathbone, so strongly identified with the character in the States following the Fox/Universal features of the late thirties and early forties. The man chosen was 36-year-old Ronald Howard (1918-96), chiefly

'An exceptionally sincere young man trying to get ahead in his profession': Ronald Howard as the detective in the TV series **Sherlock Holmes** (1954-5)

known for being the son of the far more famous British actor Leslie. Ronald had begun his film career with a bit-part in *Pimpernel Smith* (1941), which his father had produced, directed and starred in; Leslie's star had overshadowed his ever since. 'In my interpretation,' claimed Ronald, 'Holmes is not an infallible, eagle-eyed, out-of-the-ordinary personality, but an exceptionally sincere young man trying to get ahead in his profession.' Unquestionably, Ronald's Holmes – often seen

slouching, his hands in his pockets – would be far more laid-back than the Rathbone model.

His Watson was Howard Marion Crawford (1914-69), who was credited 'H Marion Crawford' in the titles, presumably to avoid any double-Howard confusion. A solid, dependable cove, Crawford's Watson makes an ideal counterpoint for Ronald's sometimes winsome Holmes – and for once, the actor's insistence that his Watson would not be 'the perennial brainless bungler who provided burlesque relief' is actually borne out in the finished programmes. The 'brainless bungler' of the Reynolds series is instead Inspector Lestrade, as played by Scots actor Archie Duncan (1914-79), very much in the Dennis Hoey mould. (Bizarrely, Duncan would also play Lestrade's Glaswegian cousin, Inspector MacDougal, in *The Case of the Jolly Hangman*.) No Mrs Hudson (or similar) appeared.

The series aired via NBC-affiliated stations on Monday nights between 7.00 and 7.30 pm from October 1954. Paul Durand's rumbustious theme was first heard introducing *The Case of the Cunningham Heritage*, a début episode that takes pains to establish the slightly altered personae of Holmes and Watson by presenting their first meeting in London in 1897. (The date isn't explicitly stated, but a character is said to have been sent to prison five years earlier, in 1892.) More or less true to A STUDY IN SCARLET (the re-reading of which had made such an impression on Reynolds), the opening scenes see a military doctor named Watson, recently returned from Afghanistan, accept the recommendation of an acquaintance, Lord Stamford, and decide to share lodgings with Sherlock Holmes, a scientific researcher whom he first meets battering corpses in a hospital lab.

Holmes and Watson (who is entirely baffled by the remarkable gaps in his new friend's otherwise vast knowledge) move into 221B Baker Street together. Soon, Holmes receives a summons from Inspector Lestrade of Scotland Yard, whom Holmes occasionally helps out. A wealthy man named Peter Cunningham has been found stabbed to death at his home, and both Cunningham's mother and brother, Ralph, have accused a young woman, Joan – who, it transpires, had secretly married Cunningham one week earlier. Joan's criminal record is enough to convince Lestrade of her guilt, but Holmes and Watson later break into the house in order to prove that Ralph, who had been blackmailing his brother, had used Joan's past to deflect suspicion of murder away from himself.

Although the case of the Cunningham heritage is of very little interest in itself, this briskly efficient episode is constructed to showcase the three regulars: the earnest, somewhat gauche and thoroughly unconventional Holmes, dedicated to creating 'a revolution in criminal investigation' and happy to housebreak in the course of a case; the

semi-admiring, semi-appalled Watson, who's nonetheless prepared to use his fists to slug Holmes out of trouble; and the stolid, cigar-chewing Lestrade, a man unburdened by any great intellect whose approach to his work is summarised by Holmes as 'trying to hammer square pegs into round holes'. 'We will sit with the good Inspector,' Holmes elaborates, 'and, with the aid of our evidence, a bit of logic, and a few simple diagrams, will attempt to persuade him that night follows day and that one and one inevitably makes two.'

Subsequent episodes continue to detail Holmes' lack of patience with the police. In *The Case of Lady Beryl* (which follows on almost directly from the end of the first instalment, just a few hours having elapsed between the two), Holmes the researcher is given reason to fulminate: 'I'll have you know, Inspector Lestrade, that if the law enforcement agencies of this country were a little – an infinitesimal amount – more advanced than ancient Neolithic Man, I would not have to be doing the basic research work that will, in time, benefit these bureaux throughout the Earth!'

The third instalment, *The Case of the Pennsylvania Gun*, sees Holmes make the acquaintance of Inspector Macleod, whom he regards in an aloof and patronising manner, almost amused by his lack of imagination. This antagonism doesn't last, however; by the time of *The Case of the Eiffel Tower*, some 30 episodes down the line, Lestrade has become very much one of the gang, revelling in Holmes and Watson's various Continental carryings-on and starting a punch-up in a can-can bar. More significantly, the idea of Holmes as scientific researcher and occasional police adviser gives way all too soon to a more conventional presentation of the character as famous consulting detective, his wider enquiries rarely glimpsed – like the chemical concoction he prepares at the beginning of *The Case of the Impromptu Performance*, for instance.

Just as *The Case of the Cunningham Heritage* draws much from A STUDY IN SCARLET, *The Case of Lady Beryl* also borrows heavily, and without acknowledgment, from Doyle. Here, an Austrian agent named Carl Oberstein is found dead in the study of Foreign Office official Lord Beryl – and Lady Beryl, found with a gun in her hand, confesses to the murder. Holmes, however, is certain that Lady Beryl is lying and, after examining the crime scene, concludes that the killer was, in fact, Lord Beryl's secretary, Ross, who had promised to sell secret documents to Oberstein. Lady Beryl, first on the scene, had confessed because she believed her husband to be the guilty party. Clearly, the story takes THE SECOND STAIN, in all bar the titular device, for much of its inspiration.

The Case of the Pennsylvania Gun almost counts as a straight adaptation of *The Tragedy of Birlstone*, the first part of THE VALLEY OF FEAR. In this episode, a body is found in the study of Squire John Douglas' moated country home, Birlstone Manor; half its head is blown off and a sawn-off Pennsylvania shotgun lies close by. Inspector Macleod assumes that Douglas met his end at the hands of his house guest, Morelle, with whom Douglas had staked a gold claim in the American West 20 years previously. But Holmes realises that the body belonged to a third gold claimant: a man who, believing himself cheated by Douglas, went to kill him and ended up shot by his own gun, causing the terrified Douglas to flee.

There is, in fact, only one 'named' Doyle adaptation in the entire series – a breezily cheerful version of THE RED-HEADED LEAGUE, which we may presume was the only title that the cost-conscious Reynolds was prepared to pay for – but it's not hard to discern the ghosted outline of specific tales behind several other instalments. *The Case of the Shoeless Engineer* (THE ENGINEER'S THUMB) and *The Case of the French Interpreter* (THE GREEK INTERPRETER) are self-evident. *The Case of the Winthrop Legend* concerns members of an old family reputed to find silver coins about their person in advance of a violent death – not dissimilar to the circumstances of the Openshaws in THE FIVE ORANGE PIPS. *The Case of the Christmas Pudding* reprises THE EMPTY HOUSE, perhaps by way of THE MAZARIN STONE and William Gillette's stage play, *Sherlock Holmes*. Here, condemned murderer Henry Norton escapes Newgate Prison by means of a Christmas pudding parcelled up with string coated in diamond dust. Disguised as a policeman, he enters Holmes' rooms and fires a round of bullets into a dummy of the detective.

The Case of the Violent Suitor – concerning a newspaper agony aunt who falls foul of one Jack Murdock, the insanely jealous fiancé of one of his correspondents, a wealthy heiress – echoes both THE ILLUSTRIOUS CLIENT (Holmes has files

detailing an unsolved murder in an Alpine pass, which he soon connects to the unsuitable suitor) and SHOSCOMBE OLD PLACE (we learn that the foul-tempered and brutal 'Murdock', actually a race-fixer called Freddie Brill, once nearly killed a jockey who double-crossed him). And THE SPECKLED BAND is invoked in *The Case of the Diamond Tooth*, in which a gemstone-smuggling sea captain uses a boa constrictor as a method of murder – a fact only revealed to Holmes and Watson when a secret compartment in his ship's hold slides open to reveal the serpent.

Despite its absurd resolution, *The Case of the Diamond Tooth* – beginning with a corpse being dredged up from a bleak Thames riverside – is one of several episodes to be realised in a mostly grim style. *The Case of the Exhumed Client*, for example, revels in a Gothic horror premise: the cruel Sir Charles Farnsworth is found dead, seemingly of natural causes, in the supposedly cursed Tower Room of Farnsworth Castle... but he's actually been poisoned in this airless chamber when supplied with candles soaked in arsenic. (It's THE DEVIL'S FOOT, of course, right down to a scene in which Holmes nearly falls victim to the lethal fumes himself.) With its jovial, rotund, permanently chortling psychopath, *The Case of the Jolly Hangman* is a blackly comic farce about a randomly murderous rope salesman who ends up hanged by his own necktie while attempting to escape through a window. *The Case of Blind Man's Bluff* is a gloomy, suspenseful episode about a killer who leaves a chicken's claw bound with black ribbon (a Trinidadian death fetish, apparently) at the scenes of his crimes, which are later revealed to be revenges on the callous masters of a slave ship called the *Gloria North*. Various of the slayings are detailed from the killer's point-of-view, and the dramatic showdown between Holmes and the sham-blind murderer, Vickers, employs *film noir*-ish angled shots.

But far and away the most successful of these darker entries is the enthralling *The Case of the Deadly Prophecy*, doomily introduced by Watson as 'a trail of events which filled four graves'. Every full moon for four consecutive months, Antoine, a pupil at a boys' boarding school in Arno, Belgium, has sleepwalked to the steps of a local church to write the name of a person in chalk – and all of those named have died within weeks. Teacher

Marie Grande calls in Holmes when the headmaster becomes the fourth victim. Despite suspicion falling on a local white witch, Holmes deduces that all four deaths have been merely the prelude to an attempt to extort 100,000 francs from a terrified nobleman, the Comte de Passevant, who has been told that his name will be next to appear if he does not pay up. The local doctor, Dimanche, has hypnotised Antoine and poisoned the four named previously, all to help create an appropriately convincing climate of supernatural dread. Beautifully staged, with more location work than usual, *The Case of the Deadly Prophecy* deserves recognition as something of a minor classic.

Quite rightly, other episodes strike an entirely different note. Some, like *The Case of the Baker Street Bachelors*, in which Holmes and Watson go on a double-date in the course of their efforts to investigate the Cupid's Bow marriage bureau, a front for an unscrupulous blackmailer, are just plain funny. (There's a priceless sequence in which Holmes brags about his violin-playing to his date, Pamela, while a tongue-tied and desperately uncomfortable Watson is fawned over by the moony and 'awfully stupid' Edna.) Similarly, *The Case of the Eiffel Tower* contrives to land Holmes, Watson and Lestrade, on the trail of stolen state secrets, inside a Parisian cabaret – where Holmes has to persuade the bashful Watson, the only one among them with any pidgin French, to invite a number of can-can girls to their table as cover. 'They'll like you, Watson,' insists Holmes. 'You *blush*. For England?' Stoically, the reluctant Watson straightens his tie: 'For England!'

Otherwise straight episodes often enjoy comic relief scenes, some more effective than others; there's a lovely routine in *The Case of the Diamond Tooth*, for example, involving a Portuguese dentist who resents people eating fish because it makes their teeth strong. The funniest joke in the series is probably a tiny visual gag in *The Case of Lady Beryl*, in which the camera tracks along a shelf of jars in Holmes' rooms, labelled 'POISON' 'DEADLY POISON', 'SNAKE POISON'... and then 'TEA'.

And those 'stinkaires'? In truth, *The Mother Hubbard Case* et al are more twee than anything else, a trait shared with other 'high concept' episodes such as *The Case of the Neurotic Detective*, which sets up the possibility that Holmes might have turned his intellectual powers to the perpetra-tion, not detection, of crime. (It turns out that the gold seals of Edinburgh Castle, naval secrets from the Admiralty and jewels belonging to Elizabeth I have indeed been stolen by a gang under Holmes' command, but all as part of a top-secret Government experiment to test the adequacy of state security.) In truth, the weaker episodes are mostly undone by ploddingly explicable 'mysteries' and one-too-many French bit-part actors attempting salt-of-the-Earth English accents – *The Night Train Riddle*, for example, in which the son of timber magnate 'Ripsaw' Windmaster (yes, really) is kidnapped *en route* to a boarding school by his only friend, a circus clown who's been commissioned to do away with the boy back at the Big Top. It's all resolved when burly bruiser Watson drops a sandbag on the clown's head before manhandling him away.

For the truly dire, we need turn only to *The Case of the Haunted Gainsborough*, in which Highland laird Malcolm MacGregan (a stereotypically tight Scotsman, massively overplayed by Lestrade actor Archie Duncan) is desperate to sell a valuable painting of his ancestor, Heather, before his castle falls into the hands of a mortgage lender. But Heather's ghost keeps materialising to scare off potential buyers, declaring 'A curse on all who dare conspire/To take me doon from o'er the fire'. It's all part of a plot cooked up by the unscrupulous mortgage-lender, who's employed an actress to play 'Heather'... but 'Heather', it's revealed in the final shot, *has been a real ghost all along!*

'You must realise,' said Ronald Howard (as quoted in Pointer, 1976), 'we were churning these films out at the rate of one every four days; it was really breakneck speed ... It was a terribly concentrated effort to keep going at all. After about six months I was becoming dead beat. There was scarcely time to learn the lines.' Certainly, the later episodes are, generally speaking, the weaker; there's almost an end-of-term air about episodes like *Eiffel Tower* and *Haunted Gainsborough*. These excesses aside, it's a shame that the series, still readily available on home video in the US, isn't more highly regarded. Howard's Holmes is exactly the 'exceptionally sincere' professional he set out to portray, and Crawford's Watson ranks among the very best of them. And it's sobering to think that, in terms of total screen time in the role, Howard ranks behind only Eille Norwood, Basil

Rathbone, Peter Cushing and Jeremy Brett. Major re-evaluation is urgently required.

Sadly, *Sherlock Holmes* did little for Howard's career – nor, indeed, Crawford's, who went on to play a very Watsonish Dr Petrie to the Nayland-Smiths of Nigel Green, Douglas Wilmer and Richard Greene in the five hugely variable Christopher Lee-starring Fu Manchu films of the late sixties. (He died of an overdose of sleeping pills in 1969.) Meanwhile, Sheldon Reynolds would look forward to doing it all again – this time not in Paris, but Warsaw. The saga of **Sherlock Holmes and Dr Watson** is, however, a different story entirely...

Sherlock Holmes

GB 1965 12 x 50m TV adaptations BBC Television bw
p David Goddard
regular cast Sherlock Holmes: **Douglas Wilmer**
Dr Watson: **Nigel Stock**

THE ILLUSTRIOUS CLIENT

tx 20 February 1965 BBC1
w Giles Cooper d Peter Sasdy
regular cast, plus Baron Grüner: **Peter Wyngarde** Kitty Winter: **Rosemary Leach** Violet de Merville: **Jennie Linden** Sir James Damery: **Ballard Berkeley** Shinwell Johnson: **Norman Mitchell** Leary: **Billy Cornelius** footman: **Martin Gordon** Billy: **Jimmy Ashton** music hall singer: **Anne Hart**

THE DEVIL'S FOOT

tx 27 February 1965 BBC1
w Giles Cooper d Max Varnel
regular cast, plus Dr Sterndale: **Carl Bernard** Mortimer Tregennis: **Patrick Troughton** Vicar: **John Glyn-Jones** Mrs Porter: **Nora Gordon** Brenda Tregennis: **Camilla Hasse** George Tregennis: **Derek Birch** Owen Tregennis: **Frank Crawshaw**

THE COPPER BEECHES

tx 6 March 1965 BBC1
w Vincent Tilsley d Gareth Davies
regular cast, plus Jephro Rucastle: **Patrick Wymark** Violet Hunter: **Suzanne Neve** Mrs Rucastle: **Alethea Charlton** Mr Toller: **Michael Robbins** Mrs Toller: **Margaret Diamond** Mr Fowler: **Paul Harris** Miss Stoper: **Sheila Keith** Alice Rucastle: **Norma Vogon** Miss Thompson: **Anna Perry** Edward Rucastle: **Garry Mason** page boy: **Ross Clear**

THE RED-HEADED LEAGUE

w Anthony Read d Peter Duguid
tx 13 March 1965 BBC1
regular cast, plus Jabez Wilson: **Toke Townley** Vincent Spaulding: **David Andrews** Duncan Ross: **Trevor Martin** Inspector Hopkins: **John Barcroft** Merryweather: **Geoffrey Wincott** Sergeant Jones: **Christopher Greatorex** Mary Jane: **Carla Challoner** old woman: **Beatrice Shaw** Mrs Shaw: **Audrey O'Flynn**

THE ABBEY GRANGE

tx 20 March 1965 BBC1
w Clifford Witting d Peter Cregeen
regular cast, plus Lady Brackenstall: **Nyree Dawn Porter** Theresa Wright: **Peggy Thorpe-Bates** Det Inspector Hopkins: **John Barcroft** Sir Eustace Brackenstall: **Michael Gover** Captain Croker: **Peter Jesson** Sergeant Mitchell: **Ken Thornett** cab driver: **Ian Anders** Porter: **Douglas Ives** William Randall: **David Harrison** Tom Randall: **Ronald Adams** Frank Randall: **Pierce McAvoy**

THE SIX NAPOLEONS

tx 27 March 1965 BBC1
w Giles Cooper d Gareth Davies
regular cast, plus Inspector Lestrade: **Peter Madden** Dr Barnicot: **James Bree** Horace Harker: **Donald Hewlett** Morse Hudson: **Martin Wyldeck** Mr Golder: **Norman Scace** Josiah Brown: **Arthur Hewlett** Mrs Brown: **Betty Romaine** Mr Sandeford: **Lloyd Pearson** Inspector Hill: **Raymond Witch** police constable: **Desmond Cullum-Jones** Beppo: **Andreas Markos** Billy: **Jimmy Ashton** Venucci: **Terry Leigh**

THE MAN WITH THE TWISTED LIP

tx 3 April 1965 BBC1
w Jan Read d Eric Tayler
regular cast, plus Hugh Boone: **Anton Rodgers** Mrs St Clair: **Anna Cropper** Inspector Lestrade: **Peter Madden** Inspector Bradstreet: **Victor Brooks** Lascar: **Olaf Pooley** Sergeant: **Manning Wilson** Constable: **Bernard Shine** shipping clerk: **Robin Parkinson** City gentleman: **Norman Pitt** Malay attendant: **John A Tinn**

THE BERYL CORONET

tx 10 April 1965 BBC1
w Nicholas Palmer d Max Varnel
regular cast, plus Holder: **Leonard Sachs** Mary: **Suzan Farmer** Arthur: **Richard Carpenter** Sir George Burnwell: **David Burke** Lucy: **Sandra Hampton** Gregory: **Denis Shaw** Hector: **Mark Singleton** the visitor: **John Melvin***

Watson (Nigel Stock) and Holmes (Douglas Wilmer) square up to the sleazy Jephro Rucastle (Patrick Wymark) in **Sherlock Holmes**: The Copper Beeches (1965)

THE BRUCE-PARTINGTON PLANS

tx 17 April 1965 BBC1

w **Giles Cooper** *d* **Shaun Sutton**

regular cast, plus Mycroft Holmes: **Derek Francis**
Colonel Valentine Walter: **Allan Cuthbertson**
Platelayer: **Bart Allison** Mrs Hudson: **Enid Lindsay**
Inspector Lestrade: **Peter Madden** station master:
John Woodnutt butler: **Walter Horsbrugh** Violet Westbury:
Sandra Payne Sydney Johnson: **Gordon Gostelow** waiter:
Erik Chitty Herr Oberstein: **Carl Duering**

CHARLES AUGUSTUS MILVERTON

tx 24 April 1965 BBC1

w **Clifford Witting** *d* **Philip Dudley**

regular cast, plus Charles Augustus Milverton:
Barry Jones Lady Eva Brackwell: **Penelope Horner**
Lady Farningham: **Stephanie Bidmead** Lord Farningham:
Tony Steedman Captain Fitzallen: **Derek Smee** Inspector
Lestrade: **Peter Madden** Agatha: **Ann Penfold** footmen:
Ralph Tovey, John Murray Scott under gardener: **Edward
Brooks** Billy: **Jimmy Ashton** newsboy: **Len Jones**

THE RETIRED COLOURMAN

tx 1 May 1965 BBC1

w **Jan Read** *d* **Michael Hayes**

regular cast, plus Josiah Amberley: **Maurice Denham**
Barker: **Peter Henchie** Inspector Lestrade: **Peter Madden**
Mrs Hudson: **Enid Lindsey** Ellen Amberley: **Lesley
Saweard** Dr Ray Ernest: **William Wilde** Rev J C Elman:
Christopher Banks choir boy: **Paul Martin** police
constable: **Robert Croudace** railway porter: **Arthur R Webb**

THE DISAPPEARANCE OF LADY FRANCES CARFAX

tx 8 May 1965 BBC1

w **Vincent Tilsley** *d* **Shaun Sutton**

regular cast, plus Inspector Lestrade: **Peter Madden**
Mrs Hudson: **Enid Lindsey** The Hon Philip Green: **Joss
Ackland** Lady Frances Carfax: **Sheila Shand**
Dr Shlessinger: **Ronald Radd** Mrs Shlessinger: **Diana King**
Moser: **Roger Delgado** Jules: **Neil Stacy** pawnbroker: **John
Woodnutt** Marie: **Karin MacCarthy** police sgt: **Ivor Salter**

Following the remarkable success of a try-out instalment (see **Detective: The Speckled Band**), the BBC wasted no time in throwing its considerable resources behind a full 12-part series of Holmes adaptations starring Douglas Wilmer as the Great Detective and Nigel Stock as Watson. The services of producer David Goddard would be retained, too; Goddard declared it his ambition to 'convey the unique sense of horror which counterpoints the straight detection in most of the stories'. Having already purchased television rights in five tales (including THE SPECKLED BAND), the Corporation formally assumed its option on a further eight on 19 June 1964 – a month and a day after broadcast of the pilot.

That's not to say that the Corporation's dealings with the Doyle estate were entirely straightforward. Henry E Lester, the Estate's London representative, had pushed for the BBC to enter into a co-production deal with an American network and make the series on film. None of the Corporation's officers were keen. Newly appointed series script editor John Gould expressed his 'private opinion' of Lester's proposal in an internal memo: 'any series in which an American company had a say in casting, production and programme slanting would inevitably mean that Mr Lester would have such a say, and I believe that this could be disastrous. I am also convinced from what Mr Lester has said to us that he wishes to be involved in these matters, but that any interference from him would be totally unnecessary ... The success of the programme will depend very largely on it being essentially English. We can always ask Mr Lester's opinion, just as long as we are not bound to act on it.'

Giles Cooper, the man who'd written The Speckled Band's teleplay, was commissioned to write four of the 12 adaptations in mid-June: he chose THE BRUCE-PARTINGTON PLANS, THE DEVIL'S FOOT, THE ILLUSTRIOUS CLIENT and THE BLUE CARBUNCLE. At this stage, it was expected that the series would begin around Christmas 1964, with Gould therefore nominating the 'festive' BLUE CARBUNCLE as a likely opening instalment. (Other stories then considered for adaptation included THE NORWOOD BUILDER and THE GREEK INTERPRETER.) By early July, the initial running order had settled as: The Illustrious Client and The Blue Carbuncle, both by Cooper; a version of THE BERYL CORONET, by Nicholas Palmer; a 'Murder/Robbery' story by Clifford Witting (soon to be determined as an adaptation of THE ABBEY GRANGE); THE MAN WITH THE TWISTED LIP and CHARLES AUGUSTUS MILVERTON, both by Jan Read; THE PRIORY SCHOOL, by Allan Prior; and then Cooper's Bruce-Partington Plans and Devil's Foot. Three further slots remained open, with two of these being pencilled in for Z

Cars creator John Hopkins; by September, Hopkins had turned them down.

Henry E Lester had by this time 'put it on record with the Corporation' that Adrian Conan Doyle, Sir Arthur's descendant, wanted Michael and Mollie Hardwick to be 'actively involved' with the series; the Hardwicks had scripted many of the BBC's radio adaptations and co-authored a guidebook to the canon, The Sherlock Holmes Companion. Early in September, Gould and Goddard discussed the possibility of a separate series of four 90-minute adaptations of the Holmes novels (A STUDY IN SCARLET, THE SIGN OF THE FOUR, THE HOUND OF THE BASKERVILLES and THE VALLEY OF FEAR) to be titled Sherlock Holmes: The Longer Stories – and, on 30 September, the Hardwicks submitted a storyline for their adaptation of THE VALLEY OF FEAR. Nothing would come of this – nor, indeed, Sherlock Holmes: The Longer Stories – and the Hardwicks wouldn't pen a television adaptation until 1968 (see **Sir Arthur Conan Doyle's Sherlock Holmes**).

The first of the series to go before the cameras was Jan Read's The Man With the Twisted Lip, five days' pre-filming for which took place between 28 September and 2 October around the run-down wharves and warehouses at Wapping, east London; the police station and the High Street were the focus of attention. (This would be the most generous filming allocation given any of the episodes, three days being the maximum thereafter.) Studio sequences were recorded on 20 October at the new Television Centre studios in White City. The Man With the Twisted Lip was the first of six episodes to feature Peter Madden (1905-76) as a dogged Inspector Lestrade. Gaunt and grim-featured, Madden once admitted: 'I'm generally cast as a baddie because I've got such a miserable bloody face...'

Wilmer watched the 25 September repeat of The Speckled Band, but was unsettled by his own performance, thinking his Holmes 'too smooth, urbane, and civilised'. Over the next few months he would develop the character, hoping to capture 'a much more primitive person, more savage and ruthless. He was a surprisingly unfashionable individual for a Victorian writer to portray, really – completely unsentimental in a very sentimental age.' Recordings continued with The Abbey Grange, which shot on location at the White Lodge, Richmond Park on 21 and 22 October, going into studio on 3 November.

Late in September, John Gould had been taken ill and had gone on sick leave; his replacement was Anthony Read, who had worked with Goddard the previous year on *Kipling*. Read's immediate task was to determine which three stories would conclude the series. By now, Cooper's *Blue Carbuncle* had been dropped in favour of the same writer's THE THREE GARRIDEBS... which would, in turn, be replaced by another Cooper adaptation, of THE SIX NAPOLEONS. For reasons unknown, Allan Prior's THE PRIORY SCHOOL would be written off early in November. Other scripts submitted to the production office included Jean Hart's adaptation of THE BOSCOMBE VALLEY MYSTERY, Robert Pollock's version of THE GOLDEN PINCE-NEZ, and Duncan Ross' teleplay for THE SUSSEX VAMPIRE – which, Read told the author on 11 November, would need 'a fair amount of revision before it is completely suitable ... I get the impression from reading it that you felt the story itself to be slight and you have therefore tried to invent a new story from the original idea ... Holmes and Watson themselves need some adjustment to fit the characters as we are presenting them and to keep away from the Basil Rathbone/Nigel Bruce interpretations which we firmly eschew.'

Ultimately, Vincent Tilsley – who'd said that he was 'sick with disappointment' not to have been given a chance to write a script thus far – would end up penning two adaptations, of THE COPPER BEECHES and THE DISAPPEARANCE OF LADY FRANCES CARFAX. The one remaining slot was soon taken by Jan Read's version of THE RETIRED COLOURMAN, who'd by now handed CHARLES AUGUSTUS MILVERTON over to Clifford Witting.

The Red-headed League was the next episode due into studio, scheduled for 17 November – but writer Harry Green's original dramatisation was considered to be unworkable on receipt. Green's version was abandoned on 4 November, and Anthony Read resigned himself to writing an entirely new teleplay from scratch in just two days. Location work for *The Beryl Coronet* was filmed on 17, 18 and 20 November, around Kingswood House, Coopers Hill Lane, Englefield Green, Surrey; studio scenes were taped on 1 December. The Baker Street exterior set, which would be seen in the closing titles for the entire series, was built at Ealing Studios for use in *The Illustrious Client*, the bulk of which was recorded on 15 December.

Cast and crew decamped to Cornwall for *The Devil's Foot* between 17 and 19 December, where they were entertained by Nigel Stock's after-hours bagpipes recitals; locations were found at Port Isaac, Penally Point, Port Quin, Doyden Castle, and finally St Agnes, at 'Wheal Friendly' and Trevaunance Point.

1965 began with studio scenes for *The Devil's Foot* on 10 January, immediately followed by two days' exteriors for *The Copper Beeches* at the Juniper Hall Field Centre, Dorking, Surrey. *Charles Augustus Milverton* had only a single day's location, at Grim's Dyke Rehabilitation Centre, Common Lane, Harrow Weald, on 25 January; the studio session was on 7 February. The series was now scheduled to begin transmission on 20 February, opening with *The Illustrious Client*, which contained an immensely strong supporting role for Peter Wyngarde as the blackguard Baron Grüner [sic].

In the run-up to the series' début, Wilmer and Stock appeared in costume at a press call at the Sherlock Holmes, a pub off Northumberland Avenue (David Goddard was also present). The following week, *The Illustrious Client* was awarded the cover of BBC listings magazine *Radio Times*. Critics weren't over-enamoured of Wilmer's Holmes; 'he is not the man for this particular job,' thundered the *Times*. 'He impersonates the character but does not penetrate him'. But they were far more well-disposed to Stock's Watson. 'Nigel Stock abetted likably,' reckoned *Variety*, 'dodging the peril of seeming too stupid ... the skein promises to combine nostalgia with well-mannered excitement in a pleasing mixture'.

Radio Times readers were uniformly delighted, the Chairman of the Sherlock Holmes Society of London writing to say that 'Douglas Wilmer's Holmes and Nigel Stock's Watson are truly magnificent, and the cast deserves full marks ... I can only voice the opinion of our members when I say that I hope we shall be treated to a second viewing later in the year.' In fact, the sternest criticism in the *Radio Times* came six weeks later, following transmission of *The Man With the Twisted Lip*, when Frank Newman of Sefton, Devon queried the accuracy of the episode's depiction of opium inhalation. 'Opium does not behave like tobacco but like sealing wax,' he noted, qualifying his assertion by stating, 'I occasionally smoked opium some years ago in China ...'

Chemistry lesson: Watson (Nigel Stock), Holmes (Douglas Wilmer) and Inspector Hopkins (John Barcroft)
in **Sherlock Holmes**: The Red-headed League *(1965)*

Rumblings of discontent were, however, heard in the upper echelons of the BBC – among the very mandarins, in fact, who had been so extravagant in their praise for *The Speckled Band* nine months previously. On 22 February, two days after *The Illustrious Client* had aired and one day after *The Six Napoleons* had entered the studio, Director of Television Kenneth Adam wrote to Drama head Sydney Newman to inform him that: 'There was strong and unanimous criticism at Board of Management today of the first of the *Sherlock Holmes* series, which felt it had not lived up at all to the promise of the pilot, and on which so many hopes were based. DG [Director-General] was particularly critical that one of the stories from the last and weakest selections of Conan Doyle's should have been chosen ... The acting was thought to have carried no conviction with the exception of Peter Wyngarde's, and Wilmer himself was thought to have been especially disappointing.' Newman for-

warded the memo to Goddard, appending by hand: 'I'm sorry I have to pass this on to you. I'm afraid to agree too that it was a great disappointment.'

The Copper Beeches' studio session was on 2 March, with *The Bruce-Partington Plans* (which had also enjoyed a limited amount of Ealing filming) following five days later. Location work for *The Retired Colourman* took place in Hertfordshire, at Bushey Parish Church and at Hillside, Brookshill Road, Harrow Weald over 8 and 9 March, with cast and crew spending 10 March at Sheffield Park Station on the Bluebell Line, Sussex; it went into studio on 21 March. An unlikely guest star had been due to appear, most probably as Holmes' rival, the detective Barker: Boris Karloff (1887-1969), who'd played proxy Sherlock 'Mr Mycroft' in the US television one-off *The Elgin Hour: Sting of Death*. In 1959, the émigré Karloff had returned to live in his native England, becoming friends with *Retired Colourman* writer Jan Read – with whom Karloff 'agreed in principle' to appear in the episode. Formal negotiations began late in November 1964, but – possibly due to the septuagenarian actor's commitments elsewhere – nothing came of it this time round, although Jan Read remained optimistic that Karloff could be 'roped in' to appear in a second series.

Finally, *The Disappearance of Lady Frances Carfax* enjoyed the most exotic of the series' locations: the inland town of Montreuil-sur-Mer, north-east France, which doubled for Switzerland and other locales. Sequences were filmed on 21 March in the town's backstreets, at the drive of the Chateau St Josse-sur-Mer, the cemetery at St Josse-sur-Mer and beside the water-mill on the Moulin de Bacon, with the exterior of the Café du Theatre, Place de General de Gaulle, being used the next day.

Sherlock Holmes' final Television Centre recordings took place on 4 April. David Goddard left the BBC later that month, to take up a new post as Assistant Head of Features and Drama at ABC Television, Australia. A new producer would have to be appointed for the hoped-for second series – which eventually reached the screen three years later, as **Sir Arthur Conan Doyle's Sherlock Holmes**. Not only would the follow-up have a new title, it would have a new star – and a very different presentation style.

Unlike its successor, however, all of the Wilmer episodes have survived the BBC's archive purges of the sixties and seventies. They display all the faults and virtues of *The Speckled Band*, although Wilmer's Holmes is noticeably less clubbable on occasion. *The Devil's Foot* is a good example, in which he is utterly inscrutable throughout the closing confrontation with the remorseless, revengeful Dr Sterndale. And despite the fact that *The Illustrious Client* remains a very odd choice of opening instalment – Peter Wyngarde's sneering, absurdly accented Baron Grüner utterly dominating the proceedings – the stories chosen for adaptation represent a strong blend of the familiar and the less well-known.

Latter-day viewers may find them oddly static, and the jumps between multi-camera studio video-tape and film inserts quaintly jarring, but it's no small thing to note that these dramatisations – together with many of those in *Sherlock Holmes'* 1968 follow-up – would stand as the definitive screen versions for nigh on 20 years. Two episodes

– *The Beryl Coronet* and *The Retired Colourman* – remain so, and the others are well-played enough to make for fascinating comparison with the later, much-garlanded Granada adaptations starring Jeremy Brett.

Sherlock Holmes

Germany 1967-8 6 x TV adaptations bw
d **Paul May**
regular cast Sherlock Holmes: **Erich Schellow**
Dr Watson: **Paul Edwin Roth** Mrs Hudson: **Manja Kafka**
Inspector Lestrade: **Hans Schellbach**

DAS GEFLECKTE BAND
adaptation [THE SPECKLED BAND]
tx 28 August 1967
guest cast includes Dr Roylott: **Fritz Tillmann**

SECHSMAL NAPOLEON
adaptation [THE SIX NAPOLEONS]
tx 2 October 1967
guest cast includes Mr Harker: **Heinz Bennent**

DIE LIGA DER ROTHHAARIGEN
adaptation [THE RED-HEADED LEAGUE]
tx 7 November 1967
guest cast includes Ross: **Walo Lüönd**
Mr Wilson: **Helmut Peine**

DIE BRUCE-PARTINGTON PLÄNE
adaptation [THE BRUCE-PARTINGTON PLANS]
tx 6 December 1967
guest cast includes Mycroft Holmes: **Hans Cossy**
Violet Westbury: **Inga Alexandra Fuhg**
Colonel Valentine: **Alf Marholm**

DAS BERYLL-DIADEM
adaptation [THE BERYL CORONET]
tx 9 January 1968
guest cast includes Holder: **Herbert Tiede**
Arthur Holder: **Christian Wolff**

DAS HAUS BEI DEN BLUTBUCHEN
tr 'The house with the copper beeches'
adaptation [THE COPPER BEECHES]
tx 13 February 1968
guest cast includes Mrs Rucastle: **Brigitte Drummer**
Mr Rucastle: **Hanns Ernst Jäger**

Largely forgotten until an impromptu repeat season in 1991, these West German teleplays, originally broadcast one per month, were apparently based on six scripts for the BBC's Douglas Wilmer-starring **Sherlock Holmes** series (1965). Recorded mostly in an old air-raid shelter in Cologne, the German versions featured Erich Schellow (1915-95), a Berlin-born stage actor rarely seen in films and television, in the lead. Sherlockian Uwe Sommerlad 'rediscovered' Schellow in 1992, learning that the actor had wanted to show Holmes '"as a little bit neglected, drug-addicted, but they didn't like the idea" ... director Paul May wanted Holmes as a contrast to the other action-orientated heroes of the 1960s, as a highly intelligent but 'clean' character ... Therefore Schellow was allowed to show the brilliance of Holmes but not the maniacal side ... His Sherlock is cold-blooded – 'cool' as one may say today – and never loses his composure.'

Previously seen on the German small screen in **Der Hund von Baskerville** (1955), Holmes would return to television sets west of Berlin in **Das Zeichen der Vier** (1974).

Sherlock Holmes

Italy 1968 2 x TV adaptations
RAI [Radiotelevisione Italiana]
w **Edoardo Anton** *d* **Guglielmo Morandi**
regular cast Sherlock Holmes: **Nando Gazzolo**
Dr Watson: **Gianni Bonagura**

LA VALLE DELLA PAURA
adaptation [THE VALLEY OF FEAR]
tx [in three parts] 25 October, 1 and 8 November 1968
Secondo Programma
guest cast includes Ettie Douglas: **Anna Miserocchi**
other roles: **Cesarina Gheraldi, Mario Erpichini, Ernesto Colli, Andrea Bosic, Leonardo Severini, Enrico Ostermann**

L'ULTIMO DEI BASKERVILLE
tr 'The last of the Baskervilles'
adaptation [THE HOUND OF THE BASKERVILLES]
tx [in three parts] 15, 22, 29 November 1968
Secondo Programma
guest cast includes **Paolo Carlini, Anna Maria Ackermann, Marina Malfatti, Franco Volpi, Adolfo Geri, Franco Scandurra**

Peter Cushing and Nigel Stock weren't the only TV Holmes and Watson team shooting on English locations during the summer of 1968. The others were Nando Gazzolo (1928-) and Gianni Bonagura (1925-), stars of *La valle della paura* and *L'ultimo dei Baskerville*, two three-parters made by Italy's equivalent of the BBC, RAI. Based at King's Lynn, a 30-strong Italian crew had Brickling Hall stand in for Baskerville Hall and Oxborough Hall, near Stoke Ferry, substituting for THE VALLEY OF FEAR's Birlstone House. (By coincidence, Cushing himself passed through the latter location for *The Dancing Men* episode of the BBC's **Sir Arthur Conan Doyle's Sherlock Holmes**.) Work was also done in the coastal resort of Cromer before studio shooting, and further locations at Lake Nemi, resumed in Italy. Though Doyle's THE HOUND OF THE BASKERVILLES was so firmly set in the West Country, RAI's choice of East Anglian locations was nevertheless apt, given that Doyle and his friend Fletcher Robinson started cooking up THE HOUND during a 1901 golfing holiday in Cromer.

Director Guglielmo Morandi (1913-) was a pioneer of Italian television particularly noted for his 'classic' adaptations, ranging from Turgenev's *Fathers and Sons* (*Padri e figli*, 1958) to Oliver Goldsmith's *The Vicar of Wakefield* (*Il vicario di Wakefield*, 1959). He was equally at home with crime dramas, however, having contributed to the series *Giallo club* (1960) and *Invito al poliziesco* (1961); in fact, he came to *Sherlock Holmes* direct from a Francis Durbridge thriller. With screen-writer Edoardo Anton, Morandi was careful to remain faithful to Doyle's originals, while Gazzolo sought to bring a touch of 007 to Holmes ('Like all indolent people,' he pronounced, 'when Holmes moves he really moves'), together with a vein of self-aware irony to offset the character's maniacal self-absorption. Touring Italy from 2001 to 2002 as King Lear, Gazzolo claimed to have been cast as Holmes because of his 'English' demeanour, though his attempts to enhance it with a more aquiline nose were consigned to the make-up room floor. He also pointed out that he was Peter Cushing's 'voice' when the latter's films were dubbed into Italian.

The RAI Holmes stories premiered on the 'Secondo Programma' (now known as RaiDue) on Friday 25 October 1968; as far as is known, they have not been repeated. (JR)

Pole stars:
Holmes (Geoffrey
Whitehead),
Lestrade (Patrick
Newell) and
Watson (Donald
Pickering) in an
episode of
**Sherlock Holmes
and Dr Watson**
(1979), filmed in
Warsaw

Sherlock Holmes and Dr Watson

*US/Poland 1979 24 x 25m TV series pastiches TVP
Poltel/Sheldon Reynolds Organization colour*
p **Sheldon Reynolds**
regular cast Sherlock Holmes: **Geoffrey Whitehead**
Dr Watson: **Donald Pickering** Inspector Lestrade: **Patrick
Newell** [various] Mrs Hudson: **Kay Walsh** [various]

A MOTIVE FOR MURDER
wd **Sheldon Reynolds**

THE CASE OF THE SPECKLED BAND
adaptation [THE SPECKLED BAND]
w **Michael Allen** *d* **Sheldon Reynolds**

MURDER ON A MIDSUMMER'S EVE
w **Michael Allen, Robin Bishop** *d* **Sheldon Reynolds**

FOUR MINUS FOUR IS ONE
w **Robin Bishop** *d* **Sheldon Reynolds**

THE CASE OF THE PERFECT CRIME
w **Joe Morheim** *d* **Ronald Stevens**

THE CASE OF HARRY RIGBY
w **Sheldon Reynolds, Ray Allen** *d* **Val Guest**

THE CASE OF BLIND MAN'S BLUFF
w **Joe Morheim, Robin Bishop** *d* **Peter Sasdy**

A CASE OF HIGH SECURITY
w **Robin Bishop** *d* **Roy Ward Baker**

THE CASE OF HARRY CROCKER
w **Harold Jack Bloom, Robin Bishop** *d* **Freddie Francis**

THE CASE OF THE DEADLY PROPHECY
w **George & Gertrude Fass** *d* **Freddie Francis**

THE CASE OF THE BAKER STREET NURSEMAIDS
w **Joseph Victor** *d* **Val Guest**

THE CASE OF THE PURLOINED LETTER
w Sheldon Reynolds, George Fowler *d* Val Guest

THE CASE OF THE FINAL CURTAIN
w Joe Morheim *d* Val Guest

THE CASE OF THE THREE BROTHERS
w Joe Morheim *d* Val Guest

THE CASE OF THE BODY IN THE CASE
w Tudor Gates *d* Roy Ward Baker

THE CASE OF THE DEADLY TOWER
w Joe Morheim *d* Roy Ward Baker

THE CASE OF SMITH & SMYTHE
w Joe Morheim, Sheldon Reynolds *d* Roy Ward Baker

THE CASE OF THE LUCKLESS GAMBLER
w Joe Morheim *d* Roy Ward Baker

THE CASE OF THE SHRUNKEN HEADS
w Tudor Gates *d* Val Guest

THE CASE OF THE MAGRUDERS' MILLIONS
w Joe Morheim *d* Val Guest

THE CASE OF THE TRAVELING KILLER
w George Fowler *d* Val Guest

THE CASE OF THE OTHER GHOST
w Tudor Gates, Julian Fellowes *d* Val Guest

THE CASE OF THE SITTING TARGET
w Sheldon Reynolds *d* Aurelio Crugnola

THE CASE OF THE CLOSE-KNIT FAMILY
w Andrea Reynolds *d* Sheldon Reynolds

Despite its relatively recent late seventies vintage, **Sherlock Holmes and Dr Watson**, filmed in Warsaw, must be the single least-seen English-language television series derived from the characters of Doyle. According to veteran British director Val Guest (1911-), responsible for nine episodes, ever-entrepreneurial producer Sheldon Reynolds – previously behind the Ronald Howard-starring **Sherlock Holmes** (1954-5) – had engineered a deal with the apparatchiks at the Communist-controlled Polish state television

station: 'in return for a piece of the action the Poles would give him their Poltel Studios with all building and production staff. For his part he would supply the actors and key technicians.' Also involved in setting up production was American International Pictures representative Steve Previn (brother of conductor André), who had directed the majority of the Howard instalments: 'It's a matter of foreign currency,' Previn told Guest. 'They need foreign currency desperately and this is one way they can get it.'

Bizarrely, the eminent Anthony Burgess (1917-93), writer of *A Clockwork Orange*, was hired as a consultant on the series. Many of the scripts were rehashes of episodes from the 1954-5 series, often under different titles (*The Case of the Perfect Crime*, for example, was originally presented as *The Case of the Neurotic Detective*). Exactly as before, only one tale from the Doyle canon was adapted – this time THE SPECKLED BAND, transplanted to a Bavarian-style castle – and even the first episode, *A Motive for Murder*, replayed the first meeting of Holmes and Watson, true to both A STUDY IN SCARLET and the Howard series' début, *The Case of the Cunningham Heritage*.

The new series also retained one of the Howard shows' key identifiers by making Inspector Lestrade an equal partner alongside Holmes and Watson. In fact, the central trio – Geoffrey Whitehead (1939-, best-known as a police sergeant in the crime series *Z Cars*) as Holmes, plus Donald Pickering (1933-) as Watson and Patrick Newell (1932-88) as Lestrade – had appeared together in the final series of *The Avengers* ten years previously. (Newell's regular character of 'Mother' had featured in the episodes *Pandora* and *Homicide and Old Lace* alongside Whitehead and Pickering respectively.) Like Guest, fellow series directors Roy Ward Baker (1916-), Freddie Francis (1917-) and Peter Sasdy (1934-) had all worked for Hammer Films beforehand, which may be an indicator of the series' house style.

One truly remarkable aspect of the series was the lavish Baker Street set, seemingly the largest yet built. Actors hired for supporting roles included Geoffrey Bayldon (1924-), Bernard Bresslaw (1934-93) and Catherine Schell (1944-). Richard Greene (1918-85), top-billed as Sir Henry in the seminal Basil Rathbone picture of 40 years before, *Sir Arthur Conan Doyle's The Hound of the*

Baskervilles (1939), appeared as 'Lord Brompton' in *The Case of the Purloined Letter* – a title itself purloined from Edgar Allan Poe.

Towards the end of shooting, Baker recalls that 'the head of Polish TV, who had sanctioned the whole enterprise, was arrested on alleged charges of corruption. He was supposedly found in possession of two country houses, three American cars and four each of heaven alone knew what else'. For his part, Guest remembers that Reynolds 'landed in some currency-changing fracas with the Polish authorities' and 'had all his film negatives confiscated'. Such circumstances may explain the series' erratic distribution: it has never aired in Britain, and has only been screened in the US on the smallest of stations – on the Oregon local network, for example, early in 1982.

Sherlock Holmes and the Great Murder Mystery

US 1908 Crescent Film Manufacturing Company
bw silent

A gorilla escapes from the ship's berth where it has been caged – and, pursued by the ship's captain, climbs through the window of a nearby house and kills a young woman who has just bade farewell to her fiancé, Jim. The captain recaptures the beast and returns to the ship. Back at the house, the butler discovers the girl's corpse; he tells the police that the last person to see her was the fiancé, who is promptly arrested. Dr Watson reads about the case in a newspaper and shows it to his friend, the detective Sherlock Holmes – who, intrigued, decides to investigate. He examines the crime scene and retires to his rooms to ponder the problem, considering the possible suspects: first, Jim; then, a burglar; and finally, having learned of its presence at the docks, the gorilla. After interrogating the ship's captain, Holmes rushes to a local courtroom, where his evidence prevents the hapless Jim from being hanged.

Although plainly a retelling of Edgar Allan Poe's short story *The Murders in the Rue Morgue* (1841), with Holmes substituting for Poe's Chevalier C Auguste Dupin, *Sherlock Holmes and the Great Murder Mystery* is, nonetheless, significant for two reasons: firstly, it marks the first confirmed

appearance of Dr Watson on film, and secondly, it features a sequence that would be repeated countless times throughout Holmes' on-screen career. The edition of *Moving Picture World* dated 28 November 1908 noted how 'Holmes returns to his study in deep thought, with his mind concentrating upon the crime. He is trying to unravel the mystery when he takes his old violin down from its peg and begins to play fantastic music which puts him in [a] trance to solve the problem. Herein are shown remarkable visions of the different clues and theories of Holmes' brain...' In this respect, *Sherlock Holmes and the Great Murder Mystery* suggests an early representation of the character based solely on his deductive abilities, not the various scrapes his investigations might lead him into.

Production company Crescent Film had been formed in the spring of 1908 by two young New Yorkers, Fred J Balshofer (1877-1969) and Herman Kolle, whose principal resources were a field model Pathé camera, the use of Kolle's father's hall-for-rent at 272 Prospect Avenue, South Brooklyn (and, on sunny days, its gardens), plus a crude laboratory. One other of Crescent's known productions, *Young Heroes of the West*, was reportedly a not-too-convincing Western starring various neighbourhood youths; might *Sherlock Holmes and the Great Murder Mystery*, therefore, have featured a cast mostly in their teens and twenties?

Crescent was dissolved later in 1908, apparently after Kolle was frightened off by detectives hired by Thomas Edison's Motion Picture Trust company – which was then busy harassing filmmakers not allied to Edison's organisations, both in and out of court. Balshofer would, however, continue in the business, becoming a founder member of the New York Motion Picture Company, which began by churning out low-budget Westerns such as *The Squaw's Revenge* (1909). Writer-director Balshofer was later responsible for the joyfully titled *The Haunted Pajamas* (1917) and the early Rudolph Valentino picture, *An Adventuress* (1920).

Sherlock Holmes and the Leading Lady

US/Italy/GB 1991 TVM pastiche Harmony
Gold/Banque et Caisse d'Epargne de l'Etat
Luxembourg/Banque Parabis Luxembourg/Silvio

Berlusconi Communications 175m colour
tx in two parts 16, 23 August 1992 [US syndication]
w **Bob Shayne**, **H R F Keating** *executive p* **Harry Alan**
Towers *p* **Frank Agrama, Alessandro Tasca, Daniele**
Lorenzano *d* **Peter Sasdy**
cast Sherlock Holmes: **Christopher Lee** Dr Watson:
Patrick Macnee Irene Adler: **Morgan Fairchild** Sigmund
Freud: **John Bennett** Eberhardt Bohm: **Engelbert**
Humperdinck Elliott Ness [Ned Elliott]: **Tom Lahm** Sir
Reginald Cholmondeley: **Ronald Hines** Michael Simpson-
Makepeace: **Nicholas Gecks** Lady Violet Cholmondeley:
Jenny Quayle Franz Winterhauser: **Michael Siberry** Capt
Von Bork: **Dominic Jephcott** Dr Froelich: **Frank**
Middlemass Margaret Froelich: **Charlotte Attenborough**
Franz Dietrich: **James Bree** Count Giddings: **John Gower**
Olga: **Mia Nadasi** Franz Hoffman: **Robert Rietty** Franz
Zimmer: **Kalman Glass** Oberstein: **Paul Humpoletz**
Zygovich: **Tom Chadbon** Kosich: **Kevin Quarmby** Serge:
Terence Beesley Karparti: **Patrick Monckton** stage door-
keeper [Mueller]: **Leon Lissek** Emperor Franz Joseph: **Cyril**
Shaps Lt Melbury: **Guy Scantlebury** Mycroft Holmes:
Jerome Willis Mrs Hudson: **Margaret John** Inspector
Schmidt: **Michael McStay** Hilda: **Amy Taylor** Heinrich:
Jeremy Beckman guard: **Anthony Marsh** maitre d': **Sandor**
Elès stage manager: **Mark Powley** chief usher: **Patrick**
Duggan nightclub doorman: **Gertan Klauber** Matilda: **Julia**
Finlay gypsy leader: **Jovica Nikolic** major domo **Marcel**
Medernach monk: **Nick Gray** Prince Orlofsky: **Peter**
Bamber Ida: **Peta Bartlett** Frank: **Phillip Dogham**
Adele: **Diane Horsley** Dr Falke: **Bruce Ogston**
Eisenstein: **Gareth Roberts** Rosalinda: **Debra Skeen**

THE MYSTERY

In 1910, Mycroft Holmes tells his brother Sherlock
of a newly developed, remote-control explosive
device which has been stolen from its inventor, Dr
Froelich, in Vienna. The device was due to be delivered up to the British government; now, with both
Russian and German agents eager to get their hands
on it, Holmes' task is to locate it before they do.

THE INVESTIGATION

In Vienna, Holmes is briefly deflected from his
purpose by an encounter with celebrated opera
singer Irene Adler. Reasoning that the detonator
may have been temporarily concealed in the opera
house, Holmes persuades Sigmund Freud to
hypnotise her in an attempt to identify the thief.
Anarchist Oberstein, worried that the diva's buried
knowledge may re-emerge, kills her maid, Hilda,

in mistake for Irene and subsequently kills
Embassy official Simpson-Makepeace. Holmes
himself kills Oberstein and then journeys with
Freud to Budapest, where he successfully
incinerates the detonator blueprint. The device
itself remains elusive.

THE SOLUTION

When Irene is kidnapped, Holmes successfully
traces the anarchists' hide-out in which she has
been concealed. Through further Freud-
administered hypnosis, it is established that the
Emperor Franz Joseph is to be assassinated that
night when he attends Irene's performance of *Die
Fledermaus*. Watson disposes of the detonator
while Holmes identifies the mystery man with his
finger on the button: snide theatre critic Franz
Hoffmann. Hoffmann having plunged to his death
from the upper reaches of the stage, Holmes
returns to London, seriously considering Irene's
proposal of marriage.

✦ ✦ ✦

Christopher Lee's aristocratic hauteur and
impressive height (6'4") were seemingly
perfect for Sherlock Holmes, but he had the
misfortune to play him under the auspices of
Berlin-based producer Artur Brauner (**Sherlock
Holmes und das Halsband des Todes**, 1962) and
then, nearly 30 years later, for the legendary fly-by-
night showman Harry Alan Towers. Lee was well
acquainted with Towers thanks to a string of
1960s potboilers that included no fewer than five
Fu Manchu pictures. The results were decidedly
mixed, and the same is true of *Sherlock Holmes and
the Leading Lady* and **Incident at Victoria Falls**, two
elephantine TV movies made back-to-back in the
closing months of 1990.

'I'm about to start work on a major television
project,' the mercurial Towers announced, 'a mini-
series called *The Golden Years of Sherlock Holmes*.
It's going to be eight one-hour adventures set in
the days when Holmes is a worldwide celebrity
and can't go anywhere without meeting equally
famous people who welcome him as a friend.
Against wonderfully exotic backgrounds he does
the good old Sherlock Holmes stuff and solves
mysteries ... Incidentally,' he added, 'Holmes will
be Christopher Lee and Watson is Patrick Macnee,
both slightly in their dotage I guess. I do believe in

'To Sherlock Holmes she was always the woman': Morgan Fairchild as Irene Adler, flanked by Patrick Macnee (Watson) and Christopher Lee (Holmes), in **Sherlock Holmes and the Leading Lady** (1991)

having the protean character actors in my movies. There aren't so many around unfortunately.'

The 'eight one-hour adventures' idea was soon supplanted by two convoluted capers running an exhausting three hours apiece and sponsored by Harmony Gold. Of the two, only *Incident at Victoria Falls* bears a prefix resembling the one originally announced (*Sherlock Holmes The Golden Years*), and both appeared on US video in drastically edited form. The full versions are no more comprehensible than the emasculated US ones, however, thanks to lazy, labyrinthine plots that often seem to be going nowhere. With a rather sketchy approach to period detail and some dodgy supporting actors, the films are no more successful than **Sherlock Holmes und das Halsband des Todes** in providing Lee's Holmes with a worthwhile framework.

Cast as an improbably youthful Irene Adler, US soap queen Morgan Fairchild got together with Lee and Macnee (both aged 68) on Friday 24 August for a London photo-call, after which *Sherlock Holmes and the Leading Lady* began in Luxembourg on Monday the 27th. Peter Sasdy, the prickly Hungarian director whom Lee had previously

worked with on *Taste the Blood of Dracula* (1969) and *Nothing But the Night* (1972), engaged not only his wife, Mia Nadasi, as Irene's bitchy understudy but also found small roles for Sandor Elès and Leon Lissek, two veterans of his *Countess Dracula* (1970). As for the leads, Macnee, last seen as a lamentable Watson in **Sherlock Holmes in New York** (1976), had Lee in involuntary stitches during filming; 'Patrick, who is one of my oldest friends, possesses a quality which convulses me,' Lee explained.

In both pictures Lee presents Holmes as an outwardly frosty but inwardly rather fruity old man, with a discreet wave in his blue-grey hair and an impressive pair of sideburns. (What he doesn't have, happily, is the enlarged nose perfected for **Sherlock Holmes und das Halsband des Todes**.) In some grievously misjudged romantic scenes, Lee and Morgan Fairchild seem to be acting in separate films, a problem made worse by the fact that Fairchild, though 40 at the time, looks closer to 30. But Holmes' response to Irene's offer of marriage, virtually choking on his champagne in misogynist alarm, remains a delightfully funny moment, and there's something genuinely touching about his subsequent account of his solitary existence.

Despite the slightly tacky presentation (and an excruciating score credited to 'Together Productions International composed and conducted by Maestro Detto Mariano'), *Leading Lady* is reasonably watchable and has some quite witty dialogue. 'Karparti is propelled by gluttony,' theorises John Bennett's impish Freud. 'He has failed to emerge from the anal stage of early development.' 'Capital,' replies Holmes. 'No doubt we should look for him in a privy.' Holmes adopts a very amusing disguise as a walrus-moustached Hungarian peasant and his vertiginous struggle with the demented Oberstein is excitingly done. Touches like this help to compensate for the acres of footage given over to entirely uninteresting opera house shenanigans and for a slew of extras who look deeply uncomfortable in their Edwardian togs. (JR)

Sherlock Holmes and the Secret Weapon

US 1942 adaptation [THE DANCING MEN]
Universal Pictures Company Inc 68m bw
w **Edward T Lowe**, **W Scott Darling**, **Edmund L Hartmann**
adaptation **W Scott Darling**, **Edward T Lowe**
assoc p **Howard Benedict** *d* **Roy William Neill**
cast Sherlock Holmes: **Basil Rathbone** Dr Watson: **Nigel Bruce** Moriarity [sic]: **Lionel Atwill** Charlotte Eberli: **Kaaren Verne** Dr Franz Tobel: **William Post Jr** Lestrade: **Dennis Hoey** Sir Reginald: **Holmes Herbert** Mrs Hudson: **Mary Gordon** pub customer: **Ted Billings*** waiter: **Paul Bryar*** aviatrix: **Vicki Campbell*** Scotland Yard man: **Gerard Cavin*** Jack Brady: **Harry Cording*** Braun: **Robert O Davis*** Peg Leg: **Harold DeBecker*** policeman: **George Eldridge*** Mueller: **Paul Fix*** London bobby: **Guy Kingsford*** Gottfried: **George Burr MacAnnan*** George: **Michael Mark*** Frederick Hoffner: **Henry Victor*** Kurt: **Harry Woods*** other roles: **John Burton***, **James Craven***, **Leslie Dennison***, **Leyland Hodgson***, **Philip Van Zandt***

THE MYSTERY
Neutral Switzerland, in wartime – where, using the guise of an antiquarian bookseller and two decoys, Sherlock Holmes enables the physicist Dr Franz Tobel to escape would-be kidnappers from the Gestapo and flee to England. Tobel is the inventor of a revolutionary bombsight that uses three sonic beams to gain a devastatingly accurate fix on its target; the device comprises four component parts, each of which is useless without the other three. A demonstration on Salisbury Plain for the benefit of senior RAF official Sir Reginald Bailey is successful – but Tobel, who has agreed to give the Allies his invention, spurns police protection. Shortly afterwards, Tobel goes missing – along with the bombsight's component parts.

THE INVESTIGATION
During his first night in Holmes' rooms, Tobel had sneaked out to visit a woman – and Holmes soon establishes that this was his lover, one Charlotte Eberli. When Holmes visits Charlotte, he discovers that Tobel had left a message with her, to be opened if anything should happen to him. The envelope is, however, found to have been opened already – and now contains a note reading simply, 'We meet again, Mr Holmes!' This, Holmes concludes, has been left by his former enemy, the criminal mastermind Professor Moriarty. Disguising himself as a Lascar called Ram Singh, Holmes trawls London's seedier streets in search of the Professor, eventually confronting him at a carpenter's. Moriarty, who is working to secure Tobel's device for the Nazis, has indeed taken the inventor – but he does not yet have the components.

Rescued from the clutches of Moriarty's hired assassins by Dr Watson and police inspector Lestrade, Holmes takes an impression of Tobel's stolen message from the pad on which it was first written, discovering a set of complex pictograms that translate into the names of three men, each of whom was given one part of Tobel's device. But all three are found killed, the bombsight parts taken by Moriarty. All hangs on the apparently untranslateable fourth line of the pictogram, which presumably gives the name of the fourth man – and the location of the crucial fourth part.

THE SOLUTION
Holmes solves the riddle first, disguising himself as the fourth man, one Frederick Hoffner – and allowing himself to be seized by Moriarty's goons and taken to the Professor's docklands hideout. There, Holmes inspires Moriarty to execute him by draining his blood, drop by drop – buying time until Lestrade and his men, who have been following a trail of paint leading to Holmes' location,

arrive. The police raid Moriarty's base, rescuing Tobel. A weakened Holmes allows Moriarty to fall victim to his own lethal trapdoor, the Professor tumbling 60 feet into the sewers... and an apparently certain doom.

✦ ✦ ✦

Lionel Atwill's Professor Moriarty steals the sequel to **Sherlock Holmes and the Voice of Terror**, despite his only entering the proceedings very late in the day. An urbane, self-aggrandising sadist with – according to female lead Charlotte Eberli – 'eyes like a snake's', this Moriarty shares an oddly perverse relationship with Basil Rathbone's Holmes, perfectly summarised by the scene in which, reclining in plushly padded sofas in Moriarty's luxuriously appointed London foxhole, the yin and yang of crime egg each other on to devise the most gruesome method possible by which the other might meet his death.

'You disappoint me, Professor,' declares Holmes. 'Somehow I always thought that in the end, you'd prove just to be an ordinary cut-throat ... Gas, poison, bullets – I assure you, Professor, were our positions reversed, I should have something much more colourful, more imaginative to offer.' With just a hint of Freudian transference, if not an outright death wish, Holmes lasciviously details how the Professor might wither away with five pints of blood being drawn from his body 'slowly, drop by drop': 'You would be aware of every exquisite second till the very end. You would be watching yourself die, scientifically noting every reaction and in full possession of your faculties ... I humbly submit, Professor, that to the very end, I have been more resourceful than yourself.' 'The needle to the last, eh, Holmes?' counters the smirking Moriarty.

At this point, the author ought to declare a personal interest: watching *Sherlock Holmes and the Secret Weapon* for the first time, aged eight or nine, he thought the ensuing sequence in which Moriarty carries out said transfusion on Holmes the most terrifying thing he'd ever witnessed – worse, even, than the robot mummies in the *Pyramids of Mars* episodes of *Doctor Who*. He's been squeamish about needles, and giving blood, ever since.

Not long after filming his red-herring role as Dr Mortimer in **Sir Arthur Conan Doyle's The Hound of the Baskervilles** (1939), Atwill had gazed into the personal and professional abyss. Fox had apparently announced that Atwill would take the role of Professor Moriarty in the follow-up, **The Adventures of Sherlock Holmes**; the part, however, went to George Zucco. Little more than 12 months into a seven-year contract with Fox, Atwill found himself more often hired out to other studios – notably playing would-be world dictator Dr Zurof opposite Rathbone in *The Sun Never Sets* (1939). Atwill would terminate his relationship with Fox in the summer of 1940, shortly after his third wife, Louise, had ended *their* arrangement, citing his 'associating with other women' among other misdemeanours.

Sometime over Christmas 1940, while engaged for Universal as another mad scientist in *Man Made Monster*, Atwill, an occasional cross-dresser, hosted one of his notorious sex parties at his Pacific Palisades home – which degenerated into a full-blown orgy shortly after the screening of two of Atwill's collection of 'stag' films, *The Plumber and the Girl* and *The Daisy Chain*. In May 1941, only weeks after Atwill's RAF pilot son, John, had been killed in action, Atwill's private proclivities were publicly exposed when one of his party guests was tried for rape. Fortunately for Atwill, the defendant was acquitted – but only after Atwill had taken the stand to deny he'd ever screened smutty pictures at his 'innocent' party.

Throughout 1942, Universal remained faithful to Atwill, casting him in serial *Junior G-Men of the Air* plus *The Mad Doctor of Market Street*, *The Ghost of Frankenstein*, *The Strange Case of Doctor Rx*, Abbott and Costello's *Pardon My Sarong* and finally *Sherlock Holmes and the Secret Weapon*. The Holmes feature, which began filming as *Sherlock Holmes Fights Back* late in June 1942, was barely underway when, on 30 June, Atwill was accused of committing perjury in the previous year's trial. Forced to confess to two charges, Atwill was eventually sentenced to five years' probation in October; his real punishment, however, was to become a Hollywood pariah. Atwill admitted that it was only 'the courage and magnaminity of one particular studio' that kept him in work. Despite his being the subject of a Hays Office veto, Universal would feature Atwill in *Frankenstein Meets the Wolf Man* (1943), *House of Frankenstein* (1944) and *House of Dracula* (1945), among others. Work was thin on the ground, and his health was desperately poor. Disgraced and embittered, Atwill died of bronchial cancer in April 1946. He was 61.

Such was the background against which *Sherlock Holmes and the Secret Weapon*'s most remarkable performer played his part. For the Holmes series, the film is more significant in that it was the first to be directed by Roy William Neill (Roland W N de Gostrie, 1887-1946), the man who'd choreograph all of the remaining entries – all bar the next as producer, too. A former war correspondent, Neill had entered the film industry circa 1915 under the eye of Inceville Studios boss Thomas H Ince, eventually directing something in the region of 40 silent pictures and gaining a contract with Columbia; his work of this period included the Boris Karloff-headlining *The Black Room* (1935). After several years labouring for Warner Bros at their Teddington Studios in the UK, Neill returned to Hollywood in 1942, when he made his first film for Universal: *Madame Spy*, a lightweight thriller about an apparent Nazi agent co-scripted by Lynn Riggs, one of the writers responsible for **Sherlock Holmes and the Voice of Terror**.

The Sherlock Holmes series was perfectly suited to Neill's style: economical but never skimpy, suspenseful but never morbid, humanised but never banal. The most obvious directorial flourish in *Sherlock Holmes and the Secret Weapon* comes when Holmes attempts to retrieve the imprint of Tobel's cryptogram from a blank pad: in just three seamless, almost-invisible cuts, Neill shifts Holmes from Charlotte Eberli's flat, to a photographic darkroom, to the sitting-room at 221B. The montage sequence representing the disguised Holmes' East End pub crawl is striking, too. And the keen eye will spot that the first of these hostelries, the absurdly named 'Cloak and Dagger', is clearly Kitty's bar as seen in the preceding Holmes picture.

Also making his series début was Dennis Hoey (Samuel David Hyams, 1893-1960) as a hopelessly dim, moustachioed Inspector Lestrade. Londoner Hoey had emigrated to America after over a decade spent in British films, including Tod Slaughter's *Maria Marten, or Murder in the Red Barn* (1935) and *The Mystery of the Mary Celeste*, a Bela Lugosi semi-horror produced by the original Hammer Films company.

The script for *Sherlock Holmes and the Secret Weapon* contains a semi-apology for spurning its source text, THE DANCING MEN, so completely.

When Holmes first shows Watson the stick-characters of Tobel's message, the doctor exclaims, 'Now I recognise that code! Do you remember a case we had some years ago? It's probably the same – alphabet substitution code.' Watson's patient and well-informed explanation of the system to Charlotte Eberli strongly suggests that the case of Elsie Cubitt remains fresh in his memory. There are several literary allusions scattered throughout the film, in fact, ranging from the disguised Holmes' mention of 'Wilhelm Shakespeare' ('an old German writer') to his comparing his methods to a plot device in Edgar Allan Poe's short story *The Purloined Letter* and a concluding speech swiped from John of Gaunt's deathbed words in Act II of the aforementioned Shakespeare's *Richard II* ('This fortress, built by nature for herself ... This blessed plot, this Earth, this realm, this England').

If the presentation of the Nazis is as patriotically cartoonish as ever, at least Moriarty has a healthy disrespect for National Socialism, addressing one of his henchmen, Kurt, as 'My dear street-brawler'. All is, of course, as it should be inside the sandbag-bedecked 221B. There's some especially admirable Rathbone/Bruce business at either end of an early scene: after Holmes casts Watson's gloves aside, explaining he's a 'very untidy fellow', Watson finds Holmes' knapsack in his armchair – and flicks it to the floor, muttering 'Untidy fellow, Holmes.'

Again usually paired with an Abbott and Costello vehicle, this time *It Ain't Hay*, on its release in December 1942, the appeal of *Sherlock Holmes and the Secret Weapon* was rather pithily summed up in *Variety*: 'plenty [of] dime novel action'. Such action would, unfortunately, be largely absent from the next in the series, **Sherlock Holmes in Washington**.

Sherlock Holmes and the Voice of Terror

US 1942 adaptation [HIS LAST BOW]
Universal Pictures Company Inc 65m bw
w **Lynn Riggs**, **John Bright** *adaptation* **Robert D Andrews**
assoc p **Howard Benedict** *d* **John Rawlins**
cast Sherlock Holmes: **Basil Rathbone** Dr Watson: **Nigel Bruce** Kitty: **Evelyn Ankers** Sir Evan Barham: **Reginald Denny** Meade: **Thomas Gomez** Anthony Lloyd: **Henry Daniell** Gen Jerome Lawford: **Montagu Love** Fabian

Holmes (Basil
Rathbone), Kitty
(Evelyn Ankers)
and Watson
(Nigel Bruce) do
their bit for the
war effort in
**Sherlock Holmes
and the Voice of
Terror** (1942)

Prentiss: **Olaf Hytten** Capt Roland Shore: **Leyland
Hodgson** 'Voice of Terror': **Edgar Barrier*** Gavin: **Robert
Barron*** Crosbie [radio technician]: **Arthur Blake*** Jill
Grandes: **Hillary Brooke*** Camberwell: **Harry Cording***
Schieler: **Robert O Davis*** Dobson [constable]: **Leslie
Dennison*** Smithson [Barham's butler]: **Herbert Evans***
Mrs Hudson: **Mary Gordon*** Grimes: **Alec Harford***
Cabby: **George Sherwood*** English officer: **Arthur
Stenning*** Grady [pub owner]: **Donald Stuart** cab driver
[Kitty's spy]: **Harry Stubbs*** Heinrich: **John Wilde***
other roles: **Ted Billings***, **Charles Jordan***, **John Rogers***

THE MYSTERY

Britain in wartime, where a German propagandist
calling himself 'The Voice of Terror' takes to the
airwaves to broadcast details of Nazi infiltrators'
latest blows against the nation: the demolition of
an aircraft factory, the destruction of an oil
refinery, the assassination of a senior official in a
train crash. The Intelligence Inner Council,
chaired by Sir Evan Barham, asks Sherlock

Holmes to silence the morale-sapping Voice and
track down the terrorists.

THE INVESTIGATION

Holmes' analysis of the broadcasts suggests that
the Voice is recorded in England and then sent to
Germany to be transmitted. After asking questions
in London's Limehouse area, Gavin, one of
Holmes' own spies, is knifed in the back – presumably by a Hamburger assassin. Holmes persuades Gavin's widow, Kitty, to mobilise the locals
to search for someone or something called
'Christopher' – the last word to pass the dying
Gavin's lips. 'Christopher' is, in fact, a reference to
an old dock where Holmes confronts a Nazi agent,
R F Meade, who escapes via a trapdoor. Holmes
deduces that there must be a German mole within
the Inner Council itself. Now working for Holmes,
Kitty agrees to spy on Meade, discovering that he
is due to go to Sevenoaks the next night.
Sevenoaks is where Sir Evan has his country

*Hande hoch!
Holmes (Basil
Rathbone)
captures sneering
Nazi R F Meade
(Thomas Gomez)
in **Sherlock
Holmes and the
Voice of Terror**
(1942)*

home; he and Holmes appear to foil an attempted landing by a German plane. Soon after, a broadcast by the Voice hints that the next day will see an all-out attack on the north-east of England...

THE SOLUTION

Kitty and Meade have been shadowed by a cab driver working for Holmes, who reports that the pair have gone to a deserted fishing village on the southern seaboard. At Holmes' instigation, the entire Council, which sought to authorise a concentration of forces in the north-east, is overruled by Downing Street. Troops escort them to the south, where Meade and his Nazi-uniformed associates are overseeing operations from a remote ruined church. Holmes reveals that the Nazis' plan was to convince the authorities of the Voice's intentions to the degree that, fearing an attack elsewhere, they would order their forces withdrawn from the south – when the south was the intended landing-point for the first stage of a German invasion. The traitor in the Council is 'Sir Evan' – actually von Bork, a German Secret Service agent who was substituted for the real Barham over 20 years before. As British Spitfires roar overhead, returning home from a surprise attack on the German forces, Meade attempts to escape – shooting Kitty dead before being gunned down himself.

✦ ✦ ✦

Were it not for an analgesic known as Bromo Quinine, there is reason to believe that the Holmes and Watson pairing of Basil Rathbone and Nigel Bruce would have spanned no more that the two 20th Century-Fox features **Sir Arthur Conan Doyle's The Hound of the Baskervilles** and **The**

Adventures of Sherlock Holmes (both 1939). Instead, Rathbone and Bruce would make 12 further appearances, becoming synonymous with the on-screen representation of the detective and the doctor. Indeed, Rathbone and Bruce are now so bound up in the post-Doyle mythology of Sherlock Holmes that it is virtually impossible to describe successive teams without making reference to their double-act, be it something to aspire to... or avoid.

Shortly after the release of the second of the two Fox pictures, Rathbone and Bruce were reunited across the airwaves of America in three series of radio adventures sponsored by Grove Laboratories, manufacturers of the aforementioned indigestion aid. Broadcast nationwide from Hollywood, the first two runs, airing on Monday evenings between October 1939 and March 1940, then on Sunday nights between September 1940 and March 1941, adapted stories from the canon. The third season, transmitted each Sunday between October 1941 and March 1942, included a number of pastiches written by regular adapter Edith Meiser – the last of which was *The Giant Rat of Sumatra*, extrapolated from a passing reference in THE SUSSEX VAMPIRE. If the number of participating radio stations is any judge, the shows were extraordinarily successful; whereas 29 broadcasters across the US signed up for the 1939-40 run, 53 took the second season.

Enter the Universal Pictures Company Inc. Founded principally by German émigré Carl Laemmle (1867-1939), the studio had prospered throughout the twenties but foundered in the early thirties, suffering massive losses despite the smash-hit, and now much-admired, horror features *Dracula* and *Frankenstein* (both 1931). His company crippled, early in 1936 Laemmle would be forced to sell out to a conglomeration of hawkish entrepreneurs, Charles R Rogers assuming control of production. Rogers' reign was an unmitigated disaster, once again prompting fears of financial ruin, but by May 1938, two ex-RKO men, Nate Blumberg and Cliff Work, had assumed key positions as company president and vice-president in charge of production respectively. *Dracula* and *Frankenstein* were re-released, to be joined soon after by a second Frankenstein sequel: *Son of Frankenstein* (1939), featuring Rathbone as the heir of Mary Shelley's modern Prometheus. Horror flicks, Abbott and Costello comedies and adventure serials such as *The Green Hornet* and *Junior G-Men* (both 1940) saved Universal. And when the company needed supporting features to be shown alongside its A-product, Blumberg and Work turned to a tried-and-tested favourite, still in the nation's ear, if not its eye: Rathbone's Holmes.

Early 1942 saw Universal strike a seven-year deal with the Doyle estate, purchasing 21 stories from the canon and extended rights in Doyle's characters. Three films would be made each year, two of which had to be adaptations of the Doyle stories (although all these would be cursory, in-name-only versions of the tales). The Doyle estate went away richer to the tune of some $300,000, a sum which must have helped alleviate any dismay felt by the estate when Universal's first production saw the updated Great Detective take on the forces of the Third Reich.

In context, this wasn't so bizarre a step: popular American film characters had fallen foul of warmongering enemy agents long before the December 1941 attack on Pearl Harbor. Columbia's thief-turned-detective the Lone Wolf, as played by Warren William, investigated a Washington-based espionage ring in *The Lone Wolf Spy Hunt* (1939), later foiling Nazis at large in London and Egypt in *Counter-Espionage* (1942) and *Passport to Suez* (1943). MGM brought pre-Great War adventurer-sleuth Nick Carter, as played by Walter Pidgeon, into the present day in *Nick Carter, Master Detective* (1939), followed by *Phantom Raiders* and *Sky Murder* (both 1940). Fox's Charlie Chan, as played by Sidney Toler, got topical in *City of Darkness* (1939) and *Charlie Chan in Panama* (1940). And Columbia had William Gargan in the self-explanatory *Enemy Agents Meet Ellery Queen* (1942). Far from setting a trend, Universal's Holmes was following it.

Another RKO alumnus, Howard Benedict, defected to Universal to oversee production of the Holmes features – the first of which, provisionally titled *Sherlock Holmes Saves London*, went before the cameras early in May 1942. Hired to direct was John Rawlins (1902-97), a former film editor turned Universal journeyman, previously responsible in part for the serials *Junior G-Men* and *The Green Hornet Strikes Back* (1941), among others. The key supporting role of Sir Evan was given to Reginald Denny (Leigh Dugmore Denny, 1891-1967), an

English actor who'd appeared as Prince Alexis in John Barrymore's **Sherlock Holmes** (1922) but had become far better known for his recurring role as Algy Longworth in eight of Paramount's Bulldog Drummond films. Stage player Thomas Gomez (Sabino Tomas Gomez, 1905-71) made his film début as nasty Nazi R F Meade, a borderline psychotic motivated by his own power-lust. In a striking, designed-to-demonise soliloquy, Meade details a childhood dream in which, dressed in shining armour, he 'rode over the bodies of underlings' whose 'blood ran out along the gutters like a river ... What if this was no dream? What if this was prophecy?'

Meade's associate Schieler was played by German-born Rudolph Anders (1895-1987) under the name 'Robert O Davis'; 'Davis' had essayed similar roles in *Confessions of a Nazi Spy* (1939) and Chaplin's *The Great Dictator* (1940). The female lead, Kitty, went to Chilean beauty Evelyn Ankers (1918-85), who'd screamed her way through two of Universal's most recent horrors, *The Wolf Man* and *The Ghost of Frankenstein* (both 1941); she would later turn up in **The Pearl of Death** and **Your Show Time: The Adventure of the Speckled Band**. Henry Daniell and Hillary Brooke, playing Intelligence officer Lloyd and Holmes' driver Jill Grandes, would be given far more to do in subsequent Rathbone Holmeses, most notably **The Woman in Green**.

Although preceded by an on-screen disclaimer ('Sherlock Holmes, the immortal character of fiction created by Sir Arthur Conan Doyle, is ageless, invincible and unchanging. In solving significant problems of the present day he remains – as ever – the supreme master of deductive reasoning'), *Sherlock Holmes and the Voice of Terror*

An east wind coming: Holmes (Basil Rathbone) and sleeper von Bork (Reginald Denny) watch the RAF return from bombing Germany in **Sherlock Holmes and the Voice of Terror** (1942)

does contain one odd little comment on the fact that neither Holmes nor Watson (nor, for that matter, Mary Gordon's Mrs Hudson) appear to have aged since they were last seen: Holmes goes to pick up his deerstalker, but Watson stops him, saying, 'No, no, no, no. Holmes, you promised.' The detective exits wearing a smart 1940s fedora instead. This apparent confirmation that the inhabitants of 221B Baker Street enjoy Methuselah-like powers is rendered doubly baffling when it is revealed that Watson and Sir Evan were at school together, presumably in the early 1900s. (Watson's nickname, we are told, was 'Blouser' – from 'big girl's blouse', perhaps?) In all significant respects, however, the two leads are quite unchanged from **The Adventures of Sherlock Holmes**, Rathbone's ridiculous, Caesar-styled coiffure notwithstanding.

Ostensibly an adaptation of HIS LAST BOW, *Sherlock Holmes and the Voice of Terror* retains only the notion of Holmes being procured for the war effort, his tracking down fifth columnists at work on the British mainland, the closing 'East wind coming' monologue and the name of German secret agent 'von Bork' from Doyle's original. Here, von Bork, his name invoked only minutes before the conclusion, has been a 'sleeper' ever since Kaiser Wilhelm II had substituted him for Sir Evan Barham over 20 years previously (a plot device which betrays a shocking lack of understanding of comparatively recent history, not to mention omitting the Weimar Republic from the timeline entirely). The 'Voice of Terror' itself is a Teuton taunter prone to exclamations such as, 'Englishmen – do you still await your doom in your stupid, stuffy little clubs? It will come, I promise you!' This aspect of the piece appears to have been inspired by the activities of 'Lord Haw-Haw', as the *Daily Express* dubbed one of two notorious propagandists broadcasting to Blitz-torn London out of Zeesen. 'Haw-Haw' is most commonly identified with an American-born Englishman called William Joyce, a Mosleyite who defected to Germany in August 1939 and was eventually hanged for high treason in January 1946.

If the film's rather uncomfortable topicality was responsible for its British release being delayed, reportedly due to the intervention of the war censor, until late in November 1943 (more than a full year after its American release, where it most often supported dimwitted Abbott and Costello timewaster *Pardon My Sarong*), then one wonders how the notion of an Intelligence establishment headed by a Nazi spy could ever have been passed for public exhibition. Writing in the *New York Times* on 19 September 1942, Bosley Crowther had picked up this idea, commenting: 'It is surprising that Universal should take such cheap advantage of the present crisis to exploit an old, respected fiction character, and that it should do so in a manner which throws suspicion on Britain's administrators. The late Conan Doyle, who obviously never wrote this story, as Universal claims, must be speculating sadly in his spirit world on this betrayal of trust.' Perhaps the British censor's liberalism was unwittingly accounted for in UK trade paper *Today's Cinema*, which remarked, in sanguine fashion, on 15 October 1943: 'The implausibilities of such a yarn ... can hardly, of course, find ready acceptance with English audiences.'

Those same audiences would, it must be said, have been likely to ridicule many other not-so-British and not-so-likely aspects of *Sherlock Holmes and the Voice of Terror*: the absurdly spacious Transylvanian-style Limehouse cellar-pub, all squeezebox music and waiting at tables; a BBC radio service primed to play a recording of Beethoven's Fifth the instant Sherlock Holmes calls to request it; a Holmes who tells Kitty to 'Take it easy.' Most grating of all is a sequence in which Kitty announces 'I'm British and I'm proud of it!' in an undisguised American accent.

Despite its frequent lapses in judgment, not to mention logic – why do the Nazis record the Voice in England and fly discs out to Germany? how does Holmes learn Meade's name? was Kitty involved with Meade from the outset? was Kitty, in fact, complicit in Gavin's murder? what were American tanks and munitions doing at the East India Dock? – *Sherlock Holmes and the Voice of Terror* possesses a breathless conviction that counterbalances most objections, and Rathbone's strident, stirring rendition of the closing 'East wind coming' monologue, delivered over a swelling, elegiac theme, has magnificence about it. Propaganda, yes; a *Triumph of the Will*, no. But some sort of triumph all the same.

The second in the series was **Sherlock Holmes and the Secret Weapon**.

Sherlock Holmes Baffled

*US 1900 parody American Mutoscope and Biograph
Company 35 seconds approx bw silent*

In a windowed room somewhere, a black-clad
burglar is helping himself to silver from a table,
stashing his loot in a sack. A man wearing a
dressing-gown over his everyday clothes, cigar
clamped between his teeth, enters the room and
taps the thief on the shoulder. The villain promptly
vanishes, leaving his swag on the table; the other
sits beside the table and lights his cigar, which
promptly explodes. Simultaneously, the burglar
reappears. Quick as a flash, the other produces a
revolver and fires it, then chases the thief around
the table before he disappears again. The other
picks up the sack and makes for the door –
whereupon the sack vanishes from his hands as
the thief winks in and out of existence for the final
time. The other, Sherlock Holmes, is baffled.

The story of Sherlock Holmes on screen begins,
ostensibly, with a silly trick film recorded in 1900
on the rooftop of 841 Broadway, New York, using a
heavy 'Mutograph' camera that punched perfora-
tions into the 35mm stock as it was cranked
through. The film was designed to be viewed on
the primitive Mutoscope peepshow device, a rival
patent to Thomas Edison's Kinetoscope. Formed in
December 1895, the American Mutoscope
Company ('and Biograph' came later) was an
agglomeration of former Edison associate W K L
Dickson with Herman Casler, Eliza Koopman and
Harry N Marvin. The Mutoscope machines and
films proved hugely successful, outselling Edison's
device and enabling the company to move to new
premises, establishing an indoor studio in 1906.

Sherlock Holmes Baffled called upon the time-
honoured technique of stop-start exposure,
enabling its preternaturally endowed thief to hop
about the static scene like some Spring-heeled Jack
of the novelty arcades; the joke is that the great
detective, Sherlock Holmes, is his victim – and
utterly unable to account for his antics. In that
sense, *Sherlock Holmes Baffled* is the first ever
filmed Holmes parody, a strain that would endure
throughout the silent era with countless titles
including *Sherlock Bonehead* (Kalem Co, 1914),
Sherlock, the Boob Detective (Thistle, 1915), *A Study*

in *Skarlit* (Comedy Combine-Sunny South, 1915)
and the wonderful *The Mystery of the Leaping Fish*,
starring Douglas Fairbanks as the doped-up 'Coke
Ennyday' (Triangle Film Corporation, 1916).
Discounting, then, the Mutoscope effort, the first
true Holmes picture was **The Adventures of
Sherlock Holmes** (1905).

Sherlock Holmes contra Professor Moryarty

*tr 'Sherlock Holmes versus Professor Moryarty'
Germany 1911 film serial Vitascope GmbH silent bw*

DER ERBE VON BLOOMROD
tr 'The heir/inheritance of Bloomrod' 2231 feet
d **Viggo Larsen**
cast unknown

By 21 April 1911, just over six weeks after the
final episode of **Arsène Lupin contra Sherlock
Holmes** had gone on release, the first chapter of a
second Vitascope Holmes serial, again directed by
the prodigious Viggo Larsen, was in the hands of
the German film censor's office. Little more is
known about *Sherlock Holmes contra Professor
Moryarty*: the fact that it bore a subtitle suggests
that further instalments were at least intended, if
not actually produced; the fact that no person or
place called 'Bloomrod' appears anywhere in the
Doyle canon suggests that these were new adventures featuring Holmes' adversary, this 'Moryarty'.
Whatever the truth of the matter, Vitascope was far
from finished with Sherlock Holmes – and, in
1914, the company would release **Der Hund von
Baskerville**, the first of a whole series of films
based on one Holmes tale in particular.

Viggo Larsen would continue to work in
Germany for Vitascope; his later pictures *Der Eid
das Stephen Huller* (1912) and *Die Sumpfblume*
(1913) both featured Wanda Truemann, the actress
who became his wife. Larsen's 'fluid' direction
would later grace *Rotterdam-Amsterdam*, a Messter-
Film picture of March 1918 in which he featured
as 'Detektivs Holms' [sic], a character charged with
investigating the disappearance of a hoard of
well-secured precious stones while in transit – a
mystery that, according to *Der Kinematograph*,

Holms solves 'with elegance and with disguises'. *Rotterdam-Amsterdam* was written by Richard Hutter, co-author of May-Films' *Herrin der Welt* ('Mistress of the world') series, and featured Robert Wüllner in a supporting role. It's impossible to say whether or not 'Holms' was named as an intentional parody of 'Holmes' – or whether a misplaced letter 'e' in the press has denied us confirmation of yet another silent German Sherlock.

Larsen died in his adopted homeland on 6 January 1957.

Sherlock Holmes en Caracas

tr 'Sherlock Holmes in Caracas'
Venezuela 1992 parody [THE SUSSEX VAMPIRE] *Big Ben Productions/Tiuna Films/Foncine 95m colour*
wd **Juan E Fresan** *p* **Juan E Fresan, Franklin Whaite**
cast includes Sherlock Holmes: **Jean Manuel Montesinos**
Dr Watson: **Gilbert Dacournan** Miss Venezuela: **Maria Eugenia Cruz** Governess: **Carolina Luzardo**
other roles: **Giles Bickford, Richard Cummings, Chippili Ruthman**

S herlock Holmes and Dr Watson fly to Venezuela after an old friend of Holmes', now living in Maracaibo, requests the detective's assistance; he thinks his children may be in danger from his young wife, an ex-beauty queen whom he has come to fear may be a vampire. Having also investigated the children's governess, whom he unmasks as a follower of pagan rites, Holmes reaches the startling conclusion that the former Miss Venezuela is, indeed, one of the bloodsucking undead.

A knockabout, quickfire English-speaking comedy in which, despite the evidence of the title, Holmes passes only fleetingly through the South American city of Caracas. The plot inverts THE SUSSEX VAMPIRE by having the suspect wife confirmed as a creature of supernatural origin, making this one of the very few occasions when the spirit world meets the characters of Holmes and Watson. But since much of this low-budget piece, described as being cast from the Monty Python mould, is designed to strip down Holmesian convention (Holmes moans about his inadequate characterisation, and is forever aggravated by Watson – who, having foregone his writing-desk,

now videotapes the detective's every move via camcorder), it's probably permissible.

Sherlock Holmes Faces Death

US 1943 adaptation [THE MUSGRAVE RITUAL]
Universal Pictures Company Inc 68m bw
w **Bertram Millhauser** *pd* **Roy William Neill**
cast Sherlock Holmes: **Basil Rathbone** Dr Watson: **Nigel Bruce** Lestrade: **Dennis Hoey** Dr Sexton: **Arthur Margetson** Sally Musgrave: **Hillary Brooke** Brunton: **Halliwell Hobbes** Mrs Howells: **Minna Phillips** Captain Vickery: **Milburn Stone** Phillip Musgrave: **Gavin Muir** Langford: **Gerald Hamer** Clavering: **Vernon Downing** Captain MacIntosh: **Olaf Hytten** Geoffrey Musgrave: **Frederic Worlock** slinking figure: **Martin Ashe*** Nora: **Joan Blair*** pub proprietor: **Harold de Becker*** Mrs Hudson: **Mary Gordon*** Grace: **Norma Varden*** Jenny: **Heather Wilde*** constables: **Charles Coleman*, Dick Rush*** sailors: **Peter Lawford*, Eric Snowden***

THE MYSTERY

Northumberland in wartime: Dr Watson has volunteered for medical service at Hurlstone Towers, formerly Musgrave Manor – a long-established, reputedly haunted estate which, with the permission of the surviving Musgrave siblings, Geoffrey, Sally and Phillip, has been temporarily converted into a convalescent home for wounded officers. One night, Watson's assistant, Dr Sexton, is found stabbed in the neck and the clock tower strikes 13, an event said to foretell the death of a member of the family. Watson travels to London to fetch Sherlock Holmes – but the pair arrive too late, discovering Geoffrey's body hidden beneath a pile of leaves...

THE INVESTIGATION

Inspector Lestrade is already at the scene, and he soon decides to arrest one of the residents, the American captain Pat Vickery – who has been romantically involved with Sally, much to the dead Geoffrey's distaste. Later, as the next in line to the estate, Sally is obliged to recite an ancient litany, 'the Musgrave Ritual', over Geoffrey's body. Brunton, the eavesdropping butler, gets drunk and is dismissed by Phillip. The clock strikes 13 again – and, next morning, Phillip's corpse is found in the boot of Sally's roadster. Examining the Ritual,

'Who first shall find it, were better dead': Holmes (Basil Rathbone) and boozy butler Brunton (Halliwell Hobbes) attempt to decode 'the Musgrave Ritual' in **Sherlock Holmes Faces Death** (1943)

Holmes realises that it suggests pieces in a game of chess to be played out on the chequered floor of the Manor's main hall. He is led to a particular square above a disused cellar – and in the spot directly underneath, finds the lost crypt of a 16th century Musgrave, Ralph. Brunton's body lies beside Ralph's sarcophagus; the dead man is clutching a box containing an old parchment, which Holmes surreptitiously pockets. Holmes announces to the household that Brunton had attempted to write the name of his killer on the floor in his own blood, and that he is going to Newcastle to collect the chemicals he needs to help reveal Brunton's full message. Watson is left to guard the inside of the Manor, but is locked out by an unknown person and arrested by the police. The killer makes his way into the crypt...

THE SOLUTION

It is Dr Sexton, who is surprised to discover Holmes in Brunton's place. Holmes confesses that the 'message in blood' was a ruse; Sexton, in turn, admits to the murders, but manages to overpower Holmes – and shoots the detective dead with his own gun. In the cellar above, Watson and the police are waiting, Sexton's own words having condemned him; the unharmed Holmes appears, pointing out that he'd loaded his weapon with blanks. The parchment, it transpires, is a long-lost land grant, confirming the Musgrave family's ownership of 'eighty thousand acres of the richest land in England'; Sexton had planned to marry Sally and thus gain a stake in the prize. Not wishing to make hundreds of families destitute by asserting the Musgraves' claim, Sally burns the document.

✦ ✦ ✦

S eldom can a more credulous bunch of characters have been assembled than at Hurlstone Towers sometime during the Second World War. Sadly, this applies to the normally sceptical Sherlock Holmes himself, for *Sherlock Holmes Faces Death* – fourth in the Universal sequence – is distinguished by its (albeit unstated) acceptance of the paranormal.

Whereas it's almost amusing to note that the first four lines of the so-called Musgrave Ritual – 'Who first shall find it, were better dead; who next shall find it, perils his head; the last to find it, defies dark powers; and brings good fortune to Hurlstone Towers' – take on the air of prophecy in light of the film's conclusion (with butler Brunton, baddie Sexton and Holmes himself representing the first, the next and the last), the fact that the confluence between the litany and later events isn't underlined in the closing reel is no indicator of subtlety on the part of scriptwriter Bertram Millhauser. Rather, it suggests a script lacking both internal clarity and sympathy for its source material.

Then there's that old chestnut, the clock that strikes 13 for reasons inexplicable; oh, and the seemingly divine bolt of lightning which contravenes all known physical laws by breaking glass in its attempt to fry the latest of the Musgrave line. Concerns about omissions from the Doyle text and, say, the presentation of an inappropriately buffoonish Watson – the two tiresome whinges that pass most often for criticism in Holmes fandom – are as nothing to such lazy touches, dumping the arch-rationalist Sherlock Holmes in a world whose fringes can only be explained by magic, not science. No producer has yet put forward a serious adaptation of, say, THE HOUND OF THE BASKERVILLES in which the legendary 'hound of Hell' is ultimately revealed to have a genuinely infernal origin – it'd be a case of quite spectacularly missing the point – but prophetic parchments and clairvoyant clocktowers are in exactly the same league. Not that *Sherlock Holmes Faces Death* is the sole offender – episodes of the 1954-5 Ronald Howard-starring **Sherlock Holmes** TV series (*The Haunted Gainsborough*, for example) and even the otherwise fine **Murder By Decree** attempt to pull off similar stunts – but it's a very black mark against an otherwise creditable, not to say credible, picture. Even Holmes' now-obligatory closing speech ('There's a new spirit abroad...') has a quasi-Biblical, lay preacher's tone about it.

One supposes that the Universal team simply got carried away in their eagerness to distinguish the piece from the rather pallid spy heroics of its immediate precursor, **Sherlock Holmes in Washington**, by dumping Basil Rathbone's Holmes and Nigel Bruce's Watson into a diluted Gothic milieu. Even if the viewer can't precisely identify the Hurlstone village set with the 19th

century mittel-European 'Vasaria' familiar from Universal's later Frankenstein films, or the Musgrave crypt with the resting-place of Bela Lugosi's Count Dracula, he or she won't miss such hokey signifiers as Charlie the raven, who squawks 'I'm a devil!' at strangers down the local pub, or the old dark house festooned with secret passageways. Claiming that the former Musgrave Manor has two camply named spectres-in-residence, Lady Florinda and Sir Gervase, is over-egging the pudding somewhat.

All of which leaves little room for the plot of THE MUSGRAVE RITUAL itself – which is a shame, because it's among the Doyle stories that lend themselves most readily to a cinematic presentation. Millhauser's substitution of a giant chessboard for the painstaking measurement of distances between trees is a marvellous conceit, but it's a pity that, in a house stuffed full of shell-shocked war veterans, drunken butlers spouting verses of William McGonagall awfulness and eavesdropping old maids with uncanny physical resemblances to 'trunk murderers', the least interesting and characterful individual of them all should be unmasked as the principal villain.

Dennis Hoey's Inspector Lestrade made only his second appearance in this, the first of Universal's second block of three Sherlock films (at which point director Roy William Neill assumed producership of the series from Howard Benedict). He seizes the opportunity to stamp his mark on the role, presenting a passive-aggressive Plod whose catchphrase is 'Let's stick to motive, that's my strong point.' Rathbone's increasingly grumpy Holmes plainly despises him, warning an unfairly targeted suspect: 'Just incriminate yourself, Captain Vickery – that's all Inspector Lestrade wants.' (Later, on discovering Lestrade to be trapped in the Manor's wainscoting, like a faint-hearted kitten caught up a tree, Holmes tells the housekeeper: 'Get him a saucer of milk.') Watson fares better than in the previous film, being presented at the outset as a medical practitioner, entirely independent of Holmes. He also gets to be the butt of a rather intriguing joke which reminds one of the fact that he and Holmes are celebrities in 'their' world. On being caught by a police sentry outside the cordoned-off Manor, he protests 'Look here, constable, I'm Dr Watson.' 'Are ye now?' grunts the other. 'Well, I'm Mrs Miniver!'

Filmed from 12 April 1943, *Sherlock Holmes Faces Death* was released in the US on 17 September. The next film in Universal's second trio was **The Spider Woman**.

Sherlock Holmes i Bondefangerkløer

tr 'Sherlock Holmes in the hands of the conmen'
at **Den Stjaalne Tegnebog** ['The stolen wallet']
aka **The Confidence Trick** [GB], **A Confidence Trick** [US]
*Denmark 1910 pastiche Nordisk Films Kompagni
873 feet bw silent*
known cast Sherlock Holmes: **Otto Lagoni** other roles:
Axel Boesen, **Rigmor Jerichau**, **Victor Fabian**

Having spent several years working in Canada, one Bill Barrett returns to his native land with substantial earnings in his wallet. At the station, he meets a number of well-dressed strangers who offer to take him out on the town to celebrate his return; they ply him with drink at both a bar and an expensive restaurant. When Barrett wakes up, he discovers that he has been robbed of his watch, his pocketbook and his wallet – the victim of a gang of confidence tricksters. Sherlock Holmes mounts a search of the bar and the restaurant, learning the location of the gang's hideout from the restaurateur; after various adventures, he retrieves the wallet and brings the gang to justice.

The only one of the Nordisk films known to have survived, **Sherlock Holmes i Bondefangerkløer** – the successor to **Den Forklædte Guvernante** – was the second of the two films to feature Otto Lagoni as the hero-detective. Utterly typical of the series, it was released in the UK on 10 December 1910 and in the US in April 1911, where it was held to be 'more than ordinarily interesting' by *Moving Picture World*. **Den Sorte Haand** came next.

Sherlock Holmes i Livsfare

tr 'Sherlock Holmes' life in danger'
aka **Sherlock Holmes** [GB/US]
*Denmark 1908 pastiche Nordisk Films Kompagni
1142 feet bw silent*
wd **Viggo Larsen**

known cast Sherlock Holmes: **Viggo Larsen**
Raffles: **Holger Madsen** Professor Moriarty: **Gustav Lund**
other roles: **Otto Detlefsen**, **Aage Brandt**

Robber Raffles' designs on a particular pearl necklace lead to his being fingered by detective Sherlock Holmes. Raffles writes to the villainous Professor Moriarty Esq, warning him that Holmes is on the trail and must be got 'out of the way'. Like Raffles, Moriarty is soon trapped and arrested – but not before the wicked Professor has made an unsuccessful attempt on Holmes' life.

Denmark was quick to take Sherlock Holmes to its cultural heart. Conan Doyle translations were on Copenhagen bookstalls from 1893 on; by 1906, authorised editions had been joined by at least one pastiche adventure, Carl Quistgaard Muusmann's *Sherlock Holmes paa Marienlyst*. That same year, kinematograph impresario Ole Olsen founded the Nordisk Films Kompagni, establishing a studio at Valby, Copenhagen. From humble beginnings – a documentary short detailing the funeral procession of Christian IX – Nordisk grew so rapidly that by 1908 it was selling films throughout Europe and, as the Great Northern Film Company, had even established a New York office. The first picture distributed in the US by Great Northern, released late in February 1908, went under the title of *Iceboat Racing on Lake St Clair*.

Heading up Nordisk's New York operation was a Norwegian called Ingvald Aaes – who, it appears, initiated the production of two linked Sherlock Holmes pictures, *Sherlock Holmes i Livsfare* and **Raffles Flugt Fra Fængslet**. Shot by cameraman Axel Sørensen sometime prior to late July, both were written and directed by, and starred, Viggo Larsen (1880-1957), a former Forces man who'd been working for Nordisk since 1906, when he'd written, directed and acted in a picture called *Anarkistens Svigermor* ('The anarchist's mother-in-law').

Larsen's Holmes was a stiff-collared, gun-toting 'tec sometimes seen in an odd raincoat and flat cap combination; he shared lodgings with both Watson and an 'office boy', Billy – the latter being the largely forgotten 'young but very wise and tactful' Baker Street page who appears in THE VALLEY OF FEAR and THE MAZARIN STONE, among others. However, THE VALLEY OF FEAR would not be written until early in 1914, the character being filched by Doyle from William Gillette's 1899 play *Sherlock Holmes* (itself filmed in 1916). So it can only be assumed that Larsen was intimately familiar with the Gillette play at the time of *Sherlock Holmes i Livsfare*'s production, even though the precise date of its first Danish staging is unknown. Certainly, the play's 'Stepney Gas Chamber' sequence would be reworked in the third Nordisk film, **Det Hemmelige Dokument**. Incidentally, there's no evidence that Watson appears in any of the subsequent Nordisk films; the character is sidelined in favour of the youthful Billy.

Not only would Holmes be pitted against Professor Moriarty in *Sherlock Holmes i Livsfare*, but also another great villain of late 19th century literature – E W Hornung's 'gentleman burglar' Raffles, anti-hero of *The Amateur Cracksman* (1899; a compilation of short stories first published in the *Strand*), plus a succession of sequels. Although presumably unintentional, and certainly 'unlicenced' in the modern sense, the 'crossover' of the two characters in *Sherlock Holmes i Livsfare* has a pleasing symmetry. Ernest William Hornung (1866-1921) was Doyle's brother-in-law, and Raffles had been consciously created as 'a kind of inversion' of Holmes; indeed, *The Amateur Cracksman* had been dedicated 'To ACD. This form of flattery.'

Raffles would return in Nordisk's sequel to *Sherlock Holmes i Livsfare*, **Raffles Flugt Fra Fængslet** – but these were not the first fictions in which the pair had been conflated. The first of an eventual ten *Remarkable Adventures of Raffles Holmes* by American parodist John Kendrick Bangs had seen print in the 22 July 1905 edition of *Harper's Weekly*; Bangs' thief-cum-detective inherited distinct characteristics from both father Sherlock and grandfather Raffles. That same year, Hornung's original 'cracksman' made his film début, as portrayed by J Barney Sherry, in an American silent, *The Adventures of Raffles, the Amateur Cracksman* (see **The Adventures of Sherlock Holmes**, 1905). Danish and Italian shorts followed the Nordisk pictures, in 1910 and 1911 respectively, before the first full-length Raffles feature – *Raffles, the Amateur Cracksman*, starring John Barrymore – appeared in 1917.

Interestingly, the notion that Doyle and Hornung should collaborate in bringing the two characters together in print had been mooted as

early as 1903. Publisher Trumbull White nearly succeeded in brokering a deal between the two in 1913, but it was the similarly disappointed theatrical agent George C Tyler who most accurately summarised the unlikelihood of such an agreement ever being reached: 'Neither author could be persuaded to let his pet character get the worst of it in a battle of wits...'

The Holmes/Raffles pairing in *Sherlock Holmes i Livsfare* proved popular. The grandiose hyperbole of Great Northern's publicity bumf – 'The season's biggest feature film ... An absorbing subject, the interest of which is enhanced by novel stage effects. The fight in the moving train is the perfection of realism' – was echoed by enthusiastic write-ups in journals such as Britain's the *Bioscope* ('Plot and counter-plot are most cleverly worked out and though the film is a long one the incidents are so exciting that there is no diminution of interest throughout') and America's *Moving Picture World* ('a masterly production in every respect ... The staging is splendid and introduces some novel effects, not claptrap contraptions'). The film was released in Great Britain early in October 1908 – seemingly ahead of both Denmark and the US, where it was issued around late November/early December.

Like all bar one of its 11 eventual sequels (they being **Raffles Flugt Fra Fængslet**, **Det Hemmelige Dokument**, **Sangerindens Diamanter**, **Droske Nr. 519**, **Den Grå Dame**, **Den Forklædte Guvernante**, **Sherlock Holmes i Bondefangerkløer**, **Den Sorte Haand**, **Milliontestamentet**, **Hotelrotterne** and **Den Sorte Hætte**), every print of *Sherlock Holmes i Livsfare* has since been lost. The significance of the series cannot, however, be overlooked; a remarkably early example of mass-marketed movie-making to an established formula, it more than adequately marks cinema's transition from gimcrack spectacle to industry-cum-artform.

Sherlock Holmes in New York

US 1976 TVM pastiche Twentieth Century-Fox Film Corporation 120m colour
tx 18 October 1976 NBC-TV
w **Alvin Sapinsley** p **John Cutts** d **Boris Sagal**
cast Sherlock Holmes: **Roger Moore** Professor Moriarty:
John Huston Dr Watson: **Patrick Macnee** Irene Adler:
Charlotte Rampling Inspector Lafferty: **David Huddleston**

Fraulein Reichenbach: **Signe Hasso** Mortimer McGraw: **Gig Young** Daniel Furman: **Leon Ames** Heller: **John Abbott** Haymarket proprietor: **Jackie Coogan** Nicole Romaine: **Maria Grimm** telegraph office manager: **William Benedict** Mrs Hudson: **Marjorie Bennett** man in the chequered suit: **Paul Sorenson** stage doorman: **John Steadman** Nickers: **Robert Ball** workman #1: **Vince Barbi** workman #2: **Roy Goldman** policeman: **Tom Denver** carriage driver: **Gil Perkins** Haymarket driver: **Harvey Perry** engineer: **Alvin Sapinsley** woman on the pier: **Shawn Mallory** telegram boy: **Meredith Cutts** Scott Adler: **Geoffrey Moore**

THE MYSTERY

March 1901: Sherlock Holmes penetrates the heart of Professor Moriarty's secret HQ in London's Victoria Docks to inform his nemesis that his plot to assassinate one Lord Brackish has failed, and all of his gang have been rounded up and arrested – but, as usual, there is no evidence to directly implicate their leader. Moriarty vows to avenge himself by perpetrating 'the crime of the century', humiliating Holmes in the eyes of all the world. Three days later, Holmes receives an envelope from New York; for the past ten years, the actress Irene Adler, with whom Holmes once spent a long week in Montenegro, has sent him two tickets to all of her first nights. This time, however, the tickets are torn in half, which Holmes takes as a signal that something is very wrong.

Travelling to New York with Dr Watson in tow, Holmes discovers that Irene's illegitimate son, Scott, has been kidnapped; he then receives a message from Moriarty instructing him to refuse to co-operate with the police when asked, or else the boy will die. Sure enough, Holmes is contacted by NY police inspector Lafferty and one Mortimer McGraw, president of the International Gold Exchange, a secret bullion store beneath Manhattan where the gold reserves of the major countries are held; the Exchange has been robbed, stripped clean. In three days' time, a transaction is due to take place between Italy and Germany. Should the robbery be discovered, a world war seems the most likely outcome. This, then, is the crime of the century: with Moriarty holding the bankrupt nations to ransom, he will be able to set himself up as ruler of the entire world. And, remembering Moriarty's warning, Holmes is forced to refuse to help...

Holmes (Roger Moore) and Watson (Patrick Macnee) enjoy a bite of the Big Apple in **Sherlock Holmes in New York** (1976)

THE INVESTIGATION

Holmes' only chance is to find and rescue the boy before the robbery is revealed. He deduces that Scott's abducter was a woman, and soon identifies a likely suspect – Nicola Romaine, a performer with whom Scott was friendly. Posing as an Italian escapologist, Holmes makes his way to Romaine's lodgings, where the drugged boy is being kept. He persuades Romaine to keep Scott's rescue secret while he pursues the case of the missing bullion, and returns the boy to Irene. Now all that remains is to work out exactly how Moriarty broke into the gold vaults and stole 360,000 50-pound ingots – a process which would have taken a hundreds-strong team 12 days to complete ...

THE SOLUTION

Using the construction of the New York subway as cover, Moriarty has, in fact, built an exact replica of the vault directly above the original – and it is that empty chamber which is assumed to have been burgled; the gold is exactly where it always was! The threat of war is averted, but Moriarty contrives to abduct Scott a second time. Holmes enters Moriarty's trap-ridden hideout alone in a bid to

Photocall for **Sherlock Holmes in New York** *(1976): Charlotte Rampling (Irene Adler), David Huddleston (Inspector Lafferty), John Huston (Moriarty), Gig Young (Mortimer McGraw) and Patrick Macnee (Watson), plus Geoffrey and Roger Moore (Scott Adler and Sherlock Holmes)*

rescue the boy, only narrowly escaping with his life. Moriarty makes his getaway, and Holmes reunites Scott and Irene, before heading back to London. Scott, it transpires, has 'a fondness for music ... and solving problems'.

✦ ✦ ✦

Very few actors could hold together a piece which, entirely seriously, sets out to depict a lovelorn Holmes battling to rescue his young son from the clutches of Professor Moriarty. Roger Moore, perhaps unsurprisingly, is not one of them. But despite its (at best) misguided casting, despite its cumbersome premise and stodgy production – despite the unequivocal wrongness of it all – *Sherlock Holmes in New York* exudes a certain gauche charm. And that's perhaps the kindest thing one can say about the whole sorry business.

There's no real reason why Holmes should not be presented as an arch, raffish and ageing English roué, but in such a role it's impossible not to regard Roger Moore – the living epitome of those qualities, through his Ivanhoe, his Saint and his irksome James Bond – as anything other than Roger Moore doing his Roger Moore schtick. Although an unlikely prospect, if *Sherlock Holmes in New York* is still around in a hundred years' time, it might just be possible for a viewer with no accumulated awareness of Moore's screen persona to fully appreciate and evaluate such an incarnation of Holmes. For the time being, however, we're stuck with Sherlock Moore – a smug eyebrow in a cape, pithily summed up by John Huston's craggy Dublin Moriarty early on: 'Damn and blast ye for the meddler that y'are, sir, with your West End ways, talkin' down yer upper-class nose and only happy when ye're dressin' up as someone else as though life was some schoolboy lark!'

Sherlock Holmes in New York was shot during an unusually lengthy gap between Bond sequels. Since filming the pedestrian *The Man with the Golden Gun* in 1974, Moore had appeared in one would-be screwball comedy (*That Lucky Touch*), one so-so adventure (*Shout at the Devil*) and a truly dire Italian thriller (*Gli esecutori*, aka *The Sicilian Cross*). Like these, the Holmes project is adrift, lacking in focus. Moore is playing in a swashbuckling comic adventure, Huston a knockabout spoof, leading lady Charlotte Rampling a romance, and Patrick Macnee appears to be solely interested in impersonating Nigel Bruce's Watson, with a wheezy rasp oddly appended to the expected bluster.

This Watson, it must be said, is shockingly poor; one wonders how Macnee ever got to reprise the role 15 years later in the TV movies **Sherlock Holmes and the Leading Lady** and **Incident at Victoria Falls**. The character serves no useful purpose whatsoever, gambolling along at Sherlock Moore's heels like an aged dog longing to be put out of its misery. He exhibits an especially irritating form of Blimpish buffoonery, too – refusing, for example, to reset his pocket watch from the Greenwich standard: 'They're cheeky buggers, I must say, making up their own time!'

Writer Alvin Sapinsley (who makes a small appearance in the film) inserts slight points of Sherlockian witticism – Holmes impersonating Colonel Moran (THE EMPTY HOUSE) at the outset, a governess named 'Fraulein Reichenbach', a 'four-pipe problem' ('Be careful you don't set the upholstery alight, like you did that night at Ashby-de-la-Zouch!') – but none to any great effect. Worse, none of the players – let alone the audience – appears to be sure whether the piece is intentionally funny; no-one does a double-take at the repeated references to a henchman named 'Nickers', for example. Quite what genre director Boris Sagal believed himself to be working on remains open to question. Russian-born Sagal had accrued a considerable reputation as a director of often down-beat, highbrow telefeatures; he met an unpleasant end as a result of an accident involving a helicopter blade in 1981. Gig Young, billed as making a 'Special Guest Appearance' as Mortimer McGraw, earned a footnote in Hollywood Babylon too, killing himself in 1978 after killing his fifth wife.

Still, the film's main point of interest is its suggestion that Sherlock Moore could have sired a son with A SCANDAL IN BOHEMIA's Irene Adler. To its credit, the question is never actually resolved; the suggestion remains to the end that Irene might, just might, be toying with Sherlock. However, the unfolding of this subplot is magnificently awful. On learning that the unmarried Irene's boy is named Scott, Holmes reveals to Watson that his own full name is 'William Sherlock Scott Holmes' – not, let it be stressed, canonical fact! – and we are given the grisly details of a week's romantic sojourn in Montenegro shared by Irene and Sherlock in 1891. (Sherlock: 'You were appearing in *Rigoletto*.' Irene: 'You were on a walking tour. What an unlikely place to find someone who is never at home outside London.' Sherlock: 'Until then...') Perhaps the strongest indicator of Scott Adler's parentage lies, in fact, in the identity of the juvenile who plays him: Geoffrey Moore, nine-year-old son of Roger.

Muddle-headed as it is, *Sherlock Holmes in New York* does have some minor compensations. The revelation that Moriarty has built an empty gold vault over the top of the still-extant one is pleasantly preposterous – and what's that statuette standing on Moriarty's desk? Could it really be the Maltese Falcon, the McGuffin which propels the plot of a certain seminal early 1940s film noir directed by one... John Huston?

Sherlock Holmes in the 22nd Century

GB/US 1999-2001 26 x 25m approx TV series adaptations Scottish Television Enterprises Ltd/DIC Productions LP colour/animation
concept by **Sandy Ross** developed by **Phil Harnage**
exec p **Andy Heyward, Robby London, Michael Maliani, Elizabeth Partyka** *d* **Scott Heming, Robert Brousseau**
voice cast Sherlock Holmes: **Jason Gray Stanford**
Dr John Watson: **John Payne** Inspector Beth Lestrade: **Akiko Morison** Wiggins: **Viv Leacock** Deirdre: **Jennifer Copping** Professor James Moriarty: **Richard Newman** Martin Fenwick: **Ian James Corlett** Chief Inspector Greyson: **William Samples** newscaster: **Jo Bates**

THE FALL AND RISE OF SHERLOCK HOLMES
adaptation [THE FINAL PROBLEM]
w **Phil Harnage**
tx 6 May 1999 ITV

THE CRIME MACHINE
adaptation [THE VALLEY OF FEAR]
w **Martha Moran**
tx 13 May 1999 ITV

THE HOUNDS OF THE BASKERVILLES
adaptation [THE HOUND OF THE BASKERVILLES]
w **Phil Harnage**
tx 20 May 1999 ITV

THE RESIDENT PATIENT
w **Robert Askin**
tx 27 May 1999 ITV

THE SCALES OF JUSTICE
adaptation [THE SPECKLED BAND]
w **Ken Pontac**
tx 4 June 1999 ITV

THE ADVENTURE OF THE DANCING MEN
w **Terence Taylor & Eleanor Burian-Mohr**
tx 11 June 1999 ITV

THE CROOKED MAN
w **Terence Taylor & Eleanor Burian-Mohr**
tx 20 June 1999 ITV

THE ADVENTURE OF THE EMPTY HOUSE
w **Marv Wolfman**
tx 27 June 1999 ITV

THE ADVENTURE OF THE DERANGED DETECTIVE
adaptation [THE DYING DETECTIVE]
w **Henry Gilroy**
tx 4 July 1999 ITV

SILVER BLAZE
w **Robert Askin**
tx 11 July 1999 ITV

THE SIGN OF FOUR
w **Phil Harnage**
tx 18 July 1999 ITV

THE ADVENTURE OF THE SUSSEX VAMPIRE LOT
adaptation [THE SUSSEX VAMPIRE]
w **Phil Harnage**
tx 25 July 1999 ITV

THE MUSGRAVE RITUAL
w **Robert Askin**
tx 1 August 1999 ITV

THE ADVENTURE OF THE BLUE CARBUNCLE
adaptation [THE BLUE CARBUNCLE]
w **Seth Kearsley**
tx 11 December 1999 [US]

THE FIVE ORANGE PIPS
w **Greg Johnson**
tx 7 February 2000 [US]

THE RED-HEADED LEAGUE
w **Martha Moran**
tx 14 February 2000 [US]

THE MAN WITH THE TWISTED LIP
w **Mark Johnson**
tx 21 February 2000 [US]

THE SECRET SAFE
adaptation [HIS LAST BOW]
w **Reed Shelley, Bruce Shelley**
tx 31 March 2001 [US]

THE ADVENTURE OF THE SECOND STAIN
adaptation [THE SECOND STAIN]
w **Reed Shelley, Bruce Shelley**
tx 21 April 2001 [US]

THE ADVENTURE OF THE ENGINEER'S THUMB
adaptation [THE ENGINEER'S THUMB]
w **Ken Pontac**
tx 28 April 2001 [US]

THE GLORIA SCOTT
w **Woody Creek**
tx 12 May 2001 [US]

THE ADVENTURE OF THE SIX NAPOLEONS
adaptation [THE SIX NAPOLEONS]
w **Martha Moran**
tx 19 May 2001 [US]

THE CREEPING MAN
w **Ken Pontac**
tx 26 May 2001 [US]

THE ADVENTURE OF THE BERYL BOARD

adaptation [THE BERYL CORONET]
w **Eleanor Burian-Mohr**, **Terence Taylor**
tx 23 June 2001 [US]

THE ADVENTURE OF THE MAZARIN CHIP

adaptation [THE MAZARIN STONE]
w **Gildart Jackson**
tx 30 June 2001 [US]

A CASE OF IDENTITY

w **Robert Askin**
tx 21 July 2001 [US]

Guaranteed to strike fear into the heart of the fustier Sherlockian, *Sherlock Holmes in the 22nd Century* is an anime-inflected children's series which manages, for the most part, to straddle two horses pulling in very different directions: the great canon of Doyle's works, and the need to engage the minute attention-spans of the Pokemon generation. Although brisk and sometimes very enjoyable, its patchy transmission history indicates that it failed its target audience of six-to-11-year-olds – and so it seems unlikely to breed a horde of future Holmes fans born after the death of Jeremy Brett.

The back-story is wonderfully imaginative. As per Doyle, Professor Moriarty died at the Reichenbach Falls... but then Sherlock Holmes recovered the body, interring it inside an ice cave nearby and rolling a rock across the entrance. Centuries pass. In the year 2103, Inspector Beth Lestrade of New Scotland Yard becomes convinced that Moriarty has returned – and so she has the deep-frozen Holmes revived and retained as a consultant to the Yard in his old rooms at Baker Street, which have since become a Sherlock Holmes Museum. Aided by Lestrade's Model 7 Law Enforcement Compudroid, which wears an 'elastomask' of Dr Watson's features, Holmes soon discovers that an unethical Parisian geneticist, Dr Martin Fenwick, has found Moriarty's perfectly preserved corpse and extracted DNA from it, with which he has created a clone of the evil Professor. The brilliant new Moriarty cannot be controlled, however – and it has used a brainwashing process to turn Fenwick into its lackey. The rejuvenated, cane-fighting Holmes is aided in his quest to bring about the destruction of the new Moriarty by his

22nd century Baker Street Irregulars – ghetto kids Wiggins and Deirdre plus the mute, hover-chair transported technowhiz Tennyson.

Moriarty's evil schemes prove every bit as grandiose as those of the original. In *The Crime Machine*, he uses a 'criminitising' ray to create an army of burglars and looters under his command. In the next episode, *The Hounds of the Baskervilles*, he terrorises a lunar community with two artificial devil-dogs (one holographic, one robotic, built with the parts his slaves had stolen in *The Crime Machine*) as part of a scheme to set up a power-base on the Moon with which he can dominate the Earth. Later episodes see Holmes tangle with Moriarty and Fenwick many times more in cases which are only loosely inspired by Doyle: in *The Resident Patient*, for example, Percy Blessington MD, 'the world's foremost authority on anatomical reconstruction', is embroiled in a plan to kidnap two world leaders and substitute the villain's placemen, wearing false faces; in *The Adventure of the Blue Carbuncle*, the Carbuncle is the latest must-have Christmas toy – a troll-like robot doll. And so on: no one will be surprised to learn that *The Speckled Band* concludes with Holmes caught in the coils of a huge, mutated snake. Interestingly, the feisty and rather lovely Lestrade is very much the second lead throughout the remaining adventures, with Watson – whom Holmes at first refuses to accept – as little more than a glorified pet.

The series was a co-production between America's DIC Entertainment (previously responsible for *Sonic the Hedgehog* and *Super Mario Bros*) and Scottish Television Enterprises. The two companies had previously collaborated on two series entitled *Captain Zed and the Zee Zone* and *Hurricanes*. STE's deputy chief executive Sandy Ross first put forward the idea of a cartoon Holmes series set in the future, initially entitled *Sherlock Holmes in the 21st Century* – soon amended when it was realised that that the series would most likely commence just short of the year 2000. (In fact, neither the title nor the idea was all that innovative; a two-part story entitled *Sherlock Holmes in the 23rd Century* had featured in the mid-eighties robot cowboy cartoon series *BraveStarr*.)

Sherlock Holmes in the 22nd Century premiered in the UK on the independent ITV network in July 1999, but only the first 13 episodes were broadcast.

In the US, 17 episodes were screened on the Fox Kids cable channel from September 1999 – albeit in a different running order, and ending with *The Man With the Twisted Lip*. The remainder aired in 2001, when the series was nominated for a Daytime Emmy Award in the category of 'Special Class Animated Program'.

Sherlock Holmes in Washington

US 1942 pastiche Universal Pictures Company Inc 71m bw

w **Bertram Millhauser** *story* **Bertram Millhauser, Lynn Riggs** *assoc p* **Howard Benedict** *d* **Roy William Neill** *cast* Sherlock Holmes: **Basil Rathbone** Dr Watson: **Nigel Bruce** Nancy Pattridge [sic]: **Marjorie Lord** William Easter: **Henry Daniell** Stanley: **George Zucco** Lt Pete Merriam: **John Archer** Bart Lang: **Gavin Muir** Detective Lt Grogan: **Edmund MacDonald** Howe: **Don Terry** Cady: **Bradley Page** Mr Ahrens: **Holmes Herbert** Senator Henry Babcock: **Thurston Hall** Army inspector/'Voice of London': **John Burton*** steward: **Eddie Coke*** Mrs Ruxton: **Caroline Cooke*** girlfriend: **Evelyn Cooke*** hotel porter: **Kernan Cripps*** bomber pilot: **Leslie Dennison*** Sir Henry Marchmont: **Gilbert Emery*** Mrs Jellison: **Alice Fleming*** Beryl Pettibone: **Mary Forbes*** Mrs Hudson: **Mary Gordon*** 'John Grayson' [Alfred Pettibone]: **Gerald Hamer*** airport official: **Leyland Hodgson*** waiter: **Tom Martin*** laboratory assistant: **Irving Mitchell*** George: **Clarence Muse*** doorman: **Jason Robards Sr*** Miss Pringle: **Margaret Seddon*** Mrs Bryce Partridge: **Regina Wallace*** young officer: **Phil Warren*** clerk: **Ian Wolfe*** Army majors: **Paul Scott***, **Lee Shumway*** reporters: **Alexander Lockwood***, **Charles Marsh***, **Gene O'Donnell***

THE MYSTERY

During the Second World War, British diplomat Sir Henry Marchmont flies to New York, apparently carrying a secret state document of huge tactical significance. The enemy agents tailing Marchmont soon become aware, however, that he is but a decoy. The papers are in fact being couriered on the same flight by British Secret Service operative Alfred Pettibone, who has adopted the guise of a Chancery Lane solicitor named 'John Grayson'. On the Washington train, Pettibone, fearing that the agents led by William Easter are about to strike, casually passes a matchbook to a young lady

named Nancy Partridge; she is unaware that the matchbook conceals the sole copy of the papers, photographed onto microfilm. Pettibone is soon whisked away by Easter's men – and, desperate to retrieve a document which, if handed to the enemy, could prove 'absolutely disastrous' to the British government and its allies, Home Office mandarin Ahrens calls in Sherlock Holmes.

THE INVESTIGATION

With Dr Watson, Holmes searches Pettibone's rooms, discovering photographic processing equipment which leads him to the conclusion that the sole copy of the document is held on microfilm and hidden inside an American matchbook. Shrugging off an assassination attempt, Holmes and Watson arrive in Washington, where they are greeted by police officer Detective-Lieutenant Grogan. Efforts have been made to misdirect Holmes to the Hotel Metropole, where a grisly discovery awaits him – a trunk containing Pettibone's corpse. Holmes surmises that the enemy agents cannot have acquired the document yet and, after interrogating George, the steward on the train from which Pettibone was taken, realises that the matchbook must be in Nancy Partridge's possession. Easter's men have reached the same conclusion, grabbing Nancy – and the matchbook – at her engagement party.

THE SOLUTION

Careful examination of the trunk in which Pettibone was found sets Holmes and Watson in search of an antiques dealership that serves as cover for the gang. They soon home in on the business owned by one 'Richard Stanley' – actually Heinrich Hinkel, formerly one of the Kaiser's most valued agents and now the head of a vast spy ring. Holmes confronts Hinkel – who, unknowingly, is now carrying the matchbook – but the spymaster orders Holmes and Nancy killed. Watson, however, has informed Grogan of Holmes' whereabouts. The police raid the shop, saving the pair, but Hinkel escapes. Holmes races to the office of Senator Henry Babcock, another passenger who travelled on the Washington Express; the detective has led Hinkel to believe that the document may actually have been passed to Babcock. Hinkel holds Holmes and Babcock at gunpoint, but the police are waiting outside. Captured, Hinkel can

Holmes (Basil Rathbone) and Senator Henry Babcock (Thurston Hall) get closer to the secret of the missing microfilm in **Sherlock Holmes in Washington** *(1942)*

only watch as Holmes takes the matchbook from his possession, revealing that the spymaster has been holding the microfilmed document all along.

✦ ✦ ✦

Neither as triumphalist as **Sherlock Holmes and the Voice of Terror** nor as unashamedly lurid as **Sherlock Holmes and the Secret Weapon**, **Sherlock Holmes in Washington**, the third of Universal's war years pictures, is a disappointing, ho-hum thing founded on one idea – Holmes' transatlantic pursuit of a matchbook. It's a good idea – and, at times, very well executed – but it's a solitary idea nonetheless. The viewer will be utterly charmed by the 'engagement party' sequence, in which the matchbook holding the secret microfilm central to the plot is passed from pillar to post, at one point being picked up by the British diplomat most desperate to have it retrieved – 'I'd give anything to get my hands on that document,' he rumbles, lighting his cigar, 'or at least know it's in safe hands' – but the trick has been played once too often by the time it's finally in Holmes' grasp.

Although the two principal baddies, William Easter and Heinrich Hinkel, are played by past and future versus-Rathbone Moriartys, neither Henry Daniell nor George Zucco make anything like the mark they would do/did in **The Woman in Green** and **The Adventures of Sherlock Holmes** (1939) respectively; the script simply doesn't give them anything to work with. Rathbone's Holmes does, at least, get the deathless line, 'She's walking around with dynamite in her handbag!' – and delivers it with the straightest of faces. Nigel Bruce's Watson is, however, condemned to spend the entire film on the sidelines, interpolating his duffer-doctor schtick wherever he can: banging on about the cricket scores; brushing up on American slang ('How are you, buddy – what's cooking?' is how he greets the Washington cops); boggling at the four-colour comic adventures of Universal Pictures' own space ace, Flash Gordon ('seems a very capable fellow'); and chewing gum. 'Oh, put it away,' sneers Holmes.

The plotting is distinctly creaky, too, with Holmes enjoying some rather suspect insights – a

Helped by a steward (Eddie Coke), Holmes (Basil Rathbone) and Watson (Nigel Bruce) discover a vital clue inside a wrecked railroad car in **Sherlock Holmes in Washington** *(1942)*

sliver of wood from a Louis XV chair telling him that the villains are hidden in an antiques shop, for example. Ten years previously, scriptwriter Bertram Millhauser had been responsible for Paramount's dire, Clive Brook-starring **Conan Doyle's Master Detective Sherlock Holmes** (1932), and this piece – a sort of lightweight, non-threatening pre-empting of *Kiss Me Deadly* – is more in the Brook mould than his four other Universal scripts.

Filmed in the autumn of 1942 under the title *Sherlock Holmes in the USA*, **Sherlock Holmes in Washington** is noticeably more coy about the identity of 'the enemy' than the previous two films in the series, the main villain being merely a former agent of the long-deposed Kaiser turned freelance. Although it received broadly positive reviews on release at the end of April 1943 (*Variety*'s only reservation being to note that the key McGuffin 'seems to hold an inexhaustible supply of matches'), this would be the last time that the war was central to the Universal series, reduced to part of the background later on (the convalescent officers in **Sherlock Holmes Faces Death**, the Adolf Hitler shooting-gallery target in **The Spider Woman**).

True to the previous two instalments, Holmes spouts a rousing polemic in the final moments, this time a slightly inaccurate quotation from the conclusion of Winston Churchill's address to Congress, as given in the Capitol on 26 December 1941: 'It is not given for us to peer into the mysteries of the future – but in the days to come, the British and American people for their own safety and the good of all will walk together in majesty and justice and in peace.' As ever, the Americans arrived late; British audiences didn't receive this message of solidarity from across the Atlantic until February 1944, leading one to suspect that the war censor had intervened (as with **Sherlock Holmes and the Voice of Terror**). They would have been appalled to hear, via the 221B wireless, a BBC announcer claiming the great Corporation to be simply a 'News Bureau'.

So Sherlock's war was, more or less, over. The fashion for bringing popular icons to the forefront of battle had been on the wane by the time of **Sherlock Holmes and the Voice of Terror**; even Johnny Weismuller's muscle-bound jungle boy Tarzan had got in on the act in *Tarzan Triumphs* and *Tarzan's Desert Mystery* (both 1943), and by the time Hollywood's top dog was abroad in Nazi-held

Norway in *Son of Lassie* (1945), the genre had completely exhausted itself. Rathbone's Holmes would begin to venture into something of an ahistorical neverwhere with Universal's next effort, **Sherlock Holmes Faces Death**.

Sherlock Holmes Solves 'The Sign of Four'

US 1913 adaptation [THE SIGN OF THE FOUR]
Thanhouser Company silent bw
cast includes Sherlock Holmes: **Harry Benham**

Despite numbering only two reels, this now-lost version of THE SIGN OF THE FOUR appears to have been remarkably faithful to its source text, the write-up in *Moving Picture World* detailing all the significant story points – 'The one-legged man, the East Indian with his blow-pipe, the Sholtos, the Baker Street lodgings, the scenes in India' – and praising the narrative's 'weird Oriental atmosphere'. Released in the US in February 1913, it featured 'a younger and heavier-built man than we usually see' as Holmes: Harry Benham (1884-1969), who had played the bestial Mr Hyde to James Cruze's Dr Jekyll in Thanhouser's 1912 version of Robert Louis Stevenson's most famous novella. Oft-credited throughout the nineteen-tens, the film career of 'Handsome Harry' didn't extend into the sound era.

The successful enterprise responsible for *Sherlock Holmes Solves 'The Sign of Four'* had been founded in 1909 at New Rochelle, New York by Edwin Thanhouser (1865-1956), formerly the manager of Milwaukee's Academy of Music Theatre. Prominent actors working exclusively for Thanhouser circa 1912 included the aforementioned James Cruze (1884-1942), William Garwood (1884-1950) and William Russell (c 1884-1929); actresses of the time included Benham's wife, Ethyle Cooke (1885-1949), Mignon Anderson (1892-1983) and the ill-fated Florence LaBadie (1888-1917). It's entirely possible that Thanhouser's Jonathan Small and Mary Morstan might be found somewhere in these lists.

In the UK, Benham's sole outing as the detective was released, bizarrely, in June 1914 as an appendage to Éclair's eight-film series ... **From the Adventures of Sherlock Holmes**.

Sherlock Holmes und das Halsband des Todes

aka **Sherlock Holmes La valle del terrore** [Italy]
Sherlock Holmes et le collier de la mort [France]
Sherlock Holmes and the Deadly Necklace
[UK theatrical/US television]
West Germany/Italy/France1962 pastiche CCC Filmkunst GmbH/INCEI Film/Critérion Film 87m bw
w **Curt Siodmak** *p* **Artur Brauner**
d **Terence Fisher, Frank Winterstein**
cast Sherlock Holmes: **Christopher Lee** Dr James [sic]
Watson: **Thorley Walters** Professor Moriarty: **Hans Söhnker** Inspector Cooper: **Hans Nielsen** Ellen Blackburn: **Senta Berger** Paul King: **Ivan Desny** Peter Blackburn: **Wolfgang Lukschy** Charles [Moriarty's chauffeur]: **Leon Askin** Mrs Hudson: **Edith Schultze-Westrum** Williams [auctioneer]: **Bruno W Panthel** American: **Heinrich Gies** French police inspector: **Bernard Lajarrige** light girl: **Linda Sini** doctor: **Roland Armontel** librarian: **Danielle Argence**

Distinctive Danish ad for **Sherlock Holmes und das Halsband des Todes** *(1962)*

Christopher Lee by gaslight in **Sherlock Holmes und das Halsband des Todes** *(1962)*

Jenkins: **Franco Giacobini** butler: **Waldemar Frahm**
waitress: **Renate Hütter** [aka **Rena Horten**]
Johnny: **Max Straasberg** Samuels: **Corrado Anicelli**∗
Wirt: **Pierre Gualdi**∗ postmaster: **Kurt Hain**∗

THE MYSTERY

An invaluable necklace, reputed to have belonged to Cleopatra, has gone missing soon after its discovery in an Ancient Egyptian burial chamber. Could the theft be connected to a recent rash of homicides, in which Holmes detects the hand of the distinguished anthropologist, Professor Moriarty? Could it also be connected to the death at 221B of a down-at-heel police informer called Jenkins, who expires on Holmes' chaise longue while making a strange fluttering motion with his hands? Watson is perplexed, but Holmes is convinced that all three circumstances are linked, despite Inspector Cooper's stern warning not to get involved without the express permission of Scotland Yard.

THE INVESTIGATION

Holmes deduces that Jenkins' dying gesture was a reference to a low-life waterfront pub called the Hare and Eagle. Watson accompanies him there, and after a quick appraisal of the unprepossessing clientele Holmes decides on a spot of rooftop eavesdropping. Overhearing a confab between Moriarty and an ex-con lieutenant of his, and seeking further confirmation from the records department of the London *Times*, Holmes establishes a connection between Moriarty and the purloined necklace. Disguising himself with moustache, spectacles and the demeanour of a prissy academic, Holmes gains entrance to Moriarty's apartment and discovers the necklace there, concealed in an Egyptian sarcophagus. Holmes promptly hands it over to Inspector Cooper, who is to guard it until its imminent sale at auction.

THE SOLUTION

Holmes knows perfectly well that Moriarty will stop at nothing in order to retrieve the necklace, and accordingly assumes another disguise, this time as a raddled old sea-dog. Visiting the Hare and Eagle again, he succeeds in getting himself recruited into Moriarty's gang. A police van transporting the necklace to the auction rooms is manoeuvred into stopping above a manhole, which is the cue for Holmes and his temporary cronies to swarm up from the sewers and appropriate the necklace once more. Holmes sees off his companions, however, and repairs to the auction rooms, where the distraught Inspector Cooper is delighted when a package is delivered – addressed by Holmes to himself – containing the missing necklace. Moriarty is stymied (though, thanks to insufficient evidence, not arrested), whereupon word comes through of a series of murders that are being attributed to Jack the Ripper...

Fresh from his success in the early Hammer horrors (including his turn as Sir Henry in that company's lurid makeover of **The Hound of the Baskervilles**), Christopher Lee found himself much in demand on the Continent – so much so

that in March 1962 he found it expedient to move from Belgravia to the northern shore of Lake Geneva. Turning 40 in May, he initially found work thinner on the ground than he had anticipated, thanks to the necessity to establish his Swiss residency by spending six months in the country out of his first 12. In July, however, he was cast in a German/Italian/French co-production called *Sherlock Holmes und das Halsband des Todes*, made by Artur Brauner's CCC (Central Cinema Company) at Brauner's extremely busy Haselhorst Atelier in Spandau. There was also the lure of a ten-day location stint in the Republic of Ireland.

There were several other inducements, not least the opportunity to play Sherlock Holmes himself. The screenplay was by Curt Siodmak (1902-2000), distinguished veteran of 1930s German classics like *Menschen am Sonntag* and *F.P.1 antwortet nicht* together with 1940s Hollywood horrors like *Black Friday*, *The Wolf Man*, *I Walked with a Zombie* and *The Beast with Five Fingers*. (He was also the author of the much-filmed novel *Donovan's Brain*.) And, presumably because of his success with **The Hound of the Baskervilles**, Lee's old friend Terence Fisher had been coaxed away from his Twickenham home to direct, bringing with him one of his favourite character actors, Thorley Walters, to play Dr Watson.

At the Spandau studio, however, it quickly became apparent that the production was not going to run smoothly. 'They were doing something that really was impossible to do,' Walters recalled. 'They would have a Frenchman playing with you in one scene speaking French, and the Germans speaking in German in the same scene ... It was impossible to tell, if you were addressing lines to somebody in English and they replied in German and somebody else replied in French, where you were ... We *all* had trouble with the management,' he added darkly. 'I can't give you more details – libel and that!'

Lee also keeps his counsel regarding the film's off-camera controversies, except to say that the tension between Brauner and his associate Heinrich von Leipziger caused the mild-mannered Fisher to lose his temper for the first and only time in Lee's experience. And though Lee, with his profusion of multi-national assignments, was becoming used to the kind of Babel described by

Holmes (Christopher Lee) finds incriminating evidence in Moriarty's apartment in **Sherlock Holmes und das Halsband des Todes** (1962)

Walters, Fisher was not and the film was eventually co-directed by his first assistant, Frank Winterstein.

The numerous production problems also put paid to a sequel in which Lee's Holmes was to tangle with Jack the Ripper; not only is this Ripper follow-up hinted at in the film's final scene, it was also announced in *Bild*, a German tabloid roughly equivalent to the *Sun*. Retaining his 'Henry E Lester' pseudonym, von Leipziger, an executive of the Conan Doyle estate, ditched the disagreeable Brauner, decamped to England and teamed up with Michael Klinger and Tony Tenser of Compton-Tekli. The resulting Holmes/Ripper film, **A Study in Terror**, can therefore be seen, in a roundabout sort of way, as the promised sequel to *Sherlock Holmes und das Halsband des Todes*.

Ruinously dubbed in an English version (*Sherlock Holmes and the Deadly Necklace*) slung together by Peter Riethof, the picture has acquired a misplaced reputation as a total disaster. In fact, there's nothing much wrong with it that the restoration of Lee and Walters' original dialogue tracks wouldn't put right; that and the removal of Martin Slavin's hideously inappropriate jazz score. The reconstruction of 221B is meticulously done

(art director: Paul Markwitz), as is the period recreation of an Edwardian capital thronged with motor cars rather than horse-drawn cabs. (As was customary during the 1960s, Dublin was used as a stand-in for turn-of-the-century London.) Though bearing virtually no relation to THE VALLEY OF FEAR as initial trade announcements suggested it would (only the film's Italian title would retain this bogus association), the screenplay is a neat enough Siodmak intrigue and Hans Söhnker makes a charmingly baleful Moriarty – or 'Moriarity' as the American dubbers insist on calling him. The shapely Austrian beauty Senta Berger, 21 at the time, is also on hand as an eye-catching, though under-employed, heroine.

Lee and Walters, meanwhile, are ideally cast as Holmes and Watson. Holmes is introduced in the guise of a lanky old sea-dog, a rather skimpy get-up that Watson and Mrs Hudson inexplicably fail to see through. Revealing his true self, we find that Lee has been fitted by make-up man Heinz Stamm with an unusually severe widow's peak and a prosthetically enlarged nose, the better to approximate Sidney Paget's original *Strand* magazine illustrations; indeed, as Holmes consults his newspaper, we're treated to several lengthy profile shots to make sure the enhanced hooter doesn't go unnoticed. If this Teutonic nose-job isn't strange enough, Lee's costumes, designed by Vera Mügge, vary from swish smoking jackets to rather comically checkered Inverness capes. Taken all in all, however, he looks close to the Paget ideal.

Lee has pointed out that his Holmes was an attempt 'to play him really as he was written, as a very intolerant, argumentative, difficult man,' and yet his performance is a relaxed and occasionally playful one, providing a blueprint for the almost skittish Holmes he would play in 1990. He indulges in a bizarre fencing match with Watson – a bread knife and a rolled-up copy of the *Times* their chosen weapons – and is all smiles as he elucidates the dying gesture of the luckless Jenkins. He also conducts a couple of interrogations with his knuckles parked nonchalantly on one cheek.

Walters (1913-1991) was here beginning a sporadic association with Watson that would encompass a walk-on with Peter Jeffrey in *The Best House in London* (1968), a stint opposite Douglas Wilmer in **The Adventure of Sherlock Holmes' Smarter Brother** (1975) and a TV partnership with Christopher Plummer in **Classics Dark and Dangerous: Silver Blaze** (1977). An expert light comedian who made his name opposite Jack Hulbert and Cicely Courtneidge in the 1940s, he makes Watson a slow but sparky individualand repeated the trick in Terence Fisher's *Frankenstein Created Woman* (1966), in which Walters' delightful Dr Hertz and Peter Cushing's ascetic Baron Frankenstein are cast unmistakeably in Holmes/Watson mould. As for *Sherlock Holmes und das Halsband des Todes*, Walters concluded mildly that 'I never saw the film, so I can make no comment on it except that my working with Terry Fisher developed into a great friendship.'

The film was made at the height of Germany's collective obsession with Edgar Wallace mysteries, which had kicked off in 1959 with Harald Reinl's *Der Frosch mit der Maske*. Lee himself had appeared in two such films in 1961 (*Das Geheimnis der gelben Narzissen* and *Das Rätsel der roten Orchidee*), and his Holmes début has something of the same thrill-a-minute tone. The ratiocination in Siodmak's script amounts to almost nothing, with Holmes presented instead as a high-handed man of action. And, presumably by coincidence, the film's introductory shot of a corpse floating in a canal is almost identical to the opening of a *British* Edgar Wallace adaptation, Walter Summers' *The Dark Eyes of London* (1939).

The film's serial-style hi-jinks, coupled with edgy monochrome photography from the aptly named Richard Angst, put one in mind also of German silent cinema. (The prolific Brauner was simultaneously involved in several films reviving the Weimar super-criminal Dr Mabuse for hip 1960s audiences.) Resorting once more to his low-life disguise – donkey jacket, eyepatch, walrus moustache etc – Holmes successfully infiltrates Moriarty's docklands gang, disabling one of the thugs by throwing a dart at him. The police van robbery is then conducted from the sewers – Lee was disconcerted to learn that the evil-smelling location for this sequence had been a poison gas factory during the war – and the cliffhanger mechanics of the heist are only compromised, for English-speaking viewers, by the ridiculously fey East End accent applied to Holmes' sea-dog persona by the anonymous dubber.

The film was rushed out in Germany on 30 November 1962, though Brauner's Italian and French co-producers delayed releasing it until 3 May 1963 and 20 May 1964 respectively. In the US, it was consigned to TV and in the UK it only crawled into cinemas in March 1968. (Distributors Golden Era bought it as part of a package that also included Brauner's Edgar Wallace shocker, *Das Phantom von Soho*, starring *Halsband* veterans Hans Söhnker and Hans Nielsen.) The word 'plodding' featured in assessments from both the *Monthly Film Bulletin* and the *Daily Cinema*. 'On the face of it,' opined the former, 'Christopher Lee and Thorley Walters ought to make a fine Holmes and Watson, but their performances here are swamped by abysmal dubbing ... Apart from some startling anachronisms the period detail is on the whole nicely done (in particular the snake motif of Moriarty's apartment). But the film itself, feebly directed by Terence Fisher, is plodding and colourless.' The *Daily Cinema*'s Marjorie Bilbow dismissed the film as 'A plodding, humourless attempt to present the greatest of all English detectives,' concluding that 'As a story woven around an unknown detective it would be forgivable, but classic characters demand more accurate handling than this.'

These judgments are too harsh, but there's no getting around the fact that, thanks to the disastrous soundtrack applied to the film's English version, Christopher Lee's first stab at Holmes has to remain a tantalising 'might-have-been'. (JR)

The Sign of Four

aka **The Sign of the Four**

GB 1923 adaptation [THE SIGN OF THE FOUR] *Stoll Picture Productions Ltd 6750 feet silent bw*
wd **Maurice Elvey** *chief of production/p* **Jeffrey Bernerd**
cast Sherlock Holmes: **Eille Norwood** Dr Watson: **Arthur Cullin** Mary Morstan: **Isobel Elsom** Prince Abdullah Khan: **Fred Raynham** Jonathan Small: **Norman Page** Dr Thaddeus Sholto: **Humberston Wright** Tonga, the pygmy: **Henry Wilson** housekeeper: **Mdme d'Esterre** Inspector Athelney Jones: **Arthur Bell**

Zippy, zestful and thoroughly engaging, Stoll's *The Sign of Four* is far, far better than the company's only other Holmes feature, **The Hound of the Baskervilles** (1921) – and the lengthy motorboat chase along the Thames with which it concludes will prove an eye-opener to all those who consider silent films irredeemably dull. Indeed, since Eille Norwood's Holmes whizzes beneath almost every major bridge on the river, the film demands to be preserved as a valuable document of 1920s London. Returning writer/director Maurice Elvey wrote: 'All the river scenes ... were taken under typical London mist conditions. Twenty-nine separate days, spread over a period of some weeks, were occupied in obtaining ideal effects ... The screen does not reveal the difficulties under which we worked, nor does it indicate the material used in obtaining what I required. Though only one yacht and four launches appear in the picture, seven yachts were requisitioned. The Thames is a tidal river, and the varying time of the tides and the varying speed and roughness of the water rendered taking difficult. Particularly did we discover the latter fact when using the light motor racing boats, brought in from Monte Carlo for the purpose. Heavy seas were often running in the lower reaches, but patience was eventually rewarded.'

Last in the still-unbeaten run of moving-picture adaptations begun in **The Adventures of Sherlock Holmes** (1921), *The Sign of Four* is not quite a valedictory effort, since Norwood's regular, white-haired Watson, Hubert Willis, was evicted in favour of the burlier Arthur Cullin – Elvey famously considering Willis too old to make a convincing beau for Mary Morstan. Although Elvey could hardly have claimed to have no personal interest in such a move – he had, after all, only recently married leading lady Isobel Elsom (Isabella Reed, 1893-1981), whom he'd known as far back as the Samuelson romance *Quinneys* (1919) – it's very hard to imagine Willis' rather ineffectual, genteel Watson rescuing the object of his affections from a blazing boat, as Cullin does here. Norwood was none too impressed with the recasting, reportedly describing Cullin's Watson as looking like 'a middle-aged provincial butler'. But the choice of Cullin was not so strange, given that he had already played the doctor to H A Saintsbury's detective in the Samuelson version of **The Valley of Fear** seven years previously. Elvey's marriage to Elsom didn't last, but his career only wound up in 1957, taking in both *High Treason* (1928), reputedly the first British 'talkie', and *Sons of the Sea* (1939), among the first British colour films. He died in 1967.

Having collared Norman Page's remarkably grumpy Jonathan Small, Norwood's reign as Holmes ends on a pleasingly bathetic note. Back at 221B, the detective glances up at the mantelpiece, upon which sits his invitation to Watson and Mary's wedding. Alone again, naturally.

The Sign of Four

GB 1987 TVM adaptation Granada Television 102m colour tx 29 December 1987 ITV
w **John Hawkesworth** *exec p* **Michael Cox**
p **June Wyndham Davies** *d* **Peter Hammond**
cast Sherlock Holmes: **Jeremy Brett** Dr John Watson: **Edward Hardwicke** Major Sholto: **Robin Hunter** McMurdo: **Alf Joint** Jonathan Small: **John Thaw** Tonga: **Kiran Shah** Miss Mary Morstan: **Jenny Seagrove** Mrs Hudson: **Rosalie Williams** Williams: **Derek Deadman** Thaddeus & Bartholomew Sholto: **Ronald Lacey** Lal Chowder [sic]: **Ishaq Bux** Captain Morstan: **Terence Skelton** Mrs Bernstone: **Marjorie Sudell** Inspector Athelney Jones: **Emrys James** Sherman: **Gordon Gostelow** Mrs Mordecai Smith: **Lila Kaye** Jack Smith: **William Ash** Wiggins: **Courtenay Roper-Knight**

boatyard workman: **Tommy Wright** Mordecai Smith:
Dave Atkins Kartar Singh: **Badi Uzzaman** Achmet: **Renu
Setna** Jagodish Singh: **Ravinder Singh Reyatt**

After filming the first series of Granada's **The
Return of Sherlock Holmes**, Jeremy Brett was
admitted to London's Maudsley Hospital,
necessitating a postponement of *The Sign of Four*, a
feature-length special designed to bridge the gap
between the two series of **The Return** – and
intended, more importantly, as Granada's
contribution to the Holmes centenary. The film
eventually started production on 19 January 1987,
ranging between Manchester, Liverpool, Yorkshire,
Norfolk, London, Gloucester-shire and Malta
before concluding on 10 March. 'Jeremy is now
fully recovered and ready to be back at work,'
disclosed a Granada spokesman the week before
production began. 'He did have what he describes
as a good old-fashioned nervous breakdown, but
he is certainly well now.'

Granada veteran Ray Goode, director of
photography on both *Brideshead Revisited* and *The
Jewel in the Crown*, explained in *American
Cinematographer* that the complexities of getting *The
Sign of Four* off the ground predated not only Brett's
hospitalisation but even the Granada sequence
itself. 'The script was presented to Granada in 1981
as a pilot film for the Sherlock Holmes series,' he
maintained. 'Various people read the script and
logistically it was so difficult that they decided not to
do it. It was put away. Then all of a sudden – after 18
or 19 episodes of Sherlock Holmes – it reappeared
as Granada's first 35mm project. It's a hell of a
project and very, very difficult to photograph.'

That Granada were prepared to shoot *The Sign
of Four* on 35mm is an indication of the deluxe
treatment lavished upon it. Both in studio and on
location, Goode's photography and Tim Wilding's
production design create an almost tangible
impression of 1890s veracity, while John
Hawkesworth's script adheres closely to Doyle's
original. (The details of Holmes' cocaine addiction
in the novel's opening paragraphs had already
been spliced into the début episode of **The
Adventures of Sherlock Holmes**, *A Scandal in
Bohemia*, and were accordingly dropped.) And it's
cast to the hilt, with John Thaw as an alternately
vengeful and mournful Jonathan Small, Emrys
James an outrageously conceited Athelney Jones,

Ronald Lacey an authentically freakish Thaddeus
Sholto (doubling as his ill-starred twin,
Bartholomew) and Jenny Seagrove a picture of
porcelain composure as Mary Morstan.

Watson's attraction towards Mary is touchingly
sketched in by Edward Hardwicke – though, in order
not to compromise the Holmes/Watson relationship
in future instalments, the Watson/Morstan marriage
is deleted. Watson is left to sigh unrequitedly at the
window of 221B while the unconcerned Holmes
subsides into a post-investigative stupor.

Characteristic Conan Doyle touches of exotic
horror are also faithfully preserved. The opening
intrusion of Small and his mysteriously
diminutive familiar is edgily done, with the
shuffling Tonga dealing Major Sholto's manservant
a smart hammer blow as he dozes obliviously in a
chair. (Veteran stuntman Alf Joint was cast as the
unlucky McMurdo, having previously doubled for
Eric Porter's Moriarty during the epic Reichenbach
plunge featured in Granada's *The Final Problem*.)
Bartholomew Sholto is subsequently discovered
frozen upright in his Norwood eyrie, a ghastly *risus
sardonicus* on his lips and with taloned hands
splayed as if in mid-conversation. Holmes'
wharfside quizzing of Mrs Mordecai Smith,
together with the climactic Thames riverboat
chase, are both highly atmospheric and intriguingly
suggestive of the cross-country hounding of Count
Dracula in Bram Stoker's novel, which THE SIGN
OF THE FOUR predated by some seven years.

The pursuit of the *Aurora* is done with a *Boy's
Own* vigour belying the logistical nightmares
outlined by Ray Goode: 'The real difficulties
became apparent when we did our original
'reccies' – the property has changed so much,
especially along the Thames, that there was
nowhere to point the camera.' The solution was to
shoot the Thames footage day-for-night and then
merge it with footage shot at the Norfolk Broads,
as Goode put it, 'night-for-night'.

Jeremy Brett's Holmes is the centrepiece, the
piercing eyes, brilliantined hair, bat ears and death-
mask pallor creating an indelible image of 'true cold
reason' personified. Whether clambering around
the upper reaches of Pondicherry Lodge (filmed at a
Gothic pile in Harrogate, rather than Norwood) or
crinkling in amused fellow-feeling as Thaddeus
explains his addiction to the hookah, he is riveting
to watch from start to finish. Some of the affecta-

On the trail of the Aurora: Sherlock Holmes (Jeremy Brett) at a Thames-side embankment in **The Sign of Four** (1987)

tions, notably the palm sliding upwards across the forehead, are meaningless bits of camp fiddle-faddle, but it's hard to disagree with Ann Mann's judgment in *Television Today* that 'Jeremy Brett would, I am sure, have warmed the cockles of Conan Doyle's heart ... Played with the shrewd neurosis which the character suggests, his manner is as taut as one of his fiddle strings, and at times he resembles a bird of prey, concentrating, twitching, then pouncing, but always with subtlety and eloquence.' Compare Mann's reference to 'a bird of prey', incidentally, with the *News Chronicle* review of Hammer's **The Hound of the Baskervilles**, in which Paul Dehn pointed out that Peter Cushing's 'questing hawk's head so swivels in the throes of observation that one can almost hear the brain brought to a fine fizz inside.' Though outwardly cooler than Cushing, exactly the same applies to Brett.

The flashback to Small's acquisition of the Agra treasure, which comes as a convoluted let-down

after the riverboat chase, was filmed in Malta. Though not required, Brett was taken along in an effort to complete his recuperation. It didn't work; a further attack of manic depression immediately followed the filming of *The Sign of Four* and Brett reappeared with a peculiar hair-cut for the second series of **The Return of Sherlock Holmes**. And when a feature-length version of **The Hound of the Baskervilles** met with across-the-board critical derision, the Granada sequence was headed straight for the doldrums. As a result, *The Sign of Four* remains its crowning achievement. (JR)

The Sign of Four

Canada 2001 TVM adaptation Muse Entertainment (Sign of Four) Inc 90m colour
tx 23 March 2001 Odyssey Channel [US]
w **Joe Wiesenfeld** *p* **Irene Litinsky** *d* **Rodney Gibbons**

cast Dr Watson: **Kenneth Welsh** Sherlock Holmes: **Matt Frewer** Miss Morstan: **Sophie Lorain** Thaddeus/Bartholomew: **Marcel Jeannin** Inspector Jones: **Michel Perron** John Small: **Edward Yankie** Williams: **Kevin Woodhouse** Sikhs: **Cas Anvar**, **Samir Mallah**, **Ganesha Rasiah** Major Sholto: **Johni Keyworth** Mrs Hudson: **Kathleen McAuliffe** Tonga: **Fernando Chien** Mrs Bernstone: **Una Kay** Achmet: **Chimwemwe Miller** Wiggins: **Daniel Brochu** Sherman: **Dennis St John** Mrs Smith: **Emma Stevens** Professor Morgan: **Noel Burton** Kitmutgar: **Kenneth Fernandez** captain's son: **Justin Bradley** policemen: **Pascal Richard**, **Denis Frane**

Sholto housekeeper Mrs Bernstone is scornful of the suggestion that the chiselled, foppish individual she's just been introduced to is the real Sherlock Holmes: 'Oh, go on. I've seen his picture in the *Strand Magazine*.' 'Those garish illustrations do distort my profile, my dear woman,' bridles Matt Frewer's Holmes, 'but surely there is some resemblance?' Well, no. As with the first of the Canadian Muse Entertainment TV movies, **The Hound of the Baskervilles** (2000), *The Sign of Four* presents a determinedly different take on the detective – and fiddles on the fringes of the text to mostly pleasing effect.

Here, Watson is given a protective, paternalistic faith in Mary Morstan, whom Holmes believes to be a cynical 'adventuress' out to ensnare the naïve, unwitting Thaddeus Sholto (and thus Thaddeus' share of the Agra treasure). Meanwhile, Holmes' fractious relationship with the belligerent Inspector Athelney Jones leads to the steamboat *Aurora* being raided by the police – 'the regulars', as Holmes puts it, as opposed to the 'auxiliaries' of the Holmes/Watson team – in dock, not on the water. (An amendment made more, one suspects, for budgetary reasons, rather than that given by director Rodney Gibbons: 'We couldn't risk anyone falling into the frigid St Lawrence River in November.') In an all-action finale, Watson falls victim to the paralysing darts of the fleet-footed but not pygmy Tonga; fortunately, Holmes has already had police surgeon Professor Morgan develop an antidote, enabling him to save Watson's life before despatching Tonga with his own barb.

Although marred by some worryingly stilted English accents among the supporting cast, *The Sign of Four* sees Muse developing a stock-in-trade as purveyors of agreeably pacy riffs on well-known

Doyle texts, bolstered no end by the increasingly impressive Watson of Kenneth Welsh. Two further Frewer/Welsh films followed soon after: **The Royal Scandal** and **Sherlock Holmes and the Case of the Whitechapel Vampire**.

The Sign of Four: Sherlock Holmes' Greatest Case

GB 1932 adaptation Associated Radio Pictures 76m bw
w **W P Lipscomb** *production supervisor* **Rowland V Lee**
d **Graham Cutts**
the players include Sherlock Holmes: **Arthur Wontner**
Mary Morstan: **Isla Bevan** Dr Watson: **Ian Hunter**
Jonathan Small: **Graham Soutten** Thaddeus Sholto: **Miles Malleson** Major Sholto: **Herbert Lomas** Atherly Jones [sic]: **Gilbert Davis** Mrs Smith: **Margaret Yarde**
the tattooed man: **Roy Emerton** Bartholomew Sholto: **Kynaston Reeves*** Captain Morstan: **Edgar Norfolk*** Mrs Hudson: **Clare Greet*** Tonga: **Togo***

A spirited and likeable rehash of THE SIGN OF THE FOUR, this third Arthur Wontner Holmes anticipates the highly regarded Basil Rathbone/ Nigel Bruce Universal sequence in more ways than one...

In the wake of his first two Sherlock pics, **The Sleeping Cardinal** and **The Missing Rembrandt**, Wontner was persuaded early in 1932 to desert Twickenham Studios for British rivals Associated Radio Pictures, with whom American producer/ director Rowland V Lee (1891-1975) was then working. Lee's interest in Holmes is unsurprising given that, just two years earlier, he'd (almost certainly) directed the *Murder Will Out* segment of feature-length revue **Paramount on Parade**, in which Clive Brook's Holmes had squared off against Warner Oland's Fu Manchu. Lee hired Graham Cutts to direct Associated's Holmes script, which was by W P Lipscomb, writer of the previous year's Raymond Massey-headlining **The Speckled Band**.

Cutts (1885-1958), who'd co-founded Gainsborough Pictures, was highly regarded for a number of 1920s adventure-romances highlighting idols such as Ivor Novello and Mae Marsh, and it was hoped that he'd add life to Wontner's plummy-voiced, paternalistic Holmes. Suggestions that Rowland V Lee and Basil Dean (writer-director of the 1929 Clive Brook vehicle, **The Return of Sherlock Holmes**) helped Cutts with the direction are in part substantiated by E G Cousins On the British Sets column in *Picturegoer* (13 February 1932). They have some excellent atmosphere in this film, in which Basil Dean is directing Arthur Wontner, Cousins observed. Whoever called the shots, it was decided to reject Wontner's former Watson, Ian Fleming, in favour of a younger man, 32-year-old Ian Hunter, who would play a dashing, blushing doctor in the mould of a matinée idol, sweeping blonde Isla Bevan's Mary Morstan off her feet – quite literally, on the characters' first meeting! 'Thank goodness you were here, Watson,' says Sherlock, as the doctor lies the swooning Mary on the sofa of 221B. 'In such embarrassing matters as fainting women I defer to you.'

This for-its-time pacy *Sign of Four*, ostentatiously subtitled *Sherlock Holmes' Greatest Case*, kicks off by relating the whole of the Agra Fort/Andaman Islands back-story told in the novel's penultimate chapter, making much melodramatic mileage out of the ominous tapping of Jonathan Small's wooden leg. Its portly, preening, wig-wearing Small is given a new sidekick in addition to the native Tonga – Meade Bailey, a towering and comically dense fellow Andaman fugitive whom Small tattoos so Bailey can hide out as 'the Tattooed Man' in the travelling funfair where the conspirators are based. (A 'Mr Burchett' is referred to as playing the 'Tattoo Artist' in certain cast lists, but he was simply the chap who drew the designs seen on actor Roy Emerton's body.) Small and Bailey are presented as gormless, aitch-dropping no-goods, much given to addressing all and sundry as 'matey' and referring to the Agra hoard as 'ver sparklers'. Their chirpy duologues become hilariously strained on occasion, as when Small scorns Bailey's distinctly unsubtle plan to murder anyone who crosses their path to the treasure. 'You can't do much of it wivout leaving some clue,' sneers Small. Bailey: 'Eh?' Small: 'Clue. You know what 'clue' is, don'tcha?' Bailey: 'Yeah. It's what you sticks paper togevver wiv.' Cue Oliver Hardy-style 'D'oh!' reaction shot from Small.

Indeed, taken as a whole, this *Sign of Four* carries a potent (and very British) class-related subtext. The lower orders, defined by Holmes as 'homo Taurus', or bull men, are swarthy,

clod-hopping scum who'd happily sell their muvvers for a quart of gin. Foreigners are mute savages who bite the heads off boa constrictors. The officers of the state, as represented by police inspector Atherly Jones, are pompous, semi-articulate poltroons given to pithy sentiment such as, 'What I always sez is, an ounce of practice makes for a ton of theory.' ('Yes, I've heard you say it,' sneers Holmes, unimpressed.) And the upper classes are either treacherous, back-stabbing swines like Major Sholto or weaselly, neurotic 'rabbit men' like Thaddeus, living off unearned inherited wealth. Which only leaves three characters on the side of the angels – Holmes, Watson and the self-proclaimed 'terribly weepy' Mary Morstan. Pointedly, the latter is no longer a governess but runs a small West End florist's, and only gains a share of the hoard once she's been through hell to earn it. The viewer is given the impression that only English middle-class entrepreneurs and professionals are worth a jot in this filthy world (a point of view which does not contradict a great deal of Doyle, it must be said).

Following a number of hilariously spontaneous and unlikely deductions by Holmes – Small's handwriting alone revealing that he has but one leg, for example ('It grieves me to think, Watson, that you've never read my treatise on the physical and mental reactions of the disabled') – the film zips to its climax once Mary and Watson have set off independently on an ill-advised recce of the King's Cross sideshow where the villains are based. ('Oh, how I'd like to put it over on Holmes!' claims Watson.) Mary is kidnapped, and Holmes and Watson pursue the fleeing speedboat *Aurora* down the Thames to a warehouse – where, despite the unidextrous Small's best efforts to clobber the good guys with strangely high kicks from his extended prosthetic leg, our hopelessly weedy heroes better the hardened criminal thugs in a straight fist-fight, and Watson takes the simpering Mary for his wife.

Blessed with all the visual tricks and tics Cutts could muster – an endless variety of picture wipes dividing scenes, newspaper headlines announcing Small's escape mixed over the image of the wretched Major, a grotesquely distorted shot from Thaddeus' point-of-view of Small throttling him – *The Sign of Four: Sherlock Holmes' Greatest Case* was given a broadly happy, if unspectacular, reception upon its release in May 1932 (ahead of **The Missing Rembrandt**, incidentally, despite the fact that the latter release was made first). Wontner returned to Twickenham to make two further pictures alongside Ian Fleming, beginning with **The Triumph of Sherlock Holmes**. Meanwhile, Lee's Hollywood stock continued to rise; over 1938-9, he cast the British actor Basil Rathbone in three successive pictures for Universal – *Son of Frankenstein*, *The Sun Never Sets* and *Tower of London*.

In 1942, Universal in turn cast Rathbone in the first of a sequence of contemporaneously set Holmes pictures, **Sherlock Holmes and the Voice of Terror**. Oddly enough, the earlier *The Sign of Four* has Wontner's gun-toting Holmes pursuing his prey through a dockside London, itself part of a modern-day world containing cars, telephones, streamlined speedboats and mechanised funfairs (the latter seen in Rathbone's **The Spider Woman**). Coincidence?

Silver Blaze

aka **Murder at the Baskervilles** [US]
GB 1936 adaptation Twickenham Film Productions Ltd 71m bw
w **Arthur Macrae, H Fowler Mear** *p* **Julius Hagen**
d **Thomas Bentley**
cast Sherlock Holmes: **Arthur Wontner** Dr Watson:
Ian Fleming Professor Moriarty: **Lyn Harding**
Inspector Lestrade: **John Turnbull** Colonel Ross: **Robert Horton** Sir Henry Baskerville: **Lawrence Grossmith**
Diana Baskerville: **Judy Gunn** Jack Trevor: **Arthur Macrae**
Colonel Sebastian Moran: **Arthur Goullet** John Straker:
Martin Walker Mrs Straker: **Eve Gray** Miles Stamford:
Gilbert Davis Mrs Hudson: **Minnie Rayner**
Silas Brown **D J Williams** Bert Prince: **Ralph Truman**
stable lad: **Ronald Shiner*** Silver Blaze: **Nagina***

I n 1937, the British film industry experienced a paralysing studio slump brought on by over-inflated, and industry-wide, attempts at expansion. You wouldn't have guessed it, however, from the buzz of activity that was going on in October 1936. Will Hay was making *Good Morning, Boys* at Gainsborough, Max Miller was in *Don't Get Me Wrong* at Teddington, Conrad Veidt was at Denham for *Dark Journey*, and Marlene Dietrich was adding exoticism to *Knight Without Armour*,

also at Denham. *London Melody* was occupying the spanking new Pinewood facility (which had formally opened on 30 September) and, miles from any conventional studio, Michael Powell was making *The Edge of the World* off the west coast of Scotland. Arthur Wontner, meanwhile, was at Twickenham for his last screen appearance as Sherlock Holmes, *Silver Blaze*, which began shooting on 28 September. By coincidence, soon-to-be-Sherlock Basil Rathbone started work the same day on a Rowland V Lee item at Denham called *Love from a Stranger*, in which he played Ann Harding's psychotic husband.

Silver Blaze saw Thomas Bentley taking over as director from Leslie Hiscott, who had handled the three previous entries in Twickenham's Holmes series, though a severe bout of flu kept Bentley away from the studio for a full two weeks. Bentley (1880-1953) had started as an actor at the turn of the century, offering lively impersonations of various Dickens characters. Fanatically devoted to bringing Dickens to the masses, he directed his first film in 1912: a short called *Leaves from the Books of Charles Dickens*. By the time of *Silver Blaze*, however, his numerous Dickens films were behind him and ahead lay a stint as technical adviser to the British Film Council.

The script was, as usual, by the ubiquitous H Fowler Mear, with help this time from Arthur Macrae, who doubled as the film's juvenile lead. Doyle's original horse-nobbling saga is followed with considerable fidelity, except for the importation of Professor Moriarty and Colonel Sebastian Moran to pad the film to feature length. Sir Henry Baskerville also appears (20 years, we're told, after his run-in with the legendary Hound), offering Holmes the chance to recuperate in the West Country after a debilitating illness. (Holmes was coaxed out of retirement in Wontner's previous film, **The Triumph of Sherlock Holmes**, but here, indisposition aside, he seems to have returned to business as usual.) Baskerville has a neighbour called Colonel Ross, whose prize horse, Silver Blaze, is hotly tipped to win the Barchester Cup. A dodgy turf accountant, Miles Stanford, expects to be ruined should Silver Blaze succeed and the nefarious Moriarty agrees to put the horse out of commission for him for £1000: a strangely parochial undertaking for the so-called Napoleon of Crime.

While Holmes is on the trail of the vanished Silver Blaze, the horse's groom and trainer are found dead in rapid succession and, when Moriarty hears that the recovered horse will be running after all, he sends Colonel Moran to assassinate Holmes with a new-fangled airgun. The attempt fails, but Moran is more successful when attending the race disguised as a newsreel cameraman, the airgun concealed in his cine-camera. Silver Blaze's jockey is picked off mid-race, the second favourite wins, and Holmes sets Watson on the trail of the shady Stanford, which he infers will also be the trail to Professor Moriarty himself. The captured Watson is rescued by Holmes and Inspector Lestrade only moments before Moriarty can hurl him down an underground lift shaft. 'Professor Moriarty (Lyn Harding) has had his headquarters in many strange places,' observed a correspondent for *The Cinema* during production, 'but never before in a disused tube station.'

Bentley's illness during production, and the resultant disruption to the shooting schedule, presumably accounts for the fact that Audrey Cameron and Aubrey Mallalieu are mentioned in trade accounts of the film's cast as late as Week Two of production but fail to turn up in the finished product. Disrupted or not, the first week was devoted to the film's Baker Street scenes, the second to the set representing the home of Colonel Ross, and on Friday 23 October a second unit journeyed to Newbury to film the race sequences while Bentley stayed at Twickenham in the studio-constructed stable. 'Here,' continued *The Cinema*, 'a racehorse named Nagina (unbeaten as a two-year-old in her day) was imported for the title role.'

Silver Blaze was issued in July 1937, the year in which Gaumont-British and Twickenham itself would become the most prominent casualties of the studio slump. *Kinematograph Weekly*, having described Wontner's Holmes as 'an unforgettable figure' and Ian Fleming's Watson as 'a prize rabbit', went on to observe that 'Scenes on the moors, in the racing stables and in Sir Henry's country mansion have been devised with an expert eye for visual effect. The racehorse sequences are suitably sensational ... and Holmes' lodgings in Baker Street present us with the looked-for surrounding and appurtenances of the detective's domestic menage.' Twickenham's art department will have been pleased to read the latter endorsement; as *The Cinema* reported in the film's first week of production, 'Art director James Carter has been to considerable trouble to reassemble the original 'props' used in Mr Hagen's previous Sherlock Holmes films for the sitting room set.'

The film only surfaced in the USA in 1941, fitted with a new title, *Murder at the Baskervilles*, as a nod to the success of the Twentieth Century-Fox Holmes films which had begun with **Sir Arthur Conan Doyle's The Hound of the Baskervilles**. As the opportunistic retitling indicates, Wontner's crown had by that time passed to Basil Rathbone. His last bow, however, remains a lively and inventive picture. The material taken from SILVER BLAZE itself is delightfully done, with Wontner prowling genuine stud farms in full deerstalker mode and mouthing dialogue lifted direct from the original. The interpolation of Sir Henry Baskerville seems reasonable, but Mear and Macrae struggle to work Moriarty and Moran into the mix while lumbering Wontner with a series of lightning assumptions rather than reasoned deductions. The attempts at modernity – Moriarty's tube station lair, Moran's newsreel camera-cum-rifle etc – also sit uneasily with Wontner's authentic Holmes, by now showing his 61 years all too clearly.

But the cliffhanger ending is terrific, bringing the curtain down on Wontner's distinguished screen association with Holmes in clichéd but engaging fashion. Rescued from the brink of the abyss, Watson ignores the fulminations of the thwarted Moriarty and tells Holmes that 'It's the most amazing case we've ever solved.' 'Elementary, Watson, elementary,' counters Holmes in reply. (JR)

Sir Arthur Conan Doyle's Sherlock Holmes

GB 1968 16 x 50m TV adaptations BBC Television bw/colour
p **William Sterling**
regular cast Sherlock Holmes: **Peter Cushing**
Dr Watson: **Nigel Stock**

THE SECOND STAIN

tx 9 September 1968 BBC1 [bw]
w **Jennifer Stuart** d **Henri Safran**

Inspector Gregson (George A Cooper) aids Watson (Nigel Stock) and Holmes (Peter Cushing) in their quest to solve the riddle of 'the Greek interpreter' in an episode of **Sir Arthur Conan Doyle's Sherlock Holmes** *(1968)*

regular cast, plus Trelawney Hope: **Daniel Massey** Lady Hilda: **Penelope Horner** Lord Bellinger: **Cecil Parker** Henri Fournaye alias Edward Lucas: **Derek Waring** Lady Emily: **Cheri Lunghi** Mme Fournaye: **Alicia Deane** Inspector Lestrade: **William Lucas** John Mitton: **Freddie Barlle** Renate: **Joan Crane** PC Macpherson: **Clifford Cox** Lucy: **Sandra June Williams** Huguette: **Marita Leslie** ticket clerk: **Ronald Forfar** Mrs Hudson: **Grace Arnold** Jacobs: **Leslie Pitt**

A Study in Scarlet

tx 16 September 1968 BBC1 [bw] 15 September 1970 BBC2 [colour]
w **Hugh Leonard** *d* **Henri Safran**
regular cast, plus Joey Daly: **Joe Melia** Inspector Gregson: **George A Cooper** Inspector Lestrade: **William Lucas** Alice Charpentier: **Edina Ronay** Jefferson Hope: **Larry Cross** Enoch Drebber: **Craig Hunter** Madame Charpentier: **Dorothy Edwards** Arthur Charpentier: **Larry Dann** Joseph Stangerson: **Edward Bishop** Police Constable Rance: **Michael Segal** commissionaire: **Henry Kaye** Mrs Hudson: **Grace Arnold** Wiggins: **Tony McLaren** Police Constable Murcher: **Michael Goldie** cabby: **Freddie Barlle***

The Dancing Men

tx 23 September 1968 BBC1 [bw] 22 September 1970 BBC2 [colour]
w **Michael & Mollie Hardwick** *d* **William Sterling**
regular cast, plus Hilton Cubitt: **Maxwell Reed** Elsie Cubitt: **Judee Morton** Saunders: **Brenda Bruce** Mrs King: **Gwen Nelson** Hunt: **Edward Brayshaw** Inspector Martin: **Richardson Morgan** Abe Slaney: **Frank Mann** Dr Armstrong: **Henry Gilbert** maid: **Annabella Johnston** Mrs Hudson: **Grace Arnold** constables: **David Simeon, Norman Caley**

The Hound of the Baskervilles

2 episodes tx 30 September & 7 October 1968 BBC1 [bw] 7 & 14 July 1970 BBC2 [colour]
w **Hugh Leonard** *d* **Graham Evans**
regular cast, plus Sir Henry Baskerville: **Gary Raymond** Beryl Stapleton: **Gabriella Licudi** Stapleton: **Philip Bond** Squire Frankland: **George Howe** Barrymore: **Christopher Burgess** Mrs Barrymore: **June Watson** Sir Hugo Baskerville: **Gerald Flood** [1] Sir Charles Baskerville: **Ballard Berkeley** [1] Dr Mortimer: **David Leland** [1] hotel manager: **David Trevena** [1] girl: **Susan Lefton** [1] coachman: **Bob Harris** [1] servant: **Alan Meadows** [1]

Holmes (Peter Cushing) and Watson (Nigel Stock) in Holmes' Dartmoor hideout in **Sir Arthur Conan Doyle's Sherlock Holmes**: The Hound of the Baskervilles (1968)

Laura Lyons: **Penelope Lee** [2] convict: **Tony Rohr** [2] landlord: **Edward Higgens** [2]

THE BOSCOMBE VALLEY MYSTERY

tx 14 October 1968 BBC1 [bw] 21 July 1970 BBC2 [colour]
w **Bruce Stewart** *d* **Viktors Ritelis**
regular cast, plus Turner: **John Tate** James McCarthy: **Nick Tate** Moran: **Jack Woolgar** Insp Lanner: **Michael Godfrey** Alice: **Heather Kyd** Bill McCarthy: **Peter Madden** Cowper: **Victor Brooks** Patience: **Caroline Ellis** fat man: **Gertan Klauber** Matlock: **Vernon Joyner** Bella: **Sally Sanders**

THE GREEK INTERPRETER

tx 21 October 1968 BBC1 [bw]
w **John Gould** *d* **David Saire**
regular cast, plus Wilson Kemp: **Peter Woodthorpe** Harold Latimer: **Nigel Terry** Mycroft Holmes: **Ronald Adam** Inspector Gregson: **George A Cooper** Sophy: **Evie Kyrol** Davenport: **Edward Hardwicke** Paul: **Alexis Mann** The real Melas: **Clive Cazes** the Greek priest: **Doros Kamenos** Crito Manikuros: **Steve Plytas***

THE NAVAL TREATY

tx 28 October 1968 BBC1 [bw] 11 August 1970 BBC2 [colour]

w **John Gould** *d* **Antony Kearey**
regular cast, plus Lord Holdhurst: **Dennis Price** Percy Phelps: **Corin Redgrave** Joseph Harrison: **Peter Bowles** Annie Harrison: **Jane Lapotaire** Charles Gorot: **Patrick Tull** Tangey: **Robin Wentworth** Inspector Forbes: **Donald Tandy** Peters: **Lane Meddick** Mrs Tangey: **Lucy Griffiths** Mrs Hudson: **Grace Arnold** ambassador: **Joseph Maxwell** constable: **Humphrey Heathcote**

THOR BRIDGE

tx 4 November 1968 BBC1 [bw] 28 July 1970 BBC2 [colour]
w **Harry Moore** *d* **Antony Kearey**
regular cast, plus Grace Dunbar: **Juliet Mills** Dolores: **Isa Miranda** Neil Gibson: **Grant Taylor** Bates: **Henry Oscar** Sergeant Coventry: **Willoughby Gray** Rose: **Anne Ogden** Mrs Hudson: **Grace Arnold** Sara: **Erin Geraghty** Emily: **Gillian Hayes**

THE MUSGRAVE RITUAL

tx 11 November 1968 BBC1 [bw] 4 August 1970 BBC2 [colour]
w **Alexander Baron** *d* **Viktors Ritelis**
regular cast, plus Rachel Howells: **Georgia Brown** John Brunton: **Brian Jackson** Reginald Musgrave: **Norman Wooland** Mrs Hudson: **Grace Arnold** Janet: **Elizabeth**

Hughes Dick Darrell: **Norman Florence** Ellen: **Sheelah Wilcocks** sergeant: **Dominic Allan**

BLACK PETER

tx 18 Nov 1968 BBC1 [bw]
w **Richard Harris** *d* **Antony Kearey**
regular cast, plus Inspector Hopkins: **James Kenney**
Rachel Carey: **Ilona Rodgers** Peter Carey: **John Tate**
Mrs Carey: **Ilona Ference** John Neligan: **Wilfrid Downing**
Patrick Cairns: **Jerold Wells** Mrs Hudson: **Grace Arnold**
landlord: **John Baskcomb** Slater: **Brian Hayes**
Allardyce: **Fred Hugh** Lancaster: **John de Marco**

WISTERIA LODGE

tx 25 November 1968 BBC1 [bw] 18 August 1970
BBC2 [colour]
w **Alexander Baron** *d* **Roger Jenkins**
regular cast, plus Inspector Baynes: **Richard Pearson**
John Scott Eccles: **Derek Francis** Henderson: **Walter Gotell**
Miss Burnet: **Tanya Robinson** Mrs Hudson: **Grace Arnold**
Garcia: **Carlos Pierre** José: **Tutte Lemkow**
Warner: **Desmond Stokes** PC Walters: **Philip Anthony**
Lucas: **Christopher Carlos** mulatto: **Roy Stewart**

SHOSCOMBE OLD PLACE

tx 2 December 1968 BBC1 [bw] 25 August 1970
BBC2 [colour]
w **Anthony Read***, **Donald Tosh*** *d* **Bill Bain**
regular cast, plus Sir Robert Norberton: **Nigel Green**
Mason: **Edward Woodward** Stephens: **David Bird**
Carrie: **Carol Macready** Barnes: **Michael Beint**
George Norlett: **Kevin Lindsay** Sam Brewer: **Peter Miles**
Josie Bootle: **Yvonne Ball** racegoers: **Jim Collier,
Maurice Quick, John Lawrence**

THE SOLITARY CYCLIST

tx 9 December 1968 BBC1 [bw] 1 September 1970
BBC2 [colour]
w **Stanley Miller** *d* **Viktors Ritelis**
regular cast, plus Violet Smith: **Carole Potter** Carruthers:
Charles Tingwell Woodley: **David Butler** Lucy: **Gillian
Bailey** Mrs Bainbridge: **Ysanne Churchman** clerk: **Alan
Tucker** Mr Trivett: **Clyde Pollitt** Williamson: **Peter Miles**
landlord: **Harry Webster** Peter: **Dean Harris**

THE SIGN OF FOUR

tx 16 December 1968 BBC1 [bw] 8 September 1970
BBC2 [colour]
w **Michael & Mollie Hardwick** *d* **William Sterling**
regular cast, plus Mary Morstan: **Ann Bell** Thaddeus and

Bartholomew Sholto: **Paul Daneman** Inspector Athelney
Jones: **John Stratton** Mrs Forrester: **Ailsa Grahame**
Jonathan Small: **Howard Goorney** Mrs Hudson: **Grace
Arnold** Lal Rao: **Ahmed Khalil** McMurdo: **Sydney Conabere**
Wiggins: **Tony McLaren** Mrs Mordecai Smith: **Annabella
Johnston** Mr Mordecai Smith: **Davis S Boliver**
Mrs Bernstone: **Ann Way** Tonga: **Zena Keller** Alice: **Sara
Clee** John Sholto: **John Dunbar** policemen: **Ves Delahunt,
David James, Kenneth Hale, Tony Leary** Toby: **Toddy**

THE BLUE CARBUNCLE

tx 23 December 1968 BBC1 [bw]
w **Stanley Miller** *d* **Bill Bain**
regular cast, plus Lady Morcar: **Madge Ryan** James Ryder:
James Beck Howard Baker: **Richard Butler** Breckinridge:
Michael Robbins Peterson: **Frank Middlemass** Windigate:
Ernest Hare Horner: **Neil Fitzpatrick** Police Sergeant:
Clyde Pollitt Mrs Hudson: **Grace Arnold** Mrs Oakshott:
Edna Dore Catherine Cusack: **Diana Chappel**

With Peter Cushing replacing Douglas Wilmer in the title role, this troubled follow-on to the BBC's 1965 **Sherlock Holmes** has the distinction of being the most-watched Holmes series of all time, gaining some 15.5 million viewers at its British peak. Ironically, it has since come to languish among the most obscure, little known about it bar the fact that it was the first to be made for colour transmission. However, a small amount of detective work reveals a twisting, turning behind-the-scenes saga no less compelling than its 16 strong instalments.

Over the late summer and early autumn of 1966, the Wilmer series was granted a much-requested repeat run – and its continued success the second time around appears to have convinced the BBC's powers-that-were to take up its option on a second run of 13 instalments. Early in December, BBC television drama chief Andrew Osborn (formerly the actor who had played the Corporation's first ever Holmes, oddly enough, in the 1951 play **For the Children: The Adventure of the Mazarin Stone**) asked Wilmer's agent John Miller about his client's availability, stating that the BBC was keen to make more Holmeses. Wilmer, then working in Hong Kong, declined Osborn's offer, being unimpressed by a proposal to cut costs by reducing the number of days allocated to rehearsal and also afraid of typecasting. Certainly, his most prominent film role in the interim – as

Sir Denis Nayland Smith, aristocratic antithesis to Christopher Lee's Yellow Peril, in *The Brides of Fu Manchu* – had tapped a very similar vein. In fact, Wilmer's Hong Kong sojourn was for a second run-in with Lee: *The Vengeance of Fu Manchu*.

The search for a new lead was now on. While the BBC informed the Doyle estate of its decision to exercise its option on another series (negotiations were completed early in January 1967), one actor's name leaped to the top of the shortlist – that of John Neville, whose Holmes-versus-the-Ripper film **A Study in Terror** had only recently departed the cinema circuit. Enquiries in mid-December had revealed that Neville was 'definitely interested' in playing the part of Holmes – and on 12 January, Osborn suggested Neville's casting to Nigel Stock, whose continued presence as Watson was never in doubt: 'I hope this idea appeals to you. Did you by any chance see the film? He was very good in it.'

It soon became clear, however, that Neville's commitments at the Nottingham Playhouse, where he was actor-manager, would prove difficult, if not impossible, to fit around the new series' necessarily lengthy production schedule. Although each episode of this new run was to be shot on a ten-day turnaround, as opposed to the 14 enjoyed by the previous set, it would still require the lead actor to be at the BBC's call for a good six months. Osborn continued to press Neville throughout January and February, when he lunched one other prospective Sherlock: Eric Porter, then in the process of becoming a household name as rigid antihero Soames, head of a middle-class Victorian dynasty in BBC2's hugely successful *The Forsyte Saga*. Neither actor would ultimately be contracted. Some 17 years later, Porter would make the role of Professor Moriarty his own opposite Jeremy Brett's Great Detective in two episodes of Granada's **The Adventures of Sherlock Holmes**.

Despite the lack of a star, planning for the new series continued throughout 1967; by 10 May, a provisional running order had been compiled (probably by Anthony Read, one of two script editors on the Wilmers). First came adaptations of THE MUSGRAVE RITUAL and WISTERIA LODGE, both by Vincent Tilsley, followed by THE BLUE CARBUNCLE by Stanley Miller; THE NAVAL TREATY by John Gould (the other script editor on the Wilmers); a two-part THE HOUND OF THE

BASKERVILLES by Clive Exton; THOR BRIDGE by Harry Moore; SHOSCOMBE OLD PLACE, then THE GREEK INTERPRETER, by either Anthony or Jan Read; THE REIGATE SQUIRES (author undetermined); THE DANCING MEN, probably by Hugh Leonard; BLACK PETER, pencilled in for Tilsley; and finally THE SECOND STAIN, most likely by Clifford Witting. THE EMPTY HOUSE was appended as a 'maybe', but it was noted that this could only be the first episode.

Real progress wasn't made until the New Year, with the appointment of William Sterling as producer. An Australian émigré, Sterling had served time on the BBC's proto-soap *Compact* before overseeing adventure serial *The Three Musketeers* and a sequel, *The Return of the Musketeers*, throughout 1966-67. He came to this latest assignment with a clear mission – as set out in an internal memo of 23 January 1968, where he noted that the overall style of production was to be 'in the Patrick Hamilton manner'. (Throughout the thirties and forties, the grossly under-rated Hamilton had written a number of bleak crime melodramas such as the novel *Hangover Square* and the plays *Gaslight* and *Rope*, the latter filmed by Alfred Hitchcock.) The memo continued, describing the approach as: 'Hard, sharp, full of tension, mystery and Victorian crime savagery ... Holmes by turns demonic and laconic in energy: athletic, mentally alert.'

Possible writers at this point were named as Alexander Baron (who had adapted the exploits of D'Artagnan and company for Sterling), plus Leo Lehman, Robert Muller, Bruce Stewart, Tilsley, Jack Pulman, Michael and Mollie Hardwick and finally Richard Harris, whose version of THE RED CIRCLE – a new addition to the list of Doyle adaptations – was being worked on by 14 February. By 9 April, Sterling had contracted a number of directors, sending an identical memo to each: 'Would you watch Hitchcock's *Psycho* on Easter Monday, 15th April, BBC1 at 9.30 pm. As I have been saying to everybody it is a starting point for my production approach to Sherlock Holmes. Enjoy it!'

Given that Sterling sought to retain the Holmesian credentials of the Wilmer series, albeit in a darker presentation style, there could scarcely be an actor better placed to play his Sherlock than Peter Cushing. Since appearing in Hammer Films' **The Hound of the Baskervilles** (1959), Cushing had continued to milk the British Gothic boom both

The game's afoot (again): Nigel Stock and Peter Cushing pose for **Sir Arthur Conan Doyle's Sherlock Holmes** *(1968)*

with Hammer and rival companies such as Amicus and Tigon, becoming almost synonymous with grim fantasy pictures at the expense of theatre and TV work – odd, given that Cushing's fame/notoriety had been founded in early fifties' BBC productions like Rudolph Cartier's still-stunning *Nineteen Eighty-Four*. As devoted to Doyle's detective as ever, Cushing signed to play the lead early in February 1968 – ordering the purchase of a number of *Strand* back numbers to aid his preparation, perusing them with the zeal of an obsessive.

The new series was intended to outdo the Wilmer run in every way possible – not the least of which was colour recording, unconfirmed until mid-May and, since nationwide colour broadcasts were not due to commence until January 1970, contingent on the BBC's contract with the Doyle estate permitting a repeat run on BBC2 up to two years on. In addition, the soon-to-be-retitled **Sir Arthur Conan Doyle's Sherlock Holmes**, now 16 episodes long, would see a much greater allocation of location filming and a glittering array of 'International Guest Stars' propping up each instalment.

On a Sterling wish-list of 30 April were names such as Raymond Massey (Holmes in the 1931 **The Speckled Band**) playing Jefferson Hope in *A Study in Scarlet*, George Sanders as Mycroft in *The Greek Interpreter*, Curt Jürgens as Henderson in *Wisteria Lodge*, Leo McKern as Black Gorgiano in *The Red Circle* and Hayley Mills as Alice Turner in *The Boscombe Valley Mystery*, plus quintessential sixties icons like Julie Christie as Lady Trelawney Hope in *The Second Stain*, Albert Finney as Sir Henry in *The Hound of the Baskervilles*, and either Peter Finch, Stanley Baker or Sean Connery as Sir Robert Norberton in *Shoscombe Old Place*. Although instructions were sent to begin negotiations with all of these, all appear to have been beyond the producer's reach – or pocket.

First to go before the cameras in the early summer was Hugh Leonard's two-part version of THE HOUND OF THE BASKERVILLES – the second to feature Cushing, and the first to include sequences filmed *in situ* on Dartmoor itself, as per Doyle. Cast and crew were based at Newton Abbot for the main shoot; however, scenes in and around the Grimpen Mire were remounted at Ealing Studios

Peter Cushing's distress was magnified daily during production of
Sir Arthur Conan Doyle's Sherlock Holmes *(1968)*

after the filmed sequences were judged unusable, and a short outdoor session took place at Regents Park, London. Studio recordings at BBC Television Centre took place on 8 and 22 July – when, elsewhere within the Corporation's Wood Lane headquarters, decisions were being taken which would impact heavily upon the remainder of the series.

Script editor John Barber left the series suddenly during production of *The Hound of the Baskervilles*. His replacement was Donald Tosh, a former story editor on *Compact* and *Doctor Who* among others; in his pre-BBC career with Granada Television, he had picked out the series outline which led to the development of *Coronation Street*. For Tosh, *Sir Arthur Conan Doyle's Sherlock Holmes* would prove to be something of an ordeal; he arrived just as the production team had completed their *Hound* only to be told that the series was already some £13,000 over-budget – an overspend which patently could not be tolerated by the drama department's heads. 'Once they'd taken so long and spent so much money on *The Hound of the Baskervilles*, Andrew Osborn and David Rose kind of summoned me,' remembers Tosh. 'They suddenly said, "Will Sterling's going to be fired. You've

got to do it yourself." I thought, "Christ, I'm going to be doing this as both editor and producer, and they're looking for the patsy" – which, indeed, they were...

'Anyway, on it went and Will Sterling sort of sat there. They discovered he couldn't be fired without enormous breaches of contract, or something, so they just left him sitting there in the office – which made life impossible, because they said, "You must pay no attention to anything he says." Wonderful – I have a producer who's not a producer, who I'm not allowed to pay attention to, and he is allowed to go on mixing it up. This is why it was a very, very unhappy experience in the main – but one just got down and thought, "Well, it's got to be got on the air. We've got to get something on the air, as good as possible" – and it was really quite successful. This is the extraordinary thing, because the production side of it was a total disaster! My first instruction was, "You must bring it in on budget at the end." And I said, "Well, this is all very well, but the scripts have all been commissioned." They were film scripts – I mean, 90 per cent of them was film, and I said there was no way they could do this. And they said, "Well it's got to be brought into studio..."'

Tosh was forced to contact the various writers, who by now had all delivered ambitious, location-intensive screenplays, and work with them – 'in some cases willingly, in some cases arm-twisting like mad' – to bring the stories back into the enclosed stages at Television Centre, with only very few exterior scenes permissible. 'The original scripts were very different to what actually, ultimately went on the air – we had to go back tight to the stories, and if we were sticking them in the studio, we couldn't sort of embellish, which they had been doing.' A case in point being *Shoscombe Old Place*, which ultimately reached the screen without a writing credit at all. 'Anthony Read had his name taken off until it was shown in Italy, where it got some sort of extraordinary award – and he went and collected it, which I thought was a bit bold!' says Tosh, claiming that Read's commitments on location for another series had meant that he was unavailable to rework the script; Tosh was forced to make the necessary changes himself. 'I sent it off to Tony and he hated it! He said, "It's not the script I wrote," and I said, "I know – the one you wrote all took place outside, filming strange girls running around the countryside with fewer and fewer clothes on and I couldn't actually see the point – very decorative I'm sure, but it wasn't quite Conan Doyle..."

'However, [director] Bill Bain joined us about two days before going into rehearsal, and on that Friday he sat down with me and went through the whole thing as to what he wanted, and that weekend I rewrote – well, I wrote an adaptation of SHOSCOMBE OLD PLACE... It was a great success, although I had only – what was it, five sets? We got a lovely performance from Edward Woodward, who sort of held the thing together – so it worked, and Bill Bain did a beautiful job on it, but some of the others were horrendous. I almost wish, in a sense, we'd had more really strong directors like Bill. What happened was, having to tie everything back into the studio concentrated the minds wonderfully of the directors, who really had only just learned about filming. At the time, everyone was going mad, thinking, "Now I can make *The Searchers* by John Ford." Well, suddenly they couldn't, and so they had to think, "Wait a minute, how do we do this?" The really good directors, like Bill Bain, came up absolutely 100 per cent and delivered us wonderful, tight productions. Antony Kearey did some very good ones, too.'

Production continued week in, week out. Directed by Sterling himself, *The Dancing Men*'s location shoot (in and around Oxborough Hall, near Swaffham, Norfolk) proceeded as planned early in August, following *A Study in Scarlet*, *Black Peter* and *The Second Stain* into studio on 2 September. Two days later, a few short scenes for *The Boscombe Valley Mystery* were filmed in and around Chilbrook Farm and Cobham Stud Stables, Cobham, and at Queensmere Lake on Wimbledon Common.

Promoted as '16 hour-long thrillers with decidedly macabre near-Gothic overtones', the series made its BBC1 début at 9.05 pm on Monday 9 September, at which point ten episodes were yet to be recorded – and, incredibly, it wasn't even certain what one of these would be! Money was so tight by 13 September that Richard Harris' *The Red Circle*, deemed too expensive to produce, was hastily dropped from the schedule, and Stanley Miller's long-since-abandoned *The Blue Carbuncle* was hurriedly pressed back into service, on the grounds that it would be a simple replacement

suitable for transmission in Christmas week as the last episode of the series.

Again, Tosh was forced to step in to expand the script. 'If we'd have done Stanley's it would have lasted about 25 minutes. Stanley was a very successful television writer – he had masses of credits going back to the fifties – and was notorious for being the most difficult writer to change. Having to rewrite *The Blue Carbuncle* – using, I must admit, great hunks of Stanley – I just put bits in so it ran the full period; the story itself is fairly slight. Anyway, I sent him the script and it was very sweet because he rang me up and he said, "Oh, this seems to be exactly the script I sent in," and I thought, "If he can't see the joins, that's all right." That was one of the happier episodes – most of the others were absolute nightmares, because of everything happening in the studio and everything being so tight.'

Recording continued throughout October and November with *The Greek Interpreter* (featuring actor Edward Hardwicke in a minor role, years before becoming Jeremy Brett's second Watson in Granada Television's **The Return of Sherlock Holmes**), then *The Naval Treaty*, *The Musgrave Ritual*, *Wisteria Lodge*, *Shoscombe Old Place* and location scenes for *The Sign of Four* on Harrow Weald Common, at Twickenham and on the Thames at Brentford, near the London Apprentice. But matters came to a head with the recording of *The Solitary Cyclist*, featuring Carole Potter as the harried Violet Smith. Potter was, in fact, Sterling's wife – 'an actress of no talent at all, and consequently has never been heard of before or since', according to Tosh – and had, of course, been cast at Sterling's insistence. But it was the quietly diligent Cushing – constantly pressurised by a remorseless ten-days-per-episode schedule alien to an actor who had spent over ten years in films, making 90 minutes of material in six weeks – who found himself at the centre of an unholy row with Tosh. 'The big thing with our series was that Peter himself was a total Holmesian, and absolutely steeped in them – if we put a word wrong, he knew,' says Tosh. 'So eventually I used this against him...'

Doyle's faintly incredible conclusion has Holmes wrapping up the adventure by confessing that he ought to have solved the case earlier ('I have been very obtuse, Watson ... When in your

Dr Mortimer (David Leland) brings Holmes (Peter Cushing) news of a terrible legend apparently made flesh in **Sir Arthur Conan Doyle's Sherlock Holmes**: The Hound of the Baskervilles *(1968)*

report you said that you had seen the cyclist as you thought arrange his necktie in the shrubbery, that alone should have told me all'). Due to the fact that this was felt to be 'the lamest get-out', Cushing apparently suggested altering the script to give it a more likely climax – much to Tosh's irritation, having accomodated all of the actor's Holmes-fan pickiness thus far. 'I said, "No, you insist we stick to Doyle, we stick to Doyle." We had a huge row about it in the studio, because he said he wouldn't say this line. I said, "Of course you'll say that line." There were huge great rows, and in front of everyone I accused him of unprofessionalism, which shook him to the core. I was by then jumping up and down! Oh dear. All too shaming, really...

'Peter was a delight – very gentle and pleasant, an awfully nice man. It was just the once we had this absolutely mammoth row. I thought, "I have had so much trouble with all this" – what with having seen how very boring what's-her-name was as an actress, thinking Will has wished this all on us and Viktors [Ritelis, director] was kind of caving

in to everybody – and I thought, "No, I dig my heels in here. Beyond this I do not go. We're doing Doyle – and that's it!" It all got out of hand. The next week we were all chums again...'

The series wrapped with the recording of the rewritten *The Blue Carbuncle*, film inserts for which were shot at Great Goodwin Farm, Merrow, near Guildford; inside the Devonshire Club, St James Street, SW1; and outside the Constitutional Club, also in St James Street. It aired on 23 December, exactly one week after recording, bringing the enormously successful series to a close. *The Sign of Four* had garnered 15.5 million viewers, with one other episode topping the chart of the top 20 programmes.

Despite this, the series won only a mixed reception from the Fourth Estate, the *Daily Mail* lambasting it as a crude attempt to 'crash the international market' and revelling in the fact that the BBC had begun transmission of an unfinished edit of *The Dancing Men*. Despite thinking Cushing 'a somewhat off beat bit of casting', *Variety*'s British correspondent 'Hawk' praised *The Hound of the Baskervilles* for its 'pinpoint feeling for accuracy in the backdrops ... costumes and other production facets'. Sadly, US audiences would be denied the chance to see the series, Stateside stations apparently thinking it 'too violent' for American tastes. Contractual issues may also have precluded its sale to the US, although the series would be shown in South Africa, New Zealand and Australia.

Given its success with viewers, one would assume that it was the series' turbulent production that scotched the chances of an immediate sequel – but for the fact that one such sequel did come close to pre-production. Back in July 1968, Adrian Conan Doyle had suggested that a further series might adapt *The Exploits of Sherlock Holmes*, a 1954 collection of pastiches which he'd co-authored with John Dickson Carr. At the time, a BBC mandarin had informed Doyle that Osborn would like to put on a further Sherlock Holmes series, but instead of dramatising existing stories wanted to acquire the rights in the basic characters and then to write new and original stories around them – nominating the BBC's use of A J Cronin's characters in *Dr Finlay's Casebook* as a successful precedent. To which Doyle had curtly replied: 'the Estates are not prepared at this stage to allow the BBC to make their own dramatisations.' However, by October 1969, the BBC had suggested that a new series of 13 might comprise nine of the 11 *Exploits* plus four canonical adaptations; Adrian Conan Doyle was reportedly 'delighted' with this proposal. Provisionally slated for the 1971-72 season, the project ran out of steam and was quietly shelved.

Twelve of the Cushing shows were repeated, this time in colour, between July and September 1970. *The Second Stain*, *The Greek Interpreter*, *Black Peter* and *The Blue Carbuncle* were omitted from the run; to this day, they have never been shown in colour in the UK. Three of them never will be. It was then standard BBC practice for tapes to be wiped and re-used once they were judged to be of no further value (in this case, since the original contract with the Doyle estate precluded any other transmissions), which, long before the advent of home video and cable television, would not have seemed quite so crass and short-sighted a course as it appears now.

By lucky chance, however, *A Study in Scarlet*, both parts of *The Hound of the Baskervilles*, *The*

Boscombe Valley Mystery, *The Sign of Four* and *The Blue Carbuncle* have survived. Watching the surviving instalments, one is delighted to see the cod-Gothic titles – in which Holmes and Watson examine daggers, knuckledusters and the like to the sound of swirling strings and mournful brasses – give way to a lush, elegant presentation style and a very fine lead performance. Cushing is far less waspish than in the Hammer *Hound*, helping to defuse the few occasions when the series' full-on approach threatens to lapse into camp histrionics with urbanity and not a little humour – clearing a sandwich-scoffing Fat Man from his railway carriage by the exercising of his deductive powers in *The Boscombe Valley Mystery*, or becoming thoroughly exasperated by the sight of Watson and Mary Morstan fawning over one another in *The Sign of Four*.

And if the budgetary cuts are pretty obvious – the film inserts being few, fleeting and far between – some real imagination has gone into disguising the fact. In the aforementioned *Boscombe Valley Mystery*, for example, farmer Turner's career as an Australian highwayman is related in a startling montage of etchings from his scrapbook, with appropriate sound effects running over the top – and there's a particularly striking moment when a very non-naturalistic splash of blood appears on one of these. Indeed, the series' very liberal use of Kensington Gore is remarkable in itself; in the same episode, Bill McCarthy's bloody head wound is displayed in unflinching detail.

Although Cushing would play Holmes one last time, in 1984's **The Masks of Death**, *Sir Arthur Conan Doyle's Sherlock Holmes* clearly dissuaded him from committing to appear in another full television series for the rest of his life. On the eve of the 1970 repeats, *Radio Times* reporter Rosemary Collins captured him conjuring up from memory what was clearly a traumatic experience: '"Television is an enormous strain, all the pressures, the pace ... very high-powered. And there were so many inconsistencies in Conan Doyle's books which we had to try and iron out ... Holmes is a very complex and difficult character ... three different coloured dressing-gowns, a variety of pipes. We did try to keep the details right." Cushing sighs, as if it were almost too much for him. His eyes are large, grey and worried. He folds and unfolds his hands...'

Sir Arthur Conan Doyle's The Hound of the Baskervilles

US 1939 adaptation Twentieth Century-Fox Film Corporation 80m colour

w **Ernest Pascal** *assoc p* **Gene Markey** *d* **Sidney Lanfield**
cast Sir Henry Baskerville: **Richard Greene**
Sherlock Holmes: **Basil Rathbone** Beryl Stapleton: **Wendy Barrie** Dr Watson: **Nigel Bruce** James Mortimer, MD: **Lionel Atwill** Barryman: **John Carradine** Frankland: **Barlow Borland** Mrs Jenifer Mortimer: **Beryl Mercer** John Stapleton: **Morton Lowry** Sir Hugo Baskerville: **Ralph Forbes** cabby: **E E Clive** Mrs Barryman: **Eily Malyon** coroner: **Lionel Pape** convict: **Nigel de Brulier** Mrs Hudson: **Mary Gordon** Sir Charles: **Ian MacLaren** Bruce: **John Burton*** Jon: **Dennis Green*** shepherd: **Ivan Simpson*** Edwin: **Evan Thomas*** Roderick: **Peter Willes*** the Hound: **Chief*** [pseudonym for **Blitzen**]

S ir Arthur Conan Doyle's The Hound of the Baskervilles – as Twentieth Century-Fox's adaptation was ostentatiously labelled, both on screen and on all its posters and publicity, presumably to underscore both its 'authorised' status and its fidelity to the Doyle text – was, in its time, the most lavish of Hollywood's efforts to visualise any part of the Holmes canon.

Filmed from 29 December 1938 and calling for the use of a spectacularly eerie fog-shrouded Dartmoor set some 300 feet long by 200 feet wide, it starred budding British matinée idol Richard Greene (1918-85) as a boyishly handsome Sir Henry romancing a Beryl Stapleton played by Wendy Barrie (Marguerite Wendy Jenkins, 1912-78), who was immortalised in literature when her godfather, J M Barrie, wrote her into his stories of the fairy Peter Pan. In a striking touch, the Dartmoor scenes ran without any kind of incidental score, just howls of wind... and (maybe) something worse. Ernest Pascal's crisp screenplay substantially deviated from Doyle only in places – most notably in adding a spooky séance scene in which Dr Mortimer's mousy wife, who supposedly has 'strong mediumistic qualities' and is 'conducive to psychic phenomena', attempts to summon up the spirit of the dead Sir Charles: 'Tell us of all the weird, horrible things that have happened on the moor.' Unusually, Mortimer himself was played as a very plausible suspect by

Lionel Atwill, later a fine Moriarty in **Sherlock Holmes and the Secret Weapon** (1942). John Carradine's no-less-creepy butler was renamed 'Barryman', presumably to avoid confusion with the prominent Barrymore clan, whose scion John had been a memorable lead in Goldwyn's **Sherlock Holmes** (1922). The scary Hound itself was played by a Great Dane called Blitzen, who suffered the indignity of being renamed 'Chief' after (as the *New York Times* reported on 21 May 1939) 'Hollywood's current distaste for Nazidom' had made it essential to 'remove the Teutonic taint'. The jarring, mildly shocking closing line – Holmes' barked, out-of-left-field entreaty to his doctor-associate to supply him henceforth with his narcotic relaxant of choice ('Oh Watson – the needle!') – was censored before release, and only reinstated when the film was reissued in June 1975.

Has anything escaped me?

Almost everything.

Accounts vary as to how Basil Rathbone came to assume the mantle of Sherlock Holmes; came to *be* Sherlock Holmes for nigh on three generations, and beyond. The Johannesburg-born Philip St John Basil Rathbone (1892-1967) had learned his trade in the Shakespearean rep company of his actor-manager cousin, Frank Benson, making his film début at the age of 28 in Stoll Picture Productions' *Innocent* (1921). Commuting back and forth across the Atlantic throughout the 1920s, Rathbone was soon picked out as Hollywood's screen villain of choice, playing opposite Errol Flynn in Warner Bros' original swashbucklers, *Captain Blood* (1935) and *The Adventures of Robin Hood* (1938). So casting Rathbone as Holmes was casting against type. Whether or not that choice was a moment's sudden inspiration on the part of Twentieth Century-Fox head Darryl F Zanuck (as some stories have it), or made at the instigation of Fox producer Gene Markey, is irrelevant. Entirely commanding (without ever having to assert that authority), unmortal and apart from the crowd (without ever having to call upon actorly tics and tricks), and fluent of movement and diction, Basil Rathbone *was* Sherlock Holmes – every bit as perfect an incarnation of Doyle's detective for talking pictures as Sidney Paget's drawings had been for the printed page, and William Gillette for the boards.

It's become fashionable to attempt to divorce Rathbone's 'superb', 'definitive' Holmes from

Dream team: Holmes (Basil Rathbone) and Watson (Nigel Bruce) commence their immortal partnership in **Sir Arthur Conan Doyle's The Hound of the Baskervilles** *(1939)*

Nigel Bruce's 'dunderheaded', 'absurd' Watson (who, at the time of the *Hound*'s release on 31 March 1939, was called 'rounded and credible' in the *New York Herald-Tribune*, one of many positive notices). In fact, theirs is an indivisible partnership: Rathbone's Holmes is the way he is in order to best complement Bruce's Watson, and vice versa. It isn't Rathbone alone who makes the lines crackle in the first Baker Street scene, in which the pair ponder Dr Mortimer's cane; it isn't Rathbone alone who makes the scene in which the strange old pedlar reveals his true identity so electrifying, so funny, so triumphant: he and Bruce are a double-act, they do it together. Indeed, if the most reliable account of how the Fox *Hound* was arrived at is to be believed, Bruce's name was invoked by Markey just one breath after Rathbone was nominated as a potential Holmes; if Rathbone was to be Holmes, Bruce simply *had* to be Watson, and that was that.

Born (surprisingly) in Mexico, Bruce (William N Bruce, 1895-1953) had played on the stage

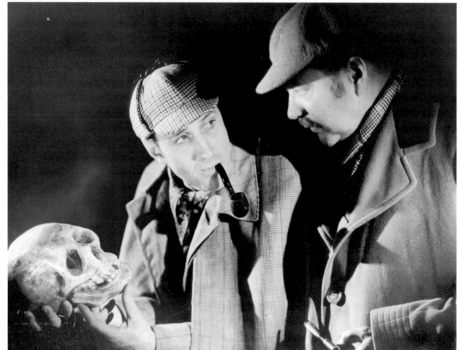

'Tell us of all the weird, horrible things that have happened on the moor': Holmes (Basil Rathbone) and Watson (Nigel Bruce) in **Sir Arthur Conan Doyle's The Hound of the Baskervilles** (1939)

throughout his English youth, graduating from often-comic appearances in British films such as *The Scarlet Pimpernel* (1934) to more prestigious American productions such as *Treasure Island* (1934) and the next year's *She*. (It's amusing to note Bruce's fellow players in *The Lady is Willing*, another important production of 1934: Leslie Howard and Cedric Hardwicke, the fathers of a notable TV Holmes and a notable TV Watson respectively.) As members of Hollywood's community of expat Brits, Rathbone and Bruce were friends long before the *Hound*. It shows. One without the other is unthinkable – Morecambe without Wise, light without shade.

Those revisionists who complain that Bruce's Watson mars this film – not to mention the 13 Rathbone pictures that followed it, starting with **The Adventures of Sherlock Holmes** (1939)·– on the grounds that Doyle didn't write Watson as an older, better-natured, funnier foil to Holmes, might ponder whether or not Bruce's Watson didn't actually rehabilitate the doctor on screen: Watson had, after all, been more or less written out of the first 20 years of Sherlock Holmes films, making only a handful of appearances throughout the silent era. Even in the first two

Hollywood-produced talking pictures, **The Return of Sherlock Holmes** (1929) and **Conan Doyle's Master Detective Sherlock Holmes**, he'd either been aged beyond recognition, with a grown-up daughter, or entirely marginalised. Before Bruce, Watson was considered dispensable; after Bruce, it would be a near-unthinkable heresy to show Holmes without him.

The Fox *Hound* would be blissful even without such a fine detective/doctor team. The fact of that team's presence makes it quite probably the only Sherlock Holmes film that can hold its head among the true classics of the cinema.

Sir Arthur Conan Doyle's The Hound of the Baskervilles

GB 1983 TVM adaptation [THE HOUND OF THE BASKERVILLES] *Mapleton Films Ltd/ Investors in Industry plc 96m colour tx 3 November 1983 HBO* [US]
w **Charles Edward Pogue** *p* **Otto Plaschkes** *d* **Douglas Hickox**
cast Sherlock Holmes: **Ian Richardson** Dr John Watson: **Donald Churchill** Dr Mortimer: **Denholm Elliott**

Beryl Stapleton: **Glynis Barber** Geoffrey Lyons: **Brian Blessed** Mrs Barrymore: **Eleanor Bron** Barrymore: **Edward Judd** Inspector Lestrade: **Ronald Lacey** Sir Henry Baskerville: **Martin Shaw** Laura Lyons: **Connie Booth** cabbie: **Eric Richard** shop owner: **Michael Burrell** maid: **Cindy O'Callaghan** young girl in mire: **Francesca Gonshaw** Sir Charles Baskerville: **David Langton** Jack Stapleton/Sir Hugo Baskerville/bearded man: **Nicholas Clay**

Like **Sir Arthur Conan Doyle's The Sign of Four**, this, the second of the two Ian Richardson-headlining TV movies, is moderately sensationalised but not entirely convincing. And this time round, the films' greatest asset, Richardson himself, becomes sidelined as a parade of very recognisable British TV faces take turns in the spotlight, among them: Martin Shaw (1945-), aka *The Professionals* bonehead Doyle, who assumes a faintly absurd Texan accent as Baskerville heir Sir Henry; Glynis Barber (1955-), aka the BBC's stripping comic-strip heroine *Jane* and *Blake's 7* gunslinger Soolin, as a jodhpur-clad Beryl Stapleton (this in the same year as her sole feature film lead, in Michael Winner's remake of highwaywoman melodrama *The Wicked Lady*); and bushy-bearded Brian Blessed (1937-), aka *Z Cars'* PC 'Fancy' Smith, bringing a surprising sensitivity to his role as drunken failed artist and wife-beater Geoffrey Lyons.

The character of Geoffrey, Laura Lyons' husband, was a new addition to the list of possible suspects courtesy returning screenwriter Charles Edward Pogue. The script has Laura strangled in her bed by Stapleton, who fears that she might reveal he had acted as a go-between for her and her lover Sir Charles Baskerville, thereby disclosing his part in Sir Charles' murder. The wretched Geoffrey is arrested for the killing of his wife, enabling Holmes to have Stapleton show his true hand. It's an entirely effective subplot. The angry Geoffrey, indeed, is given a party trick swiped from Dr Grimesby Roylott in THE SPECKLED BAND – bending a poker in half, whereupon an unimpressed Holmes, cool as you like, straightens it back. Another significant deviation from the text of THE HOUND is found in the London scenes, where a disguised Stapleton, trailing Sir Henry in a cab, takes a potshot at the new Baskerville heir using a rifle disguised as a cane – a cane topped with a sculpted dog's head...

The film was shot more or less simultaneously with its companion piece, **Sir Arthur Conan Doyle's The Sign of Four**, but the practicalities of filming on location in Dartmoor and the West Country between 12 November and 1 December 1982 precluded David Healy – who, since the spring, had been engaged every evening as show-stopper Nicely-Nicely Johnson in the National Theatre's revival of the musical *Guys and Dolls* – from playing Dr Watson in both. Executive producer Sy Weintraub refused to rock the boat by rearranging the filming schedule around Healy's availability, so his replacement was Donald Churchill (1930-91), then best known as the second Inspector Spooner in Ray Galton and Johnny Speight's police sitcom *Spooner's Patch* (1979-82).

Churchill's Watson makes more of an impact than Healy's, but his burly duffer of a doctor, each line mumbled through a mouth seemingly full of cotton wool, fails utterly as a foil to Richardson's Holmes; Richardson would himself describe the Churchill Watson as 'too common'. He does, however, have one beautiful moment: in a Dartmoor post office-cum-pub, Watson meets Inspector Lestrade (who, in another diversion from the source text, has been sent to Devon on a special assignment to head the search for escaped convict Selden, whom he'd originally arrested) – and, in an

Sherlock Holmes (Ian Richardson) spies on the Dartmoor types in **Sir Arthur Conan Doyle's The Hound of the Baskervilles** *(1983)*

Watson (Donald Churchill) is struck dumb while Holmes (Ian Richardson) analyses Dr Mortimer's cane in **Sir Arthur Conan Doyle's The Hound of the Baskervilles** *(1983)*

attempt to keep news of Holmes' involvement in the hunt for the Hound from the police, tells him: 'I am here for the sailing.' 'Sailing?' splutters Lestrade. 'There's no sailing round here!' 'Oh, what a pity,' murmurs Watson. 'I must have been misinformed...'

Director Douglas Hickox (1929-88) was previously responsibly for the camply horrible Vincent Price vehicle *Theatre of Blood* (1973), and although *Sir Arthur Conan Doyle's The Hound of the Baskervilles* doesn't quite aspire to such excesses, it wrings what Gothic juice it can from the material. Certainly, the scene in which 17th century bad boy Sir Hugo Baskerville appears to anally rape a runaway servant girl on the moor while her horse whinnies frantically as it drowns in the Grimpen Mire pushes the boundaries of good taste, and the scene where a prowling POV camera is used to show the Hound tracking and devouring Dr Mortimer's spaniel Sheba opens up the possibility of a whole new filmic sub-genre – the dog-on-dog slasher movie. Richardson told *Scarlet Street* magazine that Hickox 'had to be stopped from having blood coming out of the mouths of the gargoyles on the Hall... I said, "Dougie, why do you want this blood gushing out

of the gargoyles?" And he said, "Well, it adds a touch of the grotesque..."'

Baskerville Hall itself was Knightshayes Court, a National Trust property near Tiverton, Devon. Hickox and production designer Michael Stringer had hunted high and low for a Dartmoor house with a 'dual personality, which could be seen sometimes as happy ... and at others as spooky', and, according to Hickox, had 'just about given up and were on our way back when the art director suggested looking at this place 20 miles away ... We arrived at the most colossal Victorian house, designed by William Burge. And we couldn't believe what we saw. One side of the house overlooked a garden, and was extremely pleasant – but the other side had gargoyles on it, and was extremely sinister. Then we walked into the hall, which looked like an MGM film set – and we discovered the crest of the house was hounds! And they were everywhere – woven into the carpets, carved into the woodwork ... It's astonishing that with all the films and TV versions made before, no-one had found it.' Much of the moor itself was built at Shepperton Studios, Hickox and producer Otto Plaschkes having decided that gambling on the British winter would prove too risky: 'We'd have ended up lost in a bog, or weeks behind because of the weather.'

Pogue shadowed the unit on location and watched the following weeks' studio interiors – which, in an interview on the Writers' Guild of America website, he nominated the best experience of his professional career. 'The American producer took me to London with him for three months ... the only place I ever wanted to go and I was doing it on somebody else's dime. We had the cream of the British acting community in these films and they were incredibly respectful of the writing. Actors like Ian Richardson and Denholm Elliott were coming up to me *asking* if they might change a word. I was on set every day and my opinions and input were constantly sought. High cotton.'

Elliott (1922-92), previously Stapleton in the disasterous Peter Cook/Paul Morrissey **The Hound of the Baskervilles** parody (1977), was here cast as a cringing Dr Mortimer. He'd also appeared in the TV comedy **The Strange Case of the End of Civilisation As We Know It** alongside Connie Booth (1944-), who is almost unrecognisable in the Richardson *Hound* in an atypically serious and affecting performance as the doomed Laura Lyons. Booth would reappear in the 1987 Michael Pennington-starring TV movie **The Return of Sherlock Holmes** – and no less than four of this *Hound*'s guest cast would later turn up in Granada Television's long-running series of Holmes adaptations: Churchill as Scott Eccles in **The Return of Sherlock Holmes**: *Wisteria Lodge*; Nicholas Clay (1946-2000) as Dr Percy Trevelyan in **The Adventures of Sherlock Holmes**: *The Resident Patient*; Ronald Lacey (1935-91) as Thaddeus Sholto in **The Sign of Four**; and David Langton (1912-94) as Sir James Damery in **The Case-book of Sherlock Holmes**: *The Illustrious Client*.

If Richardson has little opportunity to show off his considerable abilities (his best scenes being in disguise as a palm-reading gypsy), he does, at least, get to close out the film in style. 'The curse of the Baskervilles,' says Watson, 'a figment of the imagination.' 'But without the imagination, Watson,' asserts a smiling Holmes, 'there would be no horror...' Richardson was supposed to appear as the detective in many more TV movies, including a Pogue-scripted versus-Moriarty pastiche, *The Prince of Crime*, which was booked to

begin filming at Pinewood Studios in March 1983 – but Sy Weintraub's grandiose plans faltered after Granada Television announced its intention to make its own series of adaptations, **The Adventures of Sherlock Holmes** (1984-5).

Having spent a considerable sum purchasing rights in the complete Holmes canon from the Doyle estate, Weintraub was naturally aghast to discover that a major British company was planning to sell its own versions of the stories to television stations across the length and breadth of his principal market, the United States. On 13 April 1984, British trade paper *Broadcast* asserted that Granada's efforts to distribute its series in the US were now imperilled following a claim of 'copyright infringement and unfair competition' brought by Weintraub in association with Doyle estate trustee Dame Jean Conan Doyle, daughter of Arthur. The report continued: 'The Conan Doyle stories published before 1907 are now in the public domain. But what his daughter is claiming is that though the stories Granada is using are out of copyright, the character of Sherlock Holmes and Dr Watson, because they feature in stories after 1907, are still under copyright ... Dame Jean and Weintraub sought financial remuneration from Granada stating that failing this they would bring an injunction against the company should it try to distribute the series in the US.'

Granada's New York lawyers disputed Weintraub and Doyle's case on the grounds that 'Dame Jean would have had to control the use of the name or character of Sherlock Holmes consistently over many years in the US which ... she hasn't.' Richardson has maintained that Weintraub was indeed able to settle out of court, reportedly for a sum large enough to cover his two films' production costs and generate a profit into the bargain. The Granada series, and its sequels, air in the US to this day.

And so ended a worthwhile if somewhat eccentric attempt to bring Sherlock Holmes into the 1980s. The films were first screened, to little interest, at the Cannes Film Festival in May 1983 (**Sir Arthur Conan Doyle's The Sign of Four** did, at least, garner Desmond Davis a 'best director' award at the MystFest event in Cattolica, Italy, later that summer) and premiered in the US on cable channel Home Box-office in November and December. In the UK, their 1984 video release by

Embassy Home Entertainment preceded their delayed TV débuts, shunted into graveyard slots several years later.

The Prince of Crime later mutated into 1990's **Hands of a Murderer**, featuring Edward Woodward as Holmes. Having been associated with two ultimately unmade Sherlockian projects – being intended to replace Peter Cushing as the lead in *The Abbot's Cry*, the projected sequel to 1984's **The Masks of Death**, and also scheduled to appear opposite a Watson played by comic actor David Jason in a planned film version of Charles Marowitz's Broadway play, *Sherlock's Last Case* – Richardson would come to play Dr Joseph Bell, supposedly the real-life template for Holmes, in **Murder Rooms: The Dark Beginnings of Sherlock Holmes** (2000-1), an intriguing series of BBC-produced fictions.

Sir Arthur Conan Doyle's The Sign of Four

GB 1983 TVM adaptation [THE SIGN OF THE FOUR]
Mapleton Films Ltd/Ross & Partners (Securities) Ltd
93m colour
tx 7 December 1983 HBO [US]
w **Charles Edward Pogue** *p* **Otto Plaschkes**
d **Desmond Davis**
cast Sherlock Holmes: **Ian Richardson** Dr John Watson: **David Healy** Major John Sholto: **Thorley Walters** Mary Morstan: **Cherie Lunghi** Jonathan Small: **Joe Melia** Inspector Layton: **Terence Rigby** Bartholomew Sholto: **Clive Merrison** Thaddeus Sholto: **Richard Heffer** Tonga: **John Pedrick** Mordecai Smith: **Michael O'Hagan** Williams: **Robert Russell** McMurdo: **John Benfield** Lal Rao: **Moti Makan** maid: **Kate Binchy** Mr Sherman: **Gordon Rollings** Mrs Smith: **Merelina Kendall** Wiggins: **Darren Michael** other roles: **P J Cassell**

O verdone but underachieving, *Sir Arthur Conan Doyle's The Sign of Four* was the first of a projected 20-plus TV movies starring Royal Shake-speare Company mainstay Ian Richardson (1934-) as the Great Detective. Derailed by production of Granada Television's lavish Jeremy Brett-headlining **The Adventures of Sherlock Holmes** (1984-5), the series ultimately numbered only two, rendering Richardson's superior interpretation a minor curio. On the available evidence, the story might have been very different.

The series was made at the instigation of executive producer Sy Weintraub (1923-2000), a New Yorker whose previous productions included a number of fifties and sixties Edgar Rice Burroughs-derived potboilers beginning with *Tarzan's Greatest Adventure* (1959). Believing it necessary to secure rights from the Doyle estate (in the UK, the Holmes stories had entered the public domain in 1980, 50 years on from the author's death), Weintraub paid, in Richardson's words, 'a lot of money' for the permissions. Intending to film in the UK with a British cast and crew, Weintraub delegated line-producing responsibilities to Otto Plaschkes, formerly a production manager on Weintraub's *Tarzan's Three Challenges* (1963); Plaschkes' solo production efforts included Swinging London taboo-buster *Georgy Girl* (1966). The director of the first film, an energetic, pulpy version of THE SIGN OF THE FOUR by first-time US screenwriter Charles Edward Pogue, was Desmond Davis (1927-), whose TV work spanned fifties episodes of *The Adventures of Sir Lancelot* and seventies instalments of *The New Avengers*. Davis' most recent feature to date was a star-strewn Ray Harryhausen-produced Greek mythology effort, *Clash of the Titans* (1981).

Weintraub's plans were first heralded on the front page of trade paper *Screen International* in February 1982. Under the headline '£20m Holmes series', the story affirmed that Weintraub had 'acquired the rights to the 56 short stories and the four novels ... he is planning to turn between 20 and 30 of them into feature-length films'. The movies, which would be privately financed and produced under the banner of Mapleton Films, were being 'shot for all markets – theatrical, TV, cable and video', and it was anticipated that 'each film will be budgeted at around £700,000'. A 'worldwide search for actors to play Holmes and Watson' was already underway.

Richardson was cast after Plaschkes had seen the actor slumming it in a 'terrible' BBC1 detective-themed *Play For Today*, A Cotswold Death (broadcast 1981, and also starring Edward Hardwicke, the second of the Granada Watsons), in which his character had attempted to emulate Holmes' methods. Richardson's performance is exemplary: deep but not tortured; light of touch but never flippant. 'I'm drawn to these sort of affairs like a magnet,' declares his Holmes, archly extending a finger in the direction of the corpse of Bartholomew Sholto (played as a thoroughly nasty piece of work by Clive Merrison, later the voice of Holmes in BBC Radio 4's nineties adaptations of the entire canon).

Richardson throws himself wholeheartedly into the spirit of the thing, revelling in Holmes' intellectual delight as he inspects Bartholomew's body and its surroundings for evidence; he's entirely convincing even in the several potentially absurd scenes, such as Holmes' fight with a fairground strongman and his tussle with Tonga, here a human-flesh-eating midget whose racially insulting representation owes more to James Bond film henchmen than Doyle. (He's Nick-nack sporting Odd-job's bowler and biting necks with Jaws' fangs, after *The Man With the Golden Gun*, *Goldfinger* and *The Spy Who Loved Me* respectively.) Perhaps most impressively, this Holmes is able to sit inside a completely hooded hansom and identify his precise location throughout a long journey's travel!

His Watson, however, is so ineffectual his presence barely registers. David Healy (1932-95) plays the doctor with a soft Irish accent but little obvious effort. Formerly an understudy at the RSC in Richardson's time, Healy had been overawed to be given the opportunity to play Falstaff opposite Richardson's Ford in *The Merry Wives of Windsor*, and apparently brought his subsequent 'hero-worship' of the actor to Watson's perception of Holmes. If so, it doesn't work – Healy's approach negating the possibility of his Watson making his own mark.

Two former on-screen Watsons fare rather better. Terence Rigby, at the time of filming fresh from his appearance opposite Tom Baker in the BBC's four-part adaptation of **The Hound of the Baskervilles** (1982), plays a pompous and thoroughly deluded 'Inspector Layton' (not Doyle's Athelney Jones, for no readily obvious reason). A source of amusement, not frustration, for Richardson's Holmes, Layton's cack-handed inspection of a crime scene and his subsequent cretinous assumptions cause Holmes to bury his face in his hands. Thorley Walters had appeared as Watson in **Sherlock Holmes und das Halsband des Todes** (1962), *The Best House in London* (1968), **The Adventure of Sherlock Holmes' Smarter Brother** (1975) and **Classics Dark and Dangerous: Silver Blaze** (1977). Despite being third-billed here, his ranting,

pop-eyed Major John Sholto is dead in the first five minutes – which is still long enough for him to blow most of the story's major revelations.

And that's the principal problem with this version of THE SIGN OF THE FOUR. Unnecessarily heavy on exposition early on, it leaves little plot for the latter stages, compensating by tacking-on added perilous scenarios to only moderate effect: Jonathan Small and Tonga mounting an assault on Thaddeus Sholto's home, murdering the aesthetic Thaddeus and nearly Mary Morstan, too, their efforts foiled only by Holmes' superheroic intervention; and, following a scrap on a moving carousel, Holmes' pursuit of the pair through a fairground ghost train and a *Lady From Shanghai/Man with the Golden Gun*-style hall of mirrors.

However, screenwriter Pogue, who clearly knows his Doyle (at one point, Cherie Lunghi's winsome Mary quotes Helen Stoner in THE SPECKLED BAND: 'It is not the cold that makes me shiver ... it is fear'), only once directly contradicts the text. Unfortunately, this comes at the very climax, where Holmes deduces that Jonathan Small has *not*, in fact, thrown the Agra treasure into the Thames – and, with a cry of 'His confession is as hollow as his wooden leg!', has Small's stump screwed off, sending a slow-motion shower of concealed gemstones all over the 221B Baker Street floor. Which looks every bit as daft as it sounds.

Sir Arthur Conan Doyle's The Sign of Four was filmed for five weeks at Shepperton Studios and at various locations along the Thames riverside. The story of its non-release is related in the entry for its follow-up, **Sir Arthur Conan Doyle's The Hound of the Baskervilles** (also 1983).

The Sleeping Cardinal

aka **Sherlock Holmes' Fatal Hour** [US]
GB 1931 adaptation [THE FINAL PROBLEM/THE EMPTY HOUSE] *Twickenham Film Studios Ltd 84m bw*
w **Cyril Twyford**, **H Fowler Mear** *p* **Julius Hagen**
d **Leslie S Hiscott**
cast Sherlock Holmes: **Arthur Wontner** Dr Watson: **Ian Fleming** Col Henslowe [Professor Robert Moriarty]: **Norman McKinnel** Kathleen Adair: **Jane Welsh**
Col Sebastian Moran: **Louis Goodrich** Inspector Lestrade: **Philip Hewland** J J Godfrey: **Charles Paton** Mrs Hudson:

Minnie Rayner Ronald Adair: **Leslie Perrins** Thomas Fisher: **William Frazer** Tony Rutherford: **Sidney King** Marstan: **Gordon Begg** No 16: **Harry Terry**

With this film, Arthur Wontner (1875-1960) made so great an impression in the Holmes role that Vincent Starrett, in his 1934 book *The Private Life of Sherlock Holmes*, claimed that 'No better Sherlock Holmes than Arthur Wontner is likely to be seen and heard in pictures in our time.'

After being told on numerous occasions how like Holmes he looked (even by Doyle himself), the role came to Wontner, ironically, only after a stage performance as Sexton Blake, the so-called 'office-boy's Sherlock Holmes' who had first appeared in *The Marvel* in 1893. 'We produced the play at the Prince Edward Theatre in 1930,' he told *Film Weekly*, 'but it was not a great success ... Within almost a month Mr Julius Hagen invited me down to the Twickenham studios and imparted the news that he was going to make a talkie of Conan Doyle's great character, and thought of me for the part. *The Sleeping Cardinal*, as the picture was called, was started at once, and with its screening in London last February [1931] my bow as Sherlock Holmes at last was made.'

The prolific Hamburg-born producer Julius Hagen (1883-1940) had taken control of the old St Margaret's Studio at Twickenham in 1929; his partners in the enterprise were directors Leslie Hiscott and Henry Edwards. Hiscott (1894-1968) is remembered today as the chief architect of the ill-famed 'quota quickies', cheap programmers pumped out in quantity to fulfil the terms of the 1927 Cinematograph Films Act. Though many of these made a nonsense of the high-flown name Hagen gave his production company – Real Art – several of them did indeed have their artful moments, and *The Sleeping Cardinal*, shot late in 1930, is a case in point.

The opening sequence is arrestingly done: in virtual silence and almost entirely in the dark, with a murdered security guard sprawling into a sliver of light illuminating the floor of a bank strongroom. We're then transported to the rooms of young Foreign Office employee Ronald Adair, whose talent for winning at cards is arousing suspicion among his fellow players and anxiety in his attractive sister Kathleen (Jane Welsh, later to

reappear in the second Wontner vehicle, **The Missing Rembrandt**). She seeks the advice of her old friend Dr Watson, a silver-haired charmer of the old school played here, and throughout the Twickenham/Holmes sequence, by Australian actor Ian Fleming (1888-1969). Amusingly, in the run-up to Holmes' artfully delayed appearance, Watson tries to impress Kathleen with a Holmesian bit of ratiocination regarding a hat left behind by one of the departing gamblers, a spiel that sounds plausible but is later discredited.

A good quarter-hour has gone by before Wontner's Holmes looks around a wing of his armchair, puffing on his pipe and declaring, 'My dear Mrs Hudson, you've always been a temptation to me.' The line is repeated verbatim in the closing stages of Wontner's last Holmes outing, **Silver Blaze** (1936), giving the series a nice sense of symmetry and drawing attention to the vein of sublimated flirtation passing between Holmes and Mrs Hudson throughout. As played by Minnie Rayner, the latter is a blowzy and warm-hearted cockney whose establishment, in a triumph of production design from Twickenham's regular art director James Carter, looks rather more déclassé than most 221Bs. After visits from Inspector Lestrade (about the bank robbery) and Kathleen Adair (about her wayward brother), Holmes is joined by a heavily muffled Moriarty in a replay of the confrontation from THE FINAL PROBLEM, though much of the detail is drawn, uncredited, from Gillette's stage version of the scene.

Young Adair, it transpires, is being blackmailed by Moriarty into using his Foreign Office status to transport the proceeds from the bank robbery to Paris. Moriarty's disembodied voice addresses Adair through a portrait of a dozing Cardinal Richelieu that has been executed on steel; his HQ in a basement bootmaker's also features artificially cobwebbed doors, secret panels and concealed speakers in the ceiling. When Adair is shot, and Holmes deduces that the bullet was fired from a neighbouring window, we enter THE EMPTY HOUSE territory, with Moriarty arranging for a similar fate to befall Holmes.

Despite the fact that Colonel Sebastian Moran, in the highly unintimidating form of actor Louis Goodrich, has appeared as a Moriarty lieutenant earlier on, it is Moriarty himself who pulls the trigger, only to be apprehended when the lights

Moriarty unmasked: Watson (Ian Fleming), Moriarty (Norman McKinnel), Holmes (Arthur Wontner), Lestrade (Philip Hewland) and Mrs Hudson (Minnie Rayner) in **The Sleeping Cardinal** *(1931)*

come up. Hiscott cuts away to Mrs Hudson in 221B, sprawled among shards of plaster from the bust of Holmes she was obligingly holding in silhouette against the window, while Moriarty's civilised front is dropped completely, with the lean and lupine stage star Norman McKinnel spitting out 'You clever, cunning swine!' as he attempts to strangle Holmes. The denouement also reveals that the kindly Colonel Henslowe, a one-armed Scottish tiger hunter in Adair's gambling circle, was Moriarty all along. Holmes ignores Moriarty's seething threats and closes the film with a violin recital designed to mollify the incommoded Mrs Hudson.

The film opened in March 1931, though *Picturegoer*'s Lionel Collier only filed his report on 25 July: 'The intricate plot is very well worked out and Arthur Wontner's rendering of Sherlock Holmes wholly convincing ... I take my hat off to Leslie Hiscott for getting so much out of a difficult screen subject.' It had appeared in the US back on 10 July, its original title deemed too somnolent and exchanged for the much racier *Sherlock Holmes' Fatal Hour*. Wontner's Holmes – detached, cerebral, even avuncular – went down a storm; the film

ran on Broadway for over a month, to the considerable chagrin of Warner Bros, who had sniffily offloaded the film onto the humble First Division for distribution purposes.

With this kind of Stateside success, unprecedented for a British film, it was obvious that Wontner's Holmes would return – sooner rather than later. (JR)

Den Sorte Haand

tr 'The Black Hand'
at **Mordet i Baker Street**
tr 'Murder in Baker Street'
aka **The Blackmailer** [GB]
Denmark 1910 pastiche Nordisk Films Kompagni
958 feet silent bw
d **Holger Rasmussen**
known cast Sherlock Holmes: **Otto Lagoni**
the rich Mr X: **Axel Boesen** Mrs X: **Ingeborg Rasmussen**
the villain: **Poul Welander** the boy Dick: **Erik Crone**

A gang known as 'The Black Hand' attempt to extort a large sum of money from a wealthy man, Mr X. On Sherlock Holmes' advice, Mr X drops an envelope stuffed with newspaper clippings at the designated point. Unaware that the leader of the gang is a police detective, Holmes waits to see who picks up the envelope, then follows them to a hide-out maintained by an old Chinese man. When Mr X is kidnapped, Holmes and his servant, Dick, disguise themselves as Orientals in order to gain entry to the gang's den, where they find a list of gang members. But the gang return; an attempt is made to poison the captive Holmes, Dick and Mr X. Holmes overpowers the old Chinese man, enabling Dick and Mr X to escape. The detective is attached to an 'infernal machine' – but Dick saves him, and they are able to present the chief of police with evidence of the detective's guilt.

A virtual reprise of **Den Forklædte Guvernante**, right down to Holmes' method for identifying the criminals' hiding-place; even the hiding-place itself appears, from surviving photographs, to be the same set redressed. The gang in both films was named 'The Black Hand' in various press sheets – a lunge at topicality, for two notorious real-life 'Black Hand Gangs' were in operation at the time: the first being a group of Sicilian blackmailers and terrorists at work in the US, the second the secret society of Slavs that would precipitate the Great War by ordering the assassination of Archduke Ferdinand in Sarajevo in June 1914. Released in Denmark in the wake of **Sherlock Holmes i Bondefangerkløer**, *Den Sorte Haand*, the third and last short to feature Otto Lagoni as Holmes, was issued in Britain on 1 October 1910 under the title *The Blackmailer*. The *Bioscope* noted it to be 'a detective story full of incidents, and is one of the sort which the public so dearly love'.

Interestingly, in the same week that *Den Sorte Haand* became available in the UK, the *Bioscope* identified another Nordisk short as a Holmes film. *The Diamond Swindler* (probably *Diamantbedrageren*, 1910) was called 'A clever detective story in which some diamond swindlers are tracked by Sherlock Holmes'. Elsewhere, the character was named 'Harry Traxton, a clever pupil of Sherlock Holmes'; in the absence of British caption cards naming the lead character, it seems safest to write this off as a misattribution on the *Bioscope*'s part. The next Nordisk Holmes film proper was **Milliontestamentet**.

Den Sorte Hætte

tr 'The Black Hood'
aka **The Conspirators** [GB/US]
Denmark 1910 pastiche Nordisk Films Kompagni
1273 feet bw silent
w **Ravn Jonson** *d* **William Augustinus**
known cast Sherlock Holmes: **Lauritz Olsen**
Mr Wilson: **Valdemar Hansen** Mrs Wilson: **Julie Henriksen**
Harry Clark: **Otto Lagoni** Lord Capetown: **Frederik Jacobsen** police constables: **Carl Schenstrøm**, **Pedersen (Tivoli's Pjerrot)** [sic]

When Lord Capetown telegraphs his solicitor, Wilson, to tell him that he is close to death and needs to consult him regarding his 'securities', Wilson's crooked clerk Harry Clark spies an opportunity to visit Capetown and take the securities for himself. Secretly, Clark is 'the Black Hood', the leader of a gang of cloaked and hooded criminals. The gang conspire to kidnap Wilson and send a message to Capetown, telling him that Wilson is ill and Clark will take his place. Wilson's servant, Billy, finds a rough draft of one of Clark's messages; when it is realised that Wilson has been taken, Sherlock Holmes is called in. By disguising himself as Capetown, Holmes is able to arrest Clark and, wearing Clark's Black Hood, trace the rest of the gang to their hideout – where he is spotted and thrown through a trapdoor into a pit. The detective has already asked Mrs Wilson to call the police, however, and they are able to rescue both Holmes and Wilson and arrest the gang.

Following **Hotelrotterne**, *Den Sorte Hætte*, the last of Nordisk's ten sequels to **Sherlock Holmes i Livsfare**, was released in the UK on 10 June 1911 and in the US during September. Evidently, the attraction of the company's slightly crude melodramas was beginning to fail: the *New York Dramatic Mirror* noted that 'The chief difficulty with this production is that it leaves too much to the imagination. One questions the whys and wherefores...' Whereas 119 copies of the second film, **Raffles Flugt Fra Fængslet**, were sold both in Denmark and overseas, only 51 prints of the penultimate *Hotelrotterne* were struck – a fact which tells a tale in itself.

The Speckled Band

*GB 1931 adaptation British & Dominions Studios 90m bw
w* **W P Lipscomb** *source* **The Speckled Band** [stage adaptation
by **Arthur Conan Doyle**] *p* **Herbert Wilcox*** *d* **Jack Raymond**
cast Dr Rylott: **Lyn Harding** Sherlock Holmes: **Raymond
Massey** Helen Stonor: **Angela Baddeley** Mrs Staunton:
Helen Price Dr Watson: **Athole Stewart** Mrs Hudson:
Marie Ault* Rodgers: **Stanley Lathbury*** Violet: **Joyce
Moore*** builder: **Charles Paton***

*The youthful
Raymond Massey,
pictured a few
years before his
one-and-only
appearance as
Holmes in* **The
Speckled Band**
(1931)

Released shortly after the first of the American-
produced Clive Brook pictures (**The Return of
Sherlock Holmes**, 1929) and the first of the British
Arthur Wontner films (**The Sleeping Cardinal**,
1931), this sometimes handsome but clearly flawed
retelling of THE SPECKLED BAND – only the third
Holmes film with sound – lacks the conviction of
either. Like other surplus-to-requirements
Sherlocks of its time – the Robert Rendel-starring
The Hound of the Baskervilles (1931) and Reginald
Owen's **A Study in Scarlet** (1933) – it made little
impact on release, and has since fallen into relative
obscurity. But unlike either of these, it has a
Holmes who might have proven a match for
Brook and, arguably, Wontner: Raymond Massey
(1896-1983).

Originally, producers British & Dominions
Studios – relative newcomers to the scene, whose
The Woman in White (1929), produced and
directed by Herbert Wilcox, also tapped a certain
classic Gothic/mystery vein – had offered the role
of Holmes to Sir Gerald du Maurier (1873-1934), a
hugely popular, naturalistic-in-style mainstay of the
English stage especially noted for his Raffles and
Bulldog Drummond. Despite the fact that he
judged it a 'fair script' and there seemed to be
'plenty of money lying about', du Maurier
declined, nominating his younger friend Massey
in his stead. The Canadian-born Massey, who
called du Maurier's getting the part for him 'one
of the kindest acts I ever knew', suspected that
the perfectionist du Maurier loathed the
pressurised atmosphere of talking picture sets.
The Speckled Band would mark Massey's first
major screen appearance, a couple of earlier bit
parts notwithstanding.

The screenplay by William P Lipscomb (1887-
1958), a former actor who would eventually write
over 50 film scripts including Wontner's **The Sign
of Four: Sherlock Holmes' Greatest Case** (1932),
was at least partly based on Doyle's own stage
version of *The Speckled Band*, which had premiered
at London's Adelphi Theatre on 4 June 1910.
Consequently, the evil Roylott becomes 'Rylott'; the
elder of his stepdaughters is not 'Julia Stoner' but
'Violet Stonor'; the housekeeper is 'Mrs Staunton';
and a butler, Rodgers, plus an Indian accomplice/
manservant, Ali, number among the villain's
household, too. Lipscomb's *Speckled Band* also
opens with a lengthy inquest into Violet's death
attended by Dr Watson, a friend of the Stonor girls'
mother – but the film, with its limited cast, would
omit many other aspects of Doyle's play.

Welshman Lyn Harding (1876-1952), a thunder-
ing Dr Rylott, was accorded the seemingly unusual
privilege of being credited above Massey in the list
of players – but it seems rather more explicable
when one considers that Harding had played
Rylott in that original 1910 stage version, reprising
the role at the Strand Theatre in 1911, at Chicago's
Studebaker Theatre in 1914, and at London's St
James's and Royalty Theatres over 1921-22. Born
David Llewellyn Harding, the actor had made his
West End début in 1897, adopting the diminutive
'Lyn' as his stage name on finding that the English
could not pronounce 'Llewellyn'. Gaining positive

notices for his roles as Bill Sikes in a version of *Oliver Twist* and Svengali in a version of *Trilby* (by George du Maurier, father of Gerald), Harding ploughed a similarly villainous furrow with his Rylott.

Legend has it that Doyle and Harding argued over the interpretation of the part, the writer having envisaged a more melodramatic, over-the-top villain than the apparently 'haunting' and 'complex' characterisation the actor chose to perform. If the film is any guide, Doyle's intention beggars belief, for Harding's eye-rolling Demon King is remarkable only in its lack of understatement. Harding would graduate to the role of Professor Moriarty in the later Wontner pictures **The Triumph of Sherlock Holmes** (1934) and **Silver Blaze** (1936).

The Speckled Band was filmed at the London Film Studios at Denham, Hertfordshire, with a small number of exteriors being recorded in the outlying countryside – including the night scene where Holmes, disguised as a builder, attempts to evade the dogs (a cheetah and a baboon in Doyle's original) which patrol the grounds of Rylott's Stoke Manor [sic]. Here, a 150-pound Alsatian was starved for a day prior to being let loose on the unfortunate Massey, whose trenchcoat concealed a 'necklace' of meat to distract the ravening hound from the actor's more tender parts. As it transpired, on being given its cue the beast chose to throw its paws around Massey's neck and smother him in kisses.

Massey's Holmes, a jug-eared, rubber-faced aesthete in a Chinese silk dressing-gown, represents a departure from the norm – as does his state-of-the-art front office, an art deco suite replete with the latest inventions: a mechanical index that is 'supposed to give details of every criminal case and the whereabouts of every criminal at any given date', for example, and a voice-recording system. The detective has office staff at '107' Baker Street, too: typists, and a stressed young secretary, Miss Pringle. 'I could not avoid a sense of guilt at my participation in this travesty of a classic,' wrote Massey in his autobiography nearly 50 years later, but in truth these lunges towards modernity are handled with a certain style, not to mention rather more sensitivity than in, say, **Conan Doyle's Master Detective Sherlock Holmes**, released one year later. Massey swings between a louche, laid-back, almost

Oscar Wilde approach (calling Rylott's barely veiled menaces 'a trifle robust, nothing more') and the glum melancholy on display in the closing scene. When a morning-suited Watson gives him news of Helen's wedding, he tells the doctor, 'Give them my congratulations – or perhaps, condolences.' 'Rubbish – we all come to it, my dear fellow!' protests his friend, exiting the room. Holmes returns to his lonely researches. 'Not all, dear Watson,' he sighs. 'Not all...'

No less innovative was the film's presentation: there are several flashbacks, plus a quite remarkable sequence in which, one by one, the heads of the suspect inhabitants at Stoke Manor materialise between Holmes and Watson, who are sitting on a swish leather sofa discussing the case. Such startling effects don't entirely mitigate against some very tedious patches; Holmes' investigation of Violet's old room, for example, seems interminable. The striking Stoke Manor interiors of art director L P Williams (Lawrence P Williams, born 1908) dwarf the actors, with bedroom doors pushing ten feet high, and much is made of these by cinematographer F A ('Freddie') Young (1902-98), whose very effective work suggests the talent that, over 30 years later, would win three Oscars for his collaborations with director David Lean: *Lawrence of Arabia* (1962), *Doctor Zhivago* (1965) and *Ryan's Daughter* (1970).

Massey would go on to bigger and better things: his first American picture, *The Old Dark House* (1932); classic bad guys in *The Scarlet Pimpernel* (1934) and *The Prisoner of Zenda* (1937); *Things to Come* (1935); *Arsenic and Old Lace* (1942), and many more. But only the hardest of hearts could fail to be charmed by his début, a picture so innocent it fails to see how amending its source text to have the hero order the nightgowned heroine to lie back in her bed and await the arrival of her father's snake might, perhaps, suggest rather more than was intended.

The Spider Woman

US 1943 pastiche Universal Pictures Company Inc
63m bw
w **Bertram Millhauser** *pd* **Roy William Neill**
cast Sherlock Holmes: **Basil Rathbone** Dr Watson: **Nigel Bruce** Adrea Spedding: **Gale Sondergaard**

Rumbled as a bogus importer of exotic fauna, Adrea Spedding's man Radlik (Alec Craig) is disarmed by Holmes (Basil Rathbone) in **The Spider Woman** *(1943)*

Lestrade: **Dennis Hoey** Norman Locke: **Vernon Downing** Radlik: **Alec Craig** Gilflower: **Arthur Hohl** Mrs Hudson: **Mary Gordon** attendant: **Frank Benson*** announcer: **John Burton*** Colonel's wife [Susan]: **Lydia Bilbrook*** Fred Garvin: **Harry Cording*** Larry: **Teddy Infuhr*** Colonel [Robert]: **Stanley Logan*** fortune teller: **Belle Mitchell*** croupier: **John Roche*** pygmy: **Angelo Rossito*** plainclothesman: **Arthur Stenning*** Artie: **Donald Stuart*** Taylor: **Gene Stutenroth*** charwomen: **Sylvia Andrews***, **Marie de Becker*** clerks: **Wilson Benge***, **John Rogers*** newsvendors: **Jimmy Aubrey***, **George Kirby***

THE MYSTERY

A spate of newspaper-sensationalised 'pyjama suicides' – men who've hurled themselves out of upper-storey bedrooms – becomes the talk of London. Though his advice on the matter is eagerly sought after, Sherlock Holmes is away on a fishing holiday with Dr Watson in the highlands of Scotland. Holmes is certain that these suicides are, in fact, murders – but professes no interest in investigating, telling Watson that he fears recent medical symptoms of his own to be indicative of an imminent cerebral haemorrhage. Soon after, to Watson's horror, Holmes' hat is seen floating at the foot of a swirling waterfall. The news breaks: Sherlock Holmes is missing, presumed dead. 'LAWLESSNESS RAMPANT' scream the headlines.

THE INVESTIGATION

When Watson and Inspector Lestrade prepare to move Holmes' criminal indexes to the British Museum, the detective is forced to break his cover, confessing that his 'death' was a ruse to help target the person responsible for the pyjama murders. Holmes divines the workings of a feline mind – a 'female Moriarty' – and, having established that all

Holmes (Basil
Rathbone)
impersonates a
hard-up Indian
Maharajah in a
bid to lure Adrea
Spedding (Gale
Sondergaard) in
**The Spider
Woman** (1943)

the victims were formerly well-to-do gamblers, he
has devised an alias to entice the killer: that of the
Maharajah Rajnee Singh, newly arrived from India
for surgery on his paralysed arm.

At the Urban Casino, 'Singh' is approached by a
woman called Adrea Spedding – who, on hearing
that the Maharajah is broke, suggests 'Singh' takes
a loan from one of her associates, using his life
insurance policy as collateral. Later, 'Singh' takes
tea with Adrea, who claims to have spent much of
her childhood in India; here, both Holmes and
Adrea identify the other as a fraud. Having
established how Adrea profits from the murders,
the exposed Holmes sets himself up for a 'pyjama
assassination' at the Langdon Flats; a poisonous
spider duly crawls through a ventilation duct onto
Holmes' pillow, but Holmes is prepared. On the
roof, he shoots one of Adrea's associates, but finds
a child's footprints nearby. Has Adrea used a child
to crawl through the ducting and deliver the spider?

Entomologist Adam Gilflower identifies the
species of spider as *lycosa carnivora*, whose venom

induces self-destructive urges – and gives Holmes
the name of the only man in England who imports
the creatures from near Africa's Obongo River:
Matthew Ordway. Before Holmes and Watson can
call on Ordway, Adrea visits 221B, ostensibly to ask
Holmes to investigate the 'disappearance' of
Rajnee Singh. She is accompanied by her strange
mute 'nephew', Larry – who deposits a lethal
devil's foot root in the Baker Street hearth, the
fumes from which nearly kill Holmes and Watson.

THE SOLUTION

One of Adrea's men, Radlik, poses as the now-
murdered Ordway, but Holmes and Watson see
him off, finding a clue to the identity of Adrea's
spider-handler: not Larry, but one of a race of
African pygmies who are naturally immune to the
poison. Holmes locates 'Obongo from the Congo,
the Prancing Pygmy' at a fairground in a High
Holborn arcade – where, behind a fortune-teller's
booth, he discovers himself to have been ensnared
by Adrea, who duly has Holmes strapped behind a

shooting gallery target. Playing the game, the unwitting Watson manages to miss his friend's heart three times – but Holmes frees himself, and soon delivers Adrea into the arms of Inspector Lestrade.

✦ ✦ ✦

Describing a media phenomenon as 'like such and such... *on acid*' has become the cliché of refuge for the incompetent commentator. So, then, *The Spider Woman*: it's like a Sherlock Holmes movie... *on acid* – a quite deranged, too-fast conflation of up to six Doyle stories peopled entirely by cartoon grotesques. Needless to say, it's a total joy, its only real fault being its oddly perfunctory closing minute, the symphony fading out when it ought to hit a high sustain.

Although Bertram Millhauser's on-screen credit claims his script to have been 'based on *a* story by Sir Arthur Conan Doyle', whichever of the most likely candidates is being referred to is debatable. THE FINAL PROBLEM clearly supplies Holmes' 'demise' in a roaring torrent; THE SPECKLED BAND, a venomous creature being fed through a ventilator as an instrument of murder; THE SIGN OF THE FOUR, a diminutive and murderous foreigner, attached to a fairground, whose footprints are mistaken for those of a child; and THE DEVIL'S FOOT is explicitly referred to when Holmes and Watson enjoy their second narrow escape from the eponymous smoking poison. ('I remember that – "The Cornish Horror",' says Watson, in a trick recycled from **Sherlock Holmes and the Secret Weapon**'s mention of the already occurred THE DANCING MEN.) Casting the net a little wider, Holmes' almost-admirable female adversary suggests an implacably murderous Irene Adler (A SCANDAL IN BOHEMIA) – but perhaps the broadest sweep of the plot can be found in THE DYING DETECTIVE, which is echoed by a Holmes who pretends to be the victim of a terminal condition in order to bring to justice a person who kills by means of an exotically originated poison.

That said, *The Spider Woman*, the first of the Universal pictures thought to be enticing enough to be released without the name 'Sherlock Holmes' somewhere in its title, is far more than just a parlour game of spot-the-reference. Millhauser's own inventions bring the piece to life, notably the scenes in which Watson, Lestrade and Mrs

Hudson mourn the loss of their friend ('Funny duck, 'e was,' murmurs Lestrade to Watson, before bursting out with, 'Why d'you let him fall in that blasted river? Why didn't you jump in after him, you big blunderhead?'); the scenes in which Adrea and 'Rajnee Singh' compete to catch out the other first over tea, and later at Baker Street, never once baldly stating what they know about the other; and the delightful inversion of the now-traditional 'Watson doesn't see that the Baker Street visitor is actually Holmes in disguise' sequence. 'Of all the transparent old fakers I ever saw!' the laughing Watson tells an aged, partially sighted entomologist. '"Gilflower" – what a name to pick! "Bullflower" ... "Bullfrog" ... "Wiggle-woggle"! Why, you can do better than that ... Those dark glasses! That preposterous wig! Come out from behind those silly whiskers – I know you!' Holmes, of course, chooses to enter the room just as Watson is yanking hard at Gilflower's chops – and the sheer horror which then crosses the features of Nigel Bruce's Watson makes for the funniest moment in the whole Universal series. Most remarkable of all, however, is Adrea's disturbed and disturbing 'nephew', Larry – part-Midwich Cuckoo before his time, part-*Dracula*'s Renfield (albeit a Renfield who *listens* to flies, which is surely more unsettling than simply *eating* them).

To claim that the finale, in which Holmes is strapped behind a fairground shooting target bearing the image of a forties dictator ('Mussolini, 'irihito or 'itler,' shouts a barker, ''it 'em where their 'earts oughta be and listen ter the 'ollow sound!') is as suspenseful as an Alfred Hitchcock set-piece would be to overstate the case, but the fact that it's Watson taking aim does electrify. Roy William Neill's direction, beginning with an unexpected and dramatic defenestration, is as unflagging as the no-nonsense script. And if the narrative does jump from time to time, only the fact that we never see 'Rajnee Singh' sign over his life insurance to Adrea's associates seems an obvious omission. Indeed, it's almost a pity that the pseudo-Greek chorus supplied by a 'disgusted of Tunbridge Wells'-type Colonel and his winsome wife isn't retained past the first ten minutes.

Fifth in the Universal sequence, *The Spider Woman* (provisionally entitled *Sherlock Holmes in Peril*) followed **Sherlock Holmes Faces Death** into production in April/May 1943. *The Spider Woman* was not, however, the next Universal film to feature Basil Rathbone's Holmes and Bruce's Watson. That distinction went to *Crazy House*, a would-be zany Hollywood-set effort released in October 1943 and showcasing the antics of Ole Olsen and Chic Johnson, stars of *Hellzapoppin'* (1942). The four-line Rathbone/Bruce sequence was filmed during the recording of *The Spider Woman*, on the set used for spider-importer Matthew Ordway's study (where Holmes and Watson discover the pygmy's skeleton, in fact). Here, Watson tells Holmes that there's a lot of excitement at the studio; on the grounds that 'I know everything,' Holmes deduces that Olsen and Johnson have arrived in Hollywood.

Gale Sondergaard (Edith Holm Sondergaard, 1899-1985), whose poised, glacially glamorous Adrea Spedding steals all bar one of her *Spider Woman* scenes, had appeared alongside Rathbone three times previously, in *Mark of Zorro* (1940), *The Black Cat* and *Paris Calling* (both 1941). Former stage actress Sondergaard had won the first-ever 'Best Supporting Actress' Academy Award for her first-ever film role, as the Machiavellian housekeeper Faith Paleologue in Warner Bros' *Anthony Adverse* (1936). The one *Spider Woman* scene stolen from Sondergaard is, of course, the 'Adrea and Larry visit Baker Street' sequence – which is clearly won by the uncredited Teddy Infuhr (1936-), a seven-year-old who featured in over 50 pictures between 1942 and 1954, among them Hitchcock's *Spellbound* (1945).

Sondergaard won critical plaudits upon the film's release on 21 January 1944 ('Gale Sondergaard is so good you almost wish she would get the best of the great detective,' wrote Wanda Hale in the *New York Daily News*), even if journalists appeared to be tiring of the Holmes series in general. 'The man-seeking, deadly spider, the poison gas, the fly-catching boy, the murderous midget ... are, when taken by themselves, conducive to mild chill. Under examination, however, they become the most arrant nonsense,' wrote Archer Winsten in the *New York Post*, before going off at a bizarre, misogynist tangent. 'The picture's sole value ... is the weird light it sheds on the true nature of women. Dangerous creatures, women ... A man must be half mad to keep one of them in the same house or room as himself. If you don't believe me, see *Spider Woman* ... There are

much worse things than being murdered in a subtle way for your life insurance.'

Universal was convinced enough of Sondergaard's popularity in the role to invest in a try-out for what was, evidently, envisaged as the first in a series of B-features of her own. But *The Spider Woman Strikes Back*, released early in 1946, bore no substantial connection to the Holmes film, featuring Sondergaard not as Adrea Spedding but instead quasi-vampiric Nevadan poisoner Zenobia Dollard. With the aid of a silent assistant played by Rondo Hatton, another notable Holmes series villain (see **The Pearl of Death**), Zenobia combines human gore and arachnoid venom in an effort to breed meat-eating plants which will then produce a sap lethal to local cattle.

Sadly, even if Universal hadn't thrown away the original character in favour of such a dismal reinvention, Sondergaard's Spider Woman would never have made it past one or two sequels at most. In October 1947, Sondergaard's husband, Herbert Biberman, was summoned to appear before Senator Joseph McCarthy's House Un-American Activities Committee, when he and his wife were accused of holding left-wing sympathies. Biberman became one of the so-called 'Hollywood Ten' gaoled as a result of McCarthy's paranoid obsession with Communism. Sondergaard, whose second film had featured her as a victim of the Salem witch-hunts, was blacklisted by the studios, and did not appear in another mainstream picture for 21 years.

Universal followed the case of Sherlock Holmes versus the Spider Woman with **The Scarlet Claw**.

Star Trek: The Next Generation

US 1988/93 2 x 45m approx TV pastiches
Paramount Pictures Corporation colour
regular cast includes Capt Jean-Luc Picard: **Patrick Stewart**
Cmdr William Riker: **Jonathan Frakes** Lt/Lt Cmdr Geordi
La Forge: **Levar Burton** Lieutenant Worf: **Michael Dorn**
Counselor Deanna Troi: **Marina Sirtis**
Lt Commander Data: **Brent Spiner**

ELEMENTARY, DEAR DATA
tx 10 December 1988
w **Brian Alan Lane** *p* **Burton Armus, Mike**

Gray & John Mason *d* Rob Bowman
regular cast above, plus Doctor Pulaski: **Diana Muldaur**
Moriarty: **Daniel Davis** Inspector Lestrade: **Alan Shearman**
ruffian: **Biff Manard** prostitute: **Diz White**
Assistant Engineer Clancy: **Anne Elizabeth Ramsay**
pie man: **Richard Merson**

Deep space, the 24th century: while the vast Starship *Enterprise* awaits a rendezvous with another craft, android officer Data persuades fellow crewmember Lt Geordi La Forge to play Dr Watson to his Sherlock Holmes inside a computer simulation of 19th century London constructed within one of the ship's recreational 'holodecks'. However, Data only intends to play Holmes inside established, canonical works – and *Enterprise* medical officer Kate Pulaski challenges Data to solve a Holmes-style mystery to which he will not know the answer beforehand. Geordi orders the creation of an opponent with the capacity to out-think Data; in that instant, the 'unreal' character of Professor Moriarty, Holmes' arch-enemy, acquires a degree of self-awareness. Abducting Pulaski, Moriarty manages to prevent the deactivation of the simulation and, in time, affects the running of the 'real' *Enterprise*, demanding an audience with its Captain, Jean-Luc Picard. Having no substance, Moriarty is unable to exist inside the 'real' world, as he desires – but since he is, nonetheless, a conscious being, Picard and Moriarty strike a bargain: Pulaski is released, and the Professor will be permanently stored in the holodeck's memory while scientists try to find a way to give him physical form.

SHIP IN A BOTTLE

tx 30 January 1993
w **René Echevarria** *p* **Peter Lauritson** *d* **Alexander Singer**
regular cast above, plus Dr Beverly Crusher: **Gates McFadden** Moriarty: **Daniel Davis** the Countess Regina Bartholomew: **Stephanie Beacham** Barclay: **Dwight Schultz** gentleman: **Clement Von Franckenstein** computer voice: **Majel Barrett**

Four years later, Moriarty is restored when an engineer, Barclay, is despatched to examine a minor glitch in the holodeck's running. He summons Picard, Data and Barclay to an audience at 221B Baker Street, where he demands to know why no progress has been made in giving him substance – and astonishes the three when he

walks out onto the decks of the *Enterprise*, something which transcends the known laws of science. Moriarty asks that the process is repeated to give form to the Countess Regina Bartholomew, the love of his life; bound by the ethics of such an act, Picard refuses. Moriarty contrives to seize control of the *Enterprise*, and sets the crew to work on realising the Countess' incarnation via the *Enterprise*'s matter transporter. However, Data realises that the *Enterprise* which he, Picard and Barclay are in is a holodeck simulation which Moriarty is controlling; they never left '221B'. The Countess achieves form, and she and Moriarty depart the *Enterprise* in a shuttlecraft. This is, however, a simulation which Picard has made – and, although continuing to believe that they are travelling the universe, the pair are trapped in a computer memory disk.

✦ ✦ ✦

Although not strictly speaking Sherlockian – not even their digitised Moriarty believes himself to be the 'real' Professor – these two science fantasies make such intriguing use of Holmes fiction that to exclude them would be churlish.

Star Trek: The Next Generation was a long-running extrapolation from the seminal sixties television series, featuring an all-new cast under the captaincy of Jean-Luc Picard; its strengths and weaknesses are adequately documented in the two instalments which draw heavily on the 221B mythos. A queer, po-faced blend of the original's covert, Cold War-derived American imperialism dressed in multi-cultural rhetoric, this new series introduced the android Data as its proxy Mr Spock; as with Leonard Nimoy's logic-devoted Vulcan in the first series, Data's sheer emotionlessness, paradoxically, is a tool to enable supposedly dispassionate Starfleet officers to give voice to issues beyond the remit of the *Enterprise*'s mission. The ship's 'virtual reality' holodecks were a gimmick of the new show, too. *Elementary, Dear Data*, an early second series instalment, appears to have been devised to expand upon both these elements.

It's very odd that a starship's Science Officer should be fascinated with Holmes, given Holmes' wilful ignorance of matters astronomical (see A STUDY IN SCARLET); nonetheless, *Elementary, Dear Data* initially promises to be a fascinatingly circular meditation: a Holmesian pastiche *about*

Holmesian pastiche. Data – whose interest in the Holmes stories as a problem-solving mechanism was introduced in the otherwise unremarkable first season episode *Lonely Among Us* (tx 11 November 1987) – is castigated for programming the holodeck to simulate only established, canonical mysteries which he might easily solve simply by recognising various plot elements; visual clues are duly swiped from The Bruce-Partington Plans, The Valley of Fear, A Scandal in Bohemia and The Speckled Band (an emerald tiepin, a copy of *Whitaker's Almanack*, a snuffbox and a serpentine bell-pull respectively). Data also observes the characters of Inspector Lestrade, The Red-headed League's Jabez Wilson and even A Scandal in Bohemia's Irene Adler. Amusingly, the viewer is never told that the bearded young man whom Lestrade brings to 221B early on is, in fact, an adventuress in drag.

However, once the program is altered to posit a Sherlockian scenario replete with a character with the capacity to out-think Data, the teleplay takes an abrupt turn from the would-be metafictional to the would-be metaphysical. For reasons that are never explained, the created Moriarty becomes aware of his own existence (presumably, this is a consequence of his being constructed solely in relation to the 'real' Data), and begins to explore his circumstances. And although the scenes where Moriarty (whose vaguely Byronic, tousle-headed incarnation is a very long way from his canonical depiction, which causes one to wonder just where the holodeck's representation is taken from) comes to realise that there is another layer of reality above his own are compelling enough, the Holmesian aspects shrivel away in favour of a very *Star Trek* seminar on 'Philosophy Lite', with much time spent debating whether or not the Latin dictum '*cogito ergo sum*' is, in fact, true (answer: erm, well – yes, probably).

Sixth series sequel *Ship in a Bottle* covers much the same territory, but at least allows Moriarty full access to the *Enterprise*'s wonders. However, despite a prominent caption claiming that the character's use is 'by arrangement with Dame Jean Conan Doyle', there is even less Holmes mythology within; as Moriarty himself puts it, 'My past is nothing but a fiction – the scribblings of an Englishman dead now for four centuries. I hope to leave his books on the shelf, as it were.' This little

speech is the greatest pity, for it is said to prove that the character is not malevolent; being *Star Trek*, Moriarty is allowed to be cunning, but not plain bad. The issue being explored is, in fact, his tragedy. Perhaps this entirely amusing but hopelessly misguided exercise provides the clearest evidence of something all Holmes fans knew in their water a long time ago: that Moriarty has no purpose minus Holmes, whose very existence gives him his reason to be – and that without him, he's nothing. QED, Captain.

The Strange Case of the End of Civilisation As We Know It

GB 1977 TVM parody Shearwater Films 54m colour
tx 18 September 1977 ITV
w Jack Hobbs, Joseph McGrath, John Cleese *from an original idea by* Jack Hobbs *and* Joseph McGrath
p Humphrey Barclay *d* Joseph McGrath
cast Arthur Sherlock-Holmes: John Cleese Dr William Watson: Arthur Lowe Dr Gropinger: Ron Moody air hostess: Holly Palance President of the USA: Joss Ackland black CIA man: Val Pringle Klein of the CIA: Bill Mitchell the other CIA man: Chris Malcolm African delegate: Christopher Asante English delegate: Denholm Elliott 1st Australian: Nick Tate Miss Hoskins: Josephine Tewson Chinese delegate: Burt Kwouk Chief Commissioner: Stratford Johns Mrs Hudson and Francine Moriarty: Connie Booth bus conductor: Derek Griffiths Constable at Scotland Yard: Billy Hamon 2nd Australian: Edmund Pegge intercom man: Robert Kingdom tea lady: Maria Charles hotel commissionaire: Delaney O'Connor receptionist: Moira Foot Hercule Poirot: Dudley Jones Columbo: Luie Caballero M: Kenneth Benda Miss Moneypacket: Charlotte Alexandra Steve McGarrett: Maurice Kaufmann Sam Spade: Mike O'Malley McCloud: Paul Chapman false Watson: Norman Atkyns* *nb* Irene Handl *is not* Orson Welles

The Mystery

T E Lawrence (of Arabia) Airport, 10:32 hrs, 18 September 1975. His diary having been pocketed by a mystery thief, confused US peace representative Dr Gropinger, uncertain where he is, greets an assembly of Arabs in Hebrew – and is promptly shot dead. Later, at the White House, CIA officials show the American President a message: 'Today Gropinger, tomorrow the world. Moriarty.'

THE INVESTIGATION

London, England, teatime, 19 September 1975. At Scotland Yard, international police delegates discuss Moriarty's threat to end civilisation as we know it in five days if control of the world is not ceded to him. A computer confirms that the original Professor Moriarty is dead, and that this new Moriarty must be his only living descendant. On the computer's advice, Chief Commissioner Blocker asks Arthur Sherlock-Holmes, grandson of the old Moriarty's detective nemesis, to investigate. A mystery assailant stabs Blocker in the back, but it is Sherlock-Holmes' idiotic part-bionic assistant, Watson, who finishes the wounded Chief Commissioner off. At Scotland Yard, Sherlock-Holmes announces his plan to bring Moriarty out into the open by assembling all the world's greatest detectives together in one place – a target too tempting for the villain to resist.

THE SOLUTION

Carlton Hotel, England, Surrey, 16:39 hrs, 22 September 1975. While Sherlock-Holmes and Watson work on a crossword, a false Watson kills the other detectives – Hercule Poirot, Columbo, Hawaii policeman Steve McGarrett, Sam Spade and McCloud among them. The two Watsons soon meet, Sherlock-Holmes only identifying the imposter by virtue of the true Watson's dimwittedness. The false Watson is revealed to be Mrs Hudson, Sherlock-Holmes' Scottish housekeeper, in disguise – but Mrs Hudson is but an alias for Francine Moriarty, the Professor's evil grand-daughter (a fact Sherlock-Holmes has been aware of since 1964). Francine shoots Sherlock-Holmes repeatedly, not knowing that Sherlock-Holmes had previously asked Watson to load Francine's gun with blanks. Unfortunately, Watson had forgotten to carry out the task, and so Sherlock-Holmes collapses, mortally injured. Watson brings half the ceiling down on top of Sherlock-Holmes and himself in his failed pursuit of Francine. Has Dr Watson fractured his skull? Will Sherlock-Holmes really die? Will Francine Moriarty escape unharmed and succeed in her plan to destroy civilisation as we know it? Yes.

✦ ✦ ✦

The second of John Cleese's two swipes at the Great Detective is even less coherent than his

Arthur Lowe and John Cleese pictured in Staines on 26 January 1977, completing location work for **The Strange Case of the End of Civilisation As We Know It**

muddled turn in **Comedy Playhouse: Elementary My Dear Watson** (also featuring actress Josephine Tewson) five years previously. Nor is it especially funny, its Henry Kissinger and Richard Nixon caricatures being mere chips at a seam of semi-political satire mined more thoroughly by *Dr Strangelove or, How I Learned to Stop Worrying and Love the Bomb* (1963) and countless undergraduate revues. (The black farce whereby a sniper casually picks off Scotland Yard visitors from a vantage point in Big Ben is the only really original bit of business here.) Racial slurs are rife, its black characters delivering phonetically scripted lines such as, 'Dis am not de work of de real late great Professor Moriarty. He been done dead dese damn 75 years, bwana.' Did 1977 audiences really find an African policeman's speech being translated into the sound of tom-tom drums, or Sherlock-Holmes' entreaty to 'cut the coon talk', hilarious? Needless to say, the supposedly rib-tickling opening, in which a US peacemaker is shot dead somewhere in the Middle East after mistakenly addressing a gun-toting Arab horde in Hebrew, simply appals.

A collection of rather laboured sketches only occasionally referring to a barely expounded plot, *The Strange Case of the End of Civilisation As We*

Sherlock-Holmes (John Cleese) transports 'a sort of model of the Chief Commissioner of Scotland Yard' in **The Strange Case of the End of Civilisation As We Know It** (1977)

Know It eventually dispenses with 'satire' in favour of bungled bungling involving Arthur Sherlock-Holmes and Dr William Watson MD, as played by Cleese and *Dad's Army* icon Arthur Lowe (1915-82). Not a coke fiend like his illustrious grandad, Cleese's Sherlock-Holmes instead prefers to fill his Meerschaum with a variety of unconventional leaves, potted in jars labelled 'Herbs Au Sherlock Holmes', 'Grand Royal African Special Selection' and 'Jeffries Old Imperial Nugget Textured Shag'.

The story turns on Watson's stupidity, Sherlock-Holmes only distinguishing the real doctor from the Watson-disguised Francine Moriarty because he's 'so consistently, relentlessly, almost magically half-witted'. Lowe's performance is easily the most enjoyable part of the film, his constant interjections of 'Good Lord!' bearing comic fruit when he meets his double: they burble 'Good Lord!' at each other for what seems like several minutes. Watson's accidental killing of Chief Commissioner Blocker – by replacing the dagger he's realised he ought not to have removed from his back – suggests a darker and altogether more profitable direction for the piece.

According to Cleese, *The Strange Case of the End of Civilisation As We Know It* was originated by

Joseph (often 'Joe') McGrath (1930-), a comedy writer-director he'd worked with on films like *The Bliss of Mrs Blossom* (1968) and *The Magic Christian* (1969): 'Joe brought the project to me, and I rewrote it with him.' McGrath is probably best known for producing the first series of the Peter Cook/Dudley Moore show *Not Only ... But Also* and for directing parts of Bond spoof *Casino Royale* (1967); his later work included *Digby the Biggest Dog in the World* (1974) and the smutty *I'm Not Feeling Myself Tonight* (1976).

Co-produced by broadcasters London Weekend Television, *Strange Case* was filmed at Shepperton Studios and on location in the capital. The starry cast included Cleese's amicably estranged wife, and *Fawlty Towers* writing partner, Connie Booth as both a Scots-accented Mrs Hudson and a leather-hotpanted Francine Moriarty; Booth would later appear in **Sir Arthur Conan Doyle's The Hound of the Baskervilles** (1983) and **The Return of Sherlock Holmes** (1987). Several filmed scenes were cut, including a lengthy sequence with Joss Ackland as another, clumsier, Jimmy Carter-esque President of the USA and actor Joseph Brady's turn as wheelchair-bound investigator Ironside, one of the many TV and film 'tecs bumped off in the finale.

Cleese enjoyed making *Strange Case* – 'Some of it, I thought, was terribly funny, particularly Arthur Lowe who played Watson. He is a wonderful English character actor who had an alarming habit of falling asleep during takes. He couldn't sleep at night, and I think he had some condition similar to narcolepsy, and he twice fell asleep during takes, which was the most amazing thing I had ever seen. The first time he was off camera, but the second time he was on camera!' – but nonetheless came to recognise this poorly received parody as 'something that I completely misjudged ... I still think, in retrospect, there were some very funny things in it, but by and large, I got it wrong.'

A Study in Scarlet

GB 1914 adaptation Samuelson Film Mfg Co
5749 feet bw silent
w **Harry Engholm** *p* **G B Samuelson** *d* **George Pearson**
cast Jefferson Hope: **Fred Paul** Lucy Ferrier: **Agnes Glynne**
Brigham Young: **Harry Paulo** Sherlock Holmes:
James Bragington John Ferrier: **James LeFre**
young Lucy Ferrier: **Winnifred Pearson**

In the 1992, the British Film Institute named the Samuelson Film Manufacturing Company's version of A STUDY IN SCARLET among the lost films it most wanted to find. Although not the first Holmes picture to be made in Britain (that distinction goes to the 1912 Éclair series, detailed under ... **From the Adventures of Sherlock Holmes**), Samuelson's effort was indeed the first British-owned Holmes film. Setting aside such parochial concerns as nationhood, the rediscovery of *A Study in Scarlet* would shed light on a film remarkable for its scale and ambition alone. Harry Engholm's adaptation re-ordered Doyle's narrative to open with the American West sequences; a flashback in the novel, here they became the film's principal focus, with the Holmes-in-London scenes figuring solely in the closing stages. *A Study in Scarlet* was, therefore, almost certainly the first in a very small sub-genre: the British Western.

Producer George Berthold Samuelson (1888-1947) was an entrepreneur who had sensed the possibilities of the moving picture business after selling a newsreel detailing the state funeral of King Edward VII. His first self-made effort was the widely distributed *60 Years a Queen* (1913), the success of which encouraged him to invest in a glass studio at a site known as Worton Hall in Isleworth, Middlesex. The first film to go before the Samuelson cameras there was *A Study in Scarlet*, but the studio sequences were not its most remarkable aspect. Samuelson and his director, George Pearson (1875-1947), sought to find 'passable replicas of the Rockies and the Salt Lake Plains' to mount the scenes showing the Mormons' trek. Cheddar Gorge, Somerset (later seen in **The Last Adventures of Sherlock Holmes**) and the beaches of Southport Sands (bordering Samuelson's home town) were duly chosen. Filming through the lens of cameraman Walter Buckstone took place over June and July 1914. Surviving photographs detailing the Mormons' caravans and encampment suggest a richly detailed piece, the sheer number of people involved being larger than any other Holmes picture to date.

The principal actor in Samuelson's effort was Fred Paul as vengeful pioneer Jefferson Hope, whose performance would be fulsomely praised in *Pictures and the Picturegoer* the following year: 'One is filled with regret when the long film comes to an end, not only because of the ingenious story, but because Mr Paul's intense acting succeeds throughout in gripping and fascinating his audience.' Paul would later play hero Sir Denis Nayland Smith in a series of films based on Sax Rohmer's Fu Manchu stories produced by Stoll, the company responsible for the Eille Norwood Holmes series beginning with **The Adventures of Sherlock Holmes** (1921). James Bragington, a worker in Samuelson's Birmingham bureau, was cast as Holmes purely for his physical resemblance to the traditional Sidney Paget-inspired depiction of the detective. Indeed, Bragington's Holmes appears remarkably unlike the William Gillette model, surely the principal visual source for the presentation of the character up to this point; it's possible, in fact, that Bragington's Holmes was the first to wear a deerstalker on screen.

Released at Christmas 1914, *A Study in Scarlet* was successful enough for Samuelson to make another Holmes picture not long afterwards. **The Valley of Fear** (1916), however, would call for the employment of a professional actor in the part of Holmes.

A Study in Scarlet

US 1914 adaptation Universal Film Manufacturing Co
2 reels bw silent
*w **Grace Cunard** d **Francis Ford***
known cast Sherlock Holmes: **Francis Ford**

Set for release just one day after Samuelson's **A Study in Scarlet**, albeit on the other side of the Atlantic, this proved an inauspicious beginning to the various Universal companies' long association with Sherlock Holmes (see **Sherlock Holmes and the Voice of Terror** et al). A trade notice issued in advance of release featured a jolly picture of 'Sir A Conan Doyle', who appeared to be giving his personal endorsement to 'a wonderful detective story that's distinctly different'.

This was distinctly cheeky, for the film was distinctly unauthorised – unlike the rather longer Samuelson effort, which was fully paid for. (Copyright infringement was rife in the early years of the film industry; in July 1910, for example, a Parisian court had declared against 'Piracy by Cinematograph' following a case brought by the playwright Georges Courteline, and in November

*James Bragington, the Birmingham office clerk who became the first British screen Sherlock Holmes in **A Study in Scarlet** (1914)*

1911 the Kalem Company was censured by the US Supreme Court over a rogue version of *Ben-Hur*.) It has been suggested that *A Study in Scarlet* was intended as the first of several Universal-produced Sherlock Holmes adventures, but this idea may well derive from a misreading of the aforementioned blurb – which described Doyle's A STUDY IN SCARLET, quite rightly, as 'The first of a series of fascinating, mysterious detective stories'.

The writer-director team responsible was Grace Cunard (Harriet Mildred Jeffries, 1893-1967) and Francis Ford (Francis Thomas O'Fearna, 1883-1953), who had met as actors in the Westerns of producer Thomas H Ince (1882-1924). In 1913, Cunard and Ford teamed up to oversee the production of a great many pictures and serials, most under the 'Gold Seal' banner, for Carl Laemmle's Universal company, then proclaiming itself the 'Largest Manufacturers of Films in the Universe'. Cunard-Ford titles included such enticements as *The Twin's Double* (1913), *The Mysterious Rose*, *The Phantom Violin*, *Lucille Love – the Girl of Mystery* (all 1914) and *Three Bad Men and a Girl* (1915). Cunard and Ford took lead roles in almost all their pictures, alongside an informal repertory company of performers that included Harry Schumm (1877-1953), Ernest Shields (1884-1954) and Lew Short (1875-1958). It's certain that Ford played Holmes himself, wearing a lattice-work-patterned dressing-gown and outsized Andy Capp-style headgear. And it seems entirely plausible that Cunard could have made an attractive Lucy Ferrier, perhaps with Schumm or Shields as, say, Joseph Stangerson or Jefferson Hope.

Most intriguingly, an actor named 'Jack Francis' is often said to have played Dr Watson. No 'Jack Francis' is known to have appeared in any other films of the period – but someone who did, and very often for Cunard and Ford (in *The Mysterious Rose*, for example, plus later productions including 1915's *The Broken Coin* and 1916's *The Purple Mask*), was Francis Ford's brother, a young man born Sean Aloysius O'Fearna in 1895. The brother, also sometimes engaged as a prop man and stunt artiste, was then using the name 'Jack', which may help explain the confusion. Francis would gradually step back from directing, being employed exclusively as an actor from 1929 on. His brother, however, took an opposite path, directing the Westerns *The Tornado* and *Straight*

Shooting for Universal in 1917. Six years later, the one-time Jack became known as 'John Ford' – and as such pursued an epic career including legendary highlights like *My Darling Clementine* (1946), *The Quiet Man* (1952) and *The Searchers* (1955). John Ford died in 1973, but the mystery remains: was the greatest director of American Westerns one of the very first John Watsons, too?

A Study in Scarlet

US 1933 pastiche KBS/World Wide Pictures 71m bw
w **Robert Florey** *continuity and dialogue* **Reginald Owen**
p **E W Hammons** *d* **Edwin L Marin**
cast Sherlock Holmes: **Reginald Owen** Mrs Pyke **Anna May Wong** Eileen Forrester: **June Clyde** Merrydew: **Allan Dinehart** John Stanford: **John Warburton** Lastrade [sic]: **Alan Mowbray** Dr Watson: **Warburton Gamble** Jabez Wilson: **J M Kerrigan** Mrs Murphy: **Doris Lloyd** Will Swallow: **Billy Bevan** Capt Pyke: **Wyndham Standing** Dearing: **Halliwell Hobbes** Daffy Dolly: **Leila Bennett** Ah Yet: **Tetsu Komai*** Mrs Hudson: **Tempe Piggott*** Baker **Cecil Reynolds***

THE MYSTERY

Forrester, Murphy and Pyke, three of the seven members of the so-called 'Scarlet Ring', have died and their share of the society's assets has been divided among the surviving members. Forrester's daughter Eileen is a distraught witness to the death of Pyke, while Murphy's widow appeals to Sherlock Holmes to redress the wrong done her regarding her late husband's legacy, all of which has been appropriated by the shady Ring leader, Merrydew. When another member, Malcolm Dearing, is found murdered, Holmes determines to bring Merrydew to justice.

THE INVESTIGATION

Holmes goes in disguise to the country home of Pyke's widow, a sinuous Chinese woman, and makes a thorough examination of its subterranean passages. Another ring member, Jabez Wilson, is in fear of his life and enlists Holmes' aid, only for the pair of them to stumble upon the corpse of Wilson's Ring associate, Baker. Holmes advises Wilson to accept Mrs Pyke's invitation to spend the night at the Grange, unaware that Eileen, too, has been lured there.

THE SOLUTION

Mrs Pyke admits a cowled figure to the Grange, who promptly makes off with the swooning Eileen. Holmes, Watson and Lastrade [sic] are on the premises, however, killing Ring member Ah Yet as he is about to murder Wilson and revealing the cowled kidnapper as Captain Pyke, whose death had been faked. Merrydew is also apprehended, and Holmes explains that the Ring was a front formed to dispose of some long-stolen Oriental jewels – and that the Pykes had murdered the other members to keep the booty for themselves.

✦ ✦ ✦

British actor Reginald Owen (1887-1972), best remembered as Scrooge in Edwin L Marin's 1938 version of *A Christmas Carol*, also had the distinction of being the only screen actor (prior to Patrick Macnee) to have played both Holmes and Watson. Having backed up Clive Brook in **Conan Doyle's Master Detective Sherlock Holmes** (1932), Owen was promoted the following year to the star role in Marin's A Study in Scarlet – actually not A STUDY IN SCARLET at all, but an Edgar Wallace-flavoured modern-dress scenario cooked up by Robert Florey and Owen himself.

'Here is a case in which the actor realised that not only must he portray his character as he saw it,' observed the film's pressbook, 'but, too, he must strive to interpret the role as the thousands of Sherlock Holmes readers had visualised the character.' No readers, however, will have visualised Holmes as Owen plays him – a slightly florid everyday detective residing at 221A [sic] Baker Street, only donning the trademark deerstalker and Inverness cape in the publicity photos, assuming a useless 'kindly old duffer' disguise when infiltrating Mrs Pyke's lair, and rapping out canonical lines like 'Come, Watson, the game is afoot' with minimum excitement. Some of the pastiche dialogue Owen wrote for himself has a certain swing, though, notably the closing exchange in which soon-to-be-married orphan Eileen Forrester says, 'Perhaps you'll give me away.' 'I appreciate the compliment,' replies Owen/Holmes smoothly, 'but I never give a lady away, except sometimes professionally.'

Owen's other line readings, however, are so ponderous and portentous he comes across more like a calculating villain than a consulting detective. Presumably unintentional, this nevertheless underlines the physical resemblance between Holmes and the odious Merrydew, whom he describes as 'London's most dangerous crook: the king of blackmailers: a gliding, slithey, venomous snake' – qualities admirably captured in Allan Dinehart's cigar-chewing performance.

Though situated on Sunset Boulevard, the Tiffany Studio, where the film was shot, was a minor operation whose main claim to fame was its importation in 1929 of the British stage director James Whale to film *Journey's End*. Whale subsequently directed Universal's groundbreaking *Frankenstein* (1931), a project originally earmarked for French-born director Robert Florey. Given Florey's initial involvement in *Frankenstein*, it's perhaps no coincidence that a minor part in the Florey-scripted *A Study in Scarlet* was reserved for Cecil Reynolds, a West Coast psychiatrist who had 'performed delicate brain operations on many prominent persons' and acted as technical adviser (!) on *Frankenstein*. Another *Frankenstein* veteran, cinematographer Arthur Edeson, claimed that 'The setting of a mystery story is obviously the most perfect medium for experiment with strange camera angles and tricky lighting effects,' proving it by giving the film touches of visual distinction in stark contrast to its hokey plot.

There's a sidelined but engaging Dr Watson from Warburton Gamble, a bald-headed Broadway import fresh from acting opposite Gloria Swanson in *Tonight or Never* and Greta Garbo in *As You Desire Me*, and a world-class femme fatale from the Chinese-American beauty Anna May Wong (1907-1961), whose interview at the Savoy Hotel with the apprehensive Jabez Wilson is artfully shot through the flames of an open-topped stove. (The Jabez Wilson name was lifted, of course, from Doyle's THE RED-HEADED LEAGUE.) There's also, unfortunately, a good deal of racial prejudice at Wong's expense, as when ubiquitous comedy cockney Billy Bevan says 'You can't make English gentry out of the heathen Chinee no-how' and dithering ladies' maid Leila Bennett describes her as 'Such a good-looker: such eyes. She walks like a cat. Such a figure, such a fine bit of goods. An English lady make her look like nothin'.'

Edwin L Marin (1899-1951) soon graduated to better things, making a couple of Philo Vance adventures for MGM and ending with some colourful Randolph Scott vehicles. His single Sherlock Holmes project, released on 31 May 1933, is marred by a tedious parade of Hollywood cockneys (the opening line of dialogue is 'Lor' love a duck!'), some stagey cliffhangers typical of Broadway mystery plays (a gas-filled chamber, the whole 'old dark house' denouement) and, of course, by Owen's uniquely bovine Holmes. (JR)

A Study in Terror

GB 1965 pastiche Compton-Tekli Film Productions Ltd/Sir Nigel Films Ltd 95m colour
w **Donald & Derek Ford**, **Herman Cohen*** & **Harry Craig***
p **Henry E Lester** *d* **James Hill**
cast Sherlock Holmes: **John Neville** Doctor Watson: **Donald Houston** Lord Carfax: **John Fraser** Doctor Murray: **Anthony Quayle** Mycroft Holmes: **Robert Morley** Annie Chapman: **Barbara Windsor** Angela: **Adrienne Corri** Inspector Lestrade: **Frank Finlay** Sally: **Judi Dench** Prime Minister: **Cecil Parker** singer: **Georgia Brown** Duke of Shires: **Barry Jones** Cathy Eddowes: **Kay Walsh** Mary Kelly: **Edina Ronay** Chunky: **Terry Downes** Joseph Beck: **Charles Regnier** Home Secretary: **Dudley Foster** Max Steiner: '**Peter Carsten**' [pseudonym for **O W Fischer**] Polly Nichols: **Christiane Maybach** simpleton/Michael Osborne: **John Cairney** landlady: **Avis Bunnage** Mrs Hudson: **Barbara Leake** PC Benson: **Patrick Newell** Liz Stride: **Norma Foster** first streetwalker: **Donna White***

THE MYSTERY
Autumn, 1888: following the vicious slashings-to-death of three streetwalkers in the stews of seedy Whitechapel, an unmarked parcel is sent from that very district to Sherlock Holmes. It contains a surgeon's toolkit; the post-mortem knife is conspicuously missing...

THE INVESTIGATION
The case belonged to Michael Osborne, the disowned and two-years-since disappeared medical student son of the Duke of Shires. Holmes and Watson discover it to have been pledged to a pawnbroker's by a woman named Angela Osborne, formerly resident at a local soup kitchen run by police surgeon Doctor Murray and financed philanthropically by the young Lord Carfax, the Duke of Shires' other son. Angela, it transpires, was a local whore who, in association with a villain

Sailors on shore leave ogle the ill-fated Liz Stride (Norma Foster) in **A Study in Terror** (1965)

named Steiner, had blackmailed Michael, threatening to disgrace his family by revealing details of their secret marriage. Meanwhile, the 'Jack the Ripper' killings continue...

THE SOLUTION

The innocent Michael, an imbecile since learning of Angela and Steiner's blackmail scheme, is being harboured by Murray. The Ripper is Carfax, determined to murder every tart in Whitechapel in his search for the treacherous Angela – an insane bid to protect his four-generations-mad family's name.

✦ ✦ ✦

A richly Eastmancolored melodrama showcasing a fine ensemble of British character actors, *A Study in Terror* – the unlikely product of an unholy alliance comprising Conan Doyle's second son, Soho's foremost distributors of cinematic smut and the man who made *I Was a Teenage Werewolf* – only occasionally reveals its roots in the shabby, sleazy world of exploitation film.

The first of two pictures in which the Great Detective is called upon to identify the most notorious killer of 'his' age, *A Study in Terror* is but a small part of sex-murderer Jack the Ripper's fictional career, which has proven every bit as diverse as Holmes'. On stage, the Ripper had debuted in the German Frank Wedekind's plays *Erdgeist* ('Earth show', 1895) and *Die Büchse der Pandora* ('Pandora's box', 1902), both of which would become the basis for his first two screen appearances proper, in 1923 and 1928 respectively; the same sources were combined in Alban Berg's 1937 opera *Lulu*. Meanwhile, in print, Marie Belloc Lowndes' 1913 novel *The Lodger* cemented an image of the Ripper as a solitary, medically skilled and vengeance-fixated tenant of a Whitechapel room – itself an early urban myth probably derived from a theory addressed to the *Times* by one Dr Lyttleton Forbes Winslow on 12 September 1888 – which would become the Ripper's dominant incarnation for four decades, from a stage adaptation titled *Who is He?* (1923) to a Hitchcock-directed silent (1926), its sound remake (1932), a

Fluent with a swordstick: John Neville's 'original caped crusader' in **A Study in Terror** (1965)

Hollywood version (1943) and *Room To Let* (1949), a proto-horror Hammer film.

The rise of Hammer's Gothic (and, significantly, colour) horrors following *The Curse of Frankenstein* (1956) precipitated a boom in grisly British fantasy pictures, aided by the progressive relaxation of censorship strictures following the introduction of the adults-only 'X' certificate, which would enable a full, no-holds-barred depiction of the Ripper's sex crimes for the first time. Sure enough, 1959 saw the release of Robert S Baker and Monty Berman's sensationalised British B-movie *Jack the Ripper* (scripted by Hammer's Jimmy Sangster), which nominated a mad surgeon as the Ripper, his homicidal career curtailed in a bizarre elevator accident. That same year, Hammer released *The Man Who Could Cheat Death*, Sangster's loose adaptation of the play *The Man in Half Moon Street*, in which a deranged scalpel-wielding doctor stalks hapless women by night in a foggy turn-of-the-century Paris. The climax has the killer consumed in a blazing building along with a once-beautiful woman whose face is now horribly scarred – a more-than-noteworthy prefiguring of the conclusion of *A Study in Terror*.

Such precedents set, it's unsurprising that neither American producer Herman Cohen nor British producer Tony Tenser failed to see the potential in a Holmes-versus-the-Ripper flick. Having associate-produced his first pictures in his early twenties (including the astonishingly titled *Bela Lugosi Meets a Brooklyn Gorilla*, 1952), Cohen had gone on to invent the 'teen-horror' film with *I Was a Teenage Werewolf* (1957) and *I Was a Teenage Frankenstein* (1958), also setting up a London office that would beget pictures such as *Horrors of the Black Museum* (1959). Cohen claims that inspiration came when, in England, he met one Henry E Lester, then copyright-protecting legal representative for the Conan Doyle estate. 'Henry Lester had talked to a pair of independent producers in London who were interested in making a Sherlock Holmes picture,' he told *Scarlet Street* magazine in 1995, 'but they didn't have the money. I got the idea of pitting Sherlock Holmes against Jack the Ripper...'

That 'pair of independent producers' were, it seems, Michael Klinger and Tony Tenser, whose West End Compton Cinema Club had, since 1960, expanded to become a hugely profitable distribution network for risqué films. Under the aegis of Compton-Cameo Films (soon after, Compton-Tekli), they'd branched out into production with saucy numbers such as *Naked – As Nature Intended*, *That Kind of Girl* and *The Yellow Teddybears*. Given the prevailing cinema trend, the horror-cum-suspense thriller was a natural (and altogether more respectable) genre for the duo to exploit. Beginning with the Hammeresque *The Black Torment*, the group had gone on to finance Roman Polanski's seminal *Repulsion*. Tenser, however, disputes Cohen's account of the genesis of *A Study in Terror*, believing that it was Gene Gutowski, *Repulsion*'s credited producer, who introduced him to Lester: 'He said he wanted to do another Sherlock Holmes film, and would I do it?' In this version, Tenser devises the Ripper angle, having already asked *The Black Torment*'s writing team of Donald and Derek Ford to pen the script. He then calls Cohen and asks him to 'come in for half the budget'.

For his part, Cohen maintains that, while researching *Horrors of the Black Museum*, he'd been 'one of the first Americans to be taken through Scotland Yard's Black Museum', where he'd learned that 'Queen Victoria sealed some secret documents on the case of Jack the Ripper ... it all points to a member of the Royal family. That's why we did what we did. We didn't get want to get too close to the Royal family, but we made the Ripper an aristocrat.' Entirely predictably, Henry E Lester might also claim to have originated *A Study in Terror* – and, seeing as 'Lester' was none other than Heinrich von Leipziger, associate producer of 1962's **Sherlock Holmes und das Halsband des Todes** (a film which ends with Christopher Lee's Holmes receiving news of the revived Ripper's exploits), he might well have reason to. Indeed, a German newspaper report explicitly stated during production on **Halsband** that Christopher Lee's 'next' Holmes film was to be a Holmes/Ripper encounter.

Whatever the true story of the film's genesis, a three-way deal would eventually be struck. Working alongside Cohen (who would ensure US distribution for the film through his association with Hollywood giant Columbia Pictures) and Compton-Tekli (which had rights to the film throughout the Eastern hemisphere) was Sir Nigel Films Ltd (after Sir Nigel Loring, the hero of ACD's historical novels *The White Company* and *Sir Nigel*), a company set up by Conan Doyle's heirs. The deal having been approved by Adrian Conan Doyle (who'd later make visits to both the Shepperton Studios set and London location), Henry Lester would be given an entirely token producer's credit. Cohen, in fact, oversaw the film's day-to-day progress solo.

As *Fog* (eventually re-titled at Columbia's insistence, and much to Cohen's chagrin; Tenser takes credit for the new title), the film went into production on location and at Shepperton Studios during the summer of 1965. Its surprisingly eclectic cast was gathered by director James Hill, a former documentarist and Children's Film Foundation mainstay with one 'serious' film under his belt (kitchen-sink drama *The Kitchen*, 1960) and just a year away from his greatest success, life-with-the-lions epic *Born Free*. Allegedly, Michael Gough, who'd played the lead in Cohen's *Horrors of the Black Museum*, *Konga* and *Black Zoo*, was 'very unhappy' not to be offered the part of Holmes –

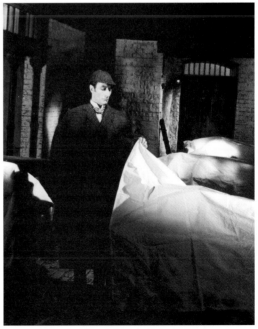

Remains of the day: Holmes (John Neville) notes the Ripper's handiwork in **A Study in Terror** *(1965)*

*Bloodhound owner Peter Couves helps John Neville to publicise **A Study in Terror** in October 1965*

which went instead to John Neville, cast in tandem with his Watson, Donald Houston.

A dashing, aquiline detective in natty threads – foppish Beau Brummell frockcoat and hat for surveying a crime scene, tuxedo and opera cape for a trip to an East End boozer – Neville's Holmes only sports a token deerstalker in *A Study in Terror*'s final third. Dervish-like in unarmed combat, and fluent in the application of a devilish swordstick, this gung-ho and 'indestructible' Sherlock is willing to be 'intrigued' into the case, but resists authority pressure to involve himself for the sake of preserving the status quo, citing pointedly political creed to brother Mycroft: 'Any government which allows the poverty of Whitechapel deserves, as far as I'm concerned, riddance.' Earlier, the Home Secretary has complained that, 'Only last week [Holmes] was grossly offensive to the governor of Pentonville Prison...'

Neville (1925-), a busy and highly regarded theatrical actor-manager, suggested the young Judi Dench, whom he knew well from her appearances opposite him at Nottingham Playhouse, for the supporting role of soup kitchen angel Sally. Neville had turned down the Holmes role in the Broadway musical *Baker Street* (Fritz Weaver played it) and, following his big-screen Holmes excursion, would be courted as a possible replacement for Douglas Wilmer in BBC Television's 1968 series **Sir Arthur Conan Doyle's Sherlock Holmes**. He subsequently played Sherlock on stage, replacing John Wood in the RSC's Broadway run of the Gillette play *Sherlock Holmes*. Rarely seen in films, Neville's most prominent cinematic role is undoubtedly the lead in Terry Gilliam's spectacular *The Adventures of Baron Munchausen* (1989).

According to Neville, Welsh-born Houston (1923-91) made 'the best Doctor Watson, ever. He wasn't a buffoon, he wasn't a joke...' Even more bullish and forceful than Holmes, Houston's have-a-go Watson doesn't blanch at barging his way into a burly blackmailer's lair – 'You're asking for trouble, aren'tcha?' says Steiner. 'No, we're giving it,' comes the reply – and is fulsome in his denunciation of wickedness: 'I feel I want to do something violent when I see a villain like Steiner enjoying the rewards of his skulduggery!' Houston played prominent parts in a number of pictures from *The Blue Lagoon* (1950) on, appearing in films as varied as *Yangtse Incident* (1957), *Room at the Top* (1958) and *Carry On Jack* (1963; *not* a Ripper spoof).

A Study in Terror's notable first is the feature film début of Holmes' brother, Mycroft, whose canonical appearances number only THE GREEK INTERPRETER and THE BRUCE-PARTINGTON PLANS. Rightly, Mycroft is accorded the role of governmental intermediary; the scene-stealing Robert Morley interprets the character in plummy, domineering fashion. The film, in fact, is positively overburdened with strong performances; exploitation stars Adrienne Corri, Edina Ronay and Barbara Windsor (not yet a regular Carry On turn) contribute just as much as their feted thespian fellows, from Morley and Neville to the acclaimed Austrian actor O W Fischer, here playing Steiner under the pseudonym Peter Carsten. As a side note, Frank Finlay would reprise his Inspector Lestrade in the second Holmes-versus-Ripper flick, **Murder By Decree** – in which Anthony Quayle, *A Study in Terror*'s Murray, would also appear.

Britain's *Monthly Film Bulletin*, mealy-mouthed as ever, begrudgingly praised the film's 'charmingly period sets' and 'pleasantly muted colour', called the plot 'agreeably tangled' but claimed that 'the film marks time lamely in the intervals between its conventionally shock-cut murders, while John Neville and Donald Houston uncomfortably mouth their lines as if suspecting that nobody will listen.' America's *Variety* thought the premise 'a neat enough gag ... Though the mixture of fiction and fact doesn't entirely click ... this provides a fair measure of amusement. An excellent cast gives the production full value. Dialog and situations sometimes teeter on the edge of parody (providing misplaced yocks)...' Reviewer 'Rich' seemed taken by the 'prosties', though.

Famously, *A Study in Terror* was luridly promoted in the States by reference to the then-hot pop cultural phenomenon of James Bond and, especially, Batman. 'Here comes the original caped crusader!' ran the poster's tagline. It flopped dreadfully, but perhaps 'caped crusader' isn't so inappropriate an assessment of Neville's agile and socially conscious Holmes, for the script's moments of (admittedly slight) political critique do give Sherlock's world a hitherto-unseen verisimilitude,

and it's a pleasure to see Holmes and Watson engaged within (and sometimes disgusted by) a less idealised projection of late 19th century London.

The film, then, has aged well – its most dated moments being the murder of Mary Kelly, shot with a prowling, lewd POV camera in the manner of a cut-price *Peeping Tom*, and those where the bizarre, bebop-inflected score completely overwhelms the action, all xylophone and bongos. Director Hill lavishes attention on the crowd scenes, cataloguing small, human moments with his documentarist's eye, such as an old lady surreptitiously swigging gin from another's glass. All human life is present in his Whitechapel, every bit the 'Sodom and Gomorrah' it's claimed to be. His London is, in fact, his biggest star, raspberry-blowing whores and all. It's almost a shame that a slightly tacky murder mystery keeps getting in the way.

Suspense: The Adventure of the Black Baronet

US 1953 TV pastiche CBS 30m bw
tx 26 May 1953 CBS
w **Michael Dyne** *source* **The Adventure of the Black Baronet** [pastiche by **Adrian Conan Doyle** & **John Dickson Carr**]
p **Himan Green** *d* **Robert Mulligan**
cast includes Sherlock Holmes: **Basil Rathbone**
Dr Watson: **Martyn Green** Lady Lavington: **Mary Howard** Lavington: **Anthony Dearden** other roles: **members of the New York branch of the Baker Street Irregulars**

'I find it's impossible to escape Holmes,' an increasingly desperate Basil Rathbone told the *New York Herald-Tribune* shortly before transmission of *The Adventure of the Black Baronet*, the half-hour teleplay that marked his comeback in the role.

The years following **Dressed to Kill**, the last of the Universal B-pictures to feature Rathbone's Holmes, had been lean ones. Selling his house in Bel-Air and moving to the East Coast, Rathbone had hoped to find fulfilment in the theatre, but had made only one truly noteworthy Broadway appearance – as Dr Sloper in *The Heiress*, a play derived from Henry James' *Washington Square* – before being forced to retreat to his more familiar Sherlock Holmes persona. Hence the 1947 radio series *Scotland Yard*, in which he played Inspector Burke; hence his cameo appearance as a police detective in *Sherlock Holmes in the Mystery of the Sen-Sen Murder, or Who Was the Louse who Shot the Grouse*, a skit featuring vaudevillian Milton Berle, broadcast as part of the NBC Television variety show *Texaco Star Theater* on 19 April 1949.

Two years later, he played Dr Jekyll in an adaptation of Robert Louis Stevenson's *Dr Jekyll and Mr Hyde* shown on 6 March 1951 as part of the CBS anthology series *Suspense*, which ran for 260 episodes between March 1949 and August 1954. *Suspense* kept a number of other faded ex-Universal stars in work, incidentally, with appearances by Boris Karloff in a version of W W Jacobs' *The Monkey's Paw* and Bela Lugosi in Edgar Allan Poe's *The Cask of Amontillado*.

Towards the end of 1952, Adrian Conan Doyle, son of Arthur, had collaborated with the prolific mystery writer John Dickson Carr (1906-77) on *The Adventure of the Seven Clocks*, the first of 12 pastiches later packaged under the title *The Exploits of Sherlock Holmes*. All of these were inspired, in some way, by throwaway references in the canon to 'unpublished' cases. The second story, *The Adventure of the Black Baronet*, was derived from a remark about 'the unfortunate Madame Montpensier', as mentioned in THE HOUND OF THE BASKERVILLES.

Here, Madame Montpensier is a former actress, now married to Sir Richard Lavington – who is accused of killing his house guest, a society blackmailer known as Colonel Buck Dalcy, found with his throat cut. An ancient silver goblet known as 'the Luck of Lavington' sits on the table before the corpse. With the help of Dr Watson and Inspector Tobias Gregson, Holmes uncovers the secret of the Luck, the invention of Lavington's ancestor, a 15th century 'black baronet': it conceals a switchblade designed to slaughter those who drink from it, a fate that befell Dalcy accidentally.

The Adventure of the Black Baronet was first published in the weekly *Collier's* magazine on 23 May 1953, three days ahead of the transmission of an adaptation of the story in *Suspense*. Rathbone had met Adrian Conan Doyle sometime the previous year to discuss the possibility of staging a new Sherlock Holmes play adapted by his wife Ouida Bergere Rathbone from a number of sources, including A SCANDAL IN BOHEMIA, THE SECOND STAIN and THE FINAL PROBLEM. It may be

that his appearance in the *Suspense* version of *Black Baronet* was a favour to Doyle Jr, who had been 'most enthusiastic' about Ouida's play. The ailing Nigel Bruce does not appear to have been called by producers CBS; following a heart attack, he died on 8 October that year. Instead, Watson was played by British singer-actor Martyn Green (1899-1975). The director was Robert Mulligan (1925-), later Oscar-nominated for *To Kill a Mockingbird* (1962).

Sadly, no recording of the show is known to survive – and so all we have to evaluate Rathbone's return are a handful of unhappy reviews. 'Sherlock is bound to seem a little awkward if he must hurry up for the middle commercial,' ruminated the *New York Times*. 'Mr Rathbone did not seem too happy with a part with which he could never really come to grips ... Mr Green had very little to do, but even so did not seem to represent sufficient contrast to Mr Holmes. The Nigel Bruce interpretation ... had much more body. Doctor Watson is basically a superb foil, but on Monday evening he was only a straight man.' Rathbone, it seems, was under the impression that *The Black Baronet* was a try-out for six more of the Doyle/Carr stories, but no such series was forthcoming. The following year, young Ronald Howard would become the first television Holmes to meet with real success in **Sherlock Holmes** (1954-5).

With Jack Raine as Watson and Thomas Gomez (from **Sherlock Holmes and the Voice of Terror**) as Moriarty, Ouida's play, *Sherlock Holmes*, premiered at Boston's Shubert Theater on 10 October 1953. Three weeks later, it opened at New York's New Century Theater – and, following wretched notices, closed after just three performances. 'Try as I would my heart was not really in it,' wrote Rathbone. 'I hoped to be carried by the volume of public opinion that had supported me so enthusiastically from 1939 to 1946. But this was 1953. Seven years had passed – yes, we were at least seven years too late! ... Then there was this new gadget television that was sweeping the country ... With our Sherlock Holmes play we were leisurely, thoughtful, and purposefully analytical, in the mood of the period. With television it happened fast, and was most times all over in about 24 minutes, allowing six minutes for introduction and closing and commercials. We were outdated, hopelessly outdated.'

Basil Rathbone, the greatest of all screen Sherlocks, would never again appear in the role.

Terror By Night

US 1946 pastiche Universal Pictures Company Inc
60m bw w **Frank Gruber** pd **Roy William Neill**
cast Sherlock Holmes: **Basil Rathbone** Dr Watson: **Nigel
Bruce** Major Duncan Bleek [Colonel Sebastian Moran]:
Alan Mowbray Inspector Lestrade: **Dennis Hoey** Vivian
Vedder: **Renee Godfrey** Professor Kilbane: **Frederic Worlock**
Lady Margaret: **Mary Forbes** Sands: **Skelton Knaggs** train
attendant: **Billy Bevan** Ronald Carstairs: **Geoffrey Steele**
steward: **Gilbert Allen*** Mock: **Harry Cording*** Inspector
McDonald: **Boyd Davis*** Alf Shallcross: **Gerald Hamer***
conductor: **Leyland Hodgson*** constable: **Colin Kenny***
baggage car guard: **Charles Knight*** Mrs Shallcross: **Janet
Murdoch*** attendant: **Tom Pilkington*** man on platform:
C Aubrey Smith* Mock Jr: **Bobby Wissler***

THE MYSTERY

In London, thieves have made an unsuccessful
attempt to steal a priceless diamond, the Star of
Rhodesia, from Lady Margaret Carstairs, whose
son, Ronald, employs Sherlock Holmes to ensure
the Star's security *en route* to Edinburgh on the
'Scotch Express'. At Euston Station, Holmes
encounters Inspector Lestrade, who will be
travelling incognito on behalf of Scotland Yard;
Dr Watson, meanwhile, has met an old army
comrade, Major Duncan Bleek. That night, Ronald
Carstairs is found dead in his compartment; the
Star has vanished. Holmes suspects Colonel
Sebastian Moran, a colleague of the 'late,
unlamented' Professor Moriarty...

THE INVESTIGATION

Holmes, Watson and Lestrade interrogate a
number of passengers: the nervous Mr and Mrs
Shallcross, whose only 'crime' is to have stolen a
teapot from a London hotel; gruff mathematician
Professor William Kilbane; and even Lady
Margaret, on the grounds that the 'theft' may have
been an insurance scam. Grieving daughter Vivian
Vedder, however, is revealed to be nothing of the
sort; she is indeed carrying her mother's corpse in

the baggage car, but the coffin contains a secret
compartment in which Moran's paid assassin,
Sands, has been smuggled aboard. After an attempt
is made on Holmes' life, the detective reveals that
the Star of Rhodesia taken from Carstairs was, in
fact, a fake; having held the real Star throughout,
Holmes entrusts the diamond to Lestrade.

THE SOLUTION

Later, Sands clubs Lestrade unconscious and takes
the Star, but his employer, Moran – aka Watson's
'chum', Major Duncan Bleek – shoots his own
henchman dead using an air pistol loaded with
poisoned darts. Holmes, however, is onto Moran –
and when the train stops, Scots police inspector
McDonald and several constables board it to
apprehend the Colonel. After a tussle, McDonald
gets his man; outside, however, McDonald's prisoner
is revealed to be Lestrade, who promptly arrests the
bogus policeman, whom Holmes has identified as
one of Moran's cronies. Holmes, meanwhile, has
the cunning Moran handcuffed in the dining car –
and the Star safely back in his possession.

✦ ✦ ✦

If the dismal **Pursuit to Algiers** suggests that, ten
films in, Universal's Sherlock Holmes series
was moribund, then *Terror By Night*, despite being
superior in every department, is not a convincing
repudiation. It's too short to cause offence, but too
slight to enthuse about.

Pursuit to Algiers' two biggest problems – lack
of mystery and lack of pace – are well addressed by
newcomer Frank Gruber's zestful screenplay,
which not only serves as an efficient whodunit
(or 'who-is-it?', once the name of Colonel Moran
has been invoked) but also compresses the story
into the space of just a few hours (not several
drawn-out days, as in **Pursuit to Algiers**). Gruber
(1904-69), best known as an author of pulp
Westerns, had previously adapted Eric Ambler's
The Mask of Dimitrios for Warners. Although the
credits declare that Gruber took 'a story' by Doyle
for his inspiration, at least three are involved: THE

EMPTY HOUSE (in which Colonel Moran first wields an air-powered weapon), with a hint of THE DISAPPEARANCE OF LADY FRANCES CARFAX (the false-bottomed coffin, big enough to hide a person) and a dash of THE SIGN OF THE FOUR (poison darts).

Worryingly, tried-and-tested ideas from earlier Universal pictures are present, too: the cursed item of jewellery from **The Pearl of Death**, and an old school friend of Watson's being unveiled as the villain, as in **Sherlock Holmes and the Voice of Terror**. But the reversals, when they come, are actually surprising – especially Moran's killing of Sands and the scenes involving the Colonel's stooge, the fake 'Inspector McDonald'. In his third Holmesian role (the first being as the detective's rival, Gore-King, in **Conan Doyle's Master Detective Sherlock Holmes**, the second being Inspector Lestrade in the 1933 **A Study in Scarlet**), British actor Alan Mowbray (1896-1969) makes a fair fist of switching between the genial 'Major Bleek' and the ruthless Moran. There's nothing particularly quotable in the film, but Lestrade's response upon finding Holmes standing over the body of the murdered Carstairs – 'That's a bit quick, even for you!' – cannot fail to raise a wry smile. *Terror By Night* was Dennis Hoey's last turn as Lestrade, incidentally, and contains his least ingratiating performance.

The *New York Times* fingered Hitchcock's *The Lady Vanishes* (1938) as *Terror By Night*'s inspiration when it was released, to little enthusiasm, on 1 February 1946. It would prove to be the penultimate Universal Holmes; the last would go under the title **Dressed to Kill**.

They Might Be Giants

US 1971 parody Universal Pictures/Newman-Foreman Company 86m colour
w **James Goldman** *p* **John Foreman**, **Paul Newman***
d **Anthony Harvey**
cast Dr Watson: **Joanne Woodward** Justin Playfair: **George C Scott** Wilbur Peabody: **Jack Gilford** Blevins Playfair: **Lester Rawlins** Daisy: **Rue McClanahan** Dr Strauss: **Ron Weyand** Grace: **Kitty Winn** Grace's boyfriend: **Peter Fredericks** Maud: **Sudie Bond** Miss Finch: **Jenny Egan** Peggy: **Theresa Merritt** messenger: **Al Lewis** Mr Small: **Oliver Clark** telephone operators: **Jane Hoffman**, **Dorothy Greener** sanitation men: **M Emmet Walsh**, **Louis Zorich** telephone guard: **Michael McGuire** policeman: **Eugene**

Roche Mr Brown: **James Tolkan** Brown's driver: **Jacques Sandalescu** Mr Bagg: **Worthington Miner** Mrs Bagg: **Frances Fuller** teenage boy: **Matthew Cowles** teenage girl: **Candy Azzara** police Lt: **John McCurry** Chief: **Tony Capodilupo** usher: **F Murray Abraham** Winthrop: **Staats Cotsworth** chestnut vendor: **Paul Benedict** store manager: **Ralph Clanton** cab driver: **Ted Beniades**

Occupying the cutting-edge of British theatre in the late fifties and early sixties, Joan Littlewood's Theatre Workshop, located at the Theatre Royal Stratford East, was responsible for such landmark plays as *A Taste of Honey*, *The Hostage* and *Fings Ain't Wot They Used T'Be*. A further gift to posterity from Theatre Workshop, oddly enough, was an extraordinary parade of future sitcom stars: Jean Boht, Anthony Booth, Yootha Joyce, Miriam Karlin, Brian Murphy, Victor Spinetti, Barbara Windsor and many more. One such, Harry H Corbett, was a year away from his signature role in *Steptoe and Son* when he took the lead in *They Might Be Giants*, which opened at Stratford East on 28 June 1961.

The play was by American writer James Goldman (1927-1998; elder brother of prolific screenwriter William) and involved a mentally unbalanced judge (Corbett), who imagines that he is Sherlock Holmes, striking up a touching relationship with his aptly named psychiatrist Dr Watson (Avis Bunnage). The show was not a success, running only for the scheduled four weeks. Broadway impresario Hal Prince decided to take it no further while Joan Littlewood, who had just seen *Sparrers Can't Sing* (written by another future sitcom favourite, Stephen Lewis) collapse on its West End transfer, was sufficiently disgruntled to abandon Stratford East, only returning in March 1963 with the triumphant *Oh! What a Lovely War*.

They Might Be Giants took a little longer to resurface. When a later Goldman play, *The Lion in Winter*, had become a well-received film directed by Anthony Harvey, producers Paul Newman and John Foreman hit upon *They Might Be Giants* as a vehicle for Newman's wife, Joanne Woodward. Retaining Harvey as director, Newman-Foreman put the film into production in New York on 24 November 1969, wrapping the project on 20 February 1970. Universal were perplexed by the whimsical result, however, and delayed releasing it until June 1971. (Its UK release was delayed even

'Why, Mr Rathbone, it's an honour, sir': a New York cop (Eugene Roche) greets 'Sherlock Holmes' (George C Scott) and Dr Watson (Joanne Woodward) in **They Might Be Giants** (1971)

longer, until March 1972.) Worse, they chopped it around unmercifully and even excised the film's exhilarating climax, in which 'Holmes' and Watson, assisted by various Greenwich Village oddballs, create slapstick chaos in a supermarket in order to evade both the pursuing police and the Mob. As a result of this, as Alexander Walker put it in the *Evening Standard*, 'The acting works more enjoyably than the allegory – though that has been fatally interfered with, as you can tell by comparing the film's anti-climaxes with the missing scenes which are described in a press synopsis someone obviously forgot to re-edit, too.'

George C Scott and Joanne Woodward, Oscar winners for *Patton* and *The Three Faces of Eve* respectively, hold the piece together with exemplary, and frequently touching, performances but even they are defeated by the slackening pace and increasing sentimentality of the film's second half. As a starry-eyed portrait of a so-called lunatic liberating robotic 'straights' from the rigours of modern life, the film looks back to Jean Giraudoux's wartime play *La folle de Chaillot* (filmed in 1968 as *The Madwoman of Chaillot*, with Harvey's *Lion in*

Winter star, Katharine Hepburn, in the title role) and forward to Terry Gilliam's *The Fisher King* (1991), with comic Robin Williams as a uniquely irksome 'Holy Fool'. But, for all Harvey's echoes of Frank Capra and even Federico Fellini, the film's concluding passages ring false; ham-fisted front-office surgery or not, it's hard to disagree with Vincent Canby's *New York Times* assessment of *They Might Be Giants* as 'a mushy movie'.

This is sad because the film starts in fine style. The Scott character, Justin Playfair, has an unscrupulous brother called Blevins, who opens the proceedings with no-nonsense narrative economy by declaring that 'My brother's lost his mind. The doctor says it's permanent. I'm putting him away. The minute he's committed I'll be rich.' Justin, meanwhile, subjects an elderly delivery boy (played by Al 'Grandpa Munster' Lewis) to an off-hand piece of Holmesian deduction. 'You » suffer from lumbago,' he pronounces. 'You're hag-ridden by your wife, you keep a sheepdog for a pet and you had chicken soup for breakfast.' Blevins' skittish wife Daisy, clad in a fluffy yellow negligée, squeals excitedly at this display and says, 'I just

Dr Watson (Joanne Woodward) and Justin Playfair (George C Scott) embark on their Greenwich Village quest in **They Might Be Giants** *(1971)*

love it when you do that.' She likes Justin just as he is – and so, the film argues, should we. A latterday Don Quixote tilting at mechanised Manhattan windmills, Justin/Holmes is a colossal figure who rapidly co-opts the mousey Mildred Watson into his strangely innocent world.

He impresses her first by effortlessly persuading a tubby mental patient to talk. He correctly identifies Mr Small (whose first name may or may not be Jonathan) as Rudolph Valentino, and strides out of the clinic with a breezy, 'Well, I must be off. My best to Vilma Banky.' In his basement laboratory, bubbling with gaily coloured test-tubes, he subjects Mildred herself to a disarmingly accurate analysis ('No one you've loved has ever loved you back') and then has a poignant moment of his own. Speaking of his former self, he points out that 'He tried to make the world a kinder place ... It drove him mad. He lost his mind. But I am not that man.' Embarking on their picaresque investigation, they encounter a cop who greets Justin with a bedazzled 'Why, Mr Rathbone, it's an honour, sir.'

This is all great stuff – wittily written, cleverly directed, and nicely scored by John Barry. The love

that subsequently develops between 'Holmes' and Watson is beautifully observed, too. But their Greenwich Village quest (in which Justin seeks to face down a generalised 'Moriarty' representing the evils of systematised modern living) is not. 'Holmes' and Watson end up at the head of a raggle-taggle deputation of gently barmy social outcasts, all seeking 'romance, excitement, danger'. 'Holmes' finally calls them to order with the words, 'Dear friends, will those of you who know what this is all about please raise your hands.' By this stage, audience members are just as unlikely to comply as the characters, while simultaneously becoming aware of a faint whiff of pretentiousness in Goldman's meandering script. The film remains chiefly memorable, in fact, for the tantalising glimpse it provides of what the monolithic Scott might have made of the character in a straight Holmes story.

As a postscript, *They Might Be Giants* was by no means the first film to present a 'fantasist' Sherlock Holmes. Buster Keaton's 45-minute masterpiece *Sherlock Jr* (1924) involves a humble projectionist who finds his way into the film he's projecting; a dazzling display of camera trickery and unfeigned daredevil stunts, it was also the picture in which Keaton inadvertently broke his neck. The Ufa production *Der Mann, der Sherlock Holmes war* ('The Man Who was Sherlock Holmes', 1937) stars Hans Albers and Heinz Rühmann as down-at-heel private detectives who boost their business by posing as Holmes and Watson; Conan Doyle himself (Paul Bildt) dogs their footsteps in what Graham Greene called (in the *Spectator*) 'an erudite and rather Pirandello-ish plot.' A later fantasy Holmes appeared in the person of British actor Rupert Frazer, invoked as a mental picture by the titular hero of ABC-TV's *Father Dowling Investigates* to help crack a case in *The Consulting Detective Mystery*, transmitted on 25 April 1991. (JR)

The Three Garridebs

1937 TV adaptation 30m approx NBC bw
tx circa 27 November 1937 NBC
w **Thomas H Hutchinson** *p* **Robert Palmer** *d* **Eustace Wyatt**
cast Sherlock Holmes: **Louis Hector** Dr Watson: **William Podmore** Mrs Hudson: **Violet Besson** John Garrideb: **Arthur Maitland** Nathan Garrideb: **James Spottswood** Inspector Lestrade: **Eustace Wyatt** Mrs Saunders: **Selma Hall**

The year 1937 saw television broadcasting arrive in the USA. Initially the province of an eager band of hobbyists and technophiles, try-out transmissions began in major cities – including New York, where, late in November, the world's first Sherlock Holmes teleplay aired to an audience numbered in hundreds.

Seeking suitable subjects for dramatic interpretation, the National Broadcasting Company had purchased rights in the Doyle story THE THREE GARRIDEBS, which, despite its limited cast of characters and restricted settings, remains an unusual choice of tale – unless one considers that the plot revolves around an American conman; indeed, one of Holmes' suspicions is confirmed by the inappropriate use of Stateside colloquialisms. Not that Holmes was an unknown quantity at NBC, which had been broadcasting radio dramas based on the Doyle stories as far back as October 1930 – the first with William Gillette (see **Sherlock Holmes**, 1916) opposite Leigh Lovell's Watson. Subsequently, Richard Gordon had taken the lead in three full seasons of plays. NBC had long since exhausted the Doyle canon, writer Edith Meiser now devising pastiches with titles like *The Haunted Bagpipes* and *The Singular Affair of the Aluminum Crutch*. From November 1934, NBC had a third Holmes – Louis Hector, and so it was he who would be awarded the distinction of being the first ever TV 'tec.

The Three Garridebs, 'the most ambitious experiment in teleshowmanship so far attempted in the air above New York' (as the *New York Times* put it), was to be the first substantial drama produced out of NBC's Radio City studios. Just three, very small, sets were constructed (Holmes' rooms, Nathan Garrideb's home, plus the office of Inspector Lestrade) and two pre-filmed inserts were featured (a shot of the London skyline, plus a sequence filmed partly in Central Park in which Holmes and Watson take a hansom cab to Nathan's house). Surviving off-screen 'telesnaps' reveal Hector as an Eille Norwood-style Holmes in black cape and widow's peak, with Violet Besson's Mrs Hudson being younger, and prettier, than the norm.

Guided by director/actor Eustace Wyatt (1882-1944), the play was performed six times during the last week of November. Remarkably faithful to its source text – a huge amount of Doyle's dialogue was recited near-verbatim – the production won the approval of the *New York Times*: 'In six performances

for members of The American Radio Relay League, the ingenious welding of film and television production offered an interesting glimpse into the future of a new form of dramatic art.'

Touha Sherlocka Holmese

tr 'The desire of Sherlock Holmes'
Czechoslovakia 1972 parody Studio Barrandov 97m colour
w **Ilja Hurník**, **Stepán Skalsky** *p* **Ilja Hurník** *d* **Stepán Skalsky**
cast Sherlock Holmes: **Radovan Lukavsky** Dr Watson: **Václav Voska** Abrahamová: **Vlasta Fialová** Lady Oberonová: **Marie Rosulková** koncertní mistr: **Bohus Záhorsky** dirigent: **Eduard Kohout** Lord Biddleton: **Miroslav Machácek** Wrubelski: **Vlastimil Brodsky** Yawayoga: **Juraj Herz** tympanista: **Josef Kemr** cellistka: **Marie Drahokoupilová** místoreditel: **Václav Lohnisky** Vrátny: **Václav Trégl** detektiv: **Vladimír Mensík** Pizzelli: **Milan Riehs** reditel opery: **Vladimír Stach** Zabiják: **Pavel Landovsky** Sir A C Doyle: **Josef Patocka** Doprovazec: **Josef Somr** Lékar: **Zdenek Hodr**

Founded on the intriguing premise that Holmes' secret wish was to be freed from the bounds of convention and apply his wits to criminal deeds, *Touha Sherlocka Holmese* is a broadly painted comedy with a vaguely postmodern twist handsomely filmed on location in Prague, Liberec and Hrádek u Nechanic. Beginning with a scene in which Doyle himself sets out the detective's secret ambitions, Holmes' quest to commit the perfect crime is eventually foiled by Watson.

Twenty-one years later, Josef Somr (1934-), who enjoyed a minor role towards the end of the cast list, would be cast as Dr Watson opposite Viktor Preiss' Sherlock Holmes in a half-hour Czech television play, *Splhající professor*. Literally 'The creeping professor', this was apparently a comic adaptation of THE CREEPING MAN (tx 16 April 1993).

The Triumph of Sherlock Holmes

GB 1934 adaptation [THE VALLEY OF FEAR]
Real Art Productions Ltd 82m bw
w **H Fowler Mear**, **Cyril Twyford** *p* **Julius Hagen** *d* **Leslie S Hiscott**

cast Sherlock Holmes: **Arthur Wontner** Professor Moriarty:
Lyn Harding John Douglas: **Leslie Perrins** Ettie Douglas:
Jane Carr Dr Watson: **Ian Fleming** Col Sebastian Moran:
Wilfrid Caithness Cecil Barker: **Michael Shepley**
Ted Balding: **Ben Welden** Boss McGinty: **Roy Emerton**
Inspector Lestrade: **Charles Mortimer** Mrs Hudson:
Minnie Rayner Ames: **Conway Dixon** Captain Marvin:
Edmund D'Alby Jacob Shafter: **Edward Lynds**

'You all know Sherlock Holmes – the whole universe knows him. He's the virile hawk-faced principal of this unique picture, engaged in unravelling the most obscure, devilish mystery that ever tested his fretting powers!'

So ran one of the advertising 'catchlines' which US exhibitors were urged to use in promoting Arthur Wontner's fourth assignment as Sherlock Holmes. The sedate, old world charm which Wontner brought to his Holmes could never be described as 'virile' – indeed, in *The Triumph of Sherlock Holmes*, the writers took account of his age (59) and presented a Holmes going into beekeeping retirement – but his resemblance to the Paget proto-type remains remarkable and his easy insouciance in explicating a hideous murder at Birlstone Castle is a pleasure to watch. Essentially a stage actor, all Wontner lacked was the cinematic dynamism, verging on mania, which Rathbone, Cushing and Brett

A rare candid shot of Arthur Wontner (1875-1960), pictured in November 1935, mid-way between filming **The Triumph of Sherlock Holmes** *and* **Silver Blaze**

would later bring to the role; in short, sex appeal.

The film was unveiled in the UK in February 1935, with *Monthly Film Bulletin* asserting that 'Arthur Wontner is the only Sherlock Holmes. His playing throughout is in perfect character and he seems to have walked straight out of the Sidney Paget illustrations.' 'Arthur Wontner is a perfect Sherlock Holmes,' *Picturegoer*'s Lionel Collier con-firmed. In America, the film opened in May along-side the George O'Brien vehicle *The Millionaire Cowboy* as the final attraction at New York's vener-able Criterion Theatre, which was demolished immediately afterwards. 'You're a sensation, Holmes!' cried Watson in speech-bubble format on the posters. 'Every record broken at the Criterion Theatre New York. It's amazing!' 'Elementary, my dear Watson!' countered Holmes. 'It's my greatest picture.' US critics seemed inclined to agree: 'One of the best Sherlock Holmes stories ever produced' (*Hollywood Reporter*), 'The goings on are grotesque, gory and gripping' (*New York Post*), 'Arthur Wontner is the best of all the Holmes imperson-ators' (*New York Evening Journal*).

Along with the first Basil Rathbone vehicle, **Sir Arthur Conan Doyle's The Hound of the Baskervilles** (1939), *The Triumph of Sherlock Holmes* remains perhaps the most faithful cinematic translation of a Doyle original, in this case THE VALLEY OF FEAR. The only notable deviations are a token appearance from Colonel Sebastian Moran of THE EMPTY HOUSE and a more substantial turn from Professor Moriarty himself. An unseen *éminence grise* in the novel, here he tops and tails the film in the fleshy, beetle-browed person of Lyn Harding, the Welsh barnstormer who, as Dr Rylott, had taken top billing in British & Dominions' **The Speckled Band** three years earlier. Swathed in scarves, Moriarty appears in Holmes' Baker Street rooms early on to wish him 'a pleasant and *perma-nent* retirement' in a confrontation (distilled from THE FINAL PROBLEM and the Gillette play) which Wontner had already performed with Norman McKinnel's Moriarty in **The Sleeping Cardinal**.

Holmes takes Mrs Hudson with him to his country retreat, resulting in some typically charming exchanges between Wontner and Minnie Rayner. (When Holmes commends her chicken casserole, she clucks, 'You let it get cold while you were deducing the age of the chicken.') Watson and Inspector Lestrade soon intrude on

Moriarty (Lyn Harding) wishes Holmes (Arthur Wontner) 'a pleasant and permanent retirement' in **The Triumph of Sherlock Holmes** *(1934)*

Holmes' Sussex lethargy, however, and a cipher message convinces Holmes that 'Some deviltry is brewing against the owner of Birlstone Castle.' So it proves. The apparent murder of US émigré John Douglas is played out in the dark (another effect repeated from **The Sleeping Cardinal**) – and just as well, since we learn later that the weapon was a sawn-off shotgun and, as Lestrade puts it, the victim's 'face [was] completely blown away.'

Ettie Douglas' quavering account of her husband's past – as a Pinkerton agent who infiltrated an American secret society called the Scowrers – ushers us into a lengthy flashback in which the Twickenham team make a surprisingly successful stab at reproducing a Pennsylvania mining community. Kate Cameron of the *New York Sunday News* was not convinced, however. 'All that part of the film concerned with Holmes' investigation of the crime is most interestingly unfolded,' she wrote. 'But that part of the story which is told in a series of flashbacks, with the action taking place in the United States, is just too ridiculous. All the Americans in the film are villains and the leader of a gang is made up to look like Abraham Lincoln.'

Whether resembling Lincoln or not, the prolific, one-eyed character actor Roy Emerton is

terrific as Boss McGinty, assaulting a minion with a feral viciousness that puts Moriarty's posturings in the shade.

Even so, *Kinematograph Weekly* was right to quibble that 'Too much footage is devoted to the American flashback' and that 'much entertainment is lost during the period the fascinating character [of Holmes] is absent' – though this is a charge that could be made against THE VALLEY OF FEAR itself.

Holmes eventually reveals, of course, that Douglas is still with us and the effaced corpse was actually that of his would-be assassin. (Now we know why Leslie Hiscott staged the murder in darkness.) Moriarty turns up, tries to kill Holmes, ascends to the battlements, holds aloft a chunk of masonry with a seething cry of 'Curse you, Holmes!', is climactically shot from his perch and plunges into the moat below – though the effect looks more like a pebble plopping into a small bowl of water. 'Good heavens, Holmes,' gasps Watson. 'It's a long drop...' 'Yes,' agrees Holmes, leaning nonchalantly against a pillar. 'It's rather longer than that required by law, I fancy, my dear Watson – but equally effective.' Whereupon Holmes contentedly lights his pipe and the credits roll. (JR)

The Valley of Fear

GB 1916 adaptation Samuelson Film Mfg Co
6500 feet bw silent
w Harry Engholm p G B Samuelson
d Alexander Butler [unconfirmed]
cast Sherlock Holmes: **H A Saintsbury** Ettie Douglas:
Daisy Burrell Professor Moriarty: **Booth Conway**
McGinty: **Jack Macaulay** John McMurdo: **Cecil Mannering**
Dr Watson: **Arthur M Cullin** Capt Marvin: **Lionel D'Aragon**
Shafter: **Bernard Vaughan** Ted Baldwin: **Jack Clair**

G B Samuelson's follow-up to **A Study in Scarlet** (1914) was a version of the other 'difficult' Holmes novel, the recently published THE VALLEY OF FEAR, also dependent on lengthy flashback sections set in the USA in which the detective does not appear. Even less is known about Samuelson's second attempt than about the first, but the fact that Professor Moriarty is third-credited suggests a slightly licentious adaptation. The director was reportedly Alexander Butler, who would oversee

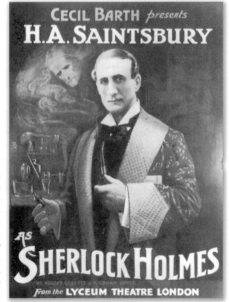

*H A Saintsbury, who appeared as the Great Detective on stage more often than even the great William Gillette, played Holmes only once on screen, in **The Valley of Fear** (1916)*

Samuelson's 1916 version of *The Sorrows of Satan* and direct the Egyptological proto-horror, *The Beetle* (1919). Some sources, however, attribute the film to Fred Paul, who had played Jefferson Hope in **A Study in Scarlet** and later played Nayland Smith in Stoll's Fu Manchu series, several instalments of which he also directed.

The film's relative obscurity probably dates from the year of its release, when it's likely to have been overshadowed by the same year's Essanay-produced **Sherlock Holmes** (1916), in which actor William Gillette played out his Holmes for posterity. If this was the case, it seems unfair given that Samuelson had hired perhaps the second most-noted stage Holmes of the time to replace the amateur James Bragington.

Between 1902 and 1905, H A [Harry Arthur] Saintsbury (1869-1939) had given over 900 recitations of his Holmes in a version of the Gillette play touring the north of England. Five years later, between July and October 1910, he reprised the part at the West End's Adelphi and Globe theatres in Doyle's own stage version of THE SPECKLED BAND, also featuring Lyn Harding as Dr Grimesby Rylott (see **The Speckled Band**, 1931). The *Times* remarked that Saintsbury 'seems to have been born to play Sherlock Holmes', but the actor would be unconvinced by his later efforts to transfer the character to celluloid: 'The character of Holmes, with his inscrutable face and passive attitude, was especially difficult to adapt to the (silent) film; I had to do just the things I had left out on stage.' *The Speckled Band*, again with Saintsbury and Harding, would be briefly revived at the St James's Theatre and the Royal Theatre between September 1921 and January 1922; Saintsbury would tour the Gillette play again towards the end of the decade.

Playing Watson in the Samuelson film was Arthur M Cullin, whose second appearance as the doctor, opposite Eille Norwood's Holmes in Stoll's **The Sign of Four** (1923), has survived. Booth Conway, who played Moriarty, would also appear versus Norwood on screen, as a wicked Oliver Cromwell in Stoll's 1920 production *The Tavern Knight*.

We Present Alan Wheatley as Mr Sherlock Holmes in ...

GB 1951 6 x 35m TV series adaptations BBC Television bw

w **C A Lejeune** *p* **Ian Atkins**
regular cast Sherlock Holmes: **Alan Wheatley**
Dr Watson: **Raymond Francis**

THE EMPTY HOUSE

tx 20 October 1951 BBC Television
regular cast, plus Inspector Lestrade: **Bill Owen**
Colonel Moran: **Eric Maturin** Mrs Hudson: **Iris Vandeleur**
tall thin man: **Clement Hamelin** unimpressed onlooker:
Sam Kydd first nursemaid: **Pamela Barnard**
second nursemaid: **Iris Williams** first errand boy: **Tony
Burton** second errand boy: **Eddie Sutch** 1st PC: **Leslie
Parker*** 2nd PC: **Cecil Petty*** 1st Detective:
Clement Hamelin* 2nd Detective: **Sam Kydd***
3rd Detective: **Charles Johnston***

A SCANDAL IN BOHEMIA

tx 27 October 1951 BBC Television
regular cast, plus the King of Bohemia: **Alan Judd**
Irene Adler: **Olga Edwards** Godfrey Norton: **John Stevens**
Mrs Hudson: **Iris Vandeleur** housekeeper: **Betty Turner**
old cabby: **Michael Raghan** young cabby: **Donald Kemp**
ostlers: **Meadows White**, **John Fitzgerald** and **Vernon Gibb**
scissors grinder: **Meadows White** Cpl guardsman:
John Fitzgerald 1st seedy loafer: **Eric Dodson**
2nd seedy loafer: **Cecil Petty** 1st suburban woman: **Pamela
Barnard** 2nd suburban woman: **Florence Viner**
coffee stall holder: **John Boddington** organ grinder: **Vernon
Gibb** nursemaid: **Alexis Milne** clergyman: **John
Boddington** 1st lounger: **Michael Raghan**
2nd lounger: **Tom Criddle*** 3rd lounger: **Donald Whittle**
guardsman: **Donald Kemp**

THE DYING DETECTIVE

tx 3 November 1951 BBC Television
regular cast, plus Inspector Lestrade: **Bill Owen**
Mr Culverton Smith: **Henry Oscar** Mrs Hudson: **Iris
Vandeleur** Staples: **A G Dennett**

THE REIGATE SQUIRES

tx 17 November 1951 BBC Television
regular cast, plus Colonel Hayter: **H G Stoker** Inspector
Forrester: **Stanley Van Beers** Mr Cunningham: **Beckett
Bould** Alec Cunningham: **Thomas Heathcote** butler: **John
Vere** cook: **Iris Vandeleur** Tweeny: **Pamela Barnard**
PC Perkins: **Victor Platt** PC Barker: **Donald Kemp**
Mr Acton: **Gordon Phillott** milkman: **Cecil Petty***

THE RED-HEADED LEAGUE

tx 24 November 1951 BBC Television
regular cast, plus Inspector Lestrade: **Bill Owen**
Jabez Wilson: **Sebastian Cabot** Vincent Spaulding: **Martin
Starkie** Duncan Ross: **Larry Burns** Mr Merryweather:
Arthur Goulett rejected applicant: **Christopher Hodge**
hopeful applicant: **Nicolas Tannar** 2nd hopeful applicant:
Cecil Petty* 3rd hopeful applicant: **Gordon Collyer**
4th hopeful applicant: **Grenville Wright** 5th hopeful
applicant: **Edmund Warwick** 6th hopeful applicant:
Max Barrett 7th hopeful applicant: **Geoffrey Chater**
PCs: **Geoffrey Chater**, **Max Barrett**

THE SECOND STAIN

tx 1 December 1951 BBC Television
regular cast, plus Inspector Lestrade: **Bill Owen**
Mr Trelawney Hope: **John Robinson** Lady Hilda Trelawney
Hope: **Alvys Maben** the Premier: **J Leslie Frith** Mrs
Hudson: **Iris Vandeleur** Eduardo Lucas: **John Le Mesurier**
PC Macpherson: **Donald Kemp** butler: **Clarence Bigge**
unknown woman: **Pamela Barnard***

Noteworthy for being television's first series of
Sherlock Holmes adaptations, no tapes of
this sextet have survived; indeed, it's highly
unlikely that telerecordings of the live broadcasts
were ever made.

*We Present Alan Wheatley as Mr Sherlock Holmes
in...* is the series title as given on the episodes'
opening caption card, although the BBC listings
magazine *Radio Times* would label them *Alan
Wheatley as Sherlock Holmes in...* There is no
evidence to link the series to BBC Television's first,
isolated Holmes interpretation of the same year
(**For the Children: The Adventure of the Mazarin**

'Practically a documentary programme': the painstakingly authentic 221B interior built for **We Present Alan Wheatley as Mr Sherlock Holmes in ...** (1951)

Stone, transmitted 29 July 1951). Instead, it seems that the series was considered part of the BBC's contribution to the Festival of Britain celebrations – a 'tribute to the great man of Baker Street'. During 1951, some 50,000 people had attended a Sherlock Holmes Exhibition in Baker Street itself.

Quoted in Pointer (1976), star Alan Wheatley recalled the series' genesis as dating from his performance in a TV version of Patrick Hamilton's *Rope*: 'C A Lejeune gave me a marvellous notice in the *Observer* and she finished up by saying, "If the BBC have got any sense they will commission a series of Sherlock Holmes stories and ask Alan Wheatley to play Sherlock Holmes." So the BBC, very unlike them, took this up and wrote to her and said, "All right, if you will do the scripts we will do the series," and that's how they came to be done...'

Wheatley (1907-91), a BBC radio newsreader during the War whose film roles had included *Brighton Rock* (1947), was given Raymond Francis as his Watson. Iris Vandeleur, as Mrs Hudson, and Bill Owen, as Inspector Lestrade, would appear in most of the six plays. In a feature written for *Radio*

Times, Lejeune claimed that 'we picked the stories that seemed likely to give a variety of subject, while rounding out the portrait of the man... We have tried, as loyally as we can, to preserve both the spirit and the high spirits of the original stories' – making this the first of many adaptations to trumpet canonical authenticity as the *sine qua non* for essays into Holmesian lore. 'Holmes, and the Victorian world in which he mainly operated, will not be modernised in this series, nor will they be guyed. The most assiduous care has been taken to see that every historical detail shall be authentic, and Ian Atkins, the producer, insists that for him the series is "practically a documentary programme".'

However high her artistic aspirations, scriptwriter Lejeune foundered when confronted by the practicalities of live television. Wheatley: 'In one particular scene she finished up with a sentence from me, and opened the next scene also with a sentence from me, in heavy disguise, with no time at all for a change! ... In the end the only thing to do was for me to play the previous scene out of camera while I was making-up in the corner of the set.' With each episode being introduced by Nona Liddell's rendition of Offenbach's 'Barcarolle', the series was accorded a high-profile Saturday night slot in the late autumn, recommencing evening transmissions (after the then-obligatory early evening closedown) at 8.00 pm. Typically, a few very brief and usually silent film sequences would be shot the day before live recording – shots of Holmes going into fog, or Holmes and Watson in a cab, for example. One indication of the series' relative crudity is that stage manager Cecil Petty and assistant stage manager Pamela Barnard would have acting roles in almost every episode – a hangover from television drama's roots in the practices of repertory theatre.

Although Wheatley would retain a damning opinion of the entire experience ('I never enjoyed anything less ... it remains a very unpleasing memory for me, because of the dialogue and construction ... In my opinion [Holmes] just seemed to be an insufferable prig'), his performance was fulsomely praised in the *Times*: 'though rather younger and fuller in the face than the Holmes of his opponents' nightmares, [Wheatley] yet catches the essential character. He is a figure, not merely of wonder or of fun, but of romantic possibility.'

Without a Clue

GB/US 1988 parody ITC Productions Ltd 107m colour
w **Gary Murphy, Larry Strawther** *p* **Marc Stirdivant**
d **Thom Eberhardt**
cast Sherlock Holmes: **Michael Caine** Dr Watson: **Ben Kingsley** Inspector Lestrade: **Jeffrey Jones** fake Leslie: **Lysette Anthony** Prof Moriarty: **Paul Freeman** Lord Smithwick: **Nigel Davenport** Mrs Hudson: **Pat Keen** Greenhough: **Peter Cook** Sebastian: **Tim Killick** Wiggins: **Matthew Savage** Peter Giles: **John Warner** real Lesley: **Matthew Sim** Mayor Johnson: **Harold Innocent** John Clay: **George Sweeney** Archie: **Murray Ewan** reporter #1: **Stephen Tiller** reporter #2: **Michael O'Hagan** reporter #3: **Ivor Roberts** photographer: **Martin Pallot** bobby at warehouse: **Gregor Fisher** Constance: **Caroline Milmoe** bartender: **Steven O'Donnell** barrister: **James Bree** singer: **Sarah Parr-Byrne** thug #1: **Clive Mantle** thug #2: **Dave Cooper** Hadlers: **Richard Henry** lady on train: **Lesley Daine** Christabel: **Jennifer Guy** Mr Andrews: **John Tordoff** Mrs Andrews: **Alexandra Spencer** landlady: **Elizabeth Kelly** local #1: **Sam Davies** local #2: **Adam Kotz** constable at Lakes: **John Surman** henchman #1: **Les White** henchman #2: **Chris Webb** dockworker: **Andy Bradford** sergeant at docks: **Evan Russell** driver: **Alan Bodenham** the Duke: **Prince, the Wonder Dog**

THE MYSTERY

The brilliant investigator Dr Watson falls out with Reginald Kincaid, a boorish drunk and failed actor who, for several years, has secretly been paid by Watson to masquerade as the doctor's once-convenient creation, the consulting detective known as 'Sherlock Holmes'. Tired of 'Holmes' taking the credit for his own deductive genius, Watson attempts to promote his own services as 'the Crime Doctor', but discovers that no-one will accept Holmes' apparently dim-witted sidekick as any kind of 'substitute'. When Chancellor of the Exchequer Lord Smithwick attempts to employ Holmes following the theft of the Bank of England's template for the £5 note, Watson is forced to ask Kincaid to lend credence to his investigation by playing Holmes one last time, lest

Mrs Hudson (Pat Keen) discovers that hopeless Holmes actor Reginald Kincaid (Michael Caine) has failed to hang himself in **Without a Clue** *(1988)*

The bungling 'Sherlock Holmes' (Michael Caine) and the brilliant Dr Watson (Ben Kingsley) in **Without a Clue** (1988)

the economy of the entire British Empire be flooded with forgeries and collapse...

THE INVESTIGATION

Watson and 'Holmes' travel to the Lake District in search of Peter Giles, a printer at the Royal Mint who has inexplicably vanished. A drowned body is discovered, and it is assumed that the plates have sunk to the bottom of the Lakes – but Watson later reveals to Giles' daughter Leslie, recently returned from Paris, that her father's 'trail' has been a carefully laid ruse planned by his own arch-enemy, Professor Moriarty. Watson and Holmes confront Moriarty at the Southwark docks, where the master criminal is receiving a smuggled shipment of

printer's ink. However, during an attempt to board Moriarty's boat, Watson is shot, and his body is lost to the Thames...

THE SOLUTION

The despairing Kincaid's chance discovery of a clue apparently placed by Giles within the serial number of one of the forged notes leads the reborn 'Holmes' to Moriarty's printing presses, hidden away under a disused theatre. There, 'Leslie' is revealed to be one of the Professor's cronies, but the alive-and-well Watson reappears, having faked his own demise – and, following a duel with Holmes, Moriarty perishes in a gas explosion. To reporters gathered outside Baker Street, Holmes announces his retirement, his place to be taken by Watson – but Watson persuades the 'Great Detective' to continue his investigations.

✦✦✦

By contriving to invert the roles usually ascribed to Holmes and Watson, then seasoning their characters with several quarts of bile, *Without a Clue* succeeds at being that rare thing – a complete, rounded and coherent full-length Sherlock parody. It might lack the sheer class of, say, **The Private Life of Sherlock Holmes**, or the moments of inspired madness which keep **The Adventure of Sherlock Holmes' Smarter Brother** rat-tat-tatting along, but its steady pace, clear intent and conformity to a traditional three-act structure – qualities more or less lacking in the other two mentioned – serve as good foundations on which to build an only slightly promising premise into a solid, workable and aesthetically pleasing 100-minute-or-so film. It don't contain a lot of Art, but it is a picture one can like.

Beginning life as *The Imposter of Baker Street*, the script would be shorn of co-writer Larry Strawther's many references to the Doyle canon upon being put into production by the independent ITC group. 'A lot was sacrificed to make it broader in appeal,' director Thom Eberhardt confirmed to magazine *Cinefantastique*. 'Mysteries in this vein tend to be very talky with constant explanations about how it happened or about the significance of clues. Audiences once had a tolerance for this but they don't anymore...' Eberhardt, an Emmy award-winning documentarist, had only three features under his belt before being hired by freelance producer Marc Stirdivant, who'd become Walt Disney's youngest-ever staff producer upon writing the silly Michael Crawford vehicle *Condorman* (1981). Claiming to like 'quirky movies about solid interpersonal relationships', the director would describe the film as '*The Odd Couple*, Victorian-style': 'And that's what we have here – two people really worlds apart...'

Shot for just $10 million under a second title, the insipid *Sherlock and Me*, the picture was made in eight weeks at a variety of English locations – Lake Windermere and Derwent Water to the north, then Gloucester, Blenheim Palace, Syon Park and London to the south, with interiors at both Pinewood and Shepperton Studios. Playing cock-er-nee actor Kincaid was cock-er-nee actor Michael Caine, whose rag-bag roster of films had spanned both dizzying highs (*The Ipcress File, Get Carter, Sleuth*) and ignominious lows (*Swarm, Blame it on Rio, Jaws: The Revenge*). Caine was enjoying a small renaissance at the time, with well-received roles in *Mona Lisa, Hannah and Her Sisters* and the comedy *Dirty Rotten Scoundrels*. For the much-admired Anglo-Indian Ben Kingsley, most noted for the lead in *Gandhi* (1982), the bitterly resentful Watson would prove a rare comic part. Other British thesps filled out the cast list, with the indefinable Peter Cook making the last of his several appearances in Sherlock-related satires (principally 1977's woeful HOUND OF THE BASKERVILLES burlesque).

The first 'act' of *Without a Clue* revels in presenting the unpalatable truth behind the fiction of the Doyle stories – to the extent of displaying a mocked-up *Strand Magazine* cover advertising SILVER BLAZE, with Caine/Kincaid's features pasted in Holmes' place. (And can it really be coincidental that the names of actors 'Caine' and 'Kincaid' share a certain homophonic ring?) Thus Mrs Hudson is reconfigured as a pious Presbyterian termagant; likewise, there's a running gag whereby the Baker Street Irregulars, like Fagin's boys, pick the pocket-watches of all they meet. The film continues to deconstruct Holmesian convention throughout its (intentionally pointless) mid-section, ultimately mocking the greatest Sherlockian shibboleth of all – that all things are connected by a chain of absolute logic – in the scenes where Kincaid performs an astonishing feat of intellectual gymnastics in order to deduce the location of Moriarty's hideout.

His train of thought is demonstrated to be entirely spurious, however – which suggests that, in this world, chance, coincidence and anti-rationalism are forces which override the science of pure reason. Or, indeed, that reading too much into anything is a Very Daft Idea.

The picture does flirt with pseudo-postmodern cleverness elsewhere – in the line, 'I was once just a figment of your imagination. Now Sherlock Holmes belongs to the whole world!' perhaps, which might be said to signal the idea that the figure of Sherlock Holmes is now infinitely more potent than the stories which begat him, and in Watson's *Strand* editor being named 'Greenhough', after Doyle's *Strand* editor Herbert Greenhough Smith. But, for the most part, the script is content to keep its discourse solely at the level of the feed and punch-line. (The sot Kincaid's 'An occasional libation enables me to stiffen my resolve' is swiftly rejoined by Mrs Hudson's 'Your resolve should be pickled by now.') The fact of Watson's genius going un-noticed while Holmes' dunderheaded pronouncements are revered runs throughout, to best effect when Holmes, having gingerly prodded a white corpse dragged from Derwent Water, says 'It's my opinion this man is dead!' – only for a flatfoot to one side to whisper, awestruck, 'He's a genius!'

Reviews ranged from the so-so in *Variety* ('This novel approach generates a few laughs and smiles, but of a markedly mild nature and with most of them provoked by the shrewdly judged antics of the two stars') to the downright scathing in

Lysette Anthony as one of Moriarty's more alluring confederates in **Without a Clue** *(1988)*

Monthly Film Bulletin ('If this premise were to be workable, it would require the casting of an actor who could actually pass as the genuine Holmes. As it is, we are simply given a buffoon'). Yes, *Without a Clue* is slightly shoddy round the edges. Yes, it does occasionally err on the side of the clunkingly, ingratiatingly obvious (comedy exploding test-tubes and charred-face make-up ahoy!). But, in its better-judged scenes, it extracts no small degree of pathos from the situation (Kincaid's hopeless despondency following Watson's apparent demise, for example). If its makers had been brave enough to risk fracturing the tone by lingering on some of its more human asides, *Without a Clue* might just have been a great film.

Or, at least, a little more than 'good'.

The Woman in Green

US 1945 pastiche Universal Pictures Company Inc
68m bw

w **Bertram Millhauser** *pd* **Roy William Neill**
cast Sherlock Holmes: **Basil Rathbone** Dr Watson: **Nigel Bruce** Lydia: **Hillary Brooke** Moriarity [sic]: **Henry Daniell** Fenwick: **Paul Cavanagh** Inspector Gregson: **Matthew Boulton** Maude: **Eve Amber** Onslow: **Frederic Worlock** Williams: **Tom Bryson** Crandon: **Sally Shepherd** Mrs Hudson: **Mary Gordon** Waring: **John Burton*** shabby man: **Harold DeBecker*** barman: **Leslie Denison*** Carter: **Tony Ellis*** victim: **Kay Harding*** Commissioner: **Alec Hartford*** newsman: **Tommy Hughes*** Norris: **Olaf Hytten*** short-tempered officer: **Boyd Irwin*** Mowbray: **Violet Seaton*** porter: **Arthur Stenning*** Dr Simnell: **Percival Vivian*** constables: **Ivo Henderson***, **Colin Hunter***

THE MYSTERY

Over several weeks, four young women are found murdered, their right forefingers cleanly severed; all London is horrified by 'the most atrocious murders since Jack the Ripper'. After a dressing-down from the Commissioner of Scotland Yard, Inspector Gregson seeks Sherlock Holmes' counsel. Holmes suspects the killings to be 'incidental to some larger and more diabolical scheme'. At the Pembroke House bar, Holmes and Gregson see widower Sir George Fenwick drinking with a beautiful woman – Lydia Marlowe, who invites Sir George back to her flat. Drugged and mesmerised, Sir George wakes in a shabby hotel

off the Edgeware Road [sic] – where another young woman has been killed. And Sir George has her finger in his pocket...

THE INVESTIGATION

Sir George's daughter, Maude, goes to Holmes after she has observed her father burying the finger in the garden. But Maude has been followed, and when they return to Sir George's house, they find him murdered, clutching a Pembroke House matchbook. Sir George had withdrawn £10,000 the day before, suggesting he was being blackmailed. Holmes suspects the hand of the presumed-dead Professor Moriarty. His suspicions are confirmed when Moriarty appears at 221B to warn the detective off – and when Holmes refuses, Moriarty sets him up for assassination, stationing a sniper, Corporal Williams, in an empty house directly opposite Holmes' rooms. The plot is foiled, but Williams is later killed.

THE SOLUTION

Holmes believes that Moriarty had employed hypnotism on both Fenwick and Williams, and following a tip-off from his brother, Mycroft, visits a private club for hypnotists, the Mesmer. He sees Lydia again – unaware that Moriarty has sent her to lure him back to her flat. There, Lydia attempts to hypnotise Holmes, and seems to have been successful; after making him sign a suicide note, Moriarty urges Holmes to walk off the roof terrace. Holmes is, however, shamming until Dr Watson, Gregson and the police arrive. Lydia is arrested, but Moriarty makes a break across the rooftops – and falls to his doom.

◆ ◆ ◆

In keeping with the Universal series' escalating ghoulishness – throat-cuttings in **The Scarlet Claw**, back-breakings in **The Pearl of Death**, incineration and dismemberment in **The House of Fear** – the ninth Basil Rathbone/Nigel Bruce picture promises to unmask a sexual psychopath given to clipping a finger off each of his attractive young victims. The year being 1945, the premise is glossed over and dropped halfway through – but it's intriguing to note that scriptwriter Bertram Millhauser's first draft, titled *Invitation to Death*, would have seen eight and nine-year-old girls falling prey to the killer.

TEMPTRESS OF PLEASURE OR MISTRESS OF MURDER?

THE WOMAN IN GREEN

Starring

BASIL RATHBONE
NIGEL BRUCE

with
HILLARY BROOKE
PAUL CAVANAGH
HENRY DANIELL
EVE AMBER
SALLY SHEPHERD
MATTHEW BOULTON

A characteristically sensational poster for Universal's **The Woman in Green** *(1945)*

Unsurprisingly, this aspect of the screenplay – submitted to the scrutineers of film industry regulator Joseph I Breen on 21 December 1944, barely three weeks prior to production – was held to be in 'flagrant violation' of the Production Code. The script was duly revised (other Bowdlerisms included the removal of villain Moriarty's clerical disguise), but the finished version remains easily the most sordid of the series: note the scene in which actress Kay Harding is stalked through London's stews, the likes of which would not be seen in a Holmes film until 1965's versus-the-Ripper entry **A Study in Terror**. (Interestingly, Harding's earlier turn as the teenage victim of a maniac in **The Scarlet Claw** had been passed for exhibition unquestioned.) Quite why the character of Dr Simnell was allowed to remain is a matter for debate. Although Millhauser artfully contrives not to state outright that this bow-tied, white-haired, outwardly benevolent old gent is Moriarty's hired murderer, the presentation of an elderly uncle type who is fascinated by children's dolls dressed in nurses' uniforms – and who carries about his person a set of scalpels 'sharp enough to split a hair' – gives the film a nasty, perverted edge.

Rathbone claimed Henry Daniell's Moriarty as his favourite ('There were other Moriartys, but none so delectably dangerous', he wrote in his autobiography, *In and Out of Character*), but it's hard to see why Daniell's cold fish of a Professor should be favoured over the George Zucco and Lionel Atwill interpretations (as seen in 1939's **The Adventures of Sherlock Holmes** and 1942's **Sherlock Holmes and the Secret Weapon** respectively). Only the adversaries' confrontation in Holmes' rooms carries any real weight. 'We shall walk together, hand in hand, through the gates of eternity,' suggests Holmes; 'What a charming picture that would make,' replies Moriarty.

The Professor's rather wet slip off a studio rooftop in the finale is no Reichenbach, either, being a dismissal far more suited to a common thug – but then he's relegated to the status of stooge throughout, consistently outshone by Hillary Brooke's luminous Lydia. Having taken a very minor role in **Sherlock Holmes and the Voice**

At the Mesmer Club, hypnotist Lydia Marlowe (Hillary Brooke) casts her spell over Club chairman Onslow (Frederic Worlock) and Holmes (Basil Rathbone) in **The Woman in Green** (1945)

of Terror, and played the goody-two-shoes Sally Musgrave in **Sherlock Holmes Faces Death**, Brooke (Beatrice Peterson, 1914-99) graduated to full-blown femme fatale as the titular 'Woman in Green', and her ice princess ranks on a level with Gale Sondergaard's **Spider Woman**. She's utterly bewitching in her trick-shot-effected mesmerism scenes; even the famously asexual Holmes is moved to tell Lydia, 'I like the way you look.' Yes, he may be shamming – but much earlier, he's given the untypically naturalistic line, 'C'mon, let's get a drink.'

Dennis Hoey's buffoonish Lestrade is here swapped for Matthew Boulton's altogether more human Inspector Gregson (after A Study in Scarlet, The Sign of the Four, The Greek Interpreter, The Red Circle and Wisteria Lodge); it's a pity that Boulton wasn't retained, for

his despairing opening voiceover gives weight to the premise. Then again, given that the upshot of losing Lestrade is that Watson remains the only possible butt of the picture's humour, perhaps it's just as well that Hoey would return in the next Universal effort, **Pursuit to Algiers**. Here, Watson's only real function is to be hypnotised into slack-jawed idiocy in a padded-out scene at the Mesmer Club; it's a very small mercy that the Breen Office, in one of its better judgments, saw fit to stop the scene short before the doctor dropped his kecks.

A film of real merit, despite some obvious deficiencies in plotting and a very lazy climax, *The Woman in Green* also manages to cram in a condensed retelling of The Empty House, where Moriarty sets a sniper opposite 221B and succeeds only in shooting a dummy detective.

O Xangô de Baker Street

tr 'The Baker Street tango'
*Portugal/Brazil 1999 pastiche MGN Filmes/Sky Light
Cinema Foto e Art Ltd 120m colour*
w **Miguel Faria Jr**, **Patrícia Melo** *source* **O Xangô de Baker
Street** [novel by **Jô Soares**] *p* **Tino Navarro** *d* **Miguel Faria Jr**
cast includes Sherlock Holmes: **Joaquim de Almeida**
Dr Watson: **Anthony O'Donnell** Sarah Bernhardt: **Maria de
Medeiros** Mello Pimenta: **Marco Nanini** Baronez Maria
Luísa: **Cláudia Abreu** Dom Pedro II: **Cláudio Marzo**
Dr Saraiva: **Emiliano Queiroz** Esperidiana: **Letícia
Sabatella** desembargador [appeals court judge]: **Jô Soares**
Marquis de Salles: **Marcello Antony** Miguel: **Caco Ciocler**

B
razilian wit Jô Soares (presenter of a popular
late-night chat show on TV Globo) published
his iconoclastic Portuguese language pastiche *O
Xangô de Baker Street* in 1995. A bestseller, it was
subsequently translated into English as *A Samba
for Sherlock*. Soares' story sees Holmes and Watson
summoned to Rio de Janiero in 1886 to investigate
the disappearance of a Stradivarius violin presented
to the Emperor Dom Pedro II by a favourite
mistress, the Baroness Maria Luísa. Their arrival is
prompted by the intervention of the French actress
Sarah Bernhardt, then appearing at Rio's

Municipal Theatre. The detective docks in Brazil to
find that a serial killer is now at work – a sexual
predator who leaves a single violin string
entangled in the pubic hair of his young female
victims. Along the way, Holmes succeeds in
inventing Brazil's national cocktail, the *caipirinha*.

The feature version, filmed over three months
on location in Oporto, London and then Rio, was
seen in Portugal in 1999 prior to opening the sixth
Festival do Rio on 27 September 2001, its
Brazilian release following on 19 October. Joaquim
de Almeida (1957-), best known to English-speaking
audiences for his villainous role in Robert
Rodriguez's remake of his own *Desperado* (1995),
played Holmes opposite British film and TV actor
Anthony O'Donnell as Watson. The 'divine' Sarah
Bernhardt was incarnated in the form of Maria de
Medeiros (1965-), the babyish Fabienne in Quentin
Tarantino's *Pulp Fiction* (1994), and Soares himself
took a minor role as an appeals court judge. At the
time of writing, this well-received film had not yet
reached British or American screens.

*Latin lust: on the
trail of a Rio
Ripper, Holmes
(Joaquim de
Almeida) meets
the divine Sarah
Bernhardt (Maria
de Medeiros) in*
**O Xângo de
Baker Street**
(1999)

Young Sherlock Holmes

aka **Young Sherlock Holmes and the Pyramid of Fear** [GB]

US 1985 pastiche Paramount Pictures Corporation/ Amblin Entertainment Inc 109m Panavision colour
w **Chris Columbus** *p* **Mark Johnson** *d* **Barry Levinson**
cast Sherlock Holmes: **Nicholas Rowe** John Watson: **Alan Cox** Elizabeth: **Sophie Ward** Rathe: **Anthony Higgins** Mrs Dribb: **Susan Fleetwood** Cragwitch: **Freddie Jones** Waxflatter: **Nigel Stock** Lestrade: **Roger Ashton-Griffiths** Dudley: **Earl Rhodes** Master Snelgrove: **Brian Oulton** Bobster: **Patrick Newell** Reverend Nesbitt: **Donald Eccles** Dudley's friends: **Matthew Ryan**, **Matthew Blakstad**, **Jonathan Lacey** Ethan Engel: **Walter Sparrow** Egyptian tavern owner: **Nadim Sawalha** Mr Holmes: **Roger Brierley** Mrs Holmes: **Vivienne Chandler** curio shop owner: **Lockwood West** cemetery caretaker: **John Scott Martin** school porter: **George Malpas** school Reverend: **Willoughby Goddard** policeman with Lestrade: **Michael Cule** policeman in shop window: **Ralph Tabakin** hotel receptionist: **Nancy Nevinson** voice of older Watson: **Michael Hordern**

THE MYSTERY

A cloaked figure carrying a blowpipe stalks an accountant named Bentley Bobster – and manages to shoot a dart into his neck unnoticed. As he sits down to eat, Bobster suffers an hallucination in which his poultry course comes to life on his plate. Back home, Bobster's bedroom fittings appear to become fire-breathing serpents; convinced the room is ablaze, Bobster leaps to his death from the window. Soon after, the Reverend Nesbitt falls victim to the same assassin; believing a knight in a stained glass church window has come to life, Nesbitt flees into the road and is run over by a carriage. Meanwhile, young John Watson is sent to a boarding school, Brompton, where he is billeted in a dormitory alongside an older student, Sherlock Holmes – the brilliant protégé of schoolmaster Rathe.

Holmes is in love with Elizabeth Hardy, the niece of Rupert T Waxflatter, a retired teacher-turned-inventor who lives on the school premises. Holmes notices that Waxflatter has kept cuttings relating to the deaths of both Bobster and Nesbitt; suspecting a connection between the two, Holmes consults Detective-Sergeant Lestrade, who dismisses his theory. Back at Brompton, Holmes' rival, Dudley Babcock, conspires to have Holmes expelled for cheating in an exam. But as Holmes exits the school gates, Waxflatter himself proves to be the killer's next victim – and accidentally stabs himself to death while attempting to beat off an illusory bronze harpy in a curio shop. Waxflatter's dying words to Holmes are entirely cryptic: 'Ehtar, Holmes, Ehtar.'

THE INVESTIGATION

Holmes trails a mysterious stranger seen at Waxflatter's funeral, but loses the track. Holmes holes up in Waxflatter's rooms; Watson reluctantly agrees to help Holmes and Elizabeth find the killer. Holmes and Watson return an Egyptian blowpipe dropped at the murder scene to the curio shop; the shopkeeper trades them the address of the man who bought the blowpipe from him some time previously. At a seedy Egyptian tavern, the pair are confronted by hostile devotees of Osiris, the Egyptian god of the dead. Beating a retreat, they analyse a piece of cloth torn from the killer's cowl by Elizabeth's dog. This leads all three to a paraffin factory in Wapping, inside which they discover a giant pyramid built by Egyptian cultists. Holmes attempts to prevent the cultists' masked high priest from mummifying a still-living girl; the attempt is unsuccessful, and all three are struck by the nightmare-inducing darts in their flight, only just escaping with their lives.

A picture showing Waxflatter and the two other victims as young men leads them to identify the next target: Chester Cragwitch, the man seen at the funeral. Cragwitch tells Holmes and Watson that in Egypt, many years previously, the four had discovered an underground pyramid containing the tombs of five Egyptian princesses; they stirred up local unrest, leading to the massacre of many

The prodigy:
Nicholas Rowe is
**Young Sherlock
Holmes** *(1985)*

local villagers by the British Army. 'Ehtar' was a surviving Anglo-Egyptian boy who, together with his sister, swore vengeance on the four. Too late, Holmes realises that 'Ehtar' backwards spells 'Rathe'. They rush back to the school – but Rathe and his secret sister, school matron Mrs Dribb (actually the assassin), have already kidnapped Elizabeth, who is to be the fifth English girl murdered by the cultists in their bid to avenge the five ancient princesses...

THE SOLUTION

Holmes and Watson pilot Waxflatter's 'flying machine' to Wapping, crashing into the frozen Thames close by. Holmes then contrives to bring the cultists' own pyramid down on them before Elizabeth can be sacrificed. Mrs Dribb is killed, but Holmes is left for dead in the burning pyramid; Watson simultaneously rescues Holmes and prevents Rathe from escaping with Elizabeth. Elizabeth is mortally wounded when she steps in front of a bullet Rathe fires at Holmes; Rathe and Holmes duel on the frozen river, where Rathe meets his apparent end, sinking into the icy depths. Elizabeth dies. Heartbroken, Holmes gathers up the things he has collected during the

adventure – a deerstalker, a pipe and Rathe's coat – and makes his lonely way out of the school. In Switzerland, a man signs into an Alpine hotel under the name 'Moriarty': it is Rathe.

✦ ✦ ✦

It comes as some surprise that *Young Sherlock Holmes*, a picture produced under the executive eye of Steven Spielberg – the director who, in the seventies and eighties, rewrote the Hollywood record books with the enormously successful *Jaws*, *Close Encounters of the Third Kind* and *ET* (the latter referenced in *Young Sherlock Holmes*, when Waxflatter's flying machine crosses the moon) – should prove quite so downbeat. Cravenly book-ended by two verbose on-screen disclaimers ('Although Sir Arthur Conan Doyle did not write about the very youthful years of Sherlock Holmes and did establish the initial meeting between Holmes and Dr Watson as adults, this affectionate speculation about what might have happened has been made with respectful admiration and in tribute to the author and his enduring works' – oh, *please*), heresy is the least of the crimes of which the film might be accused. Its single Academy Award nomination might make it a rarity in

Close encounters: the juvenile Holmes (Nicholas Rowe) and Watson (Alan Cox) take to the air in Waxflatter's flying machine in **Young Sherlock Holmes** *(1985)*

Elstree Studios, Borehamwood, Hertfordshire, with other locations including Wapping, East London and Radcliffe Square, Oxford.

Its three young principals were all virtual unknowns: as Holmes, MP's son Nicholas Rowe (born 1966), an Old Etonian who'd appeared in *Another Country* (1984), Merchant-Ivory's drama of homosexual stirrings in an English public school; as Watson, Alan Cox, the 14-year-old son of actor Brian; as Elizabeth, Sophie Ward (born 1966), daughter of actor Simon and with minor roles in *The Hunger* (1983) and *Return to Oz* (1985) to her credit.

Groundbreaking computer-assisted effects work by Industrial Light & Magic, a facility set up in the wake of *Star Wars* (1977), gave life to the 'Glass Man', the stained-glass knight which menaces the Reverend Nesbitt, but other techniques employed were rather more traditional. 'Go-motion' animated the gargoyle-like bookends that torment Waxflatter, while rod puppets were used in the scene where the contents of an imaginary pantry come to life to threaten young Watson (the realisation of which took Dr Pretorius' 'miniature people' in 1935's *Bride of Frankenstein* for its inspiration).

The many, many ways in which *Young Sherlock Holmes* contradicts the 'Sacred Writings' are glaringly obvious (Holmes and Watson first meeting nearly 20 years prior to their first meeting in A STUDY IN SCARLET, etc) – but leaving Doylean pedantry aside, the fundamental problem with Columbus' story is that it bears precious little resemblance to a Sherlock Holmes plot. Many commentators have remarked on the similarities between *Young Sherlock Holmes* and *Indiana Jones and the Temple of Doom* (1984), the Spielberg-directed prequel to *Raiders of the Lost Ark* (1981) in which Harrison Ford's adventurer-archaeologist uncovers a homicidal band of Thuggees at work in 1930s India. Although it's entirely true to say that the 'pyramid' sequences in *Young Sherlock Holmes* – in which our heroes (adventurer, his love interest and his short, round sidekick) observe a foreign cult's high priest practicing ritual sacrifice in a vast, hidden temple – are near shot-for-shot identical to the *Temple of Doom* scenes in which our heroes (adventurer, his love interest and his sidekick, Short Round) observe a foreign cult's high priest practicing ritual sacrifice in a vast,

Sherlockian cinema; that that nomination should be for visual effects trickery tells a tale in itself.

Young Sherlock Holmes was made by Amblin Entertainment, a company founded by Spielberg, Kathleen Kennedy and Frank Marshall. Amblin's previous productions had included the grotesque comedy *Gremlins* (1984) and a dismal children's treasure-hunt adventure, *The Goonies* (1985) – both of which were scripted by *Young Sherlock Holmes'* screenwriter Chris Columbus, who would later become the director responsible for the unfathomably popular family-friendly films *Home Alone* (1990) and *Mrs Doubtfire* (1993). *Young Sherlock Holmes* avoids a similar insipidity, but then it enjoys a director of a different calibre altogether: Baltimore-born former stand-up comic Barry Levinson, whose prior works had included nostalgic coming-of-age movie *Diner* (1982) and baseball drama *The Natural* (1984). Levinson was joined by Mark Johnson, producer of both of the latter, on the Holmes picture, which was filmed in the UK in the summer of 1985 at the Thorn EMI hidden temple, it's a little disingenuous to suggest, as some have, that one is simply a more child-friendly remake of the other – certainly when one considers alternative sources for *Young Sherlock Holmes...*

The blowpipe-wielding assassin might be said to derive from Tonga in THE SIGN OF THE FOUR, were it not for the fact that such a character would be equally at home in the Fu Manchu stories of Sax Rohmer, in which a foreign malefactor establishes himself as a kingpin among the immigrant workforce of a fogbound olde London; in which exotic poisons, such as 'the Zayat Kiss', cause mysterious deaths in locked rooms; in which the villain builds himself a base of operations among the creaking wharves of the eastern Thames; in which hordes of obsessive devotees of the villain menace the dogged detective on the trail of their overlord, his eternal, seemingly indestructible, adversary... (Although Rohmer is most known for his stories and novels featuring the Chinese 'devil doctor' Fu Manchu, beginning with 1913's *The Mysterious Dr Fu-Manchu*, it should also be noted that many other of his works, such as 1914's *The Romance of Sorcery*, display evidence of the writer's life-long obsession with quasi-Egyptological mysticism – another key facet of *Young Sherlock Holmes*.) Put bluntly, Columbus' screenplay is an elegant and reasonably expert pastiche of another series of early 20th century British thrillers entirely – a series so removed in concept, style, intended effect and intellectual weight as to be anathema to Doyle's Holmes.

No wonder, then, that *Young Sherlock Holmes* is held in such generally low regard by aficionados, despite its many virtues: Holmes' youthful insouciance (he believes that three days ought to be long enough to master the violin); a *tour de force* sequence in which Holmes is challenged to recover a stolen fencing trophy; Holmes' baiting of a patronising, piggy-faced Detective-Sergeant Lestrade; an utterly charming little scene in which Watson is finally persuaded to assist the expelled Holmes, so breaking school rules (Watson: 'I can't afford to jeopardise my medical career.' Holmes: 'Weasel.' Watson, huffy: 'I'm not a weasel. I'm just – practical.' Holmes, cutting: 'Weasels *are* practical...'); and, strikingly, Holmes' hallucination, in which he imagines a bizarre domestic tableau

where he fails an austere and aloof father. Altogether less successful are the film's efforts to describe the making of the man: Holmes' desire never to be alone is dashed by the strangely distant death of the strangely remote Elizabeth – an aspect doubtless distressing for a young audience, but quite in tune with the film's rather cruel, near-sadistic edge. Note also the killing of cuddly father figure Waxflatter, beautifully played by Nigel Stock – Watson in the two sixties BBC TV series **Sherlock Holmes** and **Sir Arthur Conan Doyle's Sherlock Holmes** – which is as one with the film's many gleeful, comic-horrific, special effects slayings.

Famously failing to make any real impact at the box-office (reportedly, it grossed just $4.25 million in the USA), *Young Sherlock Holmes* may have flopped in its day – but ought now to be feted as a dress rehearsal for something in an altogether different league. The terrifyingly profitable *Harry Potter and the Philosopher's Stone* (2001), based on the literary exploits of the most noted fictional character of the age, sees a precocious clever-clogs, his sort-of girlfriend and his weaselly sidekick uncover nefarious goings-on at an English public school, all orchestrated by a wicked schoolmaster devoted to devilish ways. Spearheading an ongoing franchise, *Harry Potter and the Philosopher's Stone* was, of course, directed by Chris Columbus.

Young Sherlock: The Mystery of the Manor House

GB 1982 8 x TV serial [1 x 60m/7 x 30m] pastiche Granada Television colour
w **Gerald Frow** *p* **Pieter Rogers** *d* **Nicholas Ferguson**
regular cast Sherlock: **Guy Henry** Jasper Moran: **Christopher Villiers** Dr Sowerbutts: **David Ryder-Futcher** John Whitney: **Tim Brierley** Mrs Turnbull: **June Barry** [1-4, 6-8] Ranjeet: **Lewis Fiander** [1-7] Uncle Gideon: **John Fraser** [1-4, 6-8] Aunt Rachel: **Heather Chasen** [1-4, 6-8] Charity: **Eva Griffith** [1-4, 6-8] Mrs Cunliffe: **Jane Lowe** [1-4, 7-8] Charlotte Whitney: **Zuleika Robson** [1-4, 6-8] Natty Dan: **Davy Kaye** [1] Anil: **Raj Patel** [1-2, 4, 6-7] Colonel Turnbull: **Donald Douglas** [1-7] Sergeant Grimshaw: **Tom Chatto** [1-3, 5] Newbugs: **Ian McCurrach** [1-2, 7-8] Captain Cholmondeley: **Andrew Johns** [2, 6-8]

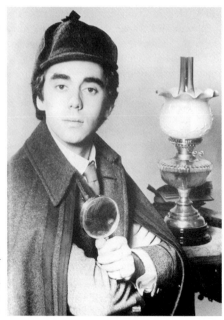

Guy Henry as the teenage hero of **Young Sherlock: The Mystery of the Manor House** *(1982)*

Tom Hudson: **Robert Grange** [3-4]
the Munshi: **Stefan Kalipha** [4] Mr Prendergast: **Dennis Edwards** [4] Albert Bates: **Brian Orrell** [5-6]
William Greasley: **Michael Irwin** [6-8]
Queen Victoria: **Marina McConnell** [8]

[1] THE YOUNG MASTER
tx 31 October 1982 ITV

[2] THE GIPSY CALLS AGAIN
tx 7 November 1982 ITV

[3] THE RIDDLE OF THE DUMMIES
tx 14 November 1982 ITV

[4] A SINGULAR THORN
tx 21 November 1982 ITV

[5] THE WOMAN IN BLACK
tx 28 November 1982 ITV

[6] THE GLASS CUTTER'S HAND
tx 5 December 1982 ITV

[7] THE UNEXPECTED VISITORS
tx 12 December 1982 ITV

[8] THE EYE OF THE PEACOCK
tx 19 December 1982 ITV

THE MYSTERY
Lancashire, November 1871: 17-year-old boarding-school pupil Sherlock Holmes returns home to Pendarg Manor, only to find the family seat in the possession of an ex-Indian Army type, Colonel Turnbull – whose 'nephew', Jasper Moran, sets a dog to chase Sherlock away. Bankruptcy has forced Sherlock's parents into exile in France, leaving their son in the care of two pious relatives, Aunt Rachel and Uncle Gideon. When a travelling patterer called Natty Dan is found dead in a forester's hut close to the manor, Sherlock resolves to investigate Pendarg and its new owners ...

THE INVESTIGATION
Local poacher 'Newbugs' helps Sherlock to conclude that Natty Dan fell victim to a poisoned thorn delivered by a Labrador. What's more, Dan's hastily-scrawled final message to the world – 'HAY BAG. OLD MO' – helps expose the supposedly-invalid 'Mrs Turnbull' as none other than an ex-music hall performer named Bessie Bright. More mysteries – such as why a stolen tailor's dummy has been found in the woods – lead Sherlock to break into the manor accompanied by a local doctor, John Whitney. There, they find an outrageous scheme being rehearsed: an attempt to drug Queen Victoria during a state visit to the local railway, temporarily replacing the monarch with her double, Bessie Bright, who has been tutored by one Professor Moriarty. Her mission? To steal the Koh-i-Noor diamond, substituting a fake in its stead.

THE SOLUTION
Captured by the villains, Sherlock and Whitney awake in hospital to discover that a whole week has passed, and the scheme since stopped – or so it seems. In truth, their 'ward' is a room in Pendarg, and the plan is still in progress. Escaping a poison gas trap, Sherlock sees that the plot is foiled. His fellow conspirators' schemes ruined, Jasper warns Sherlock that he has not heard the last of the names Moran and Moriarty. Next February, Sherlock and his allies are rewarded by a grateful Queen Victoria, who swears them all to secrecy in the affair.

✦ ✦ ✦

Autumn 1982 was a good time to be a juvenile devotee of Sherlock Holmes. No sooner had the BBC's Tom Baker ended his Sunday teatime quest for **The Hound of the Baskervilles** than – the very next week, and in an identical slot – ITV's *Young Sherlock* commenced his researches into goings-on at the manor house of his forefathers. Guy Henry, the RADA-trained 21-year-old godson of comedian Charlie Drake, played the beetle-browed 17-year-old Sherlock – a scion of the landed Lancashire gentry, surprisingly! – whose juvenile adventures, written by Gerald Frow, would fill up the next eight weeks' airtime.

Each episode opens with a pair of hands – Watson's, presumably – playing a series of Edison wire phonograph recordings marked: 'To be handed to Doctor Watson and listened to only after my death'. The voice of the since-deceased Holmes (not credited to any actor) recaps events at the outset of each instalment, the first beginning: 'You may have thought, my dear Watson, that with my demise you had heard the last of your old friend Sherlock Holmes. As you will now perceive, this is not so. Since our last meeting all those years ago, I have assiduously devoted my retirement to recording, as accurately as memory will allow, details of certain events that took place during my youth ... of which I have hitherto apprised no-one. The first of these adventures I choose to call *The Mystery of the Manor House*.'

Times reviewer Dennis Hackett summarised the opening, double-length, 'Chapter' thus: 'The story finds Holmes, home from school, to discover father and mother abroad, owing to the former's bankruptcy, the house sold and in the hands of some upper-class weirdos and an Irish wolfhound without a glimmer of Celtic charm ... Holmes, bitten but not terribly dismayed, in keeping with the overwhelming superiority of later years, has to lodge in the household of his Uncle Gideon's upstart sister, a household stocked with characters for whom, one might suppose, Mr Frow owes some debt to Dickens.' True enough – many minutes of each episode are devoted to laboured routines involving these prim provincials, not to mention the eccentric 'Dr Sowerbutts'. Several nods to Sherlockian lore are contained within. Holmes is seen to adopt both deerstalker and Meerschaum pipe during the story, and we learn that he can differentiate types of tobacco ash after studying the remains left by his father, a cigar connoisseur. Aunt Rachel's cook, Liza-Anne

Cunliffe, is a 36-year-old widow whose suitor, a mail train guard named Tom Hudson, has asked her to be his wife, and to live with him in a small Baker Street house he's inherited. Jasper Moran, we learn, has a brother called Sebastian (as appears in THE EMPTY HOUSE).

Although lacking in pace and dated in style, *Young Sherlock* builds in interest, but only as far as its penultimate Chapter, where the villains' dastardly plot is summarily halted off-screen. The only proper dramatic event from here on – Colonel Turnbull's transport being blown up – occurs out-of-vision, too, leading one to suspect that a tight budget has been allowed to dictate the unfolding of the story. (It seems bizarre that Moriarty, the mastermind behind the plot, is barely present; indeed, he is only glimpsed in a night-time long shot, riding up to the manor on horseback.) The whole of the final Chapter is a dismal coda to the main action, of no consequence save some 'There's just one thing I don't understand'-style exposition. Worse, Holmes' voiceover goes on to describe what an anticlimax the whole thing is!

A second *Young Sherlock* serial was planned – probably *The Adventure of Ferryman's Creek*, which would have paired him up with brother Mycroft – but it never appeared. Producers Granada Television instead continued to develop the rather more feted Jeremy Brett project, **The Adventures of Sherlock Holmes** (1984-5). Intriguingly, Henry went on to appear as a public schoolboy in boaters-and-buggery drama *Another Country* (1984), alongside one Nicholas Rowe – who would shortly land the starring role in the altogether more grand **Young Sherlock Holmes**.

Your Show Time: the Adventure of the Speckled Band

US 1949 TV adaptation [THE SPECKLED BAND]
Marshall Grant-Realm Television 28m bw
tx 25 March 1949 CBS
w **Walter Doniger** d **Sobey Martin**
cast includes Helen Stoner: **Evelyn Ankers**
Sherlock Holmes: **Alan Napier** Dr Watson: **Melville Cooper**
host: **Arthur Shields**

Known as *Story Theater* on some stations, *Your Show Time* was a relatively highbrow 26-part series of short story adaptations: works transferred to the small screen included Robert Louis Stevenson's *The Sire de Malétroit's Door* (tx 28 January 1949), Guy de Maupassant's *Mademoiselle Fifi* (tx 4 February 1949) and Théophile Gautier's *The Mummy's Foot* (tx 11 February 1949). Doyle's THE SPECKLED BAND came tenth in the run, with British actor Alan Napier (1903-88), now known principally for his recurring role as Wayne family butler Alfred Pennyworth in the mid-1960s *Batman* TV series, as an aristocratic Holmes. Universal horror dreamgirl Evelyn Ankers, previously seen opposite Basil Rathbone in both **Sherlock Holmes and the Voice of Terror** and **The Pearl of Death**, headed the cast as Holmes' oppressed and fearful client Helen Stoner.

Das Zeichen der Vier

Germany 1974 TV movie adaptation [THE SIGN OF THE FOUR] *Bavaria Film/Zweites Deutsches Fernsehen 55m colour*
tx 8 June 1974
w **Jean Ferry, Jacques Nahum** *d* **Jean-Pierre Decourt**
cast Sherlock Holmes: **Rolf Becker** Mary Morstan: **Gila von Weitershausen** Dr Watson: **Roger Lumont** Thaddeus Sholto: **Hans Peter Hallwachs** Lestrade: **Dieter Kirchlechner** Rao: **Osman Ragheb** Jonathan Small: **Hans Elwenspoek** Mrs Hudson: **Gisela Hoeter** Mrs Smith: **Senta Sommerfeld** Sammy: **Edgar Maschmann** Wiggins: **Helge Jacobsen**

Following on from **Der Hund von Baskerville** (1955) and the Erich Schellow-headlining **Sherlock Holmes** series (1967-8), this one-off version of THE SIGN OF THE FOUR starring the much-credited TV actor Rolf Becker (1935-) is the last Sherlockian production to have originated in Germany to date.

It's a matter of the greatest regret that *Sherlock Holmes und die sieben Zwerge* ('Sherlock Holmes and the Seven Dwarves'), an eight-part children's fantasy serial of the early 1990s, seems to have featured no Sherlock at all, headlining instead one Alfred Müller as retired detective 'Hans Holms'.

Appendix

The Lost Detektivfilms

In the last years of the Kaiser, a vast number of silent Sherlock Holmes pictures were released in Germany. Serials such as **Arsène Lupin contra Sherlock Holmes** and **Der Hund von Baskerville** (1914-20) are obscure enough, but beneath them lie whole strata of forgotten films – missing, presumed destroyed, along with substanstial contemporaneous records of their content. (Of course, precious few German films were exported to either Britain or America from 1914 on, thus restricting textual resources to a handful of German-language magazines.) Some of these were mere novelty featurettes – for example, Lloyd-Film GmbH's *Karlchens Traum als Sherlok Holmes* ('Karlchen's dream of Sherlok [sic] Holmes', 1914), the title of which strongly implies a 'fantasist' short. Others are rather more intriguing... but details are scarce, often apocryphal, and more-than-likely unreliable.

Ein Meisterstück von Sherlock Holmes
(1908)

'A Sherlock Holmes masterpiece' – a one-reel short about which no details are known.

Ein Fall für Sherlock Holmes
(1911)

'A case for Sherlock Holmes', produced by Henri Adolph Müller, was a comedy about a pickpocket who succeeds in escaping his pursuers – including Holmes? – by means of a succession of disguises.

Schlau, schlauer, am schlauesten!
(CIRCA 1912)

'Smart, smarter, smartest!' was the German title of a long-lost picture originally produced by the French company Eclipse. Presumably a parody, it featured four of the most popular pre-war screen detectives – Pathé's comic Nick Winter, plus three Éclair heroes: Nick Carter (from the literally thousands of adventures of an American investigator, written by various hands and first published in *New York Weekly* in 1886); Nat Pinkerton (a German invention of 1907, whose exploits, with titles like *The Devil's Automobile*, *In the Den of the Sea Criminals* and *Mr Kennedy's Orang-utan*, were reprinted all over Europe); and, of course, Sherlock Holmes (whose first French screen outings are noted under **... From the Adventures of Sherlock Holmes**).

An October 1912 edition of *Der Kinematograph* detailed the quite bizarre plot of *Schlau, schlauer, am schlauesten!* as follows: while staying at the Hotel Royal in Aubagne, a Countess, the Grafin Verdeuil, is robbed of her jewellery by a thief who makes his escape by aeroplane. However, the machine suffers a mechanical failure and crashes in flames near Gardane; the thief is dragged unconscious from the wreckage and taken to a hostel. Meanwhile, the Countess writes to detective Nat Pinkerton, asking him to investigate the theft. Pinker-ton receives her request while breakfasting with his fellow investigators Nik Carter, Nik Winter [both *sic*] and Sherlock Holmes. Pinkerton leaves, but his jealous colleagues, wanting a share of the finder's fee, decide to hold up his investigation; Carter has already doped Pinkerton with an opium cigar. At the Hotel Royal, Pinkerton finds an airman's suit in the room next to the Countess', and his suspicions are further aroused on reading a newspaper report about a pilot who has crashed near Gardane, but is refusing to give his name.

Disguised as a coachman, Pinkerton visits the wounded airman and finds the jewellery hidden under his pillow. When the rival detectives follow Pinkerton's trail to Gardane, they find the thief tied to his bed and a note from Pinkerton telling them that he has the jewellery already – and that they can take the thief home. The next train, however, has not yet left, and so, with the pilot in tow, they race to the station in a variety of disguises: Winters as a Russian, Holmes as his wife and Carter as a priest. But Pinkerton has anticipated that the three would attempt to swipe the jewellery en route and, donning a mask, sets up a life-sized doll in his compartment, which Winter duly robs in the night. Thinking themselves victorious, Carter, Winter and Holmes leap off the train, leaving the airman behind – whereupon the masked Pinkerton promptly arrests him, and takes both the thief and the in-fact-intact jewellery back to the Countess in triumph.

Detektiv Braun,
aka Sherlock Holmes contra Dr Mors
(CIRCA 1914)
See **Der Hund von Baskerville** (1914-20).

Ein Schrei in der Nacht
(1915)
'A scream in the night' was a 4101-foot three-reeler made by Decla-Film-Gesellschaft/Holz & Co, Berlin. Directed by Alwin Neuß, this is supposed to have seen Neuß reprise his starring role as Sherlock Holmes – after **Milliontestamentet** (1910) and the earlier instalments of **Der Hund von Baskerville**.

Sherlock Holmes auf Urlaub
(CIRCA 1916)
'Sherlock Holmes on holiday', produced and directed by Carl Schönfeld, was a series that extended to at least two episodes, one of which was called *Der Wärwolf* ('The werewolf'). It is sometimes said to have also featured Neuß, as is...

Sherlock Holmes nächtliche Begegnung
(CIRCA 1916)
... 'Sherlock Holmes' nocturnal encounter', a Vitascope GmbH four-reeler.

William Voss, der Millionendieb
(1916)
'William Voss, the thief of millions' was a three-reel feature written and produced by Rudolf Meinert, director of the first two pictures in the **Der Hund von Baskerville** series (1914-20), and released by his own company, Meinert-Film. Apparently based on a story by Turszynsky, its 'exciting' and 'constantly surprising' narrative was spelled out in great detail in a January 1916 edition of *Der Kinematograph*: William Voss is the servant of an aged and paralysed Count who has been maintained for years by a charitable association –

but the association's president, who harbours certain suspicions regarding the Count's circumstances, asks Sherlock Holmes to infiltrate the Count's castle. There, Holmes discovers that the Count has in fact been buried in a vault for ten years – during which time Voss has been using a life-sized dummy of the hermit-like Count to help him acquire a fortune.

It seems entirely possible, however, that *Der Kinematograph* got it wrong, and that the character it nominated as Sherlock Holmes was, in fact, a rival detective named Harry Higgs, as featured in several other Meinert-Film productions of the time. Other titles in the 'Harry Higgs-Serie' included *Der gelbe Ulster* ('The yellow Ulster') and *Das Geheimnis der Pagode* ('The secret of the pagoda'); *William Voss, der Millionendieb* may be an alternate title for the Higgs episode *John Rool*. Even more confusingly, a comedy film with musical numbers entitled *Peter Voss, der Millionendieb* was released in 1930; apparently based on a novel by Ewald Gerhard Seelinger, it was remade in 1946 and 1958. The *Peter* films do not appear, to the uninitiated, to have any relation to *William*.

Die Erdstrommotor
(CIRCA 1917) AND SEQUELS
Probably the most frustrating hole in the history of Sherlock Holmes on screen, *Die Erdstrommotor* ('The earthquake motor') was the first of 12 or more four-reel adventures – possibly a series, perhaps a serial – produced by Kowo Gesellschaft/Filmfabrikation GmbH between 1917 and 1919. Most appear to have been written by Paul Rosenhayn and directed by Carl Heinz Wolff (1883-1942).

The first three films are said to have all featured actor Hugo Flink as Holmes: *Die Erdstrommotor*, plus *Die Kasette* ('The casket', 3983 feet) and *Der Schlangenring* ('The snake ring', 3724 feet, perhaps a version of THE SPECKLED BAND). The titles *XYZ* (4613 feet) and *Brockhaus, Band 13* (4330 feet) are sometimes listed as episodes four and five. Stage impresario and silent film Svengali Ferdinand Bonn is believed to have played either Holmes or the villainous 'Dr Mors' (a character derived from Bonn's own Sherlock Holmes stage play of 1906; see **Der Hund von Baskerville**, 1914-20) in several instalments beginning with *Was er im Spiegel sah*

('What he saw in the mirror', 4144 feet), and then *Die Gifteplombe* ('The poisoned seal', 3999 feet), *Das Schicksal der Renate Yongk* ('The destiny of Renate Yongk', 4314 feet, perhaps written by Werner Bernhardy), *Die Dose des Kardinals* ('The Cardinal's snuffbox', between 3953 and 4354 feet). Episodes ten and eleven were *An den ersten Staatsanwalt* ('To the public prosecutor', between 4429 and 4918 feet) and *Echte Perlen* ('Real pearls', 3202 to 3379 feet).

The sequence may have concluded with *Der Mord im Splendid Hotel* ('The murder in the Hotel Splendid', 3671 to 4127 feet, possibly featuring Kurt Brenken-dorff as Holmes). A thirteenth film, *Der indische Spinne* ('The Indian spider'), is said to have been one of these films, too – but, unlike the others mentioned here, it is not numbered as part of Kowo's sequential 'Sherlock Holmes-Serie' in the *Deutsche Filmografie*.

Rotterdam-Amsterdam
(1918)
See **Sherlock Holmes contra Professor Moryarty**.

Drei Tage tot
(1919)
Or 'Three Days Dead', a 'Detektiv-Drama in 3 Akten' released by Rhein, Lichtbild-AG Bioscop-Konzern, Köln. Directed by a Swede, Nils Olaf Chrisander (1884-1947), this was supposedly based on the story of The Dying Detective.

Das Detektivduell,
aka Harry Hill contra Sherlock Holmes
(1921)
Valy Arnheim (1883-1950), who would go on to play Barrymore in **Der Hund von Baskerville** (1929), directed and co-produced this five-act 'duelling detectives' story submitted to the German film censor in January 1921.

To enable this book to be read as a continuous history, this timeline lists every A-Z entry together with the actors who played Sherlock Holmes in each case. To show the order in which Holmes' various interpreters were presented to the public, the dates given are those of release and therefore do not always correspond to the copyright dates given in the body of the book. A number of noteworthy events in Sherlockian and screen history are also referenced.

1887
- First Sherlock Holmes story, A STUDY IN SCARLET, published in *Beeton's Christmas Annual*

1888
- 'Jack the Ripper' killings in London's East End

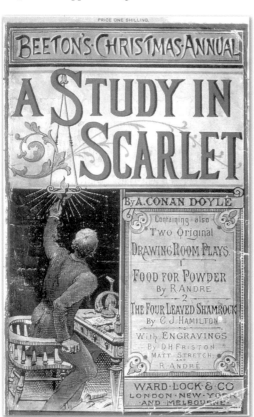

1891
- Thomas Edison patents his 'Kinetoscope'
- A SCANDAL IN BOHEMIA begins the first series of Holmes adventures in the *Strand Magazine*

1892
- Basil Rathbone born

1893
- THE FINAL PROBLEM published: Holmes 'dies' at the Reichenbach Falls

1896
- Lumière brothers open Le Cinematographé in Paris

1899
- First night of William Gillette's play *Sherlock Holmes*

1900
- **Sherlock Holmes Baffled** [unknown]

1901
- Queen Victoria dies
- THE HOUND OF THE BASKERVILLES begins serialisation in the *Strand*

1903
- Holmes returns from the 'dead' proper in THE EMPTY HOUSE

1905
- *Variety* begins publication
- **The Adventures of Sherlock Holmes** [unknown]

1908
- Death of *Strand* artist Sidney Paget
- **Sherlock Holmes and the Great Murder Mystery** [unknown]
- **Sherlock Holmes i Livsfare** [Viggo Larsen]
- **Raffles Flugt Fra Fængslet** [Viggo Larsen]
- **Det Hemmelige Dokument** [Einar Zangenberg]

1909
- Sangerindens Diamanter [Viggo Larsen]
- Droske Nr. 519 [Viggo Larsen]
- Den Grå Dame [Viggo Larsen]

1910
- Den Forklædte Guvernante [Otto Lagoni]
- Sherlock Holmes i Bondefangerkløer [Otto Lagoni]
- Arsène Lupin contra Sherlock Holmes [Viggo Larsen]

1911
- Sherlock Holmes contra Professor Moryarty [unknown]
- Den Sorte Haand [Otto Lagoni]
- Milliontestamentet [Alwin Neuß]
- Hotelrotterne [Einar Zangenberg]
- Den Sorte Hætte [Lauritz Olsen]

1912
- British Board of Film Censors established
- ... From the Adventures of Sherlock Holmes [unconfirmed]

1913
- Peter Cushing born
- Sherlock Holmes Solves 'The Sign of the Four' [Harry Benham]

1914
- Der Hund von Baskerville [Alwin Neuß, Eugen Berg, Kaiser-Titz]
- A Study in Scarlet [James Bragington]
- A Study in Scarlet [Francis Ford]

1916
- The Valley of Fear [H A Saintsbury]
- Sherlock Holmes [William Gillette]

1921
- The Adventures of Sherlock Holmes [Eille Norwood]
- The Hound of the Baskervilles [Eille Norwood]

1922
- The Further Adventures of Sherlock Holmes [Eille Norwood]
- Sherlock Holmes [John Barrymore]

1923
- The Last Adventures of Sherlock Holmes [Eille Norwood]
- The Sign of Four [Eille Norwood]

1926
- John Logie Baird demonstrates television

1927
- *The Jazz Singer* becomes the first successful sound picture
- Publication of the last Holmes adventure, SHOSCOMBE OLD PLACE

1929
- Der Hund von Baskerville [Carlyle Blackwell]
- The Return of Sherlock Holmes [Clive Brook]

1930
- Death of Sir Arthur Conan Doyle
- Paramount on Parade [Clive Brook]

1931
- The Speckled Band [Raymond Massey]
- The Sleeping Cardinal [Arthur Wontner]
- The Hound of the Baskervilles [Robert Rendel]

1932
- The Missing Rembrandt [Arthur Wontner]
- The Sign of Four: Sherlock Holmes' Greatest Case [Arthur Wontner]
- Conan Doyle's Master Detective Sherlock Holmes [Clive Brook]

1933
- Jeremy Brett born
- A Study in Scarlet [Reginald Owen]

1935
- The Triumph of Sherlock Holmes [Arthur Wontner]

1936
- The BBC starts limited television service from Alexandra Palace

1937
- William Gillette dies
- Silver Blaze [Arthur Wontner]
- Der Hund von Baskerville [Bruno Güttner]

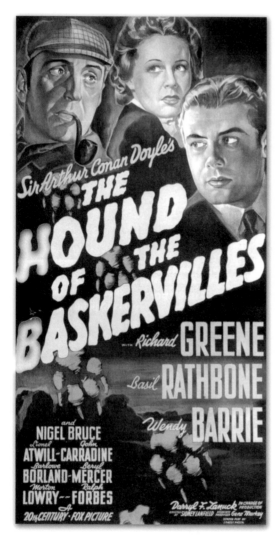

1943
- Sherlock Holmes in Washington [Basil Rathbone]
- Sherlock Holmes Faces Death [Basil Rathbone]

1944
- The Spider Woman [Basil Rathbone]
- The Scarlet Claw [Basil Rathbone]
- The Pearl of Death [Basil Rathbone]

1945
- The House of Fear [Basil Rathbone]
- The Woman in Green [Basil Rathbone]
- Pursuit to Algiers [Basil Rathbone]

1946
- Terror By Night [Basil Rathbone]
- Dressed to Kill [Basil Rathbone]

1948
- Eille Norwood dies

1949
- Your Show Time: The Adventure of the Speckled Band [Alan Napier] TV

1951
- For the Children: The Adventure of the Mazarin Stone [Andrew Osborn] TV
- The Man Who Disappeared [John Longden]
- We Present Alan Wheatley as Mr Sherlock Holmes in ... [Alan Wheatley] TV

1953
- *The Robe*, first film to be released in CinemaScope
- Suspense: The Adventure of the Black Baronet [Basil Rathbone] TV

1954
- Sherlock Holmes [Ronald Howard] TV

1955
- Independent television service commences in UK

1959
- The Hound of the Baskervilles [Peter Cushing]
- Der Hund von Baskerville [Wolf Ackva] TV

- The Three Garridebs [Louis Hector] TV
- Die graue Dame [Hermann Spielmans]

1939
- Sir Arthur Conan Doyle's The Hound of the Baskervilles [Basil Rathbone]
- The Adventures of Sherlock Holmes [Basil Rathbone]

1942
- Sherlock Holmes and the Voice of Terror [Basil Rathbone]
- Sherlock Holmes and the Secret Weapon [Basil Rathbone]

1960
- Arthur Wontner dies

1962
- Sherlock Holmes und das Halsband des Todes [Christopher Lee]

1964
- Detective: The Speckled Band [Douglas Wilmer] TV

1965
- Sherlock Holmes [Douglas Wilmer] TV
- A Study in Terror [John Neville] **1967**
- Basil Rathbone dies
- Sherlock Holmes [Erich Schellow] TV

1968
- Sir Arthur Conan Doyle's Sherlock Holmes [Peter Cushing] TV
- Sherlock Holmes [Nando Gazzolo] TV

1970
- The Private Life of Sherlock Holmes [Robert Stephens]

1971
- They Might Be Giants [none]

1972
- The Hound of the Baskervilles [Stewart Granger] TV
- Touha Sherlocka Holmese [Radovan Lukavsky]

1973
- Comedy Playhouse Presents: Elementary, My Dear Watson [John Cleese] TV

1974
- Das Zeichen der Vier [Rolf Becker] TV
- Dr Watson and the Darkwater Hall Mystery: A Singular Adventure [none] TV

1975
- The Adventure of Sherlock Holmes' Smarter Brother [Douglas Wilmer]

1976
- The Return of the World's Greatest Detective [Larry Hagman] TV

1976 *(continued)*
- Sherlock Holmes in New York [Roger Moore] TV
- The Seven-Per-Cent Solution [Nicol Williamson]

1977
- Première of *Star Wars*
- Classics Dark and Dangerous: Silver Blaze [Christopher Plummer] TV
- The Strange Case of the End of Civilisation As We Know It [John Cleese] TV

1978
- The Hound of the Baskervilles [Peter Cook]

1979
- Murder By Decree [Christopher Plummer]
- Sherlock Holmes and Dr Watson [Geoffrey Whitehead] TV
- Priklyucheniya Sherloka Kholmsa i doktora Vatsona [Vasili Livanov] TV

1981
- Children's Mystery Theater: The Treasure of Alpheus T Winterborn [Keith McConnell] TV

1982
- The Hound of the Baskervilles [Tom Baker] TV
- Young Sherlock: The Mystery of The Manor House [Guy Henry] TV

1983
- The Baker Street Boys [Roger Ostime] TV
- Sir Arthur Conan Doyle's The Hound of the Baskervilles [Ian Richardson] TV
- Sir Arthur Conan Doyle's The Sign of Four [Ian Richardson] TV

1984
- The VCR blamed for lowest-ever cinema admissions in the UK
- The Adventures of Sherlock Holmes [Jeremy Brett] TV
- The Masks of Death [Peter Cushing] TV

1985
- Young Sherlock Holmes [Nicholas Rowe]

1986
- The Return of Sherlock Holmes [Jeremy Brett] TV
- The Great Mouse Detective [Basil Rathbone]

1987
- The Return of Sherlock Holmes [Michael Pennington] TV
- The Loss of a Personal Friend [Peter Harding]
- The Sign of Four [Jeremy Brett] TV

1988
- Without a Clue [Michael Caine]
- The Hound of the Baskervilles [Jeremy Brett] TV
- Star Trek: The Next Generation [none] TV

1989
- Alfred Hitchcock Presents: My Dear Watson [Brian Bedford] TV

1990
- Hands of a Murderer [Edward Woodward] TV

1991
- The Case-book of Sherlock Holmes [Jeremy Brett] TV
- The Crucifer of Blood [Charlton Heston] TV

1992
- The Master Blackmailer [Jeremy Brett] TV
- Sherlock Holmes and the Leading Lady [Christopher Lee] TV

- Incident at Victoria Falls [Christopher Lee] TV
- Sherlock Holmes en Caracas [Jean Manuel Montesinos]

1993
- US survey reveals that less than ten per cent of films made in 1910s have survived
- The Last Vampyre [Jeremy Brett] TV
- The Eligible Bachelor [Jeremy Brett] TV
- The Hound of London [Patrick Macnee] TV
- 1994 Baker Street: Sherlock Holmes Returns [Anthony Higgins] TV

1994
- Peter Cushing dies
- The Memoirs of Sherlock Holmes [Jeremy Brett] TV
- Fu Er Mo Si Yu Zhong Guo Nu Xia [Fan Ai Li]

1995
- Jeremy Brett dies

1999
- Sherlock Holmes in the 22nd Century [Jason Gray Stanford] TV
- O Xangô de Baker Street [Joaquim de Almeida]

2000
- Murder Rooms: The Dark Beginnings of Sherlock Holmes [none] TV
- The Hound of the Baskervilles [Matt Frewer] TV

2001
- The Sign of Four [Matt Frewer] TV
- The Royal Scandal [Matt Frewer] TV

2002
- Sherlock [James D'Arcy] TV
- The Case of the Whitechapel Vampire [Matt Frewer] TV
- The Hound of the Baskervilles [Richard Roxburgh] TV

2003
- The League of Extraordinary Gentlemen [none]